Give Me Five! ENGLISH 2

TEACHER'S BOOK

Joanne Ramsden • Donna Shaw

macmillan education

Macmillan Education
4 Crinan Street
London N1 9XW
A division of Macmillan Publishers Limited

Companies and representatives throughout the world

Teacher's Book 978-1-380-02494-7
Teacher's Book Pack 978-1-380-02493-0

This edition published 2018
First edition entitled *High Five! English* published 2014 by Macmillan Publishers Limited

Original series concept design by Tom Cole
Page make-up by emc design limited
Illustrated by Ángeles Peinador
Cover design by Bigtop Design Limited
Cover photograph by **Macmillan Publishers Limited**/Tom Dick and Debbie Productions

Authors' acknowledgements
The authors would like to thank everyone at Macmillan who has given help and advice throughout this project. Special thanks from Jo to Carlos, Daniel and Alex for their patience and support during this process. Special thanks from Donna to José, Elisa, Teresa and Marina for their encouragement and enthusiasm.

The publishers would like to thank
The publishers would like to thank Amanda Morrison Prince, Colegio El Parque, La Navata, Madrid; Amaya Carrera García, Colegio Santa Teresa de Jesús, Valladolid; Ana Isabel Fernández Sáez, CEIP La Encina, Las Rozas, Madrid; Aránzazu Sánchez Rodríguez, CEIP Rosa Luxemburgo, Madrid; Beatriz García Vaquero, CEIP Mariano José de Larra, Madrid; Carme Tena, Col·legi Sagrada Familia, Tortosa, Tarragona; Carmen María Largo Muñoz, CEIP Federico García Lorca, Colmenar Viejo, Madrid; Cristina Nieto Ruiz de Gaona, CEIP Margarita Salas, Arroyo de la Encomienda, Valladolid; David García Martínez, CEIP Amador de los Ríos, Madrid; Estíbaliz Medina Martín, CEIP Virgen de Navalazarza, San Agustín de Guadalix, Madrid; Francisco Javier Navarro Pineda, Colegio Tajamar, Madrid; Iratxe Zabaleta Zendagorta, Ikastola San Fidel, Guernica, Vizcaya; Jesús Javier de Andrés Urraca, CEIP Esperanza, Madrid; Juana Rego Freire, CEIP Padre Poveda, Madrid; Judith Muñoz Díaz, CEIP Rodríguez Sahagún, Madrid; Lucía Manso Estébanez, CEIP Ciudad de Guadalajara, Madrid; Lucía López Sánchez, CEIP San Juan de la Cruz, Madrid; Lucía Soria García, CEIP Alberto Alcocer, Madrid; María Jesús Pérez Pérez, CEIP Alberto Alcocer, Madrid; Mario Merino Fernández, CEIP María Martín, Madrid; Marta Moreno Arroyo, CEIP Vicente Aleixandre, Móstoles, Madrid; Miren Itziar Ispizua Mintegui, CEIP Ramiro de Maetzu, Madrid; Paula Reyes García, CEIP Alberto Alcocer, Madrid; Susana Espinel Beneitez, Colegio Grazalema, El Puerto de Santa María, Cádiz; Susana García Pizarro, Ateneu Instructiu, Sant Joan Despí, Barcelona; Virginia Escalona Monreal, CEIP La Encina, Las Rozas, Madrid.
Commissioned photography by Lisa Payne p14, Redhill Media Ltd p21 (br) and Tom Dick and Debbie Productions p16.

Full acknowledgments for illustrations and photographs in the facsimile pages can be found in the Pupil's Book 978-1-380-01357-6, the Activity Book ISBN 978-1-380-01377-4.

Printed and bound in Brazil

2022
27

Give Me Five!

TEACHER'S BOOK 2

Syllabus

Unit	Key Competences and Key Learning Outcomes	Contents Lexis
Starter Unit Let's go back to school!	• Identify and say eight school subjects (Lesson 2) • Ask and answer about school subjects (Lesson 2) • Read, listen and understand a story about a magic bike (Lesson 4) • Ask and answer about the weather (Lesson 4) • Use the Pupil's App on Navio • Identify and say vocabulary from Level 1 (Lesson 1) • Say the alphabet in English (Lesson 3) • Ask and answer how to spell out words (Lesson 3) • Make a cut-out and review your learning (Lesson 4) • Ask and answer questions about your / your friends' names (Lesson 1) • Work with a Talk Partner to practise and reinforce learning (all lessons) • Sing two songs (Lessons 1 and 3) • Understand, act out and give an opinion on a story (Lesson 4)	**Core vocabulary** • *Arts and Crafts, English, ICT, Maths, Music, PE, Science, Spanish* • *cloudy, raining, snowy, stormy, sunny, windy* • the alphabet **Extension vocabulary (optional)** • *cold, cool, hot, warm* **Recycled vocabulary** • Level 1: classroom objects; clothes; family members; farm animals; food; instructions; numbers 1–20; places in town; shapes; toys; transport
Unit 1 Move your body	• Identify and say ten sports (Lesson 1) • Use present simple 'I' and 'you' (Lesson 2) • Read, listen and understand a story about Molly's activities (Lesson 3) • Identify and say six action verbs (Lesson 4) • Read about Sports Day in Britain (Lesson 6) • Watch and understand a video about Sports Day (Video and 21st Century Skills) • Use the Pupil's App on Navio • Use a strategy to practise spelling key words (Lesson 1) • Say a tongue twister and practise 'ai' and 'ay' spellings (Lesson 5) • Review language in the unit and reflect on own learning (Lesson 8) • Practise activity types found in the Cambridge Exams: Pre A1 Starters • Understand the importance of organising personal possessions (Lesson 3) • Work with a Talk Partner to practise and reinforce learning (all lessons) • Play a communication game about sports (Lesson 5) • Sing three songs (Lessons 1, 4 and 8) • Understand, act out and give an opinion on a story (Lesson 3) • Think about the sports you play at school (Lesson 6) • Read, understand and act out a poem (Lesson 7)	**Core vocabulary** • *baseball, basketball, cycling, football, hockey, rollerblading, skateboarding, swimming, tennis, volleyball* • *bounce, catch, hit, jump, kick, throw* **Extension vocabulary (optional)** • *(go) climbing, (go) fishing, (go) sailing, (play) badminton, (play) golf, (play) table tennis; (do) athletics, (do) ballet, (do) gymnastics, (do) karate* **Other vocabulary** • *indoors, outdoors* • *bat, football boots, goggles, mess, rollerblades, sports centre, tennis racket* • *underarm, overarm* **Recycled vocabulary** • Days of the week; *ball, balloon, big, fast, hands, legs, run, small, swimsuit*
Unit 2 Let's go shopping!	• Identify and say ten food items (Lesson 1) • Use indefinite articles: *a / an / some* (Lesson 2) • Read, listen and understand a story about a naughty parrot (Lesson 3) • Ask and answer questions about the price of food (Lesson 4) • Read about Pancake Day in Britain (Lesson 6) • Watch and understand a video about recipes (Video and 21st Century Skills) • Count to fifty (numbers 10–50) (Lesson 4) • Use the Pupil's App on Navio • Use a strategy to practise spelling key words (Lesson 1) • Say a tongue twister and practise 'ee' and 'ea' spellings (Lesson 5) • Review language in the unit and reflect on own learning (Lesson 8) • Practise activity types found in the Cambridge Exams: Pre A1 Starters • Understand the importance of saying 'please' when you ask for something (Lesson 3) • Work with a Talk Partner to practise and reinforce learning (all lessons) • Play a communication game about shopping (Lesson 5) • Sing four songs (Lessons 1, 4, 5 and 8) • Understand, act out and give an opinion on a story (Lesson 3) • Think about special food days where you live (Lesson 6) • Read, understand and write a recipe (Lesson 7)	**Core vocabulary** • *bread, carrots, green beans, lemons, peaches, pineapples, potatoes, sweets, tomatoes, yoghurt* • numbers 1–50 **Extension vocabulary (optional)** • *blackberry, broccoli, coconut, lettuce, lime, peas, plum; sixty, seventy, eighty, ninety* **Other vocabulary** • *food, shopping* • *money, naughty, shop, shopping list* • *bowl, chocolate, cook, flour, make, mix, pancake, put, races, sugar, toss* • *olives, sandwich, slices; first, then, now, finally* **Recycled vocabulary** • *apples, cake, cheese, chicken, chips, eggs, fish, grapes, ice cream, meat, milk, oranges, pasta, pears, pineapple, rice, salad, water* • *delicious* • *breakfast, lunch, dinner* • *eyes, hair, mouth, nose*

Competence in linguistic communication · Competence in mathematics, science and technology · Digital competence
Learning to learn · Social and civic competences · Sense of initiative and entrepreneurship · Cultural awareness and expression

Contents					Cross-curricular links
Structures	**Phonics**	**Sociocultural aspects**	**British Culture and Literacy**	**21st Century Skills**	
Core structures • *What's your favourite subject? My favourite subject is (English). What's yours?* • *How do you spell (English)?* **Other structures** • *We've got … We're ready (to) …* • *We (read / listen / write / sing / speak English).* • *What colour (is / are) …* **Recycled structures** • *What's your / his / her name? Your / His / Her name is (Jake / Molly).* • *What colour is the …? What can you see? I can see …* • *What's the weather like? It's (sunny) today. Is it (raining)? Yes, it is.*		**Cooperative learning** **Skills** • Listening to your classmates (Lesson 1) • Friends as a resource (Lesson 2) • Working together (Lesson 3)			
Core structures • *Do you play any sports? I play (tennis). I go (rollerblading).* • *I go (swimming) (on Saturday).* • *Do you (play football / go cycling)? Yes, I do. / No, I don't.* • *He / She (plays) (tennis).* • *He / She (kicks / throws / hits) the ball.* **Other structures** • *What's your favourite sport? My favourite sport is (football).* • *What sports do you play at school?* **Recycled structures** • *I (like / love) … I don't (like / love) …* • *Do you like (hockey)? Yes, I do. / No, I don't.*	• Alternative vowel spellings **'ai'** / **'ay'** (sn**ai**ls, pl**ay**, r**ai**n, d**ay**)	**Cooperative learning** **Song** • *Well Done!* (Lesson 8) **Skills** • Encouraging participation (Lesson 2) • Think-Pair-Share (Lessons 3 and 8) • Working together as a team (Lesson 5) • Working together as a class (Lesson 7) **Values** • Organising your things	**British Culture** • Sports Day **Literacy** **Text type** • A poem (text to express) **Reading skills** • Predicting from pictures • Scanning and sequencing • Reading a poem	**21st Century Skills** • **Ways of working:** learn to join in	**Links to Science** **The human body** • Joints that move when we play different sports • Safety equipment for sports • Muscles pull our bones to help us move **Arts and Crafts** • Identifying and using lines, shapes and colours • Creating a matching game
Core structures • *Can I have (a / an / some) …, please? Yes, of course. Here you are. Thank you very much.* • *How much is this (lemon)? How much are these (carrots)?* • *It's (50 cents). They're (25 cents). Great! I'll take it / them.* **Other structures** • *Can I help you?* • *I help / put …* • *She puts in (flour). / She tosses (the pancake).* • *We have (pancake races).* **Recycled structures** • *I like / I love / I don't like … Do you like …? Yes, I do. No, I don't. We've got …*	• Alternative vowel spellings **'ee'** / **'ea'** (Qu**ee**n, J**ea**n, **ea**ts, m**ea**t, gr**ee**n, sh**ee**p, ch**ee**se)	**Cooperative learning** **Songs** • *What do I need to do?* (Lesson 5) • *Well Done!* (Lesson 8) **Skills** • Listening to others (Lesson 2) • Working together as a team (Lessons 4, 5) • Encouraging one another (Lesson 7) • Think-Pair-Share (Lesson 8) **Values** • Saying please	**British Culture** • Pancake Day **Literacy** **Text type** • A recipe (instructional text) **Reading skills** • Predicting from pictures • Reviewing information • Sequencing • Matching	**21st Century Skills** • **Digital skills:** finding information online	**Links to Science** **Food** • The five food groups • Health, growth and energy • Balanced meals • Wheat, eggs and milk **Arts and Crafts** • Identifying and using natural shapes and colours of food • Making and playing a shopping game

Syllabus

Unit	Key Competences and Key Learning Outcomes	Contents
		Lexis
Unit 3 At the zoo	• Identify and say ten wild animals (Lesson 1) • Use *Has it got …? / Have they got …?* and short answers (Lesson 2) • Read, listen and understand a story about a mysterious egg (Lesson 3) • Describe and guess animals (Lesson 4) • Read about garden wildlife in Britain (Lesson 6) • Watch and understand a video about animals (Video and 21st Century Skills) • Use animal body parts vocabulary to compare animals (Lesson 4) • Read and understand animal fact files (Lesson 7) • Learn to sort information (Video and 21st Century Skills) • Use the Pupil's App on Navio • Use a strategy to practise spelling key words (Lesson 1) • Say a tongue twister and practise 'oo' and 'ui' spellings (Lesson 5) • Review language in the unit and reflect on own learning (Lesson 8) • Practise activity types found in the Cambridge Exams: Pre A1 Starters • Understand the importance of helping your friends and family (Lesson 3) • Work with a Talk Partner to practise and reinforce learning (all lessons) • Play a communication game describing animals (Lesson 5) • Sing four songs (Lessons 1, 4, 5 and 8) • Understand, act out and give an opinion on a story (Lesson 3) • Think about wild animals where you live (Lesson 6)	**Core vocabulary** • *crocodile, elephant, giraffe, hippo, lion, lizard, monkey, penguin, snake, tiger; beak, body, face, tail, teeth, wings* **Extension vocabulary (optional)** • *bear, camel, dolphin, kangaroo, turtle, whale; feathers, fur, spots, stripes* **Other vocabulary** • *dangerous, grasslands, jungle, wild animal* • *ground, hatches, inside, lost, sign, strange* • *fox, goose, hedgehog, kangaroo, squirrel* • *dish, garden, grass, night, nuts, seeds* • *fact file, gorilla, ice, insects, leaves, polar bear, rainforest, snow* **Recycled vocabulary** • *bird, cat, chicken, cow, dog, duck, goat, horse, mouse, parrot, sheep, zebra, zoo* • *arms, ears, face, fingers, hair, legs, mouth, neck, toes, big, fat, long, tall* • *climb, fly, tree; fish, fruit, meat*
My project 1: Pets	• Identify and name animals we keep as pets (Lesson 1) • Do a survey to find out what pets the class have (Lesson 1) • Write and present a page about your pet (Lesson 2) • Understand and complete a simple graph about pets (Lesson 1) • Use the Pupil's App on Navio • Plan your pets class book page (Lesson 1) • Think about your project (Lesson 2) • Work as a class to make a class book about pets (Lesson 2) • Sing a cooperative learning song (Lesson 2)	**Core vocabulary** • *goldfish, guinea pig, hamster, mouse, rabbit, spider, stick insect, turtle, in water, in a cage, in a tank, in a house* **Recycled vocabulary** • *bird, cat, dog, fish*
Unit 4 The nature trail	• Identify and say ten features of a nature trail (Lesson 1) • Use present continuous to describe actions (Lesson 2) • Read, listen and understand a story about Toby on a nature trail (Lesson 3) • Ask and answer questions to find out what people are doing (Lesson 4) • Use prepositions of movement (Lesson 4) • Write a guided adventure story (Lesson 7) • Watch and understand a video about the environment (Video and 21st Century Skills) • Read about forest schools in Britain (Lesson 6) • Use the Pupil's App on Navio • Use a strategy to practise spelling key words (Lesson 1) • Say a tongue twister and practise 'or' and 'al' spellings (Lesson 5) • Review language in the unit and reflect on own learning (Lesson 8) • Practise activity types found in the Cambridge Exams: Pre A1 Starters • Understand the importance of not touching wild animals (Lesson 3) • Learn to look after the environment (Video and 21st Century Skills) • Work with a Talk Partner to practise and reinforce learning (all lessons) • Play a communication game about a nature trail (Lesson 5) • Sing four songs (Lessons 1, 4 and 8) • Understand, act out and give an opinion on a story (Lesson 3) • Read and understand an adventure story (Lesson 7)	**Core vocabulary** • *bridge, forest, grass, hill, lake, leaves, path, river, road, sand* • *across, along, down, up* **Extension vocabulary (optional)** • *field, mud, sea, stream, village, waterfall; around, into, out of, through* **Other vocabulary** • *deep, nature trail; chasing, crazy, cycle path, spines; rolling* • *branches, butterflies, caterpillars, den, forest, minibeast hunt, mud pies, rocks, stones, twigs, worms* • *afraid, beach, cave, giant spiders, hero, key, map, monster, mummies, pool, secret passage, torch, treasure* **Recycled vocabulary** • *catch, climb, jump, play, ride (a horse / a bike), run, sail (a boat), swim, walk; flowers, grass, leaves, sheep* • *in, on*

Competence in linguistic communication | Competence in mathematics, science and technology | Digital competence
Learning to learn | Social and civic competences | Sense of initiative and entrepreneurship | Cultural awareness and expression

Contents					Cross-curricular links
Structures	**Phonics**	**Sociocultural aspects**	**British Culture and Literacy**	**21st Century Skills**	
Core structures • *It's got (long hair).* • *Has it got (long hair)? Yes, it has. / No, it hasn't.* • *They've got (four legs).* • *Have they got (four legs)? Yes, they have. / No, they haven't.* • *It hasn't got (a beak). They haven't got (wings).* **Other structures** • *I haven't got …* • *Have you got …?* • *They live … They eat …* **Recycled structures** • *I've got … I'm … I can / can't (swim). I live … It's (an elephant). It's got (four legs). A (lion) has got … (Hippos) have got … They're (small).*	• Alternative vowel spellings **'oo'** / **'ui'** (kangar**oo**, g**oo**se, swims**ui**t, fruit j**ui**ce, p**oo**l)	**Cooperative learning** **Songs** • *Let's take turns!* (Lesson 5) • *Well Done!* (Lesson 8) **Skills** • Listening to others (Lesson 2) • Working together as a team (Lesson 5) • Encouraging one another (Lesson 7) • Think-Pair-Share (Lesson 8) **Values** • Helping your friends and family	**British Culture** • Garden wildlife **Literacy** **Text type** • Fact files (informative text) **Reading skills** • Remembering facts • Predicting from pictures • Using mind maps • Scanning • Reviewing information • Sequencing • Matching	**21st Century Skills** • **Ways of thinking:** learning to sort information	**Links to Science** **Animals** • Animal habitats • Classifying animals by their diet • The difference between vertebrate and invertebrate animals • Describing mammals **Arts and Crafts** • Identifying and using primary and secondary colours to colour animals and their habitats • Making and colouring an animal game
Core structures • *Its name is (Bob).* • *Its favourite food is (meat).* • *Its favourite toy is (a ball).* • *It lives in (my house).* **Recycled structures** • *This is my (dog). It's brown.* • *It's got (four legs) and (short hair).* • *How many (rabbits) are there? There are (three rabbits). Have you got any pets? Yes, I have, I've got (two dogs and a turtle). No, I haven't.*		**Cooperative learning** **Song** • *Listen to others* (Lesson 2) **Skills** • Working together (Lessons 1 and 2)			**Links to Science** **Animals** • Classifying animals • How animals are born **Arts and Crafts** • Observing and identifying lines, shapes and colours • Making an insect poster
Core structures • *What are you doing? I'm (walking) (on the path).* • *Are you (swimming) (in the lake)? Yes, I am. / No, I'm not. What's he / she doing? He's / She's (running) (up the hill). Is he / she running up a hill? Yes, he / she is. / No, he / she isn't.* **Other structures** • *Breathe in. Breathe out. Let's calm down. Let's count. I can touch and smell (the tree), but I can't see it. We learn how to (make a den). We make (mud pies). We go on (a minibeast hunt).* **Recycled structures** • *There's a … There are … He sails / crosses / goes / finds …*	• Alternative vowel spellings **'or'** / **'al'** (h**or**se, sh**or**ts, w**al**ks, t**al**ks, st**or**m)	**Cooperative learning** **Songs** • *Calm down* (Lesson 4) • *Well Done!* (Lesson 8) **Skills** • Listening to others (Lesson 2) • Working together as a team (Lesson 5) • Encouraging one another (Lesson 7) • Think-Pair-Share (Lesson 8) **Values** • Not touching wild animals	**British Culture** • Forest schools **Literacy** **Text type** • An adventure story (text to entertain) **Reading skills** • Remembering facts • Scanning • Sequencing • Relating pictures to new vocabulary	**21st Century Skills** • **Living in the world:** learning to look after the environment	**Links to Science** **Plant life** • The characteristics of plants • The features of trees, bushes and grass • Evergreen and deciduous trees **Arts and Crafts** • Identifying and using shapes and colours present in nature • Making and colouring a nature trail game

Syllabus

Unit	Key Competences and Key Learning Outcomes	Contents
		Lexis
Unit 5 The frozen lake	• Identify and say ten action verbs (Lesson 1) • Use present continuous: 'we' and 'you' (Lesson 2) • Read, listen and understand a story about a snowman (Lesson 3) • Describe and guess snowmen (Lesson 4) • Use adjectives, present continuous verbs and 'has got' (Lesson 4) • Read about winter activities in Britain (Lesson 6) • Write a guided conversation (Lesson 7) • Watch and understand a video about making snowmen (Video and 21st Century Skills) • Use the Pupil's App on Navio • Use a strategy to practise spelling key words (Lesson 1) • Say a tongue twister and practise 'oa' and 'ow' spellings (Lesson 5) • Review language in the unit and reflect on own learning (Lesson 8) • Practise activity types found in the Cambridge Exams: Pre A1 Starters • Understand the importance of wearing warm clothes when it's cold (Lesson 3) • Work with a Talk Partner to practise and reinforce learning (all lessons) • Play a communication game about what snowmen are doing (Lesson 5) • Learn to be creative (Video and 21st Century Skills) • Sing four songs (Lessons 1, 4, 5 and 8) • Understand, act out and give an opinion on a story (Lesson 3) • Think about winter activities you can do where you live (Lesson 6) • Read and understand a fable (Lesson 7)	**Core vocabulary** • *dance, drink, eat, listen to music, make a snowman, play, skate, smile, take a photo, wave* • *clean, dirty, fat, short, tall, thin* **Extension vocabulary (optional)** • *cry, fall, laugh, move, shout, skip; beautiful, strong, ugly, weak* **Other vocabulary** • *alive, moving, park, sledge, sledging, snowing* • *snow, stones; dry ski slope, ice rink, skiing, toboggan, tubing* • *autumn, spring, summer, winter; ant, grasshopper; cold, hot, hungry, silly* **Recycled vocabulary** • Body parts; Food; *hat, scarf* • *big, fast, new, old, slow, small* • *circle, oval, rectangle, square, star, triangle*
Unit 6 All year round	• Identify and say eight seasonal activities (Lesson 1) • Use present simple: 'we', 'you' and 'they' (Lesson 2) • Understand and act out a conversation (Lesson 2) • Read, listen and understand a story about the four seasons (Lesson 3) • Ask and answer about dates (Lesson 4) • Read about seasonal festivals in Britain (Lesson 6) • Watch and understand a video about seasons (Video and 21st Century Skills) • Use ordinal numbers (Lesson 4) • Use the Pupil's App on Navio • Use a strategy to practise spelling key words (Lesson 1) • Say a tongue twister and practise 'ir' and 'ur' spellings (Lesson 5) • Review language in the unit and reflect on own learning (Lesson 8) • Practise activity types found in the Cambridge Exams: Pre A1 Starters • Understand the importance of working together (Lesson 3) • Ask and answer about your birthday (Lesson 4) • Work with a Talk Partner to practise and reinforce learning (all lessons) • Do a class survey about birthdays (Lesson 5) • Learn to do a survey (Video and 21st Century Skills) • Sing four songs (Lessons 1, 4, 5 and 8) • Understand, act out and give an opinion on a story (Lesson 3) • Think about seasonal festivals where you live (Lesson 6) • Read, understand and complete a traditional rhyme (Lesson 7)	**Core vocabulary** • *celebrate Halloween, eat chestnuts, finish school, go to the beach, open presents, plant seeds, smell flowers, wear warm clothes* • *first – thirty-first* • *spring, summer, autumn, winter* **Extension vocabulary (optional)** • *spring: look at baby animals; summer: go on holiday, eat ice cream; autumn: play in the leaves, pick apples; winter: play in the snow; eat special food, have a party, send cards, wear a costume* **Other vocabulary** • *cold, cool, hot, warm; America, cousins, postcard; camera, pedalling backwards, poster, project, wheels;* Months of the year; *birthday, party* • *April Fools' Day, carnival, Christmas, crackers, drum, jokes, parade, remember, turkey; leap year* **Recycled vocabulary** • *Bonfire Night; cake, doll, hat*

Competence in linguistic communication · Competence in mathematics, science and technology · Digital competence
Learning to learn · Social and civic competences · Sense of initiative and entrepreneurship · Cultural awareness and expression

Contents					Cross-curricular links
Structures	**Phonics**	**Sociocultural aspects**	**British Culture and Literacy**	**21st Century Skills**	
Core structures • *What are you doing? We're (skating).* • *Are you (dancing)? Yes, we are. / No, we aren't.* • *Are they (skating)? Yes, they are. / No, they aren't.* • *He's a (fat) snowman. He's got a (dirty) (hat).* **Other structures** • *Are you ready? We're working. We're collecting food. Winter is coming. I'm (hungry).* • *He's / She's got (a tall hat / thin arms).* • *You share with me. I share with you.* **Recycled structures** • *Are you (climbing)? Yes, I am. / No, I'm not.* • *There's a … We can … We go (tubing).* • *This is … These are …* • *He's (taking / moving) … They're (dancing).*	• Alternative vowel spellings **'oa'** / **'ow'** (sn**ow**man, g**oa**t, c**oa**t, r**ow**, yell**ow**, b**oa**t, rainb**ow**)	**Cooperative learning** **Songs** • *Sharing is a good thing to do* (Lesson 5) • *Well Done!* (Lesson 8) **Skills** • Working together as a team (Lesson 5) • Think-Pair-Share (Lesson 8) **Values** • Wearing warm clothes when it's cold	**British Culture** • Winter activities **Literacy** **Text type** • A fable (text to entertain and educate) **Reading skills** • Scanning for specific information • Sequencing • Reflecting on a moral	**21st Century Skills** • **Ways of thinking:** learning to be creative	**Links to Science** **Water, land and air** • Identifying the different forms of water • The names of the different forms of water • How water changes state • Different types of land **Arts and Crafts** • Identifying and using different materials to represent winter • Making and playing a communication game
Core structures • *What do you / they do (in summer)?* • *We (go to the beach). They (go to the beach).* • *Do they (celebrate Halloween)? Yes, they do. / No, they don't.* • *When's your birthday? My birthday is on the (eighteenth) of (June).* **Other structures** • *Do you (eat chestnuts in America), too? Yes, we do.* • *Do you want to come to my party?* • *We pull crackers. We play jokes. We wear (paper hats). We have (a bonfire).* • *What festivals do you celebrate? What do you do on festival days?* **Recycled structures** • *I / We can … It's / We've got … It hasn't got … There are …* • *When's your birthday? My birthday is on …*	• Alternative vowel spellings **'ir'** / **'ur'** (p**ur**ple, t**ur**tle, b**ir**thday, f**ir**st, th**ir**d)	**Cooperative learning** **Songs** • *We can do it!* (Lesson 5) • *Well Done!* (Lesson 8) **Skills** • Working together as a team (Lesson 5) • Learning strategies (Lesson 7) • Think-Pair-Share (Lesson 8) **Values** • Working together	**British Culture** • Seasonal festivals **Literacy** **Text type** • A traditional rhyme (text to express) **Reading skills** • Scanning for specific information • Sequencing	**21st Century Skills** • **Ways of working:** learning to do a survey	**Links to Science** **Seasons and the Sun** • The position of the Sun in the different seasons • Characteristics of the seasons and position of the Sun • The months in each season **Arts and Crafts** • Identifying and using different patterns, lines, spaces and colours to reflect things in nature • Making and carrying out a survey

Syllabus

Unit	Key Competences and Key Learning Outcomes	Contents
		Lexis
My project 2: Jobs	• Identify and name different jobs (Lesson 1) • Ask and answer questions about jobs (Lesson 1) • Write and present your jobs poster (Lesson 2) • Use the Pupil's App on Navio • Work in small groups to plan a jobs poster (Lesson 1) • Think about your project (Lesson 2) • Sing a cooperative learning song (Lesson 2)	**Core vocabulary** • *artist, cook, dancer, doctor, firefighter, footballer, pilot, police officer, teacher, vet; boots, helmet, white coat; cook, dance, fly a plane, paint pictures, put out fires*
Unit 7 My house	• Identify and say ten rooms in the house (Lesson 1) • Use *There's a / There are / There isn't a / There aren't any* (Lesson 2) • Read, listen and understand a story about a haunted house (Lesson 3) • Ask and answer about who objects belong to (Lesson 4) • Watch and understand a video about unusual homes (Video and 21st Century Skills) • Use the Pupil's App on Navio • Use a strategy to practise spelling key words (Lesson 1) • Say a tongue twister and practise 'ou' and 'ow' spellings (Lesson 5) • Review language from the unit and reflect on own learning (Lesson 8) • Practise activity types found in the Cambridge Exams: Pre A1 Starters • Understand the importance of being kind to your friends (Lesson 3) • Learn to help at home (Video and 21st Century Skills) • Work with a Talk Partner to practise and reinforce learning (all lessons) • Play a communication game about where objects are (Lesson 5) • Sing three songs (Lessons 1, 4 and 8) • Understand, act out and give an opinion on a story (Lesson 3) • Learn about children's bedrooms in Britain (Lesson 6) • Think about what you've got in your bedroom (Lesson 6) • Read and understand a play script (Lesson 7) • Complete and act out a conversation from a play (Lesson 7)	**Core vocabulary** • *bathroom, bedroom, dining room, flat, garage, garden, hall, house, kitchen, living room* • *box, camera, clock, phone, radio, watch* **Extension vocabulary (optional)** • *chimney, roof, wall, window, upstairs, downstairs; key, lamp, rug, towel* **Other vocabulary** • *floor, shut, watching TV, watering the flowers; armchair, funfair, ghost, haunted, mirror, piano, scared, sofa* • *board games, bookcase, drum, guitar, pop music, pyjama, stickers, sticker collection, upstairs* • *dragon, fairy godmother, get married, glass, midnight, play, prince, sad, script, wicked* **Recycled vocabulary** • *bed, bread, door, eating, food, having a shower, mouse, running, shoes* • *skeleton, witch; bath, bed, run, shower* • *mess; big, small; books, music* • *car, dress, horse, mice, phone, pumpkin, sister; clean, dirty, new, old*
Unit 8 All around the town	• Identify and say ten places in a town (Lesson 1) • Use *Is there a …? / Are there any …?* and short answers • Read, listen and understand a story about a dark night (Lesson 3) • Ask for and give directions (Lesson 4) • Read and write about the emergency services in Britain (Lesson 6) • Watch and understand a video about road safety (Video and 21st Century Skills) • Act out a conversation giving simple directions (Lesson 4) • Use the Pupil's App on Navio • Use a strategy to practise spelling key words (Lesson 1) • Say a tongue twister and practise 'y' and 'igh' spellings (Lesson 5) • Review language from the unit and reflect on own learning (Lesson 8) • Practise activity types found in the Cambridge Exams: Pre A1 Starters • Understand the importance of remembering where you put your things (Lesson 3) • Learn to cross the road safely (Video and 21st Century Skills) • Work with a Talk Partner to practise and reinforce learning (all lessons) • Play a communication game about giving directions (Lesson 5) • Sing three songs (Lessons 1, 4 and 8) • Understand, act out and give an opinion on a story (Lesson 3) • Read, understand and write an invitation (Lesson 7)	**Core vocabulary** • *baker's, bank, bus station, car park, chemist's, fire station, museum, police station, post office, train station* • *go straight on, turn (left / right), from, to* **Extension vocabulary (optional)** • *airport, butcher's, hotel, library, market, university; go along, go past the …, on the corner, opposite* **Other vocabulary** • *dinosaurs, exploring, holidays; dark, hungry, night* • *doctor, emergency, fire engine, firefighter, helmet, loud, police officer, safety, siren, uniform, wheels; candles, face painting, games, invitation* **Recycled vocabulary** • Places in the town; Seasons; *between, in front of, next to; balloons, big, birthday, cake, car, party, presents, red, ride a bike, sweets*

Competence in linguistic communication · Competence in mathematics, science and technology · Digital competence · Learning to learn · Social and civic competences · Sense of initiative and entrepreneurship · Cultural awareness and expression

Contents					Cross-curricular links
Structures	**Phonics**	**Sociocultural aspects**	**British Culture and Literacy**	**21st Century Skills**	
Core structures • *He's / She's a (teacher). He / She wears (a uniform).* • *A (doctor) (helps) (people). A (pilot) (flies a plane).* • *I want to be (a vet).*		**Cooperative learning** **Song** • *It's fun to work together!* (Lesson 2) **Skills** • Working together (Lessons 1 and 2)			**Links to Science** **People who help us** • Types of job and places of work **Arts and Crafts** • Reviewing elements of art: lines, shapes, colours, textures, forms, patterns and movement • Making a cityscape at night
Core structures • *There's / isn't a (garage).* • *There are / aren't any (bedrooms).* • *Whose is this (watch)?* • *It's (mine / yours / his / hers). Is it his / hers / yours?* **Other structures** • *There's a haunted (bedroom). There aren't any (skeletons). There's a (camera) in my (garage).* **Recycled structures** • *There's a … There are … I've got (a guitar). I love (music). Today, I'm making … We play / listen to …*	• Alternative vowel spellings **'ou'** / **'ow'** (br**ow**n, c**ow**, l**ou**d, m**ou**se, ar**ou**nd, h**ou**se)	**Cooperative learning** **Songs** • *Well Done!* (Lesson 8) **Skills** • Think-Pair-Share (Lessons 2 and 8) • Listening to others (Lesson 3) • Working together as a team (Lesson 5) **Values** • Being kind to your friends	**British Culture** • Bedrooms **Literacy** **Text type** • A play script (text to entertain) **Reading skills** • Predicting from title • Scanning for specific information • Remembering facts • Acting out conversations	**21st Century Skills** • **Living in the world:** learn to help at home	**Links to Science** **Materials** • Different materials • Properties of materials • Natural and manufactured materials • The properties of glass **Arts and Crafts** • Observing and identifying lines, shapes, colours, patterns, textures and forms in art and the environment • Making and playing a game
Core structures • *Is there a (bank)? Yes, there is. No, there isn't.* • *Are there any (museums)? Yes, there are. No, there aren't.* • *How do I get to the (post office)?* • *Go straight on. Turn left / right. How do I get from the (bank) to the (post office)?* **Other structures** • *Here's / There's the cinema.* • *Call this number if you need …* • *Come to my party. I hope you can come! My (dad)'s a (firefighter). He / She works / drives / wears …* **Recycled structures** • *It's (between / in front of / next to) …* • *He / She wears / rides / drives …*	• Alternative vowel spellings **'igh'** / **'y'** (fl**y**, l**igh**t, n**igh**t)	**Cooperative learning** **Song** • *Well Done!* (Lesson 8) **Skills** • Listening to others (Lesson 1) • Working together as a team (Lesson 5) • Think-Pair-Share (Lesson 8) **Values** • Remembering where you put your things	**British Culture** • The emergency services **Literacy** **Text type** • An invitation (persuasive text) **Reading skills** • Scanning for specific information • Remembering facts	**21st Century Skills** • **Living in the world:** learn to cross the road safely	**Links to Science** **Forces** • Sources of light and sound • Natural and artificial light sources • Changing direction • Using maps **Arts and Crafts** • Observing and identifying movement in sculptures • Making and playing a game

Syllabus

Unit	Key Competences and Key Learning Outcomes	Contents
		Lexis
Unit 9 Holiday fun	• Identify and say ten holiday places (Lesson 1) • Use past simple: 'I' and 'you' (Lesson 2) • Understand and act out a conversation (Lesson 2) • Ask and answer questions about where you were yesterday (Lesson 2) • Read, listen and understand a story about a magic trip (Lesson 3) • Use irregular plurals (Lesson 4) • Ask and answer about people (Lesson 4) • Read about summer holidays in Britain (Lesson 6) • Read, understand and write a diary extract (Lesson 7) • Watch and understand a video about weekend activities (Video and 21st Century Skills) • Use the Pupil's App on Navio • Learn to use a digital camera (Video and 21st Century Skills) • Use a strategy to practise spelling key words (Lesson 1) • Say a tongue twister and practise 'ear' and 'air' spellings (Lesson 5) • Review the language from the unit and reflect on own learning (Lesson 8) • Practise activity types found in the Cambridge Exams: Pre A1 Starters • Understand the importance of playing outside with your friends (Lesson 3) • Work with a Talk Partner to practise and reinforce learning (all lessons) • Play a communication game about where you were (Lesson 5) • Sing three songs (Lessons 1, 4 and 8) • Understand, act out and give an opinion on a story (Lesson 3) • Think about what you do in your summer holidays (Lesson 6)	**Core vocabulary** • *aquarium, castle, chocolate factory, circus, funfair, safari park, science museum, sports centre, theatre, water park* • *child, children, man, men, woman, women* **Extension vocabulary (optional)** • *amusement arcade, art gallery, climbing wall, ice rink, royal palace, skateboard park; person, people, parent, grandparent* **Other vocabulary** • *dolphin; bored, magic, tower, trip; arts and crafts, butterfly house, giant chess, hide and seek, maze, paint a cup / plate, summer holidays* • *badge, clown, diary, roller coaster, stilts, ticket* **Recycled vocabulary** • Places in the town, Describing hair and eyes, Family members, Days of the week • *fish, fly, holiday, hungry, slide* • *birthday, games, garden; cloudy, cold, hot, sunny; fast, tall*
My project 3: Time	• Ask and answer about the time (Lesson 1) • Associate time with daily routines (Lesson 1) • Present your project (Lesson 2) • Use the Pupil's App on Navio • Follow instructions (Lesson 1) • Think about your project (Lesson 2) • Work together to practise the time (Lesson 1) • Ask and answer about the time other pupils do things (Lesson 2) • Sing a cooperative learning song (Lesson 2) • Make a clock (Lesson 2)	**Core vocabulary** • Numbers 1–50; *o'clock, quarter past, half past, quarter to* **Recycled vocabulary** • *get dressed, get up, go to bed, go to school, have breakfast, have dinner, have lunch, have a shower, play*
Festivals: Harvest Festival	• Listen, read and say a poem • Learn about traditional Harvest Festival activities in Britain • Think about food festivals in your country • Make a harvest basket	**Core vocabulary** • *autumn, baskets, celebrate, cheer, food, fruit, ground, grow, harvest, moon, round, summer, vegetables*
Festivals: Carnival	• Listen, read and say a rhyme • Talk about dressing up • Learn about carnival • Make a carnival mask	**Core vocabulary** • *cape, carnival, competition, costume, face, mask, paint, parade, wig*

Competence in linguistic communication · Competence in mathematics, science and technology · Digital competence
Learning to learn · Social and civic competences · Sense of initiative and entrepreneurship · Cultural awareness and expression

Contents				21st Century Skills	Cross-curricular links
Structures	**Phonics**	**Sociocultural aspects**	**British Culture and Literacy**		
Core structures • *Where were you yesterday / last weekend?* • *I was at the (circus). We were at the (chocolate factory). Were you at the (castle)? Yes, I was. No, I wasn't.* • *Who's that (woman)? He's / She's … Who are those (men)? They're …* **Other structures** • *It was fun / great! Yesterday was (Saturday). It was (sunny).* **Recycled structures** • *Let's go to … Where's (Beth)? Here I am.* • *He's / She's got (short) (hair). There is / are …* • *He's / She's my (cousin). They're my (grandparents).* • *We can (play hide and seek). We love (the maze). Our favourite place is … In this photo, we're playing …*	• Alternative vowel spellings '**air**' / '**ear**' (b**ear**, p**ear**, st**air**s, funf**air**)	**Cooperative learning** **Songs** • *We can do it!* (Lesson 7) • *Well Done!* (Lesson 8) **Skills** • Listening to others (Lesson 1) • Working together as a team (Lesson 5) • Think-Pair-Share (Lesson 8) **Values** • Playing outside with your friends	**British Culture** • Summer holidays **Literacy** **Text type** • A diary (text to retell event) **Reading skills** • Scanning for specific information • Remembering facts	**21st Century Skills** • **Digital skills:** learn to use a digital camera	**Links to Science** **Electricity** • Machines that use electricity **Arts and Crafts** • Observing and identifying the effect of colour; shade; and warm and cool colours in art • Making and playing a game
Core structures • *What time is it? It's (eight) o'clock. It's a quarter past (eight). It's half past (eight). It's a quarter to (nine).* • *I (get up) at …* • *What time do you (go to school)?* • *I (go to school) at (nine o'clock).*		**Cooperative learning** **Song** • *Listen to others* (Lesson 2) • *Well done!* (Lesson 2) **Skills** • Working together (Lessons 1 and 2)			**Links to Science** **Time** • Clocks in the past; measuring time • Timelines **Arts and Crafts** • Reviewing elements of art: lines, shapes, colours, textures, forms, patterns and movement • Making a photo exhibition
Core structures • *We celebrate (Harvest Festival). We make (big baskets).*					
Core structures • *Put on (your costume). Paint (your face). Wear (a wig).*					

Introduction to *Give Me Five!*

Give Me Five! is a six-level course for pupils who have an extended English timetable and are being taught at a faster pace. It is designed to develop pupils' communicative competences in a systematic and comprehensive manner and to provide a basis for life-long learning.

With *Give Me Five!* 2, pupils ...

- **identify language patterns** and be creative with grammar.
- **use new technologies and multimedia** as tools for learning.
- **develop 21st Century Skills** through engaging and real-world videos to explore ways of thinking, ways of working and living in the world.
- **develop their social and civic competences** through cooperative learning projects, songs and activities.
- **develop literacy skills** through a range of enjoyable and motivating real-world texts.
- **communicate confidently and fluently** through well-supported speaking tasks.
- **participate fully** in fun and engaging activities such as songs, stories, games and chants.
- **prepare for Cambridge Exams** through the systematic integration of exam practice and a dedicated Exams Practice lesson in each unit.
- **develop their thinking skills and multiple intelligences** through challenging activities.
- **become independent and reflective learners** through the integration of learning-to-learn strategies and activities.
- **develop reading, writing, listening and speaking** in a balanced and integrative manner.
- **learn about British culture** and think about their own culture through lively culture lessons.
- **develop strategies for spelling** through the systematic practice of alternative spellings of long vowel sounds.
- **link their learning to other subjects in the curriculum** such as Science and Arts and Crafts.

Meet the characters in *Give Me Five! 2*

Molly and **Jake** are brother and sister. They are seven years old and have got a mischievous dog called **Toby**. They are the lucky owners of a magic bike. Their bike looks like a normal tandem, but when they ring the bell amazing things happen!

Beth is Jake and Molly's friend, and she's seven years old, too. She uses her scooter to accompany her friends on their adventures.

Tom and **Anna** are two British children who introduce us to their favourite traditions and cultural activities.

Cooperative learning

Give Me Five! 2 incorporates a variety of **cooperative learning tasks and strategies** which require the pupils to work together in a structured way. Working in pairs and small groups has many benefits. The pupils are prepared to spend more time on the tasks, are motivated to produce more language and are more likely to use creative and logical thinking. Cooperative learning also helps develop a positive classroom environment as the pupils have a greater sense of belonging and learn to understand and value all the members of the group. Finally, cooperative tasks require the pupils to be active and more independent learners, building their self-confidence and their ability to cope with uncertainty and unpredictability.

Give Me Five! 2 makes use of common and well-researched cooperative learning strategies. The pupils are taught how to work with **Talk Partners,** learning that the Talk Partners Task flashcard means they should turn to the person sitting next to them and form a pair. The teacher then sets the task, e.g. practising a question and answer exchange or saying a tongue twister together. Alternatively, during **Think-Pair-Share** activities, learners listen to a question, think about it individually, discuss the answer with a partner and then share their ideas with the rest of the class. In addition to these strategies, the Teacher's Book lesson plans provide a selection of **easy-to-use cooperative learning activities** which require no or minimal preparation. There is also a simple, clearly-staged **cooperative project** at the end of each term where the pupils plan, create and then evaluate a piece of work in groups and as a class.

In order for cooperative learning to be successful, the pupils need to learn and practise interpersonal skills such as turn taking, listening to others and sharing. *Give Me Five! 2* provides an **innovative cooperative learning songs bank** which supports the teacher in this task. The ***Well Done!* song** is introduced at the end of Unit 1 and is played at the end of each unit. Other cooperative songs are presented in the following units in Terms 1 and 2, and can be reused throughout the year when needed.

Cooperative learning songs bank

Well Done!

Well done!
Well done!
Well done everyone!
Let's do a high five!
Well done everyone!
(Repeat)

Sharing is a good thing to do

Pencils, rubbers, scissors, too.
You share with me,
I share with you.
Sharing is a good thing to do.
Yes! Sharing is a good thing to do.
(Repeat)

We can do it!

We can do it!
We can do it!
Yeah!
We can do it!
We can do it!
Yeah!
Come on everybody!
Come on everybody!
We can do it!
We can do it!
Yeah!

It's fun to work together

Together, together,
It's fun to work together.
You and me,
Me and you.
It's fun to work together.
(Repeat)

Calm down

Let's calm down.
Let's calm down.
Breathe in,
Breathe out.
Now let's count.
One, two, three, four, five
Let's calm down.

Let's take turns!

Let's take turns.
Let's take turns.
Come on everybody.
Let's take turns.
It's my turn.
It's your turn.
Let's have fun!
(Repeat)

Listen to others

Listen to others.
Listen, please.
Listen with your ears.
Listen, please.
Listen to others.
Listen, please.
Listen, everybody.
(Repeat)

What do I need to do?

What do I need to do?
What do I need to do?
Read instructions,
They help you.
What do I need to do?
What do I need to do?
Listen to instructions,
They help you.

21st Century learning

Give Me Five! 2 and 21st Century learning

Today's learners are growing up in a complex, changing world where an enormous amount of information is available at the touch of a button and where social media allows them to communicate with people all around the world. Technology is transforming the way we live and the way we learn. A key objective of *Give Me Five! 2* is to support learners in developing the necessary skills for the digital age. Apart from using digital technology, skills such as communicating and collaborating with others, thinking creatively and critically, and working to become a caring global citizen are an essential part of this course.

Give Me Five! 2 takes an integrated approach to the use of digital technology and the teaching of **digital skills**. In each unit there is a comprehensive set of digital practice material for the learner, helping them to become autonomous and digitally confident. Pupils are also supported in developing specific ICT skills. There are tips on how to use the internet to find, select and present information, and there is a selection of projects with digital outcomes. Guided web quests also support pupils in using the internet to explore new places around the world.

There are multiple opportunities for **communication** and **collaboration** in *Give Me Five! 2*. Learners are encouraged to work together to discover and build knowledge through quizzes and questionnaires, whole-class discussions and a wide range of *Talk Partner* activities. Pupils also work with *Writing Partners* to plan, write and evaluate pieces of written work, and are encouraged to work cooperatively to review learning and reflect on progress at the end of each unit. Finally, there are structured cooperative projects which by providing opportunities for authentic communication, they encourage the development of interpersonal skills and enable learners to celebrate achievement.

Each unit of *Give Me Five! 2* provides a range of tasks to build the pupil's **critical and creative thinking skills**. These include problem-solving, evaluating information, and using imaginative thinking. The Video and 21st Century Skills lessons also focus on a selection of discrete thinking skills. They provide practical tips and thinking strategies.

The interconnectivity of the 21st century and the increasing diversity of our communities mean that pupils need to learn how to respect and value other cultures. *Give Me Five! 2* provides learners with cultural information about the UK. This rich content provides opportunities for **intercultural learning**, where learners identify cultural differences and similarities and build a positive attitude toward their own and other cultures. Finally, a dedicated *Values* section in each unit supports learners in developing their **social and civic competencies** and helps them to make a positive difference in the world.

Video and 21st Century Skills lessons

Video generates interest and supports learners' listening skills by providing a clear visual context and model to practise speaking. It is also a flexible tool, allowing teachers to pause the recording or turn off the sound, and can be used as a stimulus for thinking, language practice and communication. Each unit in *Give Me Five! 2* concludes with a Video and 21st Century Skills lesson. These video lessons help to build key 21st century skills, develop visual literacy and provide a springboard for authentic communication.

The stars of the videos are the children Sophie and Tom, and the adult Abby, who are the presenters of *Channel 21*. They begin each programme by introducing a new topic and then share a selection of related video clips that they have gathered. These visually rich videos bring images of the world into the classroom and offer insights into British culture. The children and the adult then discuss the clips and highlight a 21st century skill in the material. This serves to contextualise the 21st century skill and show the learner how it is relevant in their learning and in their lives.

The 21st Century Skills selected for this level are the following:

Ways of thinking: these skills focus on critical and creative thinking and include sorting information (Unit 3) and being creative (Unit 5).

Ways of working: these skills focus on collaboration, organisation and communication and include joining in (Unit 1) and doing a survey (Unit 6).

Digital skills: these skills focus on evaluating information and using digital technology and include finding information online (Unit 2) and using a digital camera (Unit 9).

Living in the world: these skills focus on values, responsibility and cultural awareness and include looking after the envrionment (Unit 4), helping at home (Unit 7) and crossing the road safely (Unit 8).

Multiple Intelligences

According to this theory, each human being possesses a set of intelligences. Some of these may be more dominant than others, but all of them can be nurtured and developed. In *Give Me Five!*, seven key intelligences are highlighted:

Linguistic intelligence

The pupils are supported on their journey to becoming confident and **accurate speakers**, listeners, readers and writers of the English language through a wide variety of activities. The **four language skills** are carefully integrated into the material and the pupils are given opportunities to use this language in familiar communicative contexts.

Visual-spatial intelligence

The engaging **artwork** in *Give Me Five!* helps the pupils to visualise contexts for language. **Graphic organisers**, such as simple charts, help the pupils form their own conceptual links and order new information.

Musical intelligence

The pupils are exposed to **songs, chants, tongue twisters, rhymes, riddles** and **poems**. These help them to appreciate and produce natural-sounding rhythm, stress and intonation.

Logical-mathematical intelligence

The pupils' understanding of **numbers, shapes and space** is reinforced. The pupils are encouraged to notice and use the **rules and patterns** of language.

Bodily-kinaesthetic intelligence

The pupils are encouraged to use **mime, gesture** and **acting out**. They develop their fine motor skills through **projects, games** and **cut-out activities**.

Interpersonal intelligence

The Values sections give the pupils the opportunity to reflect on their relationship with people around them. **Cooperative learning songs and activities** reinforce positive classroom behaviour such as sharing.

Intrapersonal intelligence

The pupils are encouraged to think about their feelings and beliefs through questionnaires and discussion questions. The pupils are also encouraged to **reflect on their learning and progress** throughout the course.

Tips for teaching pupils with Special Educational Needs

Setting up the class and working together

- Change the groupings regularly to make sure the SEN pupils have an opportunity to work with all their classmates. Check *Give Me Five! Teacher's Book* for pair and group work suggestions.
- Keeping routines is highly important for SEN pupils. Use visuals to reinforce rules and routines and the task cards to show different parts of the lesson.
- Make instructions clear and on a step-by-step basis. Check understanding by giving an example and getting an example from the pupils.
- Use positive classroom language. Say what you want pupils to do, not what you don't want them to do. For example, say ***Look at the board*** not ***Don't keep turning round***.
- Develop a peer mentoring system to encourage pupils to help each other and share skills.

Hearing Impaired (HI) pupils

- Write instructions on the board or highlight them on the IWB. Make sure you have your pupil's attention before you read out the instructions or speak.
- Seat your hearing impaired (HI) pupil facing you to make lip reading and following instruction gestures easier.
- Assign or ask for a volunteer helper or note-taker depending on the level. The helper can point out the instructions in the Pupil's Book and a note-taker can take note of the key ideas of a listening to support the hearing impaired pupil.

Visually Impaired (VI) learners

- Say every word you write on the board and use realia to teach vocabulary. Realia allows the visually impaired pupils to use all their senses.
- *Give Me Five!* offers plenty of songs, stories and dialogues with lesson tips on how to include total physical response (TPR) activities.
- Encourage other pupils to describe experiences to give plenty of exposure to personal and shared interests and create an active and engaging learning environment.

Dyslexic learners

- Provide enough scaffolding in every lesson. For brainstorming activities, do the first few examples with the class. Ask the pupils to do the first part of an activity and check their answers before moving on to the next part. For writing activities, provide the pupils with a model which can be done as a whole class first.
- If pupils can't write in their books, provide photocopies to allow pupils with dyslexia to mark the text or cut it and move it around. This allows for information to be processed in manageable chunks.

Key Competences and Key Learning Outcomes

The **Key Competences and Key Learning Outcomes** outline the **knowledge**, **skills** and **behaviour** that the pupils need to develop in order to achieve their full personal potential, participate in an effective and constructive way in society and become responsible and autonomous life-long learners.

Competence in linguistic communication: the ability to use language to express and interpret concepts, facts, feelings and ideas.

Cultural awareness and expression: the ability to understand and appreciate different art and cultural forms.

Competence in mathematics, science and technology: the ability to apply mathematical thinking to solve everyday problems and to use scientific knowledge to explain the natural world and understand the consequences of human action.

Sense of initiative and entrepreneurship: the ability to apply qualities and skills such as creativity, critical thinking and perseverance, and to plan and manage projects.

Digital competence: the ability to use digital technology confidently, critically and responsibly.

Social and civic competences: the ability to understand and appreciate diversity in society and to develop personal and interpersonal competences.

Learning to learn: the ability to organise one's own learning and work efficiently and autonomously as an individual or in a group.

How *Give Me Five! 2* develops the Key Competences and Key Learning Outcomes

Competence in linguistic communication

Give Me Five! 2 develops the pupils' linguistic skills in a systematic and integrative manner. The pupils learn to identify the meaning, sounds and rhythms of words and phrases through **songs**, **chants** and **stories**. The use of short **listening texts** helps them develop the ability to understand simple communicative messages in everyday contexts. There is systematic practice of tricky sounds which helps the pupils develop clear and natural pronunciation. In addition, the structured use of **games**, **personalisation activities** and simple **conversations** provide the pupils with the opportunity to practise real-world exchanges in the classroom and express their feelings and opinions in English.

A clearly structured **cooperative project** each term involving pair or group work further develops the pupils' speaking skills and also their presentation skills, as they share their completed work with the class.

Give Me Five! 2 also helps support the pupils' **emergent reading and writing** by systematically focusing on **key letter sounds** in English and their different **spelling patterns**. In the **Literacy Lessons**, the pupils have the opportunity to read a variety of rich and engaging real-world texts, while the Activity Book provides ample opportunities for **written production** through a range of guided writing activities.

Competence in mathematics, science and technology

In *Give Me Five! 2*, mathematical competence is developed in a number of ways. **Language patterns** are highlighted. Activities and tasks that require the pupils to use **mathematical and logical thinking skills** are integrated into the material. These include sequencing, counting, finding differences and solving riddles. Each unit of *Give Me Five! 2* is **linked to an area of learning in Science**, reinforcing key concepts and language across the curriculum. In addition, **real-world factual texts**, such as a fact file or a lunch menu, introduce the pupils to different ways of presenting and processing information. The pupils are also given the opportunity to work with simple **charts, diagrams** and **graphic organisers**.

Digital competence

Give Me Five! 2 uses digital resources as tools to support learning, familiarising the pupils with **computer technology** and showing them how technology can be used for learning purposes. The **Pupil's App on Navio** serves to consolidate classwork and allows the pupils to work independently outside the classroom. Within the classroom, the **Teacher's Resource Bank** provides enhanced digital resources for presentation and practice, integrated audio and phonics videos and interactive activities.

Learning to learn

Give Me Five! 2 introduces a variety of **learning strategies** to help the pupils become more independent and reflective learners. Learning objectives are set at the beginning and reviewed at the end of each lesson using **Task flashcards**. The pupils are encouraged to reflect on their learning and progress at the end of each unit through the use of a **self-evaluation traffic light cut-out**.

In each unit, the pupils also use the **Look-Copy-Cover-Write strategy to practise spelling** ten core vocabulary words.

Social and civic competences

Developing the ability to understand how somebody else is feeling and knowing how to respond appropriately is an important objective of *Give Me Five!*, and emphasis is placed on **cooperative learning** and **positive classroom behaviour**.

A bank of **cooperative learning songs** is provided to teach and reinforce the importance of active participation, cooperation and respect and support for others in the classroom. In addition, each unit of the Teacher's Book suggests one or more easy-to-use **cooperative learning activities**.

A **Values** section in each unit encourages the pupils to reflect on their natural, social and cultural environment, integrating topics such as wearing warm clothes when it is cold, being kind to your friends and the importance of working together.

Sense of initiative and entrepreneurship

Give Me Five! 2 develops a sense of initiative and entrepreneurship through the inclusion of a **cooperative project** in each term. These require the pupils to work in groups to successfully plan and complete a task, such as designing and making a class wall display or a group poster. Working together to complete a task helps the pupils to take responsibility for their work and gain confidence in their abilities.

Regular **Talk Partner** activities and a **communicative game using a cut-out** in each unit offer the pupils the opportunity to practise speaking in pairs, personalise the language and work independently. Initiative is also encouraged through regular **personalisation activities**, as well as activities which encourage the pupils to be creative and use their imagination.

Cultural awareness and expression

In *Give Me Five! 2*, the pupils are introduced to **British culture** through lively and age-appropriate culture lessons. These help the pupils understand and respect different customs. A **Think about your culture** section encourages the pupils to reflect on their own culture and have a clearer idea of their own cultural identity.

Give Me Five! 2 also provides the opportunity to experience and appreciate a range of **art forms** such as poems, songs, stories, craft activities, miming and performance and encourages the pupils to express their ideas, experiences and emotions through these mediums.

Give Me Five! 2 Pupil's components

Pupil's Book

This is a 120-page, full-colour, write-in book that contains a Starter Unit and nine thematic units, each with photographic stickers. It also comprises three fun and easy-to-use cooperative projects and material for two festivals sections. Each unit is divided into eight lessons and provides vocabulary input and practice, a short dialogue to contextualise and practise chunks of language and a double-page story for language input and consolidation. It also contains a humorous tongue twister to practise a long vowel sound, a photographic British culture lesson, an engaging real-world literacy text and a unit review. At the end of each unit there is a Video and 21st Century Skills lesson, and at the back of the book there is practice material for Cambridge English Young Learners exams.

Activity Book

This 120-page write-in book works in tandem with the Pupil's Book to reinforce and practise the unit language and to develop the pupil's literacy, listening and speaking skills. Guided writing activities provide the support the pupils need at the start of the second year of Primary with the level of challenge progressing gradually through the book. Each unit comprises a variety of activities which are devised to engage and challenge the pupils, activate different intelligences, encourage creativity and allow the pupils to use language in a personal and meaningful way. At the end of each unit there is a spelling page. At the back of the Activity Book there is practice material for Cambridge English Young Learners exams and a vocabulary review section.

Pupil's App on Navio

Powered By NAVIO

The Pupil's App on Navio is designed to accompany the course and provide extra practice in class or at home. Pupils can create avatars and then explore Navio's immersive worlds. Pupils complete game-based activities designed to practise and review the language and content learnt in class. As they do so, they earn rewards, points and badges. The App tracks pupils' progress so the teacher can see how they are doing and provide extra support where it is needed. The App also includes all the songs, stories and animations from the course so that pupils can review them at home and share them with their family. The access code for the Pupil's App can be found inside the front cover of the Pupil's Book.

PERFECT PARTNERS WITH

BY ME

Social Science Primary 2 **Natural Science Primary 2**

Arts and Crafts Primary 2

Grammar Goals 2

Give Me Five! 2 Teacher's components

Teacher's Book

This user-friendly, spiral-bound book provides teachers with as much or as little support as they need. The At a Glance Lesson Plans, illustrated with images of the Pupil's Book and Activity Book, clearly highlight the learning aims, key language, materials required, learning routines, key activities and a range of optional extra activities, including Links to Science and cooperative learning activities. These are accompanied by Detailed Lesson Plans which provide complete and concise teaching notes for each activity and answer keys. Full audioscripts can be found at the back of the book. In addition, there is a Reflective Teacher page at the end of each unit for documenting learning, noting ideas and planning actions.

Teacher's App on Navio

The Teacher's App on Navio offers one-stop access to all the many resources which accompany the course. **Tap and Teach Lessons** with **integrated audio and video** ensure that everything you need to teach each lesson is in one place. You can use the **Classroom Management tool** to award points for good behaviour or success in class, and track your pupils' marks and progress using the **Progress Tracker**. You'll find additional resources in the **Teacher's Resource Bank** (see opposite) and **Test Generator**. For Levels 1–2 you'll also have access to additional phonics activities on Magic Phonics.

Class CDs

Four class CDs provide all the recorded material for the Pupil's Book and Activity Book: songs, chants, conversations, listening tasks, stories, games, tongue twisters, culture lessons, literacy texts, review material, 21st Century Skills lessons and Cambridge Young Learner Exams practice material. They also include recordings of the cooperative learning songs and a karaoke version of the Lesson 1 song in each unit.

Flashcards

A set of 110 full-colour flashcards with photographic images of the key vocabulary from Lesson 1 of each unit. Suggestions for using the flashcards are given in the Detailed Lesson Plans and in the Flashcards games bank on page 23.

Teacher's Resource Bank: Course Resources

The Teacher's Resource Bank, located within the Teacher's App on Navio, contains a wealth of resources that complement *Give Me Five!* In addition to providing downloads for all class audio and video, the resource bank contains:

- **Letters to parents:** an introductory letter, followed by a letter to present each unit.
- **Talk flashcards:** a set of 19 cards showing a word and a picture to support the pupils' understanding of key activity instructions.

- **Vocabulary and Grammar Booster worksheets:** to reinforce and extend the vocabulary and grammar syllabus.
- **Evaluation Rubrics:** one grid per unit to evaluate pupils' level of achievement of the Unit Key learning outcomes, as well as their cooperative learning skills.
- **Tests:** a Diagnostic Test, Unit Tests, Term Tests and an End-of-Year Test with audio and Teacher's Notes. Each test has a standard and a higher level version.

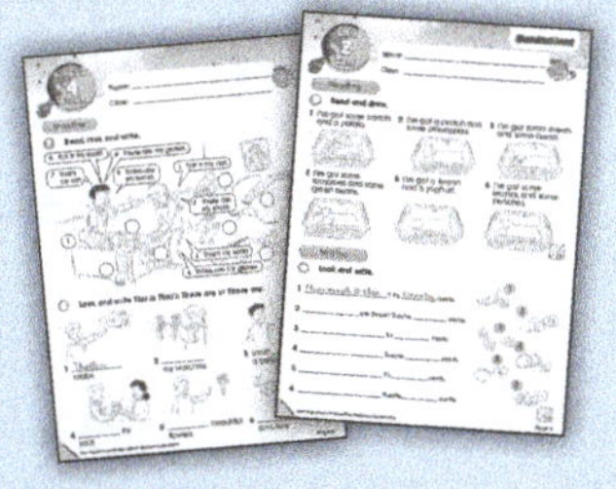

- **Word cards:** a set of 110 word cards, written in handwriting font. Suggestions for using the word cards can be found in the Detailed Lesson Plans and in the Word cards games bank on page 23.

Teacher's Resource Bank: External Exams Resources

This component supports teachers who are preparing their pupils for the ***Trinity Graded Exam in Spoken English*** (Grades 2 and 3) or the ***Cambridge English Young Learners Starters Test***. These resources contain the following:

- **Videos** of children doing speaking practice.
- **Teacher's Notes** on how to exploit these videos in the classroom and tips for teachers.
- **Trinity Exam Practice Worksheets**.
- Extra Cambridge Exam **practice material** and **practice tests**.
- A set of **Trinity Exam Practice cards** for optional Trinity-type speaking practice at the start of each lesson.

Teacher's and Pupil's Apps on Navio

The Navio app which accompanies this course offers one-stop access to the huge range of resources that come with *Give Me Five! 2*. **Tap and Teach Lessons** enable you to move seamlessly between the book and digital components, and you can track your pupils' marks and review their progress using the **Progress Tracker**, and find additional resources in the **Resource Bank** and **Test Generator**.

Accessing the app

To access Navio:

1. Go to www.MacmillanNavio.com/givemefive
2. Follow the onscreen instructions

If you haven't got a Macmillan Education account, you need to create a profile. Then you can enter your access code and download the app for your device (see System Requirements: www.macmillannavio.com/systemrequirements).

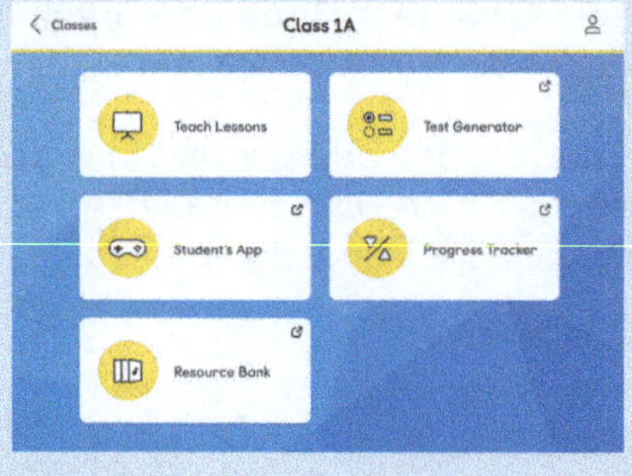

Setting up a class

You, or your school administrator, will need to set up a class and register pupils with their names and the email address of their parents or guardians. Once the class is created, login details can be given to parents. Parents can then log in to the Pupil's App and enter the access code from the inside cover of the Pupil's Book to access the 3D worlds and practise content.

Managing your downloads

Navio makes it easy to manage the storage space on your device, as you can control how much material you download at one time. Navio makes it clear how much storage space your chosen content will need. You can download the complete Teacher's and Pupil's Apps at once, or, if your device has limited storage capacity, you can choose to download only one or two units. And after you finish a unit, you can safely delete the content from your device. You won't lose your pupils' data, as this information is stored online.

Using the Progress Tracker

All the work your pupils complete in the app is recorded in the **Progress Tracker**. You can monitor the progress of a whole class or any individual pupil. Every activity in the App is mapped against the course Learning Outcomes and Skills, so you can easily identify where your pupils need extra support.

Teaching a lesson

Navio makes it easy to plan and teach your lessons with fully interactive **Tap and Teach Lessons** for every lesson in *Give Me Five! 2*. Go to your Class Dashboard and choose Teach Lessons. Find the lesson you want to teach and click to open it. Click on the Toolbar along the bottom of the screen to expand it to Thumbnail view. The Toolbar also contains the Tap and Teach tools you need to teach heads-up, whole-class activities, including a Timer, Pen tool and Mask tool.

Lessons follow the lesson plans in the Teacher's Book, and provide everything you need to teach from your device in one place. They include digital versions of all the activities in the Pupil's Book and Activity Book, with their answer keys. They also include all the audio and video you need for the lesson, as well as some extra tools such as digital Flashcards. All relevant pages from all three books are also provided so that you can project them in class, to help your pupils and to encourage heads-up participation.

When you teach, move through the lesson slide by slide using the arrows, or double click on a thumbnail to jump straight to a particular activity. If you prefer, you can Filter activities to customise the lesson so it includes only the content you want to teach.

Using the Rewards tool

Navio's new **Rewards tool** is a great way to keep your pupils engaged in class. Much more than just a record of attendance, you can also use it to award points for good behaviour or success in activities. You can even organise your class into teams, and you can award points to individuals, groups or the whole class at any time. When pupils earn points, they appear in the Pupil's App next time they log in, so parents can see their performance.

Pupil's App

As a teacher you can also access a version of the Pupil's App from the Class Dashboard. This has all the same content that your pupils can access at home, but your version is set in **Teacher Mode**. This means that all the activities and worlds are already unlocked, and the App does not record any marks to the Progress Tracker.

We recommend using Teacher Mode when pupils share devices to avoid mixing up pupils' grades and progress. However, if pupils have individual devices or are using the app at home, they should always log in with their own username and password. In this way they can earn points and badges, set up and customise their avatar and build a record of their progress in the Progress Tracker.

Flashcards and Word cards games bank

Flashcard games

1 *Class chain*

Organise the class into a large circle. Show the pupil on your right one of the flashcards and ask a question: **Do you (play tennis / like bananas / like tigers)?** *(Yes, I do. / No, I don't.)* Pass the card to the pupil, who then turns to the person on his / her left and repeats the question. The card is passed around the chain, the pupils asking and answering each time, until it returns to you. When the pupils are more confident, pass several cards around the chain at the same time. Praise the class for working so well together.

2 *Definitions game*

Stick the unit flashcards up on the board. Choose one of the items and describe it. The pupils guess the answer. The pupils continue the game with a Talk Partner.

3 *Disappearing words*

Stick five flashcards in a row on the board. Point to the cards one by one and ask the pupils to name the item. Turn over the last card. Ask the pupils to name all the items again, including the item on the card you turned over. Turn over another card and repeat the procedure. Continue until all the cards are face down and the pupils are naming them from memory. Turn the cards face up again and name them one last time. **Optional:** Play again with the other five items in the lexical set.

4 *Memory!*

Stick the flashcards face down on the left-hand side of the board and the corresponding word cards face down on the right-hand side. Choose a volunteer to pick up a card from each side. The pupil names the item, reads the word and decides if it is a match. If it doesn't match, the pupil replaces the cards in the same place. If it matches, he / she removes the two cards and continues playing. Repeat with other volunteers until all the cards are matched.

5 *Quick flash*

Hold the unit flashcards in a pile facing you. Quickly, turn the pack around to face the pupils, then turn it back again. The pupils name the item they see.

6 *Guessing game*

Select a volunteer and ask him / her to step outside the classroom for a moment and secretly show him / her one of the flashcards. When the pupil comes back in, elicit questions to help the class guess the flashcard. For sports, the class asks *Do you play (volleyball / go cycling)?* For place names, the class asks *Where were you?* The pupil answers *I was at (the sports centre).* Repeat with different volunteers each time, changing the flashcard.

7 *Mime game*

Stick the flashcards up on the board. Whisper one of the items to a volunteer. He / She mimes the word(s). The class guess the correct word, using the flashcards on the board for support. The pupils can also play with a Talk Partner, taking turns to mime and guess the words.

8 *Slowly, slowly*

Hold up a flashcard, but cover the picture with a piece of paper so the pupils can't see it. Slowly reveal the flashcard from behind the paper until the pupils see enough of the picture to guess the item.

9 *Which one's missing?*

Stick all the flashcards face up on the board. Ask the pupils to name them as you do so. Say **Close your eyes**. Remove one of the flashcards and hide it behind your back. Say **Open your eyes! Which one's missing?** The pupils guess which one is missing by asking questions, for example, *Is it the (circus)?*

Word card games

1 *Stop!*

Say one of the words from the lexical set that you want to practise, for example **carrots**. Then hold up the food word cards one by one, allowing enough time for the pupils to read each word. The pupils should say *Stop!* when you hold up the corresponding card.

2 *Clever parrots*

Hold up a word card and say a word. The pupils should repeat the word if it is the same as the word on the card. If it isn't the same, the pupils should stay silent. To add an element of fun to the game, encourage the class to do a mime or make a noise (e.g. imitate a squawking parrot) when they repeat the word.

3 *Bit by bit*

Cover a word card with a piece of paper. Then slide the paper to reveal the word's first letter. Ask **Which word is it?** The pupils say the words they know starting with that letter. Continue revealing more letters, one by one, until the pupils guess the word.

4 *Splat!*

Stick the word cards on the board in random order. Invite two pupils to the board and say one of the words. The pupils point to the corresponding word card as quickly as possible. Repeat the procedure with different pupils. To add an element of fun, give each pupil a plastic fly swatter to 'swat' the corresponding card.

5 *Board pelmanism*

Stick a set of flashcards and the corresponding word cards face down on the board in random order. Number all the cards. Then divide the class into two teams. The teams take turns to choose two numbers. The teacher turns over the corresponding cards each time. If the cards match, the teacher removes them from the board and awards the team a point. If the cards do not match, the teacher returns them face down to their original positions. Encourage the class to try to remember where the different cards are located. The team with the most points, when all the cards have been removed, is the winner.

Using the Pupil's Book and Activity Book

Lessons 1 and 2

Eight to ten items of vocabulary are introduced and practised using **photographic flashcards**.

Attractive artwork engages the pupils and helps contextualise language.

A **fun and easy-to-sing song** builds fluency and makes language more memorable.

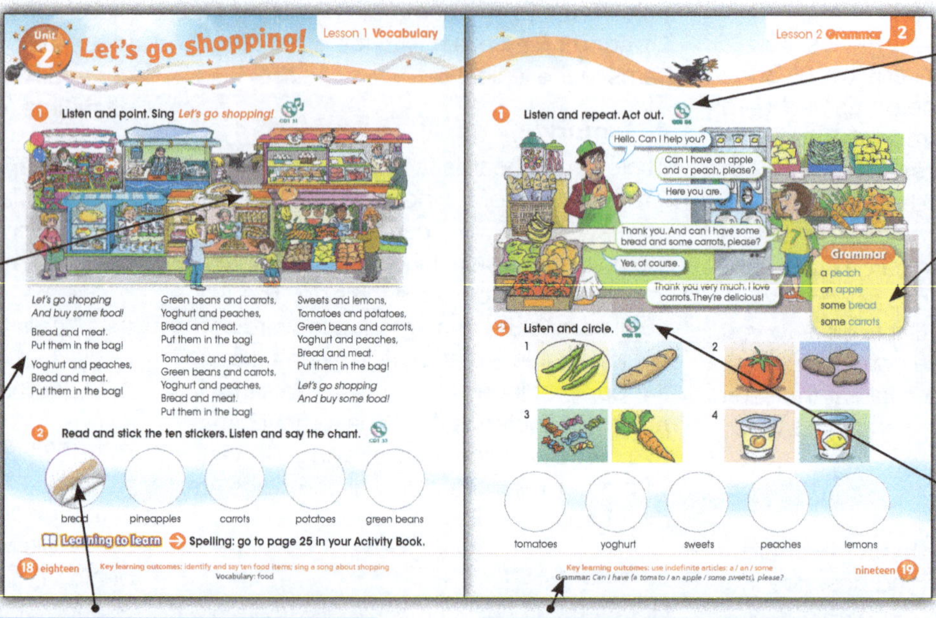

A short conversation places grammar in a fun and familiar context.

Key language is highlighted in the **grammar box**.

A variety of **engaging listening tasks** build the pupils' confidence in understanding the new language. All the audioscripts can be found at the back of the Teacher's Book.

The pupils use **real-world photographic stickers** to create a record of the vocabulary across the bottom of the spread. The pupils then say a **catchy vocabulary chant**.

The key learning outcomes and the key language are given at the bottom of the page.

Activities are devised to engage the pupils and provide practice in reading and writing the new vocabulary items.

Fun, game-like activities motivate the pupils to write.

The pupils **review and recycle** an item of vocabulary at the bottom of each Activity Book page.

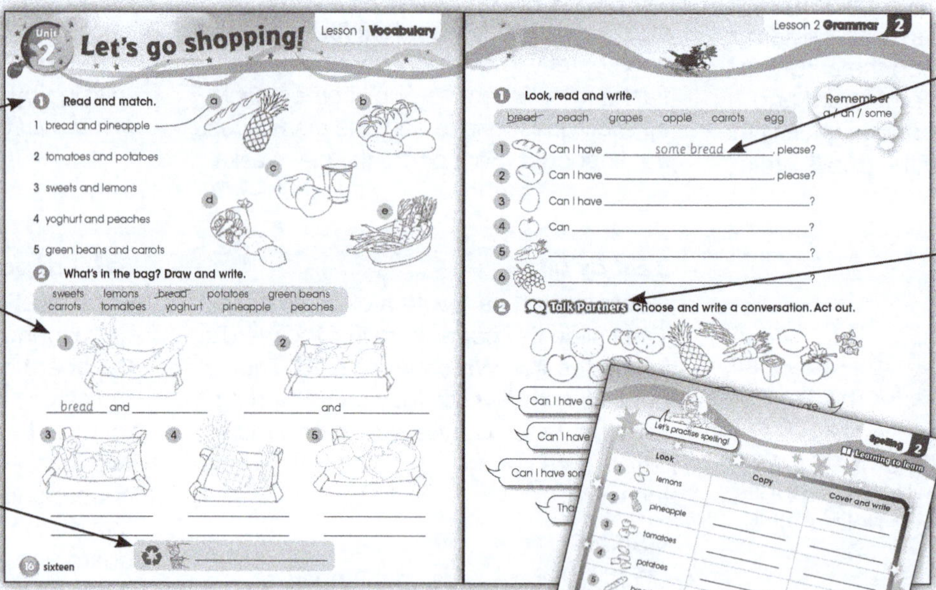

A range of activities give the pupils practice in reading the new grammar.

Talk Partners icon indicates when the pupils have the opportunity to practise speaking in pairs.

The pupils use the **Look-Copy-Cover-Write technique** to learn how to spell. The pupils first copy the word. Then they cover the first two columns and write the word from memory. Finally, they uncover the columns and check their spelling.

Digital resources

Teacher's Digital: Don't forget you can teach these lessons using the Teacher's App on Navio.

Pupil's Digital: Encourage your pupils to use the Pupil's App on Navio to practise the vocabulary from these lessons.

Powered By NAVIO

Lesson 3

A pre-reading task helps prepare the pupils for reading and listening to the story.

In each unit, the pupils enjoy a **magical adventure** with Molly, Jake, Beth, Toby the dog and their magic bike. A list of frame-by-frame comprehension questions for each story are provided in the Detailed Lesson Plan in the Teacher's Book.

Attractive and humorous pictures and an **exciting audio recording** support the pupils' understanding of the narrative.

Pupils watch an **exciting, animated video** to consolidate their understanding of the story.

The story reinforces language introduced in Lessons 1 and 2 and previews language from Lesson 4.

The ***Give Me Five!* Values** section uses photos to encourage the pupils to reflect on the story and relate a personal, social or civic value to their own lives.

A wide range of engaging story activities reinforce and check the pupils' understanding of the story and encourage them to use key language from it.

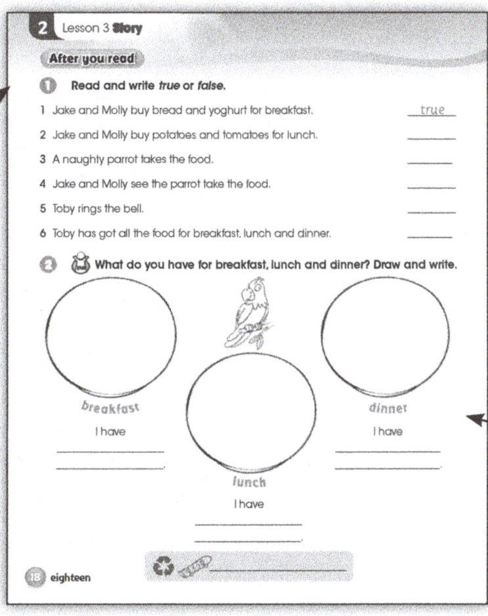
2 Lesson 3 **Story**

After you read

1 **Read and write *true* or *false*.**

1 Jake and Molly buy bread and yoghurt for breakfast. true
2 Jake and Molly buy potatoes and tomatoes for lunch. ______
3 A naughty parrot takes the food. ______
4 Jake and Molly see the parrot take the food. ______
5 Toby rings the bell. ______
6 Toby has got all the food for breakfast, lunch and dinner. ______

2 **What do you have for breakfast, lunch and dinner? Draw and write.**

breakfast — I have ______
lunch — I have ______
dinner — I have ______

18 eighteen

The activities encourage the pupils to respond to the story in a **personal and creative way**.

Digital resources

Teacher's Digital: Don't forget you can teach this lesson using the Teacher's App on Navio.

Pupil's Digital: Encourage your pupils to use the Pupil's App on Navio to practise the vocabulary from these lessons.

Powered By NAVIO

Using the Pupil's Book and Activity Book

Lessons 4 and 5

Four to six new items of vocabulary are introduced and practised (dates in Unit 6), using **photos or colourful illustrations**.

The **Toby's tongue twister** section gives the pupils practice in recognising and producing long vowel sounds. The pupils are encouraged to investigate two different ways of spelling each vowel sound.

A **lively song or chant** gives further practice of the vocabulary and introduces additional grammar.

Simple **games** allow the pupils to practise the new language and encourage them to work independently.

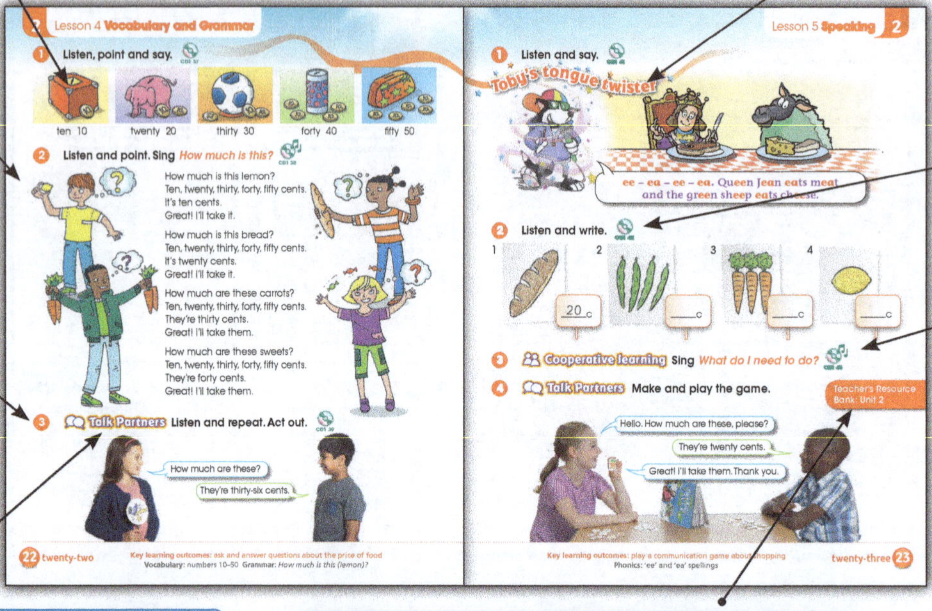

A listening task prepares the pupils for a communicative game. The pupils listen to children playing the game.

Cooperative learning songs are introduced to teach and practise interpersonal skills. In this example, the pupils are reminded to follow instructions.

Talk Partners icons indicate when the pupils have the opportunity to practise speaking in pairs. These activities build confidence, encourage cooperative learning and ensure full participation.

The pupils make one **cut-out** in each unit and play a **communicative game** in pairs. These cut-outs can be found in the Teacher's Resource Bank.

Listening activities have a clear and meaningful purpose. In this activity, the pupils listen and write the numbers.

An enjoyable range of writing activities encourage the pupils to **notice and play with language patterns**.

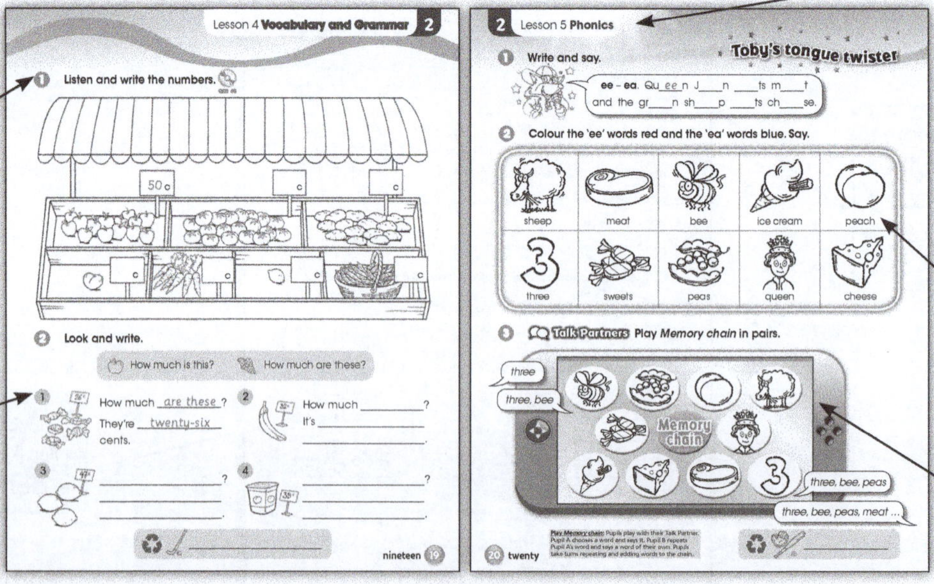

The pupils enjoy a **full page of phonics** activities to practise reading, writing and saying the key grapheme.

The activities use recycled words to build the pupils' confidence and link new information to existing knowledge.

The pupils play simple **phonics games** with their Talk Partner.

Digital resources

Teacher's Digital: Don't forget you can teach these lessons using the Teacher's App on Navio.

Pupil's Digital: Encourage your pupils to use the Pupil's App on Navio to practise the vocabulary from these lessons.

Powered By NAVIO

Lessons 6 and 7

The pupils are introduced to **interesting and age-appropriate cultural content** through two British children, Tom and Anna.

Photos of the Culture Kids doing **real-world cultural activities** really bring the culture to life. This helps foster a positive attitude towards British culture and English language learning.

Think about your culture encourages the pupils to identify similarities and differences between the two cultures and to begin to form their own cultural identity.

The **Before you read activities** help prepare the pupils to read. These include activating the pupils' existing knowledge, exploiting visuals, asking questions to raise interest and making predictions.

The pupils are introduced to a **wide range of text types**. These are selected to reflect the interests and experiences of the age group and have an **authentic appearance** that will appeal to learners.

All texts are supported by an audio recording.

Lesson 6 British culture

1 Listen and read. Answer.

In Britain, there's a special day called Pancake Day. We make pancakes and we have races with them!

We help Mum make the pancakes. We put flour, milk and two eggs in a bowl. Then, we mix it.

Mum cooks the pancakes. She tosses a pancake in the air. Then, she catches it again.

We eat our pancakes. I put chocolate on my pancake. My sister puts sugar and lemon on hers.

At school, we have pancake races. We run and toss the pancake at the same time. It's good fun!

Think about your culture

Do you have a special food day in your country?

24 twenty-four

Lesson 7 Literacy 2

Text type: A recipe

Before you read

1 Look at the picture of the funny face sandwich. What do you think you need to make it?

2 Listen and read the recipe.

Funny face sandwich

This sandwich is easy and fun to make. It's delicious, too!

To make this sandwich you need:
- one slice of bread
- three slices of cheese
- two slices of egg
- three olives
- one piece of carrot
- some salad

Ask an adult to help you.

Instructions

First, put the slices of cheese on the slice of bread.

Then, add the eggs for eyes. Put an olive in the centre of each egg.

Now, add an olive for the nose and a piece of carrot for the mouth.

Finally, add the salad for the hair.

After you read

Go to page 22 in your Activity Book.

twenty-five 25

The pupils are directed to the **After you read activities** in the Activity Book.

Understanding of the cultural content is consolidated through a listening activity.

A question asked by Tom or Anna encourages the pupils to think more about their own culture.

Me icons indicate when the pupils have the opportunity to use language to write about themselves and their lives. These **personalisation tasks** help make language more meaningful and memorable for the pupils.

A range of **After you read activities** reinforce and check the pupils' understanding of the literacy text.

A variety of **enjoyable writing activities** allow the pupils to respond to the text in a personal and creative way.

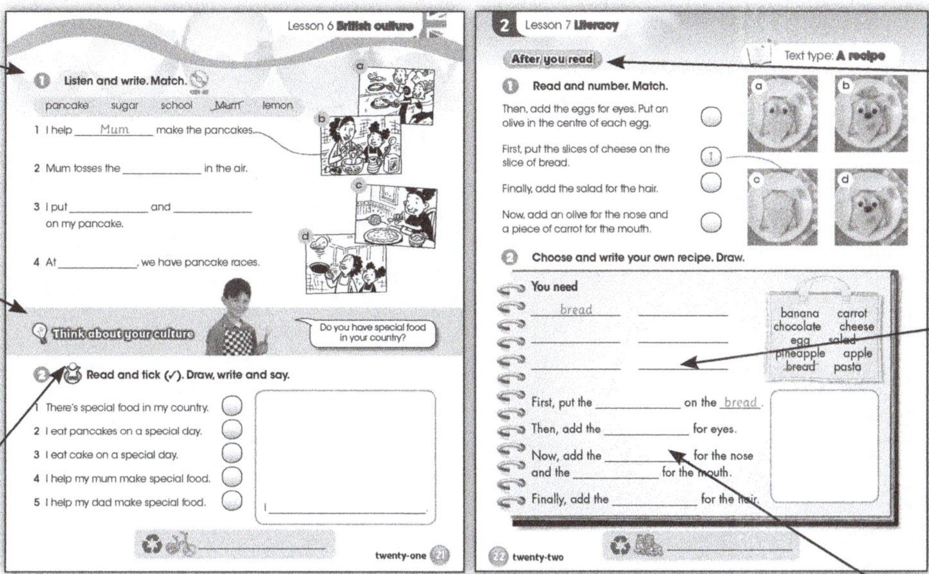

Lesson 6 British culture

1 Listen and write. Match.

pancake sugar school Mum lemon

1 I help Mum make the pancakes.

2 Mum tosses the ________ in the air.

3 I put ________ and ________ on my pancake.

4 At ________, we have pancake races.

Think about your culture

Do you have special food in your country?

2 Read and tick (✓). Draw, write and say.

1 There's special food in my country.

2 I eat pancakes on a special day.

3 I eat cake on a special day.

4 I help my mum make special food.

5 I help my dad make special food.

twenty-one 21

2 Lesson 7 Literacy

After you read

Text type: A recipe

1 Read and number. Match.

Then, add the eggs for eyes. Put an olive in the centre of each egg.

First, put the slices of cheese on the slice of bread.

Finally, add the salad for the hair.

Now, add an olive for the nose and a piece of carrot for the mouth.

2 Choose and write your own recipe. Draw.

You need

bread

banana carrot chocolate cheese egg salad pineapple apple bread pasta

First, put the ________ on the bread.

Then, add the ________ for eyes.

Now, add the ________ for the nose and the ________ for the mouth.

Finally, add the ________ for the hair.

22 twenty-two

The pupils have the opportunity to **create their own text**, similar to the one in the Pupil's Book. This writing is guided to help ensure success.

Digital resources

Teacher's Digital: Don't forget you can teach these lessons using the Teacher's App on Navio.

Pupil's Digital: Encourage your pupils to use the Pupil's App on Navio to practise the vocabulary from Lesson 7.

Powered By NAVIO

Using the Pupil's Book and Activity Book

Lesson 8, Review and 21st Century Skills video lesson

A **full-page review** in both the Pupil's Book and the Activity Book checks and reinforces all of the unit vocabulary and grammar.

Review activities develop **thinking skills** such as logical thinking. In this activity, the pupils identify the food items and write them in the correct column.

Achievement is recognised by singing a ***Well done!*** **cooperative learning song** and sticking the ***Give Me Five!*** **sticker**.

The children introduce the video lesson and spark the pupils' interest in a wide range of topics.

The pupils watch an engaging **video** related to the topic of the unit and 21st Century Skills.

Finding information online is a good way to practise 21st Century Digital Skills. Pupils are set fascinating tasks to promote the skills needed in the modern world.

The Activity Book Review activities help to reinforce reading and writing of the unit vocabulary and grammar.

The pupils use the **traffic light cut-out** in the Teacher's Resource Bank at the end of each Activity Book Review to **reflect and feed back on their learning** in the unit. The teacher reads each statement in turn (from the 'Key' box at the bottom of the page) and the pupils point to the colour / face that best describes how they feel.

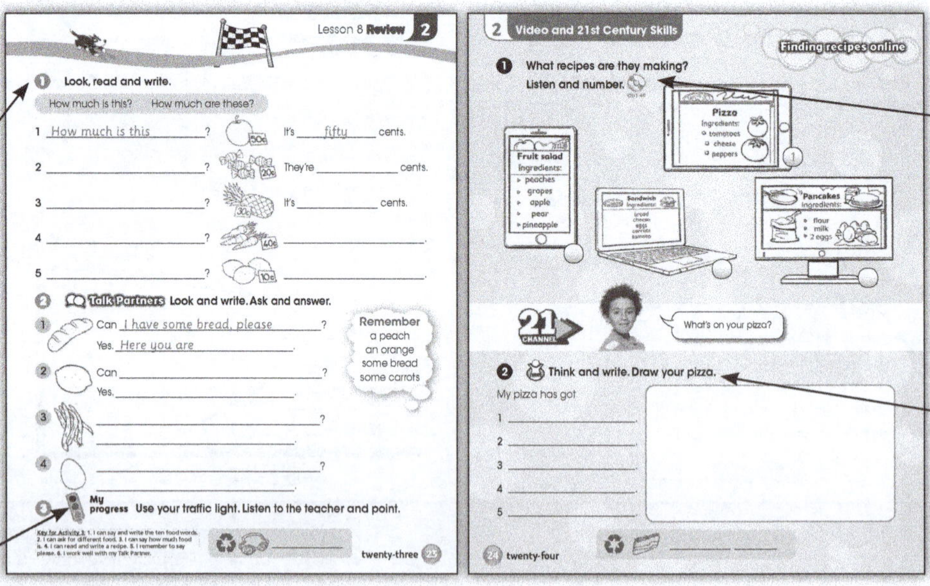

The pupils do a **listening task** to further develop their understanding of the 21st Century Skill.

The pupils do a personalised **21st Century Skills** task.

Digital resources

Teacher's Digital: Don't forget you can teach these lessons using the Teacher's App on Navio.

Pupil's Digital: Encourage your pupils to use the Pupil's App on Navio to practise the vocabulary from these lessons.

Powered By NAVIO

Jsing the projects

Give Me Five! 2 provides three fun and highly doable **projects**. These provide an opportunity for the pupils to **work cooperatively** and develop their speaking skills in a structured way, building autonomy and promoting creativity.

Each project introduces a **new lexical set**, while also **recycling vocabulary** from earlier units. All new vocabulary is recorded on the Class audio.

Listening and speaking activities **introduce the topic** of the project by **recycling** vocabulary and grammar from previous units.

Pupils are encouraged to do further internet research by answering a question.

Enjoyable hands-on activities develop the pupils' fine motor skills and encourage creativity.

Cooperative learning songs develop interpersonal skills and group work skills.

An **attractive final class or group display** creates a sense of achievement and builds confidence.

The project is broken down into stages and pupils follow a step-by-step guide to complete it.

Simple instructions guide pupils in the preparation of their project highlighting the importance of planning and preparing their work.

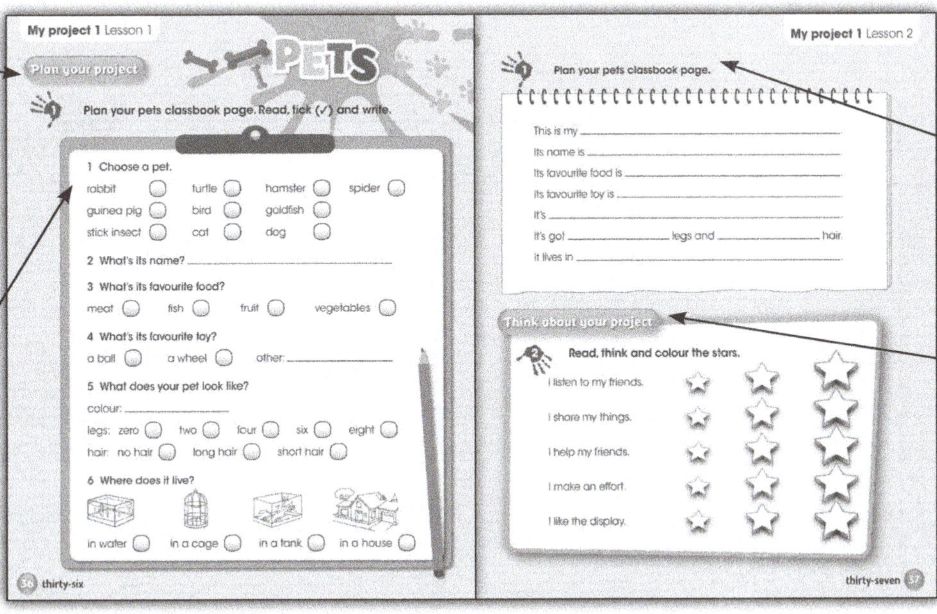

These activities provide a model for the pupils' own writing in the project.

The pupils **reflect on their cooperative skills and their work**.

Digital resources

Teacher's Digital: Don't forget you can teach these lessons using the Teacher's App on Navio.

Pupil's Digital: Encourage your pupils to use the Pupil's App on Navio to practise the vocabulary from these lessons.

Powered By NAVIO

Using the Exams Practice

The Cambridge Exams Practice section at the end of both the Pupil's Book and Activity Book introduces the pupils to the activity types found in the different parts of the three papers of the Cambridge English Young Learners Starter Tests: Listening, Reading and Writing and Speaking.

The Cambridge Exams Practice pages at the back of the Pupil's Book will help the pupils to **develop the necessary** skills to do the Listening and Speaking papers.

The **shield** highlights **the skill** practised in each activity.

An **engaging, achievable listening** activity, requiring a non-linguistic response. Pupils, typically, demonstrate their understanding by **colouring or ticking**.

After listening, the pupils, with their Talk Partners, have the opportunity to **activate the production** of the core vocabulary and grammar.

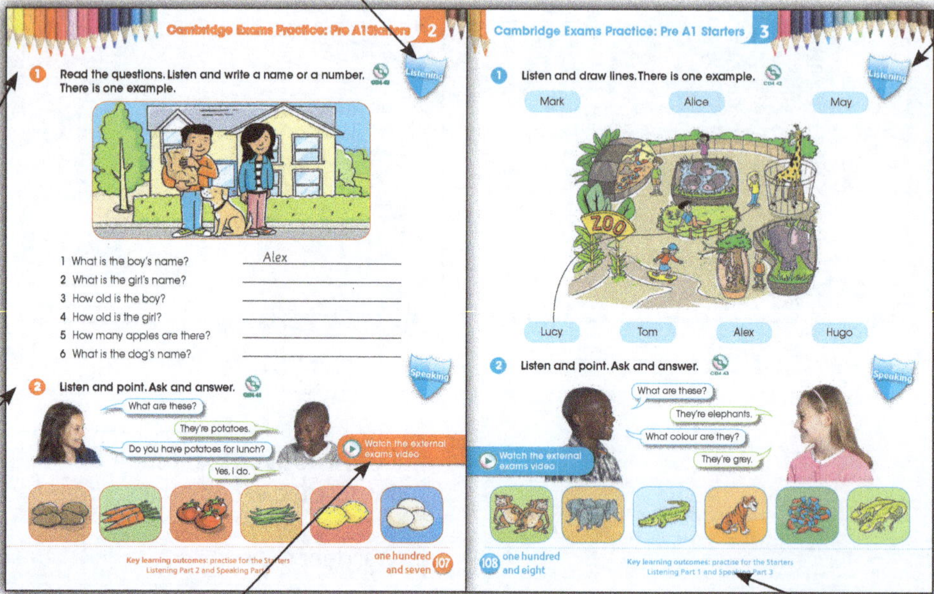

Cambridge Exams Practice: Pre A1 Starters 2

1 Read the questions. Listen and write a name or a number. There is one example.

1 What is the boy's name? Alex
2 What is the girl's name?
3 How old is the boy?
4 How old is the girl?
5 How many apples are there?
6 What is the dog's name?

2 Listen and point. Ask and answer.

What are these?
They're potatoes.
Do you have potatoes for lunch?
Yes, I do.

Watch the external exams video

Key learning outcomes: practice for the Starters Listening Part 2 and Speaking Part

one hundred and seven 107

Cambridge Exams Practice: Pre A1 Starters 3

1 Listen and draw lines. There is one example.

Mark Alice May
Lucy Tom Alex Hugo

2 Listen and point. Ask and answer.

What are these?
They're elephants.
What colour are they?
They're grey.

Watch the external exams video

108 one hundred and eight

Key learning outcomes: practice for the Starters Listening Part 1 and Speaking Part 3

For further practice, watch the **External Exams Video** which you can find in the Teacher's Resource Bank.

The **key learning outcomes** and **parts of the exam** practised are given at the bottom of the page.

The Cambridge Exams Practice pages at the back of the Activity Book will help the pupils to **develop the necessary** skills to do the Reading and Writing papers.

These activities focus on the **vocabulary from the unit. Clear visual cues** provide support and **guide** the pupils' reading and writing.

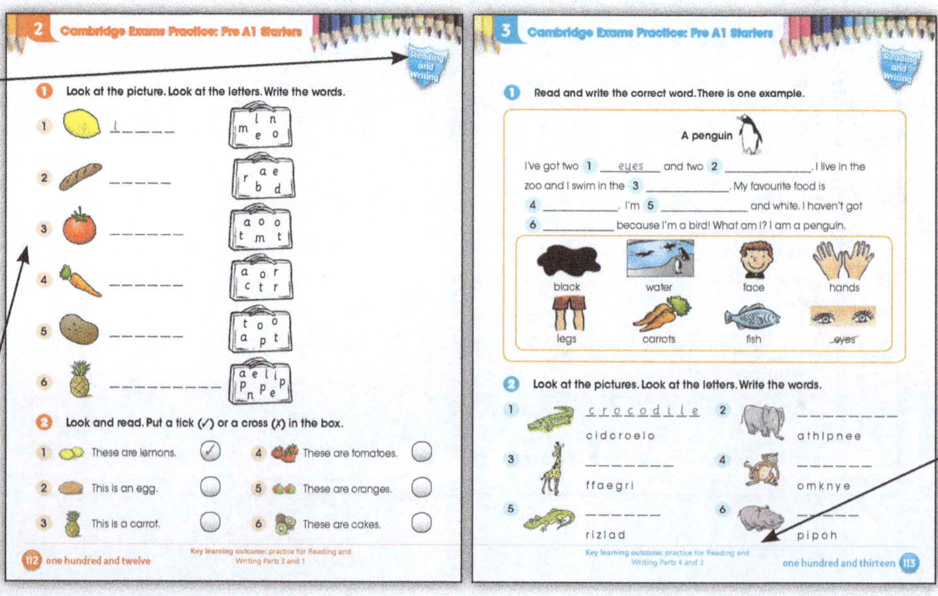

2 Cambridge Exams Practice: Pre A1 Starters

1 Look at the picture. Look at the letters. Write the words.

2 Look and read. Put a tick (✓) or a cross (✗) in the box.

1 These are lemons. ✓
2 This is an egg.
3 This is a carrot.
4 These are tomatoes.
5 These are oranges.
6 These are cakes.

112 one hundred and twelve

Key learning outcome: practice for Reading and Writing Parts 3 and 1

3 Cambridge Exams Practice: Pre A1 Starters

1 Read and write the correct word. There is one example.

A penguin

I've got two 1 eyes and two 2 ______. I live in the zoo and I swim in the 3 ______. My favourite food is 4 ______. I'm 5 ______ and white. I haven't got 6 ______ because I'm a bird! What am I? I am a penguin.

black water face hands legs carrots fish eyes

2 Look at the pictures. Look at the letters. Write the words.

1 crocodile cidcroelo
2 athlpnee
3 ffaegri
4 omknye
5 rizlad
6 pipoh

Key learning outcome: practice for Reading and Writing Parts 4 and 3

one hundred and thirteen 113

The **key learning outcomes** and **parts of the exam** practised are given at the bottom of the page.

Digital resources

Teacher's Digital: Don't forget you can teach these lessons using the Teacher's App on Navio.

Pupil's Digital: Encourage your pupils to use the Pupil's App on Navio to practise the vocabulary from these lessons.

Powered By NAVIO

Exams Practice

Give Me Five! 2 and the external exams

Give Me Five! 1 and *2* provide a wide range of materials to support teachers who are preparing their pupils for the ***Cambridge English Young Learners Starters Test***. Reading, writing and listening activity types found in the ***Cambridge English Young Learners Starters Tests*** are integrated into the material and each book ends with Cambridge Exams Practice lessons in the Pupil's Book and Activity Book. This material is adapted to match the linguistic and cognitive level of the pupils, and language is systematically extended as the course progresses.

There are also the **External Exams Resources** which contain videos of children doing speaking exams, and provide Teacher's Notes on how to exploit these videos in the classroom. The resources, which are part of the Teacher's Resource Bank, also includes additional External Exams material and practice tests, for both the *Cambridge English Young Learners Starters* and the *Trinity Graded Exam in Spoken English* (Elementary Stage, Grades 2 and 3), material focused on developing specific exam related skills and a set of **Trinity Exam Practice cards**.

Trinity Exam Practice cards

The **Trinity Exam Practice cards** are a set of photocopiable cards. They can be used to build the pupils' confidence in asking and answering questions. On each card is a question based on the ***Trinity Graded Exam in Spoken English*** syllabus (Grades 2 and 3). Some cards may also contain other language from *Give Me Five!* These cards should be printed out, laminated if possible and filed by unit. They can then be used during the Starting the lesson stage, which systematically recycles language, transferring it to the pupils' long-term memory. For the Trinity Exam Practice cards routine, the teacher selects several cards from <u>previous</u> units. The teacher should choose a different set of cards for each lesson, and tricky questions and recent topics should be revisited more frequently. The teacher then uses the cards to practise asking and answering questions by doing one of the following suggested activities:

Trinity Exam Practice cards activity bank

1 *Ask and answer in Talk Partners*

Point to the Talk Partners Task flashcard and ask the class to get into their pairs. Then hold up one of the selected Trinity Exam Practice cards and ask the class the question. Invite a pupil to answer and repeat their answer for the class. The pupils then ask and answer the same question with their Talk Partner. Repeat the procedure with other cards.

2 *Question bounce*

Select a Trinity Exam Practice card, read out the question and ask the class to think of an answer. Then point around the room, finally choosing one pupil. This pupil should answer the question. If the pupil answers correctly, he / she should take another card and ask the question to the class. Once again, the class should think of the answer and then the pupil with the card selects another pupil to answer. Repeat the procedure as many times as you wish, ensuring that the questions are 'bounced' to a range of pupils in the class.

3 *Walking questions*

Select six to eight Trinity Exam Practice cards. Drill each question as a class and invite a different pupil to answer each time. Hand out the cards to different pupils. These pupils must move around the class and ask their question to five other pupils. When they have asked five pupils, they should return to their seats. When all the pupils have returned to their seats, hand out the cards to six different pupils and repeat the procedure.

4 *Pass the questions around the circle*

Organise the class so that the pupils are sitting in a circle. Hold up a Trinity Exam Practice card and ask the question to the pupil on your left. Once the pupil has answered, give him / her the card. The pupil then turns to his / her left and asks the next pupil the same question. The card gets passed around the circle. As the pupils become more confident, introduce more cards.

5 *Pass the questions around the circle (variation)*

Organise the class so that the pupils are sitting in a circle. Then drill each question as a class and invite a different pupil to answer each time. Play some music and have the pupils pass several cards around the circle at the same time. Use the pause button to stop the music. When the music stops, the pupils with the cards ask the question they are holding to the pupil on their right. Play the music again and repeat the procedure.

6 *Bag and ball*

For this game you need a bag containing a selection of Trinity Exam Practice cards and a soft ball. Organise the class so that the pupils are sitting in a circle. Then play some music. The pupils pass the bag and ball around the circle separately while the music is playing. When the music stops, the pupil holding the bag takes out and reads a question. The pupil holding the ball should answer the question. Play the music again and repeat the procedure.

7 *Snakes and ladders*

Draw a simple snakes and ladders board on the board and draw a question mark in eight to ten of the squares. Divide the class into two teams and ask each team to throw the dice. The team with the highest number should begin the game. The teams take turns to throw the dice and move along the board. When a team lands on a question mark, read out one of the Trinity Exam Practice cards. The team has to answer correctly to stay on the square. If they don't answer correctly, they move back to their last square. The game continues until a team reaches the 'finish' square.

8 *Card race*

Select two sets of five questions and stick them face down on the board in two 'lanes', with a flag or 'finish' line drawn at the end. Divide the class into two teams. Invite a pupil from Team A to come to the board, turn over the first card and read the question to his / her team. If Team A answers the question correctly, the card remains face up. If the team answers incorrectly, the card is turned face down again and must be repeated on the next turn. Then invite a pupil from Team B to come up and do the same. The team that turns over all the cards first, reaching the 'finish' flag or line, is the winner.

Using the Teacher's Book

The Teacher's Notes have a clear, user-friendly design, offering both an **At a Glance Lesson Plan** and a **Detailed Lesson Plan**. These mirror each other, enabling teachers to move between the two lesson plans with ease.

This box clearly shows the learning objectives, key active language and materials required for the lesson. The lesson objectives are mapped to the **Key Competences and Key Learning Outcomes**.

The **At a Glance Lesson Plan** provides a brief overview of all the activities in the lesson, including **Starting** and **Ending the lesson activities**, and **Extra activities**. Class audio references are also provided.

Fast Forward icons indicate the **fast route** through the lesson for teachers who have shorter lessons or fewer hours of English.

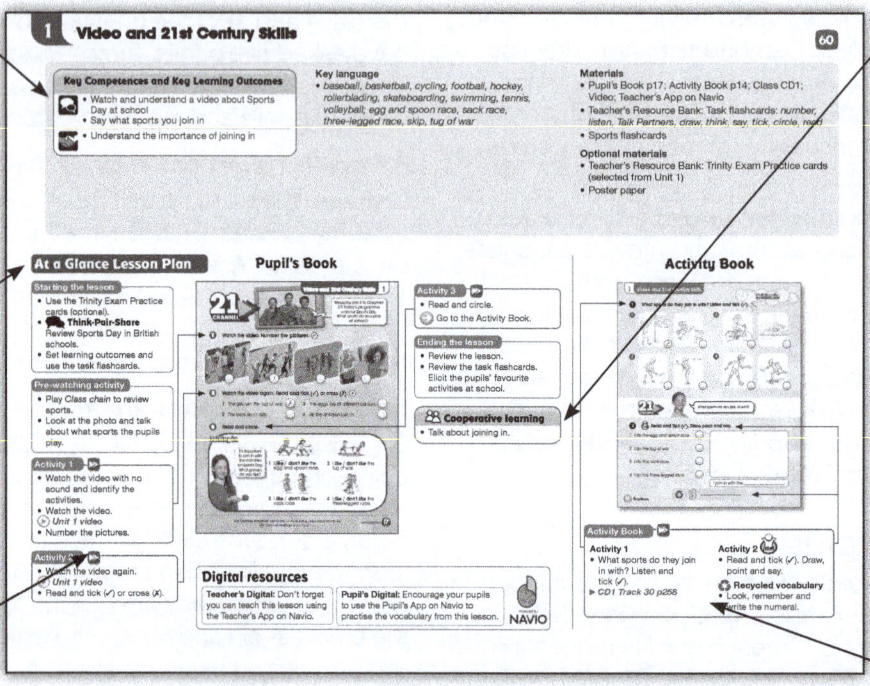

1 Video and 21st Century Skills

60

Key Competences and Key Learning Outcomes

- Watch and understand a video about Sports Day at school
- Say what sports you join in
- Understand the importance of joining in

Key language

- *baseball, basketball, cycling, football, hockey, rollerblading, skateboarding, swimming, tennis, volleyball; egg and spoon race, sack race, three-legged race, skip, tug of war*

Materials

- Pupil's Book p17; Activity Book p14; Class CD1; Video; Teacher's App on Navio
- Teacher's Resource Bank: Task flashcards: *number, listen, Talk Partners, draw, think, say, tick, circle, read*
- Sports flashcards

Optional materials

- Teacher's Resource Bank: Trinity Exam Practice cards (selected from Unit 1)
- Poster paper

At a Glance Lesson Plan

Pupil's Book

Starting the lesson
- Use the Trinity Exam Practice cards (optional).
- **Think-Pair-Share** Review Sports Day in British schools.
- Set learning outcomes and use the task flashcards.

Pre-watching activity
- Play *Class chain* to review sports.
- Look at the photo and talk about what sports the pupils play.

Activity 1
- Watch the video with no sound and identify the activities.
- Watch the video. *Unit 1 video*
- Number the pictures.

Activity 2
- Watch the video again. *Unit 1 video*
- Read and tick (✓) or cross (✗).

Activity 3
- Read and circle.
- Go to the Activity Book.

Ending the lesson
- Review the lesson.
- Review the task flashcards. Elicit the pupils' favourite activities at school.

Cooperative learning
- Talk about joining in.

Digital resources

Teacher's Digital: Don't forget you can teach this lesson using the Teacher's App on Navio.

Pupil's Digital: Encourage your pupils to use the Pupil's App on Navio to practise the vocabulary from this lesson.

NAVIO

Activity Book

Activity Book

Activity 1
- What sports do they join in with? Listen and tick (✓).
- *CD1 Track 30 p258*

Activity 2
- Read and tick (✓). Draw, point and say.

Recycled vocabulary
- Look, remember and write the numeral.

Each unit includes a number of enjoyable **Cooperative learning activities**, which require no or minimal preparation.

Optional **Link to Science** activities in each unit review and reinforce learning from the Science curriculum.

There is also a brief overview of the Activity Book activities.

The **Detailed Lesson Plan** provides more detailed **step-by-step instructions** for each activity.

The activities for **Starting the lesson** include optional use of the **Trinity Exam Practice cards** (see page 31) and the **Task flashcards** (see page 21) to give the pupils a clear idea of what they are going to do in the lesson.

Activity Book teaching notes always appear in a shaded box so they can be easily identified.

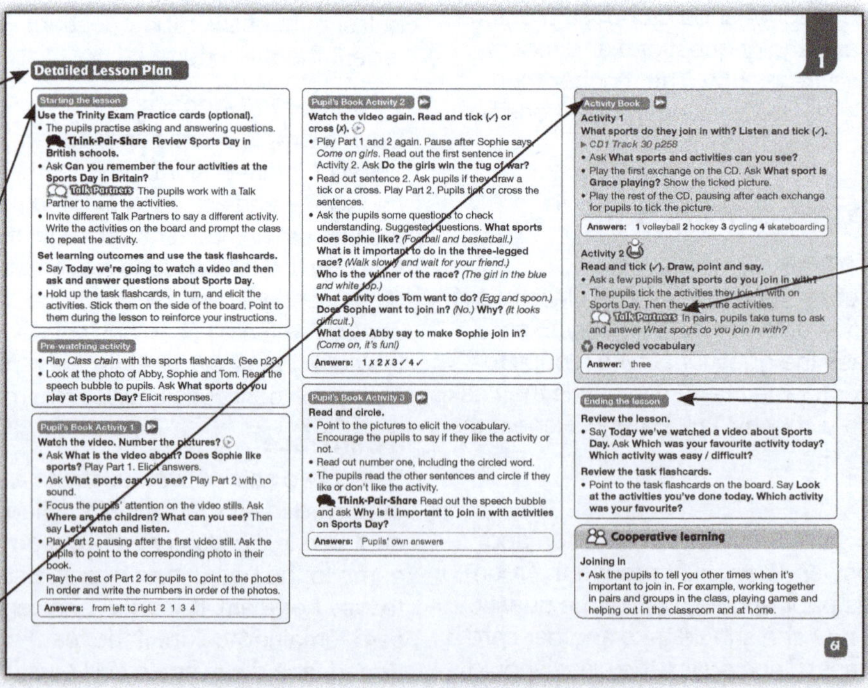

1

Detailed Lesson Plan

Starting the lesson

Use the Trinity Exam Practice cards (optional).
- The pupils practise asking and answering questions.
  Think-Pair-Share Review Sports Day in British schools.
- Ask **Can you remember the four activities at the Sports Day in Britain?**
  Talk Partners The pupils work with a Talk Partner to name the activities.
- Invite different Talk Partners to say a different activity. Write the activities on the board and prompt the class to repeat the activity.

Set learning outcomes and use the task flashcards.
- Say **Today we're going to watch a video and then ask and answer questions about Sports Day**.
- Hold up the task flashcards, in turn, and elicit the activities. Stick them on the side of the board. Point to them during the lesson to reinforce your instructions.

Pre-watching activity
- Play *Class chain* with the sports flashcards. (See p23.)
- Look at the photo of Abby, Sophie and Tom. Read the speech bubble to pupils. Ask **What sports do you play at Sports Day?** Elicit responses.

Pupil's Book Activity 1

Watch the video. Number the pictures?
- Ask **What is the video about? Does Sophie like sports?** Play Part 1. Elicit answers.
- Ask **What sports can you see?** Play Part 2 with no sound.
- Focus the pupils' attention on the video stills. Ask **Where are the children? What can you see?** Then say **Let's watch and listen.**
- Play Part 2 pausing after the first video still. Ask the pupils to point to the corresponding photo in their book.
- Play the rest of Part 2 for pupils to point to the photos in order and write the numbers in order of the photos.

Answers: from left to right 2 1 3 4

Pupil's Book Activity 2

Watch the video again. Read and tick (✓) or cross (✗).
- Play Part 1 and 2 again. Pause after Sophie says *Come on girls*. Read out the first sentence in Activity 2. Ask **Do the girls win the tug of war?**
- Read out sentence 2. Ask pupils if they draw a tick or a cross. Play Part 2. Pupils tick or cross the sentences.
- Ask the pupils some questions to check understanding. Suggested questions. **What sports does Sophie like?** *(Football and basketball.)*
  What is it important to do in the three-legged race? *(Walk slowly and wait for your friend.)*
  Who is the winner of the race? *(The girl in the blue and white top.)*
  What activity does Tom want to do? *(Egg and spoon.)*
  Does Sophie want to join in? *(No.)* **Why?** *(It looks difficult.)*
  What does Abby say to make Sophie join in? *(Come on, it's fun!)*

Answers: 1 ✗ 2 ✗ 3 ✓ 4 ✓

Pupil's Book Activity 3

Read and circle.
- Point to the pictures to elicit the vocabulary. Encourage the pupils to say if they like the activity or not.
- Read out number one, including the circled word.
- The pupils read the other sentences and circle if they like or don't like the activity.
  Think-Pair-Share Read out the speech bubble and ask **Why is it important to join in with activities on Sports Day?**

Answers: Pupils' own answers

Activity Book

Activity 1

What sports do they join in with? Listen and tick (✓).
CD1 Track 30 p258
- Ask **What sports and activities can you see?**
- Play the first exchange on the CD. Ask **What sport is Grace playing?** Show the ticked picture.
- Play the rest of the CD, pausing after each exchange for pupils to tick the picture.

Answers: 1 volleyball 2 hockey 3 cycling 4 skateboarding

Activity 2

Read and tick (✓). Draw, point and say.
- Ask a few pupils **What sports do you join in with?**
- The pupils tick the activities they join in with on Sports Day. Then they draw the activities.
  Talk Partners In pairs, pupils take turns to ask and answer *What sports do you join in with?*

Recycled vocabulary

Answer: three

Ending the lesson

Review the lesson.
- Say **Today we've watched a video about Sports Day.** Ask **Which was your favourite activity today? Which activity was easy / difficult?**

Review the task flashcards.
- Point to the task flashcards on the board. Say **Look at the activities you've done today. Which activity was your favourite?**

Cooperative learning

Joining in
- Ask the pupils to tell you other times when it's important to join in. For example, working together in pairs and groups in the class, playing games and helping out in the classroom and at home.

61

Talk Partner activities are clearly signposted.

The activities for **Ending the lesson** include reviewing the lesson objectives using the **Task flashcards**.

Each lesson includes optional **Extra activities** to reinforce and extend learning.

Let's go back to school!

Unit overview

Key Competences and Key Learning Outcomes

- Identify and say eight school subjects (Lesson 2)
- Ask and answer about school subjects (Lesson 2)
- Read, listen and understand a story about the magic bike (Lesson 4)

- Ask and answer about the weather (Lesson 4)

- Use the Pupil's App on Navio

- Identify and say vocabulary from Level 1 (Lesson 1)
- Say the alphabet in English (Lesson 3)
- Spell out words (Lesson 3)
- Make a cut-out and review your learning (Lesson 4)

- Ask and answer questions about your name and your friends' names (Lesson 1)

- Work with a Talk Partner to practise and reinforce learning (all lessons)

- Sing two songs (Lessons 1 and 3)
- Read, listen and understand a story (Lesson 4)

Vocabulary

Core vocabulary
Arts and Crafts, English, ICT, Maths, Music, PE, Science, Spanish; cloudy, raining, snowy, stormy, sunny, windy; the alphabet

Extension vocabulary (optional)
cold, cool, hot, warm

Recycled vocabulary
Level 1: classroom objects; clothes; family members; farm animals; food; instructions; numbers 1–20; places in town; shapes; toys; transport

Structures

Core structures
What's your favourite subject?
My favourite subject is (English).
How do you spell …?

Other structures
We've got … We're ready to …
We (read / listen / write / sing / speak English).
What colour (is / are) …

Recycled structures
What's your / his / her name? My / His / Her name is (Jake / Molly).
What colour is the …? What can you see?
I can see …
What's the weather like? It's very (sunny) today.
Is it (raining)?
Yes, it is.

Cooperative learning

Skills: Listening to one another (Lesson 1); Friends as a resource (Lesson 2); Working together (Lesson 3)

Key Competences and Key Learning Outcomes

- Identify and say vocabulary from Level 1
- Listen and act out a conversation

- Say your name
- Ask and answer about your name and your friends' names

- Sing a song

Key language

Recycled: *animals, toys, classroom objects, places, clothes, food, shapes*

- *What colour is / are the … I can see … What's your / his / her name? My / His / Her name is …*

Materials

- Pupil's Book p4; Activity Book p2; Class CD1; Teacher's App on Navio
- Character flashcards
- Teacher's Resource Bank: Task flashcards: *find, say, Talk Partners, listen, sing, read, write, act out, circle*

At a Glance Lesson Plan

Pupil's Book

Starting the lesson

- Greet the class and introduce yourself.
- Set learning outcomes using the task flashcards.

Cooperative learning

Listening to your classmates

- Play *The name chain* game.

Activity 1

- Find and say.

Activity 2

- Talk Partners
  Find and say the numbers.

Activity 3

- Listen and point.
- Sing *We've got our school bags.*

▶ *CD1 Track 1 p256*

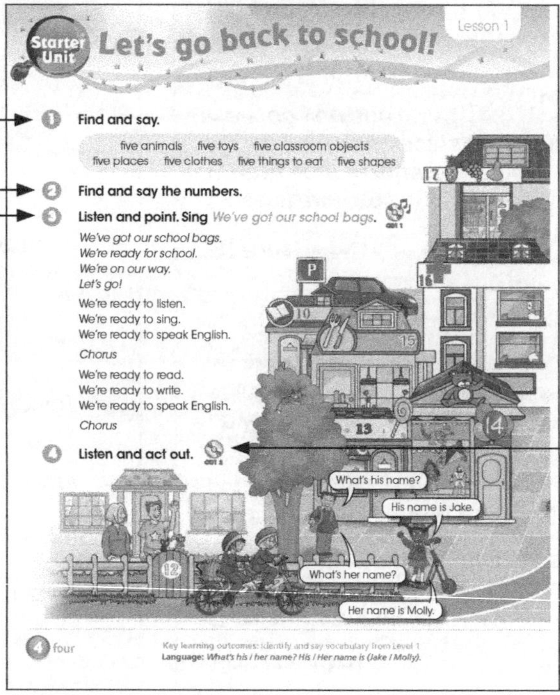

Activity 4

- Talk Partners
  Listen and act out.

▶ *CD1 Track 3 p256*

Go to the Activity Book.

Ending the lesson

- Review the lesson.
- Review the task flashcards.

Extra activity

Reinforcement

- Review shapes.

Activity Book

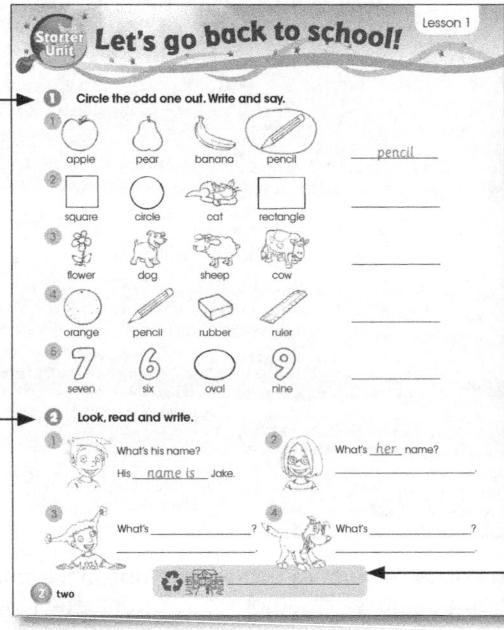

Activity Book

Activity 1

- Circle the odd one out.
- Write and say.

Activity 2

- Look, read and write.

Recycled vocabulary

- Look, remember and write the word.

Digital resources

Teacher's Digital: Don't forget you can teach this lesson using the Teacher's App on Navio.

Pupil's Digital: Encourage your pupils to use the Pupil's App on Navio to practise the vocabulary from this lesson.

Powered By NAVIO

Starting the lesson

Greet the class and introduce yourself.

- Say **My name's (your name).** Ask **What's your name?** Elicit a response from individuals.

Set learning outcomes using the task flashcards.

- Stick the task flashcards for the lesson on one side of the board. Point to them and say the task during the lesson to reinforce your instructions.

Cooperative learning

Listening to your classmates

- Play *The name chain* to learn each others' names. Sit in a circle. Ask the pupil on your left **What's your name?** The pupil answers and asks the next pupil the same question. Continue around the circle.

Pupil's Book Activity 1

Find and say.

- (Books open.) Ask **Who can you see?** *(Jake, Molly, Beth and Toby.)* Ask **Can you see Mum and Dad? Where are they?** *(In front of the house.)* Ask **What can you see?** Elicit the names of items from Level 1: *I can see (a cat / a car / a hospital),* etc.
- Ask about the different lexical sets in turn. **Can you find five animals? Can you name any more animals?** The pupils point to and name the animals in the scene. Elicit the names of other animals from Level 1. Review the other lexical sets in the same way.
- Review colours. Ask **What colour is the bike? What colour are the flowers?**, etc.
- Review shapes. Ask **Can you see a (triangle)?** Elicit the different shapes in the picture: circles, rectangles, squares, triangles, stars and ovals.

Pupil's Book Activity 2

Find and say the numbers.

- Explain to the class that the numbers 1–20 are hidden in the picture. Challenge the pupils to find them. Ask **Can you find the numbers?**
- Talk Partners The pupils take turns to find, point to and say the hidden numbers with a Talk Partner.

Answers: **1** girl's school bag **2** maths poster **3** maths poster **4** maths poster **5** maths poster **6** maths poster **7** farm gate **8** maths poster **9** whiteboard in classroom **10** on bookshop **11** T-shirt **12** front gate **13** sweet shop **14** toyshop **15** restaurant **16** hospital **17** fruit shop **18** school gate **19** whiteboard in classroom **20** bus

Pupil's Book Activity 3

Listen and point. Sing *We've got our school bags.*

▸ *CD1 Track 1 p256*

- Introduce the task flashcards. Hold up the 'listen' card and say **Now we're going to listen to a song.** Ask the pupils to predict the task flashcards that will be in the song. Stick those they suggest on the board.
- Say **Let's listen to the song**. Play the CD. The pupils listen and point to the cards they guessed correctly. Remove any that were not in the song. Reposition the cards in order *(listen, sing, read, write).*
- Point to the 'sing' task flashcard and say **Now we're going to sing *We've got our school bags.***
- Play the CD. The pupils sing and do the actions.

Pupil's Book Activity 4

Listen and act out.

▸ *CD1 Track 3 p256*

- Show the flashcard of Jake / Toby and ask **What's his name?** Show the flashcard of Molly / Beth and ask **What's her name?** Use scaffolding to help the pupils to say *His name is* (*Jake / Toby*). *Her name is* (*Molly / Beth*).
- (Books open.) Say **Let's listen.** Play the CD. The pupils listen and follow the conversation.
- Play the CD again, pausing for the pupils to repeat.
- Talk Partners The pupils ask about the names of different members of the class with a Talk Partner. They take turns to point and ask *What's his / her name?* Remind them that we use 'his' for boys and 'her' for girls.

Activity Book

Activity 1

Circle the odd one out. Write and say.

- (Books open.) Elicit the four items in the first group. Ask **Which is the odd one out?** Elicit *pencil*. Confirm that 'pencil' is the odd one out because it isn't a fruit. Repeat for the remaining groups. Pupils circle the odd one out each time and write the word on the line.

Answers: **1** pencil **2** cat **3** flower **4** orange **5** oval

Activity 2

Look, read and write.

- (Books open.) Encourage a confident child to read the example question and answer. Remind the pupils that we use 'his' for boys and 'her' for girls. The pupils complete the questions and answers individually.

Answers: **1** name is **2** her**,** Her name is Molly. **3** her name, Her name is Beth. **4** his name, His name is Toby.

Recycled vocabulary

- The pupils look at the picture, remember and write the word.

Answer: school

Ending the lesson

Review the lesson.

- Say **Today we've asked and answered about our friends' names.** Elicit the questions and answers from the pupils and praise them for their effort. Reinforce the use of 'his' for boys and 'her' for girls.

Review the task flashcards.

- Point to the task flashcards on the board. Say **Look at the activities you've done today. Which was your favourite?**

Extra activity

Reinforcement

- Ask pupils to review, find and point to different shapes in the classroom, for example, circle (CD), etc. Alternatively, ask **What shape is the (CD)?** for them to answer.

Key Competences and Key Learning Outcomes

- Identify and say eight school subjects
- Say a vocabulary chant
- Ask and answer questions about school subjects

Key language

- *Arts and Crafts, English, ICT, Maths, Music, PE, Science, Spanish*
- *What's your favourite subject? My favourite subject is (English). What's yours?*

Materials

- Pupil's Book p5; Activity Book p3; Class CD1; Teacher's App on Navio
- School subjects flashcards
- Teacher's Resource Bank: Task flashcards: *listen, say, act out, follow, colour, write, Talk Partners*

At a Glance Lesson Plan

Pupil's Book

Starting the lesson

- Review the *We've got our school bags* song.

▶ ***CD1 Track 1 p256***

- Set learning outcomes using the task flashcards.

Activity 1

- Listen and point.
- Say *The school subjects* chant.

▶ ***CD1 Track 4 p256***

Activity 2

- Listen and repeat.
- Talk Partners Act out.

▶ ***CD1 Track 5 p256***

Activity 3

- Listen and point.

▶ ***CD1 Track 6 p256***

Go to the Activity Book.

Ending the lesson

- Review the lesson.
- Review the task flashcards.

Extra activity

Reinforcement

- Make a *What's your favourite subject?* living graph.

Cooperative learning

Friends as a resource

- Talk Partners Ask and answer *What's this?*

Activity Book

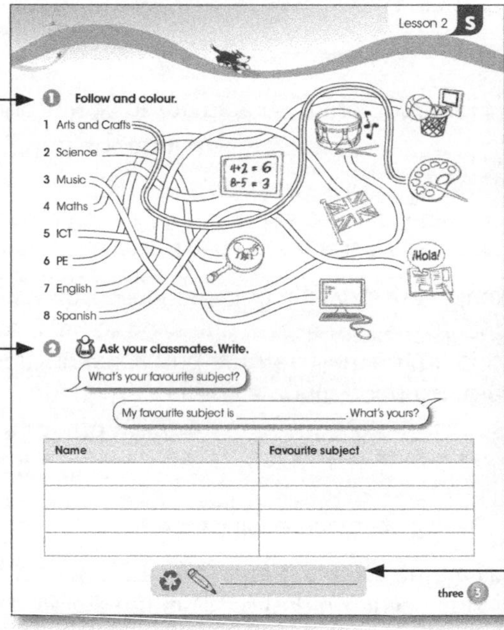

Activity Book

Activity 1

- Follow and colour.

Activity 2

- Ask your classmates. Write.

Recycled vocabulary

- Look, remember and write the word.

Digital resources

Teacher's Digital: Don't forget you can teach this lesson using the Teacher's App on Navio.

Pupil's Digital: Encourage your pupils to use the Pupil's App on Navio to practise the vocabulary from this lesson.

Powered By NAVIO

Starting the lesson

Review the *We've got our school bags* song.

▶ *CD1 Track 1 p256*

▶ *CD1 Track 2 p256 (optional karaoke version)*

- Give out the task flashcards from the song (*listen, sing, read, write*) to different groups of pupils.
- Play the CD (or use the karaoke version). The groups hold up their flashcard when they hear it in the song.

Set learning outcomes using the task flashcards.

- Explain the aims of the lesson. Say **Today we're going to learn about school subjects.**
- Stick the task flashcards for the lesson on one side of the board. Point to them and say the action during the lesson to reinforce your instructions.

Pupil's Book Activity 1

Listen and point. Say *The school subjects* chant.

▶ *CD1 Track 4 p256*

- Ask the pupils to name the subjects they study at school. Say the English word for any they say in their mother tongue and hold up the corresponding flashcard as you do so. Stick the flashcard on the board, naming it again. The pupils repeat the school subject after you. Repeat with the remaining school subjects. Point out that PE stands for Physical Education and we usually say PE; and that ICT stands for Information and Communication Technology (or computer studies). Pupils use the computer in these lessons.
- (Books open.) Focus the class on the school in the picture. Play the CD. The pupils listen to the chant and point to the corresponding school subject posters inside the school.
- Play the CD again. The pupils listen and say the chant.

Pupil's Book Activity 2

Listen and repeat. Act out.

▶ *CD1 Track 5 p256*

- Say **Can you see the pupils in the playground? Let's listen.**
- Play the CD. The pupils listen and follow the conversation.
- Play the CD again, pausing after each sentence for the pupils to repeat.
- Talk Partners When the pupils are confident with the language, ask them to practise the conversation with a Talk Partner.

Pupil's Book Activity 3

Listen and point.

▶ *CD1 Track 6 p256*

- Spread the school subject flashcards around the classroom. Tell the pupils that they are going to try and guess the subject by listening to the sounds in the different classrooms.
- Play the CD. The pupils point to and name the school subject as they hear it. If necessary, pause the CD after the sound effects to give the pupils time to think.

Answers: **1** Music **2** English **3** Maths **4** PE

Activity Book

Activity 1

Follow and colour.

- (Books open.) Read the first school subject collectively *(Arts and Crafts).* Ask the pupils to follow the maze with their finger to reach the corresponding picture. Repeat for the remaining school subjects. The pupils colour the path from the subject to the picture using a different colour for each subject.

Answers: **1** paint palette **2** magnifying glass **3** drum **4** sums **5** computer **6** basketball hoop **7** Union Jack **8** ¡Hola!

Activity 2 (me)

Ask your classmates. Write.

- Read the question. Encourage a confident pupil to answer with his / her favourite subject. Ask the class to complete the answer speech bubble with their own favourite subject. The pupils should then survey their classmates to find out their favourite subjects, completing the chart with names and subjects.
- If you have a confident class, encourage them to use the information gathered to introduce one of their friends. Encourage them to say *This is my friend. (Her) name's (Maria). (Her) favourite subject is (Music)*, etc.

Recycled vocabulary

- The pupils look at the picture, remember and write the vocabulary word.

Answer: a pencil

Ending the lesson

Review the lesson.

- Say **Today we've talked about our favourite subjects at school. Can you remember the question?** Elicit the question and possible answers from the pupils.

Review the task flashcards.

- Point to the task flashcards on the board. Say **Look at the activities you've done today. Which activity was your favourite?** Elicit the pupils' favourite activities.

Extra activity

Reinforcement

- Make a *What's your favourite subject?* living graph. Stick the eight school subject flashcards in a line along the board. Ask the class **What's your favourite subject?** As the pupils raise their hands and answer in turn, ask them to come out and line up in front of the corresponding flashcard. Count the pupils and see which subject is the most popular in the class.

Cooperative learning

Friends as a resource

- Help pupils to understand that they can ask each other for help in the classroom as well as asking the teacher.
- Talk Partners The pupils point to different objects in the classroom and ask and answer the question *What's this?* with a Talk Partner.

Key Competences and Key Learning Outcomes

- Say the alphabet
- Ask and answer how to spell words
- Sing an alphabet song

Key language
- *the alphabet*
- *How do you spell (English)?*

Materials
- Pupil's Book p6, Activity Book p4, Class CD1; Teacher's App on Navio
- School subjects flashcards
- Teacher's Resource Bank: Task flashcards: *listen, say, read, Talk Partners, colour, write*

Optional materials
- The letters of the alphabet out of coloured paper or card

At a Glance Lesson Plan

Pupil's Book

Starting the lesson
- Review school subjects.
- Set learning outcomes using the task flashcards.

Activity 1
- Listen and point. Say the alphabet.
- ▶ *CD1 Track 7 p256*

Activity 2
- Listen and sing *The alphabet.*
- ▶ *CD1 Track 8 p256*

Activity 3
- Listen and read.
- Talk Partners Ask and answer.
- ▶ *CD1 Track 9 p256*

Go to the Activity Book.

Ending the lesson
- Review the lesson.
- Review the task flashcards.

Extra activities

Reinforcement
- Review *The alphabet* song.

Extension
- Talk Partners Play *The spelling game.*

Cooperative learning

Working together
- Talk Partners Practise the alphabet and spelling.
- Talk Partners Play *Back writing.*

Activity Book

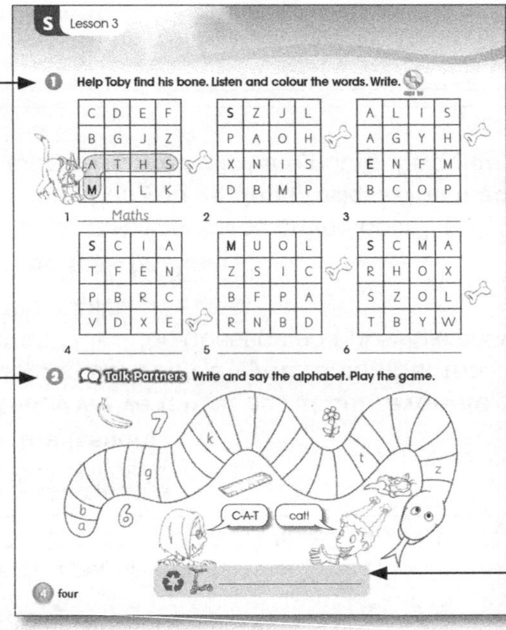

Activity Book

Activity 1
- Help Toby find his bone. Listen and colour the words.
- Write.
- ▶ *CD1 Track 10 p256*

Activity 2
- Write and say the alphabet.
- Talk Partners Play the game.

Recycled vocabulary
- Look, remember and write the word.

Digital resources

Teacher's Digital: Don't forget you can teach this lesson using the Teacher's App on Navio.

Pupil's Digital: Encourage your pupils to use the Pupil's App on Navio to practise the vocabulary from this lesson.

Powered By NAVIO

Starting the lesson

Review school subjects.

- Review school subjects by playing *Slowly, slowly* (see p23) with the unit flashcards.

Set learning outcomes using the task flashcards.

- Say **Today we're going to learn to say the alphabet and spell in English.**
- Hold up the task flashcards in turn and elicit the words. Stick them on one side of the board. Point to them during the lesson to reinforce your instructions.

Pupil's Book Activity 1

Listen and point. Say the alphabet.

▶ *CD1 Track 7 p256*

- (Books open.) Say **Let's learn the alphabet in English.** Point to each letter of the alphabet in the picture in turn, naming it as you do so. The pupils repeat after you.
- Say **Let's listen and repeat the letters.** Play the CD. The pupils repeat and point to each letter.
- Play the CD again and repeat the activity.

Pupil's Book Activity 2

Listen and sing *The alphabet.*

▶ *CD1 Track 8 p256*

- Play the CD. The pupils listen and point to the letters.
- Play the CD again. The pupils join in and point to the letters.
- Divide the class into four groups. Each group is responsible for one of the sets of letters. Play the CD again. The groups stand up to sing when they hear their letters.

Pupil's Book Activity 3

Listen and read. Ask and answer.

▶ *CD1 Track 9 p256*

- Play the CD. The pupils listen and read the conversation.
- Play the CD again, pausing for the pupils to repeat.
- Talk Partners The pupils practise the conversation with a Talk Partner. Encourage them to ask about and spell the other school subjects using the posters to help them gain confidence.

Activity Book

Activity 1

Help Toby find his bone. Listen and colour the words. Write.

▶ *CD1 Track 10 p256*

- (Books open.) Tell the pupils they are going to help Toby find his bone. They listen to and colour the letters they hear. After each word, the pupils name it and write it on the line.

Answers: **1** Maths **2** Spanish **3** English **4** Science **5** Music **6** school

Activity 2

Write and say the alphabet. Play the game.

- (Books open.) Ask the pupils to name the letters that are missing in the alphabet snake. They complete the alphabet individually.
- Talk Partners The pupils choose a picture and take turns to spell out the word to a partner. Their partner points to the letters in the word snake and then says the complete word.

Recycled vocabulary

- The pupils look at the picture, remember and write the word.

Answer: a scooter

Ending the lesson

Review the lesson.

- Say **Today we've learnt the alphabet in English.** Elicit the question *How do you spell …?* and encourage the pupils to say the alphabet again.

Review the task flashcards.

- Point to the task flashcards on the board. Say **Look at the activities you've done today. Which activity was your favourite?**

Extra activities

Review *The alphabet* song.

▶ *CD1 Track 8 p256*

- Cut out letters of the alphabet and give one to each pupil. Ask the class to line up in alphabetical order. Play the CD and ask the pupils to hold up their letter when they hear it.

Extension

- Play *The spelling game*. Ask the pupils to look at pages 4 and 5 of their Pupil's Books. Spell out some of the items. The pupils point to and say the items, for example, say **C-A-T.** The pupils say *cat* and point to the cat in the tree. Say **T-O-B-Y.** The pupils point to and say *Toby*. If you have a confident class, spell out more complex and irregular words, for example, *S-C-H-O-O-L.*
- Talk Partners The pupils continue the game with a Talk Partner.

Cooperative learning

Working together

- Talk Partners The pupils help each other learn to say the alphabet in English. They take turns to say the letters and help each other if they get stuck (Pupil A: a; Pupil B: b; Pupil A: c, etc.).
- Talk Partners The pupils play *Back writing,* a multisensory game, to practise the alphabet further. One pupil turns their back towards his / her partner. Pupil A traces letters with a finger on the back of Pupil B. Pupil B says the letter. After four or five letters the pupils change roles and repeat.

Key Competences and Key Learning Outcomes

- Read, listen and understand a story about a magic bike
- Read the story with some fluency

- Ask and answer about the weather

- Make the traffic light cut-out and evaluate your learning

- Read, listen and understand a story
- Act out a story

Key language

Recycled: *cloudy, raining, snowy, stormy, sunny, windy*

Recycled: *What's the weather like? It's (sunny) today. Is it (raining)? Yes, it is.*

Extension vocabulary

- *cold, cool, hot, warm*

Materials

- Pupil's Book p7; Activity Book p5; Class CD1; Teacher's App on Navio
- School subjects flashcards, Weather flashcards
- Teacher's Resource Bank: Weather word cards
- Teacher's Resource Bank: Task flashcards: *listen, read, act out, number, write, draw, think, colour, cut out, Talk Partners*
- Teacher's Resource Bank: Traffic light cut-out
- Scissors, red, yellow and green crayons or coloured pencils

At a Glance Lesson Plan

Starting the lesson

- **Talk Partners** Review the alphabet and spelling.
- Set learning outcomes using the task flashcards.

Vocabulary review

- Review Level 1 weather vocabulary.

Word cards

- Read the word cards. Match them to the flashcards.

Activity 1

- Explain the story title.
- Listen and read.

▶ ***CD1 Track 11 p256***

- Act out.

Now watch the animated story!

Go to the Activity Book.

Pupil's Book

Ending the lesson

- Review the task flashcards.

Extra activity

Vocabulary extension

- Present four additional vocabulary items.

Digital resources

Teacher's Digital: Don't forget you can teach this lesson using the Teacher's App on Navio.

Pupil's Digital: Encourage your pupils to use the Pupil's App on Navio to practise the vocabulary from this lesson.

Powered By NAVIO

Activity Book

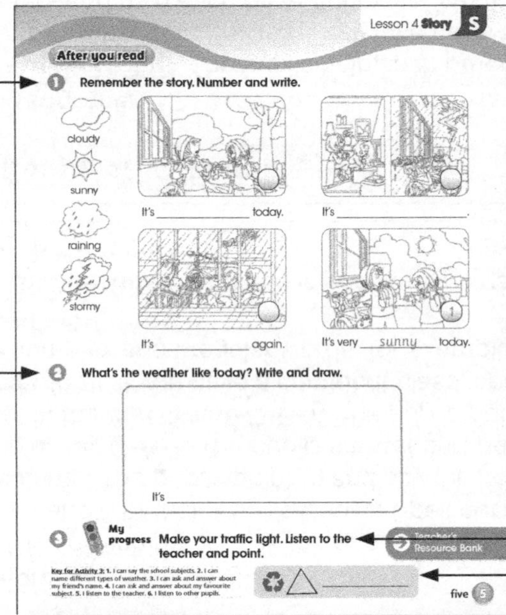

Activity Book

After you read: Activity 1

- Remember the story. Number and write.

Activity 2

- What's the weather like today? Write and draw.

Activity 3 My progress

- Make your traffic light.
- Listen to the teacher and point.

Recycled vocabulary

- Look, remember and write the word.

Starting the lesson

Review the alphabet and spelling.

- Play *The spelling game.* Spell out one of the school subjects. The pupils name the subject. Alternatively, ask **How do you spell *Music*?**
- Talk Partners The pupils play the game with a Talk Partner. Stick the school subject flashcards on the board for reference.

Set learning outcomes using the task flashcards.

- Say **Today we're going to ask and answer about the weather and read a story.**
- Hold up the task flashcards in turn and elicit the words. Stick them on one side of the board. Point to them during the lesson to reinforce your instructions.

Vocabulary review

Review Level 1 weather vocabulary.

- (Books closed.) Ask the pupils to look out of the window. Ask **What's the weather like today?** Show the weather flashcards in turn, leaving the flashcard that corresponds to the weather until last. Ask **Is it (windy)?** Stick the flashcards on the board.

Word cards

Read the word cards. Match them to the flashcards.

- Hold up a weather word card. The pupils read together. A pupil sticks the word card next to the corresponding flashcard. Repeat for the other weather cards.
- Point to each word card. The pupils read the words.

Pupil's Book Activity 1

Explain the story title.

- (Books open.) Focus on the title. Elicit or explain what a storm is. Encourage the pupils to mime a storm.

Listen and read. Act out.

▸ *CD1 Track 11 p256*

- (Books open.) Ask **Who can you see? What can you see? What's the weather like?** Encourage different pupils to answer.
- Prepare the pupils for reading and listening by asking them to put their finger on the first frame. Play the CD. The pupils follow the text with their finger. Pause between each frame to check understanding.

Suggested comprehension questions

- Frame 1: **What's the weather like?** *(It's very sunny and very hot.)*
- Frame 2: **What can Jake hear?** *(A storm.)*
- Frame 3: **Is the bike OK?** *(No. It's wet and dirty.)*
- Frame 4: **What can you see?** *(A rainbow.)*
- Frame 5: **Where are Jake and Molly?** *(At home.)*
- Frame 6: **Where's the bike?** *(It's inside.)*
- Talk about the importance of looking after belongings. Say **Do Jake and Molly take care of their bike in the story? What happens?** *(The bike gets wet and dirty. The bell doesn't work.)* Remind them that things get broken if you don't look after them.
- Ask **Have you got a bike? Do you clean it?**
- Organise the class into four groups (Beth, Molly, Jake and Dad).
- Play the CD. Each group joins in when their character speaks. If necessary, pause the CD after each sentence for the pupils to repeat.
- The pupils swap roles and join in with their new character.

Activity Book

After you read: Activity 1

Remember the story. Number and write.

- (Books open.) Ask **What's the weather like?** Elicit the answer for each frame in turn. The pupils write the correct weather individually and sequence the pictures according to the story. Ask **Which picture is first? Which picture is next?**

Answers: cloudy 3 stormy 2 raining 4 sunny 1

Activity 2

What's the weather like today? Write and draw.

- Ask **What's the weather like today? Look through the window.** Elicit the answer. The pupils draw a picture and write the weather.

Activity 3

Make your traffic light. Listen to the teacher and point. (Teacher's Resource Bank)

- Explain that the pupils are going to make a traffic light. Point to each circle and ask **What colour is this?** The pupils cut out and colour the traffic light.
- (Books closed.) Say **Let's think about our work in this unit.** Point to the green circle, nod your head, smile a lot and say **I can do this very well.** Point to the orange circle, move your head a little and smile a little and say **I can do this.** Finally, point to the red circle, shake your head and say **I can't do this very well.**
- Read out the self-assessment statements. The pupils point to the colour on their traffic light that matches how they feel about their learning. Praise the class for their hard work.

Self-assessment statements

1. I can say the school subjects.
2. I can name different types of weather.
3. I can ask and answer about my friend's name.
4. I can ask and answer about my favourite subject.
5. I listen to the teacher.
6. I listen to other pupils.

Recycled vocabulary

- The pupils look, remember and write the word.

Answer: triangle

Ending the lesson

Review the task flashcards.

- Point to the task flashcards on the board. Say **Look at the activities you've done today. Which activity was your favourite?**

Extra activity

Vocabulary extension

- Present four words for temperature: *hot, warm, cool* and *cold*. Ask **Is it (hot / warm / cool / cold) today?** Mime each one as you do so. To show the difference, draw a thermometer on the board. Colour red at the top and blue at the bottom. Write the words on the thermometer in the appropriate place and draw a picture alongside each one to illustrate it, for example, a snowman to represent *cold*.

Date: ____________ **Unit:** ____________

1 What did my pupils learn in this unit?

2 How did my pupils work? (✓)

individually ☐ in pairs ☐ in small groups ☐

in large groups ☐ as a class ☐

3 Which key competences did my pupils develop?

- Competence in linguistic communication ☐
- Competence in mathematics, science and technology ☐
- Digital competence ☐
- Learning to learn ☐
- Social and civic competences ☐
- Sense of initiative and entrepreneurship ☐
- Cultural awareness and expression ☐

4 Which lessons / activities were the most successful and why?

5 Which lessons / activities did my pupils find the most difficult and why?

6 What did I try in the classroom for the first time? How did it go?

7 Which resources did I find most useful? (including webpages)

8 What could I do differently next time I teach this unit?

Unit 1

Move your body

Unit overview

Key Competences and Key Learning Outcomes

- Identify and say ten sports (Lesson 1)
- Talk about the sports you play (Lesson 1)
- Use the present simple 'I' and 'you' (Lesson 2)
- Read, listen and understand a story about Molly's activities (Lesson 3)
- Identify and say six action verbs (Lesson 4)
- Read about Sports Day in Britain (Lesson 6)
- Watch and understand a video about Sports Day (Video and 21st Century Skills)

- Use the Pupil's App on Navio

- Use a strategy to practise spelling key words (Lesson 1)
- Say a tongue twister and practise 'ai' and 'ay' spellings (Lesson 5)
- Review language in the unit and reflect on your own learning (Lesson 8)
- Practise activity types found in the Cambridge Exams: Pre A1 Starters

- Understand the importance of organising personal possessions (Lesson 3)
- Learn to join in (Video and 21st Century Skills)

- Work with a Talk Partner to practise and reinforce learning (all lessons)
- Play a communication game about sports (Lesson 5)

- Sing three songs (Lessons 1, 4 and 8)
- Understand, act out and give an opinion on a story (Lesson 3)
- Think about the sports you play at school (Lesson 6)
- Read, understand and act out a poem (Lesson 7)

Vocabulary

Core vocabulary
baseball, basketball, cycling, football, hockey, rollerblading, skateboarding, swimming, tennis, volleyball; bounce, catch, hit, jump, kick, throw

Extension vocabulary (optional)
(go) climbing, (go) fishing, (go) sailing, (play) badminton, (play) golf, (play) table tennis; (do) athletics, (do) ballet, (do) gymnastics, (do) karate

Other vocabulary
indoors, outdoors; bat, football boots, goggles, mess, rollerblades, sports centre, tennis racket; underarm, overarm

Recycled vocabulary
I like, I love, I don't like; Days of the week; *ball, balloon, big, fast, hands, legs, run, small, swimsuit*

Structures

Core structures
Do you play any sports?
I play (tennis). I go (swimming) (on Saturday).
Do you (play football / go cycling)? Yes, I do. No, I don't.
He / She (plays) (tennis) (on Monday). He / She (kicks / throws / hits) the ball.

Other structures
What's your favourite sport?
My favourite sport is (football).
What sports do you play at school?

Recycled structures
I (like / love) … I don't (like / love) …
Do you like (hockey)? Yes, I do. No, I don't.

Phonics

Alternative vowel spellings **'ai'** / **'ay'** (sn**ai**ls, pl**ay**, r**ai**n, d**ay**)

British Culture

Sports Day

Literacy

Text type: a poem (text to express)
Reading skills: predicting from pictures; scanning; sequencing; reading a poem

21st Century Skills

Ways of working: learn to join in

Cooperative learning

- **Song:** *Well Done!* (Lesson 8)
- **Skills:** Encouraging participation (Lesson 2); Think-Pair-Share (Lessons 3, 8); Working together as a team (Lesson 5); Working together as a class (Lesson 7)

Values

The importance of organising personal possessions.

Cross-curricular links

Links to Science
The human body: joints that move when we play different sports; safety equipment for sports; muscles pull our bones to help us move.

Suggested Arts and Crafts concepts
Identifying and using lines, shapes and colours; creating a matching game.

Key Competences and Key Learning Outcomes

- Identify and say ten different sports
- Say the vocabulary chant
- Stick the sports stickers

- Identify joints that move when we play sports (optional)

- Use a strategy to practise spelling key words

- Sing a song about sports

Key language
- *baseball, basketball, cycling, football, hockey, rollerblading, skateboarding, swimming, tennis, volleyball*
- *Do you play any sports? I go (cycling). I play (football).*

Extension vocabulary
- *(go) climbing, (go) fishing, (go) sailing, (play) badminton, (play) golf, (play) table tennis*

Recycled: *cloudy, foggy, rainy, snowy, stormy, sunny, windy*

Other vocabulary: *indoors, outdoors*

Materials
- Pupil's Book p8; Activity Book pp6 and 15; Class CD1; Teacher's App on Navio; Unit 1 stickers
- Weather flashcards; sports flashcards
- Teacher's Resource Bank: Sports word cards
- Teacher's Resource Bank: Task flashcards: Think-Pair-Share, *listen, sing, read, stick, say, match, write, tick, Talk Partners*

Optional materials
- Teacher's Resource Bank: Five Trinity Exam Practice cards (selected from the Starter Unit)

At a Glance Lesson Plan

Starting the lesson
- Use the Trinity Exam Practice cards (optional).
- **Think-Pair-Share** Review weather words.
- Set learning outcomes using the task flashcards.

Vocabulary presentation
- Present the new vocabulary.

Activity 1
- Listen and point.
- ▶ ***CD1 Track 12 p256***
- Sing *Do you play any sports?*

Word cards
- Read the word cards.
- Match them to the flashcards.

Activity 2
- Read and stick the ten stickers.
- Listen and say the chant.
- ▶ ***CD1 Track 14 p257***

Go to the Activity Book.

Pupil's Book

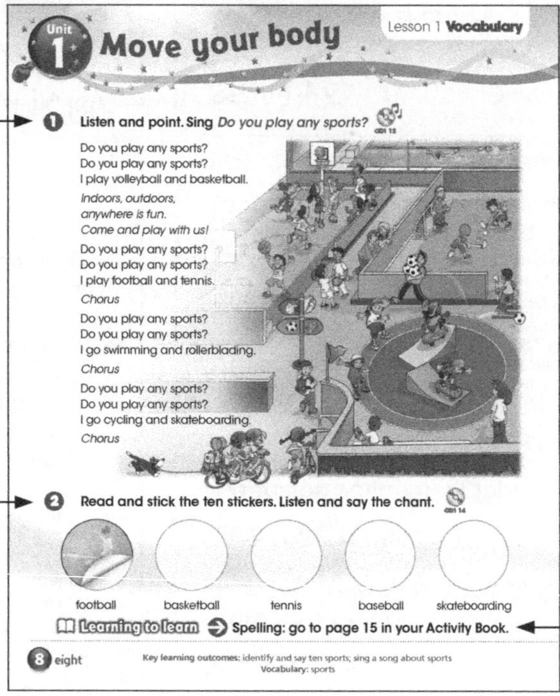

Ending the lesson
- Review the lesson.
- Review the task flashcards.

Extra activities
Reinforcement
- Play *Which one's missing?*

Vocabulary extension
- Present six additional vocabulary items.

Link to Science
- **The human body:** joints that move when we play sports

Learning to learn
Spelling
- Practise spelling at any time during this unit (Activity Book p15).

Digital resources

Teacher's Digital: Don't forget you can teach this lesson using the Teacher's App on Navio.

Pupil's Digital: Encourage your pupils to use the Pupil's App on Navio to practise the vocabulary from this lesson.

Powered By NAVIO

Activity Book

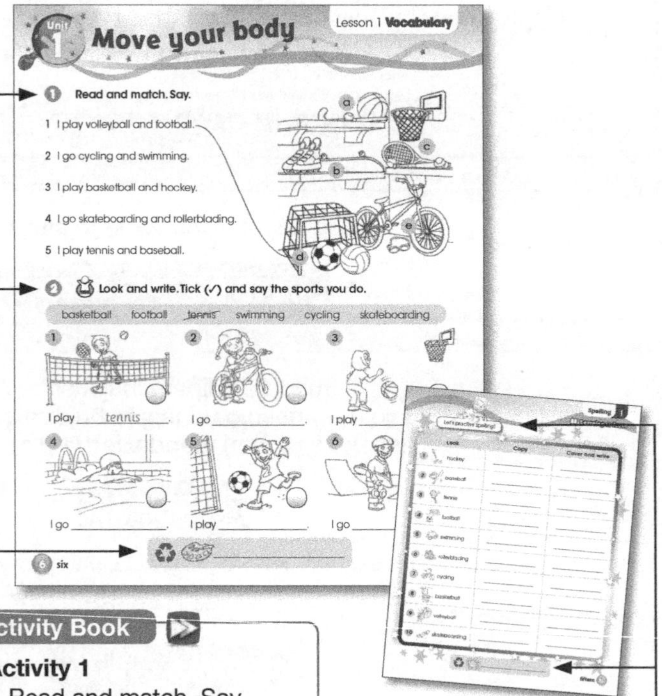

Activity Book
Activity 1
- Read and match. Say.

Activity 2
- Look and write.
- Tick (✓) and say the sports you do.

Recycled vocabulary
- Look, remember and write the word.

Spelling
Let's practise spelling!
- Use the *Look-Copy-Cover-Write* technique.

Recycled vocabulary
- Look, remember and write the phrase.

Starting the lesson

Use the Trinity Exam Practice cards (optional).

- The pupils practise asking and answering questions. (See p31.)

Think-Pair-Share Review weather words.

- Ask **Can you remember the weather words?** The class thinks silently for a minute.
- **Talk Partners** The pupils work with a Talk Partner to name the weather words.
- Invite pairs to say a different weather word. Hold up the flashcard. The class repeats. Ask **What's the weather like today?** The pupils complete a weather chart.

Set learning outcomes using the task flashcards.

- Explain the aims of the lesson. Say **Today we're going to learn the names of different sports.**
- Hold up the task flashcards in turn and elicit the words. Stick them on one side of the board. Point to them during the lesson to reinforce your instructions.

Vocabulary presentation

Present the new vocabulary.

- (Books closed.) Ask **What sports do you like?** Elicit the names of sports the pupils know.
- Stick the flashcards of any sports the pupils name on the board. Slowly reveal the remaining flashcards naming them as you do so.
- Prompt the class to mime playing each sport. Stick the flashcards on the board. Point to each one in turn and say the word with the pupils.

Pupil's Book Activity 1

Listen and point. Sing *Do you play any sports?*

▶ *CD1 Track 12 p256*

- (Books open.) Ask **Where are Molly and Jake?** *(At the sports centre.)* **What sports can you see?** The class points to and names the different sports.
- Play the CD. The pupils listen and point to the sports on the page.
- Play the CD again. The pupils sing and do the actions.

Word cards

Read the word cards. Match them to the flashcards.

- (Books closed.) Hold up a sports word card. The pupils read collectively. A pupil sticks the word card next to the flashcard on the board. Repeat.
- Point to each word card. The pupils read the words.

Pupil's Book Activity 2

Read and stick the ten stickers. Listen and say the chant.

▶ *CD1 Track 14 p257*

- Ask a pupil to read the first word. The pupils stick the corresponding sticker above the word.
- **Talk Partners** The pupils find and stick the remaining stickers. Encourage them to help each other using cooperative language (*Is this hockey? Yes. Where does this go? Here.*)
- Play the CD. The pupils listen and say the chant, pointing to the stickers in turn.

Activity Book

Activity 1

Read and match. Say.

- (Books open.) Ask different pupils to read out the sentences. The class points to the picture.
- The pupils read and match individually.

Answers: **1** d **2** e **3** a **4** b **5** c

Activity 2

Look and write. Tick (✓) and say the sports you do.

- (Books open.) Invite different pupils to name the sports. The pupils complete the sentences. Point to picture 5 and say **I play football. Do you play football?** The pupils tick this sport if they play it. Repeat for the other sports.
- **Talk Partners** The pupils tell a Talk Partner which sports they play.

Answers: **1** tennis **2** cycling **3** basketball **4** swimming **5** football **6** skateboarding

Recycled vocabulary

- The pupils look at the picture and write the phrase.

Answer: Arts and Crafts

Ending the lesson

Review the lesson.

- Say **Today we've learnt the names of sports. Which sports do you remember?** Elicit the sports.

Review the task flashcards.

- Point to the task flashcards. Say **Look at the activities you've done today. Which was your favourite?** Elicit the pupils' favourite activities.

Extra activities

Reinforcement

- Play *Which one's missing?* (See p23.)

Vocabulary extension

- Present six additional sports words: *(go) climbing*, *(go) fishing, (go) sailing, (play) badminton, (play) golf, (play) table tennis.*
- Use the Vocabulary Booster on Navio to practise these new words.

Link to Science

- If you are studying the Science topic of **the human body** in English, you could review the joints the pupils move to play each sport.
- Say one of the sports. In pairs, one pupil mimes the sport and the other one points to and names the joints that are moving. Change roles and repeat.

Spelling (Activity Book p15)

Let's practise spelling!

- The pupils can practise spelling the ten sports words using the *Look-Copy-Cover-Write* technique at any time during this unit before the Lesson 8 Review.

Recycled vocabulary

- The pupils look at the picture and write the word.

Answer: sunny

Key Competences and Key Learning Outcomes

- Understand and act out a conversation
- Complete and practise a conversation
- Use the present simple 'I' and 'you'

- Listen for specific information

Key language

Recycled: *baseball, basketball, cycling, football, hockey, rollerblading, skateboarding, swimming, tennis, volleyball*

Recycled: *Do you play any sports? I play tennis, I go swimming. Do you (play football)? Yes, I do. No, I don't.*

Other vocabulary: *goggles, mess*

Materials

- Pupil's Book p9; Activity Book p7; Class CD1; Teacher's App on Navio
- Sports flashcards
- Teacher's Resource Bank: Task flashcards: *listen, act out, tick, read, write, follow, circle, Talk Partners*

Optional materials

- Teacher's Resource Bank: Five Trinity Exam Practice cards (selected from the Starter Unit)

At a Glance Lesson Plan

Pupil's Book

Starting the lesson

- Use the Trinity Exam Practice cards (optional).
- Review the *Do you play any sports?* song.
- ▶ *CD1 Track 12 p256*
- ▶ *CD1 Track 13 p257 (optional karaoke version)*
- Talk Partners Review sports vocabulary.
- Set learning outcomes using the task flashcards.

Activity 1

- Listen and repeat.
- ▶ *CD1 Track 15 p257*
- Talk Partners Act out.

Activity 2

- Listen and tick (✓).
- ▶ *CD1 Track 16 p257*

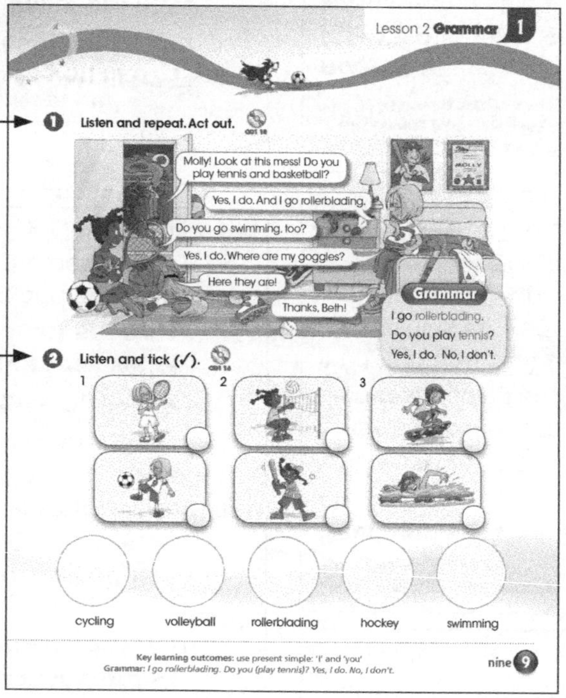

Grammar focus

- *go* or *play*?
- Go to the Activity Book.

Ending the lesson

- Review the lesson.
- Review the task flashcards.

Cooperative learning

Encouraging participation

- Play *Class chain*.

Activity Book

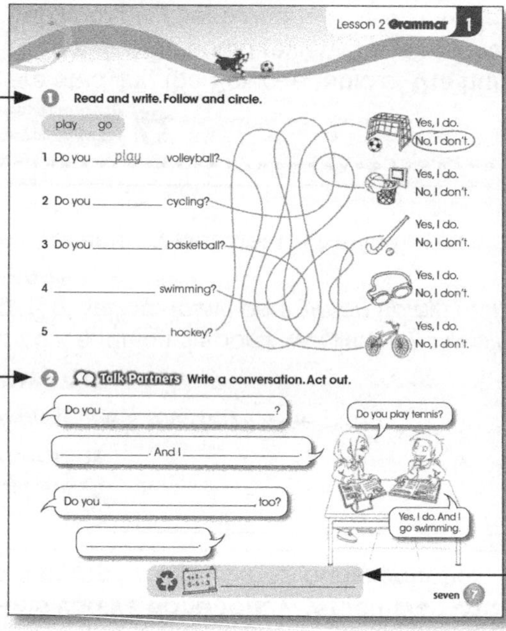

Activity Book

Activity 1

- Read and write. Follow and circle.

Activity 2

- Write a conversation.
- Talk Partners Act out.

Recycled vocabulary

- Look, remember and write the word.

Digital resources

Teacher's Digital: Don't forget you can teach this lesson using the Teacher's App on Navio.

Pupil's Digital: Encourage your pupils to use the Pupil's App on Navio to practise the vocabulary from this lesson.

Powered By NAVIO

Starting the lesson

Use the Trinity Exam Practice cards (optional).

- The pupils practise asking and answering questions. (See p31.)

Review the *Do you play any sports?* song.

▶ *CD1 Track 12 p256*

▶ *CD1 Track 13 p257 (optional karaoke version)*

- Sing the *Do you play any sports?* song from Lesson 1 (or use the karaoke version). Hand out the sports flashcards to ten pupils and tell them to stand in a line. The class sings and the pupils hold up the flashcards when they hear the sports in the song.

Review sports vocabulary.

- Play *Quick flash.* (See p23.)
- Talk Partners The pupils take turns to mime and guess the sports.

Set learning outcomes using the task flashcards.

- Explain the aims of the lesson. Say **Today we're going to ask and answer about sports you play.**
- Hold up the task flashcards and elicit the words. Stick them on one side of the board. Point to them during the lesson to reinforce your instructions.

Pupil's Book Activity 1

Listen and repeat. Act out.

▶ *CD1 Track 15 p257*

- (Books open.) Ask **Where are Molly and Beth? Is Molly's bedroom tidy?** Explain **Beth is helping Molly sort out her sports equipment.**
- Play the CD. The children listen and read the conversation. Ask **Does Molly play tennis? Does Molly play basketball? Does Molly go swimming? What does Beth find?**
- Play the CD again. Pause for the pupils to repeat.
- Talk Partners The pupils practise the conversation with a Talk Partner.
- Ask the children if their bedroom is a mess.

Pupil's Book Activity 2

Listen and tick (✓).

▶ *CD1 Track 16 p257*

- (Books open.) Name the sports in each scene. Ask **What sport does Molly play?**
- Play the CD. Pause and elicit the answer. Check that the pupils have ticked the correct box. Repeat for Beth and Jake.

Answers: Molly: football, Beth: volleyball, Jake: skateboarding

Grammar focus

***go* or *play*?**

- Point out that for some sports we say 'go' and for others we say 'play'. Draw a two-column chart on the board. *Go: cycling, swimming, rollerblading, skateboarding; Play: football, tennis, basketball, volleyball, hockey, baseball.*
- Show the sports flashcards or word cards and elicit: *I play tennis / I go cycling,* etc. Place the flashcards in the corresponding column. Ask what the sports in each column have in common (play: they use a ball; go: they end with *-ing*).

Activity Book

Activity 1

Read and write. Follow and circle.

- (Books open.) Hold up your book and read out the first question. Follow the path with your finger to the answer. Ask a pupil to complete the second question orally and read it out.
- Prompt the whole class to follow the path with their finger and elicit the correct answer.
- The pupils work on their own to complete the questions, draw the paths and circle the correct answers.

Answers: **1** No, I don't. **2** go; No, I don't. **3** play; Yes, I do. **4** Do you go; Yes I do. **5** Do you play; No, I don't.

Activity 2

Write a conversation. Act out.

- Point to the picture of Molly and Jake. Invite a pupil to act out the conversation with you.
- Focus the class on the incomplete speech bubbles. Invite a pupil to read the first speech bubble and add a sport. Repeat for the other speech bubbles.
- Talk Partners The pupils write and practise their own conversation with a Talk Partner. Invite different pairs of pupils to act out their conversations for their classmates.
- If you introduced any additional sports vocabulary in Lesson 1, encourage the pupils to use some of this in their conversations: *Do you play badminton?*

Recycled vocabulary

- The pupils look at the picture and write the word.

Answer: Maths

Ending the lesson

Review the lesson.

- Say **Today you've asked and answered about sports.** Elicit the question and short answers from the pupils: *Do you play tennis / go rollerblading? (Yes, I do. / No, I don't.)*

Review the task flashcards.

- Point to the task flashcards. Say **Look at the activities you've done today. Which activity was your favourite?** Elicit the pupils' favourite activities.

Cooperative learning

Encouraging participation

- Play *Class chain*. Organise the class into a large circle. Show the pupil on your right one of the sports flashcards and ask **Do you (play tennis)?** Elicit *Yes, I do. / No, I don't.* Pass the flashcard to the pupil, who turns to the pupil on his / her right and repeats the question. The flashcard is passed around the circle, with pupils asking and answering each time, until it returns to you. When the pupils are more confident, pass several flashcards around the chain at the same time. Praise the class for working so well together.

Key Competences and Key Learning Outcomes

- Read, listen and understand a story about Molly's activities
- Read the story with some fluency
- Become familiar with the story through a pre-reading task
- Understand the importance of organising personal possessions
- Understand and act out the story
- Give an opinion on the story

Key language

- *I play baseball. Molly plays tennis on Monday.*

Recycled: *baseball, basketball, cycling, football, hockey, rollerblading, skateboarding, swimming, tennis, volleyball; ball, run; swimsuit;* days of the week

Recycled: *Do you (play tennis / go cycling)? Yes, I do. No, I don't.*

Other vocabulary: *bat, football boots, rollerblades, sports centre, tennis racket*

Materials

- Pupil's Book pp10–11; Activity Book p8; Class CD1; Teacher's App on Navio
- Sports flashcards
- Teacher's Resource Bank: Task flashcards: *listen, read, act out, write, match, draw, Talk Partners*
- Teacher's Resource Bank: Unit 1 Lesson 3 Animated Story

Optional materials

- Teacher's Resource Bank: Five Trinity Exam Practice cards (selected from the Starter Unit)

At a Glance Lesson Plan

Starting the lesson

- Use the Trinity Exam Practice cards (optional).
- Review the *Do you play any sports?* song.
- ▶ ***CD1 Track 12 p256***
- ▶ ***CD1 Track 13 p257 (optional karaoke version)***
- Set learning outcomes using the task flashcards.

Before you read

- Explain the story title.
- Read and answer the question.

Activity 1

- Listen and read.
- ▶ ***CD1 Track 17 p257***
- **Talk Partners** Act out.

Now watch the animated story!

After you read : Activity 2

- Go to page 8 in your Activity Book.
- Values: Read and write.

Pupil's Book

Ending the lesson

- Review the lesson.
- Review the task flashcards.

Cooperative learning

Think-Pair-Share

- Remember ten sports words.

Digital resources

Teacher's Digital: Don't forget you can teach this lesson using the Teacher's App on Navio.

Pupil's Digital: Encourage your pupils to use the Pupil's App on Navio to practise the vocabulary from this lesson.

Powered By NAVIO

Activity Book

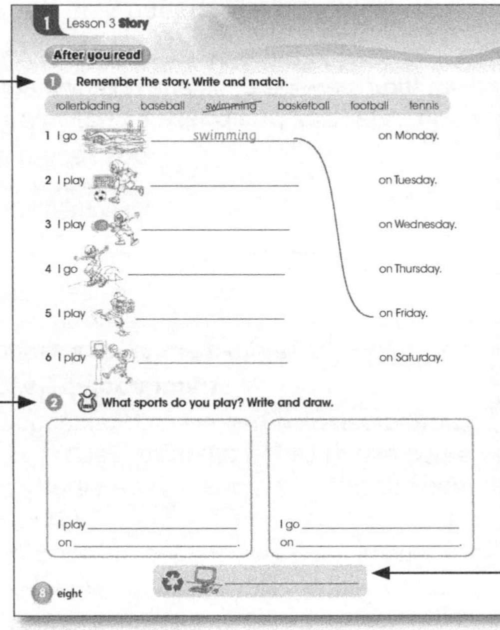

Activity Book

After you read: Activity 1

- Remember the story. Write and match.

Activity 2

- What sports do you play? Write and draw.

Recycled vocabulary

- Look, remember and write the word.

Starting the lesson

Use the Trinity Exam Practice cards (optional).

- The pupils practise asking and answering questions. (See p31.)

Review the *Do you play any sports?* song.

▶ ***CD1 Track 12 p256***

▶ ***CD1 Track 13 p257 (optional karaoke version)***

- Stick the sports flashcards from the *Do you play any sports?* song around the room. Play the CD (or use the karaoke version). The pupils sing and point to the flashcard of each sport as it appears in the song.

Set learning outcomes using the task flashcards

- Say **Today we're going to listen to a story.**
- Hold up the task flashcards and elicit the words. Stick them on one side of the board. Point to them during the lesson to reinforce your instructions.

Before you read

Explain the story title.

- (Books open.) Focus on the title and explain that Molly is very busy.

Read and answer the question.

- Read the speech bubble. The pupils scan the story to find the different sports that Molly does.
- Talk Partners The pupils feed back to a Talk Partner. The class names the sports.

Answers: tennis, football, basketball, rollerblading, swimming, baseball

Pupil's Book Activity 1

Listen and read. Act out.

▶ ***CD1 Track 17 p257***

- (Books open.) Play the CD. The pupils follow the text with their finger. Pause the CD between each story frame to check understanding.

Suggested comprehension questions

- Frame 1: **What does Molly love?** *(She loves sport.)*
- Frame 2: **What day does Molly play tennis?** *(Monday.)*
- Frame 3: **What sport does Molly do on Tuesday?** *(Football.)*
- Frame 4: **What day does Molly play basketball?** *(Wednesday.)*
- Frame 5: **What sport does Molly do on Thursday?** *(Rollerblading.)*
- Frame 6: **What has Molly got?** *(Her tennis racket.)*
- Frame 7: **What can the magic bike do?** *(Help Molly organise her things.)*
- Frame 8: **What sport does Molly do on Saturday?** *(Baseball.)*
- Ask **Did you like the story? What part did you like best?**
- Talk Partners The pupils choose their favourite frame.
- Organise the class into four groups (Beth, Molly, Jake and the narrator).
- Play the CD. Each group joins in when their character speaks. If necessary, pause the CD after each sentence for the pupils to repeat.
- The pupils swap roles and repeat the activity.

After you read

Pupil's Book Activity 2

Go to page 8 in your Activity Book.

Activity Book

After you read: Activity 1

Remember the story. Write and match.

- (Books open.) Say **Do you remember the story? Molly is talking about the sports she does.** Read out the first sentence and ask one of the pupils to match it to the corresponding day.
- Talk Partners The pupils read the completed sentences with a Talk Partner.

Answers: **1** swimming on Friday **2** football on Tuesday **3** tennis on Monday **4** rolllerblading on Thursday **5** baseball on Saturday **6** basketball on Wednesday

Activity 2 (me)

What sports do you play? Write and draw.

- (Books open.) Read out the start of the first sentence and elicit a sport from the story that the pupils do themselves. The pupils write the day and draw themselves doing the sport.
- Talk Partners The pupils show their work to a Talk Partner and say which sports they do. Encourage them to ask each other **Do you play (football)?**

Recycled vocabulary

- The pupils look at the picture and write the word.

Answer: ICT

Pupil's Book Activity 2

Values: Read and write.

- Read the value and prompt the class to choose the correct word to complete the sentence. Ask **Do you organise your things?**

Answer: organise

Ending the lesson

Review the lesson.

- Say **Today we listened to a story about Molly's busy week.** Elicit some of Molly's activities.

Review the task flashcards.

- Point to the task flashcards. Say **Look at the activities you've done today. Which activity was your favourite?** Elicit the pupils' favourite activities.

Cooperative learning

Think-Pair-Share

- Ask **Can you remember the ten sports?** Ask the class to think silently on their own for a minute.
- Talk Partners The pupils work with a Talk Partner to remember and name all ten items.
- Invite a pair to say one of the sports. Hold up the corresponding flashcard and prompt the class to repeat the word.
- Repeat the procedure, asking different pairs each time, until all ten sports have been named. Encourage the pupils to say 'play' or 'go' with each sport.

Key Competences and Key Learning Outcomes

- Describe and guess a sport
- Identify and say six action verbs
- Identify safety equipment for sports (optional)
- Sing a song

Key language
- *bounce, catch, hit, jump, kick, throw*
- *He (throws) the ball. She (catches) the ball.*

Extension vocabulary
- *(do) athletics, (do) ballet, (do) gymnastics, (do) karate*

Recycled: *He / She goes / plays …*

Materials
- Pupil's Book p12; Activity Book p9; Class CD1; Teacher's App on Navio
- Teacher's Resource Bank: Task flashcards: *listen, say, sing, Talk Partners, circle, write*

Optional materials
- Teacher's Resource Bank: Five Trinity Exam Practice cards (selected from the Starter Unit)
- Balls for catching

At a Glance Lesson Plan

Starting the lesson
- Use the Trinity Exam Practice cards (optional).
- Review the Lesson 3 story.
- Set learning outcomes using the task flashcards.

Vocabulary presentation
- Present the new vocabulary.

Activity 1
- Listen, point and say.
- ▶ *CD1 Track 18 p257*
- Play *Disappearing words.*

Activity 2
- Listen and point. Sing *He's a superstar!*
- ▶ *CD1 Track 19 p257*

Activity 3
- Listen and repeat.
- Talk Partners Play a game.
- ▶ *CD1 Track 20 p257*
- Go to the Activity Book.

Pupil's Book

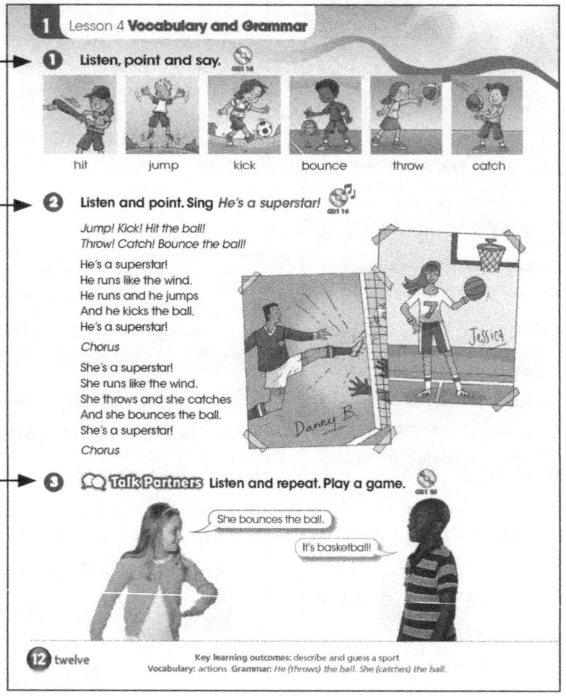

Ending the lesson
- Review the lesson.
- Review the task flashcards.

Extra activities
Reinforcement
- Play a ball game.

Vocabulary extension
- Present four additional vocabulary items.

Link to Science
- **The human body:** safety equipment for sports

Digital resources

Teacher's Digital: Don't forget you can teach this lesson using the Teacher's App on Navio.

Pupil's Digital: Encourage your pupils to use the Pupil's App on Navio to practise the vocabulary from this lesson.

Powered By NAVIO

Activity Book

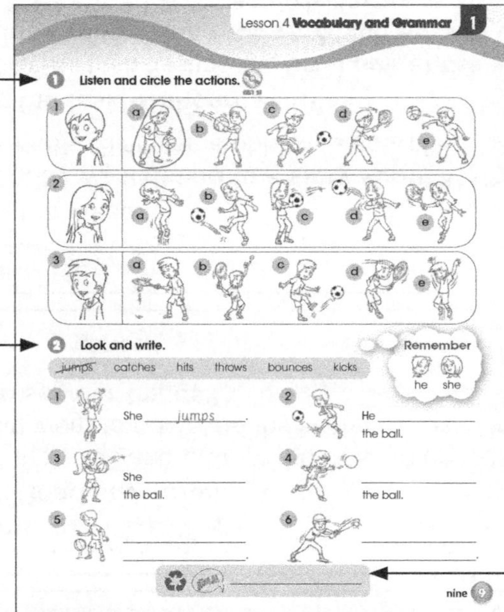

Activity Book

Activity 1
- Listen and circle the actions.
- ▶ *CD1 Track 21 p257*

Activity 2
- Look and write.

Recycled vocabulary
- Look, remember and write the word.

Starting the lesson

Use the Trinity Exam Practice cards (optional).

- The pupils practise asking and answering questions. (See p31.)

Review the Lesson 3 story.

- Randomly name the sports activities that Molly does each day. The pupils scan the story and name the day, e.g. say **Molly plays basketball**. Pupils reply *On Wednesday!*

Set learning outcomes using the task flashcards.

- Say **Today we're going to talk about actions we do when we play sports.**
- Hold up the task flashcards in turn and elicit the words. Stick them on one side of the board. Point to them during the lesson to reinforce your instructions.

Vocabulary presentation

Present the new vocabulary.

- (Books closed.) Say **When we play sport, we move our bodies and do different actions. When we play baseball or tennis, we hit the ball.**
- Repeat the verb and mime the action. Prompt the class to do the same. Then, repeat the process with the other verbs (*bounce, catch, jump, kick* and *throw*).

Pupil's Book Activity 1

Listen, point and say.

▶ ***CD1 Track 18 p257***

- (Books open.) Say **Let's listen and repeat the words**. Play the CD. The pupils repeat each word, pointing to the corresponding illustration each time. Play the CD again and repeat the activity.
- Play *Disappearing words* with the verbs *bounce*, *catch*, *hit*, *jump*, *kick* and *throw.* (See p23.)

Pupil's Book Activity 2

Listen and point. Sing *He's a superstar!*

▶ ***CD1 Track 19 p257***

- (Books open.) Point to the picture of the football star. Ask **Which sport does he play?** Repeat for the basketball star.
- Play the CD. The pupils listen and point to the corresponding superstar in their books. Play the CD again. The pupils sing and do the actions.
- Ask the pupils if they have a favourite football or basketball star.

Pupil's Book Activity 3

Listen and repeat. Play a game.

▶ ***CD1 Track 20 p257***

- Say **Let's listen and repeat the sentences.** Play the CD.
- (Books open.) Mime kicking a ball and say **He kicks the ball**. Elicit *It's football*. Then say **She bounces the ball**. Elicit *It's basketball*. Repeat the activity, using different verbs to make statements about the sports.
- **Talk Partners** Encourage the pupils to mime and name other sports that use these verbs with a Talk Partner, for example, *hit: hockey, baseball, tennis. Bounce the ball: basketball, tennis.*

Activity Book

Activity 1

Listen and circle the actions.

▶ ***CD1 Track 21 p257***

- (Books open.) Ask the class to identify the verbs. Elicit that number 1 is about a boy and number 2 is about a girl. Remind the pupils that 'he' is for boys and 'she' is for girls.
- Play the CD. Pause after the first sentence to check understanding. Repeat. The pupils circle the correct information.

Answers: **1** a, b, e **2** b, c, d **3** a, b, d

Activity 2

Look and write.

- (Books open.) Focus attention on the *Remember* box and ask which pictures need 'he' and which need 'she'. Pupils complete the sentences individually.

Answers: **1** jumps **2** kicks **3** catches **4** She throws **5** He bounces the ball. **6** He hits the ball.

Recycled vocabulary

- The pupils look at the picture and write the word. If necessary, they look back at the previous unit.

Answer: Spanish

Ending the lesson

Review the lesson.

- Say **Today we've talked about sports actions**. Elicit the verbs from the pupils.

Review the task flashcards.

- Point to the task flashcards. Say **Look at the activities you've done today. Which activity was your favourite?** Elicit the pupils' favourite activities.

Extra activities

Reinforcement

- Play a game with an imaginary ball. Give instructions for the pupils to mime: **Throw the ball up in the air and catch it. Bounce the ball three times. Throw the ball to your partner. Throw it up in the air and clap before you catch it!**
- If possible, play the game outside with real balls. After a few turns, the pupils give each other instructions.

Vocabulary extension

- Use the Vocabulary Booster on Navio and present and practise four additional sports words: *(do) athletics, (do) ballet, (do) gymnastics, (do) karate.*

Link to Science

- If you are studying the Science topic of **the human body** in English, you could review safety measures. Discuss the safety equipment for each sport in the Lesson 3 story: helmet (cycling, rollerblading, riding a scooter), pads (rollerblading), boots (football), etc.

Key Competences and Key Learning Outcomes

- Say a tongue twister with the 'ai' sound
- Learn and practise 'ai' and 'ay' spellings
- Listen for specific information
- Play a communication game about sports

Key language

- *day, May, play, rain, rainbow, say, snail, Spain, train, Tuesday*

Recycled: days of the week, *sports*

Recycled: *Beth (goes swimming) on (Wednesday). (Jake) (plays tennis) on (Saturday).*, etc.

Materials

- Pupil's Book p13; Activity Book p10; Class CD1; Teacher's App on Navio
- Teacher's Resource Bank: Task flashcards: *listen, say, match, cut out, write, colour, Talk Partners*
- Teacher's Resource Bank: Unit 1 Lesson 5 Activity 3
- Coloured pencils, scissors, large sheet of paper or card and glue

Optional materials

- Teacher's Resource Bank: Five Trinity Exam Practice cards (selected from the Starter Unit)

At a Glance Lesson Plan

Pupil's Book

Starting the lesson

- Use the Trinity Exam Practice cards (optional).
- Review the *He's a superstar!* song.

▶ *CD1 Track 19 p257*

- Set learning outcomes using the task flashcards.

Activity 1

- Listen and say.

▶ *CD1 Track 22 p257*

Go to the Activity Book.

Go to Magic Phonics.

Activity 2

- Listen and match.

▶ *CD1 Track 23 p257*

Activity 3

- Talk Partners Make and play the game (Teacher's Resource Bank: Unit 1).

Ending the lesson

- Review the lesson.
- Review the task flashcards.

Cooperative learning

Working together as a team

- Talk Partners Play *Beat the clock.*
- Make a pronunciation wall display.

Activity Book

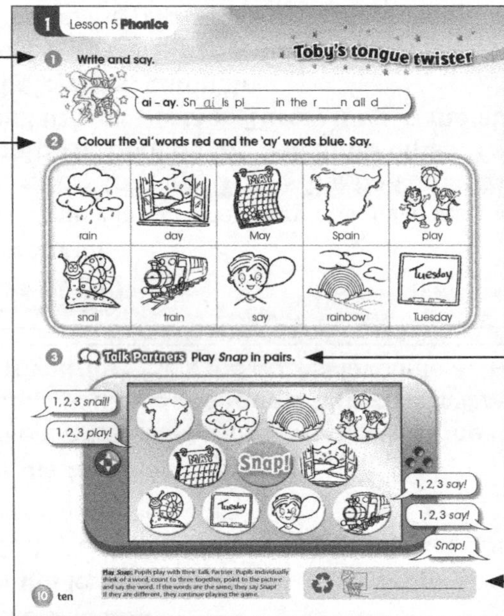

Activity Book

Activity 1

- Write and say.

Activity 2

- Colour the 'ai' words red and the 'ay' words blue. Say.

Go to Magic Phonics.

Activity 3

- Talk Partners Play *Snap* in pairs.

Recycled vocabulary

- Look, remember and write the word.

Digital resources

Teacher's Digital: Don't forget you can teach this lesson using the Teacher's App on Navio.

Pupil's Digital: Encourage your pupils to use the Pupil's App on Navio to practise the vocabulary from this lesson.

Powered By NAVIO

Starting the lesson

Use the Trinity Exam Practice cards (optional).

- The pupils practise asking and answering questions. (See p31.)

Review the *He's a superstar!* song.

▶ *CD1 Track 19 p257*

- Play the *He's a Superstar!* song from Lesson 4. The pupils stand in two lines – boys facing girls. The girls sing the first verse while the boys mime the actions. The boys sing the second verse while the girls mime the actions. All join in on the chorus.

Set learning outcomes using the task flashcards.

- Say **Today we're going to say a tongue twister and make a cut-out and talk about it.**
- Hold up the task flashcards in turn and elicit the activities. Stick them on one side of the board. Point to them during the lesson to reinforce your instructions.

Pupil's Book Activity 1

Listen and say.

▶ *CD1 Track 22 p257*

- Write the words 'play' and 'rain' on the board and ask the pupils which sound they can hear in both words ('ai'). Circle the target grapheme in each word ('ai' and 'ay') and model the sound. The pupils say the sound with you.
- Say **It's time for Toby's tongue twister! What can you see?** *(snails, play, rain)*
- Play the CD. The pupils listen and repeat the target sound, then the words and then the entire tongue twister, faster and faster.

Go to Magic Phonics.

Activity Book

Activity 1

Write and say.

- (Books open.) Say **Look at Toby's tongue twister! The letters for 'ai' are missing.** The pupils complete the tongue twister.
- Talk Partners The pupils say Toby's tongue twister and point to the 'ai' sounds. They play *Faster and faster.* The pupils take turns to say the tongue twister faster each time.

Answers: Snails, play, rain, day

Activity 2

Colour the 'ai' words red and the 'ay' words blue. Say.

- Ask the pupils to say the words and then colour them.

Answers: red: rain, Spain, snail, train, rainbow
blue: day, May, play, say, Tuesday

Go to Magic Phonics.

Activity 3

Play *Snap* in pairs.

- Demonstrate the game with a volunteer. You each think of a word, count to three together, point to the picture and say the word. If the words are the same, say *Snap!* If they are different, continue playing.
- Talk Partners The pupils play the game with a Talk Partner.

Recycled vocabulary

- The pupils look at the picture and write the word.

Answer: PE / (play) basketball

Pupil's Book Activity 2

Listen and match.

▶ *CD1 Track 23 p257*

- (Books open.) Tell the pupils that they are going to listen and find out about Beth's sports timetable.
- Play the CD. Pause after the first piece of information. Ask **What does Beth do on Monday?**
- Repeat. The pupils match the pictures to the days.

Answers: Monday: Tennis, Tuesday: swimming, Wednesday: rollerblading, Thursday: baseball, Friday: cycling, Saturday: hockey, Sunday: football

Pupil's Book Activity 3

Make and play the game (Teacher's Resource Bank).

- Focus the pupils on Activity 3. They cut out and colour the cards.
- Demonstrate the activity. Position one of the sports on each day of the week. Choose either Jake, Beth or Molly to describe. The pupils listen and place the sports on the correct day. Next, a pupil takes your part.
- Talk Partners The pupils play the game with a Talk Partner. When they have placed all the cards, they check the answers with their partner: *Is this right? Yes, it is.* The pupils change roles and play again.

Ending the lesson

Review the lesson.

- Say **Today we've practised a tongue twister**. Ask pupils to say it again.
- Then ask **Did you enjoy the *Snap!* game?**

Review the task flashcards.

- Point to the task flashcards. Say **Look at the activities you've done today. Which activity was your favourite?** Elicit the pupils' favourite activities.

Cooperative learning

Working together as a team

- Talk Partners Play *Beat the clock* to practise pronunciation. Pairs work together as a team to say as many words with the 'ai' / 'ay' sound as possible in 30 seconds. Feed back to the group. The pupils include any words from their Science lessons that contain the sound.
- Make a pronunciation wall display. Use a raindrop to represent 'ai' and a speech bubble to represent 'ay'. The pupils write and illustrate words with 'ai' or 'ay'. They stick them in the corresponding shape.

Key Competences and Key Learning Outcomes

- Read about Sports Day in Britain
- Learn that muscles pull our bones to help us move (optional)
- Listen for general understanding
- Think about the sports you play at school

Key language

- *balloon toss, egg and spoon race, sack race, wheelbarrow race*
- *What sports do you play at school?*

Recycled: *balloon, catch, fast, hands, jump, legs, run, throw*

Recycled: *I play / do … I like … My favourite … This is the …*

Materials

- Pupil's Book p14; Activity Book p11; Class CD1; Teacher's App on Navio
- Teacher's Resource Bank: Task flashcards: *listen, read, think, number, write, draw, say, tick, Talk Partners*

Optional materials

- Teacher's Resource Bank: Five Trinity Exam Practice cards (selected from the Starter Unit)

At a Glance Lesson Plan

Pupil's Book

Starting the lesson

- Use the Trinity Exam Practice cards (optional).
- **Talk Partners** Review *Toby's tongue twister*.

▶ *CD1 Track 22 p257*

- Set learning outcomes using the task flashcards.

Activity 1

- Listen and read. Answer.

▶ *CD1 Track 24 p258*

Think about your culture

- What sports do you play at school?

Go to the Activity Book.

Ending the lesson

- Review the lesson.
- Review the task flashcards.

Extra activities

Reinforcement

- Play *Can you guess?*

Extension

- Play Sports Day games.

Link to Science

- **The human body:** muscles pull our bones to help us move

Digital resources

Teacher's Digital: Don't forget you can teach this lesson using the Teacher's App on Navio.

Powered By NAVIO

Activity Book

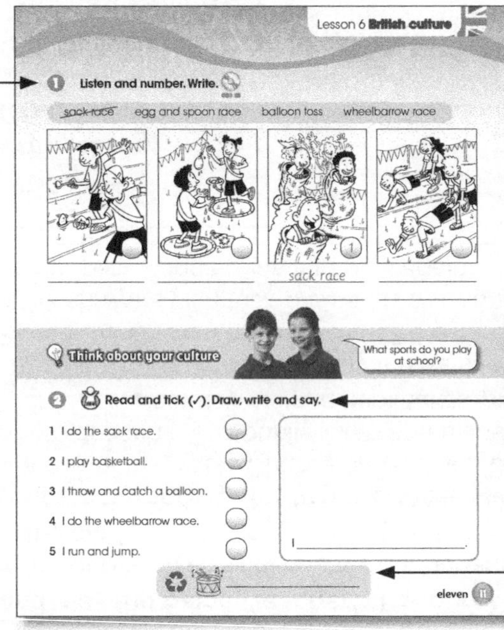

Activity Book

Activity 1

- Listen and number.
- Write.

▶ *CD1 Track 25 p258*

Activity 2: Think about your culture

- Read and tick (✓).
- Draw, write and say.

Recycled vocabulary

- Look, remember and write the word.

Starting the lesson

Use the Trinity Exam Practice cards (optional).

- The pupils practise asking and answering questions. (See p31.)

Review Toby's tongue twister.

▶ *CD1 Track 22 p257*

- Ask the class **What sound did you practise in Toby's tongue twister?** *('ai')*. Ask if they can remember the tongue twister. *(Snails play in the rain all day.)*
- Talk Partners The pupils practise the tongue twister as a class and then with a Talk Partner. The pairs practise saying it as fast as possible, reading from the Pupil's Book (page 13) if necessary. Choose a fast pair to say the tongue twister for the class.
- Draw a chart with two columns ('ai' and 'ay') on the board. Elicit words with both spellings. Ask pupils to write the words in the corresponding column, e.g. 'ai': *rain, Spain;* 'ay': *day, play.*

Set learning outcomes using the task flashcards.

- Say **Today we're going to learn about Sports Day in schools in Britain.**
- Hold up the task flashcards in turn and elicit the activities. Stick them on one side of the board. Point to them during the lesson to reinforce your instructions.

Background information

- Sports Days are organised once a year by schools in Britain. A wide variety of games are played ranging from the more straightforward sprint to the traditional egg and spoon race, wheelbarrow race, balloon toss and sack race. Other activities include parent races and the three-legged race.

Pupil's Book Activity 1

Listen and read. Answer.

▶ *CD1 Track 24 p258*

- (Books open.) Say **Let's find out about Sports Day in Britain. What can you see?**
- Play the CD. Check understanding by pointing to each photo and asking the pupils to name the activity.

Pupil's Book Think about your culture

What sports do you play at school?

- Read the question and ask the class what sports they play at school.

Activity Book

Activity 1

Listen and number. Write.

▶ *CD1 Track 25 p258*

- The pupils name the activities on the Sports Day posters. Play the CD. Pause to check pupils' answers. The pupils point to and number the correct Sports Day activity each time. After checking their answers, pupils write the name of each sport under the corresponding poster.

Answers: egg and spoon race 2, balloon toss 4, sack race 1, wheelbarrow race 3

Activity 2: Think about your culture

Read and tick (✓). Draw, write and say.

- Read out the question in the speech bubble. Elicit the pupils' answers.
- Read out the first sentence as a class and ask the pupils to tick the box if they do the sack race at school. Repeat with the other sentences.
- Ask the pupils to design a Sports Day poster and draw one of the sports they do at school.
- Invite pupils to show the class their posters and prompt them to say what they do.

Recycled vocabulary

- The pupils look at the picture and write the word.

Answer: Music

Ending the lesson

Review the lesson.

- Say **Today you've learnt about Sports Day in Britain. Do you think Sports Day is a good idea? Would you like to have Sports Day in your school?**

Review the task flashcards.

- Point to the task flashcards. Say **Look at the activities you've done today. Which activity was your favourite?** Elicit the pupils' favourite activities.

Extra activities

Reinforcement

- Play *Can you guess?* The pupils take turns to choose and mime activities from the lesson, asking and answering questions to guess the chosen action. Include verbs the pupils know from Level 1: *fly, walk, swim, sit down, stand up,* etc.:

  Pupil A: (mimes swimming)
  Pupil B: *Are you flying?*
  Pupil A: *No, I'm not.*
  Pupil B: *Are you swimming?*
  Pupil A: *Yes, I am.*

Extension

- Play Sports Day games. Remind the pupils of the rules for each game:

  Balloon toss game: In this game, you throw and catch a balloon with your partner.

  Egg and spoon race: Use a golf ball or ping pong ball. In this race, try to keep the 'egg' on the spoon. Run as fast as you can!

  Wheelbarrow race: Hold your friend's legs. Don't go too fast!

  Sack race: You jump and jump to the finish line.

Link to Science

- If you are studying the Science topic of **the human body** in English, remind the pupils that muscles pull our bones to help us move. Muscles are elastic and soft and they contract and relax to help us move.
- In pairs, pupils perform the Sports Day activities. Ask them to move in slow motion, concentrating on their muscle movements.

Key Competences and Key Learning Outcomes

- Read for specific information

- Read and understand a poem
- Write and act out a poem

Key language

- *overarm, underarm*

Recycled: *big, small; basketball, bounce, catch, football, hockey, kick, tennis, throw, volleyball*

Materials

- Pupil's Book p15; Activity Book p12; Class CD1; Teacher's App on Navio
- Teacher's Resource Bank: Task flashcards: *think, circle, listen, read, Talk Partners, number, act out*

Optional materials

- Teacher's Resource Bank: Five Trinity Exam Practice cards (selected from the Starter Unit)

At a Glance Lesson Plan

Pupil's Book

Starting the lesson

- Use the Trinity Exam Practice cards (optional).
- Play *On Sports Day*.
- Set learning outcomes using the task flashcards.

Before you read: Activity 1

- Talk about ball games.
- Which balls do you think are in the poem? Circle.

Activity 2

- Listen and read the poem.

▶ *CD1 Track 26 p258*

After you read

Go to page 12 in your Activity Book.

Ending the lesson

- Review the lesson.
- Review the task flashcards.

Extra activity

- Sing a song (optional).

Cooperative learning

Working together as a class

- Write a class poem.

Activity Book

Activity Book

After you read: Activity 1

- Remember the poem. Number.

Activity 2

- Choose and write your own poem.

- **Talk Partners** Act out.

Recycled vocabulary

- Look, remember and write the word.

Digital resources

Teacher's Digital: Don't forget you can teach this lesson using the Teacher's App on Navio.

Pupil's Digital: Encourage your pupils to use the Pupil's App on Navio to practise the vocabulary from this lesson.

Powered By NAVIO

Starting the lesson

Use the Trinity Exam Practice cards (optional).

- The pupils practise asking and answering questions. (See p31.)

Play *On Sports Day.*

- Ask the pupils what they remember about Sports Days in Britain. Say **On Sports Day he jumps**. Choose a pupil to repeat your statement and add another action: *On Sports Day, he throws the balloon and he jumps.* The next pupil repeats both statements and adds another: *On Sports Day, he runs and he throws the balloon and he jumps.* Repeat until a mistake is made. Encourage the pupils to include everyday sports in their Sports Day as well.
- Talk Partners The pupils play the game with a Talk Partner, this time talking about a girl, e.g. *On Sports Day, she plays football.*

Set learning outcomes using the task flashcards.

- Say **Today we're going to read a poem.**
- Hold up the task flashcards in turn and elicit the activities. Stick them on one side of the board. Point to them during the lesson to reinforce your instructions.

Before you read: Pupil's Book Activity 1

Talk about ball games.

- (Books closed.) Encourage the pupils to name as many ball games as they can. Ask individuals which ball games they play.

Which balls do you think are in the poem? Circle.

- (Books open.) Tell the pupils that they are going to read a poem. Ask **Do you know any poems?** The pupils name any poems they have read in English or in L1.
- Tell the pupils the title of the poem (Ball!) and ask them to predict the kinds of balls they will read about. They name different balls and circle those they think will be in the poem.
- Ask **What action words do you think are in the poem?** The pupils predict the actions.

Pupil's Book Activity 2

Listen and read the poem.

▶ *CD1 Track 26 p258*

- Read the poem collectively.
- After reading, ask **What balls are in the poem? What action words are in the poem?** Elicit the types of balls and action words to see if the pupils guessed correctly. Ask **Do you like the poem?** Say **My favourite line is (Bounce me!).**
- Talk Partners Pupils select and say their favourite line with a Talk Partner.
- Go through the poem again line by line creating actions with the pupils (see below). The pupils stand up and act out the poem, saying the lines and performing the actions at the same time.

Suggested actions

- Big ball (Open arms wide)
- Small ball (Hold finger and thumb close together)
- Tennis ball (Mime serving the ball in tennis)
- Hockey ball (Mime hitting a hockey ball)
- Football (Mime kicking a ball)
- Basketball (Mime shooting a basket)
- Volleyball (Mime punching a ball up into the air with two fists)
- Any ball! (Arms out)
- Catch me! (Mime catching a ball)
- Bounce me! (Mime bouncing a ball on the floor)
- Kick me! (Mime kicking a ball)
- Throw me! (Mime throwing a ball)
- Underarm (Mime an underarm throw)
- Overarm (Mime an overarm throw)
- Ball! (Cup both hands together in the shape of a ball)

Activity Book

After you read: Activity 1

Remember the poem. Number.

- Invite the class to identify and read out the first verse of the poem. Then ask **What's next?** The class reads out and numbers the next section of the poem. Repeat for the remaining sections.

Answers: 4 2 1 3

Activity 2

Choose and write your own poem. Act out.

- Explain that the pupils are going to write their own poem. The pupils should select words to complete each line. Remind them to think about which spaces require an action, an adjective or a sport.
- Talk Partners Pupils take turns reading and performing their poem with a Talk Partner.

Recycled vocabulary

- The pupils look at the picture and write the word.

Answer: Science

Ending the lesson

Review the lesson.

- Say **Today we read a poem about balls.** Then say **Today you wrote a poem about balls.**

Review the task flashcards.

- Point to the task flashcards. Say **Look at the activities you've done today. Which activity was your favourite?** Elicit the pupils' favourite activities.

Extra activity

Sing a song (optional).

- Choose a song. The class sings and does the actions. Alternatively, invite the class to choose a song to sing.

Cooperative learning

Working together as a class

- Write a class poem about a ball. Elicit types of balls and write them on one side of the board. Elicit words to describe the balls, e.g. *big, small, old, new, fast, slow, red, black, white.*
- Encourage the pupils to suggest new lines for the poem. Write them on the board in the form of a poem, e.g. *Fast ball / Slow ball / New ball / Old ball …*
- Read the poem once it is finished. Congratulate the class on their team effort.

Key Competences and Key Learning Outcomes

- Review language in the unit
- Reflect on own learning
- Sing a cooperative learning song

Key language

- *Well done (everyone)!*

Recycled: *baseball, basketball, bounce, catch, cycling, football, hit, hockey, jump, kick, rollerblading, run, skateboarding, swimming, tennis, throw, volleyball*

Recycled: *I play / go … Do you play / go …? Yes, I do. / No, I don't. He / She (kicks)*

Materials

- Pupil's Book p16; Activity Book p13; Class CD1; Teacher's App on Navio
- Sports flashcards
- Teacher's Resource Bank: Task flashcards: *listen, number, write, say, sing, Talk Partners, think, stick*
- Teacher's Resource Bank: Traffic light cut-out
- *Give Me Five!* sticker

Optional materials

- Teacher's Resource Bank: Five Trinity Exam Practice cards (selected from the Starter Unit)

At a Glance Lesson Plan

Pupil's Book

Starting the lesson

- Use the Trinity Exam Practice cards (optional).
- Review the unit vocabulary.
- Set learning outcomes using the task flashcards.

Activity 1

- Listen and number. Write and say.
- ▶ ***CD1 Track 27 p258***

Activity 2

- Listen. Look at Activity 1.
- ▶ ***CD1 Track 28 p258***
- **Talk Partners** Ask and answer.

Activity 3 Cooperative learning

- Sing *Well done!*
- ▶ ***CD1 Track 29 p258***
- Stick the *Give Me Five!* sticker.
- Go to the Activity Book.

Ending the lesson

- Review the task flashcards.
- Sing a song (optional).

Cooperative learning

- **Think-Pair-Share** Remember the ten sports words.

Activity Book

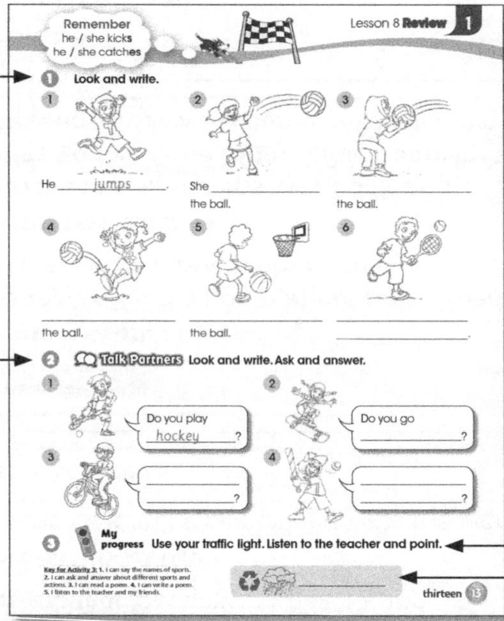

Activity Book

Activity 1

- Look and write.

Activity 2

- Look and write.
- **Talk Partners** Ask and answer.

Activity 3 My progress

- Use your traffic light. Listen to the teacher and point.

Recycled vocabulary

- Look, remember and write the word.

Digital resources

Teacher's Digital: Don't forget you can teach this lesson using the Teacher's App on Navio.

Pupil's Digital: Encourage your pupils to use the Pupil's App on Navio to practise the vocabulary from this lesson.

Powered By NAVIO

Starting the lesson

Use the Trinity Exam Practice cards (optional).

- The pupils practise asking and answering questions. (See p31.)

Review the unit vocabulary.

- Play *Quick flash* (see p23) and stick the flashcards on the board once the pupils have guessed them. Choose one and ask the pupils to guess which it is by asking **Do you play volleyball / go cycling?** Answer **No, I don't.** until the pupils guess the correct card.
- Talk Partners The pupils play with a Talk Partner.

Set learning outcomes using the task flashcards.

- Say **Today we're going to remember what we've learnt in Unit 1.**
- Hold up the task flashcards in turn and elicit the words. Stick them on one side of the board. Point to them during the lesson to reinforce your instructions.

Pupil's Book Activity 1

Listen and number. Write and say.

▶ *CD1 Track 27 p258*

- (Books open.) Point to each of the sports and elicit the words.
- Play the CD. Pause after each sentence. The pupils write the correct number in the circles.
- Play the CD again. The pupils write the correct word under each picture. Then they say the words.

Answers: **1** football **2** basketball **3** swimming **4** volleyball **5** baseball **6** cycling **7** rollerblading **8** tennis **9** hockey **10** skateboarding

Pupil's Book Activity 2

Listen. Look at Activity 1. Ask and answer.

▶ *CD1 Track 28 p258*

- Play the CD as a model. Invite two confident pupils to act out the conversation.
- Talk Partners The pupils ask and answer questions about the sports with a Talk Partner.

Pupil's Book Activity 3: Cooperative learning

- **Sing *Well done!***

▶ *CD1 Track 29 p258*

- Praise the class for their hard work and play the *Well done!* song. The pupils listen and do the actions with you. Play the CD a second time and encourage the pupils to join in and do the actions.

Stick the *Give Me Five!* sticker.

- The pupils stick the *Give Me Five!* sticker on the Pupil's Book page.
- Variation: Sing the song and stick the *Give Me Five!* sticker after the pupils have also completed the Activity Book Lesson 8 Review.

Activity Book

Activity 1

Look and write.

- Look at the first picture and read the sentence. Then ask the pupils to write in the missing words.

Talk Partners The pupils read the sentences to a Talk Partner.

Answers: **1** jumps **2** throws **3** She catches **4** She kicks **5** He bounces **6** He hits the ball.

Activity 2

Look and write. Ask and answer.

- Look at the pictures and elicit the missing words. The pupils complete the questions.

Talk Partners The pupils ask and answer the questions with a Talk Partner.

Answers: **1** hockey **2** skateboarding **3** Do you go cycling? **4** Do you play baseball?

Activity 3 My progress

Use your traffic light. Listen to the teacher and point.

- (Books closed.) Ask the class to take out their traffic light cut-out. Say **Let's think about our work in this unit.** Read the first self-assessment statement. Point to the green circle and say **Yes, I can do this very well.** Point to the orange circle and say **Yes, I can do this.** Point to the red circle and say **No, I can't do this.**
- Read the statements. For each one, the pupils point to the colour on their traffic light that shows how they feel about their own learning.

Self-assessment statements

1. I can say the names of sports.
2. I can ask and answer about different sports and actions.
3. I can read a poem.
4. I can write a poem.
5. I listen to the teacher and my friends.

Recycled vocabulary

- The pupils look at the picture and write the word.

Answer: stormy

Ending the lesson

Review the task flashcards.

- Point to the task flashcards. Say **Look at the activities you've done today. Which activity was your favourite?** Elicit the pupils' favourite activities.

Sing a song (optional).

- The class chooses their favourite song from the unit. The class sings and does the actions.

Cooperative learning

Think-Pair-Share

- Ask **Can you remember the ten sports?** Ask the class to think silently on their own for a minute.

Talk Partners The pupils work with a Talk Partner to remember and name all ten items.

- Invite a pair to say one of the sports. Hold up the corresponding flashcard and prompt the class to repeat the word.
- Finally, repeat the procedure, asking different pairs of pupils each time, until all ten sports have been named. Encourage the pupils to say *play* or *go* with each sport.

Key Competences and Key Learning Outcomes

- Watch and understand a video about Sports Day at school
- Say what sports you join in
- Understand the importance of joining in

Key language

- *baseball, basketball, cycling, football, hockey, rollerblading, skateboarding, swimming, tennis, volleyball; egg and spoon race, sack race, three-legged race, skip, tug of war*

Materials

- Pupil's Book p17; Activity Book p14; Class CD1; Video; Teacher's App on Navio
- Teacher's Resource Bank: Task flashcards: *number, listen, Talk Partners, draw, think, say, tick, circle, read*
- Sports flashcards

Optional materials

- Teacher's Resource Bank: Trinity Exam Practice cards (selected from Unit 1)
- Poster paper

At a Glance Lesson Plan

Pupil's Book

Starting the lesson

- Use the Trinity Exam Practice cards (optional).
- **Think-Pair-Share** Review Sports Day in British schools.
- Set learning outcomes and use the task flashcards.

Pre-watching activity

- Play *Class chain* to review sports.
- Look at the photo and talk about what sports the pupils play.

Activity 1

- Watch the video with no sound and identify the activities.
- Watch the video.
  Unit 1 video p278
- Number the pictures.

Activity 2

- Watch the video again.
  Unit 1 video
- Read and tick (✓) or cross (✗).

Video and 21st Century Skills 1

21 CHANNEL

Welcome back to Channel 21! Today's programme is about Sports Day. What sports do you play at school?

1 Watch the video. Number the pictures.

2 Watch the video again. Read and tick (✓) or cross (✗).

1 The girls win the tug of war. ✗ 3 The eggs are all different colours.

2 The boys can't skip. 4 All the children join in.

3 Read and circle.

Joining in

It's important to join in with the activities on Sports Day. What games do you like?

1 I (like) / don't like the egg and spoon race. 2 I like / don't like the tug of war.

3 I like / don't like the sack race. 4 I like / don't like the three-legged race.

Key learning outcomes: watch and understand a video about sports day. Ways of working: learn to join in

seventeen 17

Activity 3

- Read and circle.
- Go to the Activity Book.

Ending the lesson

- Review the lesson.
- Review the task flashcards. Elicit the pupils' favourite activities at school.

Cooperative learning

- Talk about joining in.

Digital resources

Teacher's Digital: Don't forget you can teach this lesson using the Teacher's App on Navio.

Pupil's Digital: Encourage your pupils to use the Pupil's App on Navio to practise the vocabulary from this lesson.

Powered By NAVIO

Activity Book

1 Video and 21st Century Skills

Joining in

1 What sports do they join in with? Listen and tick (✓).

21 CHANNEL What sports do you join in with?

2 Read and tick (✓). Draw, point and say.

1 I do the egg and spoon race.

2 I do the tug of war.

3 I do the sack race.

4 I do the three-legged race.

I join in with the ______

3 ______

14 fourteen

Activity Book

Activity 1

- What sports do they join in with? Listen and tick (✓).
- ▶ *CD1 Track 30 p258*

Activity 2

- Read and tick (✓). Draw, point and say.

Recycled vocabulary

- Look, remember and write the numeral.

Starting the lesson

Use the Trinity Exam Practice cards (optional).

- The pupils practise asking and answering questions.
  Think-Pair-Share Review Sports Day in British schools.
- Ask **Can you remember the four activities at the Sports Day in Britain?**
  Talk Partners The pupils work with a Talk Partner to name the activities.
- Invite different Talk Partners to say a different activity. Write the activities on the board and prompt the class to repeat the activity.

Set learning outcomes and use the task flashcards.

- Say **Today we're going to watch a video and then ask and answer questions about Sports Day**.
- Hold up the task flashcards, in turn, and elicit the activities. Stick them on the side of the board. Point to them during the lesson to reinforce your instructions.

Pre-watching activity

- Play *Class chain* with the sports flashcards. (See p23.)
- Look at the photo of Abby, Sophie and Tom. Read the speech bubble to pupils. Ask **What sports do you play at Sports Day?** Elicit responses.

Pupil's Book Activity 1

Watch the video. Number the pictures? *p278*

- Ask **What is the video about? Does Sophie like sports?** Play Part 1. Elicit answers.
- Ask **What sports can you see?** Play Part 2 with no sound.
- Focus the pupils' attention on the video stills. Ask **Where are the children? What can you see?** Then say **Let's watch and listen.**
- Play Part 2 pausing after the first video still. Ask the pupils to point to the corresponding photo in their book.
- Play the rest of Part 2 for pupils to point to the photos in order and write the numbers in order of the photos.

Answers: from left to right 2 1 3 4

Pupil's Book Activity 2

Watch the video again. Read and tick (✓) or cross (✗).

- Play Part 1 and 2 again. Pause after Sophie says, *Come on girls*. Read out the first sentence in Activity 2. Ask **Do the girls win the tug of war?**
- Read out sentence 2. Ask pupils if they draw a tick or a cross. Play Part 2. Pupils tick or cross the sentences.
- Ask the pupils some questions to check understanding. Suggested questions. **What sports does Sophie like?** *(Football and basketball.)*
  What is it important to do in the three-legged race? *(Walk slowly and wait for your friend.)*
  Who is the winner of the race? *(The girl in the blue and white top.)*
  What activity does Tom want to do? *(Egg and spoon.)*
  Does Sophie want to join in? *(No.)* **Why?** *(It looks difficult.)*
  What does Abby say to make Sophie join in? *(Come on, it's fun!)*

Answers: 1 ✗ 2 ✗ 3 ✓ 4 ✓

Pupil's Book Activity 3

Read and circle.

- Point to the pictures to elicit the vocabulary. Encourage the pupils to say if they like the activity or not.
- Read out number one, including the circled word.
- The pupils read the other sentences and circle if they like or don't like the activity.
  Think-Pair-Share Read out the speech bubble and ask **Why is it important to join in with activities on Sports Day?**

Answers: Pupils' own answers

Activity Book

Activity 1

What sports do they join in with? Listen and tick (✓).

▶ *CD1 Track 30 p258*

- Ask **What sports and activities can you see?**
- Play the first exchange on the CD. Ask **What sport is Grace playing?** Show the ticked picture.
- Play the rest of the CD, pausing after each exchange for pupils to tick the picture.

Answers: **1** volleyball **2** hockey **3** cycling **4** skateboarding

Activity 2

Read and tick (✓). Draw, point and say.

- Ask a few pupils **What sports do you join in with?**
- The pupils tick the activities they join in with on Sports Day. Then they draw the activities.
  Talk Partners In pairs, pupils take turns to ask and answer *What sports do you join in with?*

Recycled vocabulary

Answer: three

Ending the lesson

Review the lesson.

- Say **Today we've watched a video about Sports Day.** Ask **Which activity was easy / difficult?**

Review the task flashcards.

- Point to the task flashcards on the board. Say **Look at the activities you've done today. Which activity was your favourite?**

Cooperative learning

Joining in

- Ask the pupils to tell you other times when it's important to join in. For example, working together in pairs and groups in the class, playing games and helping out in the classroom and at home.

Date: ____________ Unit: ________

1 What did my pupils learn in this unit?

2 How did my pupils work? (✓)

individually ☐ in pairs ☐ in small groups ☐

in large groups ☐ as a class ☐

3 Which key competences did my pupils develop?

- Competence in linguistic communication ☐
- Competence in mathematics, science and technology ☐
- Digital competence ☐
- Learning to learn ☐
- Social and civic competences ☐
- Sense of initiative and entrepreneurship ☐
- Cultural awareness and expression ☐

4 Which lessons / activities were the most successful and why?

5 Which lessons / activities did my pupils find the most difficult and why?

6 What did I try in the classroom for the first time? How did it go?

7 Which resources did I find most useful? (including webpages)

8 What could I do differently next time I teach this unit?

Unit 2

Let's go shopping!

Unit overview

Key Competences and Key Learning Outcomes

- Identify and say ten food items (Lesson 1)
- Use indefinite articles: a / an / some (Lesson 2)
- Read, listen and understand a story about a naughty parrot (Lesson 3)
- Ask and answer questions about the price of food (Lesson 4)
- Read about Pancake Day in Britain (Lesson 6)
- Watch and understand a video about recipes (Video and 21st Century Skills)

- Count to fifty (numbers 10–50) (Lesson 4)

- Use the Pupil's App on Navio
- Find recipes online (Video and 21st Century Skills)

- Use a strategy to practise spelling key words (Lesson 1)
- Say a tongue twister and practise 'ee' and 'ea' spellings (Lesson 5)
- Review language in the unit and reflect on own learning (Lesson 8)
- Practise activity types found in the Cambridge Exams: Pre A1 Starters

- Understand the importance of saying 'please' when you ask for something (Lesson 3)

- Work with a Talk Partner to practise and reinforce learning (all lessons)
- Play a communication game about shopping (Lesson 5)

- Sing four songs (Lessons 1, 4, 5 and 8)
- Understand, act out and give an opinion on a story (Lesson 3)
- Learn about Pancake Day in Britain (Lesson 6)
- Think about special food days where you live (Lesson 6)
- Read, understand and write a recipe (Lesson 7)

Vocabulary

Core vocabulary
bread, carrots, green beans, lemons, peaches, pineapples, potatoes, sweets, tomatoes, yoghurt; numbers 1–50

Extension vocabulary (optional)
blackberry, broccoli, coconut, lettuce, lime, peas, plum; sixty, seventy, eighty, ninety

Other vocabulary
food, shopping; money, naughty, shop, shopping list; bowl, chocolate, cook, flour, make, mix, pancake, put, races, sugar, toss; olives, sandwich, slices

Recycled vocabulary
apples, cake, cheese, chicken, chips, eggs, fish, grapes, ice cream, meat, milk, oranges, pasta, pears, pineapple, rice, salad, water; delicious; breakfast, lunch, dinner; eyes, hair, mouth, nose

Structures

Core structures
Can I have (a / an / some) ..., please?
Yes, of course. Here you are. Thank you very much.
How much is this (lemon)? How much are these (green beans)?
It's (50 cents). They're (25 cents). Great! I'll take it / them.

Other structures
Let's go (shopping). Can I help you? Put them in the bag. We've got (bread) for lunch. I help / put … She puts in (flour). She tosses (the pancake). We have (pancake races). There isn't any food in the bag.

Recycled structures
I like / I love / I don't like … Do you like …? Yes, I do. No, I don't.

Phonics

Alternative vowel spellings **'ee'** / **'ea'** (Qu**ee**n, J**ea**n, **ea**ts, m**ea**t, gr**ee**n, sh**ee**p, ch**ee**se)

British Culture

Pancake Day

Literacy

Text type: a recipe (instructional text)
Reading skills: predicting from pictures; reviewing information; sequencing; matching

21st Century Skills

Digital skills: finding information online

Cooperative learning

Songs: *What do I need to do?* (Lesson 5); *Well Done!* (Lesson 8)
Skills: Listening to others (Lesson 2); Working together as a team (Lessons 4 and 5); Encouraging one another (Lesson 7); Think-Pair-Share (Lesson 8)

Values

The importance of saying please when you ask for something.

Cross-curricular links

Links to Science
Food: The five food groups; health, growth and energy; balanced meals: wheat, eggs and milk

Suggested Arts and Crafts concepts
Identifying and using natural shapes and colours of food; making and playing a shopping game

Key Competences and Key Learning Outcomes

- Identify and say ten food items
- Say the vocabulary chant
- Stick the food stickers
- Identify the five food groups (optional)
- Use a strategy to practise spelling key words
- Sing a song about shopping

Key language
- *bread, carrots, green beans, lemons, peaches, pineapples, potatoes, sweets, tomatoes, yoghurt*

Extension vocabulary
- *blackberry, broccoli, coconut, lettuce, lime, peas, plum*

Recycled: *bag, meat*

Recycled: *I like, I love, I don't like … Do you like …? Yes, I do. No, I don't. Let's go (shopping).*

Other vocabulary: *food, shopping*

Materials
- Pupil's Book p18; Activity Book pp16 and 25; Class CD1; Teacher's App on Navio; Unit 2 stickers
- Food flashcards
- Teacher's Resource Bank: Food word cards
- Teacher's Resource Bank: Task flashcards: *listen, sing, read, stick, say, Talk Partners, read, match, write*

Optional materials
- Teacher's Resource Bank: Five Trinity Exam Practice cards (selected from the Starter Unit and Unit 1)

At a Glance Lesson Plan

Pupil's Book

Starting the lesson
- Use the Trinity Exam Practice cards (optional).
- **Think-Pair-Share** Review food words.
- Set learning outcomes using the task flashcards.

Vocabulary presentation
- Present the new vocabulary.

Activity 1
- Listen and point.
- ▶ *CD1 Track 31 p258*
- Sing *Let's go shopping!*

Word cards
- Read the word cards.
- Match them to the flashcards.

Activity 2
- Read and stick the ten stickers.
- Listen and say the chant.
- ▶ *CD1 Track 33 p258*
- Go to the Activity Book.

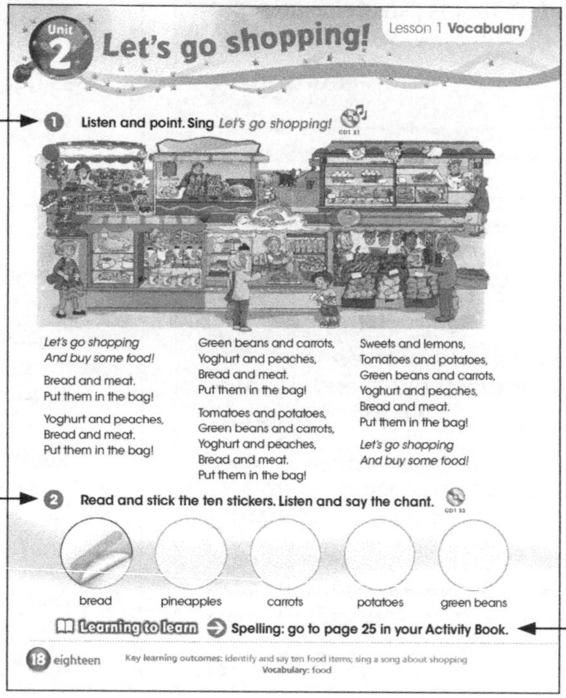

Ending the lesson
- Review the lesson.
- Review the task flashcards.

Extra activities

Reinforcement
- Play *Memory!*

Vocabulary extension
- Present seven additional vocabulary items.

Link to Science
- **Food:** the five food groups

Learning to learn

Spelling
- Practise spelling at any time during this unit (Activity Book p25).

Digital resources

Teacher's Digital: Don't forget you can teach this lesson using the Teacher's App on Navio.

Pupil's Digital: Encourage your pupils to use the Pupil's App on Navio to practise the vocabulary from this lesson.

Powered By NAVIO

Activity Book

Activity Book

Activity 1
- Read and match.

Activity 2
- What's in the bag? Draw and write.

Recycled vocabulary
- Look, remember and write the word.

Spelling

Let's practise spelling!
- Use the *Look-Copy-Cover-Write* technique.

Recycled vocabulary
- Look, remember and write the word.

Starting the lesson

Use the Trinity Exam Practice cards (optional).

- The pupils practise asking and answering questions. (See p31.)

Think-Pair-Share Review food words.

- Review the food words from Level 1. Ask **What do you like to eat? I like fish. Do you like fish?** *(Yes, I do. / No, I don't.)* Use mime if necessary.
- List the food the pupils name on the board.
- **Talk Partners** The pupils talk about the food they love, like and don't like with a Talk Partner.
- Discuss which food is good for them and which isn't. They say (*Fish / Apples*) (*is / are*) *good for me*.

Set learning outcomes using the task flashcards.

- Explain the aims of the lesson. Say **Today we're going to learn the names of different food.**
- Hold up the task flashcards and elicit the words. Stick them on one side of the board. Point to them during the lesson to reinforce your instructions.

Vocabulary presentation

Present the new vocabulary.

- (Books closed.) Show the pupils the food flashcards in turn. Ask **Do you like (bread)?** Elicit full sentences: *I (love / like / don't like) (bread, carrots)*, etc.
- (Books open.) Ask **Who can you see?** *(Jake, Molly, Mum and Dad.)* **Where are they?** *(At the market.)* **What food can you see?** The class points to and names the food items.

Pupil's Book Activity 1

Listen and point. Sing *Let's go shopping!*

▶ *CD1 Track 31 p258*

- Say **Let's listen to the song.** Play the CD.
- Play the CD again. The pupils sing and mime putting the food in a bag.

Word cards

Read the word cards. Match them to the flashcards.

- (Books closed.) Hold up a food word card. The pupils read collectively. A pupil sticks the word card next to the flashcard on the board. Repeat.
- Point to each word card. The pupils read the words.

Pupil's Book Activity 2

Read and stick the ten stickers. Listen and say the chant.

▶ *CD1 Track 33 p258*

- A pupil reads the first word. The pupils stick the corresponding sticker above the word.
- **Talk Partners** The pupils find and stick the remaining stickers. They ask and help each other using cooperative language, e.g. *(Where's the (bread)? Here! Where does this go?)*
- Play the CD. The pupils listen and say the chant, pointing to the stickers in turn.

Activity Book

Activity 1

Read and match.

- (Books open.) Ask a pupil to read the first sentence and point to the picture. The pupils read and match.

Answers: **1** a **2** b **3** d **4** c **5** e

Activity 2

What's in the bag? Draw and write.

- (Books open.) Read out the instructions. The pupils complete the drawings and write the words.

Answers: **1** bread and carrots **2** tomatoes and lemons **3** sweets and yoghurt **4** pineapple and green beans **5** potatoes and peaches

Recycled vocabulary

- The pupils look at the picture and write the word.

Answer: basketball

Ending the lesson

Review the lesson.

- Say **Today we've learnt the names of some food. What words do you remember?** Elicit the names.

Review the task flashcards.

- Point to the task flashcards. Say **Look at the activities you've done today. Which was your favourite?** Elicit the pupils' favourite activities.

Extra activities

Reinforcement

- Play *Memory!* (See p23.)

Vocabulary extension

- Present seven additional food words: *blackberry, broccoli, coconut*, *lettuce, lime, peas* and *plum.*
- Use the Vocabulary Booster on Navio to practise these new words.

Link to Science

- If you are studying the Science topic of **food** in English, you could review the five food groups. Write them on the board in columns. Show the flashcards one by one. The pupils classify them, e.g. *Peaches are fruit. Sweets are sugary food.*

Spelling (Activity Book p25)

Let's practise spelling!

- The pupils can practise spelling the ten food items using the *Look-Copy-Cover-Write* technique at any time during this unit before the Lesson 8 Review.

Recycled vocabulary

- The pupils look and write the word. If necessary, they look back at the previous unit.

Answer: volleyball

Key Competences and Key Learning Outcomes

- Use indefinite articles: a / an / some
- Complete and practise a conversation
- Identify foods for health, growth and energy (optional)
- Listen for specific information

Key language

- *Can I have (a tomato / an apple / some sweets), please?*

Recycled: *bread, carrots, green beans, lemons, peaches, pineapples, potatoes, sweets, tomatoes, yoghurt*

Materials

- Pupil's Book p19; Activity Book p17; Class CD1; Teacher's App on Navio
- Food flashcards
- Teacher's Resource Bank: Task flashcards: *listen, act out, circle, read, write, Talk Partners*

Optional materials

- Teacher's Resource Bank: Five Trinity Exam Practice cards (selected from the Starter Unit and Unit 1)

At a Glance Lesson Plan

Starting the lesson

- Use the Trinity Exam Practice cards (optional).
- Review food vocabulary. Play *Disappearing words*.
- Review the *Let's go shopping!* song.
- ▶ ***CD1 Track 31 p258***
- ▶ ***CD1 Track 32 p258 (optional karaoke version)***
- Set learning outcomes using the task flashcards.

Activity 1

- Listen and repeat.
- ▶ ***CD1 Track 34 p258***
- Talk Partners Act out.

Grammar focus

- *a, an, some*

Activity 2

- Listen and circle.
- ▶ ***CD1 Track 35 p259***
- Go to the Activity Book.

Pupil's Book

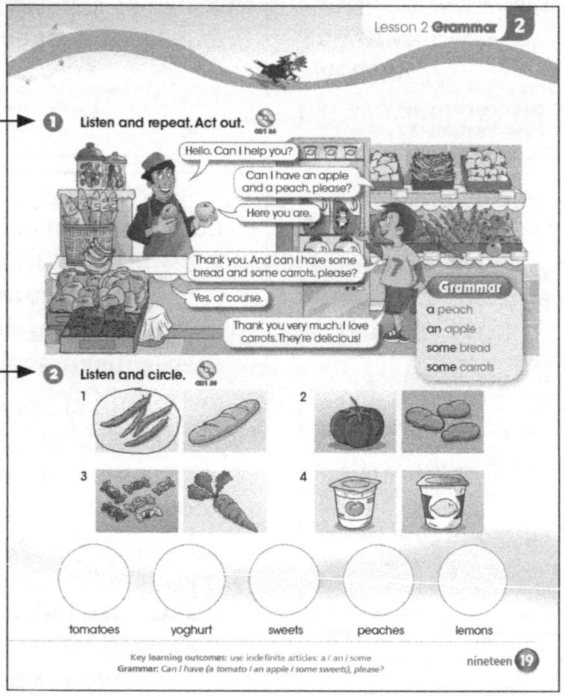

Ending the lesson

- Review the lesson.
- Review the task flashcards.

Cooperative learning

Listening to others

- Play *Memory chain.*

Link to Science

- **Food:** health, growth and energy

Digital resources

Teacher's Digital: Don't forget you can teach this lesson using the Teacher's App on Navio.

Pupil's Digital: Encourage your pupils to use the Pupil's App on Navio to practise the vocabulary from this lesson.

Powered By NAVIO

Activity Book

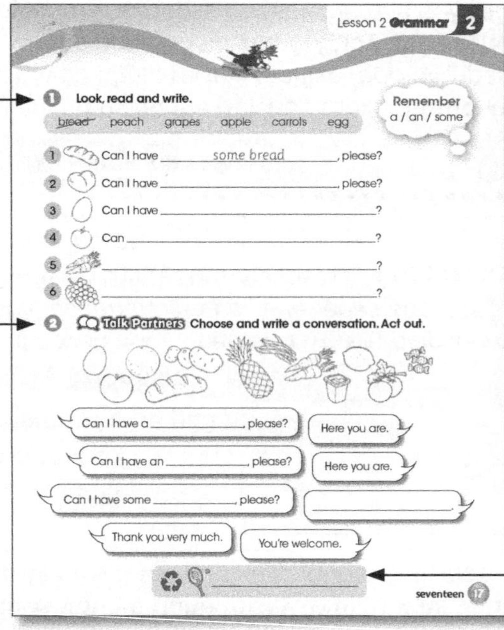

Activity Book

Activity 1

- Look, read and write.

Activity 2

- Choose and write a conversation.
- Talk Partners Act out.

Recycled vocabulary

- Look, remember and write the word.

Starting the lesson

Use the Trinity Exam Practice cards (optional).

- The pupils practise asking and answering questions. (See p31.)

Review food vocabulary.

- Play *Disappearing words.* (See p23.)

Review the *Let's go shopping!* song.

▶ *CD1 Track 31 p258*

▶ *CD1 Track 32 p258 (optional karaoke version)*

- Hand out the food flashcards to ten pupils and ask them to line up in the order of the song.
- Play the CD (or use the karaoke version). Pupils hold up their food cards as they hear the items in the song, miming putting them in a shopping bag at the end of each verse.

Set learning outcomes using the task flashcards.

- Explain the aims of the lesson. Say **Today we're going to learn how to ask for things when we go shopping.**
- Hold up the task flashcards and elicit the words. Stick them on one side of the board. Point to them during the lesson to reinforce your instructions.

Pupil's Book Activity 1

Listen and repeat. Act out.

▶ *CD1 Track 34 p258*

- (Books open.) Ask **Who can you see? Where are they?**
- Play the CD. The pupils listen and read the conversation. Check understanding. Ask **What does Jake ask for?**
- Play the CD again. Pause for the pupils to repeat.
- **Talk Partners** The pupils practise the conversation with a Talk Partner.

Grammar focus

a, an, some

- Remind the pupils that we use 'a' and 'an' to talk about one item that we can see and count. We use 'an' before a vowel.
- We use 'some' for more than one thing or items we can't count, e.g. *bread.*
- Draw a chart on the board with three columns ('a', 'an, 'some'). The pupils classify the items from the conversation. Say **apple**. Elicit *an apple*. Write 'apple' in the 'an' column, highlighting the initial vowel with a different colour. Repeat with the other items.

Pupil's Book Activity 2

Listen and circle.

▶ *CD1 Track 35 p259*

- (Books open.) Ask the pupils to name the food in the pictures. Ask **What food does Jake buy?**
- Play the CD. Pause after each conversation. The pupils circle the correct food.

Answers: **1** green beans **2** potatoes **3** a carrot **4** a peach yoghurt

Activity Book

Activity 1

Look, read and write.

- (Books open.) A pupil reads the example. Remind the class why we say *'some' bread*. The pupils complete the sentences individually, using 'a', 'an' or 'some' with each food word.

Answers: **1** some bread **2** a peach **3** an egg, please **4** I have an apple, please **5** Can I have some carrots, please **6** Can I have some grapes, please

Activity 2

Choose and write a conversation. Act out.

- A pupil reads the first speech bubble saying one of the food items.
- Another pupil reads out the second speech bubble. Repeat.

- **Talk Partners** The pupils write and practise their own conversation with a Talk Partner. Pairs read their conversations for their classmates.

Recycled vocabulary

- The pupils look at the picture and write the word.

Answer: tennis

Ending the lesson

Review the lesson.

- Say **Today you learnt to ask for food politely. Today you acted out a shopping conversation together.** Elicit some sentences.

Review the task flashcards.

- Point to the task flashcards. Say **Look at the activities you've done today. Which activity was your favourite?** Elicit the pupils' favourite activities.

Cooperative learning

Listening to others

- Play *Memory chain* to raise awareness of the importance of listening to classmates. Say **Can I have (some beans), please?** The pupil to your left repeats the question and adds another item *Can I have (some beans and some carrots), please*? Continue and then organise the pupils into small groups. Elicit food items from Level 1: *Can I have (an apple), please? Can I have (a banana), please?*

Link to Science

- If you are studying the Science topic of **food** in English, you could remind pupils that some foods help us grow, some keep us healthy and others give us energy.

Health: *apples, beans, carrots, grapes, lemons, oranges, peaches, pears, pineapple, salad, tomatoes, watermelon, fruit, vegetables*

Growth: *cheese, chicken, eggs, fish, meat, milk, yoghurt*

Energy: *bread, pasta, rice*

Key Competences and Key Learning Outcomes

- Read, listen and understand a story about a naughty parrot
- Read the story with some fluency
- Describe balanced meals (optional)
- Become familiar with the story through a pre-reading task
- Understand the importance of saying 'please' when you ask for something
- Understand and act out the story
- Give an opinion on the story

Key language

- *Can I have some bread, please? How much are these (green beans)? They're (twenty-five cents).*

Recycled: *breakfast, lunch, dinner; bread, carrots, green beans, potatoes, tomatoes, yoghurt*

Recycled: *We've got (bread and a peach yoghurt).*

Other vocabulary: *list, money, naughty, shop, shopping list*

Materials

- Pupil's Book pp20–21; Activity Book p18; Class CD1; Teacher's App on Navio
- Teacher's Resource Bank: Task flashcards: *listen, read, act out, write, draw, Talk Partners*
- Teacher's Resource Bank: Unit 2 Lesson 3 Animated Story

Optional materials

- Teacher's Resource Bank: Five Trinity Exam Practice cards (selected from the Starter Unit and Unit 1)

At a Glance Lesson Plan

Starting the lesson

- Use the Trinity Exam Practice cards (optional).
- Review the *Let's go shopping!* song.
- ▶ ***CD1 Track 31 p258***
- ▶ ***CD1 Track 32 p258 (optional karaoke version)***
- Set learning outcomes using the task flashcards.

Before you read

- Explain the story title.
- Read and answer the question.

Activity 1

- Listen and read.
- ▶ ***CD1 Track 36 p259***
- Act out.
- ***Now watch the animated story!***

After you read: Activity 2

- Go to page 18 in your Activity Book.
- Values: Read and write.

Pupil's Book

Ending the lesson

- Review the lesson.
- Review the task flashcards.

Link to Science

- **Food:** balanced meals

Activity Book

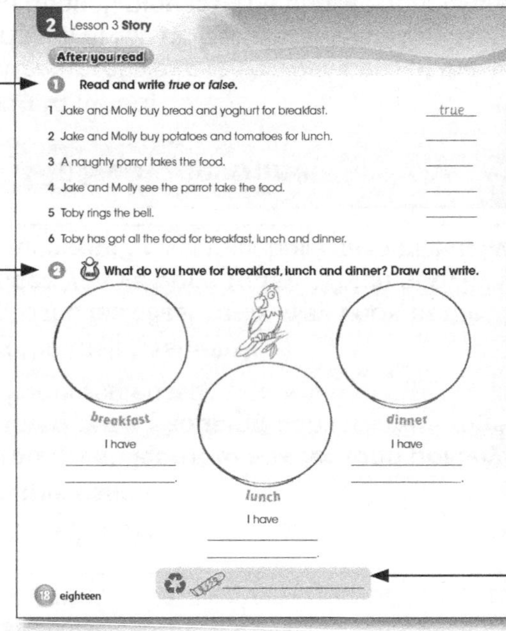

Activity Book

After you read: Activity 1

- Read and write *true* or *false*.

Activity 2

- What do you have for breakfast, lunch and dinner? Draw and write.

Recycled vocabulary

- Look, remember and write the word.

Digital resources

Teacher's Digital: Don't forget you can teach this lesson using the Teacher's App on Navio.

Pupil's Digital: Encourage your pupils to use the Pupil's App on Navio to practise the vocabulary from this lesson.

Powered By NAVIO

Starting the lesson

Use the Trinity Exam Practice cards (optional).

- The pupils practise asking and answering questions. (See p31.)

Review the *Let's go shopping!* song.

▶ *CD1 Track 31 p258*

▶ *CD1 Track 32 p258 (optional karaoke version)*

- Replace some of the food items in the song with others from Level 1: apples, bananas, fish, rice, etc. If you introduced extra vocabulary in Lesson 1, draw the items on the board and include them (*blackberry, broccoli, coconut, lettuce, lime, peas* and *plum*). Play the CD (or use the karaoke version). The pupils sing along.

Set learning outcomes using the task flashcards.

- Say **Today we're going to listen to a story.**
- Hold up the task flashcards and elicit the words. Stick them on one side of the board. Point to them during the lesson to reinforce your instructions.

Before you read

Explain the story title.

- (Books open.) Focus on the title and explain the meaning of *naughty*.

Read and answer the question.

- Ask the pupils to scan the story to find the food that Mum asks Jake and Molly to buy.
- Talk Partners The pupils feed back to a Talk Partner. The class names the food.

Answers: bread, potatoes, carrots, tomatoes, yoghurt, green beans

Pupil's Book Activity 1

Listen and read. Act out.

▶ *CD1 Track 36 p259*

- (Books open.) Play the CD. The pupils follow the text with their finger. Pause the CD between each story frame to check understanding. If necessary, ask questions after each frame.

Suggested comprehension questions

- Frame 1: **What does Mum give Jake and Molly?** *(A shopping list and some money.)*
- Frame 2: **What does Jake ask for?** *(Some bread and some potatoes.)*
- Frame 3: **What does Jake ask for?** *(Carrots, tomatoes and a yoghurt.)*
- Frame 4: **What happens to the bread and yoghurt?** *(A parrot takes them.)*
- Frame 5: **What have Jake and Molly got for lunch?** *(Green beans and carrots.)*
- Frame 6: **What happens to the potatoes and tomatoes?** *(The parrot takes them.)*
- Frame 7: **What does Toby do?** *(He rings the bell.)*
- Frame 8: **Have Jake and Molly got all the food now?** *(Yes.)*
- Ask **Did you like the story? What part did you like best?**
- Talk Partners The pupils choose their favourite frame.
- Organise the class into five groups (the narrator, Mum, Jake, Molly and the shopkeeper).
- Play the CD. Each group joins in when their character speaks. The pupils swap roles and repeat the activity.

After you read

Pupil's Book Activity 2

Go to page 18 in your Activity Book.

Activity Book

After you read: Activity 1

Read and write *true* or *false*.

- (Books open.) Read out the first sentence and elicit the answer *(true)*. Repeat with the other sentences, inviting a different pupil to read out the sentence each time.

Answers: **1** true **2** false **3** true **4** false **5** true **6** false

Activity 2 (me)

What do you have for breakfast, lunch and dinner? Draw and write.

- (Books open.) Ask **What do you have for (breakfast)?** Elicit food for each meal, reviewing vocabulary from the unit and from Level 1: *I have milk for breakfast*, etc. The pupils draw food they have for each meal and write a sentence.
- Talk Partners The pupils ask and answer about food they eat for each meal: *What do you have for (breakfast)? I have …* They comment on how healthy the meals are.

Recycled vocabulary

- The pupils look at the picture and write the word.

Answer: skateboarding

Pupil's Book Activity 2

Values: Read and write.

- Elicit that the child is at the toyshop and he wants to buy a car. Ask the pupils to tell you what word is important when you are asking for things *(please)*. Read the value and prompt the class to choose the correct word to complete the sentence.
- **Teacher's Tip:** British people use 'please' all the time when asking for things.

Ending the lesson

Review the lesson.

- Say **Today we listened to a story. Today we learnt to say 'please' when you ask for something.**

Review the task flashcards.

- Point to the task flashcards. Say **Look at the activities you've done today. Which activity was your favourite?** Elicit the pupils' favourite activities.

Link to Science

- If you are studying the Science topic of **food** in English, you could review balanced meals. A balanced meal should include a large portion of fruit and vegetables, a large portion of bread and cereals, some meat and fish or milk and dairy and only a little sugary food. The pupils look at the meals they drew in Activity 2 (Activity Book p18). Ask **Have you got fruit or vegetables? Have you got bread and cereals? What have you got?**

Key Competences and Key Learning Outcomes

- Ask and answer questions about the price of food
- Count to fifty (numbers 10–50)
- Sing a song

Key language

- numbers 1–50
- *How much is this (lemon)? How much are these (sweets)? It's (fifty) cents. They're (twenty-seven) cents. Great! I'll take it / them.*

Extension vocabulary

- *sixty, seventy, eighty, ninety*

Materials

- Pupil's Book p22; Activity Book p19; Class CD1; Teacher's App on Navio
- Teacher's Resource Bank: Task flashcards: *listen, say, sing, act out, Talk Partners, write*

Optional materials

- Teacher's Resource Bank: Five Trinity Exam Practice cards (selected from the Starter Unit and Unit 1)
- Prepare a large grid with the numbers 1–50 to display during the lesson.

At a Glance Lesson Plan

Pupil's Book

Starting the lesson

- Use the Trinity Exam Practice cards (optional).
- Review the Lesson 3 story.
- Play Can *I have some (apples), please?*
- Set learning outcomes using the task flashcards.

Activity 1

- Listen, point and say.

▶ *CD1 Track 37 p259*

Vocabulary presentation

- Present the new vocabulary.

Activity 2

- Listen and point. Sing *How much is this?*

▶ *CD1 Track 38 p259*

Grammar focus

- *This or these?*

Activity 3

- Listen and repeat.
- Talk Partners Act out.

▶ *CD1 Track 39 p259*

Go to the Activity Book.

Ending the lesson

- Review the lesson.
- Review the task flashcards.

Cooperative learning

Working together as a team

- Do a team dictation.

Extra activity

Vocabulary extension

- Present four additional vocabulary items.

Digital resources

Teacher's Digital: Don't forget you can teach this lesson using the Teacher's App on Navio.

Pupil's Digital: Encourage your pupils to use the Pupil's App on Navio to practise the vocabulary from this lesson.

Powered By NAVIO

Activity Book

Activity Book

Activity 1

- Listen and write the numbers.

▶ *CD1 Track 40 p259*

Activity 2

- Look and write.

Recycled vocabulary

- Look, remember and write the word.

Starting the lesson

Use the Trinity Exam Practice cards (optional).

- The pupils practise asking and answering questions. (See p31.)

Review the Lesson 3 story.

- Randomly name the food items that Jake and Molly buy on their shopping trip. The pupils scan the story and name the meal each item is for. Say **yoghurt.** *(Yoghurt is for breakfast.)* **Potatoes.** *(Potatoes are for dinner.)*

Play *Can I have some (apples), please?*

- Review the use of 'an', 'a' and 'some'. Say a food item (*apples*) and elicit the correct question. *Can I have some (apples), please?* Repeat with food items from Level 1 and the unit at random.

Set learning outcomes using the task flashcards.

- Say **Today we're going to learn the numbers up to fifty and ask about prices.**
- Hold up the task flashcards in turn and elicit the words. Stick them on one side of the board. Point to them during the lesson to reinforce your instructions.

Pupil's Book Activity 1

Listen, point and say.

▶ *CD1 Track 37 p259*

- (Books open.) Play the CD. The pupils repeat each word, pointing to the corresponding illustration each time.
- Play the CD again. Ask the pupils to flash their fingers in groups of ten.
- Display the grid you prepared with the numbers 1–50. Point to numbers at random and ask the pupils to say them. Ask **What number's this? Is this number twenty?** *(Yes, it is. / No, it isn't.)*

Vocabulary presentation

Present the new vocabulary.

- (Books open.) Point to the 10 cent coin. Say **Ten cents. Ten. Can you count to ten?** Count to ten with the pupils. Point to the next picture and say **Twenty cents. Twenty. Can you count to twenty?** Count to twenty with the pupils. Repeat for the remaining numbers.

Pupil's Book Activity 2

Listen and point. Sing *How much is this?*

▶ *CD1 Track 38 p259*

- (Books open.) Say **What can you see?** Point to the lemon and ask **How much is this?** Shrug your shoulders and say **I don't know.** Repeat for the carrots. Ask **How much are these?**
- Play the CD. The pupils listen and point to the food. Play the CD again. The pupils sing and do the actions.

Grammar focus

***This* or *these*?**

- Point out that we say *How much is **this**?* for one item or an item we can't count: *How much is this lemon? / How much is this bread?* We use ***these*** for more than one item: *How much are these lemons?*
- Draw a 'this' and 'these' chart on the board. Ask the pupils to classify the items from the song.

Pupil's Book Activity 3

Listen and repeat. Act out.

▶ *CD1 Track 39 p259*

- Play the CD. Ask the pupils to repeat the questions and answers.
- Talk Partners The pupils practise the conversation and act out with a Talk Partner. Encourage them to point to or collect different things in the classroom and invent the price.

Activity Book

Activity 1

Listen and write the numbers.

▶ *CD1 Track 40 p259*

- (Books open.) Ask the pupils to identify the food on the fruit and vegetable stall.
- Play the CD. Pause to check understanding. Repeat. The pupils write the price they hear on the price tags.

Answers: **1** apples 50¢ **2** potatoes 39¢ **3** green beans 23¢ **4** carrots 32¢ **5** peach 13¢ **6** lemon 47¢ **7** tomatoes 30¢

Activity 2

Look and write.

- (Books open.) Ask the pupils to name the food items. Ask **What's the question?** Ask a different pupil to tell you the answer (*It's / They're …*)
- The pupils complete the questions and answers individually.

Answers: **1** are these, twenty-six **2** is this, thirty-two cents **3** How much are these, They're forty-seven cents **4** How much is this, It's thirty-nine cents

Recycled vocabulary

- The pupils look at the picture and write the word.

Answer: hockey

Ending the lesson

Review the lesson.

- Say **Today we've talked about numbers and asked about prices.** Elicit the words from the pupils.

Review the task flashcards.

- Point to the task flashcards. Ask **Which was your favourite activity?** Elicit the activities.

Cooperative learning

Working together as a team

- Prepare a list of ten numbers on a sheet of paper. Organise four groups and select team leaders. They come to the front, read the first number on your list, return to their team and tell them it. The other team members write the number. The team leader returns and reads the next number on the list. The first team to write all the numbers correctly wins.

Extra activity

Vocabulary extension

- Use the Vocabulary Booster on Navio to present and practise four additional number words: *sixty, seventy, eighty, ninety.*

Key Competences and Key Learning Outcomes

- Say a tongue twister with the 'ee' sound
- Learn and practise 'ee' and 'ea' spellings
- Listen for specific information
- Sing a cooperative learning song
- Play a communication game about shopping

Key language

- *bee, cheese, ice cream, meat, peach, peas, queen, sheep, sweets, three*
- *What do I need to do? Read / Listen to instructions.*

Recycled: *bread, carrots, cheese, green beans, ice cream, lemons, peaches, peas, pineapples; ten, twenty, thirty, forty, fifty*

Recycled: *How much is this? How much are these? It's / They're (twenty) cents.*

Materials

- Pupil's Book p23; Activity Book p20; Class CD1; Teacher's App on Navio
- Teacher's Resource Bank: Task flashcards: *listen, say, write, sing, cut out, Talk Partners, colour*
- Teacher's Resource Bank: Unit 2 Lesson 5 Activity 4 cut-out
- Coloured pencils and scissors

Optional materials

- Teacher's Resource Bank: Five Trinity Exam Practice cards (selected from the Starter Unit and Unit 1)

At a Glance Lesson Plan

Pupil's Book

Starting the lesson

- Use the Trinity Exam Practice cards (optional).
- Review the *How much is this?* song.
- ▶ ***CD1 Track 38 p259***
- Set learning outcomes using the task flashcards.

Activity 1

- Listen and say.
- ▶ ***CD1 Track 41 p259***
- Go to the Activity Book.
- Go to Magic Phonics.

Activity 2

- Listen and write.
- ▶ ***CD1 Track 42 p259***

Activity 3 – Cooperative learning

- Sing *What do I need to do?*
- ▶ ***CD1 Track 43 p260***

Activity 4

- **Talk Partners** Make and play the game (Teacher's Resource Bank).

Ending the lesson

- Review the lesson.
- Review the task flashcards.

Cooperative learning

Working together as a team

- **Talk Partners** Play *Beat the clock.*
- Continue the pronunciation wall display.

Activity Book

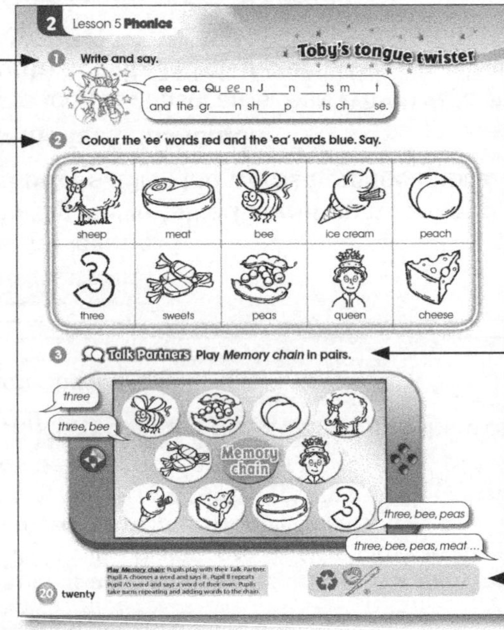

Activity Book

Activity 1

- Write and say.

Activity 2

- Colour the 'ee' words red and the 'ea' words blue. Say.
- Go to Magic Phonics.

Activity 3

- **Talk Partners** Play *Memory chain* in pairs.

Recycled vocabulary

- Look, remember and write the word.

Digital resources

Teacher's Digital: Don't forget you can teach this lesson using the Teacher's App on Navio.

Pupil's Digital: Encourage your pupils to use the Pupil's App on Navio to practise the vocabulary from this lesson.

Powered By NAVIO

Starting the lesson

Use the Trinity Exam Practice cards (optional).

- The pupils practise asking and answering questions. (See p31.)

Review the *How much is this?* song.

▶ *CD1 Track 38 p259*

- Divide the class into two halves. Half the class takes Jake's role and the other half sings along with the shopkeeper. Play the CD.

Set learning outcomes using the task flashcards.

- Say **Today we're going to say a tongue twister. We're going to make a cut-out and do the shopping role-play.**
- Hold up the task flashcards in turn and elicit the activities. Stick them on one side of the board. Point to them during the lesson to reinforce your instructions.

Pupil's Book Activity 1

Listen and say.

▶ *CD1 Track 41 p259*

- Write the words *cheese* and *meat* on the board. The pupils say the sound they can hear in both words: 'ee'. Circle the target graphemes ('ee' and 'ea') and model the sound. Ask the pupils to say the sound with you.
- Say **It's time for Toby's tongue twister! What can you see? What's the queen's name? What colour is the sheep? What does Queen Jean eat? What does the green sheep eat?**
- Play the CD. The pupils listen and repeat the target sound, then the words and then the entire tongue twister, faster and faster.

Go to Magic Phonics.

Activity Book

Activity 1

Write and say.

- (Books open.) Say **Look at Toby's tongue twister! The letters for the 'ee' sound are missing.** The pupils complete the tongue twister.

Answers: Jean, eats, meat, green, sheep, eats, cheese

- Talk Partners The pupils say *Toby's tongue twister* with a Talk Partner and point to the 'ee' sounds. They play *Faster and faster*, taking turns to say the tongue twister faster each time.

Activity 2

Colour the 'ee' words red and the 'ea' words blue. Say.

- Ask the pupils to colour and say the words.

Answers: red: sheep, bee, three, sweets, queen, cheese
blue: meat, ice cream, peach, peas

Go to Magic Phonics.

Activity 3

Play *Memory chain* in pairs.

- Demonstrate the game with a volunteer. Say **three**. The pupil repeats your word and adds another *(three, bee)*. Continue adding words to the chain.
- Talk Partners The pupils play the game with a Talk Partner.

Recycled vocabulary

- The pupils look at the picture and write the word.

Answer: baseball

Pupil's Book Activity 2

Listen and write.

▶ *CD1 Track 42 p259*

- (Books open.) The pupils listen and write the prices. Pause to check the pupils' answers.

Answers: **1** 20 cents **2** 50 cents **3** 47 cents **4** 30 cents

Pupil's Book Activity 3: **Cooperative learning**

Sing *What do I need to do?*

▶ *CD1 Track 43 p260*

- Play the CD. The pupils listen and do the actions with you. Play the CD again. The pupils join in.

Pupil's Book Activity 4

Make and play the game (Teacher's Resource Bank).

- (Books open.) Check that the pupils have got coloured pencils and scissors. The pupils colour the food and then cut out the cards. Demonstrate with a volunteer. Place each food card next to a price card. Hide the cards by placing a book as a barrier. The volunteer chooses three items to buy. Carry out the exchange from the Pupil's Book.
- Talk Partners The pupils play the game with a Talk Partner. After practising with the numbered cards, they write new prices using the numbers 1–50 on the blank price tags.

Ending the lesson

Review the lesson.

- Say **Today we've practised a tongue twister**. Ask the pupils to say it again.
- Then say **Today you did a role-play.**

Review the task flashcards.

- Point to the task flashcards. Say **Look at the activities you've done today. Which was your favourite?** Elicit the pupils' favourite activities.

Cooperative learning

Working together as a team

- Talk Partners Play *Beat the clock* to practise pronunciation of the 'ee' / 'ea' sound (see p53).
- Add to the pronunciation wall display, adding a tree ('ee') and a peach ('ea').

Key Competences and Key Learning Outcomes

- Read about Pancake Day in Britain
- Review foods that are made with eggs, flour and milk (optional)
- Listen for general understanding
- Think about special food days where you live

Key language

- *chocolate, flour, pancake, special day / food, sugar*
- *bowl, cook, make, mix, put, toss*
- *I help / put ... She puts in (flour). / She tosses (the pancake). We have (pancake races).*

Recycled: *catch, egg, lemon, milk, run*

Materials

- Pupil's Book p24; Activity Book p21; Class CD1; Teacher's App on Navio
- Teacher's Resource Bank: Task flashcards: *listen, read, think, write, match, tick, draw, say, Talk Partners*

Optional materials

- Teacher's Resource Bank: Five Trinity Exam Practice cards (selected from the Starter Unit and Unit 1)

At a Glance Lesson Plan

Pupil's Book

Starting the lesson

- Use the Trinity Exam Practice cards (optional).
- Talk Partners
  Review *Toby's tongue twister.*
  ▶ *CD1 Track 41 p259*
- Set learning outcomes using the task flashcards.

Activity 1

- Listen and read. Answer.
  ▶ *CD1 Track 44 p260*

Think about your culture

- Do you have a special food day in your country?
  Go to the Activity Book.

Ending the lesson

- Review the lesson.
- Review the task flashcards.

Extra activity

Reinforcement

- Find out more information about Pancake Day using the Internet.

Link to Science

- **Food:** eggs, flour and milk

Activity Book

Activity Book

Activity 1

- Listen and write. Match.
  ▶ *CD1 Track 45 p260*

Activity 2: Think about your culture

- Read and tick (✓). Draw, write and say.

Recycled vocabulary

- Look, remember and write the word.

Digital resources

Teacher's Digital: Don't forget you can teach this lesson using the Teacher's App on Navio.

Powered By NAVIO

Starting the lesson

Use the Trinity Exam Practice cards (optional).

- The pupils practise asking and answering questions. (See p31.)

Review Toby's tongue twister.

▶ *CD1 Track 41 p259*

- Ask the class **What sound did you practise in Toby's tongue twister?** ('ee'). Ask if they can remember the tongue twister. (*Queen Jean eats meat and the green sheep eats cheese.*)
- **Talk Partners** The pupils practise the tongue twister as a class and then with a Talk Partner. The pairs play *Faster and faster,* reading from the Pupil's Book (page 23) if necessary.
- Draw a chart with two columns ('ee' and 'ea') on the board. Elicit words with both spellings. Ask pupils to classify the words, e.g. 'ee': *queen, green, sheep, cheese*; 'ea': *Jean, eats, meat.*

Set learning outcomes using the task flashcards.

- Say **Today we're going to learn about Pancake Day in Britain.**
- Hold up the task flashcards in turn and elicit the activities. Stick them on one side of the board. Point to them during the lesson to reinforce your instructions.

Background information

- In Britain, the Tuesday before Lent is known as Pancake Day or Shrove Tuesday. It is traditional to eat pancakes, toss pancakes and have pancake races. (A pancake in a (cold) frying pan is tossed while running to the finish line.)
- Traditionally, before the fasting period of Lent, Christians used all the rich foods in their cupboards. During Lent, eggs, sugar and butter could not be eaten. These are the ingredients for pancakes.

Pupil's Book Activity 1

Listen and read. Answer.

▶ *CD1 Track 44 p260*

- (Books open.) Ask **What can you see? Let's listen and read.**
- Play the CD. Check understanding by pointing to the first photo. Ask **What do they put in the pancake?** (*Flour, milk and two eggs.*) Then **What does Mum do with the pancake?** (*She cooks it, then she tosses it and catches it.*) **What does the boy put on the pancake?** (*Chocolate.*) Ask **What does his sister put on the pancake?** (*Lemon and sugar.*) Ask **What do they do at school on Pancake Day?** (*They have pancake races.*)

Pupil's Book Think about your culture

Do you have a special food day in your country?

- Read the question and ask the class about special food days.

Activity Book

Activity 1

Listen and write. Match.

▶ *CD1 Track 45 p260*

- Say **Let's read about Pancake Day.** Read the words in the word box as a class. Play the CD. The pupils listen and write the missing words. Check comprehension.
- Read the sentences again and says the missing words. The pupils match them to the pictures.

Answers: **1b** Mum **2d** pancake **3c** sugar, lemon **4a** school

Activity 2: Think about your culture

Read and tick (✓). Draw, write and say.

- Read out the question in the speech bubble. Elicit the pupils' answers.
- Read out the first sentence as a class and ask the pupils to tick the box if there's special food in their country. Ask the pupils to name the food (if any) and ask them if they like it. Repeat with the other sentences, eliciting comments. Help the pupils express themselves by scaffolding their sentences or reflecting back their anecdotes in English.
- Ask the pupils to draw the special food they have. Invite them to show the rest of the class their drawings and read out their sentences.

Recycled vocabulary

- The pupils look at the picture and write the word.

Answer: cycling

Ending the lesson

Review the lesson.

- Say **Today you've learnt about Pancake Day in Britain. Do you like the idea of Pancake Day?**

Review the task flashcards.

- Point to the task flashcards. Say **Look at the activities you've done today. Which activity was your favourite?** Elicit the pupils' favourite activities.

Extra activity

Reinforcement

- If available, take the pupils to the computer room and guide them in using the internet to find out more information about Pancake Day.

Link to Science

- If you are studying the Science topic of **food** in English, you could review products that can be made with eggs, flour or milk: pancakes, omelette, milkshake, yoghurt and cheese.
- Remind the pupils that flour is made from wheat and is also used to make bread. Encourage them to talk about the process of making bread: First, the farmer plants the seeds. The seeds grow into plants. The farmer harvests the plants. Grain is ground into flour. The flour is made into bread. Bread is taken to the shops.

Key Competences and Key Learning Outcomes

- Read for specific information

- Read and understand a recipe
- Write a recipe

Key language

olives, sandwich, slices; first, then, now, finally

Recycled: *eyes, hair, mouth, nose; bread, carrot, cheese, egg, salad*

Materials

- Pupil's Book p25; Activity Book p22; Class CD1; Teacher's App on Navio
- Food flashcards
- Teacher's Resource Bank: Task flashcards: *Talk Partners, think, listen, read, number, match, write, draw*

Optional materials

- Teacher's Resource Bank: Five Trinity Exam Practice cards (selected from the Starter Unit and Unit 1)
- Recipe books

At a Glance Lesson Plan

Pupil's Book

Starting the lesson

- Use the Trinity Exam Practice cards (optional).
- Review food vocabulary.
- Review food vocabulary. Play the *Definitions game*.
- Set learning outcomes using the task flashcards.

Before you read: Activity 1

- Look at the picture of the funny face sandwich. What do you think you need to make it?

Activity 2

- Listen and read the recipe.
- CD1 Track 46 p260

After you read

- Go to page 22 in your Activity Book.

Lesson 7 Literacy 2

Text type: A recipe

Before you read

1 Look at the picture of the funny face sandwich. What do you think you need to make it?

2 Listen and read the recipe.

Funny face sandwich

This sandwich is easy and fun to make. It's delicious, too!

To make this sandwich you need:
- one slice of bread
- three slices of cheese
- two slices of egg
- three olives
- one piece of carrot
- some salad

Ask an adult to help you.

Instructions:

1 First, put the slices of cheese on the slice of bread.

2 Then, add the eggs for eyes. Put an olive in the centre of each egg.

3 Now, add an olive for the nose and a piece of carrot for the mouth.

4 Finally, add the salad for the hair.

After you read

Go to page 22 in your Activity Book.

Key learning outcomes: read and understand a recipe

twenty-five 25

Ending the lesson

- Review the lesson.
- Review the task flashcards.
- Sing a song (optional).

Extra activity

Extension

- Play *Hot seat.*

Cooperative learning

Encouraging one another

- Using collaborative language.

Activity Book

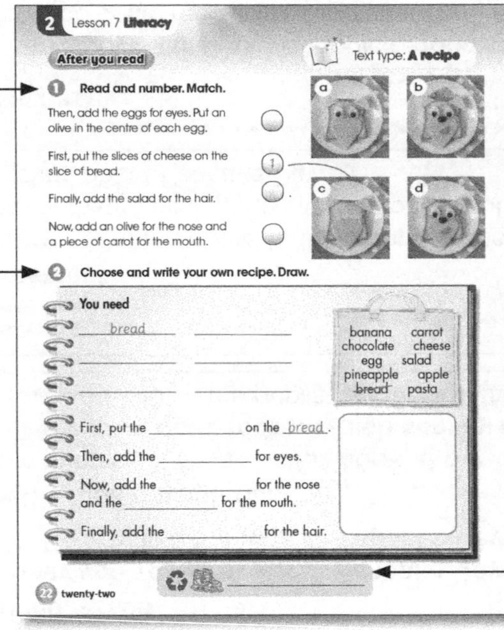
2 Lesson 7 Literacy

After you read

Text type: A recipe

1 Read and number. Match.

Then, add the eggs for eyes. Put an olive in the centre of each egg.

First, put the slices of cheese on the slice of bread. 1

Finally, add the salad for the hair.

Now, add an olive for the nose and a piece of carrot for the mouth.

2 Choose and write your own recipe. Draw.

You need

bread

banana, carrot, chocolate, cheese, egg, salad, pineapple, apple, bread, pasta

First, put the ______ on the bread.

Then, add the ______ for eyes.

Now, add the ______ for the nose and the ______ for the mouth.

Finally, add the ______ for the hair.

22 twenty-two

Activity Book

After you read: Activity 1

- Read and number. Match.

Activity 2

- Choose and write your own recipe. Draw.

Recycled vocabulary

- Look, remember and write the word.

Digital resources

Teacher's Digital: Don't forget you can teach this lesson using the Teacher's App on Navio.

Pupil's Digital: Encourage your pupils to use the Pupil's App on Navio to practise the vocabulary from this lesson.

Powered By NAVIO

Starting the lesson

Use the Trinity Exam Practice cards (optional).

- The pupils practise asking and answering questions. (See p31.)

Review food vocabulary.

- Slowly, draw simple pictures of food items from the unit and Level 1 on the board. The pupils try to name the food before you finish drawing.

Review food vocabulary. Play the *Definitions game*.

- Use the unit flashcards to play the *Definitions game* (See p23.)
- Talk Partners The pupils play the game with a Talk Partner.

Set learning outcomes using the task flashcards.

- Say **Today we're going to read a recipe.**
- Hold up the task flashcards in turn and elicit the activities. Stick them on one side of the board. Point to them during the lesson to reinforce your instructions.

Before you read: Pupil's Book Activity 1

Look at the picture of the funny face sandwich. What do you think you need to make it?

- (Optional) If you have brought in a recipe book, show it to the class. Show them how a recipe has a photo of the finished meal, a list of ingredients and instructions to make it. Some recipe books have step-by-step instructions. Ask the pupils if they have used a recipe to make anything.
- (Books closed.) Tell the pupils that they are going to read a recipe for making a special sandwich. Ask them what type of sandwiches they like. Ask **What's your favourite sandwich?**
- (Books open.) The pupils look at the photo of the funny face sandwich and name the items they think they need to make it. Write their suggestions on the board.

Pupil's Book Activity 2

Listen and read the recipe.

▶ *CD1 Track 46 p260*

- Ask **Do you know how to make a sandwich? Let's read the recipe.**
- Read the recipe collectively. After reading, return to the predicted ingredients on the board. Ask which items appear in the sandwich. Rub out any incorrect suggestions and elicit any missing items. If necessary, explain to the pupils that when we are cooking, we use a knife to slice things. Mime slicing and say **a slice of bread, a slice of cheese**. Explain that a slice is a thin piece.

Activity Book

After you read: Activity 1

Read and number. Match.

- The class identifies and reads out the first instruction from the recipe. Ask **What's next?** The class reads out and numbers the next instruction. Repeat for the remaining stages.
- Once the pupils have put the recipe in order, they match each stage to the corresponding photo.

Answers: **2** a **1** c **4** b **3** d

Activity 2

Choose and write your own recipe. Draw.

- The pupils may select ingredients to design a different sandwich. After completing their recipe they draw the finished sandwich.

Recycled vocabulary

- The pupils look at the picture and write the word.

Answer: rollerblading

Ending the lesson

Review the lesson.

- Say **Today we read a recipe.** Then say **Today you wrote your own recipe.**

Review the task flashcards.

- Point to the task flashcards. Say **Look at the activities you've done today. Which activity was your favourite?** Elicit the pupils' favourite activities.

Sing a song (optional).

- Choose a song. The class sings and does the actions. Alternatively, invite the class to choose a song to sing.

Extra activity

Extension

- Play *Hot seat.* Choose a volunteer to come out to the front and follow the instructions given by the class to make the funny face sandwich. The pupil mimes adding the ingredients to make the sandwich. Encourage individuals to direct the volunteer either by reading from the recipe in the Pupil's Book or by recalling the instructions from memory.

Cooperative learning

Encouraging one another

- Pupils encourage the hot seat volunteer by praising his / her efforts using collaborative language: *Very good! Fantastic! Well done!*, etc.

Key Competences and Key Learning Outcomes

- Review language in the unit
- Reflect on your learning
- Sing a cooperative learning song

Key language

Recycled: *apples, bread, carrots, eggs, green beans, lemons, peaches, pineapples, potatoes, sweets, tomatoes, yoghurt;* Numbers 1–50

Recycled: *Can I have a / an / some …, please? Yes. Here you are. How much is this? How much are these? It's / They're (fifty) cents.*

Materials

- Pupil's Book p26; Activity Book p23; Class CD1; Teacher's App on Navio
- Food flashcards
- Teacher's Resource Bank: Task flashcards: *listen, number, write, say, sing, read, think, Talk Partners*
- Teacher's Resource Bank: Traffic light cut-out
- *Give Me Five!* sticker

Optional materials

- Teacher's Resource Bank: Five Trinity Exam Practice cards (selected from the Starter Unit and Unit 1)

At a Glance Lesson Plan

Pupil's Book

Starting the lesson

- Use the Trinity Exam Practice cards (optional).
- Review the unit vocabulary.
- Set learning outcomes using the task flashcards.

Activity 1

- Listen and number. Write and say.

▶ *CD1 Track 47 p260*

Activity 2

- Write the food in the correct column.

Activity 3

Cooperative learning

- Sing *Well Done!*

▶ *CD1 Track 48 p260*

- Stick the *Give Me Five!* sticker.

Go to the Activity Book.

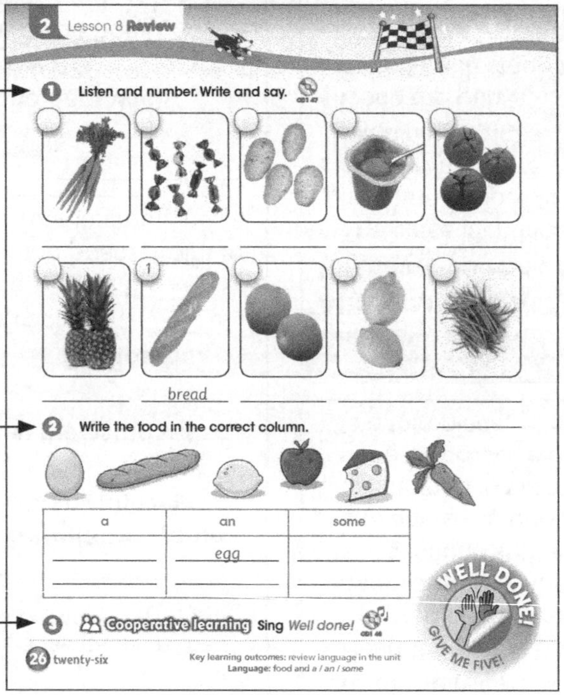

Ending the lesson

- Review the task flashcards.
- Sing a song (optional).

Cooperative learning

Think-Pair-Share

- Remember the ten food words.

Activity Book

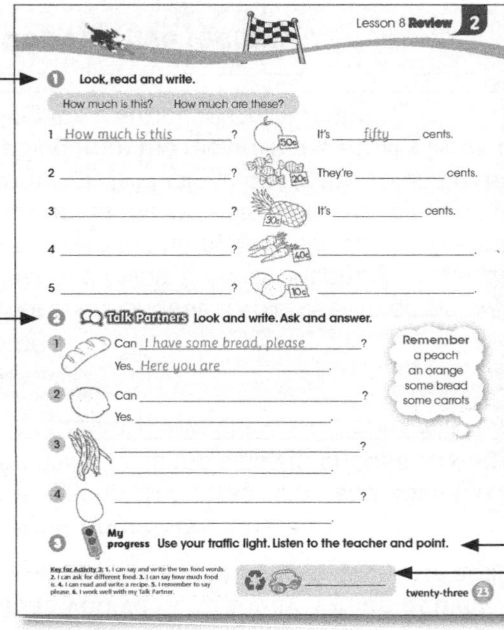

Activity Book

Activity 1

- Look, read and write.

Activity 2

- Look and write.
- **Talk Partners** Ask and answer.

Activity 3 My progress

- Use your traffic light. Listen to the teacher and point.

Recycled vocabulary

- Look, remember and write the word.

Digital resources

Teacher's Digital: Don't forget you can teach this lesson using the Teacher's App on Navio.

Pupil's Digital: Encourage your pupils to use the Pupil's App on Navio to practise the vocabulary from this lesson.

Powered By NAVIO

Starting the lesson

Use the Trinity Exam Practice cards (optional).

- The pupils practise asking and answering questions. (See p31.)

Review the unit vocabulary.

- Use the unit flashcards to review the food vocabulary. (See p23.)

Set learning outcomes using the task flashcards.

- Say **Today we're going to remember what we've learnt in Unit 2.**
- Hold up the task flashcards in turn and elicit the words. Stick them on one side of the board. Point to them during the lesson to reinforce your instructions.

Pupil's Book Activity 1

Listen and number. Write and say.

▶ *CD1 Track 47 p260*

- (Books open.) Point to each of the foods in turn and elicit the words.
- Play the CD. Pause after each sentence. The pupils write the correct number in the circles.
- Play the CD again. The pupils write the correct word under each picture. Then they say the words.

Answers: **1** bread **2** tomatoes **3** yoghurt **4** green beans **5** potatoes **6** peaches **7** pineapples **8** lemons **9** carrots **10** sweets

Pupil's Book Activity 2

Write the food in the correct column.

- (Books open.) Elicit the names of the foods with the corresponding article. The pupils write each item in the correct column: 'a', 'an' or 'some'.

Answers: a: lemon, carrot; an: egg, apple; some: bread, cheese

- Talk Partners Fast finishers name additional foods for their Talk Partner to add the correct article, 'a', 'an' or 'some', e.g. P1: tomato; P2: *a tomato*. P2: *green beans*; P1: *some green beans*, etc.

Pupil's Book Activity 3: **Cooperative learning**

Sing *Well done!*

▶ *CD1 Track 48 p260*

- Praise the class for their hard work and play the *Well done!* song. The pupils listen and do the actions with you. Play the CD again and encourage the pupils to join in and do the actions.

Stick the *Give Me Five!* sticker.

- The pupils stick the *Give Me Five!* sticker on the Pupil's Book page.

Activity Book

Activity 1

Look, read and write.

- Ask the pupils to name the food items. Say **What's the question?** (*How much is this?* or *How much are these?*) Elicit the price of each item. Pupils complete the questions and answers.
- Talk Partners The pupils role-play the exchange with a Talk Partner.

Answers: **1** How much is this? fifty **2** How much are these? twenty **3** How much is this? thirty **4** How much are these? They're forty cents. **5** How much are these? They're ten cents.

Activity 2

Look and write. Ask and answer.

- The pupils use the pictures to complete the questions and answers.

Talk Partners The pupils role-play the exchange.

Answers: **1** Can I have some bread, please? Here you are. **2** I have a lemon, please? Here you are. **3** Can I have some green beans, please? Yes. Here you are. **4** Can I have an egg, please? Yes. Here you are.

Activity 3 My progress

Use your traffic light. Listen to the teacher and point.

- (Books closed.) Ask the class to take out their traffic light cut-out. Say **Let's think about our work in this unit.** Read the first self-assessment statement. Point to the green circle and say **Yes, I can do this very well.** Then point to the orange circle and say **Yes, I can do this.** Point to the red circle and say **No, I can't do this.**
- Read the rest of the statements. For each one, the pupils point to the colour on their traffic light that shows how they feel about their own learning.

Self-assessment statements

1. I can say and write the ten food words.
2. I can ask for different food.
3. I can say how much food is.
4. I can read and write a recipe.
5. I remember to say please.
6. I work well with my Talk Partner.

Recycled vocabulary

- The pupils look at the picture and write the word.

Answer: swimming

Ending the lesson

Review the task flashcards.

- Point to the task flashcards. Say **Look at the activities you've done today. Which activity was your favourite?** Elicit the pupils' favourite activities.

Sing a song (optional).

- The class chooses their favourite song from the unit. The class sings and does the actions.

Cooperative learning

Think-Pair-Share

- Ask **Can you remember the ten food words?** Ask the class to think silently on their own for a minute.
- Talk Partners The pupils work with a Talk Partner to remember and name all ten words.
- Invite a pair to say one of the food words. Hold up the corresponding flashcard and prompt the class to repeat the word.
- Finally, repeat, asking different pairs of pupils each time, until all ten food words have been named.

Key Competences and Key Learning Outcomes

- Watch and understand a video about making pizza
- Learn to find information online
- Think and choose the ingredients for a pizza

Key language

- *cheese, flour, ingredients, milk, onion, online, peppers, pizza, recipe, tomatoes, water*

Materials

- Pupil's Book p27; Activity Book p24; Class CD1; Video; Teacher's App on Navio
- Teacher's Resource Bank: Task flashcards: *tick, read, circle, think, listen, number, write, draw, Talk Partners*
- Food flashcards

Optional materials

- Teacher's Resource Bank: Trinity Exam Practice cards (selected from Unit 2)

At a Glance Lesson Plan

Pupil's Book

Starting the lesson

- Use the Trinity Exam Practice cards (optional).
- **Think-Pair-Share** Review recipes.
- Set learning outcomes and use the task flashcards.

Pre-watching activity

- Look at the photo and talk about favourite pizzas.

Activity 1

- Watch the video.
  Unit 2 video p278
- Tick (✓) or cross (✗). Which toppings can you see?

Activity 2

- Watch the video again.
  Unit 2 video
- Read and circle.

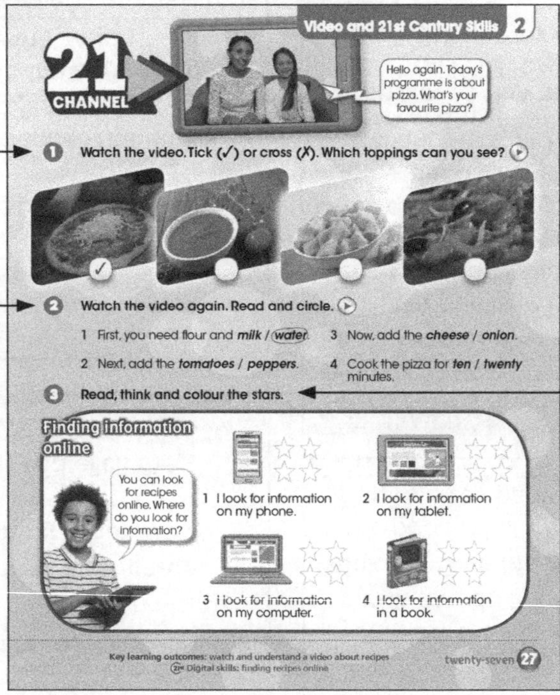

Activity 3

- Read, think and colour the stars.
- Go to the Activity Book.

Ending the lesson

- Review the lesson.
- Review the task flashcards. Elicit the pupils' favourite activities.

Extra activity

Extension

- Pupils create a pizza recipe.

Digital resources

Teacher's Digital: Don't forget you can teach this lesson using the Teacher's App on Navio.

Pupil's Digital: Encourage your pupils to use the Pupil's App on Navio to practise the vocabulary from this lesson.

Powered By NAVIO

Activity Book

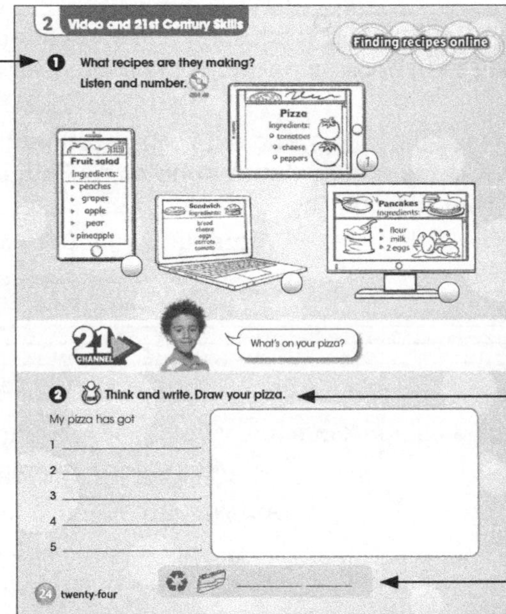

Activity Book

Activity 1

- What recipes are they making? Listen and number.
- ▶ *CD1 Track 49 p260*

Activity 2

- Think and write. Draw your pizza.

Recycled vocabulary

- Look, remember and write the word.

Starting the lesson

Use the Trinity Exam Practice cards (optional).

- The pupils practise asking and answering questions. (See p31.)

Review recipes.

Think-Pair-Share Ask **Can you remember the recipe and how to make the funny face sandwich?**

Talk Partners The pupils work with a Talk Partner to name the ingredients and the steps to make the sandwich for two minutes.

Set learning outcomes and use the task flashcards.

- Say **Today we're going to watch a video and then ask and answer questions about making a pizza**.
- Hold up the task flashcards, in turn, and elicit the activities. Stick them on the side of the board. Point to them during the lesson to reinforce your instructions.

Pre-watching activity

- Look at the photo and read the speech bubble to pupils. Ask **What's your favourite pizza?** Elicit responses.

Pupil's Book Activity 1

Watch the video. Tick (✓) or cross (✗). Which toppings can you see? *p278*

- Ask **How do you make pizza?** Play Part 1, pausing after Tom says *You need lots of delicious ingredients to put on top of the pizza.*
- Ask **What other ingredients do you need to make a pizza?** Write the pupils' ideas on the board.
- Focus on the video stills. Ask **Which toppings can you see?** Say **Let's watch and listen**.
- Explain that the pupils tick or cross the toppings as they watch. Play Part 2. Pause the video after the first video still. Ask the pupils to point to the corresponding photo in their book.
- Play the rest of Part 2 for pupils to tick or cross the photos.

Answers: From left to right: ✓ ✓ ✗ ✓

Pupil's Book Activity 2

Watch the video again. Read and circle.

- Play Part 2 again. Pause after Sophie says, *Then you add water.* Read out the first sentence in Activity 2. **Do you need flour and milk or flour and water?** Show water circled.
- Read out the sentences for the pupils to follow.
- Play the video all the way through for pupils to circle the words. Ask **Where can you find recipes and information about ingredients?**
- Ask the pupils some questions to check understanding. Suggested questions.

What is it important to do before you cook? *(Wash your hands.)*
What ingredients does Tom suggest for the topping? *(Tomatoes, peppers and onions.)*
What can Sophie and Tom use to help them make pizza? *(Their tablets.)*
What ingredients have Tom and Sophie got? *(Flour, milk, eggs.)*
What can they make with these ingredients? *(Pancakes.)*

Answers: **1** water **2** tomatoes **3** cheese **4** ten minutes

Pupil's Book Activity 3

Read, think and colour the stars.

- Point to the pictures and elicit the vocabulary.
- Read out the speech bubble. Tell the pupils to colour the stars. The more stars they colour for each picture means the more they use it.
- Say **I look for information on my phone and my computer.** Ask **Where do you look for information?** Encourage full answers.

Think-Pair-Share The pupils ask and answer the question with their Talk Partner. Encourage full answers, as in your model.

Activity Book

Activity 1

What recipes are they making? Listen and number.
► *CD1 Track 49 p260*

- On the board stick the food flashcards and elicit the words. Ask **Which foods do you hear?** Play the whole track. Elicit answers.
- Point to each list of ingredients and ask **What are the people making?** Play the CD, pausing after the first exchange. Show the number one on the pizza recipe.
- Play the rest of the track for pupils to number the ingredients.

Answers: **1** pizza **2** pancakes **3** sandwich **4** fruit salad

Activity 2

Think and write. Draw your pizza.

- Read out the speech bubble. Tell the pupils to draw their favourite pizza.
- Say **What's on your pizza?** for the pupils to repeat.

Talk Partners In pairs, pupils take turns to ask and answer *What's on your pizza?* Encourage the pupils to use full sentences.

Recycled vocabulary

Answer: pencil case

Ending the lesson

Review the lesson.

- Say **Today we've watched a video about making pizza. What did we learn about ingredients and recipes?** *(We can find lots of information online.)*

Review the task flashcards.

- Point to the task flashcards on the board. Say **Look at the activities you've done today. Which activity was your favourite?**

Extra activity

Extension

- Pupils work individually to create a funny pizza topping recipe. Tell them to use different food ingredients, for example a banana pizza. Then they share their pizzas with their partners and ask each other *What's on your pizza?*

Date: ____________ Unit: ____________

1 What did my pupils learn in this unit?

2 How did my pupils work? (✓)

individually ☐ in pairs ☐ in small groups ☐

in large groups ☐ as a class ☐

3 Which key competences did my pupils develop?

- Competence in linguistic communication ☐
- Competence in mathematics, science and technology ☐
- Digital competence ☐
- Learning to learn ☐
- Social and civic competences ☐
- Sense of initiative and entrepreneurship ☐
- Cultural awareness and expression ☐

4 Which lessons / activities were the most successful and why?

5 Which lessons / activities did my pupils find the most difficult and why?

6 What did I try in the classroom for the first time? How did it go?

7 Which resources did I find most useful? (including webpages)

8 What could I do differently next time I teach this unit?

Unit 3

At the zoo

Unit overview

Key Competences and Key Learning Outcomes

- Identify and say ten wild animals (Lesson 1)
- Use *Has it got …? / Have they got …?* and short answers (Lesson 2)
- Read, listen and understand a story about a mysterious egg (Lesson 3)
- Describe and guess animals (Lesson 4)
- Read about garden wildlife in Britain (Lesson 6)
- Watch and understand a video about animals (Video and 21st Century Skills)

- Use animal body parts vocabulary to compare animals (Lesson 4)
- Read and understand animal fact files (Lesson 7)
- Learn to sort information (Video and 21st Century Skills)

- Use the Pupil's App on Navio

- Use a strategy to practise spelling key words (Lesson 1)
- Say a tongue twister and practise 'oo' and 'ui' spellings (Lesson 5)
- Review language in the unit and reflect on own learning (Lesson 8)
- Practise activity types found in the Cambridge Exams: Pre A1 Starters

- Understand the importance of helping your friends and family (Lesson 3)

- Work with a Talk Partner to practise and reinforce learning (all lessons)
- Play a communication game describing animals (Lesson 5)

- Sing four songs (Lessons 1, 4, 5 and 8)
- Understand, act out and give an opinion on a story (Lesson 3)
- Think about wild animals where you live (Lesson 6)

Vocabulary

Core vocabulary
crocodile, elephant, giraffe, hippo, lion, lizard, monkey, penguin, snake, tiger; beak, body, face, tail, teeth, wings

Extension vocabulary (optional)
bear, camel, dolphin, kangaroo, turtle, whale; feathers, fur, spots, stripes

Other vocabulary
dangerous, grasslands, jungle, wild animal; ground, hatches, inside, lost, sign, strange; fox, goose, hedgehog, kangaroo, squirrel; dish, garden, grass, night, nuts, seeds; fact file, gorilla, ice, insects, leaves, polar bear, rainforest, snow

Recycled vocabulary
bird, cat, chicken, cow, dog, duck, goat, horse, mouse, parrot, sheep, zebra, zoo; arms, ears, face, fingers, hair, legs, mouth, neck, toes; big, fat, long, tall; climb, fly, tree; fish, fruit, meat

Structures

Core structures
It's got (long hair). Has it got (long hair)? Yes, it has. No, it hasn't. They've got (four legs). Have they got (four legs)? Yes, they have. No, they haven't.
It hasn't got (a beak). They haven't got (wings).

Other structures
I haven't got … Have you got …? They live … They eat … We've got …

Recycled structures
I've got … I'm … I can / can't (swim). I live … It's (an elephant). It's got (four legs). They're (small).

Phonics

Alternative vowel spellings **'oo'** / **'ui'** (kangar**oo**, g**oo**se, swims**ui**t, fr**ui**t j**ui**ce, p**oo**l)

British Culture

Garden wildlife

Literacy

Text type: fact files (informative text)
Reading skills: remembering facts; predicting from pictures; using mind maps; scanning; reviewing information; sequencing; matching

21st Century Skills

Ways of thinking: learning to sort information

Cooperative learning

Songs: *Let's take turns!* (Lesson 5); *Well Done!* (Lesson 8)
Skills: Listening to others (Lesson 2); Working together as a team (Lesson 5); Encouraging one another (Lesson 7); Think-Pair-Share (Lesson 8)

Values

The importance of helping your friends and family.

Cross-curricular links

Links to Science
Animals: animal habitats; classifying animals by their diet; the difference between vertebrate and invertebrate animals; describing mammals
Suggested Arts and Crafts concepts
Identifying and using primary and secondary colours to colour animals and their habitats; making and colouring an animal game

Key Competences and Key Learning Outcomes

- Identify and say ten wild animals
- Say the vocabulary chant
- Stick the animal stickers
- Identify animal habitats (optional)
- Use a strategy to practise spelling key words
- Sing a song about animals

Key language

- *crocodile, elephant, giraffe, hippo, lion, lizard, monkey, penguin, snake, tiger*

Extension vocabulary

- *bear, camel, dolphin, kangaroo, turtle, whale*

Recycled: *bird, cat, chicken, cow, dog, duck, goat, horse, mouse, sheep;* Colours; *arms, big, climb, ears, hair, legs, long, mouth, fat, fly, tall; tree*

Recycled: *I've got (four legs). I'm (a wild animal). I live (in the jungle). I can / can't (swim).*

Other vocabulary: *dangerous, grasslands, jungle, wild animal*

Materials

- Pupil's Book p28; Activity Book pp26 and 35; Class CD1; Teacher's App on Navio; Unit 3 stickers
- Animal flashcards
- Teacher's Resource Bank: Animal word cards
- Teacher's Resource Bank: Task flashcards: *listen, sing, read, stick, say, Talk Partners, write, match*

Optional materials

- Teacher's Resource Bank: Five Trinity Exam Practice cards (selected from the Starter Unit and Units 1 and 2)

At a Glance Lesson Plan

Starting the lesson

- Use the Trinity Exam Practice cards (optional).
- Review domestic animal words. Play *The guessing game*.
- Set learning outcomes using the task flashcards.

Vocabulary presentation

- Present the new vocabulary.

Activity 1

- Listen and point.
- ▶ *CD1 Track 50 p260*
- Sing *I'm a wild animal.*

Word cards

- Read the word cards.
- Match them to the flashcards.

Activity 2

- Read and stick the ten stickers.
- Listen and say the chant.
- ▶ *CD1 Track 52 p261*
- Go to the Activity Book.

Pupil's Book

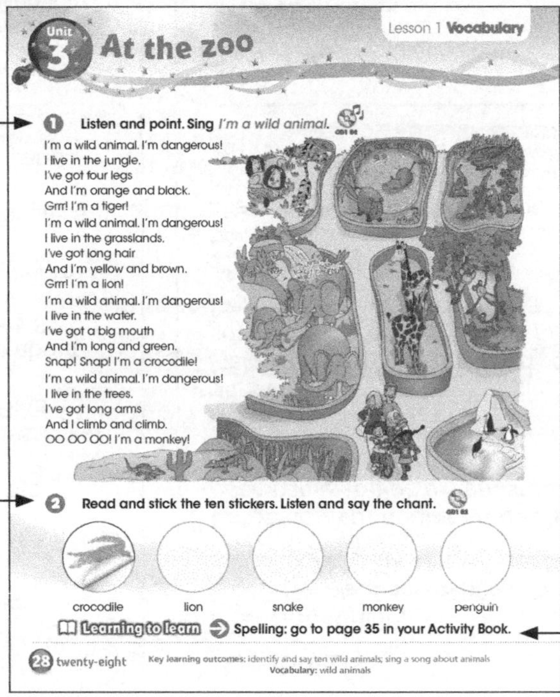
Unit 3 At the zoo

Lesson 1 Vocabulary

1 Listen and point. Sing *I'm a wild animal.*

I'm a wild animal. I'm dangerous!
I live in the jungle.
I've got four legs
And I'm orange and black.
Grrr! I'm a tiger!
I'm a wild animal. I'm dangerous!
I live in the grasslands.
I've got long hair
And I'm yellow and brown.
Grrr! I'm a lion!
I'm a wild animal. I'm dangerous!
I live in the water.
I've got a big mouth
And I'm long and green.
Snap! Snap! I'm a crocodile!
I'm a wild animal. I'm dangerous!
I live in the trees.
I've got long arms
And I climb and climb.
OO OO OO! I'm a monkey!

2 Read and stick the ten stickers. Listen and say the chant.

crocodile lion snake monkey penguin

Learning to learn ➔ Spelling: go to page 35 in your Activity Book.

28 twenty-eight Key learning outcomes: identify and say ten wild animals; sing a song about animals
Vocabulary: wild animals

Ending the lesson

- Review the lesson.
- Review the task flashcards.

Extra activity

Vocabulary extension

- Present six additional vocabulary items.

Link to Science

- **Animals:** animal habitats

Learning to learn

Spelling

- Practise spelling at any time during this unit (Activity Book p35).

Digital resources

Teacher's Digital: Don't forget you can teach this lesson using the Teacher's App on Navio.

Pupil's Digital: Encourage your pupils to use the Pupil's App on Navio to practise the vocabulary from this lesson.

Powered By NAVIO

Activity Book

Unit 3 At the zoo

Lesson 1 Vocabulary

1 Look and write.

elephant lion giraffe penguin snake crocodile lizard tiger hippo monkey

1 lion 2 3 4 5 6 7 8 9

2 Read and match. Write.

I've got two legs. I can't fly. I'm black and white. I'm a penguin.

I've got four legs. I'm very big. I've got big ears. I'm grey.

26 twenty-six

Spelling 3

Let's practise spelling!

Look Copy Cover and write

1 crocodile 2 lion 3 elephant 4 penguin 5 tiger 6 lizard 7 snake 8 monkey 9 hippo 10 giraffe

thirty-five 35

Activity Book

Activity 1

- Look and write.

Activity 2

- Read and match. Write.

Recycled vocabulary

- Look, remember and write the word.

Spelling

Let's practise spelling!

- Use the *Look-Copy-Cover-Write technique.*

Recycled vocabulary

- Look, remember and write the word.

Starting the lesson

Use the Trinity Exam Practice cards (optional).

- The pupils practise asking and answering questions. (See p31.)

Review domestic animal words.

- Review domestic animals from Level 1. Play *The guessing game.* Say **I've got four legs. I can walk and run. I can't fly. I'm white. What am I?** *(A sheep.)*
- Repeat with the other animals (cat, cow, bird, dog, duck, goat, horse, chicken), using mime if necessary.

Set learning outcomes using the task flashcards.

- Explain the aims of the lesson. Say **Today we're going to learn the names of some wild animals.**
- Hold up the task flashcards and elicit the words. Stick them on one side of the board. Point to them during the lesson to reinforce your instructions.

Vocabulary presentation

Present the new vocabulary.

- (Books closed.) Remind the pupils that the animals they learnt in Level 1 are domestic animals. They live on a farm. Say **Let's learn about wild animals!** Describe the wild animals. Say **I'm a wild animal. I've got four legs. I'm orange and black. I'm a tiger!** Show the flashcard and say **tiger**. Elicit the word. Repeat for all the animals.
- (Books open.) Ask **Who can you see? Where are they? What animals can you see?** The pupils point to and name the animals. Ask **What's your favourite animal?**

Pupil's Book Activity 1

Listen and point. Sing *I'm a wild animal.*

▶ *CD1 Track 50 p260*

- Play the CD. The pupils listen and point to the animals.
- Play the CD again. The pupils sing and do the actions.
- Play *Which one's missing?* with animal vocabulary. (See p23.)

Word cards

Read the word cards. Match them to the flashcards.

- (Books closed.) Hold up an animal word card. The pupils read collectively. A pupil sticks the word card next to the flashcard on the board. Repeat.
- Point to each word card. The pupils read the words.

Pupil's Book Activity 2

Read and stick the ten stickers. Listen and say the chant.

▶ *CD1 Track 52 p261*

- Ask a pupil to read the first word. The pupils stick the corresponding stickers above the word.
- Talk Partners The pupils find and stick the remaining stickers. Encourage them to use cooperative language: *(Where's the (tiger)? Here! Where does this go?)*
- Play the CD. The pupils listen and say the chant, pointing to the stickers in turn.

Activity Book

Activity 1

Look and write.

- (Books open.) Point to the animals and elicit their names. The pupils label the pictures with the correct words.

Answers: **1** lion **2** snake **3** hippo **4** tiger **5** crocodile **6** elephant **7** monkey **8** giraffe **9** penguin **10** lizard

Activity 2

Read and match. Write.

- (Books open.) Read the first animal riddle and elicit the answer. Invite individuals to read the riddles and elicit the animal each time. The pupils complete the riddles and match them to the corresponding picture.

Answers: **1** penguin (picture 3) **2** I'm a giraffe. (picture 4) **3** I'm an elephant. (picture 1) **4** I'm a hippo. (picture 2)

Recycled vocabulary

- The pupils look at the picture and write the word.

Answer: carrots

Ending the lesson

Review the lesson.

- Say **Today we've learnt the names of some wild animals. What animals do you remember?** Elicit the names from the pupils.

Review the task flashcards.

- Point to the task flashcards. Say **Look at the activities you've done today. Which was your favourite?** Elicit the pupils' favourite activities.

Extra activity

Vocabulary extension

- Present six additional wild animals: *bear, camel, dolphin, kangaroo, turtle* and *whale.*
- Use the Vocabulary Booster on Navio to practise these new words.

Link to Science

- If you are studying the Science topic of **animals** in English, you could review habitats. Some animals live in the *grasslands* (lion, hippo, snake, monkey, elephant, giraffe and zebra). Some live in a *lake* (hippo), some live in a *tree* (monkey, parrots, lizards) and some live in the *grass* (elephant, lion, snake, giraffe, zebra). Talk about other animals in the unit: tiger (jungle), crocodile (river). Draw the habitats on the board. The pupils stick the animal flashcards in the correct place.

Spelling (Activity Book p35)

Let's practise spelling!

- The pupils can practise spelling the ten animals using the *Look-Copy-Cover-Write* technique at any time before the Lesson 8 Review.

Recycled vocabulary

- The pupils look at the picture and write the word.

Answer: potatoes

Key Competences and Key Learning Outcomes

- Use *Has it got …? / Have they got …?* and short answers
- Complete and practise a conversation
- Listen for specific information

Key language

- *Has it got (big ears)? Yes, it has. / No, it hasn't. Have they got (four legs)? Yes, they have. / No, they haven't.*

Recycled: *crocodile, elephant, giraffe, hippo, lion, lizard, monkey, penguin, snake, tiger; big, black, ears, grey, hair, legs, white*

Recycled: *It's (an elephant). It's got (four legs). They're (small). They've got (a long tongue). A (lion) has got … (Hippos) have got …*

Materials

- Pupil's Book p29; Activity Book p27; Class CD1; Teacher's App on Navio
- Animal flashcards
- Teacher's Resource Bank: Task flashcards: *listen, read, write, Talk Partners, think, draw*

Optional materials

- Teacher's Resource Bank: Five Trinity Exam Practice cards (selected from the Starter Unit and Units 1 and 2)

At a Glance Lesson Plan

Pupil's Book

Starting the lesson

- Use the Trinity Exam Practice cards (optional).
- Review the *I'm a wild animal* song.
- ▶ ***CD1 Track 50 p260***
- ▶ ***CD1 Track 51 p261 (optional karaoke version)***
- Review animal vocabulary. Play *Slowly, slowly.*
- Set learning outcomes using the task flashcards.

Activity 1

- Listen and repeat.
- ▶ ***CD1 Track 53 p261***
- Talk Partners Act out.

Activity 2

- Listen and number.
- ▶ ***CD1 Track 54 p261***
- Go to the Activity Book.

Ending the lesson

- Review the lesson.
- Review the task flashcards.

Extra activity

Reinforcement

- Play *The guessing game.*

Cooperative learning

Listening to others

- Play *At the zoo.*

Activity Book

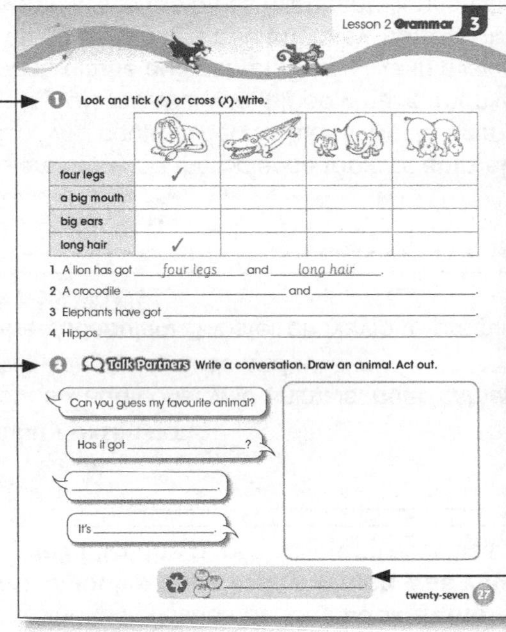

Activity Book

Activity 1

- Look and tick (✓) or cross (✗).
- Write.

Activity 2

- Write a conversation. Draw an animal.
- Talk Partners Act out.

Recycled vocabulary

- Look, remember and write the word.

Digital resources

Teacher's Digital: Don't forget you can teach this lesson using the Teacher's App on Navio.

Pupil's Digital: Encourage your pupils to use the Pupil's App on Navio to practise the vocabulary from this lesson.

Powered By NAVIO

Starting the lesson

Use the Trinity Exam Practice cards (optional).

- The pupils practise asking and answering questions. (See p31.)

Review the *I'm a wild animal* song.

▶ *CD1 Track 50 p260*

▶ *CD1 Track 51 p261 (optional karaoke version)*

- Divide the class into four groups. Give each group one of the animal flashcards from the song. Play the CD (or use the karaoke version). Groups take turns to do the mime for their animal and sing the corresponding verse.

Review animal vocabulary.

- Play *Slowly, slowly.* (See p23.)

Set learning outcomes using the task flashcards.

- Explain the aims of the lesson. Say **Today we're going to ask and answer questions about wild animals.**
- Hold up the task flashcards and elicit the words. Stick them on one side of the board. Point to them during the lesson to reinforce your instructions.

Pupil's Book Activity 1

Listen and repeat. Act out.

▶ *CD1 Track 53 p261*

- (Books open.) Ask **Who can you see? Where are they?**
- Play the CD. The pupils listen and read the conversation. Check understanding. Ask **What is Beth's favourite animal? What are Jake's favourite animals?**
- Play the CD again. Pause for the pupils to repeat.
- Talk Partners The pupils practise the conversation with a Talk Partner.

Pupil's Book Activity 2

Listen and number.

▶ *CD1 Track 54 p261*

- (Books open.) Elicit the names of the animals in the scene. Say **Let's listen.**
- Play the CD. Pause after each conversation. The pupils write the correct number.

Answers: **1** lizards **2** a crocodile **3** a snake **4** monkeys

Activity Book

Activity 1

Look and tick (✓) or cross (✗). Write.

- (Books open.) Say **Look at the lion. Has it got four legs?** The box is ticked as the example. Then say **Has it got a big mouth?** *(No, it hasn't.)* The pupils write a cross in the corresponding box. Repeat for big ears and long hair. Repeat for the other animals.
- The pupils complete the descriptions of the lion, crocodile, elephants and hippos saying what they have got.

Answers: **1** four legs, long hair **2** has got four legs, a big mouth **3** four legs and big ears **4** have got four legs and a big mouth

Activity 2

Write a conversation. Draw an animal. Act out.

- Encourage a volunteer to think of an animal and choose one of the characteristics from the table above to complete the first speech bubble.
- Another pupil completes the second speech bubble. Repeat.
- Talk Partners The pupils write, draw and practise their own conversation. Pairs read their conversations for their classmates.

Recycled vocabulary

- The pupils look at the picture and write the word.

Answer: tomatoes

Ending the lesson

Review the lesson.

- Say **Today you've described animals.** Elicit some descriptive sentences.

Review the task flashcards.

- Point to the task flashcards. Say **Look at the activities you've done today. Which activity was your favourite?** Elicit the pupils' favourite activities.

Extra activity

Reinforcement

- Play *The guessing game.* Choose one of the wild animals from the unit and say **I've got four legs. I'm dangerous. I can't fly. I'm orange and black. What am I?** *(A tiger.)*

Talk Partners After a few turns, the pupils play with a Talk Partner.

Cooperative learning

Listening to others

- Play *At the zoo.* Start off a chain by saying **At the zoo I can see (a tiger).** A pupil repeats your animal and adds a new one *(an elephant).* The pupils continue adding animals to the chain, remembering those that have been said before. Pupils must listen to each other and remember the order of the animals.
- If you have a confident class, encourage the pupils to play in small groups.

Key Competences and Key Learning Outcomes

- Read, listen and understand a story about a mysterious egg
- Read the story with some fluency
- Classify animals by their diet (optional)
- Become familiar with the story through a pre-reading task
- Understand the importance of helping your friends and family
- Understand and act out the story
- Give an opinion on the story

Key language

- *Has it got (a long neck)? No, it hasn't. This (baby animal) hasn't got (big teeth). It's got (feathers).*

Recycled: *birds, crocodiles, egg, giraffe, hippos, lions, lizards, penguin, snakes, zoo; ears, egg*

Other vocabulary: *ground, hatches, inside, lost, sign, strange*

Materials

- Pupil's Book pp30–31; Activity Book p28; Class CD1; Teacher's App on Navio
- Teacher's Resource Bank: Task flashcards: *listen, read, act out, write, circle, Talk Partners*
- Teacher's Resource Bank: Unit 3 Lesson 3 Animated Story

Optional materials

- Teacher's Resource Bank: Five Trinity Exam Practice cards (selected from the Starter Unit and Units 1 and 2)
- Animal flashcards

At a Glance Lesson Plan

Pupil's Book

Starting the lesson

- Use the Trinity Exam Practice cards (optional).
- Review the *I'm a wild animal* song.
- ▶ ***CD1 Track 51 p261 (optional karaoke version)***
- Set learning outcomes using the task flashcards.

Before you read

- Explain the story title.
- Read and answer the question.

Activity 1

- Listen and read.
- ▶ ***CD1 Track 55 p261***
- Act out.
- ***Now watch the animated story!***

After you read: Activity 2

- Values: Read and write.
- Go to page 28 in your Activity Book.

Ending the lesson

- Review the lesson.
- Review the task flashcards.

Extra activity

Extension

- Story extension.

Link to Science

- **Animals:** classifying animals by their diet

Digital resources

Teacher's Digital: Don't forget you can teach this lesson using the Teacher's App on Navio.

Pupil's Digital: Encourage your pupils to use the Pupil's App on Navio to practise the vocabulary from this lesson.

Powered By NAVIO

Activity Book

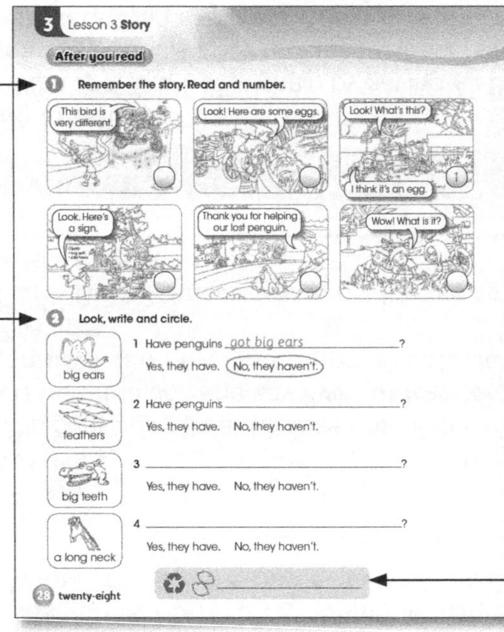

Activity Book

After you read: Activity 1

- Remember the story. Read and number.

Activity 2

- Look, write and circle.

Recycled vocabulary

- Look, remember and write the word.

Starting the lesson

Use the Trinity Exam Practice cards (optional).

- The pupils practise asking and answering questions. (See p31.)

Review the *I'm a wild animal* song.

▶ *CD1 Track 51 p261 (optional karaoke version)*

- Use the karaoke version to sing *I'm a wild animal* from Lesson 1. The pupils choose four new animals. Adapt the song to the new animals and sing it with the class.

Set learning outcomes using the task flashcards.

- Say **Today we're going to listen to a story.**
- Hold up the task flashcards and elicit the words. Stick them on one side of the board. Point to them during the lesson to reinforce your instructions.

Before you read

Explain the story title.

- (Books open.) Focus on the title. Ask the class **Why do you think the egg is mysterious?**

Read and answer the question.

- Read the speech bubble. Give the pupils 30 seconds to scan the story and find the animals.
- Talk Partners The pupils feed back to a Talk Partner and then to the class.

Pupil's Book Activity 1

Listen and read. Act out.

▶ *CD1 Track 55 p261*

- (Books open.) Play the CD. The pupils follow the text with their finger. Pause between each story frame to check understanding.

Suggested comprehension questions

- Frame 1: **Where are Jake, Molly and Beth today?** *(At the zoo.)*
- Frame 2: **What do they find?** *(An egg.)*
- Frame 3: **What comes out of the egg?** *(A strange animal.)*
- Frame 4: **What animal do they see first?** *(Giraffes.)*
- Frame 5: **What do they find next?** *(Crocodile eggs.)*
- Frame 6: **Which animal does Jake find next?** *(A bird.)*
- Frame 7: **Can they see the baby's mum now? What animal is it?** *(A penguin.)*
- Frame 8: **Does the story have a happy ending?** *(Yes.)*
- Ask **Did you like the story? What part did you like best?**
- Talk Partners The pupils choose their favourite frame.
- Organise the class into four groups (Jake, Molly, Beth and the zookeeper).
- Play the CD. Each group joins in when their character speaks. If necessary, pause the CD after each sentence for the pupils to repeat.
- The pupils swap roles and join in with their new character.

After you read

Pupil's Book Activity 2

Go to page 28 in your Activity Book.

Activity Book

After you read: Activity 1

Remember the story. Read and number.

- (Books open.) Invite individual pupils to read out the story frames in order. The pupils number the frames.

Answers: 5 4 1 3 6 2

Activity 2

Look, write and circle.

- (Books open.) Read the first question and point to the corresponding illustration. Ask a pupil to read the answer. Pupils complete the questions and circle the correct answer.

Answers: **1** got big ears; No, they haven't. **2** got feathers; Yes, they have. **3** Have crocodiles got big teeth? Yes, they have. **4** Have giraffes got a long neck? Yes, they have.

Recycled vocabulary

- The pupils look at the picture and write the word.

Answer: lemons

Pupil's Book Activity 2

Values: Read and write.

- Remind the pupils that they should help their friends and family. Read the information in the speech bubble and elicit the correct word to complete the sentence. Ask the pupils if they help their friends and family.

Ending the lesson

Review the lesson.

- Say **Today we listened to a story about a mysterious egg. Today we learnt that it is important to help your friends and family when they need you.**

Review the task flashcards.

- Point to the task flashcards. Say **Look at the activities you've done today. Which activity was your favourite?** Elicit the pupils' favourite activities.

Extra activity

Extension

- Story extension. Invite volunteers to play the parts of Jake, Beth and Molly in the story. Stick all the animal flashcards on the board. Ask the class to choose different animals for the story and act out the new conversations, e.g.
  Jake: Is this right?
  Molly: No! This baby animal hasn't got (big teeth / four legs / a long neck).

Link to Science

- If you are studying the Science topic of **animals** in English, you could remind the pupils how animals are classified by their diet. Talk about the food the animals from the story eat. Draw a three-column chart on the board (*carnivore, herbivore, omnivore*). Elicit the food that each animal eats and classify them in the chart. Include the remaining animals from the unit by showing the flashcards.

Answers: Herbivore: elephant, giraffe; Omnivore: monkey, parrot; Carnivore: penguin, crocodile

Key Competences and Key Learning Outcomes

- Describe and guess animals
- Describe animal features
- Use animal body parts vocabulary to compare animals
- Review the difference between mammals and birds (optional)
- Sing a song

Key language
- *beak, body, face, tail, teeth, wings*

Extension vocabulary
- *feathers, fur, spots, stripes*

Recycled: *It hasn't got (wings). They haven't got (beaks). It's a (giraffe). They're (crocodiles).*

Materials
- Pupil's Book p32; Activity Book p29; Class CD2; Teacher's App on Navio
- Teacher's Resource Bank: Task flashcards: *listen, say, sing, Talk Partners, number, write, draw*

Optional materials
- Teacher's Resource Bank: Five Trinity Exam Practice cards (selected from the Starter Unit and Units 1 and 2)

At a Glance Lesson Plan

Starting the lesson
- Use the Trinity Exam Practice cards (optional).
- Review the Lesson 3 story.
- Set learning outcomes using the task flashcards.

Vocabulary presentation
- Present the new vocabulary.

Activity 1
- Listen, point and say.
- ▶ *CD2 Track 1 p261*

Activity 2
- Listen and point. Sing *The animal song.*
- ▶ *CD2 Track 2 p261*

Activity 3
- Listen and repeat.
- Talk Partners Play a game.
- ▶ *CD2 Track 3 p261*
- Go to the Activity Book.

Pupil's Book

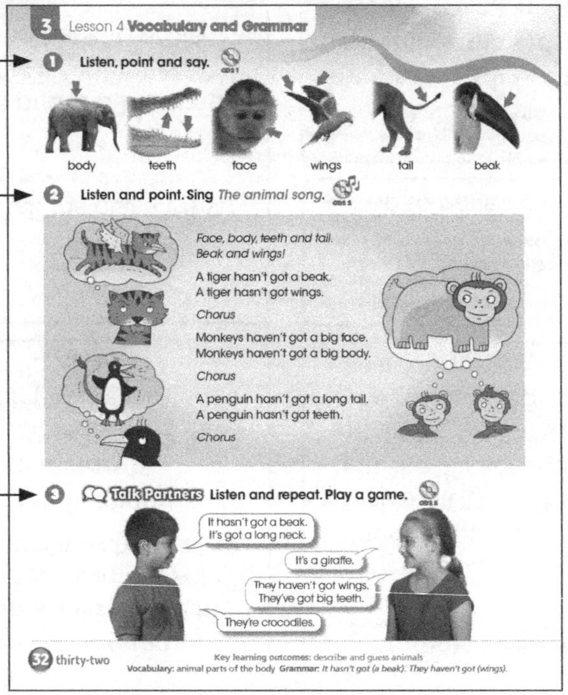
3 Lesson 4 Vocabulary and Grammar

1 Listen, point and say.

body teeth face wings tail beak

2 Listen and point. Sing *The animal song.*

Face, body, teeth and tail.
Beak and wings!
A tiger hasn't got a beak.
A tiger hasn't got wings.
Chorus
Monkeys haven't got a big face.
Monkeys haven't got a big body.
Chorus
A penguin hasn't got a long tail.
A penguin hasn't got teeth.
Chorus

3 Talk Partners Listen and repeat. Play a game.

32 thirty-two

Key learning outcomes: describe and guess animals
Vocabulary: animal parts of the body Grammar: *It hasn't got (a beak). They haven't got (wings).*

Ending the lesson
- Review the lesson.
- Review the task flashcards.

Extra activities

Reinforcement
- Review animal body parts.

Vocabulary extension
- Present four additional vocabulary items.

Link to Science
- **Animals:** the difference between mammals and birds

Digital resources

Teacher's Digital: Don't forget you can teach this lesson using the Teacher's App on Navio.

Pupil's Digital: Encourage your pupils to use the Pupil's App on Navio to practise the vocabulary from this lesson.

Powered By NAVIO

Activity Book

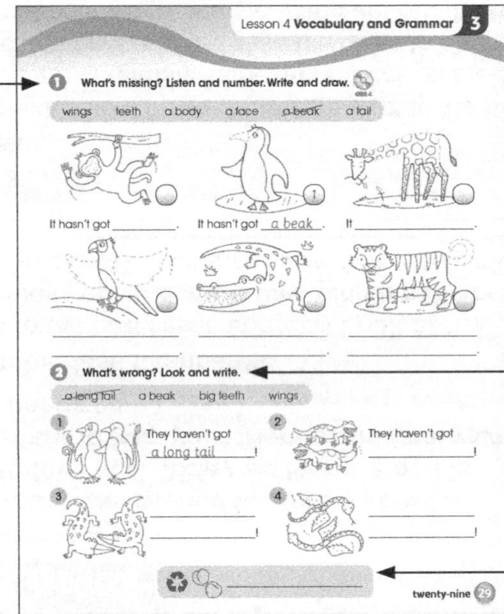
Lesson 4 Vocabulary and Grammar 3

1 What's missing? Listen and number. Write and draw.

wings teeth a body a face a beak a tail

It hasn't got ____. It hasn't got a beak. It ____.

2 What's wrong? Look and write.

a long tail a beak big teeth wings

1 They haven't got a long tail
2 They haven't got ____

twenty-nine 29

Activity Book

Activity 1
- What's missing? Listen and number. Write and draw.
- ▶ *CD2 Track 4 p261*

Activity 2
- What's wrong? Look and write.

Recycled vocabulary
- Look, remember and write the word.

Starting the lesson

Use the Trinity Exam Practice cards (optional).

- The pupils practise asking and answering questions. (See p31.)

Review the Lesson 3 story.

- Read out one of the speech bubbles. The pupils listen, scan the story and identify the frame in the story. Repeat with the other lines. Summarise what happens in the story with the class.

Set learning outcomes using the task flashcards.

- Say **Today we're going to talk about animal body parts.**
- Hold up the task flashcards in turn and elicit the words. Stick them on one side of the board. Point to them during the lesson to reinforce your instructions.

Vocabulary presentation

Present the new vocabulary.

- (Books open.) Point to the first picture and say **Look at the body.** Point to your own body and say **I've got a body. Animals have got a body, too.** Repeat for teeth and face. **Point to the tail.** Position your hands behind you and wave them like a tail. The class does the same. Repeat the word 'tail' and ask the class to say it with you. Ask **Which animals have got a tail?** Elicit *Tigers have got a tail. Monkeys have got a tail.*, etc. Repeat with the remaining animal body parts.

Pupil's Book Activity 1

Listen, point and say.

▶ *CD2 Track 1 p261*

- *Say* **Let's listen and repeat the words.** Play the CD. The pupils repeat each word, pointing to the corresponding photo. Play the CD again. The pupils repeat and do the action.

Pupil's Book Activity 2

Listen and point. Sing *The animal song.*

▶ *CD2 Track 2 p261*

- (Books open.) Say **What animals can you see?** Point to the tiger and ask **Has a tiger got (a body / teeth)?** Repeat for the other animals.
- Play the CD. The pupils listen and point to the animals. Play the CD again. The pupils sing and do the actions.

Pupil's Book Activity 3

Listen and repeat. Play a game.

▶ *CD2 Track 3 p261*

- Play the CD. Ask the pupils to repeat the sentences. A pair of pupils acts out the conversation.
- **Talk Partners** The pupils practise the conversation with a Talk Partner, naming and describing different animals each time.

Activity Book

Activity 1

What's missing? Listen and number. Write and draw.

▶ *CD2 Track 4 p261*

- (Books open.) Play the CD. The pupils order the sentences by numbering the boxes.
- They name the missing body part for each animal, complete the sentences and the drawings.

Answers: **1** penguin, a beak **2** tiger; It hasn't got a tail. **3** giraffe; hasn't got a body **4** monkey, a face **5** crocodile; It hasn't got teeth. **6** bird; It hasn't got wings.

Activity 2

What's wrong? Look and write.

- (Books open.) Say **Look at the penguins. What's wrong?** Elicit *Penguins haven't got a long tail!* Repeat with the remaining animals. The pupils cross out the incorrect body parts and complete the sentences.

Answers: **1** a long tail **2** big teeth **3** They haven't got a beak! **4** They haven't got wings!

Recycled vocabulary

- The pupils look at the picture and write the word.

Answer: peaches

Ending the lesson

Review the lesson.

- Say **Today we've talked about animal body parts.** Elicit the words from the pupils.

Review the task flashcards.

- Point to the task flashcards. Say **Look at the activities you've done today. Which activity was your favourite?** Elicit the pupils' favourite activities.

Extra activities

Reinforcement

- **Talk Partners** The pupils draw animals with the wrong body parts and show a Talk Partner. The pupils comment, e.g. *Tigers haven't got a beak!*

Vocabulary extension

- Use the Vocabulary Booster on Navio to present and practise four additional words to describe animal features: *feathers, fur, spots, stripes.*

Link to Science

- If you are studying the Science topic of **animals** in English, you could review the difference between mammals and birds.
- Draw a chart and list the characteristics of birds in one column as the pupils say them. Repeat for the mammals in the other column. Point out that we can say 'have' or 'have got' when we are talking about animal characteristics.

Key Competences and Key Learning Outcomes

- Say a tongue twister with the 'oo' sound
- Learn and practise 'oo' and 'ui' spellings
- Listen for specific information
- Sing a cooperative learning song
- Play a communication game describing animals

Key language

- *fruit, goose, juice, kangaroo; balloon, food, moon, pool, spoon, swimsuit, zoo*
- *Let's take turns. It's my turn. It's your turn.*

Recycled: *crocodile, elephant, giraffe, hippo, lion, lizard, monkey, penguin, snake, tiger; body, face, legs, neck, tail, teeth, wings*

Recycled: *It's got (a tail). It hasn't got (a beak). Is it a …? Yes, it is. No, it isn't. They've got (wings). They haven't got (hair). Are they …? Yes, they are. No, they aren't.*

Materials

- Pupil's Book p33; Activity Book p30; Class CD2; Teacher's App on Navio
- Teacher's Resource Bank: Task flashcards: *listen, say, number, sing, Talk Partners, write, colour*
- Teacher's Resource Bank: Unit 3 Lesson 5 Activity 4 cut-out
- Coloured pencils and scissors

Optional materials

- Teacher's Resource Bank: Five Trinity Exam Practice cards (selected from the Starter Unit and Units 1 and 2)

At a Glance Lesson Plan

Pupil's Book

Starting the lesson

- Use the Trinity Exam Practice cards (optional).
- Review animal vocabulary. Play *Odd one out*.
- Set learning outcomes using the task flashcards.

Activity 1

- Listen and say.
- ▶ *CD2 Track 5 p261*
- Go to the Activity Book.
- Go to Magic Phonics.

Activity 2

- Listen and number.
- ▶ *CD2 Track 6 p261*

Activity 3 Cooperative learning

- Sing *Let's take turns!*
- ▶ *CD2 Track 7 p262*

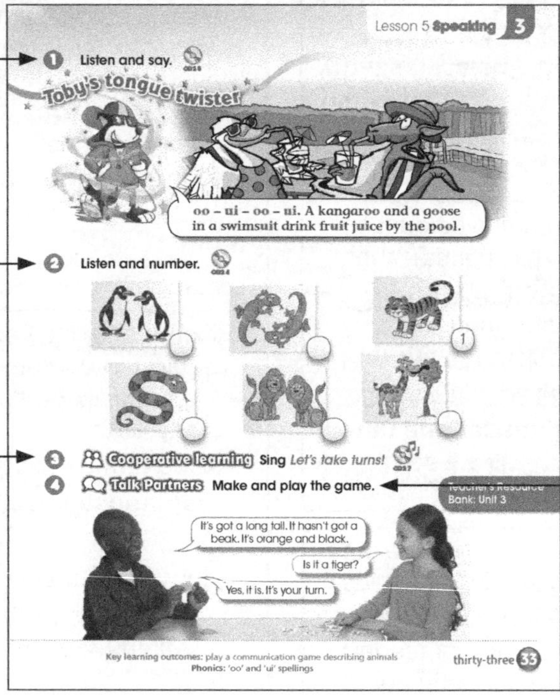

Activity 4

- Talk Partners Make and play the game (Teacher's Resource Bank).

Ending the lesson

- Review the lesson.
- Review the task flashcards.

Cooperative learning

Working together as a team

- Talk Partners Play *Beat the clock.*
- Add to the pronunciation wall display.

Activity Book

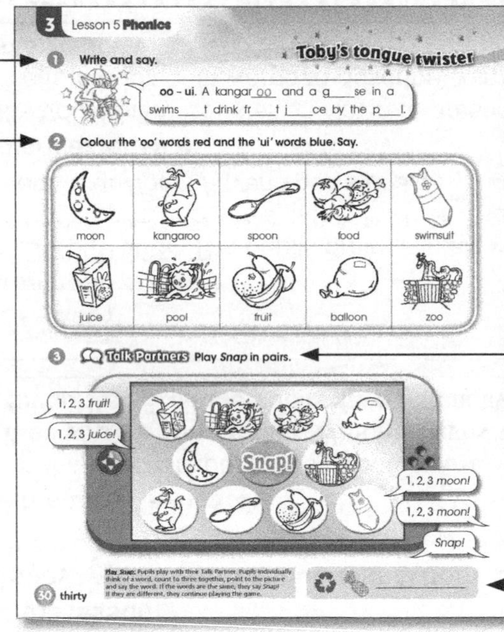

Activity Book

Activity 1

- Write and say.

Activity 2

- Colour the 'oo' words red and the 'ui' words blue. Say.
- Go to Magic Phonics.

Activity 3

- Talk Partners Play *Snap* in pairs.

Recycled vocabulary

- Look, remember and write the word.

Digital resources

Teacher's Digital: Don't forget you can teach this lesson using the Teacher's App on Navio.

Pupil's Digital: Encourage your pupils to use the Pupil's App on Navio to practise the vocabulary from this lesson.

Powered By NAVIO

Starting the lesson

Use the Trinity Exam Practice cards (optional).

- The pupils practise asking and answering questions. (See p31.)
- Review animal vocabulary. Play *Odd one out* with animal vocabulary. Say **Parrot, penguin, tiger. Which is the odd one out?** *(It's tiger. Tigers haven't got a beak.)*
- Sample groupings: Hippo, snake, elephant; Lizard, crocodile, lion; Lion, monkey, penguin.

Set learning outcomes using the task flashcards.

- Say **Today we're going to say a tongue twister. We're going to make and play a game.**
- Hold up the task flashcards in turn and elicit the activities. Stick them on one side of the board. Point to them during the lesson to reinforce your instructions.

Pupil's Book Activity 1

Listen and say.

▶ ***CD2 Track 5 p261***

- Write *pool* and *fruit* on the board. Ask the pupils which sound they can hear in both words. Circle the target grapheme in each word ('oo' and 'ui') and model the sound. The pupils say the sound with you.
- Say **It's time for Toby's tongue twister! What can you see?** *(fruit juice, a pool)* Introduce the new animal vocabulary 'goose' and 'kangaroo'. Ask **What's the goose wearing?**
- Play the CD. The pupils listen and repeat the target sound, then the words and then the entire tongue twister, faster and faster.

Go to Magic Phonics.

Activity Book

Activity 1

Write and say.

- (Books open.) Say **Look at Toby's tongue twister! The letters for 'oo' are missing.** The pupils complete the tongue twister.

Answers: kangaroo, goose, swimsuit, fruit juice, pool

- **Talk Partners** The pupils say Toby's tongue twister and point to the 'oo' sounds. They play *Faster and faster.*

Activity 2

Colour the 'oo' words red and the 'ui' words blue. Say.

- Ask pupils to say the words. The pupils then colour 'oo' words red and 'ui' words blue.

Answers: red: moon, kangaroo, spoon, food, pool, balloon, zoo; blue: swimsuit, juice, fruit

Go to Magic Phonics.

Activity 3

Play *Snap* in pairs.

- Demonstrate the game with a volunteer. You each think of a word, count to three together, point to the picture and say the word. If the words are the same, say *Snap!* If they are different, continue playing the game.
- **Talk Partners** The pupils play the game with a Talk Partner.

Recycled vocabulary

- The pupils look at the picture and write the word.

Answer: pineapple

Pupil's Book Activity 2

Listen and number.

▶ ***CD2 Track 6 p261***

- (Books open.) Say **Jake and Molly are at the zoo talking about the animals.** Pupils number the animals as they hear the descriptions.
- Play the CD. Pause to check the answers.

Answers: **1** tiger **2** penguins **3** snake **4** lizards **5** giraffe **6** lions

Pupil's Book Activity 3: **Cooperative learning**

Sing *Let's take turns!*

▶ ***CD2 Track 7 p262***

- Play the CD. The pupils listen with you. Play the CD again. The pupils join in.

Pupil's Book Activity 4

Make and play the game (Teacher's Resource Bank).

- Check that the pupils have got scissors and coloured pencils and show them how to cut out the cards. Demonstrate the activity.
- (Books open.) Choose one of the cut-outs to describe (the tiger). Read the speech bubble. Elicit *Is it a tiger?* and confirm *Yes, it is*. Repeat with a different animal.
- **Talk Partners** The pupils play the game using the language from the Pupil's Book as a model. The pupils use the cards and take turns to describe and guess.

Ending the lesson

Review the lesson.

- Say **Today we've practised a tongue twister**. Ask the pupils to say it again.
- Then say **Today you played a game with cards.**

Review the task flashcards.

- Point to the task flashcards. Say **Look at the activities you've done today. Which was your favourite?** Elicit the pupils' favourite activities.

Cooperative learning

Working together as a team

- **Talk Partners** Play *Beat the clock* to practise pronunciation of the 'oo' / 'ui' sound. (See p53.)
- Add to the pronunciation wall display, adding a moon ('oo') and a swimsuit ('ui').

Key Competences and Key Learning Outcomes

- Read about garden wildlife in Britain
- Listen for general understanding
- Think about wild animals where you live

Key language

- *dish, fox, garden, grass, hedgehog, night, nuts, seeds, squirrel, tail, tree, water*

Recycled: *climb, table*

Recycled: *Squirrels climb trees. They eat nuts. We put water in a dish. They've got a long tail.*

Materials

- Pupil's Book p34; Activity Book p31; Class CD2; Teacher's App on Navio
- Teacher's Resource Bank: Task flashcards: *Talk Partners, listen, read, think, number, write, tick, draw, say*

Optional materials

- Teacher's Resource Bank: Five Trinity Exam Practice cards (selected from the Starter Unit and Units 1 and 2)

At a Glance Lesson Plan

Pupil's Book

Starting the lesson

- Use the Trinity Exam Practice cards (optional).
- Talk Partners
  Review *Toby's tongue twister*.
  ▶ *CD2 Track 5 p261*
- Set learning outcomes using the task flashcards.

Activity 1

- Listen and read. Answer.
  ▶ *CD2 Track 8 p262*

Think about your culture

- Are there wild animals near your house?

Go to the Activity Book.

Lesson 6 British culture

1 Listen and read. Answer.

Our house has got a big garden. Lots of wild animals come to visit.

1 Lots of different birds come into our garden. We put seeds and nuts on a table for the birds.

2 Hedgehogs come into the garden, too. We can see them at night.

3 Sometimes, a fox comes into the garden. It plays on the grass. We put water in a dish for it.

4 Squirrels climb the trees in our garden. They've got a long tail. They're naughty. They eat the bird food.

Think about your culture
Are there wild animals near your house?

34 thirty-four

Key learning outcomes: read about garden wildlife in Britain, think about wild animals where you live

Ending the lesson

- Review the lesson.
- Review the task flashcards.

Extra activity

Extension

- Describing animals.

Digital resources

Teacher's Digital: Don't forget you can teach this lesson using the Teacher's App on Navio.

Powered By NAVIO

Activity Book

Lesson 6 British culture

1 Listen and number. Write.

birds fox hedgehogs squirrels

1 birds

Think about your culture

What animals can you see near your house?

2 Read and tick (✓). Draw, write and say.

1 I can see birds.
2 I can see hedgehogs.
3 I can see pets.
4 I can see squirrels.
5 I can see lizards.

I ___

thirty-one 31

Activity Book

Activity 1

- Listen and number. Write.
  ▶ *CD2 Track 9 p262*

Recycled vocabulary

- Look, remember and write the word.

Activity 2: Think about your culture

- Read and tick (✓). Draw, write and say.

Starting the lesson

Use the Trinity Exam Practice cards (optional).

- The pupils practise asking and answering questions. (See p31.)

Review Toby's tongue twister.

▶ *CD2 Track 5 p261*

- Ask the class **What sound did you practise in Toby's tongue twister?** *('oo').* Ask if they can remember the tongue twister. *(A kangaroo and a goose in a swimsuit drink fruit juice by the pool.)*
- Talk Partners The pupils practise the tongue twister as a class and then with a Talk Partner. The pairs play *Faster and faster,* reading from the Pupil's Book if necessary. A fast pair says the tongue twister for the class.
- Draw a chart with two columns ('oo' and 'ui') on the board. Elicit words with both spellings. Ask pupils to classify the words, e.g. 'oo': *moon, pool*; 'ui': *fruit, juice.*

Set learning outcomes using the task flashcards.

- Say **Today we're going to learn about the wild animals you can see in a British garden.**
- Hold up the task flashcards in turn and elicit the activities. Stick them on one side of the board. Point to them during the lesson to reinforce your instructions.

Background information

- In Britain, many people have a garden. This usually has a lawn, flowerbeds and some trees. Wild animals come into the gardens, particularly foxes, hedgehogs, squirrels and birds. Some people leave food out for the birds as winters can be very cold.

Pupil's Book Activity 1

Listen and read. Answer.

▶ *CD2 Track 8 p262*

- (Books open.) Say **Let's find out about animals in British gardens.**
- Focus the pupils' attention on the photographs and ask **What can you see? Let's listen and read.**
- Play the CD. Check understanding. Point to the first photo and point out the bird table. Ask **What animal can you see here?** Repeat with the other photos.

Pupil's Book Think about your culture

Are there wild animals near your house?

- Read the question and encourage the class to tell you if they can see wild animals near their homes and what animals they see. Are they the same or different?

Activity Book

Activity 1

Listen and number. Write.

▶ *CD2 Track 9 p262*

- (Books open.) Focus attention on the garden scene. Ask the pupils what they can see *(hedgehogs, a fox, squirrels and some birds).* Point out the pond and the bird table. Say **Let's listen to some pupils looking at the animals in their garden. Which animal do they see first?**
- Play the CD, pausing after the first conversation to check understanding. Play the remaining conversations. The pupils number the correct animal each time. On completion, they write the name of each animal.

Answers: **1** birds **2** hedgehogs **3** fox **4** squirrels

Activity 2: Think about your culture

Read and tick (✓). Draw, write and say.

- Read out the question in the speech bubble. Elicit the pupils' answers.
- Read out the first sentence as a class and ask the pupils to tick the box if they can see birds near where they live. Repeat with the other sentences.
- Ask the pupils to draw an animal they have seen near their home and write a sentence. Invite different pupils to show the rest of the class their drawings and prompt them to say which animals live near them.

Recycled vocabulary

- The pupils look at the picture and write the word.

Answer: yoghurt

Ending the lesson

Review the lesson.

- Say **Today you've learnt about garden wildlife in Britain.**

Review the task flashcards.

- Point to the task flashcards. Say **Look at the activities you've done today. Which activity was your favourite?** Elicit the pupils' favourite activities.

Extra activity

Extension

- Ask the pupils to look closely at the photos of the wild animals. Encourage them to describe the characteristics of these animals: *Look at the squirrels. They haven't got wings. They've got a long tail.*, etc.
- If you have access to the internet, explain to the pupils how in Britain there is a special society for the protection of birds. Pupils are encouraged to count the birds they see in their gardens. For more information visit the web page: http://www.rspb.org.uk/birdwatch/.

Key Competences and Key Learning Outcomes

- Write an animal fact file
- Read and understand animal fact files
- Read for specific information

Key language

- *fact file, gorilla, polar bear; ice, insects, leaves, rainforest, snow*

Recycled: *arms, body, ears, fingers, hair, legs, tail, teeth, toes; fish, fruit, meat*

Recycled: *They've got … They haven't got … They live … They eat …*

Materials

- Pupil's Book p35; Activity Book p32; Class CD2; Teacher's App on Navio
- Animal flashcards
- Teacher's Resource Bank: Task flashcards: *think, say, listen, read, write, draw, Talk Partners*

Optional materials

- Teacher's Resource Bank: Five Trinity Exam Practice cards (selected from the Starter Unit and Units 1 and 2)
- A sheet of coloured paper for each pair

At a Glance Lesson Plan

Pupil's Book

Starting the lesson

- Use the Trinity Exam Practice cards (optional).
- Review *The animal song.*

▶ *CD2 Track 2 p261*

- Set learning outcomes using the task flashcards.

Before you read: Activity 1

- What do you know about gorillas and polar bears? Think and say.

Activity 2

- Listen and read the animal fact files.

▶ *CD2 Track 10 p262*

After you read

Go to page 32 in your Activity Book.

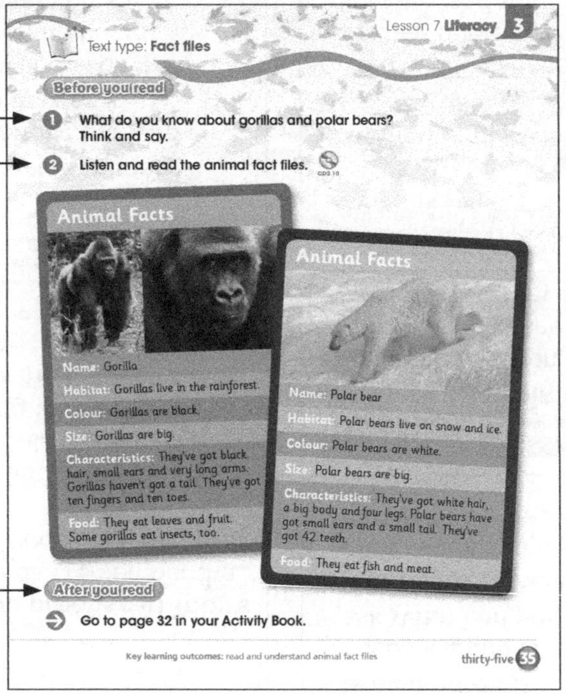
Lesson 7 Literacy 3

Text type: Fact files

Before you read

1 What do you know about gorillas and polar bears? Think and say.

2 Listen and read the animal fact files.

Animal Facts

Name: Gorilla
Habitat: Gorillas live in the rainforest.
Colour: Gorillas are black.
Size: Gorillas are big.
Characteristics: They've got black hair, small ears and very long arms. Gorillas haven't got a tail. They've got ten fingers and ten toes.
Food: They eat leaves and fruit. Some gorillas eat insects, too.

Animal Facts

Name: Polar bear
Habitat: Polar bears live on snow and ice.
Colour: Polar bears are white.
Size: Polar bears are big.
Characteristics: They've got white hair, a big body and four legs. Polar bears have got small ears and a small tail. They've got 42 teeth.
Food: They eat fish and meat.

After you read

Go to page 32 in your Activity Book.

Key learning outcomes: read and understand animal fact files

thirty-five 35

Ending the lesson

- Review the lesson.
- Review the task flashcards.
- Sing a song (optional).

Extra activity

Extension

- Prepare another animal fact file.

Cooperative learning

Encouraging one another

- Using positive language.

Link to Science

- **Animals:** describing mammals

Digital resources

Teacher's Digital: Don't forget you can teach this lesson using the Teacher's App on Navio.

Pupil's Digital: Encourage your pupils to use the Pupil's App on Navio to practise the vocabulary from this lesson.

Powered By NAVIO

Activity Book

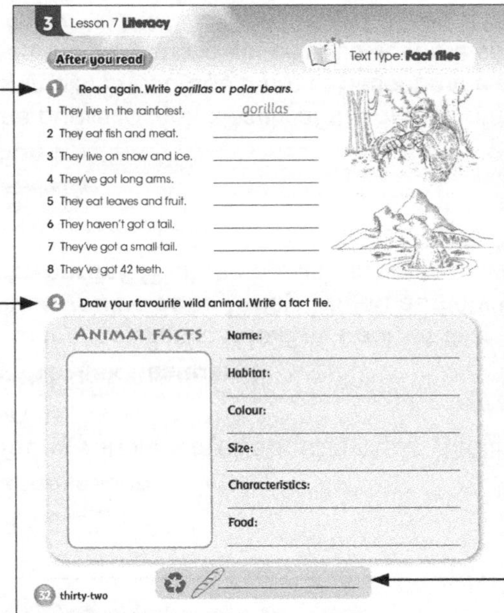
3 Lesson 7 Literacy

After you read

Text type: Fact files

1 Read again. Write *gorillas* or *polar bears.*

1 They live in the rainforest. gorillas
2 They eat fish and meat.
3 They live on snow and ice.
4 They've got long arms.
5 They eat leaves and fruit.
6 They haven't got a tail.
7 They've got a small tail.
8 They've got 42 teeth.

2 Draw your favourite wild animal. Write a fact file.

ANIMAL FACTS

Name:
Habitat:
Colour:
Size:
Characteristics:
Food:

32 thirty-two

Activity Book

After you read: Activity 1

- Read again. Write *gorillas* or *polar bears.*

Activity 2

- Draw your favourite wild animal. Write a fact file.

Recycled vocabulary

- Look, remember and write the word.

Starting the lesson

Use the Trinity Exam Practice cards (optional).

- The pupils practise asking and answering questions. (See p31.)

Review *The animal song*.

▶ *CD2 Track 2 p261*

- Divide the class into three groups. Give each group one of the animal flashcards from the song. Play the CD. Groups take turns to do the mime for their animal and sing the corresponding verse.

Set learning outcomes using the task flashcards.

- Say **Today we're going to read a fact file about animals.**
- Hold up the task flashcards in turn and elicit the activities. Stick them on one side of the board. Point to them during the lesson to reinforce your instructions.

Before you read: Pupil's Book Activity 1

What do you know about gorillas and polar bears? Think and say.

- (Books open.) Read out the question. Ask the pupils to cover the text and look at the two photos. Brainstorm any information the pupils already know or can guess by looking at the photos.
- Talk Partners The pupils discuss what they know with a Talk Partner first. Elicit the information and write it on a mind map on the board.

Pupil's Book Activity 2

Listen and read the animal fact files.

▶ *CD2 Track 10 p262*

- Play the CD and read the fact files together. After reading, return to the mind map on the board. Compare the information with the text. Change any incorrect suggestions and ask the pupils if they found anything surprising. Complete the mind map with the information that the pupils learnt.

Activity Book

After you read: Activity 1

Read again. Write *gorillas* or *polar bears*.

- Read the first sentence together and invite a pupil to say if it refers to gorillas or polar bears.
- Talk Partners The pupils take turns to read the facts and decide if they refer to gorillas or polar bears. Pupils then write the answers individually.

Answers: gorillas: 1, 4, 5, 6 polar bears: 2, 3, 7, 8

Activity 2

Draw your favourite wild animal. Write a fact file.

- Ask the pupils to choose their favourite of the two animals from the fact files in their Pupil's Book. They complete the information and draw the animal. Encourage them to close their Pupil's Book and refer to it only if they can't remember the facts.
- If you have a confident class, encourage the pupils to write their fact file about an animal of their choice. Demonstrate first by choosing a different animal to discuss together. Copy the fact file frame onto the board and complete it as you discuss ideas with the pupils. If you have access to the internet and an interactive whiteboard, research any necessary information together before completing the chart.

Recycled vocabulary

- The pupils look at the picture and write the word.

Answer: bread

Ending the lesson

Review the lesson.

- Say **Today we read a fact file.** Then say **You've written a fact file about an animal.**

Review the task flashcards.

- Point to the task flashcards. Say **Look at the activities you've done today. Which activity was your favourite?** Elicit the pupils' favourite activities.

Sing a song (optional).

- Choose a song. The class sings and does the actions. Alternatively, invite the class to choose a song to sing.

Extra activity

Extension

- Take the pupils to the computer room to find more information about animals. Encourage them to work with a partner to choose a new animal and print out a photo. They should write a new fact file for this animal on coloured paper. Display the pupils' work in a prominent place.

Cooperative learning

Encouraging one another

- Invite different pupils to share their drawings and fact files with a Talk Partner. Pupils should comment positively on each other's work: *It's lovely. Very good! Fantastic! Good job. Great work! Brilliant!*, etc.

Link to Science

- If you are studying the Science topic of **animals** in English, you could review describing mammals. Polar bears and gorillas are both mammals. Encourage the pupils to use their knowledge of mammals to extend the description of each animal: *Gorillas / Polar bears have live babies. They are vertebrate animals. They have got hair. They breathe with their lungs.*, etc.
- Encourage the pupils to use this information in their fact files.

Key Competences and Key Learning Outcomes

- Review language in the unit
- Reflect on own learning
- Sing a cooperative learning song

Key language

Recycled: *crocodile, elephant, giraffe, hippo, lion, lizard, monkey, penguin, snake, tiger; beak, body, face, tail, teeth, wings*

Recycled: *It's got … They've got … Has it got …? Yes, it has. / No, it hasn't. Have they got …? Yes, they have. / No, they haven't. It hasn't got … They haven't got …*

Materials

- Pupil's Book p36; Activity Book p33; Class CD2; Teacher's App on Navio
- Animal flashcards
- Teacher's Resource Bank: Task flashcards: *listen, number, write, say, read, sing, find, Talk Partners, Think-Pair-Share*
- Teacher's Resource Bank: Traffic light cut-out
- *Give Me Five!* sticker

Optional materials

- Teacher's Resource Bank: Five Trinity Exam Practice cards (selected from the Starter Unit and Units 1 and 2)
- A4 paper

At a Glance Lesson Plan

Pupil's Book

Starting the lesson

- Use the Trinity Exam Practice cards (optional).
- Review the unit vocabulary.
- Set learning outcomes using the task flashcards.

Activity 1

- Listen and number.
- Write and say.
- ▶ *CD2 Track 11 p262*

Activity 2

- Read and write the animals.

Activity 3 Cooperative learning

- Sing *Well done!*
- ▶ *CD2 Track 12 p262*
- Stick the *Give Me Five!* sticker.
- Go to the Activity Book.

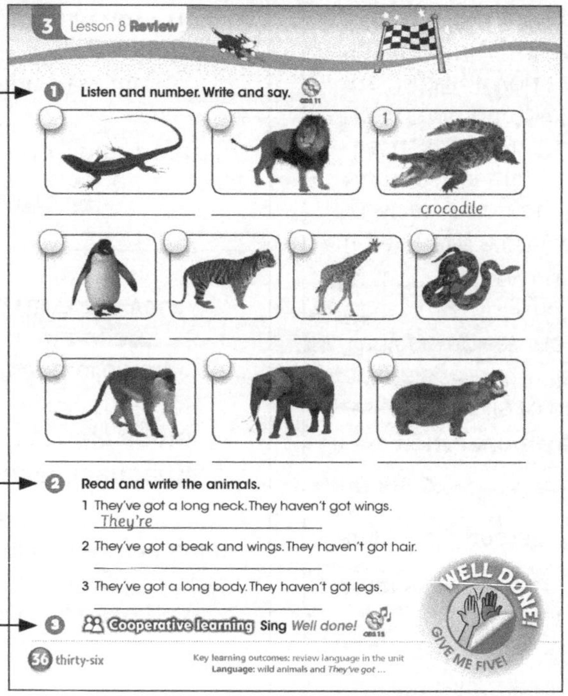

Ending the lesson

- Review the task flashcards.
- Sing a song (optional).

Extra activity

Reinforcement

- Animal descriptions.

Cooperative learning

Think-Pair-Share

- Remember ten animal words.

Digital resources

Teacher's Digital: Don't forget you can teach this lesson using the Teacher's App on Navio.

Pupil's Digital: Encourage your pupils to use the Pupil's App on Navio to practise the vocabulary from this lesson.

Powered By NAVIO

Activity Book

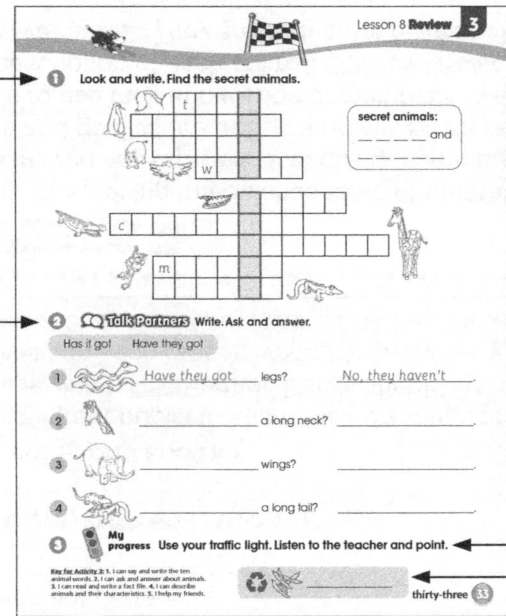

Activity Book

Activity 1

- Look and write. Find the secret animals.

Activity 2

- Write.
- Talk Partners Ask and answer.

Activity 3 My progress

- Use your traffic light. Listen to the teacher and point.

Recycled vocabulary

- Look, remember and write the phrase.

Starting the lesson

Use the Trinity Exam Practice cards (optional).

- The pupils practise asking and answering questions. (See p31.)

Review the unit vocabulary.

- Play *Disappearing words* (see p23) with the unit flashcards to review animal vocabulary.
- **Option:** Play the game in two teams. The teams take it in turns to remember the words.

Set learning outcomes using the task flashcards.

- Say **Today we're going to remember what we've learnt in Unit 3.**
- Hold up the task flashcards in turn and elicit the words. Stick them on one side of the board. Point to them during the lesson to reinforce your instructions.

Pupil's Book Activity 1

Listen and number. Write and say.

▶ *CD2 Track 11 p262*

- (Books open.) Point to each of the animals and elicit the words.
- Play the CD. Pause after each sentence. The pupils write the number next to the correct animal.
- Play the CD again. The pupils write the correct word under each picture. Then they say the words.

Answers: **1** crocodile **2** penguin **3** snake **4** giraffe **5** hippo **6** elephant **7** monkey **8** lion **9** lizard **10** tiger

Pupil's Book Activity 2

Read and write the animals.

- (Books open.) Read the sentences together and ask the class to guess the animal. Pupils write the answers.

Answers: **1** giraffes **2** They're penguins. **3** They're snakes.

Pupil's Book Activity 3: Cooperative learning

Sing *Well done!*

▶ *CD2 Track 12 p262*

- Praise the class for their hard work and play the *Well done!* song. The pupils listen and do the actions with you. Play the CD again and the pupils join in.

Stick the *Give Me Five!* sticker.

- The pupils stick the *Give Me Five!* sticker.

Activity Book

Activity 1

Look and write. Find the secret animals.

- (Books open.) Elicit the first illustrated animal characteristic *(tail)*. Ask **How do you spell that?** The pupils spell the word and write the letters in the crossword. Once the crossword is complete, the two secret animals will be revealed in the centre. Pupils write them in the gaps.

Answers: tail, penguin, hippo, wings; teeth, crocodile, giraffe, monkey, lizard **Secret animals:** lion and tiger

Activity 2

Write. Ask and answer.

- Read out the instructions. The pupils complete the questions and answers.
- **Talk Partners** The pupils practise asking and answering with a Talk Partner.

Answers: **1** Have they got; No, they haven't **2** Have they got; Yes, they have. **3** Have they got; No, they haven't. **4** Have they got; Yes, they have.

Activity 3 My progress

Use your traffic light. Listen to the teacher and point.

- (Books closed.) Ask the class to take out their traffic light cut-out. Say **Let's think about our work in this unit.** Read the first self-assessment statement. Point to the green circle and say, **Yes, I can do this very well.** Point to the orange circle and say, **Yes, I can do this.** Point to the red circle, shake your head and say, **No, I can't do this.**
- Read the remaining statements. The pupils point to the corresonding colour on their traffic light.

Self-assessment statements

1. I can say and write the ten animal words.
2. I can ask and answer about animals.
3. I can read and write a fact file.
4. I can describe animals and their characteristics.
5. I help my friends.

Recycled vocabulary

- The pupils look at the picture and write the phrase.

Answer: green beans

Ending the lesson

Review the task flashcards.

- Point to the task flashcards. Ask **Which activity was your favourite?**

Sing a song (optional).

- The class chooses their favourite song from the unit. The class sings and does the actions.

Extra activity

Reinforcement

- Give each pupil a piece of paper. They write a description of an animal using the model on Pupil's Book page 36, but they do not write the name of the animal. Give the pupils a few minutes to complete their description. Collect all the papers, shuffle and redistribute. Pupils guess the animals.

Cooperative learning

Think-Pair-Share

- Ask **Can you remember the ten animal words?** Ask the class to think silently on their own for a minute.
- **Talk Partners** Then the pupils work with a Talk Partner to remember and name all ten words.
- Invite a pair to say one of the animals. Hold up the corresponding flashcard and prompt the class to repeat the word.
- Repeat the procedure, asking different pairs each time, until all ten animals have been named.

Key Competences and Key Learning Outcomes

- Watch and understand a video about animals

- Learn to sort information
- Find similarities and differences

Key language

- *beaks, crocodile, elephant, hippo, lion, monkey, parrots, penguins, similarities, tails, tiger, Venn Diagram*

Materials

- Pupil's Book p37; Activity Book p34; Class CD2; Video; Teacher's App on Navio
- Teacher's Resource Bank: Task flashcards: *number, read, circle, listen, tick, write*

Optional materials

- Teacher's Resource Bank: Trinity Exam Practice cards (selected from Unit 3)

At a Glance Lesson Plan

Pupil's Book

Starting the lesson

- Use the Trinity Exam Practice cards (optional).
- **Think-Pair-Share** Review the animal fact files.
- Set learning outcomes and use the task flashcards.

Pre-watching activity

- Talk about favourite animals.

Activity 1

- Watch the video.
  Unit 3 video p278
- Number the pictures.

Activity 2

- Watch the video again.
  Unit 3 video
- Read and tick (✓) or cross (✗).

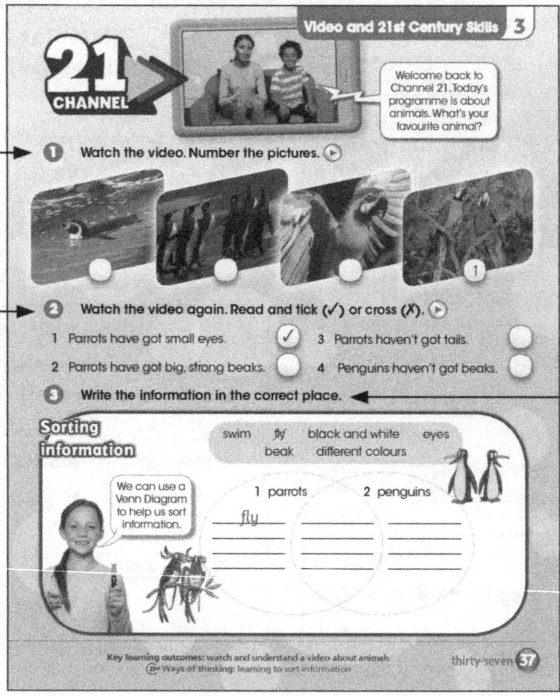

Video and 21st Century Skills 3

21 CHANNEL

Welcome back to Channel 21. Today's programme is about animals. What's your favourite animal?

1 Watch the video. Number the pictures.

2 Watch the video again. Read and tick (✓) or cross (✗).

1 Parrots have got small eyes.

2 Parrots have got big, strong beaks.

3 Parrots haven't got tails.

4 Penguins haven't got beaks.

3 Write the information in the correct place.

Sorting information

swim fly black and white eyes beak different colours

We can use a Venn Diagram to help us sort information.

1 parrots 2 penguins

fly

Key learning outcomes: watch and understand a video about animals

Ways of thinking: learning to sort information

thirty-seven 37

Activity 3

- Write the information in the correct place.
  Go to the Activity Book.

Ending the lesson

- Review the lesson.
- Review the task flashcards. Elicit the pupils' favourite activities.

Extra activity

Extension

- Pupils work in groups to create a Venn Diagram

Digital resources

Teacher's Digital: Don't forget you can teach this lesson using the Teacher's App on Navio.

Pupil's Digital: Encourage your pupils to use the Pupil's App on Navio to practise the vocabulary from this lesson.

Powered By NAVIO

Activity Book

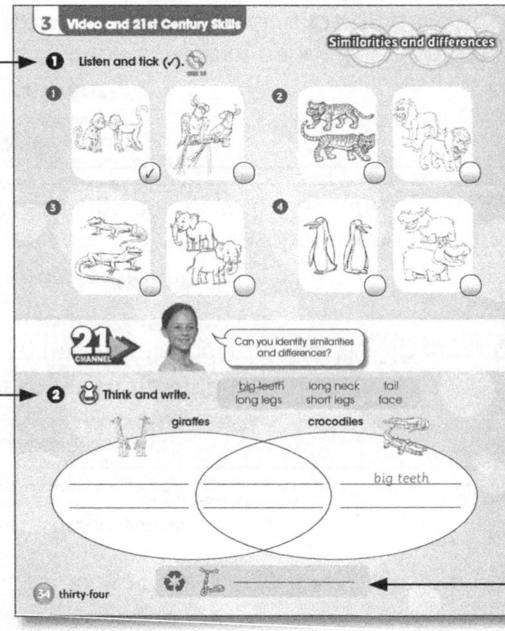

3 Video and 21st Century Skills

Similarities and differences

1 Listen and tick (✓).

21 CHANNEL

Can you identify similarities and differences?

2 Think and write.

big teeth long legs long neck short legs tail face

giraffes crocodiles

big teeth

34 thirty-four

Activity Book

Activity 1

- Listen and tick (✓).
  ▶ *CD2 Track 13 p262*

Activity 2

- Think and write.

Recycled vocabulary

- Look, remember and write the word.

Starting the lesson

Use the Trinity Exam Practice cards (optional).

- The pupils practise asking and answering questions. (See p31.)

Review the animal fact files.

- **Think-Pair-Share** Divide the class into pairs or groups of about four to six and assign each group 'gorilla' or 'polar bear'. On the board write habitat, colour, size, characteristics and food.
- Tell the pairs/groups they have two minutes to remember as many facts as they can about their assigned animal.

Set learning outcomes and use the task flashcards.

- Say **Today we're going to watch a video and then ask and answer questions about animals.**
- Hold up the task flashcards, in turn, and elicit the activities. Stick them on the side of the board. Point to them during the lesson to reinforce your instructions.

Pre-watching activity

- Read out the speech bubble and ask **What's your favourite animal?** Ask the pupils to talk about their favourite animals.

Pupil's Book Activity 1

Watch the video. Number the pictures. *p278*

- Play Part 1. Ask **What's Tom's favourite animal?** Elicit answers.
- Focus the pupils' attention on the video stills. Ask **What do you know about these animals?**
- Play Part 2, pausing after the first video still. Ask the pupils to point to the corresponding photo in their book.
- Play the rest of the video for pupils to write the numbers in order of the photos. Ask **Are penguins and parrots similar or different? Why?**

Answers: from left to right: 3 4 2 1

Pupil's Book Activity 2

Watch the video again. Read and tick (✓) or cross (✗).

- Play Part 2. Pause after Tom says, *They've got small eyes.* Read out the first sentence in Activity 2. Ask **Do parrots have small eyes?** Show the tick in the circle.
- Play Part 2 again. Pupils tick or cross the sentences.
- Ask the pupils some questions to check understanding. Suggested questions.
  Which are Tom and Sophie's favourite animals? *(Penguins and parrots.)*
  What colour are the parrots? *(Red, green, blue and yellow.)*
  What can parrots do? *(Fly.)*
  Where do parrots live? *(In the rainforest.)*
  What can penguins do? *(Swim and walk.)*
  Where do penguins live? *(In the snow and ice.)*
  What information does the diagram show about penguins and parrots? *(What's the same and what's different.)*

Answers: 1 ✓ 2 ✓ 3 ✗ 4 ✗

Pupil's Book Activity 3

Write the information in the correct place.

- Read out the speech bubble and copy the Venn Diagram on the board. Explain that they write the things in the word box that are unique to the penguin or parrot in the respective circles. Any facts which are the same go in the overlapping circle.
- Say **Fly** and ask **Which bird?** Show the example *fly* written in the parrot circle.
- Check answers as a class.

Answers: 1 **Parrots:** fly, different colours 2 **Penguins:** swim, black and white **Both:** eyes, beak

Activity Book

Activity 1

Listen and tick (✓).

▶ *CD2 Track 13 p262*

- The pupils look at the pictures. Ask **What animals can you see?**
- Play the first exchange on the CD. Ask **Which picture?** Show the tick in the circle.
- Play the rest of the CD for pupils to number the pictures.

Answers: 1 monkeys 2 tigers 3 elephants 4 hippos

Activity 2

Think and write.

- Ask a few pupils **How are giraffes and crocodiles similar / different?**
- Elicit some responses from the pupils and write one or two examples on the board. The pupils complete the Venn Diagram.
  Talk Partners Pupils compare their Venn Diagrams with their partner.

Answers: **giraffes:** long necks, long legs
crocodiles: big teeth, short legs
both: tail, face

Recycled vocabulary

Answer: scooter

Ending the lesson

Review the lesson.

- Say **Today we've watched a video about animals.** Ask **Which activity was easy / difficult?**

Review the task flashcards.

- Point to the task flashcards on the board. Say **Look at the activities you've done today. Which activity was your favourite?**

Extra activity

Extension

- Divide the class into small groups. Ask each group to think of two animals. They draw a large Venn Diagram and complete the diagram with facts about their two animals. The groups take turns to present their Venn Diagram to the class or another group. The pupils listen and try to guess the two animals.

My project 1: Pets

Key Competences and Key Learning Outcomes

- Identify and name animals we keep as pets
- Do a survey to find out what pets the class have got

- Understand and complete a simple graph about pets

- Plan your pets class book page

Key language

- *goldfish, guinea pig, hamster, rabbit, spider, stick insect, turtle; cage, tank*
- *There are (rabbits). This is a (hamster).*

Recycled: *bird, cat, dog, fish, parrot; fruit, meat, vegetables; long hair, short hair*

Recycled: *Have you got any pets? Yes, I have. No, I haven't. I've got (two dogs and a turtle).*

Materials

- Pupil's Book p38; Activity Book p36; Class CD2; Teacher's App on Navio
- Teacher's Resource Bank: Task flashcards: *listen, tick, plan, think, Talk Partners, read, write*

Optional materials

- Teacher's Resource Bank: Five Trinity Exam Practice cards (selected from the Starter Unit and Units 1, 2 and 3)

At a Glance Lesson Plan

Pupil's Book

Starting the lesson

- Use the Trinity Exam Practice cards (optional).
- Review animal vocabulary.
- Set learning outcomes using the task flashcards.

Learn: Activity 1

- Listen, point and repeat.

▶ *CD2 Track 14 p262*

Activity 2

- Ask your classmates. Tick (✓) or cross (✗).

Plan your project

- Plan your pets class book page.

Go to page 36 in your Activity Book.

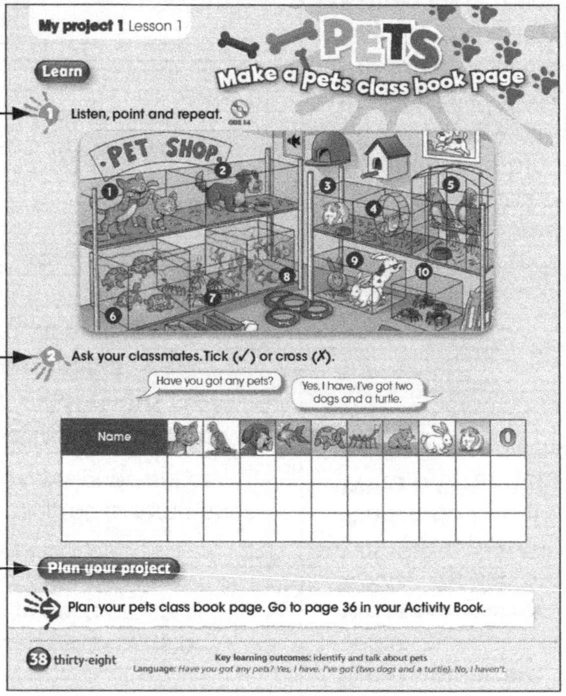

Ending the lesson

- Review the lesson.
- Review the task flashcards.

Link to Science

- **Animals:** classifying animals

Activity Book

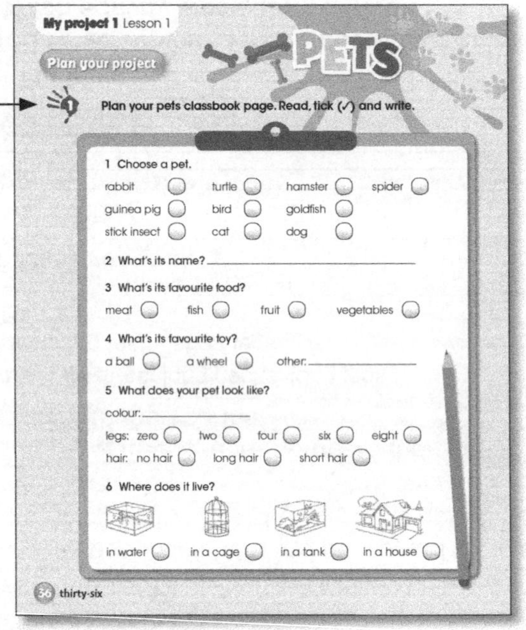

Plan your project: Activity Book

Activity 1

- Plan your pets class book page. Read, tick (✓) and write.

Digital resources

Teacher's Digital: Don't forget you can teach this lesson using the Teacher's App on Navio.

Pupil's Digital: Encourage your pupils to use the Pupil's App on Navio to practise the vocabulary from this lesson.

Powered By NAVIO

Starting the lesson

Use the Trinity Exam Practice cards (optional).

- The pupils practise asking and answering questions. (See p31.)

Review animal vocabulary.

- (Books open.) Ask the class to name any animals they know. Point to the pet shop. Ask **What can you see?** Ask the class to name the animals they know.
- Introduce the new vocabulary. Say **Look at number 3. This is a guinea pig. Look at number 9. These are rabbits.** Encourage the pupils to repeat after you.

Set learning outcomes using the task flashcards.

- Explain the aims of the lesson. Say **Today we're going to learn about pets.** Check understanding.
- Hold up the task flashcards and elicit the words. Stick them on one side of the board. Point to them during the lesson to reinforce your instructions.

Learn: Pupil's Book Activity 1

Listen, point and repeat.

▶ ***CD2 Track 14 p262***

- (Books open.) Play the CD. The pupils listen and point to the different animals as they hear them.
- Play the CD again. The pupils repeat the phrases, pointing to the different pets.
- Name different pets in a random order. The pupils point to the corresponding picture each time.
- **Talk Partners** The pupils repeat the activity with a Talk Partner, taking turns to say and point to the different pets.

Pupil's Book Activity 2

Ask your classmates. Tick (✓) or cross (✗).

- Tell the pupils that they are going to ask different friends about their pets. They can ask about each animal *Have you got a (cat)?* or they can ask *Have you got any pets?*
- The pupils tick or cross the animals on the chart.
- Once the pupils have completed their survey, ask **How many of your friends haven't got any pets? How many friends have got (one / two / a lot of) pets?**

Plan your project: Activity Book

Activity 1

Plan your pets class book page. Read, tick (✓) and write.

- Tell the class that they are going to make a pets class book. First, they need to work individually to plan their page.
- (Books open.) Ask the class to look at the clipboard. Choose a volunteer to read out the first question and the options. The pupils choose an animal for their pets class book page. Encourage as much variety as possible. Pupils who do not have a pet can choose an ideal pet or an unusual pet.
- Read the remaining questions and discuss the names of the pets, their favourite food, toys, characteristics and habitat. The pupils tick the corresponding options in preparation for the writing activity in Lesson 2.
- Encourage the children to take photos of their pets to print and bring in to class for their class book.

Ending the lesson

Review the lesson.

- (Books closed.) Say **Today we've talked about pets. What pets have we got in this class?** Encourage the pupils to respond and praise them for their effort.

Review the task flashcards.

- Point to the task flashcards. Say **Look at the activities you've done today. Which was your favourite?** Elicit the pupils' favourite activities.

Link to Science

- If you are studying the Science topic of **animals** in English, remind the pupils about the classification of animals (mammal: cat, dog, guinea pig, hamster, mouse, rabbit; birds: bird, parrot; fish: goldfish; insects: stick insect; reptiles: tortoise, turtle).
- Encourage the pupils to recall the characteristics of each animal group focusing on vertebrate animals (mammals, birds, fish, reptiles) and invertebrate animals (insects and the spider). Remind them that a spider is not an insect.

My project 1: Pets

Key Competences and Key Learning Outcomes

- Write and present a page about your pet
- Think about your project
- Work as a class to make a class book about pets
- Sing a cooperative learning song

Key language

- *Its name is (Bob). Its favourite food is (meat). Its favourite toy is (a ball). It lives in (my house).*
- *Listen to others. Listen with your ears.*

Recycled: *bird, cat, dog, fish, goldfish, guinea pig, hamster, parrot, rabbit, spider, stick insect, turtle*

Recycled: *This is my (dog). It's brown. It's got (four legs) and (short hair).*

Materials

- Pupil's Book p39; Activity Book p37; Class CD2; Teacher's App on Navio
- Teacher's Resource Bank: Task flashcards: *sing, listen, plan, read, think, colour, Talk Partners*
- Coloured pencils, A4 paper or card, glue

Optional materials

- Teacher's Resource Bank: Five Trinity Exam Practice cards (selected from the Starter Unit and Units 1, 2 and 3)
- Photos of your pets

At a Glance Lesson Plan

Pupil's Book

Starting the lesson
- Use the Trinity Exam Practice cards (optional).
- Play *Guess which pet I'm thinking of.*
- Set learning outcomes using the task flashcards.

Think about your project
- Go to page 37 in your Activity Book.

Create: Activity 1
- Make your pets class book page.

Show and tell: Activity 2: Cooperative learning
- Sing *Listen to others.*
- ▶ *CD2 Track 15 p263*

My project 1 Lesson 2

Create

1 Make your pets class book page.

Digital tip! Take lots of photos of your pet and choose the best one.

Choose a photo of your pet. Add it to your document.

Type your text. Check your spelling.

Show and tell

2 Cooperative learning Sing *Listen to others.*

3 Listen. Present your document to the class.

This is my dog. Its name is Bob.

It's lovely!

Think about your project — Go to page 37 in your Activity Book.

Key learning outcomes: make and present your pets class book page
Language: *Its name is (Bob). Its favourite food is (meat).*

thirty-nine 39

Activity 3: Show and tell
- Listen. Present your document to the class.
- ▶ *CD2 Track 16 p263*

Ending the lesson
- Review the lesson.
- Sing *Well done!*
- ▶ *CD2 Track 12 p262*
- Review the task flashcards.

Link to Science
- **Animals:** how animals are born

Activity Book

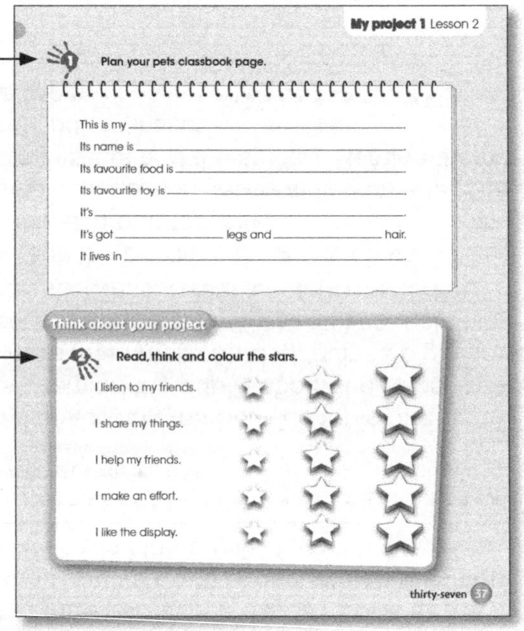

My project 1 Lesson 2

1 Plan your pets classbook page.

This is my ______
Its name is ______
Its favourite food is ______
Its favourite toy is ______
It's ______
It's got ______ legs and ______ hair.
It lives in ______

Think about your project

2 Read, think and colour the stars.

I listen to my friends.
I share my things.
I help my friends.
I make an effort.
I like the display.

thirty-seven 37

Activity Book

Activity 1
- Plan your pets class book page.

Think about your project: Activity 2
- Read, think and colour the stars.

Digital resources

Teacher's Digital: Don't forget you can teach this lesson using the Teacher's App on Navio.

Pupil's Digital: Encourage your pupils to use the Pupil's App on Navio to practise the vocabulary from this lesson.

Powered By NAVIO

Starting the lesson

Use the Trinity Exam Practice cards (optional).

- The pupils practise asking and answering questions. (See p31.)

Play *Guess which pet I'm thinking of.*

- Ask the pupils to look at the pet shop illustration (Pupil's Book p38). Describe one of the pets. The pupils guess the pet you are describing.
- Talk Partners The pupils play the game with a Talk Partner.

Set learning outcomes using the task flashcards.

- Explain the aims of the lesson. Say **Today we're going to make our class book about pets.**
- Hold up the task flashcards and elicit the words. Stick them on one side of the board. Point to them during the lesson to reinforce your instructions.

Activity Book

Activity 1

Plan your pets class book page.

- (Books open.) Focus on the outline and read it together.
- Explain that in this lesson the pupils are going to make their page for the pets class book. First they need to write a draft. Explain that writing a draft will help them to organise their ideas and give them confidence. The pupils use Activity Book p36 from the previous lesson to help them complete their draft.

Create: Pupil's Book Activity 1

Make your pets class book page.

- Focus on the instructions and invite different pupils to read them out. Explain that now the pupils are going to type and create their final document. Pupils can either draw and colour a picture of their pet or use digital photos of their pet. Remind them to choose their best photo.
- Take the pupils to the computer room to type out their text. They copy the text they drafted in Activity Book Activity 1. Encourage them to check their spelling. Print out the pupils' documents. Finally, they stick their text and a photo of their drawing of their pet onto another piece of paper or card.

Show and tell: Pupil's Book Activity 2:
Cooperative learning

Sing *Listen to others.*

▶ *CD2 Track 15 p263*

- Explain that different pupils are going to present their pets page to the class. Highlight that it's very important to listen carefully to your classmates when they are talking.
- Play the CD. The pupils listen and do the actions with you. Play the CD again and encourage the pupils to sing and do the actions.

Pupil's Book Activity 3

Listen. Present your document to the class.

▶ *CD2 Track 16 p263*

- Play the CD. The pupils listen to the boy presenting his pets class book page.
- Encourage different pupils to come up to the front and present their pet to the rest of the class. Remind the class to listen carefully.

Activity Book

Think about your project: Activity 2

Read, think and colour the stars.

- (Books open.) Read the first sentence and ask the class to look at their project.
- Say **Let's think about how we work.** Read each sentence and ask the class to colour the star for how they work. (Small star: sometimes; medium-sized star: usually; big star: always.) Praise the class for their efforts.

Ending the lesson

Review the lesson.

- Ask the class to close their books and say **Today we've worked together. What have we made?** *(A class book about pets.)* Praise the class for their hard work. Display the book where the pupils can read it.

Sing *Well done!*

▶ *CD2 Track 12 p262*

- (Books closed.) Praise the class for working together and for following instructions well. Play the CD. The pupils sing and do the actions.

Review the task flashcards.

- Point to the task flashcards. Say **Look at the activities you've done today. Which was your favourite?** Elicit the pupils' favourite activities.

Link to Science

- If you are studying the Science topic of **animals** in English, remind the pupils that some animals lay eggs and some don't. Discuss which of the pets lay eggs (goldfish, turtle, spider).
- Personalise by asking the pupils if any of their pets have had babies or laid eggs. Review baby animal names (kitten, puppy, etc.).

Date: ____________________ Unit: __________

1 What did my pupils learn in this unit?

2 How did my pupils work? (✓)

individually ☐ in pairs ☐ in small groups ☐

in large groups ☐ as a class ☐

3 Which key competences did my pupils develop?

- Competence in linguistic communication ☐
- Competence in mathematics, science and technology ☐
- Digital competence ☐
- Learning to learn ☐
- Social and civic competences ☐
- Sense of initiative and entrepreneurship ☐
- Cultural awareness and expression ☐

4 Which lessons / activities were the most successful and why?

5 Which lessons / activities did my pupils find the most difficult and why?

6 What did I try in the classroom for the first time? How did it go?

7 Which resources did I find most useful? (including webpages)

8 What could I do differently next time I teach this unit?

Unit 4

The nature trail

Unit overview

Key Competences and Key Learning Outcomes

- Identify and say ten features of a nature trail (Lesson 1)
- Use present continuous to describe actions (Lesson 2)
- Read, listen and understand a story about Toby on a nature trail (Lesson 3)
- Ask and answer questions to find out what people are doing (Lesson 4)
- Use prepositions of movement (Lesson 4)
- Write a guided adventure story (Lesson 7)
- Watch and understand a video about the environment (Video and 21st Century Skills)

- Read about forest schools in Britain (Lesson 6)

- Use the Pupil's App on Navio

- Use a strategy to practise spelling key words (Lesson 1)
- Say a tongue twister and practise 'or' and 'al' spellings (Lesson 5)
- Review language in the unit and reflect on own learning (Lesson 8)
- Practise activity types found in the Cambridge Exams: Pre A1 Starters

- Understand the importance of not touching wild animals (Lesson 3)
- Learn to look after the environment (Video and 21st Century Skills)

- Work with a Talk Partner to practise and reinforce learning (all lessons)
- Play a communication game about a nature trail (Lesson 5)

- Sing four songs (Lessons 1, 4 and 8)
- Understand and act out a story (Lesson 3)
- Think about your own culture (Lesson 6)
- Read and understand an adventure story (Lesson 7)

Vocabulary

Core vocabulary
bridge, forest, grass, hill, lake, leaves, path, river, road, sand; across, along, down, up

Extension vocabulary (optional)
field, mud, sea, stream, village, waterfall; around, into, out of, through

Other vocabulary
deep, nature trail; chasing, crazy, cycle path, spines; rolling; branches, butterflies, caterpillars, den, forest, minibeast hunt, mud pies, rocks, stones, twigs, worms; afraid, beach, cave, giant spiders, hero, key, map, monster, mummies, pool, secret passage, torch, treasure

Recycled vocabulary
catch, climb, jump, play, ride (a horse / a bike), run, sail (a boat), swim, walk; in, on; flowers, grass, leaves, sheep

Structures

Core structures
What are you doing? I'm (walking) (on the path).
Are you (swimming) (in the lake)? Yes, I am. No, I'm not. What's he / she doing? He's / She's (running) (up the hill). Is he / she running up a hill? Yes, he / she is. No, he / she isn't.

Other structures
What's the matter? He's coming this way. Catch him! That's better! Poor (Toby).; Breathe in. Breathe out. Let's calm down. Let's count.

Recycled structures
There's a … There are …

Phonics

Alternative vowel spellings **'or'** / **'al'** (h**or**se, sh**or**ts, w**al**ks, t**al**ks, st**or**m)

British Culture

Forest schools

Literacy

Text type: An adventure story (text to entertain)
Reading skills: remembering facts; scanning; sequencing; relating pictures to new vocabulary

21st Century Skills

Living in the world: learning to look after the environment

Cooperative learning

Songs: *Calm down* (Lesson 4); *Well done!* (Lesson 8)
Skills: Listening to others (Lesson 2); Working together as a team (Lesson 5); Encouraging one another (Lesson 7); Think-Pair-Share (Lesson 8)

Values

The importance of not touching wild animals.

Cross-curricular links

Links to Science
Plant life: the characteristics of plants; the features of trees, bushes and grass; evergreen and deciduous trees

Suggested Arts and Crafts concepts
Identifying and using shapes and colours present in nature; making and colouring a nature trail game

Key Competences and Key Learning Outcomes

- Identify and say ten features of a nature trail
- Say the vocabulary chant
- Stick the nature stickers
- Identify characteristics of plants (optional)
- Use a strategy to practise spelling key words
- Sing a song about a nature trail

Key language
- *bridge, forest, grass, hill, lake, leaves, path, river, road, sand*

Extension vocabulary
- *field, mud, sea, stream, village, waterfall*

Recycled: *climb, jump, play, run, swim, walk; grass*

Other vocabulary: *deep, nature trail*

Materials
- Pupil's Book p40; Activity Book pp38 and 47; Class CD2; Teacher's App on Navio; Unit 4 stickers
- Countryside flashcards
- Teacher's Resource Bank: Countryside word cards
- Teacher's Resource Bank: Task flashcards: *listen, sing, read, stick, say, match, write, Talk Partners*

Optional materials
- Teacher's Resource Bank: Five Trinity Exam Practice cards (selected from the Starter Unit and Units 1, 2 and 3)

At a Glance Lesson Plan

Pupil's Book

Starting the lesson
- Use the Trinity Exam Practice cards (optional).
- Review action verbs.
- Set learning outcomes using the task flashcards.

Vocabulary presentation
- Present the new vocabulary.

Activity 1
- Listen and point.
- ▶ *CD2 Track 17 p263*
- Sing *I'm going on a nature trail.*

Word cards
- Read the word cards.
- Match them to the flashcards.

Activity 2
- Read and stick the ten stickers.
- Listen and say the chant.
- ▶ *CD2 Track 19 p263*
- Go to the Activity Book.

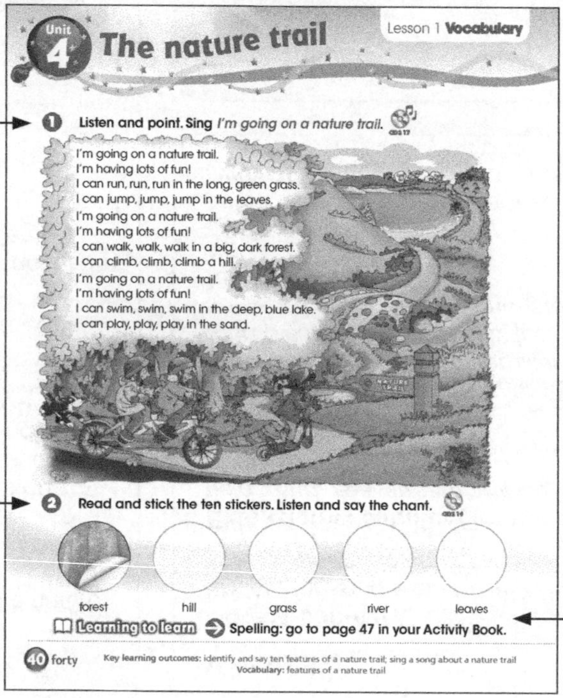

Ending the lesson
- Review the lesson.
- Review the task flashcards.

Extra activity

Vocabulary extension
- Present six additional vocabulary items.

Link to Science
- **Plant life:** the characteristics of plants

Learning to learn

Spelling
- Practise spelling at any time during this unit (Activity Book p47).

Digital resources

Teacher's Digital: Don't forget you can teach this lesson using the Teacher's App on Navio.

Pupil's Digital: Encourage your pupils to use the Pupil's App on Navio to practise the vocabulary from this lesson.

Powered By NAVIO

Activity Book

Activity Book

Activity 1
- Read and match.

Activity 2
- Look, read and write.

Recycled vocabulary
- Look, remember and write the word.

Spelling

Let's practise spelling!
- Use the *Look-Copy-Cover-Write* technique.

Recycled vocabulary
- Look, remember and write the word.

Starting the lesson

Use the Trinity Exam Practice cards (optional).

- The pupils practise asking and answering questions. (See p31.)

Review action verbs.

- Play *Can you guess?* (see p55) to review action verbs from Unit 1 and Level 1 (e.g. *run, jump, swim, walk, eat*).

Set learning outcomes using the task flashcards.

- Explain the aims of the lesson. Say **Today we're going to learn the names of things you can see on a nature trail.**
- Hold up the task flashcards and elicit the words. Stick them on one side of the board. Point to them during the lesson to reinforce your instructions.

Vocabulary presentation

Present the new vocabulary.

- (Books closed.) Say **Let's go for a walk on the nature trail!** Walk around in a circle with the class following behind you. Say **What can you see?** Encourage the pupils to suggest items they can see in nature. Remind them to use sentences: *I can see (flowers).*, etc. As they name each item, say **Take a photo!** Mime taking a photo. Show the flashcard of the lake and say **I can see a lake!** The class repeats the word. Repeat for the remaining flashcards.

Pupil's Book Activity 1

Listen and point. Sing *I'm going on a nature trail.*

▶ *CD2 Track 17 p263*

- (Books open.) Ask **Where are Beth, Molly, Jake and Toby?** *(Outside, on a nature trail.)* Ask **What can you see?** The class point to and name the different features.
- Stick the flashcards on the board in the order that they appear in the song.
- Play the CD and do the actions.
- Play the CD again. The pupils sing and do the actions.

Word cards

Read the word cards. Match them to the flashcards.

- (Books closed.) Hold up one of the word cards. The pupils read collectively. A pupil sticks the word card next to the flashcard on the board. Repeat.
- Point to each word card. The pupils read the words.

Pupil's Book Activity 2

Read and stick the ten stickers. Listen and say the chant.

▶ *CD2 Track 19 p263*

- A pupil reads the first word. The pupils stick the corresponding sticker above the word.
- Talk Partners The pupils find and stick the remaining stickers. Encourage them to use cooperative language: *Where's the (forest)? Here! Where does this go? Here!* Repeat with the other stickers.
- Play the CD. The pupils listen and say the chant, pointing to the stickers in turn.

Activity Book

Activity 1

Read and match.

- (Books open.) A volunteer reads out the first sentence and points to the corresponding illustration. Repeat for the remaining sentences. The pupils read and match individually.

Answers: **1** e **2** f **3** b **4** a **5** c **6** d

Activity 2

Look, read and write.

- (Books open.) Read out the instructions. Say **Look at the pictures. What can you see?** The pupils name the features and write the words below.
- Talk Partners The pupils check their answers with a Talk Partner: *What's number 1? (path) What's number 2? (road)*

Answers: **1** path **2** road **3** grass **4** leaves **5** river **6** forest **7** bridge **8** sand **9** lake **10** hill

Recycled vocabulary

- The pupils look at the picture and write the word.

Answer: crocodile

Ending the lesson

Review the lesson.

- Say **Today we've learnt the names of things we see in nature. What words do you remember?** Elicit the names from the pupils.

Review the task flashcards.

- Point to the task flashcards. Ask **Which was your favourite activity?**

Extra activity

Vocabulary extension

- Present six additional nature trail words: *field, mud, sea, stream, village, waterfall.*
- Use the Vocabulary Booster on Navio to practise these new words.

Link to Science

- If you are studying the Science topic of **plant life** in English, you could review some of the main characteristics of plants. Ask which of the items in today's lesson are plants *(flowers, trees, forest, grass and bushes).* Elicit the characteristics of plants, collating all the information on the board.

Spelling (Activity Book p47)

Let's practise spelling!

- The pupils can practise spelling the ten nature words using the *Look-Copy-Cover-Write* technique at any time before the Lesson 8 Review.

Recycled vocabulary

- The pupils look at the picture and write the word.

Answer: snake

Key Competences and Key Learning Outcomes

- Use present continuous to describe actions
- Complete and practise a conversation
- Identify features of trees, bushes and grass (optional)
- Listen for specific information

Key language

Recycled: *bridge, forest, grass, hill, lake, leaves, path, river, road, sand*

Recycled: *What are you doing? I'm (climbing). Are you (swimming)? Yes, I am. No, I'm not.*

Materials

- Pupil's Book p41; Activity Book p39; Class CD2; Teacher's App on Navio
- Countryside flashcards
- Teacher's Resource Bank: Countryside word cards
- Teacher's Resource Bank: Task flashcards: *listen, read, act out, tick, write, Talk Partners, think, draw*

Optional materials

- Teacher's Resource Bank: Five Trinity Exam Practice cards (selected from the Starter Unit and Units 1, 2 and 3)

At a Glance Lesson Plan

Pupil's Book

Starting the lesson

- Use the Trinity Exam Practice cards (optional).
- Review the *I'm going on a nature trail* song.
- ▶ *CD2 Track 17 p263*
- ▶ *CD2 Track 18 p263 (optional karaoke version)*
- Review nature trail vocabulary. Play *Memory!*
- Set learning outcomes using the task flashcards.

Activity 1

- Listen and repeat.
- ▶ *CD2 Track 20 p263*
- Talk Partners Act out.

Activity 2

- Listen and tick (✓).
- ▶ *CD2 Track 21 p263*
- Go to the Activity Book.

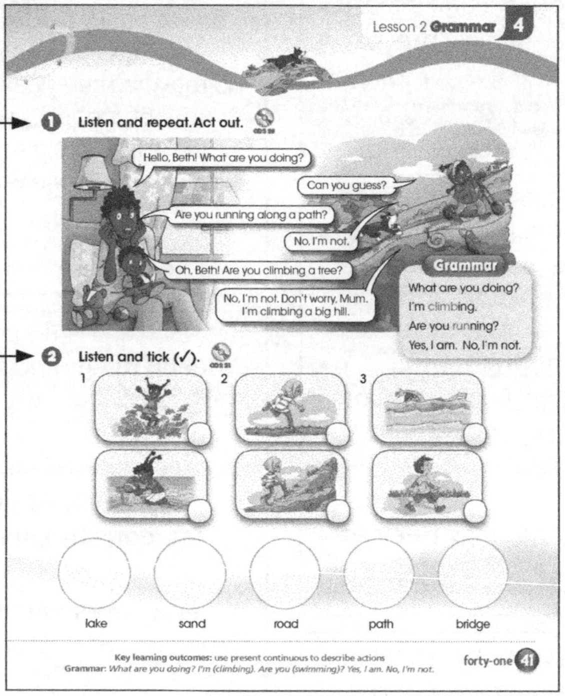

Ending the lesson

- Review the lesson.
- Review the task flashcards.

Cooperative learning

Listening to others

- Talk Partners
Play *Can you guess?*

Link to Science

- **Plant life:** the features of trees, bushes and grass

Activity Book

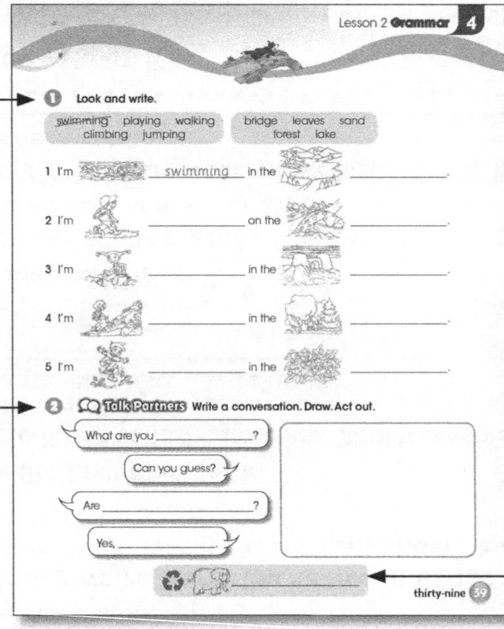

Activity Book

Activity 1

- Look and write.

Activity 2

- Write a conversation. Draw.

- Talk Partners
Act out.

Recycled vocabulary

- Look, remember and write the word.

Digital resources

Teacher's Digital: Don't forget you can teach this lesson using the Teacher's App on Navio.

Pupil's Digital: Encourage your pupils to use the Pupil's App on Navio to practise the vocabulary from this lesson.

Powered By NAVIO

Starting the lesson

Use the Trinity Exam Practice cards (optional).

- The pupils practise asking and answering questions. (See p31.)

Review the *I'm going on a nature trail* song.

▶ *CD2 Track 17 p263*

▶ *CD2 Track 18 p263 (optional karaoke version)*

- Divide the class into three groups: Jake, Molly and Beth. Give each group the two flashcards that correspond to their verse. Play the CD (or use the karaoke version). Groups take turns to sing their verse and do the actions.

Review nature trail vocabulary.

- Play *Memory!* (See p23.)

Set learning outcomes using the task flashcards.

- Explain the aims of the lesson. Say **Today, we're going to talk about actions we can do on a nature trail.**
- Hold up the task flashcards and elicit the words. Stick them on one side of the board. Point to them during the lesson to reinforce your instructions.

Pupil's Book Activity 1

Listen and repeat. Act out.

▶ *CD2 Track 20 p263*

- (Books open.) Ask **Who can you see? What else can you see?**
- Play the CD. The pupils listen and read the conversation. Check understanding. Ask **What is Beth doing?**
- Play the CD again. Pause for the pupils to repeat.
- Talk Partners The pupils practise the conversation with a Talk Partner.

Pupil's Book Activity 2

Listen and tick (✓).

▶ *CD2 Track 21 p263*

- (Books open.) Ask the pupils to name the nature trail words in the pairs of pictures.
- Play the CD. Pause after each conversation. The pupils tick the correct picture. Repeat with the remaining conversations, pausing after each one to check the pupils' answers.

Answers: **1** playing in the sand **2** running in the grass **3** walking along the path

Activity Book

Activity 1

Look and write.

- (Books open.) Explain that the pupils are going to complete the sentences with words from the word boxes. Read the example together. The pupils work individually to complete the sentences.
- Talk Partners The pupils check their answers with a Talk Partner.

Answers: **1** swimming, lake **2** walking, bridge **3** playing, sand **4** climbing, forest **5** jumping, leaves

Activity 2

Write a conversation. Draw. Act out.

- Talk Partners The pupils write and practise their own conversation with a Talk Partner. Pairs act out their conversations for their classmates.

Recycled vocabulary

- The pupils look at the picture and write the word.

Answer: elephant

Ending the lesson

Review the lesson.

- Say **Today you asked and answered questions about activities.** Elicit some questions.

Review the task flashcards.

- Point to the task flashcards. Say **Look at the activities you've done today. Which activity was your favourite?** Elicit the pupils' favourite activities.

Cooperative learning

Listening to others

- Talk Partners Play *Can you guess?* The pupils take turns to choose and mime activities from the lesson, asking and answering questions to guess the chosen action:

Pupil A: (mimes running on the sand)
Pupil B: *Are you running on the hill?*
Pupil A: *No, I'm not.*
Pupil B: *Are you running on the sand?*
Pupil A: *Yes, I am.*

Link to Science

- If you are studying the Science topic of **plant life** in English, you could ask the pupils to name the plants on a nature trail. Review features of trees, bushes and grass. Trees have a thick hard stem called a trunk. Bushes have a lot of stems and leaves. Grass is thin and bendy.

Key Competences and Key Learning Outcomes

- Read, listen and understand a story about Toby on a nature trail
- Read the story with some fluency
- Recognise evergreen and deciduous trees (optional)
- Become familiar with the story through a pre-reading task
- Understand the importance of not touching wild animals
- Understand and act out the story
- Give an opinion on the story

Key language

- *What are you doing? What's (Toby) doing? He's (running up the hill).*

Recycled: *catch, flowers, hedgehog, hill, lake, leaves, nose, path, river, sheep*

Other vocabulary: *chasing, crazy, cycle path, spines*

Materials

- Pupil's Book pp42–43; Activity Book p40; Class CD2; Teacher's App on Navio
- Teacher's Resource Bank: Task flashcards: *listen, read, act out, write, number, Talk Partners*
- Teacher's Resource Bank: Unit 4 Lesson 3 Animated Story

Optional materials

- Teacher's Resource Bank: Five Trinity Exam Practice cards (selected from the Starter Unit and Units 1, 2 and 3)

At a Glance Lesson Plan

Starting the lesson

- Use the Trinity Exam Practice cards (optional).
- Review the *I'm going on a nature trail* song.
- ▶ ***CD2 Track 18 p263 (optional karaoke version)***
- Set learning outcomes using the task flashcards.

Before you read

- Explain the story title.
- Read and answer the question.

Activity 1

- Listen and read.
- ▶ ***CD2 Track 22 p263***
- Act out.
- ***Now watch the animated story!***

After you read: Activity 2

- Go to page 40 in your Activity Book.
- Values: Read and write.

Pupil's Book

Ending the lesson

- Review the lesson.
- Review the task flashcards.

Link to Science

- **Plant life:** evergreen and deciduous trees

Digital resources

Teacher's Digital: Don't forget you can teach this lesson using the Teacher's App on Navio.

Pupil's Digital: Encourage your pupils to use the Pupil's App on Navio to practise the vocabulary from this lesson.

Powered By NAVIO

Activity Book

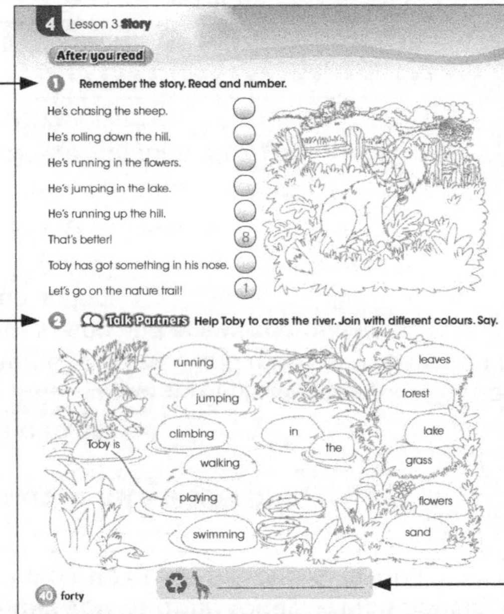

Activity Book

After you read: Activity 1

- Remember the story. Read and number.

Activity 2

- Help Toby to cross the river.
- **Talk Partners** Join with different colours. Say.

Recycled vocabulary

- Look, remember and write the word.

Starting the lesson

Use the Trinity Exam Practice cards (optional).

- The pupils practise asking and answering questions. (See p31.)
- **Review the *I'm going on a nature trail* song.**

▶ *CD2 Track 18 p263 (optional karaoke version)*

- Use the karaoke version to sing *I'm going on a nature trail* from Lesson 1.
- Play the CD. Add extra verses using other unit vocabulary: *jump in the river, ride on the road, walk on the path, walk on the bridge,* etc.

Set learning outcomes using the task flashcards.

- Say **Today we're going to listen to a story.**
- Hold up the task flashcards and elicit the words. Stick them on one side of the board. Point to them during the lesson to reinforce your instructions.

Before you read

Explain the story title.

- (Books open.) Focus on the title and elicit guesses.

Read and answer the question.

- Ask the pupils to scan the story to identify the things the children see on their nature trail.
- Talk Partners The pupils feed back to a Talk Partner.

Pupil's Book Activity 1

Listen and read. Act out.

▶ *CD2 Track 22 p263*

- (Books open.) Play the CD. The pupils follow the text with their finger. Pause between each story frame to check understanding.

Suggested comprehension questions

- Frame 1: **Where are Jake, Molly and Beth?** *(On the nature trail.)*
- Frame 2: **What's Toby doing?** *(Running up the hill.)*
- Frame 3: **Is Toby running along the path?** *(No, he isn't.)*
- Frame 4: **Is Toby jumping in the sea?** *(No, he isn't.)*
- Frame 5: **What's Toby doing?** *(He's chasing sheep.)*
- Frame 6: **Where is Toby now?** *(In the flowers.)*
- Frame 7: **What's the matter with Toby?** *(He's got spines in his nose.)*
- Frame 8: **What's has the magic bike got?** *(A first-aid kit.)*
- Ask **Did you like the story? What part did you like best?**

Talk Partners The pupils choose their favourite frame.

- Organise the class into three groups (Jake, Molly and Beth). Play the CD. Each group joins in when their character speaks. If necessary, pause the CD after each sentence for the pupils to repeat.
- The pupils swap roles and repeat the activity.

After you read

Pupil's Book Activity 2

Go to page 40 in your Activity Book.

Activity Book

After you read: Activity 1

Remember the story. Read and number.

- (Books open.) Encourage a pupil to find the first sentence from the story. Ask the pupils to read out the sentences in the order they appear in the story. The pupils number the sentences individually.

Answers: 5 3 6 4 2 8 7 1

Activity 2

Help Toby to cross the river. Join with different colours. Say.

- (Books open.) The pupils have to help Toby across the river by joining the stepping-stones. Give an example sentence, moving a finger from stone to stone as you do so. Say **Toby is playing in the forest.**
- Talk Partners Ask the pupils to make sentences, hopping their finger from stone to stone as they do so. The pupils then draw lines joining the stones. Finally, one pupil reads their finished sentences and the other mimes Toby's actions.

Recycled vocabulary

- The pupils look at the picture and write the word.

Answer: giraffe

Pupil's Book Activity 2

Values: Read and write.

- Read the value and elicit the correct word to complete the sentence.
- Ask the pupils if they are careful around wild animals when they go to the countryside.

Ending the lesson

Review the lesson.

- Say **Today we've listened to a story about a nature trail. Today you've learnt that it's important not to touch wild animals.**

Review the task flashcards.

- Point to the task flashcards. Say **Look at the activities you've done today. Which activity was your favourite?** Elicit the pupils' favourite activities.

Link to Science

- If you are studying the Science topic of **plant life** in English, ask the pupils to look back at the story and name all the plants they can see. Remind them that trees can be deciduous or evergreen and elicit the characteristics of each: deciduous trees lose their leaves in autumn; evergreen trees have green leaves all year round.

Key Competences and Key Learning Outcomes

- Use prepositions of movement
- Use present continuous verbs to describe actions through a pre-reading task
- Ask and answer questions to find out what people are doing

- Sing a cooperative learning song

- Sing a song

Key language

- *across, along, down, up; rolling, running, sailing, walking*
- *Is he / she (walking along a path)? Yes, he / she is. No, he / she isn't. Let's calm down. Let's count. Breathe in / out.*

Extension vocabulary

- *around, into, out of, through*

Recycled: *in, on*

Recycled: *What's he / she doing? He's / She's (running up a hill).*

Materials

- Pupil's Book p44; Activity Book p41; Class CD2; Teacher's App on Navio
- Teacher's Resource Bank: Task flashcards: *listen, say, sing, Talk Partners, write, match, read*

Optional materials

- Teacher's Resource Bank: Five Trinity Exam Practice cards (selected from the Starter Unit and Units 1, 2 and 3)

At a Glance Lesson Plan

Pupil's Book

Starting the lesson

- Use the Trinity Exam Practice cards (optional).
- Review the Lesson 3 story.
- Set learning outcomes using the task flashcards.

Vocabulary presentation

- Present the new vocabulary.

Activity 1

- Listen, point and say.
- ▶ *CD2 Track 23 p263*

Activity 2

- Listen and point. Sing *What's he doing?*
- ▶ *CD2 Track 24 p263*

Activity 3

- Listen and repeat.
- Talk Partners Play a game.
- ▶ *CD2 Track 25 p263*

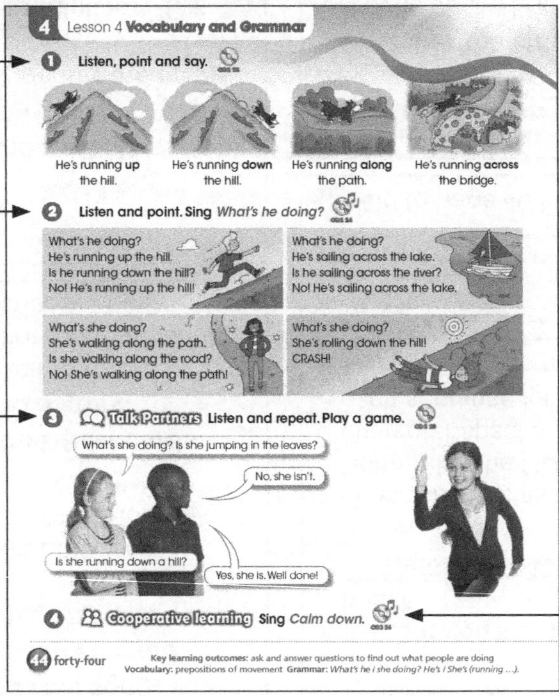

Activity 4 Cooperative learning

- Sing *Calm down.*
- ▶ *CD2 Track 26 p264*
- Go to the Activity Book.

Ending the lesson

- Review the lesson.
- Review the task flashcards.

Extra activities

Reinforcement

- Play *Toby's actions.*

Vocabulary extension

- Present four additional vocabulary items.

Digital resources

Teacher's Digital: Don't forget you can teach this lesson using the Teacher's App on Navio.

Pupil's Digital: Encourage your pupils to use the Pupil's App on Navio to practise the vocabulary from this lesson.

Powered By NAVIO

Activity Book

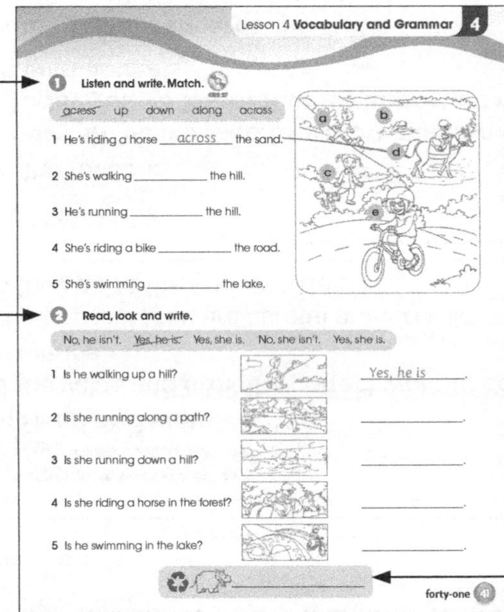

Activity Book

Activity 1

- Listen and write. Match.
- ▶ *CD2 Track 27 p264*

Activity 2

- Read, look and write.

Recycled vocabulary

- Look, remember and write the word.

Starting the lesson

Use the Trinity Exam Practice cards (optional).

- The pupils practise asking and answering questions. (See p31.)

Review the Lesson 3 story.

- Read out statements about Toby's activities in the story in random order. The pupils scan the story and say the frame number. Say **He's rolling down the hill!** The pupils reply *Number 3.*

Set learning outcomes using the task flashcards.

- Say **Today we're going to talk about different actions.**
- Hold up the task flashcards in turn and elicit the words. Stick them on one side of the board. Point to them during the lesson to reinforce your instructions.

Vocabulary presentation

Present the new vocabulary.

- (Books open.) Point to the first picture and say **Look at Toby. He's running up the hill.** Repeat the preposition **up (the hill)** and move your hands upwards. Prompt the class to repeat after you and do the action. Then, elicit the whole sentence. Repeat with the other prepositions.

Pupil's Book Activity 1

Listen, point and say.

▶ *CD2 Track 23 p263*

- Say **Let's listen and repeat the words.** Play the CD. The pupils repeat each word, pointing to the corresponding drawing. Play the CD again. The pupils repeat and do the action.

Pupil's Book Activity 2

Listen and point. Sing *What's he doing?*

▶ *CD2 Track 24 p263*

- (Books open.) Focus the group's attention on the illustrations. Ask **What's the boy doing? Is he going up or down the hill?**
- Play the CD. The pupils listen and point to the boy or the girl. Play the CD again. The pupils sing and do the actions.

Pupil's Book Activity 3

Listen and repeat. Play a game.

▶ *CD2 Track 25 p263*

- Play the CD. Play the CD again and ask the pupils to repeat the sentences. Choose a girl to help you demonstrate the activity. Ask her to mime one of the activities from the lesson. Ask **What's she doing?** The pupils ask a question to discover the activity *(Is she swimming across a lake?)* Repeat the activity with a boy. Ask **What's he doing?**
- **Talk Partners** When the pupils are confident with the activity, organise them into groups of three – a mix of boys and girls and encourage them to take turns miming and asking questions.

Pupil's Book Activity 4: **Cooperative learning**

Sing *Calm down.*

▶ *CD2 Track 26 p264*

- Explain that we can sing the *Calm down* song when we get too excited while playing a game. Play the CD. The pupils listen and do the actions with you.

Activity Book

Activity 1

Listen and write. Match.

▶ *CD2 Track 27 p264*

- (Books open.) Play the CD, pausing after the first sentence to give the pupils time to write the missing word. Repeat with the remaining sentences.
- The pupils write the missing preposition in each sentence. Then, they match each sentence to the corresponding illustration.

Answers: **1d** across **2c** down **3a** up **4e** along **5b** across

Activity 2

Read, look and write.

- (Books open.) Ask a pupil to read the first question and ask a different pupil to read the answer. Repeat for the remaining questions. Pupils write the short answers individually.

Answers: **1** Yes, he is. **2** Yes, she is. **3** No, she isn't. **4** Yes, she is. **5** No, he isn't.

Recycled vocabulary

- The pupils look at the picture and write the word.

Answer: hippo

Ending the lesson

Review the lesson.

- Say **Today we've asked and answered questions about actions.** Elicit some questions and answers from the pupils.

Review the task flashcards.

- Point to the task flashcards. Say **Look at the activities. Which was your favourite?**

Extra activities

Reinforcement

- If you have space in the classroom, ask the pupils to stand up in a group behind you. Say **We're going to play *Toby's actions.*** Start with the actions from the beginning of the lesson. Say **He's running (up / down) the hill.** The pupils mime Toby's actions. Move around the classroom. Vary the actions to include other unit vocabulary.

Vocabulary extension

- Use the Vocabulary Booster on Navio and present and practise four additional prepositions of movement: *around*, *into*, *out of*, *through*.

Key Competences and Key Learning Outcomes

- Say a tongue twister with the 'or' sound
- Learn and practise 'or' and 'al' spellings
- Listen for specific information
- Play a communication game about a nature trail

Key language

- *chalk, corn, fork, horse, short, shorts, sport, storm, talk, walk*

Recycled: *Is he / she (climbing)? Yes, he / she is. No, he / she isn't. Where's (Sally)? He's / She's (walking along the path).*

Materials

- Pupil's Book p45; Activity Book p42; Class CD2; Teacher's App on Navio
- Teacher's Resource Bank: Task flashcards: *listen, say, match, sing, Talk Partners, write, colour*
- Teacher's Resource Bank: Unit 4 Lesson 5 Activity 3
- Scissors

Optional materials

- Teacher's Resource Bank: Five Trinity Exam Practice cards (selected from the Starter Unit and Units 1, 2 and 3)

At a Glance Lesson Plan

Pupil's Book

Starting the lesson

- Use the Trinity Exam Practice cards (optional).
- Review the *What's he doing?* song.

▶ *CD2 Track 24 p263*

- Set learning outcomes using the task flashcards.

Activity 1

- Listen and say.

▶ *CD2 Track 28 p264*

Go to the Activity Book.

Go to Magic Phonics.

Activity 2

- Listen and match.

▶ *CD2 Track 29 p264*

Activity 3

- Talk Partners Make and play the game (Teacher's Resource Bank).

Ending the lesson

- Review the lesson.
- Review the task flashcards.

Cooperative learning

Working together as a team

- Talk Partners

Play *Beat the clock*.

- Continue the pronunciation wall display.

Digital resources

Teacher's Digital: Don't forget you can teach this lesson using the Teacher's App on Navio.

Pupil's Digital: Encourage your pupils to use the Pupil's App on Navio to practise the vocabulary from this lesson.

Powered By NAVIO

Activity Book

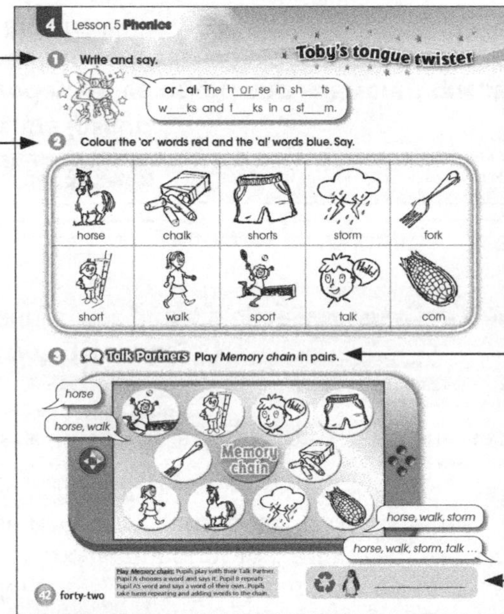

Activity Book

Activity 1

- Write and say.

Activity 2

- Colour the 'or' words red and the 'al' words blue. Say.

Go to Magic Phonics.

Activity 3

- Talk Partners

Play *Memory chain* in pairs.

Recycled vocabulary

- Look, remember and write the word.

Starting the lesson

Use the Trinity Exam Practice cards (optional).

- The pupils practise asking and answering questions. (See p31.)

Review the *What's he doing?* song.

▶ *CD2 Track 24 p263*

- Divide the class into two teams and line them up so that one team is facing the other. Team A sings the questions in the song and Team B sings the answers.

Set learning outcomes using the task flashcards.

- Say **Today we're going to say a tongue twister. We're going to make and play a game.**
- Hold up the task flashcards in turn and elicit the activities. Stick them on one side of the board. Point to them during the lesson to reinforce your instructions.

Pupil's Book Activity 1

Listen and say.

▶ *CD2 Track 28 p264*

- Write the words *horse* and *walk* on the board. Ask the pupils which sound they can hear in both words *('or')*. Circle the target grapheme in each word ('or' and 'al') and model the sound. The pupils repeat the sound with you.
- Say **It's time for Toby's tongue twister! What can you see?** *(horse, storm)* Ask **What's the horse doing?** *(walking and talking).*
- Play the CD. The pupils listen and repeat the target sound, then the words and then the entire tongue twister, faster and faster.

Go to Magic Phonics.

Activity Book

Activity 1

Write and say.

- (Books open.) Say **Look at Toby's tongue twister! The letters for 'or' are missing.** The pupils complete the tongue twister.

Answers: horse, shorts, walks, talks, storm

- Talk Partners The pupils say Toby's tongue twister and point to the 'or' sounds. They play *Faster and faster,* taking turns to say the tongue twister faster each time.

Activity 2

Colour the 'or' words red and the 'al' words blue. Say.

- Ask pupils to say the words and then colour the 'or' words red and 'al' words blue.

Answers: red: horse, shorts, storm, fork, short, sport, corn; blue: chalk, walk, talk

Go to Magic Phonics.

Activity 3

Play *Memory chain* in pairs.

- Play *Memory chain* with words from the activity.
- Talk Partners The pupils play the game with a Talk Partner.

Recycled vocabulary

- The pupils look at the picture and write the word.

Answer: penguin

Pupil's Book Activity 2

Listen and match.

▶ *CD2 Track 29 p264*

- (Books open.) Explain that some children are talking about their activities. Pupils draw a line to match the names to the activities in the picture.
- Play the CD. Pause to check the answers.

Answers: **1** Sally: walking along the path **2** Ben: running down the hill **3** May: jumping in the leaves **4** Sue: climbing a tree **5** Bill: sailing along the river **6** Nick: swimming in the lake

Pupil's Book Activity 3

Make and play the game (Teacher's Resource Bank).

- Check that the pupils have got a pair of scissors and show them how to cut out the names and place them on the picture. Demonstrate the activity.
- (Books open.) Place a barrier between the two pupils. Pupil A asks *Where's (Sally)?* Pupil B looks at his / her picture and answers accordingly. Pupil A places names on their version of the cut-out according to Pupil B's answers.

Talk Partners The pupils play the game with a Talk Partner taking turns to place and find the characters.

Ending the lesson

Review the lesson.

- Say **Today we've practised a tongue twister**. Ask the pupils to say it again.
- Then say **Today you played a game with cards.**

Review the task flashcards.

- Point to the task flashcards. Say **Look at the activities you've done today. Which was your favourite?** Elicit the pupils' favourite activities.

Cooperative learning

Working together as a team

- Talk Partners Play *Beat the clock* to practise pronunciation of the 'or' / 'al' sound. (See p53.)
- Add to the pronunciation wall display, adding a storm cloud ('or') and a piece of chalk ('al').

Key Competences and Key Learning Outcomes

- Read about forest schools in Britain
- Listen for general understanding
- Learn about school trips to a forest school in Britain
- Think about your favourite outdoor activity

Key language

- *branches, butterflies, caterpillars, den, forest, minibeast, mud pies, rocks, stones, twigs, worms*
- *I can touch and smell (the tree), but I can't see it. We learn how to (make a den). We make (mud pies). We go on (a minibeast hunt).*

Recycled: *flowers, forest, leaves, path, sweets, trees*

Materials

- Pupil's Book p46; Activity Book p43; Class CD2; Teacher's App on Navio
- Teacher's Resource Bank: Task flashcards: *Talk Partners, listen, read, think, tick, draw, write*

Optional materials

- Teacher's Resource Bank: Five Trinity Exam Practice cards (selected from the Starter Unit and Units 1, 2 and 3)

At a Glance Lesson Plan

Pupil's Book

Starting the lesson

- Use the Trinity Exam Practice cards (optional).
- **Talk Partners**
  Review *Toby's tongue twister.*
  ▶ *CD2 Track 28 p264*
- Review the *What's he doing?* song.
  ▶ *CD2 Track 24 p263*
- Set learning outcomes using the task flashcards.

Activity 1

- Listen and read. Answer.
  ▶ *CD2 Track 30 p264*

Think about your culture

- What's your favourite outdoor activity?

Go to the Activity Book.

Ending the lesson

- Review the lesson.
- Review the task flashcards.

Extra activity

Extension

- Make a forest trail.

Digital resources

Teacher's Digital: Don't forget you can teach this lesson using the Teacher's App on Navio.

Powered By NAVIO

Activity Book

Activity Book

Activity 1

- Listen and tick (✓).
  ▶ *CD2 Track 31 p264*

Activity 2: Think about your culture

- Read and tick (✓). Draw, write and say.

Recycled vocabulary

- Look, remember and write the word.

Starting the lesson

Use the Trinity Exam Practice cards (optional).

- The pupils practise asking and answering questions. (See p31.)

Review Toby's tongue twister.

▶ *CD2 Track 28 p264*

- Ask the class **What sound did you practise in Toby's tongue twister?** *('or')*. Ask if they can remember the tongue twister *(The horse in shorts walks and talks in a storm)*.
- Talk Partners The pupils practise the tongue twister as a class and then with a Talk Partner. The pairs play *Faster and faster,* reading from the Pupil's Book (page 45) if necessary. A fast pair says the tongue twister for the class.
- Draw a chart with two columns ('or' and 'al') on the board. Elicit words with both spellings. Ask pupils to classify the words, e.g. 'or': *shorts, horse*; 'al': *walk, talk*.

Review the *What's he doing?* song.

▶ *CD2 Track 24 p263*

- Sing *What's he doing?* from Lesson 4, substituting actions and places with other vocabulary from the unit.

Set learning outcomes using the task flashcards.

- Say **Today we're going to learn about a forest school.**
- Hold up the task flashcards in turn and elicit the activities. Stick them on one side of the board. Point to them during the lesson to reinforce your instructions.

Pupil's Book Activity 1

Listen and read. Answer.

▶ *CD2 Track 30 p264*

- (Books open.) Focus the pupils' attention on the photographs and ask **What can you see? Where are they?** Then say **Let's listen and read.**
- Play the CD. Check understanding by pointing to each photo and asking the pupils to name the activity.

Pupil's Book Think about your culture

What's your favourite outdoor activity?

- Read the question and encourage the class to tell you about their favourite outdoor activity.

Activity Book

Activity 1

Listen and tick (✓).

▶ *CD2 Track 31 p264*

- (Books open.) Play the CD, pausing after the first piece of information to check the answers.
- Play the CD again and encourage the class to say the complete sentence: *We make a den from branches, twigs and leaves.* Repeat with the other sentences.

Answers: **1** branches, twigs and leaves **2** leaves and flowers **3** caterpillars, butterflies and worms

Activity 2: Think about your culture

Read and tick (✓). Draw, write and say.

- Read the question in the speech bubble. Elicit the pupils' answers.
- Read the first sentence as a class and ask the pupils to tick the box if they walk in the forest. Repeat with the other sentences.
- Ask the pupils to draw their favourite outdoor activity and write a sentence about it. Invite different pupils to show the rest of the class their drawings and read out their sentences.

Recycled vocabulary

- The pupils look at the picture and write the word.

Answer: tiger

Ending the lesson

Review the lesson.

- Say **Today you've learnt about going on a trip to a forest school in Britain.**

Review the task flashcards.

- Point to the task flashcards. Say **Look at the activities you've done today. Which activity was your favourite?** Elicit the pupils' favourite activities.

Extra activity

Extension

- If possible, ask the pupils to collect and bring in some twigs and stones to make a forest trail. Take them out into the playground and organise them to work in groups, making a trail of arrows from the twigs and stones. After the groups have made their trail, they should try to follow another group's trail. Encourage them to say *It's this way! Come on!,* etc. as they follow the trail.

Key Competences and Key Learning Outcomes

- Write a guided adventure story
- Read for specific information
- Read and understand an adventure story

Key language

- *afraid, beach, cave, giant spiders, hero, key, map, monsters, mummies, pool, secret passage, torch, treasure*
- *He sails / crosses / goes / finds …*

Recycled: *bridge, grass, lake, monkey, path, river, road, sand*

Recycled: *He's walking (along the beach). There's a (secret passage). There are (giant spiders).*

Materials

- Pupil's Book p47; Activity Book p44; Class CD2; Teacher's App on Navio
- Teacher's Resource Bank: Task flashcards: *circle, say, Talk Partners, listen, read, number, write*

Optional materials

- Teacher's Resource Bank: Five Trinity Exam Practice cards (selected from the Starter Unit and Units 1, 2 and 3)
- Coloured paper

At a Glance Lesson Plan

Pupil's Book

Starting the lesson

- Use the Trinity Exam Practice cards (optional).
- Talk Partners Play *Toby's actions* in pairs.
- Set learning outcomes using the task flashcards.

Before you read: Activity 1

- What can you see in an adventure story? Circle and say.

Activity 2

- Listen and read the adventure story.

▶ *CD2 Track 32 p264*

After you read

- Go to page 44 in your Activity Book.

Ending the lesson

- Review the lesson.
- Review the task flashcards.
- Sing a song (optional).

Cooperative learning

Encouraging one another

- Talk Partners Using positive language.

Activity Book

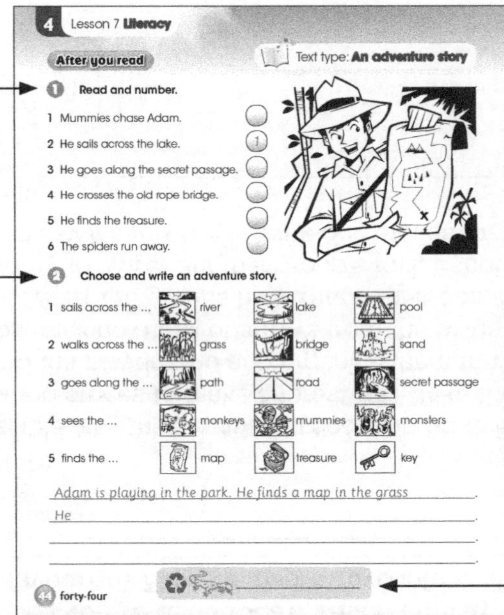

Activity Book

After you read: Activity 1

- Read and number.

Activity 2

- Choose and write an adventure story.

Recycled vocabulary

- Look, remember and write the word.

Digital resources

Teacher's Digital: Don't forget you can teach this lesson using the Teacher's App on Navio.

Pupil's Digital: Encourage your pupils to use the Pupil's App on Navio to practise the vocabulary from this lesson.

Powered By NAVIO

Starting the lesson

Use the Trinity Exam Practice cards (optional).

- The pupils practise asking and answering questions. (See p31.)

Play *Toby's actions* in pairs.

- Talk Partners Remind the pupils of the game *Toby's actions* from Lesson 4. (See p115.) Elicit the prepositions of movement and write them on the board. The pupils should use them when miming and describing Toby's actions, taking turns to make sentences and mime. After a few turns, say **Let's play 'Molly's actions' now.** Remind the pupils to use 'she' in their sentences.

Set learning outcomes using the task flashcards.

- Say **Today we're going to read an adventure story.**
- Hold up the task flashcards in turn and elicit the activities. Stick them on one side of the board. Point to them during the lesson to reinforce your instructions.

Before you read: Pupil's Book Activity 1

What can you see in an adventure story? Circle and say.

- (Books closed.) Tell the pupils that they are going to read an adventure story. Ask if they know any adventure stories. Elicit names of any they are familiar with.
- (Books open.) Focus the pupils' attention on the pre-reading activity. Ask **What's in an adventure story?** Point to each picture in turn and read the words. Ask the pupils if they think the items appear in an adventure story or not.
- Talk Partners The pupils work with a Talk Partner to scan the story and circle the items that appear.

Pupil's Book Activity 2

Listen and read the adventure story.

▶ *CD2 Track 32 p264*

- Say **Let's read and listen to the adventure story.** Play the CD.
- Use the pictures to check the pupils' understanding.
- Ask **Do you like the story? What part do you like?** Encourage the pupils to read out the part of the story they like best.
- Discuss with the class what they think will happen in the next story (Adam and the pirate ship).

Activity Book

After you read: Activity 1

Read and number.

- Invite individual pupils to read out the story frames in the correct order. The pupils number the sentences.

Answers: **1** 4 **2** 1 **3** 3 **4** 2 **5** 6 **6** 5

Activity 2

Choose and write an adventure story.

- The pupils choose one of the three items for each sentence to write a different story. Work as a class and go through the options, selecting items together. Create a new story as a class.
- Working individually, the pupils choose options for their own story. The pupils then write their new story in the space provided.
- Refer the pupils to the sentences in Activity 1 and the story in the Pupil's Book to help them.

Recycled vocabulary

- The pupils look at the picture and write the word.

Answer: lizard

Ending the lesson

Review the lesson.

- Say **Today you've read an adventure story.** Then say **You've written an adventure story.**

Review the task flashcards.

- Point to the task flashcards. Say **Look at the activities you've done today. Which activity was your favourite?** Elicit the pupils' favourite activities.

Sing a song (optional).

- Choose a song. The class sings and does the actions. Alternatively, invite the class to choose a song to sing.

Cooperative learning

Encouraging one another

- Give out coloured paper for the pupils to write their stories on and illustrate them.
- Talk Partners The pupils read their stories to a Talk Partner. Partners should use positive language and be encouraging and enthusiastic: *Very good! It's fantastic!*, etc. Display the stories in a prominent place.

Key Competences and Key Learning Outcomes

- Review language in the unit
- Reflect on own learning
- Sing a cooperative learning song

Key language

Recycled: *bridge, forest, grass, hill, lake, leaves, path, river, road, sand; across, along, down, in, on, up*

Recycled: *What are you doing? I'm (walking) (along the path). Are you (swimming) (in the lake)? Yes, I am. No, I'm not. What's he / she doing? He's / She's (running) (up the hill). Is he / she running up a hill? Yes, he / she is. No, he / she isn't.*

Materials

- Pupil's Book p48; Activity Book p45; Class CD2; Teacher's App on Navio
- Countryside flashcards
- Teacher's Resource Bank: Task flashcards: *listen, number, write, say, Talk Partners, act out, sing, stick, Think-Pair-Share*
- Teacher's Resource Bank: Traffic light cut-out
- *Give Me Five!* sticker
- Dice and counters

Optional materials

- Teacher's Resource Bank: Five Trinity Exam Practice cards (selected from the Starter Unit and Units 1, 2 and 3)

At a Glance Lesson Plan

Pupil's Book

Starting the lesson

- Use the Trinity Exam Practice cards (optional).
- Review the unit vocabulary.
- Set learning outcomes using the task flashcards.

Activity 1

- Listen and number. Write and say.

▶ *CD2 Track 33 p264*

Activity 2

- Listen.
- Talk Partners
  Act out. Ask and answer.

▶ *CD2 Track 34 p264*

Activity 3 — Cooperative learning

- Sing *Well done!*

▶ *CD2 Track 35 p264*

- Stick the *Give Me Five!* sticker.

Go to the Activity Book.

Ending the lesson

- Review the task flashcards.
- Sing a song (optional).

Cooperative learning

Think-Pair-Share

- Remember ten nature trail words.

Activity Book

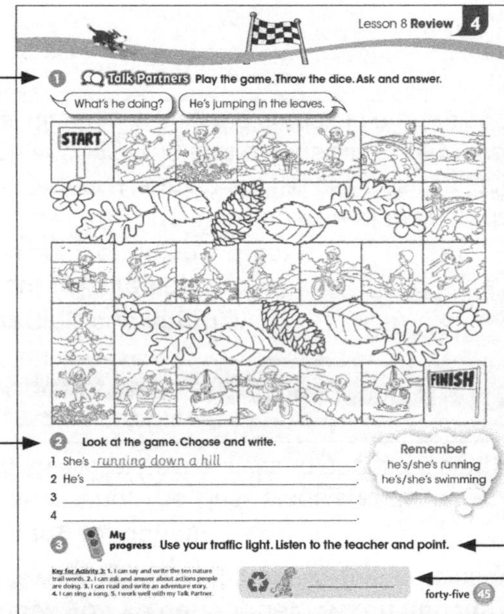

Activity Book

Activity 1

- Talk Partners
  Play the game. Throw the dice. Ask and answer.

Activity 2

- Look at the game. Choose and write.

Activity 3 My progress

- Use your traffic light. Listen to the teacher and point.

Recycled vocabulary

- Look, remember and write the word.

Digital resources

Teacher's Digital: Don't forget you can teach this lesson using the Teacher's App on Navio.

Pupil's Digital: Encourage your pupils to use the Pupil's App on Navio to practise the vocabulary from this lesson.

Powered By NAVIO

Starting the lesson

Use the Trinity Exam Practice cards (optional).

- The pupils practise asking and answering questions. (See p31.)

Review the unit vocabulary.

- Play *Definitions game* (see p23) with the unit flashcards to review the nature trail vocabulary.
- **Option:** Play the game in two teams. The teams take it in turns to remember the words.

Set learning outcomes using the task flashcards.

- Say **Today we're going to remember what we've learnt in Unit 4.**
- Hold up the task flashcards in turn and elicit the words. Stick them on one side of the board. Point to them during the lesson to reinforce your instructions.

Pupil's Book Activity 1

Listen and number. Write and say.

▶ *CD2 Track 33 p264*

- (Books open.) Point to each of the photographs and elicit the words.
- Play the CD. Pause after each sentence. The pupils number the correct photo.
- Play the CD again. The pupils write the correct word under each picture. Then they say the words.

Answers: **1** river **2** bridge **3** sand **4** road **5** hill **6** path **7** leaves **8** lake **9** grass **10** forest

Pupil's Book Activity 2

Listen. Act out. Ask and answer.

▶ *CD2 Track 34 p264*

- (Books open.) Ask the pupils to look at the photographs. Read the conversation together.
- Talk Partners The pupils take turns to mime and ask questions to guess the activity.

Pupil's Book Activity 3: **Cooperative learning**

Sing *Well done!*

▶ *CD2 Track 35 p264*

- Praise the class for their hard work and play the *Well done! song.* The pupils join in the song and do the actions with you.

Stick the *Give Me Five!* sticker.

- The pupils stick the *Give Me Five!* sticker on the Pupil's Book page.

Activity Book

Activity 1

Play the game. Throw the dice. Ask and answer.

- Talk Partners (Books open.) Demonstrate the game with a volunteer. The pupils play in twos or threes. They need a dice and counters to play. The pupils throw the dice, move their counters, asking and answering about the character in the square they land on. The first pupil to the finish line is the winner.
- Encourage the pupils to use cooperative language while they play: *It's my turn! It's your turn. Throw the dice. Move (two squares).*

Activity 2

Look at the game. Choose and write.

- Read the example sentence and ask the pupils to point to the corresponding square in the game above. Encourage pupils to choose different squares to write about.

Activity 3 My progress

Use your traffic light. Listen to the teacher and point.

- (Books closed.) Ask the class to take out their traffic light cut-out. Say **Let's think about our work in this unit.** Read the first self-assessment statement. Point to the green circle and say **Yes, I can do this very well.** Point to the orange circle and say **Yes, I can do this.** Point to the red circle and say **No, I can't do this.**
- Read the remaining statements. For each one, the pupils point to the colour on their traffic light that shows how they feel about their own learning.

Self-assessment statements

1. I can say and write the ten nature trail words.
2. I can ask and answer about actions people are doing.
3. I can read and write an adventure story.
4. I can sing a song.
5. I work well with my Talk Partner.

Recycled vocabulary

- The pupils look at the picture and write the word.

Answer: monkey

Ending the lesson

Review the task flashcards.

- Point to the task flashcards. Say **Look at the activities you've done today. Which activity was your favourite?** Elicit the pupils' favourite activities.

Sing a song (optional).

- The class chooses their favourite song from the unit. The class sings and does the actions.

Cooperative learning

Think-Pair-Share

- Ask **Can you remember the ten nature trail words?** Ask the class to think silently on their own for a minute.
- Talk Partners The pupils work with a Talk Partner to remember and name all ten items.
- Invite a pair to say one of the words. Hold up the corresponding flashcard and prompt the class to repeat the word.
- Finally, repeat the procedure, asking different pairs of pupils each time, until all ten words have been named.

Key Competences and Key Learning Outcomes

- Watch and understand a video about the environment.
- Say how you look after the environment
- Looking after the environment

Key language

- *along, bin, bridge, forest, hill, lake, lead, over, path, pick, respect, river, road, rubbish, signs*

Materials

- Pupil's Book p49; Activity Book p46; Class CD2; Video; Teacher's App on Navio
- Teacher's Resource Bank: Task flashcards: *tick, read, circle, listen, write, draw, Talk Partners*
- Countryside flashcards

Optional materials

- Teacher's Resource Bank: Trinity Exam Practice cards (selected from Unit 3)
- Poster paper

At a Glance Lesson Plan

Starting the lesson

- Use the Trinity Exam Practice cards (optional).
- Play a TPR game to review nature places.
- Set learning outcomes and use the task flashcards.

Pre-watching activity

- Look at the photo and talk about favourite places.

Activity 1

- Watch the video.
  Unit 4 video p278
- Tick (✓) or cross (✗). Are these places in the video?

Activity 2

- Watch the video again.
  Unit 4 video
- Read and circle.

Pupil's Book

Video and 21st Century Skills 4

21 CHANNEL

Hello again. Today's programme is about nature. What's your favourite natural place?

1 Watch the video. Tick (✓) or cross (✗). Are these places in the video?

2 Watch the video again. Read and circle.

1 They are walking along a **road** / **path**. 3 They are riding their **horses** / **bikes**.

2 The bridge goes **over** / **along** the river. 4 They're having a **picnic** / **party**.

3 Read and match.

Looking after the environment

It's important to keep natural places clean and tidy.

1 Respect the signs.

2 Keep your dog on a lead.

3 Put your rubbish in the bin.

4 Don't pick wild flowers.

5 Don't feed wild animals.

Key learning outcomes: watch and understand a video about the environment. Living in the world: learning to look after the environment

forty-nine 49

Activity 3

- Read and match.
- Go to the Activity Book.

Ending the lesson

- Review the lesson.
- Review the task flashcards. Elicit the pupils' favourite activities.

Extra activity

Extension

- In groups, pupils plan, draw and present signs.

Activity Book

4 Video and 21st Century Skills

Looking after the environment

1 Read, listen and match. Write.

1 I walk on the path in the forest

2 I don't feed wild animals at the

3 I respect the signs in the

4 I put my rubbish in the bin at the

What do you do to look after the environment?

2 Read and tick (✓). Draw a sign.

1 I put my rubbish in the bin.

2 I walk on the path.

3 I don't feed wild animals.

4 I respect the signs.

5 I don't touch wild flowers.

two

46 forty-six

Activity Book

Activity 1

- Read, listen and match. Write.

▶ *CD2 Track 36 p265*

Activity 2

- Read and tick (✓). Draw a sign.

Recycled vocabulary

- Look, remember and write the word.

Digital resources

Teacher's Digital: Don't forget you can teach this lesson using the Teacher's App on Navio.

Pupil's Digital: Encourage your pupils to use the Pupil's App on Navio to practise the vocabulary from this lesson.

Powered By NAVIO

Starting the lesson

Use the Trinity Exam Practice cards (optional).

- The pupils practise asking and answering questions. (See p31.)
- Stick the bridge, forest, hill, lake, path, river and road countryside flashcards around the room. Tell the pupils to stand up. **Say Go to (the forest).** The pupils go to the forest flashcard. Repeat the activity with all the flashcards. To challenge the pupils you could say two places, for example, **Go to the forest and then walk over the bridge.**

Set learning outcomes and use the task flashcards.

- Say **Today we're going to watch a video and then ask and answer questions about nature.**
- Hold up the task flashcards, in turn, and elicit the activities. Stick them on the side of the board. Point to them during the lesson to reinforce your instructions.

Pre-watching activity

- Look at the photo and read the speech bubble to pupils. Ask **What's your favourite natural place?** Elicit responses.

Pupil's Book Activity 1

Watch the video. Tick (✓) or cross (✗). Are these places in the video? *p278*

- Ask **What places do Abby and Tom like?** Play Part 1. (Tom says, *Me too. And I love the beach!*)
- Focus the pupils on the video stills. Ask **What places can you see?** Then say **Let's watch and listen.**
- Play Part 2. Pause the video after the first video still. Show the tick in the circle.
- Play the video again for pupils to tick the places they see and cross the ones they don't see.

Answers: ✓ ✗ ✓ ✓

Pupil's Book Activity 2

Watch the video again. Read and circle.

- Play Part 2. Pause after Tom says, *You can walk along the path in the park.* Read out the first sentence in Activity 2. Ask **Do they walk along a road or a path?** Show *path* circled.
- Play Part 2 all the way through for pupils to circle the words.
- Ask the pupils some questions to check understanding. Suggested questions.
  What can you do in the leaves? *(Jump.)*
  What are they doing by the lake? *(Having a picnic.)*
  What rubbish is by the lake? *(Bottles and cans.)*
  What are the family doing? *(Tidying up.)*
  What is it a good idea to have in the park? *(Lots of bins and signs.)*
  What are Tom and Sophie going to do? *(Make a poster to tell people to tidy up.)*

Answers: **1** path **2** over **3** bikes **4** picnic

Pupil's Book Activity 3

Read and match.

- Read the first sentence. Show the matching line from the first sentence to the sign. Pupils match the sentences and pictures.
  Think-Pair-Share Read out the speech bubble. Ask **Why is it important to keep natural places clean and tidy?**

Answers: **1** picture 3 **2** picture 4 **3** picture 2 **4** picture 5 **5** picture 1

Activity Book

Activity 1

Read, listen and match. Write.

▶ *CD2 Track 36 p265*

Talk Partners In pairs, the pupils look at the pictures of the nature places and take turns to say where they are and what they can see.

- Play the first exchange on the CD. Ask **Which picture are they talking about?** Show the matching line to picture c. Play the rest of the track for pupils to match the sentences and pictures.
- Point out the word *forest* in number one. Pupils write the words to complete the sentences. Play the track again for pupils to check their answers.

Answers: **1** c forest **2** b lake **3** d park **4** a river

Activity 2

Read and tick (✓). Draw a sign.

- Ask a few pupils **What do you do to look after the environment?**
- Read out the sentences for the pupils to follow. The pupils tick the things they do and don't do to look after the environment. The pupils choose one sentence and draw a sign to illustrate it.
  Talk Partners In pairs, pupils take turns to show each other their signs and tell their partner what they mean.

Recycled vocabulary

Answer: arms

Ending the lesson

Review the lesson.

- Say **Today we've watched a video about the environment. What did we learn?** *(It's important to respect signs and take care of the environment.)*

Review the task flashcards.

- Point to the task flashcards on the board. Say **Look at the activities you've done today. Which activity was your favourite?**

Extra activity

Extension

- Pupils create and draw a sign for the classroom, for example *Be quiet, Don't sit on your desk, Tidy up after class.* The pupils take turns to present their signs in small groups.

Date: ____________ Unit: ____________

1 **What did my pupils learn in this unit?**

2 **How did my pupils work? (✓)**

individually ☐ in pairs ☐ in small groups ☐

in large groups ☐ as a class ☐

3 **Which key competences did my pupils develop?**

Competence in linguistic communication ☐

Competence in mathematics, science and technology ☐

Digital competence ☐

Learning to learn ☐

Social and civic competences ☐

Sense of initiative and entrepreneurship ☐

Cultural awareness and expression ☐

4 **Which lessons / activities were the most successful and why?**

5 **Which lessons / activities did my pupils find the most difficult and why?**

6 **What did I try in the classroom for the first time? How did it go?**

7 **Which resources did I find most useful? (including webpages)**

8 **What could I do differently next time I teach this unit?**

Unit 5

The frozen lake

Unit overview

Key Competences and Key Learning Outcomes

- Identify and say ten action verbs (Lesson 1)
- Use present continuous: 'we' and 'you' (Lesson 2)
- Read, listen and understand a story about a snowman (Lesson 3)
- Use adjectives, present continuous verbs and 'has got' (Lesson 4)
- Read about winter activities in Britain (Lesson 6)
- Write a guided conversation (Lesson 7)
- Watch and understand a video about making snowmen (Video and 21st Century Skills)

- Use the Pupil's App on Navio

- Understand the importance of wearing warm clothes when it's cold (Lesson 3)

- Use a strategy to practise spelling key words (Lesson 1)
- Say a tongue twister and practise 'oa' and 'ow' spellings (Lesson 5)
- Review language in the unit and reflect on own learning (Lesson 8)
- Practise activity types found in the Cambridge Exams: Pre A1 Starters

- Work with a Talk Partner to practise and reinforce learning (all lessons)
- Play a communication game about what snowmen are doing (Lesson 5)
- Learn to be creative (Video and 21st Century Skills)

- Sing four songs (Lessons 1, 4, 5 and 8)
- Understand, act out and give an opinion on a story (Lesson 3)
- Think about winter activities you can do where you live (Lesson 6)
- Read and understand a fable (Lesson 7)

Vocabulary

Core vocabulary
dance, drink, eat, listen to music, make a snowman, play, skate, smile, take a photo, wave; clean, dirty, fat, short, tall, thin

Extension vocabulary (optional)
cry, fall, laugh, move, shout, skip; beautiful, strong, ugly, weak

Other vocabulary
alive, moving, park, sledge, sledging, snowing; snow, stones; dry ski slope, ice rink, skiing, toboggan, tubing; autumn, spring, summer, winter; ant, grasshopper; cold, hot, hungry, silly

Recycled vocabulary
Body parts; Food; *hat, scarf; big, fast, new, old, slow, small; circle, oval, rectangle, square, star, triangle*

Structures

Core structures
What are you doing? We're (skating). Are you (dancing)? Yes, we are. No, we aren't.
Are they (skating)? Yes, they are. No, they aren't.
He's a (fat) snowman. He's got a (dirty) (hat).

Other structures
Are you ready? We're working. We're collecting food. Winter is coming. I'm (hungry). He's / She's got (a tall hat / thin arms). You share with me. I share with you.

Recycled structures
This is … These are …; He's (taking / moving) … They're (dancing).

Phonics

Alternative vowel spellings **'oa'** / **'ow'** (sn**ow**man, g**oa**t, c**oa**t, r**ow**, yell**ow**, b**oa**t, rainb**ow**)

British Culture

Winter activities

Literacy

Text type: a fable (text to entertain and educate)
Reading skills: scanning for specific information; sequencing; reflecting on a moral

21st Century Skills

Ways of thinking: learning to be creative

Cooperative learning

Songs: *Sharing is a good thing to do* (Lesson 5); *Well done!* (Lesson 8)
Skills: Working together as a team (Lesson 5); Think-Pair-Share (Lesson 8)

Values

The importance of wearing warm clothes when it's cold.

Cross-curricular links

Links to Science
Water, land and air: identifying the different forms of water; the names of the different forms of water; how water changes state; different types of land

Suggested Arts and Crafts concepts
Identifying and using different materials to represent winter; making and playing a communication game

Key Competences and Key Learning Outcomes

- Identify and say ten action verbs
- Say the vocabulary chant
- Stick the activity stickers
- Identify different forms of water (optional)
- Use a strategy to practise spelling key words
- Sing a song about a frozen lake

Key language
- *dance, drink, eat, listen to music, make a snowman, play, skate, smile, take a photo, wave*
- *Are you ready?*

Extension vocabulary
- *cry, fall, laugh, move, shout, skip*

Recycled: *What are you doing? Are you (climbing)? Yes, I am. No, I'm not.*

Materials
- Pupil's Book p50; Activity Book pp48 and 57; Class CD2; Teacher's App on Navio; Unit 5 stickers
- Action verbs flashcards
- Teacher's Resource Bank: Action verbs word cards
- Teacher's Resource Bank: Task flashcards: *listen, sing, read, stick, say, Talk Partners, circle, write*

Optional materials
- Teacher's Resource Bank: Five Trinity Exam Practice cards (selected from the Starter Unit and Units 1, 2, 3 and 4)

At a Glance Lesson Plan

Pupil's Book

Starting the lesson
- Use the Trinity Exam Practice cards (optional).
- Review action verbs. Play *Can you guess?*
- Set learning outcomes using the task flashcards.

Vocabulary presentation
- Present the new vocabulary.

Activity 1
- Listen and point.

▶ *CD2 Track 37 p265*
- Sing *We're going to the lake.*

Word cards
- Read the word cards.
- Match them to the flashcards.

Activity 2
- Read and stick the ten stickers.
- Listen and say the chant.

▶ *CD2 Track 39 p265*

Go to the Activity Book.

Ending the lesson
- Review the lesson.
- Review the task flashcards.

Extra activity

Vocabulary extension
- Present six additional vocabulary items.

Link to Science
- **Water, land and air:** identifying the different forms of water

Learning to learn

Spelling
- Practise spelling at any time during this unit (Activity Book p57).

Digital resources

Teacher's Digital: Don't forget you can teach this lesson using the Teacher's App on Navio.

Pupil's Digital: Encourage your pupils to use the Pupil's App on Navio to practise the vocabulary from this lesson.

Powered By NAVIO

Activity Book

Activity Book

Activity 1
- Look, read and circle.

Activity 2
- Look, read and write.

Recycled vocabulary
- Look, remember and write the word.

Spelling

Let's practise spelling!
- Use the *Look-Copy-Cover-Write* technique.

Recycled vocabulary
- Look, remember and write the word.

Starting the lesson

Use the Trinity Exam Practice cards (optional).

- The pupils practise asking and answering questions. (See p31.)

Review action verbs.

- Play *Can you guess?* to review action verbs and vocabulary from Unit 4. Mime an action and ask **What am I doing? Can you guess?** Elicit the question from the pupils and write up a question frame on the board: *Are you … ing?*
- Talk Partners Encourage the pupils to play with a Talk Partner.

Set learning outcomes using the task flashcards.

- Explain the aims of the lesson. Say **Today we're going to learn the names of different action verbs.**
- Hold up the task flashcards and elicit the words. Stick them on one side of the board. Point to them during the lesson to reinforce your instructions.

Vocabulary presentation

Present the new vocabulary.

- (Books closed.) Tell the pupils that this unit is about winter fun. Ask them to describe winter. Say **Let's go to the lake! What can you do at the lake in winter?**
- Introduce the vocabulary by showing the verb flashcards in turn. Say **We can make a snowman. We can take a photo. We can skate.** Repeat the verb and mime the action. Prompt the class to do the same. Then, repeat with the other verbs.
- (Books open.) **Who can you see? Where are they? Is it summer? What are the children on the lake doing? What are they wearing?**

Pupil's Book Activity 1

Listen and point. Sing *We're going to the lake.*

▶ *CD2 Track 37 p265*

- Play the CD. The pupils listen and point to the actions.
- Stick the flashcards on the board in the order that they appear in the song.
- Play the CD again. The pupils sing and do the actions.

Word cards

Read the word cards. Match them to the flashcards.

- (Books closed.) Hold up one of the word cards. The pupils read collectively. A pupil sticks the word card next to the flashcard on the board. Repeat.
- Point to each word card. The pupils read the words.

Pupil's Book Activity 2

Read and stick the ten stickers. Listen and say the chant.

▶ *CD2 Track 39 p265*

- Ask a pupil to read the first word. The pupils stick the corresponding stickers above the word.
- Talk Partners The pupils find and stick the remaining stickers. Encourage them to use cooperative language. Repeat with the other stickers.
- Say **Let's listen and say the words.** Play the CD. The pupils listen and say the chant, pointing to the stickers in turn.

Activity Book

Activity 1

Look, read and circle.

- (Books open.) The pupils look at the illustrations and circle the correct verb in the speech bubble.

Answers: **1** skating **2** smiling **3** making a snowman **4** waving **5** eating **6** drinking hot chocolate

Activity 2

Look, read and write.

- (Books open.) Say **What activities can you see?** The pupils name different activities and point to them. Ask **What's number (1)?** The pupils then write each activity in the correct place.

Answers: **1** skating **2** dancing **3** listening **4** drinking **5** taking **6** playing

Recycled vocabulary

- The pupils look and write the word.

Answer: lake

Ending the lesson

Review the lesson.

- Say **Today we've learnt the names of action words. What words do you remember?** Elicit the names from the pupils.

Review the task flashcards.

- Point to the task flashcards. Say **Look at the activities you've done today. Which was your favourite?** Elicit the pupils' favourite activities.

Extra activity

Vocabulary extension

- Present six additional verbs: *cry, fall, laugh, move, shout, skip.*
- Use the Vocabulary Booster on Navio to practise these new words.

Link to Science

- If you are studying the Science topic of **water, land and air** in English, you could review the different forms of water. Ask the pupils to look at the frozen lake scene. Ask **Can you see any water?** Remind them that ice is solid water. Ask if they can see water in the other states (water vapour from the hot chocolate).

Spelling (Activity Book p57)

Let's practise spelling!

- The pupils can practise spelling the actions using the *Look-Copy-Cover-Write* technique at any time before the Lesson 8 Review.

Recycled vocabulary

- The pupils look and write the word.

Answer: hill

Key Competences and Key Learning Outcomes

- Use present continuous: 'we' and 'you'
- Complete and practise a conversation
- Identify names of different forms of water (optional)
- Listen for specific information

Key language

- *dance, drink, eat, listen to music, make a snowman, play, skate, smile, take a photo, wave*
- *What are you doing? We're (taking a photo). Are you (skating)? Yes, we are. No, we aren't.*

Materials

- Pupil's Book p51; Activity Book p49; Class CD2; Teacher's App on Navio
- Action verbs flashcards
- Teacher's Resource Bank: Task flashcards: *read, listen, Talk Partners, act out, number, write, draw, think*

Optional materials

- Teacher's Resource Bank: Five Trinity Exam Practice cards (selected from the Starter Unit and Units 1, 2, 3 and 4)

At a Glance Lesson Plan

Pupil's Book

Starting the lesson

- Use the Trinity Exam Practice cards (optional).
- Review the *We're going to the lake* song.
- ▶ ***CD2 Track 37 p265***
- ▶ ***CD2 Track 38 p265 (optional karaoke version)***
- Play *Let's go to the lake!*
- Set learning outcomes using the task flashcards.

Activity 1

- Listen and repeat.
- ▶ ***CD2 Track 40 p265***
- **Talk Partners** Act out.

Activity 2

- Listen and number.
- ▶ ***CD2 Track 41 p265***
- Go to the Activity Book.

Ending the lesson

- Review the lesson.
- Review the task flashcards.

Extra activity

Reinforcement

- Play *Guessing game.*

Link to Science

- **Water, land and air:** the names of the different forms of water

Activity Book

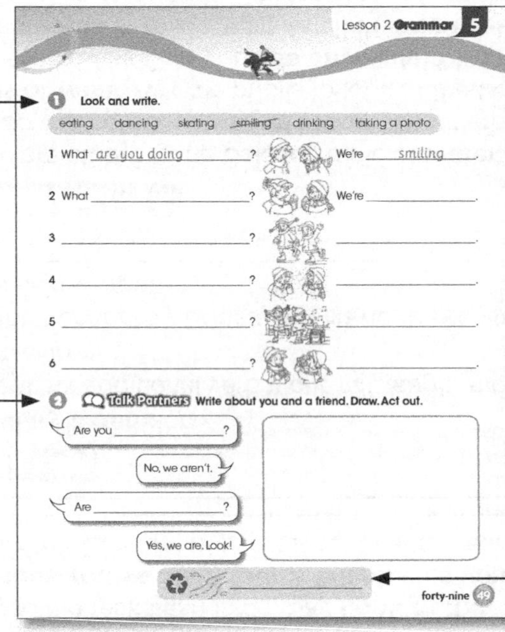

Activity Book

Activity 1

- Look and write.

Activity 2

- Write about you and a friend. Draw.
- **Talk Partners** Act out.

Recycled vocabulary

- Look, remember and write the word.

Digital resources

Teacher's Digital: Don't forget you can teach this lesson using the Teacher's App on Navio.

Pupil's Digital: Encourage your pupils to use the Pupil's App on Navio to practise the vocabulary from this lesson.

Powered By NAVIO

Starting the lesson

Use the Trinity Exam Practice cards (optional).

- The pupils practise asking and answering questions. (See p31.)

Review the *We're going to the lake* song.

▶ *CD2 Track 37 p265*

▶ *CD2 Track 38 p265 (optional karaoke version)*

- Organise the pupils into groups. Seat four pupils as if they were in the car going to the lake. Divide the remaining pupils into four groups (skating, making a snowman, drinking hot chocolate and taking a photo). Play the CD (or use the karaoke version). Encourage the pupils to sing along and do the actions.

Play *Let's go to the lake!*

- Set up the game by saying **Come on! Let's go to the lake. It's cold! Put your hat on!** (Mime putting your hat on and encourage the pupils to join in.) Say **Put your boots on! Put your scarf on!** Mime rubbing your arms and shivering. Name different actions from Lesson 1 and encourage the pupils to do the actions and repeat your statements.

Set learning outcomes using the task flashcards.

- Explain the aims of the lesson. Say **Today we're going to ask and answer about different actions.**
- Hold up the task flashcards and elicit the words. Stick them on one side of the board. Point to them during the lesson to reinforce your instructions.

Pupil's Book Activity 1

Listen and repeat. Act out.

▶ *CD2 Track 40 p265*

- (Books open.) Ask **Who can you see? Where are they?**
- Play the CD. The pupils listen and read the conversation. Check understanding. Ask **What are Beth and Molly doing?**
- Play the CD again. Pause for the pupils to repeat.

Talk Partners The pupils practise the conversation with a Talk Partner.

Pupil's Book Activity 2

Listen and number.

▶ *CD2 Track 41 p265*

- (Books open.) Ask the pupils to name each of the actions.
- Say **Let's listen.** Play the CD. Pause after each conversation. The pupils number the pictures. Repeat the conversations, pausing after each one to check the pupils' answers.

Answer: 4 1 3 2

Activity Book

Activity 1

Look and write.

- (Books open.) Explain that the pupils are going to write questions and answers. Read the example together.
- The pupils work individually to complete the sentences.
- **Talk Partners** The pupils check their answers with a Talk Partner.

Answers: **1** are you doing; smiling **2** are you doing; eating **3** What are you doing; We're skating **4** What are you doing; We're drinking hot chocolate **5** What are you doing; We're dancing **6** What are you doing; We're taking a photo

Activity 2

Write about you and a friend. Draw. Act out.

- The pupils draw themselves and a friend doing one of the activities at the frozen lake.
- **Talk Partners** The pupils complete and practise their own conversation and act it out with a Talk Partner, miming the activities they have chosen.

Recycled vocabulary

- The pupils look at the picture and write the word.

Answer: road

Ending the lesson

Review the lesson.

- Say **Today you asked and answered questions about different activities.** Elicit some questions and answers.

Review the task flashcards.

- Point to the task flashcards. Say **Look at the activities you've done today. Which activity was your favourite?** Elicit the pupils' favourite activities.

Extra activity

Reinforcement

- Choose a volunteer and play *Guessing game* (see p23) with the verb flashcards. Once the action has been guessed, change the volunteer.

Link to Science

- If you are studying the Science topic of **water, land and air** in English, you could remind the pupils of the names of the different forms of water. Draw a chart with three columns on the board *(solid, liquid, gas).* Elicit names of solid water, liquid and gas and complete the chart: solid: ice, snow; liquid: river, lake, waterfall, sea, ocean; gas: water vapour.

Key Competences and Key Learning Outcomes

- Read, listen and understand a story about a snowman
- Read the story with some fluency
- Recognise how water changes state (optional)
- Become familiar with the story through a pre-reading task
- Understand the importance of wearing warm clothes when it's cold
- Understand and act out the story
- Give an opinion on the story

Key language
- *What are you doing? We're making a snowman. He's got a fat tummy.*

Recycled: *arms, body, carrot, eyes, hat, head, nose*

Other vocabulary: *alive, moving, park, sledge, sledging, snowing*

Materials
- Pupil's Book pp52–53; Activity Book p50; Class CD2; Teacher's App on Navio
- Teacher's Resource Bank: Task flashcards: *listen, read, act out, write, number, tick, draw, Talk Partners*
- Teacher's Resource Bank: Unit 5 Lesson 3 Animated Story

Optional materials
- Teacher's Resource Bank: Five Trinity Exam Practice cards (selected from the Starter Unit and Units 1, 2, 3 and 4)

At a Glance Lesson Plan

Starting the lesson
- Use the Trinity Exam Practice cards (optional).
- Review the *We're going to the lake* song.
- ▶ *CD2 Track 37 p265*
- ▶ *CD2 Track 38 p265 (optional karaoke version)*
- Set learning outcomes using the task flashcards.

Before you read
- Read and answer the question.

Activity 1
- Listen and read.
- ▶ *CD2 Track 42 p265*
- Act out.
- *Now watch the animated story!*

After you read: Activity 2
- Go to page 50 in your Activity Book.
- Values: Read and write.

Ending the lesson
- Review the lesson.
- Review the task flashcards.

Pupil's Book

Extra activity
Extension
- Talk Partners Play *Hot seat.*

Link to Science
- **Water, land and air:** how water changes state

Activity Book

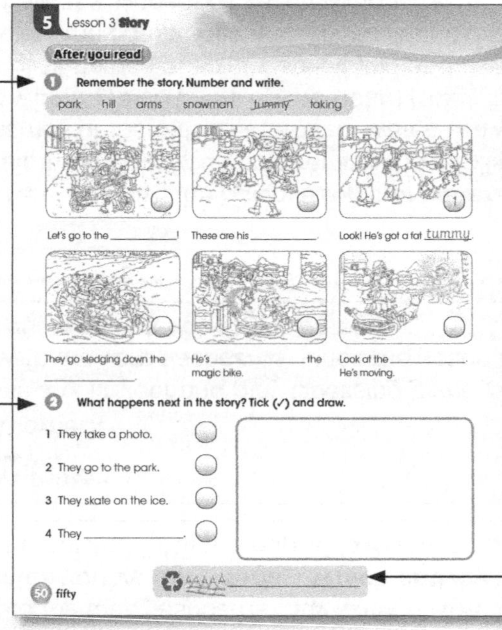

Activity Book
After you read: Activity 1
- Remember the story. Number and write.

Activity 2
- What happens next in the story? Tick (✓) and draw.

Recycled vocabulary
- Look, remember and write the word.

Digital resources

Teacher's Digital: Don't forget you can teach this lesson using the Teacher's App on Navio.

Pupil's Digital: Encourage your pupils to use the Pupil's App on Navio to practise the vocabulary from this lesson.

Powered By NAVIO

Starting the lesson

Use the Trinity Exam Practice cards (optional).

- The pupils practise asking and answering questions. (See p31.)

Review the *We're going to the lake* song.

▶ *CD2 Track 37 p265*

▶ *CD2 Track 38 p265 (optional karaoke version)*

- Sing *We're going to the lake* from Lesson 1.
- Divide the class into three groups to sing a verse each. Play the CD (or use the karaoke version).

Set learning outcomes using the task flashcards.

- Say **Today we're going to listen to a story.**
- Hold up the task flashcards and elicit the words. Stick them on one side of the board. Point to them during the lesson to reinforce your instructions.

Before you read

Read and answer the question.

- (Books open.) Focus the class on the pre-reading task. Ask **What are Jake and Molly making in the story?** Ask the pupils to look at the illustrations of the snowman and describe him: *He's got (a head). He's wearing (a hat).*

Pupil's Book Activity 1

Listen and read. Act out.

▶ *CD2 Track 42 p265*

- (Books open.) Play the CD. The pupils follow the text with their finger. Pause between each story frame to check understanding.

Suggested comprehension questions

- Frame 1: **What are Jake and Molly doing?** *(Making a snowman.)*
- Frame 2: **What has the snowman got?** *(He's got a body, a head, arms, eyes, a mouth and a nose.)*
- Frame 3: **Can the children go to the park on the bike?** *(No. It's snowing.)*
- Frame 4: **What happens to the bike?** *(It's a sledge now.)*
- Frame 5: **What happens to the snowman?** *(He's alive!)*
- Frame 6: **What is the snowman doing?** *(He's taking the magic bike.)*
- Frame 7: **Can they catch the snowman?** *(No, they can't.)*
- Frame 8: **What are they doing now?** *(They go sledging down the hill.)*

After you read

- Ask **Did you like the story? What part did you like best?**
- Talk Partners The pupils choose their favourite frame.
- Organise the class into three groups (Jake, Molly and Beth).
- Play the CD. Each group joins in when their character speaks. If necessary, pause the CD after each sentence for the pupils to repeat.
- The pupils swap roles and repeat the activity.

After you read

Pupil's Book Activity 2

Go to page 50 in your Activity Book.

Activity Book

After you read: Activity 1

Remember the story. Number and write.

- (Books open.) Ask a pupil to find the first picture from the story. The pupils write numbers to order the pictures and then complete the sentences with words from the box.

Answers: **1** tummy **2** arms **3** park **4** snowman **5** taking **6** hill

Activity 2

What happens next in the story? Tick (✓) and draw.

- (Books open.) Refer the pupils to the last frame of the story again in their Pupil's Books. Ask **What do you think happens next?** Elicit ideas, writing any key words from their suggestions on the board. If necessary, focus their ideas with questions. Ask **Do you think they take a photo? Do you think they go to the park? Do you think they skate on the ice?**
- The pupils choose one of the endings for the story, or invent their own and draw a picture in their Activity Books.

Recycled vocabulary

- The pupils look at the picture and write the word.

Answer: forest

Pupil's Book Activity 2

Values: Read and write.

- Read the value and prompt the class to choose the correct clothes to complete the sentence.
- Ask them if they do up their coat when it's cold. Mime to help with understanding.

Ending the lesson

Review the lesson.

- Say **Today we've listened to a story about a snowman. Today you've learnt that it's important to wear warm clothes on a cold day.**

Review the task flashcards.

- Point to the task flashcards. Say **Look at the activities you've done today. Which activity was your favourite?** Elicit the pupils' favourite activities.

Extra activity

Extension

- Play *Hot seat.* Choose a volunteer to come out to the front and sit in the 'Hot seat'. The pupils read out the parts of the story about making the snowman. The pupil in the hot seat mimes these actions. Encourage them to add different parts of the body.
- Talk Partners The pupils do the activity with a Talk Partner.

Link to Science

- If you are studying the Science topic of **water, land and air** in English, you could review how water changes state. Ask the pupils to imagine it's warm now at the lake. Ask **Is there snow and ice now? Why not?** Encourage them to tell you that snow and ice turn to water when it's warm.

Key Competences and Key Learning Outcomes

- Describe and guess snowmen
- Use adjectives, present continuous verbs and 'has got'
- Sing a song

Key language

- *clean, dirty, fat, short, tall, thin*
- *He's a (short) snowman. He's got a (dirty) hat.*

Extension vocabulary

- *beautiful, strong, ugly, weak*

Recycled: *big, fast, new, old, slow, small; carrot, hat, nose, orange, scarf;* Shapes: *circle, oval, rectangle, square, star, triangle*

Materials

- Pupil's Book p54; Activity Book p51; Class CD2; Teacher's App on Navio
- Teacher's Resource Bank: Task flashcards: *listen, say, sing, Talk Partners, tick, write, draw*

Optional materials

- Teacher's Resource Bank: Five Trinity Exam Practice cards (selected from the Starter Unit and Units 1, 2, 3 and 4)
- Coloured paper, cotton wool and small pieces of scrap material

At a Glance Lesson Plan

Starting the lesson

- Use the Trinity Exam Practice cards (optional).
- Review the Lesson 3 story.
- Set learning outcomes using the task flashcards.

Vocabulary presentation

- Present the new vocabulary.

Activity 1

- Listen, point and say.

▶ *CD2 Track 43 p265*

Activity 2

- Listen and point. Sing *What are they doing?*

▶ *CD2 Track 44 p265*

Activity 3

- Listen and repeat.
- Talk Partners Play a game.

▶ *CD2 Track 45 p265*

Go to the Activity Book.

Pupil's Book

Ending the lesson

- Review the lesson.
- Review the task flashcards.

Extra activities

Reinforcement

- Review shapes.
- Talk Partners Write a description and draw and decorate a snowman.

Vocabulary extension

- Present four additional vocabulary items.

Digital resources

Teacher's Digital: Don't forget you can teach this lesson using the Teacher's App on Navio.

Pupil's Digital: Encourage your pupils to use the Pupil's App on Navio to practise the vocabulary from this lesson.

Powered By NAVIO

Activity Book

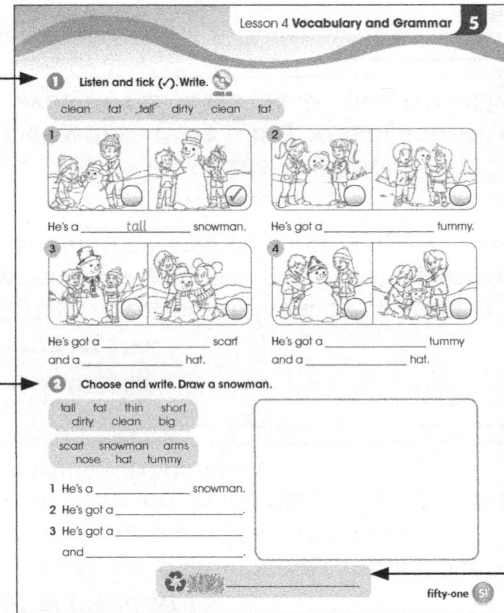

Activity Book

Activity 1

- Listen and tick (✓). Write.

▶ *CD2 Track 46 p265*

Activity 2

- Choose and write. Draw a snowman.

Recycled vocabulary

- Look, remember and write the word.

Starting the lesson

Use the Trinity Exam Practice cards (optional).

- The pupils practise asking and answering questions. (See p31.)

Review the Lesson 3 story.

- Read out lines from the story in random order.
- The pupils scan the story and say the frame number. Say, e.g. **These are his arms.** The pupils reply *Number 2.*
- Then, say the beginning of some of the lines and ask the pupils to complete them. Say **Here's a carrot for his** *(nose).* **Let's go to the** *(park).*

Set learning outcomes using the task flashcards.

- Say **Today we're going to describe a snowman.**
- Hold up the task flashcards in turn and elicit the words. Stick them on one side of the board. Point to them during the lesson to reinforce your instructions.

Vocabulary presentation

Present the new vocabulary.

- (Books open.) Point to the first picture and say **Look at the snowman. He's a fat snowman.** (Mime fat). Ask the class to name something else that is big *(a hippo, an elephant).* Praise the class for their ideas and then repeat the process with the other adjectives.

Pupil's Book Activity 1

Listen, point and say.

▶ *CD2 Track 43 p265*

- *Say* **Let's listen and repeat the words.** Play the CD. The pupils repeat each word, pointing to the corresponding illustration. Play the CD again. The pupils repeat and do the mimes.
- Ask the pupils if they can remember any other words we use for describing. Elicit *big, small, old, new, fast, slow.* Use mime if necessary to remind them.

Pupil's Book Activity 2

Listen and point. Sing *What are they doing?*

▶ *CD2 Track 44 p265*

- (Books open.) Point to the illustration. Ask **What are they doing?** Ask the pupils to describe the snowman. Ask questions to help **Is the snowman (fat or thin)? Look at his (hat).**
- Play the CD. The pupils listen and point. Play the CD again. The pupils sing and do the actions.

Pupil's Book Activity 3

Listen and repeat. Play a game.

▶ *CD2 Track 45 p265*

- Ask the pupils to look at the activity and describe the four snowmen. Play the CD. Play the CD again and ask the pupils to repeat the question and answer.
- **Talk Partners** The pupils describe the snowmen with a Talk Partner.

Activity Book

Activity 1

Listen and tick (✓). Write.

▶ *CD2 Track 46 p265*

- (Books open.) Play the CD, pausing after the first conversation to check understanding. Repeat with the remaining exchanges. The pupils tick the snowman the children are describing and then write the adjectives in the correct place.
- **Talk Partners** The pupils take turns to describe the snowmen from the activity to a Talk Partner.

Answers: **1** tall (picture 2) **2** fat (picture 1) **3** clean, clean (picture 2) **4** fat, dirty (picture 1)

Activity 2

Choose and write. Draw a snowman.

- (Books open.) Copy the text (with gaps) onto the board. Read the first sentence and ask the pupils to select one of the adjectives from the box to complete the sentence.
- Continue until you have a complete description. Read a description together and draw the snowman on the board.
- Pupils then work individually to complete the description of a snowman, using the adjectives. The pupils then draw a snowman according to their text.

Recycled vocabulary

- The pupils look at the picture and write the word.

Answer: grass

Ending the lesson

Review the lesson.

- Say **Today we've described a snowman.** Elicit some adjectives from the pupils.

Review the task flashcards.

- Point to the task flashcards. Say **Look at the activities you've done today. Which activity was your favourite?** Elicit the pupils' favourite activities.

Extra activities

Reinforcement

- Review shapes by asking the pupils to look at the picture of the snowman on Pupil's Book p54, Activity 2. Ask **What shapes can you see? Can you see a (circle)?** Repeat until all the shapes have been named, asking different pupils in turn.
- **Talk Partners** Give out coloured paper, cotton wool and small pieces of scrap material. Pupils work with a Talk Partner to write a description of a snowman by following the model in the Activity Book. They then draw the snowman and decorate it with cotton wool and pieces of fabric. Display the finished snowmen.

Vocabulary extension

- Use the Vocabulary Booster on Navio and present and practise four additional adjectives: *beautiful, strong, ugly, weak.*

Key Competences and Key Learning Outcomes

- Say a tongue twister with the 'oa' sound
- Learn and practise 'oa' and 'ow' spellings
- Listen for specific information
- Sing a cooperative learning song
- Play a communication game about what snowmen are doing

Key language

- *boat, coat, goat, rainbow, road, row, slow, snow, snowman, soap, toad, window, yellow; sharing*
- *You share with me. I share with you.*

Recycled: *They're (dancing). They're (listening to music).*

Materials

- Pupil's Book p55; Activity Book p52; Class CD2; Teacher's App on Navio
- Teacher's Resource Bank: Task flashcards: *listen, say, write, sing, Talk Partners, colour*
- Teacher's Resource Bank: Unit 5 Lesson 5 Activity 4 cut-out
- Scissors

Optional materials

- Teacher's Resource Bank: Five Trinity Exam Practice cards (selected from the Starter Unit and Units 1, 2, 3 and 4)

At a Glance Lesson Plan

Pupil's Book

Starting the lesson

- Use the Trinity Exam Practice cards (optional).
- Review the *What are they doing?* song.
- ▶ *CD2 Track 44 p265*
- Set learning outcomes using the task flashcards.

Activity 1

- Listen and say.
- ▶ *CD2 Track 47 p266*
- Go to the Activity Book.
- Go to Magic Phonics.

Activity 2

- Listen and write *T* (true) or *F* (false).
- ▶ *CD2 Track 48 p266*

Activity 3 – Cooperative learning

- Sing *Sharing is a good thing to do.*
- ▶ *CD2 Track 49 p266*

Activity 4

- Make and play the game (Teacher's Resource Bank).

Ending the lesson

- Review the lesson.
- Review the task flashcards.

Cooperative learning

Working together as a team

- Talk Partners
  Play *Beat the clock.*
- Add to the pronunciation wall display.

Activity Book

Activity Book

Activity 1

- Write and say.

Activity 2

- Colour the 'ow' words red and the 'oa' words blue. Say.

Go to Magic Phonics.

Activity 3

- Talk Partners
  Play *Snap* in pairs.

Recycled vocabulary

- Look, remember and write the word.

Digital resources

Teacher's Digital: Don't forget you can teach this lesson using the Teacher's App on Navio.

Pupil's Digital: Encourage your pupils to use the Pupil's App on Navio to practise the vocabulary from this lesson.

Powered By NAVIO

Starting the lesson

Use the Trinity Exam Practice cards (optional).

- The pupils practise asking and answering questions. (See p31.)

Review the *What are they doing?* song.

▶ *CD2 Track 44 p265*

- Sing *What are they doing?* from Lesson 4. Invent a new verse by encouraging the pupils to replace some of the adjectives with different ones: *He's got (a new hat / thin tummy / dirty scarf). He's got (fat arms).*, etc.

Set learning outcomes using the task flashcards.

- Say **Today we're going to say a tongue twister. We're going to make and play a game.**
- Hold up the task flashcards in turn and elicit the activities. Stick them on one side of the board. Point to them during the lesson to reinforce your instructions.

Pupil's Book Activity 1

Listen and say.

▶ *CD2 Track 47 p266*

- Write the words *snow* and *boat* on the board. Ask the pupils which sound they can hear in both words *('oa')*. Circle the target grapheme in each word ('ow' and 'oa') and model the sound. The pupils say the sound.
- Say **It's time for Toby's tongue twister! What can you see?** *(A snowman, a boat, a goat and a rainbow.)*
- Play the CD. The pupils listen and repeat the target sound, then the words and then the entire tongue twister, faster and faster.

Go to Magic Phonics.

Activity Book

Activity 1

Write and say.

- (Books open.) Say **Look at Toby's tongue twister! The letters for 'oa' are missing.** The pupils complete the tongue twister.
- Talk Partners The pupils say Toby's tongue twister and point to the 'oa' sounds. They play *Faster and faster,* taking turns to say the tongue twister faster each time.

Answers: snowman, goat, coat, row, yellow, boat, rainbow

Activity 2

Colour the 'ow' words red and the 'oa' words blue. Say.

- Ask pupils to say the words and then colour 'ow' words red and 'oa' words blue.

Answers: red: snow, window, slow, rainbow
blue: road, toad, soap, coat, boat, goat

Go to Magic Phonics.

Activity 3

Play *Snap* in pairs.

- Demonstrate the game with a volunteer. You each think of a word, count to three together, point to the picture and say the word. If the words are the same, say *Snap!* If they are different, continue playing the game.

Talk Partners The pupils play the game with a Talk Partner.

Recycled vocabulary

- The pupils look at the picture and write the word.

Answer: leaves

Pupil's Book Activity 2

Listen and write *T* (true) and *F* (false).

▶ *CD2 Track 48 p266*

- (Books open.) Explain that they are going to listen to children talking about the snowmen's actions. They write *T* if it's a true description and *F* if it isn't.
- Play the CD. Pause after each sentence to give the pupils time to write and to check their answers.

Answers: **1** T **2** F **3** T **4** F **5** F **6** T

Pupil's Book Activity 3: **Cooperative learning**

Sing *Sharing is a good thing to do.*

▶ *CD2 Track 49 p266*

- Explain that sharing is a good thing to do. Play the CD. The pupils listen. Play the CD again and encourage the pupils to sing along.

Pupil's Book Activity 4

Make and play the game (Teacher's Resource Bank).

- Show the pupils how to cut out the cards. Demonstrate the activity.

Talk Partners The pupils mix both their sets of cards together. They place both sets face down on the table. The pupils pick up a card each and say what the snowmen are doing. If the cards are the same, the pupils say *Snap!* If the cards are different, they replace them and try again. Demonstrate the activity with a volunteer first.

Ending the lesson

Review the lesson.

- Say **Today we've practised a tongue twister**. Ask the pupils to say it again.
- Then say **Today you played a game with cards.**

Review the task flashcards.

- Point to the task flashcards. Say **Look at the activities you've done today. Which was your favourite?** Elicit the pupils' favourite activities.

Cooperative learning

Working together as a team

- Talk Partners Play *Beat the clock* to practise pronunciation of the 'oa' / 'ow' sound. (See p53.)
- Add to the pronunciation wall display, adding a boat ('oa') and a rainbow ('ow').

Key Competences and Key Learning Outcomes

- Read about winter activities in Britain
- Listen for general understanding
- Think about winter activities you can do where you live

Key language

- *dry ski slope, ice rink, skiing, toboggan, tubing, winter*
- *I / We go (skating / skiing / tubing). I / We ride (on a toboggan).*

Recycled: *There's a … We can … We go (tubing). What are they doing? They're (tubing) down a hill. They're (dancing) on the ice.*

Materials

- Pupil's Book p56; Activity Book p53; Class CD2; Teacher's App on Navio
- Teacher's Resource Bank: Task flashcards: *Talk Partners, listen, read, think, number, tick, draw, write, say*

Optional materials

- Teacher's Resource Bank: Five Trinity Exam Practice cards (selected from the Starter Unit and Units 1, 2, 3 and 4)

At a Glance Lesson Plan

Pupil's Book

Starting the lesson

- Use the Trinity Exam Practice cards (optional).
- Talk Partners
  Review *Toby's tongue twister.*
  ▶ *CD2 Track 47 p266*
- Set learning outcomes using the task flashcards.

Activity 1

- Listen and read. Answer.
  ▶ *CD2 Track 50 p266*

Think about your culture

- What winter activities can you do where you live?

Go to the Activity Book.

Ending the lesson

- Review the lesson.
- Review the task flashcards.

Extra activity

Reinforcement

- Sing *What are they doing?*
  ▶ *CD2 Track 44 p265*

Digital resources

Teacher's Digital: Don't forget you can teach this lesson using the Teacher's App on Navio.

Powered By NAVIO

Activity Book

Activity Book

Activity 1

- Listen and number. Write.
  ▶ *CD2 Track 51 p266*

Activity 2: Think about your culture

- Read and tick (✓). Draw, write and say.

Recycled vocabulary

- Look, remember and write the word.

Starting the lesson

Use the Trinity Exam Practice cards (optional).

- The pupils practise asking and answering questions. (See p31.)

Review Toby's tongue twister.

▶ *CD2 Track 47 p266*

- Ask the class **What sound did you practise in Toby's tongue twister?** ('oa'). Ask if they can remember the tongue twister. *(A snowman and a goat in a coat row a yellow boat to the rainbow.)*
- **Talk Partners** The pupils practise the tongue twister as a class and then with a Talk Partner. The pairs play *Faster and faster,* reading from the Pupil's Book (page 55) if necessary. A fast pair says the tongue twister for the class.
- Draw a chart with two columns ('oa' and 'ow') on the board. Elicit words with both spellings. Ask pupils to classify the words, e.g. 'oa': *goat, coat*; 'ow': *snow, yellow.*

Set learning outcomes using the task flashcards.

- Say **Today we're going to learn about winter activities in Britain.**
- Hold up the task flashcards in turn and elicit the activities. Stick them on one side of the board. Point to them during the lesson to reinforce your instructions.

Pupil's Book Activity 1

Listen and read. Answer.

▶ *CD2 Track 50 p266*

- (Books open.) Focus the pupils' attention on the photographs and ask **What can you see?** Then say **Let's listen and read.**
- Play the CD. At the end of the text, check understanding by pointing to the photos one by one and asking **What are the children doing in this photo?**

Pupil's Book Think about your culture

What winter activities can you do where you live?

- Read the question and encourage the class to tell you about their favourite outdoor activities and places where they do winter activities.

Activity Book

Activity 1

Listen and number. Write.

▶ *CD2 Track 51 p266*

- (Books open.) Say **Let's listen.** Play the CD, pausing after the first conversation for the pupils to follow the example.
- Repeat with the remaining conversations, pausing after each one to check that the pupils have identified and numbered the correct picture. Pupils then write the correct word under each picture.

Answers: **1** skiing **2** riding (on a toboggan) **3** tubing **4** They're skating

Activity 2: Think about your culture

Read and tick (✓). Draw, write and say.

- Read the question in the speech bubble. Elicit the pupils' answers.
- Read the first sentence as a class and ask the pupils to tick the box if they ride on a toboggan. Repeat with the other sentences.
- Ask the pupils to draw their favourite outdoor activity and write a sentence about it. Invite different pupils to show the rest of the class their drawings and read out their sentences.

Recycled vocabulary

- The pupils look at the picture and write the word.

Answer: path

Ending the lesson

Review the lesson.

- Say **Today you've learnt about winter activities in Britain.**

Review the task flashcards.

- Point to the task flashcards. Say **Look at the activities you've done today. Which activity was your favourite?** Elicit the pupils' favourite activities.

Extra activity

Reinforcement

▶ *CD2 Track 44 p265*

- Sing *What are they doing?* from Lesson 4. Divide the class into two teams. Team A sings one line and Team B sings the next. Sing again, and this time Team A misses out an adjective and Team B sings the missing word.

  Team A: *He's got a … hat.*

  Team B: *Dirty!*
- Swap the teams and sing again.

Key Competences and Key Learning Outcomes

- Write a guided conversation
- Identify different types of land (optional)
- Read for specific information
- Read and understand a fable

Key language

- *autumn, spring, summer, winter; ant, grasshopper; cold, happy, hungry, silly*
- *We're working. We're collecting food. Winter is coming. I'm (hungry).*

Recycled: *What are you doing? He's / She's / We're / They're (singing); Can I have (some food)?*

Materials

- Pupil's Book p57; Activity Book p54; Class CD2; Teacher's App on Navio
- Teacher's Resource Bank: Task flashcards: *find, circle, Talk Partners, listen, read, number, match, write, draw*

Optional materials

- Teacher's Resource Bank: Five Trinity Exam Practice cards (selected from the Starter Unit and Units 1, 2, 3 and 4)
- Coloured paper

At a Glance Lesson Plan

Starting the lesson

- Use the Trinity Exam Practice cards (optional).
- Play *Can you guess?*
- Set learning outcomes using the task flashcards.

Before you read: Activity 1

- Look at the fable quickly. Find and circle the season words.

Activity 2

- Listen and read the fable.
- ▶ *CD2 Track 52 p266*

After you read

- Go to page 54 in your Activity Book.

Ending the lesson

- Review the lesson.
- Review the task flashcards.
- Sing a song (optional).

Pupil's Book

Lesson 7 Literacy 5

Text type: A fable

Before you read

1 Look at the fable quickly. Find and circle the season words.

spring summer autumn winter

2 Listen and read the fable.

The ants and the grasshopper

It's summer. A grasshopper sees some ants. The grasshopper is singing and dancing. The ants are working.
"Hello, ants! What are you doing?" asks the grasshopper.
"We're working. We're collecting food for winter," answer the ants.
"You're silly!" says the grasshopper.
"It's summer! Come and play."
"No," answer the ants. "Winter is coming."

In autumn, the grasshopper is still singing and dancing. The ants are still working.
"Hello, ants! What are you doing?" asks the grasshopper.
"We're working. We're collecting food for winter," answer the ants.
"You're so silly!" says the grasshopper.
In winter, the ants are happy. They're eating their food. The grasshopper is cold and hungry.
"I'm hungry!" says the grasshopper. "Can I have some food?"
"No," answer the ants. "Go and look for food in the snow!"

After you read

Go to page 54 in your Activity Book.

Key learning outcomes: read and understand a fable

fifty-seven 57

Extra activity

Reinforcement

- Draw and write about two animals.

Link to Science

- **Water, land and air:** different types of land

Activity Book

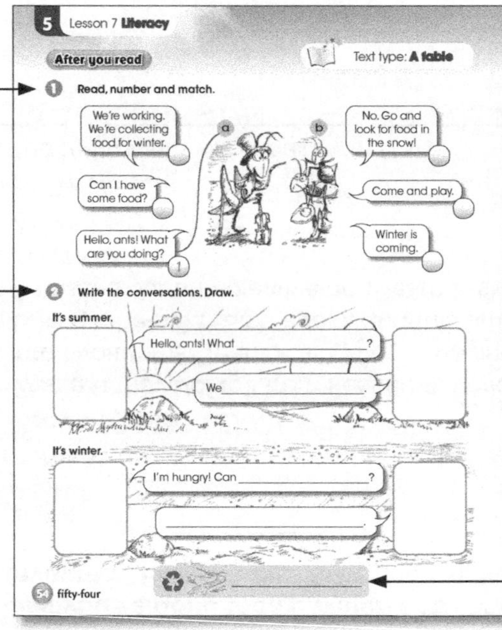
5 Lesson 7 Literacy

Text type: A fable

After you read

1 Read, number and match.

We're working. We're collecting food for winter.

Can I have some food?

Hello, ants! What are you doing?

No. Go and look for food in the snow!

Come and play.

Winter is coming.

2 Write the conversations. Draw.

It's summer.

Hello, ants! What ______?

We ______

It's winter.

I'm hungry! Can ______?

54 fifty-four

Activity Book

After you read: Activity 1

- Read, number and match.

Activity 2

- Write the conversations. Draw.

Recycled vocabulary

- Look, remember and write the word.

Digital resources

Teacher's Digital: Don't forget you can teach this lesson using the Teacher's App on Navio.

Pupil's Digital: Encourage your pupils to use the Pupil's App on Navio to practise the vocabulary from this lesson.

Powered By NAVIO

Starting the lesson

Use the Trinity Exam Practice cards (optional).

- The pupils practise asking and answering questions. (See p31.)

Play *Can you guess?*

- Play *Can you guess?* (see p55) with vocabulary from the unit (*skate, take a photo, wave, smile, eat, drink, listen to music, make a snowman, play, dance*).
- Include any additional verbs the pupils are familiar with from earlier units: *ride a horse / bike, swim, run, jump, climb, roll, fly,* etc.

Set learning outcomes using the task flashcards.

- Say **Today we're going to read a fable.**
- Hold up the task flashcards in turn and elicit the activities. Stick them on one side of the board. Point to them during the lesson to reinforce your instructions.

Before you read: Pupil's Book Activity 1

Look at the fable quickly. Find and circle the season words.

- (Books open.) Tell the pupils they are going to read and listen to a fable. Explain to them that a fable is a short story that is usually about animals. The story teaches a lesson or 'moral'.
- Focus their attention on the title and say **Point to the ants. Point to the grasshopper.** Focus their attention on the pre-reading task.
- **Talk Partners** The pupils quickly scan the text to find the seasons mentioned in the fable (summer, autumn and winter).

Pupil's Book Activity 2

Listen and read the fable.

▶ *CD2 Track 52 p266*

- Say **Let's read the fable.** Play the CD.
- Ask **Do you like the story? What part do you like?** Encourage the pupils to read out the part of the story they like best.
- Ask the pupils some questions about the fable. **Do you like this fable? Who do you like best: the ants or the grasshopper? Is the grasshopper working hard in the fable? What is the grasshopper doing? Have the ants got food in winter? Has the grasshopper got food in winter? Do the ants help the grasshopper? Do you think the ants should help the grasshopper?**
- Explain the moral to the pupils: *First work, then play.* Personalise by asking if at home they play first or do their homework.

Activity Book

After you read: Activity 1

Read, number and match.

- Invite individual pupils to read out the speech bubbles one by one and match them to the corresponding character (the ants or the grasshopper). The pupils then read the speech bubbles again in order and number them according to the story.

Answers: **1** a Hello, ants! … **2** b We're working **3** a Come and play **4** b Winter is coming **5** a Can I have … **6** b No. Go and look …

Activity 2

Write the conversations. Draw.

- The pupils complete the conversations and draw the ants and grasshopper in each scene. Encourage the pupils to adapt the end of the story if they wish so that the ants help the grasshopper.

Recycled vocabulary

- The pupils look at the picture and write the word.

Answer: river

Ending the lesson

Review the lesson.

- Say **Today you've read a fable.** Then say **Today you've learnt a moral: 'First work, then play.' Do you finish your work before you play?**

Review the task flashcards.

- Point to the task flashcards. Say **Look at the activities you've done today. Which activity was your favourite?** Elicit the pupils' favourite activities.

Sing a song (optional).

- Choose a song. The class sings and does the actions. Alternatively, invite the class to choose a song to sing.

Extra activity

Reinforcement

- Encourage the pupils to choose two new animals for the fable. They should draw the animals in one of the seasons from the fable and complete a speech bubble for each.

Link to Science

- If you are studying the Science topic of **water, land and air** in English, you could review different types of land. Focus the pupils' attention on the ant and grasshopper's habitat. Ask **Have you seen ants and grasshoppers at the park?** Tell them that they live on the land. Ask the pupils if they can name different types of land *(soil, rock, sand).* Reaffirm the importance of looking after the environment so that we don't harm living things.

Key Competences and Key Learning Outcomes

- Review language in the unit
- Reflect on own learning
- Sing a cooperative learning song

Key language

Recycled: *dance, drink, eat, listen to music, make a snowman, play, skate, smile, take a photo, wave; clean, dirty, fat, short, tall, thin*

Recycled: *We're (drinking). They're (eating). Are you (eating)? Are they (drinking)? Yes (we / they) are. No, (we / they) aren't.*

Materials

- Pupil's Book p58; Activity Book p55; Class CD2; Teacher's App on Navio
- Action verbs flashcards
- Teacher's Resource Bank: Action verbs word cards
- Teacher's Resource Bank: Task flashcards: *listen, number, write, say, act out, Talk Partners, sing, stick, find, circle, Think-Pair-Share*
- Teacher's Resource Bank: Traffic light cut-out
- *Give Me Five!* sticker

Optional materials

- Teacher's Resource Bank: Five Trinity Exam Practice cards (selected from the Starter Unit and Units 1, 2, 3 and 4)

At a Glance Lesson Plan

Pupil's Book

Starting the lesson

- Use the Trinity Exam Practice cards (optional).
- Review the unit vocabulary.
- Set learning outcomes using the task flashcards.

Activity 1

- Listen and number.
- Write and say.
- ▶ *CD2 Track 53 p266*

Activity 2

- Listen.
- ▶ *CD2 Track 54 p266*
- Talk Partners
- Act out. Ask and answer.

Activity 3 Cooperative learning

- Sing *Well done!*
- ▶ *CD2 Track 55 p266*
- Stick the *Give Me Five!* sticker.

Go to the Activity Book.

5 Lesson 8 Review

1 Listen and number. Write and say.

play

2 Talk Partners Listen. Act out. Ask and answer.

3 Cooperative learning Sing *Well done!*

58 fifty-eight

Key learning outcomes: review language in the unit
Language: action verbs and *Are you ....+ing?*

Ending the lesson

- Review the task flashcards.
- Sing a song (optional).

Extra activities

Reinforcement

- Play *Memory!*

Extension

- Word search adjectives.

Cooperative learning

Think-Pair-Share

- Remember ten action words.

Activity Book

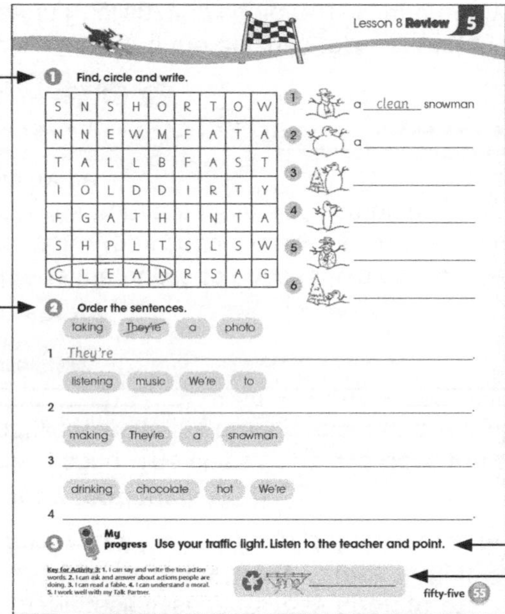

Lesson 8 Review 5

1 Find, circle and write.

S	N	S	H	O	R	T	O	W
N	N	E	W	M	F	A	T	A
T	A	L	L	B	F	A	S	T
I	O	L	D	D	I	R	T	Y
F	G	A	T	H	I	N	T	A
S	H	P	L	T	S	L	S	W
C	L	E	A	N	R	S	A	G

1 a clean snowman
2 a ______
3 ______
4 ______
5 ______
6 ______

2 Order the sentences.

taking / They're / a / photo
1 They're ______

listening / music / We're / to
2 ______

making / They're / a / snowman
3 ______

drinking / chocolate / hot / We're
4 ______

3 My progress Use your traffic light. Listen to the teacher and point.

fifty-five 55

Activity Book

Activity 1

- Find, circle and write.

Activity 2

- Order the sentences.

Activity 3 My progress

- Use your traffic light. Listen to the teacher and point.

Recycled vocabulary

- Look, remember and write the word.

Digital resources

Teacher's Digital: Don't forget you can teach this lesson using the Teacher's App on Navio.

Pupil's Digital: Encourage your pupils to use the Pupil's App on Navio to practise the vocabulary from this lesson.

Powered By NAVIO

Starting the lesson

Use the Trinity Exam Practice cards (optional).
- The pupils practise asking and answering questions. (See p31.)

Review the unit vocabulary.
- Play *Mime game* (see p23) with the unit flashcards to review the verbs.

Set learning outcomes using the task flashcards.
- Say **Today we're going to remember what we've learnt in Unit 5.**
- Hold up the task flashcards in turn and elicit the words. Stick them on one side of the board. Point to them during the lesson to reinforce your instructions.

Pupil's Book Activity 1

Listen and number. Write and say.

▶ *CD2 Track 53 p266*
- (Books open.) Point to each of the photos and elicit the words.
- Play the CD. Pause after each sentence. The pupils write the correct number in the circles.
- Play the CD again. The pupils write the correct verb under each photo. Then they say the verbs.

Answers: **1** play **2** make **3** drink **4** take **5** skate **6** wave **7** dance **8** listen **9** eat **10** smile

Pupil's Book Activity 2

Listen. Act out. Ask and answer.

▶ *CD2 Track 54 p266*
- (Books open.) Ask the pupils to look at the photographs. Read the conversation together.
- **Talk Partners** In threes, the pupils take turns to mime and ask questions to guess the activity.

Pupil's Book Activity 3: Cooperative learning

Sing *Well done!*

▶ *CD2 Track 55 p266*
- Praise the class for their hard work and play the *Well done!* song. The pupils join in.

Stick the *Give Me Five!* sticker.
- The pupils stick the *Give Me Five!* sticker on the Pupil's Book page.

Activity Book

Activity 1

Find, circle and write.
- (Books open.) First, encourage the pupils to name all the adjectives in the illustrations. Then focus their attention on the word search. Say **Can you find the words?** The pupils work individually to circle the words and write them next to the corresponding illustration to complete the description of the snowman.
- **Talk Partners** The pupils check their answers with a Talk Partner.

Answers: **1** clean **2** fat **3** tall **4** thin **5** dirty **6** short

Activity 2

Order the sentences.
- Ask a volunteer to try to read the words in the first sentence in the correct order. Repeat for the remaining examples. Pupils write the words.
- **Talk Partners** The pupils check answers with a Talk Partner.

Answers: **1** They're taking a photo. **2** We're listening to music. **3** They're making a snowman. **4** We're drinking hot chocolate.

Activity 3 My progress

Use your traffic light. Listen to the teacher and point.
- (Books closed.) Ask the class to take out their traffic light cut-out. Say **Let's think about our work in this unit.** Read the first self-assessment statement. Point to the green circle and say **Yes, I can do this very well.** Point to the orange circle and say **Yes, I can do this.** Point to the red circle, shake your head, and say **No, I can't do this.**
- Read the remaining statements. For each one, the pupils point to the colour on their traffic light that shows how they feel about their own learning.

Self-assessment statements
1. I can say and write the ten action words.
2. I can ask and answer about actions people are doing.
3. I can read a fable.
4. I can understand a moral.
5. I work well with my Talk Partner.

Recycled vocabulary
- The pupils look at the picture and write the word.

Answer: bridge

Ending the lesson

Review the task flashcards.
- Point to the task flashcards. Say **Look at the activities you've done today. Which was your favourite?** Elicit the pupils' favourite activity.

Sing a song (optional).
- The class chooses their favourite song from the unit. The class sings and does the actions.

Extra activities

Reinforcement
- Play *Memory!* (see p23) with the word cards and flashcards.

Extension
- Ask the pupils to look again at the word search (Activity Book Activity 1). Can they see any more adjectives?

Cooperative learning

Think-Pair-Share
- Ask **Can you remember the ten action words?** Ask the pupils to think silently on their own for a minute.
- **Talk Partners** The pupils work with a Talk Partner to remember and name all ten words.
- Invite a pair to say one of the activities. Hold up the corresponding flashcard and prompt the class to repeat the word.
- Finally, repeat the procedure, asking different pairs of pupils each time, until all ten words have been named.

Key Competences and Key Learning Outcomes

- Watch and understand a video about making snowmen
- Say what your snowman is like
- Learn to be creative

Key language

- *apple, arms, body, carrot, clean, creative, dirty, fat, hat, head, lemon, make a snowman, nose, scarf, short, tall, thin, twigs*

Materials

- Pupil's Book p59; Activity Book p56; Class CD2; Video; Teacher's App on Navio
- Teacher's Resource Bank: Task flashcards: *number, read, tick, listen, write, draw*

Optional materials

- Teacher's Resource Bank: Trinity Exam Practice cards (selected from Unit 5)

At a Glance Lesson Plan

Starting the lesson

- Use the Trinity Exam Practice cards (optional).
- Sing the *What are they doing?* song.

▶ ***CD2 Track 44 p265***

- Set learning outcomes and use the task flashcards.

Pre-watching activity

- Look at the photos and talk about playing in the snow.

Activity 1

- Watch the video.

Unit 5 video p279

- Number the pictures.

Activity 2

- Watch the video again.

Unit 5 video

- Read and tick (✓) or cross (✗).

Activity 3

- Read and think. Colour.

Go to the Activity Book.

Pupil's Book

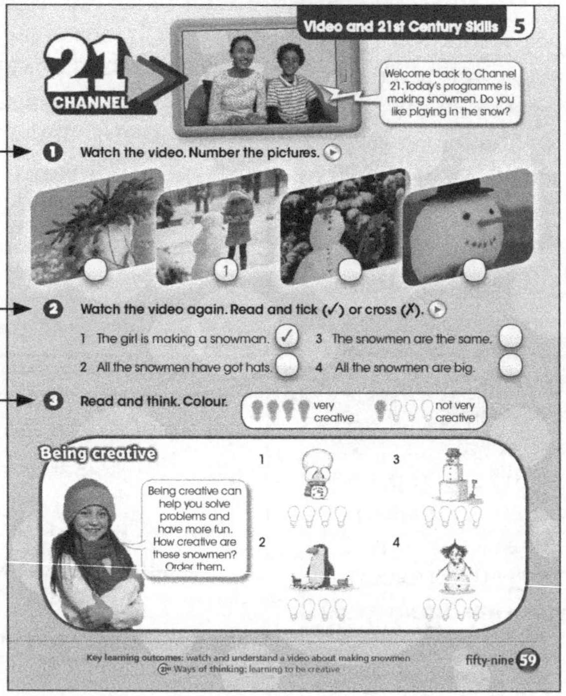

Ending the lesson

- Review the lesson.
- Review the task flashcards. Elicit the pupils' favourite activities.

Extra activity

Extension

- Picture dictation.

Digital resources

Teacher's Digital: Don't forget you can teach this lesson using the Teacher's App on Navio.

Pupil's Digital: Encourage your pupils to use the Pupil's App on Navio to practise the vocabulary from this lesson.

Powered By NAVIO

Activity Book

Activity Book

Activity 1

- Listen and number.

▶ ***CD2 Track 56 p266***

Activity 2

- Think and write. Draw your snowman.

Recycled vocabulary

- Look, remember and write the word.

Starting the lesson

Use the Trinity Exam Practice cards (optional).

- The pupils practise asking and answering questions. (See p31.)

Sing the *What are they doing?* song.

- Sing the *What are they doing?* song from Lesson 4 page 54. Ask the pupils to make up some actions to do as they sing along.

▶ *CD2 Track 44 p265*

Set learning outcomes and use the task flashcards.

- Say **Today we're going to watch a video and then ask and answer questions about snowmen**.
- Hold up the task flashcards, in turn, and elicit the activities. Stick them on the side of the board. Point to them during the lesson to reinforce your instructions.

Pre-watching activity

- Read out the speech bubble. Ask **Do you like playing in the snow?** Elicit answers.

Pupil's Book Activity 1

Watch the video. Number the pictures. *p279*

- Ask **What is the weather like in England? What does Sophie like doing in the snow?** Play Part 1 to find out.
- Focus the pupils' attention on the video stills. Ask **What do the children use to make the snowmen?**
- Play Part 2, pausing after the first video still. Ask the pupils to point to the corresponding photo in their book. Point out the number one.
- Play the rest of Part 2 for pupils to number the pictures.

Answers: 3 1 4 2

Pupil's Book Activity 2

Watch the video again. Read and tick (✓) or cross (✗).

- Read out the sentences for the pupils to follow.
- The pupils draw a tick or a cross next to the sentences. Play Part 2 for the pupils to check their answers.
- Ask the pupils some questions to check understanding. Suggested questions.
  How does the girl make the snowman's body? *(She rolls the snow into a big ball.)*
  What's the snowman's nose made from? *(A carrot.)*
  What colour are the snowmen's scarves? *(Blue and pink.)*
  What does Sophie want to use for the snowman's nose? *(An orange.)*
  What does Tom want to use for the snowman's hair? *(Leaves.)*

Answers: 1 ✓ 2 ✗ 3 ✗ 4 ✗

Pupil's Book Activity 3

Read and think. Colour.

- On the board copy the creative key. Draw a snowman on the board and describe your snowman, for example, **It's tall. It has got flowers for hair. It's wearing a woolly hat.** Point to the key and explain what it means and colour the light bulbs to represent how creative the pupils think your snowman is.
- Read out the speech bubble. The pupils look at the pictures of the snowman, think how creative they are, colour the key and then order them from not creative to very creative.

Answers: Pupils' own answers

Activity Book

Activity 1

Listen and number.

▶ *CD2 Track 56 p266*

- Ask different pupils to describe a snowman. Make sure they use full sentences, for example, *It's wearing a hat. It's got a carrot for a nose.*
- Explain they will hear people describing the snowmen and they have to number the pictures in the order they hear them. Play the first exchange on the CD. Ask **Which picture? Why?** *(The snowman is tall and thin. He's got twigs for arms and leaves for hair. He's got an apple for a nose.)*
- Play the rest of the CD, pausing after each exchange, for pupils to number the pictures.

Answers: Top row left to right: 4, 1
Bottom row left to right: 3, 2

Activity 2

Think and write. Draw your snowman.

- Read out the speech bubble and explain that the pupils plan their snowman and complete the description. The pupils then draw their snowman.
  Talk Partners Pupils take turns to point to their pictures and describe their snowman to their partner.

Recycled vocabulary

Answer: eggs

Ending the lesson

Review the lesson.

- Ask **Which activity was easy / difficult?**

Review the task flashcards.

- Point to the task flashcards on the board. Say **Look at the activities you've done today. Which activity was your favourite?**

Extra activity

Extension

- Do a picture dictation. Tell the pupils you are going to describe a snowman and they have to listen and draw what you say. Example dictation: **My snowman has got a fat body and a small head. It's got a tomato for a mouth. It's got potatoes for eyes and an apple for a nose. It has got flowers for hair and long, thin twigs for its arms.**

Date: ______________________ Unit: ____________

1 What did my pupils learn in this unit?

2 How did my pupils work? (✓)

individually ☐ in pairs ☐ in small groups ☐

in large groups ☐ as a class ☐

3 Which key competences did my pupils develop?

- Competence in linguistic communication ☐
- Competence in mathematics, science and technology ☐
- Digital competence ☐
- Learning to learn ☐
- Social and civic competences ☐
- Sense of initiative and entrepreneurship ☐
- Cultural awareness and expression ☐

4 Which lessons / activities were the most successful and why?

5 Which lessons / activities did my pupils find the most difficult and why?

6 What did I try in the classroom for the first time? How did it go?

7 Which resources did I find most useful? (including webpages)

8 What could I do differently next time I teach this unit?

Unit 6 All year round

Unit overview

Key Competences and Key Learning Outcomes

- Identify and say eight seasonal activities (Lesson 1)
- Use present simple: 'we', 'you' and 'they' (Lesson 2)
- Understand and act out a conversation (Lesson 2)
- Read, listen and understand a story about the four seasons (Lesson 3)
- Ask and answer about dates (Lesson 4)
- Read about seasonal festivals in Britain (Lesson 6)
- Watch and understand a video about seasons (Video and 21st Century Skills)

- Use ordinal numbers (Lesson 4)

- Use the Pupil's App on Navio

- Use a strategy to practise spelling key words (Lesson 1)
- Say a tongue twister and practise 'ir' and 'ur' spellings (Lesson 5)
- Review language in the unit and reflect on own learning (Lesson 8)
- Practise activity types found in the Cambridge Exams: Pre A1 Starters

- Understand the importance of working together (Lesson 3)
- Ask and answer about your birthday (Lesson 4)

- Do a class survey about birthdays (Lesson 5)
- Learn to do a survey (Video and 21st Century Skills)

- Sing four songs (Lessons 1, 4, 5 and 8)
- Understand, act out and give an opinion on a story (Lesson 3)
- Think about seasonal festivals where you live (Lesson 6)
- Read, understand and complete a traditional rhyme (Lesson 7)

Vocabulary

Core vocabulary
celebrate Halloween, eat chestnuts, finish school, go to the beach, open presents, plant seeds, smell flowers, wear warm clothes; first – thirty-first; spring, summer, autumn, winter

Extension vocabulary (optional)
spring: look at baby animals; summer: go on holiday, eat ice cream; autumn: play in the leaves, pick apples; winter: play in the snow; eat special food, have a party, send cards, wear a costume

Other vocabulary
cold, cool, hot, warm; America, cousins, postcard; camera, pedalling backwards, poster, project, wheels; Months of the year; *birthday, party; April Fools' Day, carnival, Christmas, crackers, drum, jokes, parade, remember, turkey; leap year*

Recycled vocabulary
Bonfire Night; cake, doll, hat

Structures

Core structures
What do you / they do (in summer)? We (go to the beach). They (go to the beach). Do they (celebrate Halloween)? Yes, they do. No, they don't. When's your birthday? My birthday is on the (eighteenth) of (June).

Other structures
Do you (eat chestnuts in America)? Do you want to come to my party? We pull crackers. We play jokes. We wear (paper hats). We have (a bonfire). What festivals do you celebrate? What do you do on festival days?

Recycled structures
I / We can … It's / We've got … It hasn't got … There are … When's your birthday? My birthday is on …

Phonics

Alternative vowel spellings **'ir'** / **'ur'** (p**ur**ple, t**ur**tle, b**ir**thday, f**ir**st, th**ir**d)

British Culture

Seasonal festivals

Literacy

Text type: a traditional rhyme (text to express)
Reading skills: scanning for specific information; sequencing

21st Century Skills

Ways of working: learning to do a survey

Cooperative learning

Songs: *We can do it!* (Lesson 5); *Well done!* (Lesson 8)
Skills: Working together as a team (Lesson 5); Learning strategies (Lesson 7); Think-Pair-Share (Lesson 8)

Values

The importance of working together.

Cross-curricular links

Links to Science
Seasons and the Sun: the position of the Sun in the different seasons; characteristics of the seasons and position of the Sun; the months in each season

Suggested Arts and Crafts concepts
Identifying and using different patterns, lines, spaces and colours to reflect things in nature; making and carrying out a survey

Key Competences and Key Learning Outcomes

- Identify and say eight seasonal activities
- Say the vocabulary chant
- Stick the seasonal activities stickers

- Use a strategy to practise spelling key words

- Sing a song about seasons

Key language

- *celebrate Halloween, eat chestnuts, finish school, go to the beach, open presents, plant seeds, smell flowers, wear warm clothes*

Extension vocabulary

- *spring: look at baby animals; summer: go on holiday, eat ice cream; autumn: play in the leaves, pick apples; winter: play in the snow*

Recycled: *autumn, spring, summer, winter*

Other vocabulary: *cold, cool, hot, warm*

Materials

- Pupil's Book p60; Activity Book pp58 and 67; Class CD3; Teacher's App on Navio; Unit 6 stickers
- Seasonal activities flashcards; seasons flashcards
- Teacher's Resource Bank: Seasonal activities word cards
- Teacher's Resource Bank: Task flashcards: *listen, sing, read, stick, say, circle, write*

Optional materials

- Teacher's Resource Bank: Five Trinity Exam Practice cards (selected from the Starter Unit and Units 1, 2, 3, 4 and 5)

At a Glance Lesson Plan

Pupil's Book

Starting the lesson

- Use the Trinity Exam Practice cards (optional).
- Review action verbs. Play *Can you guess?*
- Set learning outcomes using the task flashcards.

Vocabulary presentation

- Present the new vocabulary.

Activity 1

- Listen and point.

▶ *CD3 Track 1 p267*

- Sing *What's your favourite season?*

Word cards

- Read the word cards.
- Match them to the flashcards.

Activity 2

- Read and stick the eight stickers.
- Listen and say the chant.

▶ *CD3 Track 3 p267*

Go to the Activity Book.

Unit 6 All year round

Lesson 1 Vocabulary

1 Listen and point. Sing *What's your favourite season?*

What's your favourite season?
Is it spring?
Spring, when it's warm outside.
We smell flowers.
We plant seeds.
My favourite season is spring.
What's your favourite season?
Is it summer?
Summer, when it's hot outside.
We finish school.
We go to the beach.
My favourite season is summer.

What's your favourite season?
Is it autumn?
Autumn, when it's cool outside.
We eat chestnuts.
We celebrate Halloween.
My favourite season is autumn.
What's your favourite season?
Is it winter?
Winter, when it's cold outside.
We wear warm clothes.
We open presents.
My favourite season is winter.

spring summer autumn winter

2 Read and stick the eight stickers. Listen and say the chant.

smell flowers plant seeds finish school go to the beach

Learning to learn: Spelling: go to page 67 in your Activity Book.

60 sixty

Ending the lesson

- Review the lesson.
- Review the task flashcards.

Extra activity

Vocabulary extension

- Present six additional vocabulary items.

Learning to learn

Spelling

- Practise spelling at any time during this unit (Activity Book p67).

Digital resources

Teacher's Digital: Don't forget you can teach this lesson using the Teacher's App on Navio.

Pupil's Digital: Encourage your pupils to use the Pupil's App on Navio to practise the vocabulary from this lesson.

Powered By NAVIO

Activity Book

Unit 6 All year round

Lesson 1 Vocabulary

1 Read and circle.

1 We finish school in ...	autumn.	summer.
2 We plant seeds in ...	summer.	spring.
3 We open presents in ...	winter.	summer.
4 We smell flowers in ...	autumn.	spring.
5 We wear warm clothes in ...	summer.	winter.
6 We eat chestnuts in ...	autumn.	spring.

2 Look and write.

plant seeds wear warm clothes go to the beach

1 We plant seeds in spring. 2 We

3 We in autumn. 4 We

58 fifty-eight

Spelling 6 Learning to learn

Let's practise spelling!

Look	Copy	Cover and write
1 plant seeds		
2 smell flowers		
3 finish school		
4 go to the beach		
5 eat chestnuts		
6 celebrate Halloween		
7 wear warm clothes		
8 open presents		

sixty-seven

Activity Book

Activity 1

- Read and circle.

Activity 2

- Look and write.

Recycled vocabulary

- Look, remember and write the phrase.

Spelling

Let's practise spelling!

- Use the *Look-Copy-Cover-Write technique.*

Recycled vocabulary

- Look, remember and write the phrase.

Starting the lesson

Use the Trinity Exam Practice cards (optional).

- The pupils practise asking and answering questions. (See p31.)

Review action verbs. Play *Can you guess?*

- Play *Can you guess?* (See p55.)

Set learning outcomes using the task flashcards.

- Explain the aims of the lesson. Say **Today we're going to learn about the activities we do in each season.**
- Hold up the task flashcards and elicit the words. Stick them on one side of the board. Point to them during the lesson to reinforce your instructions.

Vocabulary presentation

Present the new vocabulary.

- (Books closed.) If you have a calendar, show it to the pupils and ask **What season are we in? How many seasons are there in a year?** Elicit the four seasons and stick the flashcards up as the pupils name them. Ask **What do we do in summer?** Show the first summer activity flashcard and say **We finish school in summer.** Show the beach flashcard and say **We go to the beach in summer.** Repeat for the remaining seasons and activities. Stick the flashcards on the board in the order they appear in the song.
- (Books open.) Ask **Where are Molly, Jake, Beth and Toby? What can you see?** The pupils point to and name the different features in the scene. Ask the pupils to point to each season on the page.

Pupil's Book Activity 1

Listen and point. Sing *What's your favourite season?*

▶ ***CD3 Track 1 p267***

- Say **Let's listen to the song.** Play the CD and point to the flashcards of the seasons as you hear them.
- Play the CD again. The pupils sing and do the actions.

Word cards

Read the word cards. Match them to the flashcards.

- (Books closed.) Hold up one of the activity word cards. The pupils read collectively. A pupil sticks the word card next to the flashcard on the board. Repeat.
- Point to each word card. The pupils read the words.

Pupil's Book Activity 2

Read and stick the eight stickers. Listen and say the chant.

▶ ***CD3 Track 3 p267***

- Ask a pupil to read the first phrase. The pupils stick the corresponding sticker above the phrase.
- **Talk Partners** The pupils find and stick the remaining stickers. Encourage them to use cooperative language.
- Say **Let's listen and say the words.** Play the CD. The pupils listen and say the chant, pointing to the stickers in turn.

Activity Book

Activity 1

Read and circle.

- (Books open.) Ask a volunteer to read out the first sentence and complete it with the correct season. Repeat for the remaining sentences. The pupils work individually to circle the correct seasons.
- **Talk Partners** The pupils check their answers with a Talk Partner.

Answers: **1** summer **2** spring **3** winter **4** spring **5** winter **6** autumn

Activity 2

Look and write.

- (Books open.) Ask the pupils to decide which activity we do in spring and look at the example answer. Repeat for the other seasons. The pupils write the words.

Answers: **1** plant seeds **2** go to the beach **3** celebrate Halloween **4** wear warm clothes

Recycled vocabulary

- The pupils look at the picture and write the phrase.

Answer: listen to music

Ending the lesson

Review the lesson.

- Say **Today we've learnt the activities we do each season. What activities do you remember?** Elicit activities from the pupils.

Review the task flashcards.

- Point to the task flashcards. Say **Look at the activities you've done today. Which was your favourite?** Elicit the pupils' favourite activities.

Extra activity

Vocabulary extension

- Present six additional activities for each season: *spring: look at baby animals; summer: go on holiday, eat ice cream; autumn: play in the leaves, pick apples; winter: play in the snow.*
- Use the Vocabulary Booster on Navio to practise these new words.

Spelling (Activity Book p67)

Let's practise spelling!

- The pupils can practise spelling the eight phrases using the *Look-Copy-Cover-Write* technique at any time before the Lesson 8 Review.

Recycled vocabulary

- The pupils look at the picture and write the phrase.

Answer: take a photo

Key Competences and Key Learning Outcomes

- Use present simple: 'we', 'you' and 'they'
- Understand and act out a grammar conversation
- Complete and practise a conversation
- Identify the position of the Sun in different seasons (optional)
- Listen for specific information

Key language
- *celebrate Halloween, eat chestnuts, finish school, go to the beach, open presents, plant seeds, smell flowers, wear warm clothes*
- *What do you / they do (in spring)? We / They (go to the beach). Do they (celebrate Halloween)? Yes, they do. No, they don't.*

Other vocabulary: *America, cousin, postcard*

Materials
- Pupil's Book p61; Activity Book p59; Class CD3; Teacher's App on Navio
- Seasonal activities flashcards; seasons flashcards
- Teacher's Resource Bank: Task flashcards: *listen, act out, tick, match, write, think, draw, Talk Partners*

Optional materials
- Teacher's Resource Bank: Five Trinity Exam Practice cards (selected from the Starter Unit and Units 1, 2, 3, 4 and 5)

At a Glance Lesson Plan

Pupil's Book

Starting the lesson
- Use the Trinity Exam Practice cards (optional).
- Review the *What's your favourite season?* song.
- ▶ *CD3 Track 1 p267*
- ▶ *CD3 Track 2 p267 (optional karaoke version)*
- Set learning outcomes using the task flashcards.

Activity 1
- Listen and repeat.
- ▶ *CD3 Track 4 p267*
- Talk Partners Act out.

Activity 2
- Listen and tick (✓).
- ▶ *CD3 Track 5 p267*
- Go to the Activity Book.

Ending the lesson
- Review the lesson.
- Review the task flashcards.

Extra activity

Reinforcement
- Play *Pick up two.*

Link to Science
- **The Sun:** the position of the Sun in the different seasons

Digital resources

Teacher's Digital: Don't forget you can teach this lesson using the Teacher's App on Navio.

Pupil's Digital: Encourage your pupils to use the Pupil's App on Navio to practise the vocabulary from this lesson.

Powered By NAVIO

Activity Book

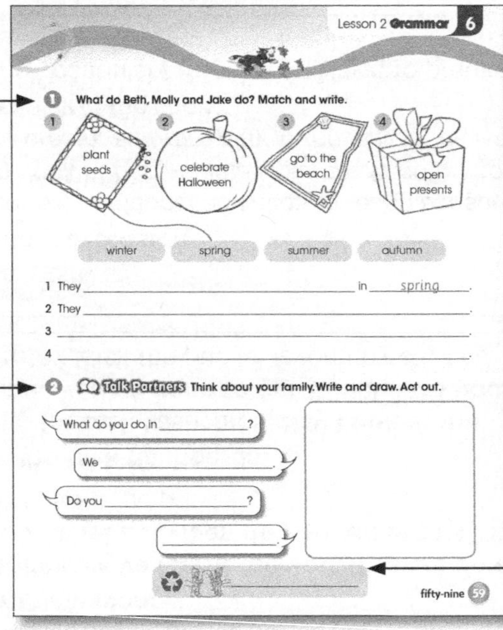

Activity Book

Activity 1
- What do Beth, Molly and Jake do? Match and write.
- Talk Partners Act out.

Activity 2
- Think about your family. Write and draw.

Recycled vocabulary
- Look, remember and write the phrase.

Starting the lesson

Use the Trinity Exam Practice cards (optional).

- The pupils practise asking and answering questions. (See p31.)

Review the *What's your favourite season?* song.

▶ *CD3 Track 1 p267*

▶ *CD3 Track 2 p267 (optional karaoke version)*

- Organise the pupils into four groups. Allocate a season to each group. Play the CD (or use the karaoke version). Encourage the pupils to sing along and do the actions for their season. Change the groups around and sing the song again.

Set learning outcomes using the task flashcards.

- Explain the aims of the lesson. Say **Today we're going to ask and answer about the activities that we do in the different seasons.**
- Hold up the task flashcards and elicit the words. Stick them on one side of the board. Point to them during the lesson to reinforce your instructions.

Pupil's Book Activity 1

Listen and repeat. Act out.

▶ *CD3 Track 4 p267*

- (Books open.) Ask **Who can you see? What's Beth got?**
- Play the CD. The pupils listen and read the conversation. Check understanding. Ask **Who's the postcard from? Where do they live? What do they do in America in summer and autumn?**
- Play the CD again. Pause for the pupils to repeat.
- Organise the class into groups of three (Beth, Jake and Molly). The groups practise the conversation.

Pupil's Book Activity 2

Listen and tick (✓).

▶ *CD3 Track 5 p267*

- (Books open.) Focus attention on the second activity and name the activities in each pair.
- Say **Let's listen. What do they do each season?** Play the CD. Pause after each conversation. The pupils tick the corresponding activity for each month. Repeat with the remaining conversations, pausing after each one to check the pupils' answers.

Answers: **1** eat chestnuts **2** smell flowers **3** open presents

Activity Book

Activity 1

What do Beth, Molly and Jake do? Match and write.

- (Books open.) Focus the pupils' attention on the illustrated word boxes. Ask **Which season do Beth, Molly and Jake do each activity?** Encourage the pupils to complete the sentences using the verbs and the corresponding season.

Answers: **1** They plant seeds in spring. **2** They celebrate Halloween in autumn. **3** They go to the beach in summer. **4** They open presents in winter.

Activity 2

Think about your family. Write and draw. Act out.

- The pupils write and ask and answer about activities they do with their own families. Invite a pupil to read the first speech bubble and add a season. A second pupil adds an appropriate activity for that season and then the first pupil asks their partner about it.
- **Talk Partners** The pupils complete and practise their own conversation with a Talk Partner. Invite different pairs of pupils to read out their conversations for their classmates.

Recycled vocabulary

- The pupils look at the picture and write the phrase.

Answer: make a snowman

Ending the lesson

Review the lesson.

- Say **Today you've talked about different activities people do during the year.** Elicit some activities.

Review the task flashcards.

- Point to the task flashcards. Say **Look at the activities you've done today. Which activity was your favourite?** Elicit the pupils' favourite activities.

Extra activity

Reinforcement

- Play *Pick up two.* Stick the seasonal activity flashcards face down on the left-hand side of the board. Stick the seasons flashcards face down on the right-hand side of the board. Divide the class into two teams. Teams take turns to select a volunteer to pick two cards – one from the left and one from the right. The pupils should make the corresponding sentence. If it's true, they gain a point and the activity card is removed from the game. If it's false, both cards are replaced where they were. Continue until no activity cards remain. The team with the most points wins.

Link to Science

- If you are studying the Science topic of **the Sun** in English, you could talk about the characteristics of each season in more detail and describe the position of the Sun in each one. Say **In summer, the Sun is high in the sky. In winter, the Sun is low in the sky.**

Key Competences and Key Learning Outcomes

- Read, listen and understand a story about the four seasons
- Read the story with some fluency
- Identify characteristics of seasons and position of the Sun (optional)
- Become familiar with the story through a pre-reading task
- Understand the importance of working together
- Understand and act out the story
- Give an opinion on the story

Key language

- *Do you (eat chestnuts in America), too? Yes, we do.*

Recycled: *January, February, March, April, May, June, July, August, September, October, November, December;* Seasons; *eat chestnuts, smell flowers, take photos*

Recycled: *I can (smell the flowers). We can (help you). We've got (our camera). It's (spring) now. There are (chestnuts). The tree has got (leaves). It hasn't got (leaves).*

Other vocabulary: *camera, pedalling backwards, poster, project, wheels*

Materials

- Pupil's Book pp62–63; Activity Book p60; Class CD3; Teacher's App on Navio
- Teacher's Resource Bank: Task flashcards: *listen, read, Talk Partners, act out, write, number, draw*
- Teacher's Resource Bank: Unit 6 Lesson 3 Animated Story

Optional materials

- Teacher's Resource Bank: Five Trinity Exam Practice cards (selected from the Starter Unit and Units 1, 2, 3, 4 and 5)

At a Glance Lesson Plan

Starting the lesson

- Use the Trinity Exam Practice cards (optional).
- Review the *What's your favourite season?* song.
- ▶ ***CD3 Track 1 p267***
- ▶ ***CD3 Track 2 p267 (optional karaoke version)***
- Set learning outcomes using the task flashcards.

Before you read

- Read and answer the question.

Activity 1

- Listen and read.
- ▶ ***CD3 Track 6 p267***
- **Talk Partners** Act out.
- ***Now watch the animated story!***

After you read: Activity 2

- Go to page 60 in your Activity Book.
- Values: Read and write.

Ending the lesson

- Review the lesson.
- Review the task flashcards.

Pupil's Book

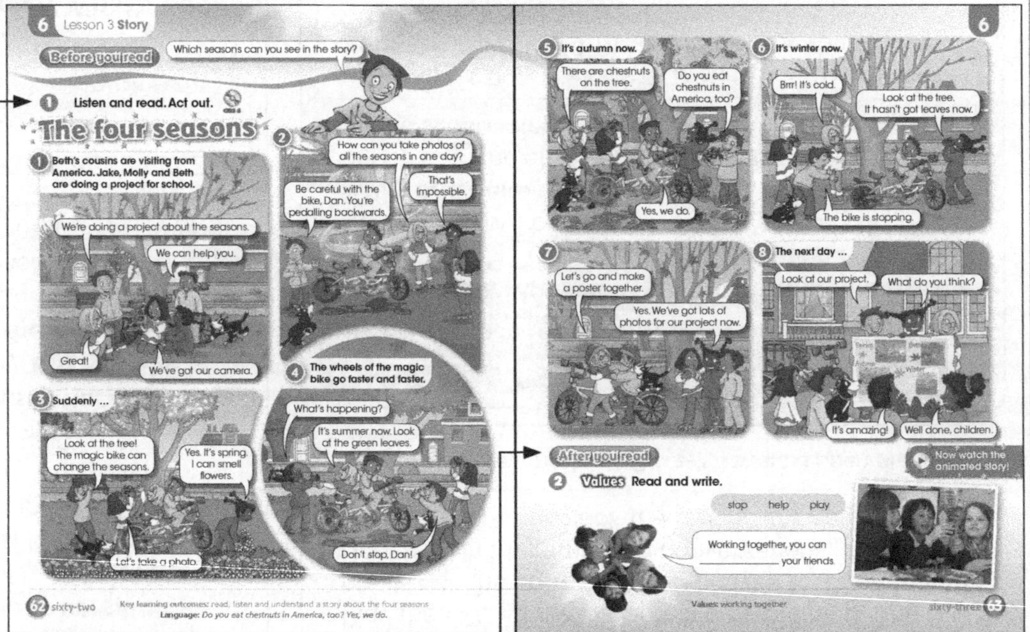

Extra activity

Extension

- Make a seasons chart.

Link to Science

- **The Sun:** characteristics of the seasons and position of the Sun

Digital resources

Teacher's Digital: Don't forget you can teach this lesson using the Teacher's App on Navio.

Pupil's Digital: Encourage your pupils to use the Pupil's App on Navio to practise the vocabulary from this lesson.

Powered By NAVIO

Activity Book

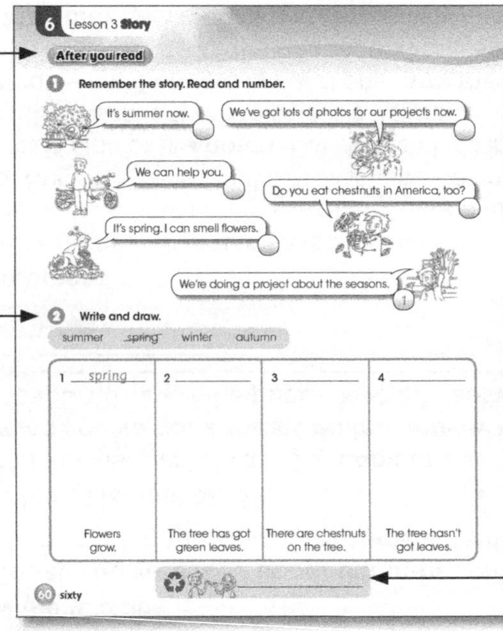

Activity Book

After you read: Activity 1

- Remember the story. Read and number.

Recycled vocabulary

- Look, remember and write the word.

Activity 2

- Write and draw.

Starting the lesson

Use the Trinity Exam Practice cards (optional).

- The pupils practise asking and answering questions. (See p31.)

Review the *What's your favourite season?* song.

▶ *CD3 Track 1 p267*

▶ *CD3 Track 2 p267 (optional karaoke version)*

- Sing *What's your favourite season?* from Lesson 1.
- Divide the class into two groups. Ask one group to sing the questions and the other to sing the responses. All the pupils join in with the last line of each verse. Play the CD (or use the karaoke version).

Set learning outcomes using the task flashcards.

- Say **Today we're going to listen to a story.**
- Hold up the task flashcards and elicit the words. Stick them on one side of the board. Point to them during the lesson to reinforce your instructions.

Before you read

Read and answer the question.

- (Books open.) Focus the class on the pre-reading task. Ask **Which seasons can you see in the story?** The pupils scan the text to find the answer. *(Spring, summer, autumn and winter.)*

Pupil's Book Activity 1

Listen and read. Act out.

▶ *CD3 Track 6 p267*

- (Books open.) Play the CD. The pupils follow the text with their finger. Pause between each story frame to check understanding.

Suggested comprehension questions

- Frame 1: **Who is visiting?** *(Beth's cousins.)*
- Frame 2: **Where are the children?** *(In the park.)*
- Frame 3: **What happens to the tree?** *(It changes.)*
- Frame 4: **What season is it now? How do you know?** *(It's summer. The tree has got green leaves.)*
- Frame 5: **What colour are the leaves now? Why?** *(They're yellow and brown. It's autumn now.)*
- Frame 6: **What season is it now? Has the tree got leaves?** *(It's winter. The tree hasn't got leaves.)*
- Frame 7: **Can the children do their homework now?** *(Yes, they can.)*
- Frame 8: **Is the project finished? It is good?** *(Yes. It's amazing!)*
- Ask **Did you like the story? What part did you like best?**
- Talk Partners The pupils choose their favourite frame.
- Organise the class into five groups. (Jake, Molly, Beth, Dan and Grace, the American cousins).
- Play the CD. Each group joins in when their character speaks. If necessary, pause the CD after each sentence for the pupils to repeat.
- The pupils swap roles and repeat the activity.

After you read

Pupil's Book Activity 2

Go to page 60 in your Activity Book.

Activity Book

After you read: Activity 1

Remember the story. Read and number.

- (Books open.) Ask the pupils to read the speech bubbles from the story to find the first one. The pupils read and order the speech bubbles individually.

Answers: 4 6 2 5 3 1

Activity 2

Write and draw.

- (Books open.) The pupils read the text in each box and decide if the corresponding season is spring, summer, autumn or winter. Encourage the pupils to draw the tree from the story as it appears in each season.

Recycled vocabulary

- The pupils look at the picture and write the word.

Answer: wave

Pupil's Book Activity 2

Values: Read and write.

- Focus attention on the photograph and discuss how by working together we can help our friends.
- Ask the pupils if they help each other.

Ending the lesson

Review the lesson.

- Say **Today we've listened to a story about the four seasons. Today you've learnt that it's important to work together and help our friends.**

Review the task flashcards.

- Point to the task flashcards. Say **Look at the activities you've done today. Which activity was your favourite?** Elicit the pupils' favourite activities.

Extra activity

Extension

- Make a seasons chart on the board to compare the seasonal differences. Spring: flowers grow; summer: trees have got green leaves; autumn: trees have got brown leaves; winter: trees haven't got leaves.

Link to Science

- If you are studying the Science topic of **the Sun** in English, you could talk to the pupils about why we have seasons. Remind them that we have seasons because the Earth is tilted.
- Remind them that the Earth is a planet that turns causing us to experience day and night. Remind them that when it's daytime in England, it's the night in Australia, because it is on the other side of the planet.

Lesson 4

Key Competences and Key Learning Outcomes

- Ask and answer about dates
- Use ordinal numbers
- Ask and answer about your birthday
- Sing a song

Key language

- *first, second, third, fourth, fifth, sixth … thirty-first*
- *When's your birthday? My birthday is on the (eighteenth) of (June).*

Extension vocabulary

- *eat special food, have a party, send cards, wear a costume*

Recycled: *cake*

Other vocabulary: Months of the year; *birthday, party*

Materials

- Pupil's Book p64; Activity Book p61; Class CD3; Teacher's App on Navio
- Teacher's Resource Bank: Task flashcards: *listen, say, sing, Talk Partners, circle, read, write, find*

Optional materials

- Teacher's Resource Bank: Five Trinity Exam Practice cards (selected from the Starter Unit and Units 1, 2, 3, 4 and 5)
- A calendar
- Coloured pencils or crayons

At a Glance Lesson Plan

Pupil's Book

Starting the lesson

- Use the Trinity Exam Practice cards (optional).
- Review the Lesson 3 story.
- Set learning outcomes using the task flashcards.

Vocabulary presentation

- Present the new vocabulary.
- Play *Line up*.

Activity 1

- Listen, point and say.

▶ *CD3 Track 7 p267*

Activity 2

- Listen and point. Sing *When's your birthday?*

▶ *CD3 Track 8 p267*

Activity 3

- Listen and repeat.
- Talk Partners Ask and answer.

▶ *CD3 Track 9 p267*

Go to the Activity Book.

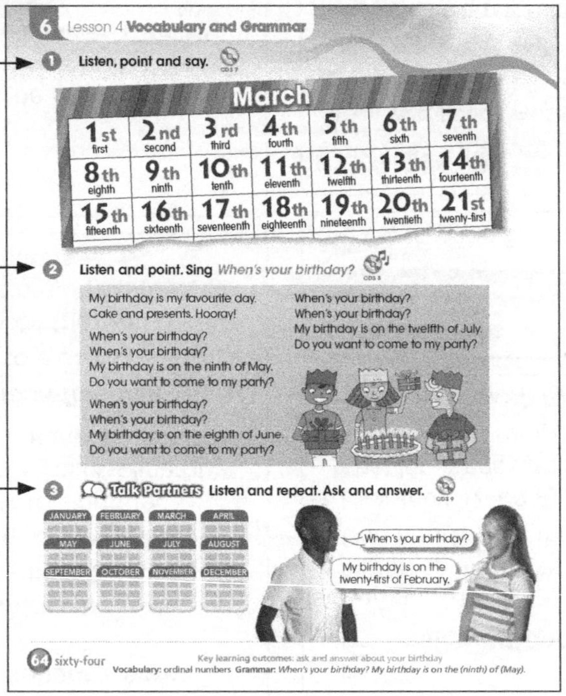

Ending the lesson

- Review the lesson.
- Review the task flashcards.

Extra activities

Reinforcement

- Practise ordinal numbers.

Vocabulary extension

- Present four additional vocabulary items.

Digital resources

Teacher's Digital: Don't forget you can teach this lesson using the Teacher's App on Navio.

Pupil's Digital: Encourage your pupils to use the Pupil's App on Navio to practise the vocabulary from this lesson.

Powered By NAVIO

Activity Book

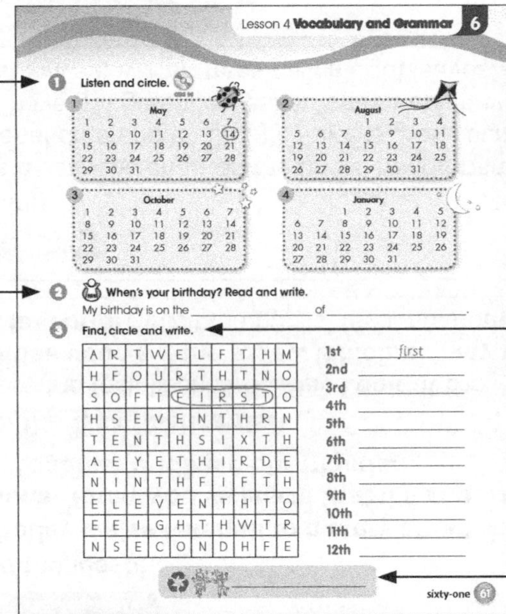

Activity Book

Activity 1

- Listen and circle.

▶ *CD3 Track 10 p267*

Activity 2

- When's your birthday? Read and write.

Activity 3

- Find, circle and write.

Recycled vocabulary

- Look, remember and write the word.

Starting the lesson

Use the Trinity Exam Practice cards (optional).

- The pupils practise asking and answering questions. (See p31.)

Review the Lesson 3 story.

- Read one of the speech bubbles from the story and ask the pupils to scan the story to locate the corresponding frame, e.g. **Be careful with the bike, Dan. You're pedalling backwards.** *(Frame 2.)*

Set learning outcomes using the task flashcards.

- Say **Today we're going to ask and answer questions about birthdays.**
- Hold up the task flashcards in turn and elicit the words. Stick them on one side of the board. Point to them during the lesson to reinforce your instructions.

Vocabulary presentation

Present the new vocabulary.

- (Books open.) Point to the illustration and say **Look at the calendar. Let's say the dates.** If you have a calendar, show it to the pupils. Point to the dates in turn and say them. Encourage the pupils to repeat.
- (Books closed.) Play *Line up.* Choose a pupil to be first in line and elicit *I'm first.* Repeat for second to sixth, e.g. *I'm second, I'm third,* etc. Point to each pupil and ask the class to state the order.
- Add another pupil to the line and tell the pupils that this pupil is seventh. Point to the pupils fourth, fifth, sixth and seventh in turn emphasising the 'th' sound. Continue until you have 20 pupils. Emphasise the pronunciation of 'twentieth'. For the 21st, 22nd and 23rd pupils, point out that we say twenty-first, twenty-second and twenty-third.

Pupil's Book Activity 1

Listen, point and say.

▶ *CD3 Track 7 p267*

- Say **Let's listen and repeat the words.** Play the CD. The pupils repeat each word, pointing to the corresponding date each time. Play the CD again and repeat the activity.

Pupil's Book Activity 2

Listen and point. Sing *When's your birthday?*

▶ *CD3 Track 8 p267*

- (Books open.) Point to the illustration. Ask **What can you see?**
- Play the CD. The pupils listen and point to the dates on the calendar. Play the CD again. The pupils sing.

Pupil's Book Activity 3

Listen and repeat. Ask and answer.

▶ *CD3 Track 9 p267*

- Ask the pupils to look at the activity and play the CD. Play the CD again and ask the pupils to repeat the question and answer.
- **Talk Partners** The pupils ask and answer about the date of their own birthdays with a Talk Partner.

Activity Book

Activity 1

Listen and circle.

▶ *CD3 Track 10 p267*

- (Books open.) Focus attention on the first activity. Play the CD. Pause after the first exchange to check understanding. Repeat with the remaining exchanges. The pupils circle the correct dates on the calendars.

Answers: **1** 14th **2** 17th **3** 16th **4** 13th

Activity 2 (me)

When's your birthday? Read and write.

- (Books open.) Ask the pupils to read the question, state their own birthday and write it in the space.

Activity 3

Find, circle and write.

- Tell the pupils to look at the word search to find the dates.
- **Talk Partners** They can work with a Talk Partner to find the words together. Encourage them to say *Look, here's (twelfth). Let's write it down.*

Recycled vocabulary

- The pupils look at the picture and write the word.

Answer: dance

Ending the lesson

Review the lesson.

- Say **Today we've talked about birthdays.** Ask the pupils to say when their birthday is.

Review the task flashcards.

- Point to the task flashcards. Say **Look at the activities you've done today. Which activity was your favourite?** Elicit the pupils' favourite activities.

Extra activities

Reinforcement

- Practise ordinal numbers. Ask the pupils to line up their coloured pencils or crayons.
- **Talk Partners** The pupils take turns to state the order *(first, second, third).*

Vocabulary extension

- Use the Vocabulary Booster on Navio and present and practise four additional seasonal activities: *eat special food, have a party, send cards, wear a costume.*

Key Competences and Key Learning Outcomes

- Say a tongue twister with the 'ir' sound
- Learn and practise 'ir' and 'ur' spellings
- Listen for specific information
- Sing a cooperative learning song
- Do a class survey about birthdays

Key language

- *bird, birthday, first, girl, nurse, purple, shirt, surf, third, thirty, Thursday, turn, turtle*

Recycled: Ordinal numbers, Months of the year

Recycled: *How do you spell …? When's your birthday? My birthday is on the (eighteenth of July). When's yours?*

Materials

- Pupil's Book p65; Activity Book p62; Class CD3; Teacher's App on Navio
- Teacher's Resource Bank: Task flashcards: *listen, say, sing, write, cut out, colour, think, Talk Partners*
- Teacher's Resource Bank: Unit 6 Lesson 5 Activity 4 cut-out
- Scissors

Optional materials

- Teacher's Resource Bank: Five Trinity Exam Practice cards (selected from the Starter Unit and Units 1, 2, 3, 4 and 5)

At a Glance Lesson Plan

Pupil's Book

Starting the lesson

- Use the Trinity Exam Practice cards (optional).
- Review the *When's your birthday?* song.
- ▶ *CD3 Track 8 p267*
- Set learning outcomes using the task flashcards.

Activity 1

- Listen and say.
- ▶ *CD3 Track 11 p268*
- Go to the Activity Book.
- Go to Magic Phonics.

Activity 2 – Cooperative learning

- Sing *We can do it!*
- ▶ *CD3 Track 12 p268*

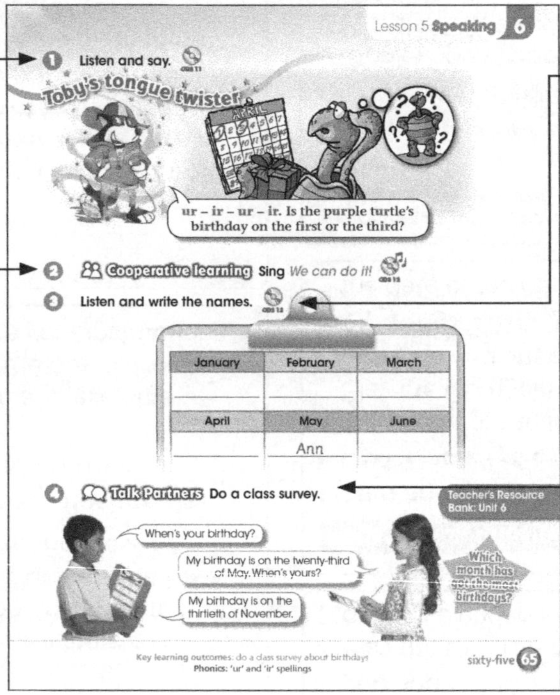

Activity 3

- Listen and write the names.
- ▶ *CD3 Track 13 p268*

Activity 4

- Talk Partners
  Do a class survey (Teacher's Resource Bank).

Ending the lesson

- Review the lesson.
- Review the task flashcards.

Cooperative learning

Working together as a team

- Talk Partners
  Play *Beat the clock.*
- Add to the pronunciation wall.

Activity Book

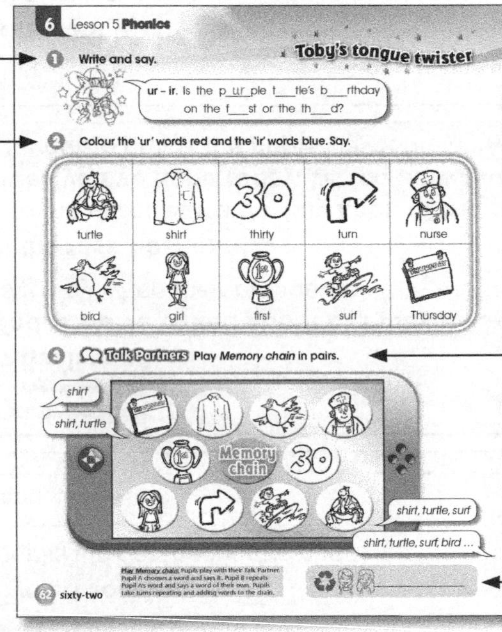

Activity Book

Activity 1

- Write and say.

Activity 2

- Colour the 'ur' words red and the 'ir' words blue. Say.

Activity 3

- Talk Partners
  Play *Memory chain* in pairs.

Recycled vocabulary

- Look, remember and write the word.

Digital resources

Teacher's Digital: Don't forget you can teach this lesson using the Teacher's App on Navio.

Pupil's Digital: Encourage your pupils to use the Pupil's App on Navio to practise the vocabulary from this lesson.

Starting the lesson

Use the Trinity Exam Practice cards (optional).

- The pupils practise asking and answering questions. (See p31.)

Review the *When's your birthday?* song.

▶ *CD3 Track 8 p267*

- Play the CD. Encourage the pupils to sing along. Choose three pupils to come to the front and replace the birthdays in the song with their own.

Set learning outcomes using the task flashcards.

- Say **Today we're going to say a tongue twister. We're going to make and use the cut-out.**
- Hold up the task flashcards in turn and elicit the activities. Stick them on one side of the board. Point to them during the lesson to reinforce your instructions.

Pupil's Book Activity 1

Listen and say.

▶ *CD3 Track 11 p268*

- Write the words *purple and first* on the board and ask the pupils which sound they can hear in both words. ('ir') Circle the target grapheme in each word ('ir' and 'ur') and model the sound. Encourage the pupils to say the sound with you. Check for accuracy.
- Say **It's time for Toby's tongue twister! What can you see?**
- Play the CD. The pupils listen and repeat the target sound, then the words and then the entire tongue twister, faster and faster.

Go to Magic Phonics.

Activity Book

Activity 1

Write and say.

- (Books open.) Say **Look at Toby's tongue twister! The letters for 'ir' and 'ur' are missing.** The pupils complete the tongue twister.
- Talk Partners The pupils say Toby's tongue twister and point to the 'ir' sounds. They play *Faster and faster,* taking turns to say it faster each time.

Answers: purple, turtle, birthday, first, third

Activity 2

Colour the 'ur' words red and the 'ir' words blue. Say.

- Ask the pupils to say the words and then colour 'ur' words red and 'ir' words blue.

Answers: red: turtle, turn, nurse, surf, Thursday
blue: shirt, thirty, bird, girl, first

Go to Magic Phonics.

Activity 3

Play *Memory chain* in pairs.

- Play *Memory chain* (see bottom of Activity Book p62 for instructions) with words from the activity.
- Talk Partners The pupils play the game with a Talk Partner.

Recycled vocabulary

- The pupils look at the picture and write the word.

Answer: smile

Pupil's Book Activity 2: Cooperative learning

Sing *We can do it!*

▶ *CD3 Track 12 p268*

- It can be difficult for young learners to sustain concentration and motivation, especially when a task is challenging. In a cooperative classroom, children help, support and encourage each other as they learn. Sing *We can do it!* when the class or individual members are finding a task difficult.
- Play the CD. The pupils listen. Play the CD again and the pupils join in.

Pupil's Book Activity 3

Listen and write the names.

▶ *CD3 Track 13 p268*

- (Books open.) Explain that some children are asking about each others' birthdays. Pupils write the names under the correct months.
- Play the CD. Pause after each conversation to give the pupils time to write and to check their answers.

Answers: **1** Ann, May **2** Tony, April **3** Lucy, March **4** Nick, January

Pupil's Book Activity 4

Do a class survey (Teacher's Resource Bank).

- (Books open.) Explain to pupils that they are going to use the survey sheet to find out their classmates' birthdays. The pupils ask everyone in the class *When's your birthday?* Encourage them to answer with the complete birth date and write the name on the survey.
- When the class has finished, ask **Which month has got the most birthdays?**

Ending the lesson

Review the lesson.

- Say **Today we've practised a tongue twister**. Ask the pupils to say it again.

Review the task flashcards.

- Point to the task flashcards. Say **Look at the activities you've done today. Which was your favourite?** Elicit the pupils' favourite activities.

Cooperative learning

Working together as a team

- Talk Partners Play *Beat the clock* to practise pronunciation of the 'ir' / 'ur' sound. (See p53.)
- Add to the pronunciation wall display, adding a shirt ('ir') and a turtle ('ur').

Key Competences and Key Learning Outcomes

- Read about seasonal festivals in Britain
- Listen for general understanding
- Think about seasonal festivals where you live

Key language

- *April Fools' Day, Bonfire Night, carnival, Christmas; celebrate, crackers, drum, jokes, parade, remember, turkey*
- *We pull crackers. We play jokes. We wear (paper hats). We have (a bonfire). What festivals do you celebrate? What do you do on festival days?*

Recycled: Months of the year; Ordinal numbers; Seasons; *lunch*

Recycled: *There's a (parade). We make (a doll). We eat (turkey).*

Materials

- Pupil's Book p66; Activity Book p63; Class CD3; Teacher's App on Navio
- Teacher's Resource Bank: Task flashcards: *Talk Partners, listen, read, think, match, tick, draw, write, say*

Optional materials

- Teacher's Resource Bank: Five Trinity Exam Practice cards (selected from the Starter Unit and Units 1, 2, 3, 4 and 5)

At a Glance Lesson Plan

Pupil's Book

Starting the lesson

- Use the Trinity Exam Practice cards (optional).
- Talk Partners
  Review *Toby's tongue twister.*
  ▶ *CD3 Track 11 p268*
- Set learning outcomes using the task flashcards.

Activity 1

- Listen and read. Answer.
  ▶ *CD3 Track 14 p268*

Think about your culture

- Do you have festivals in the four seasons? What festivals do you celebrate?
- Go to the Activity Book.

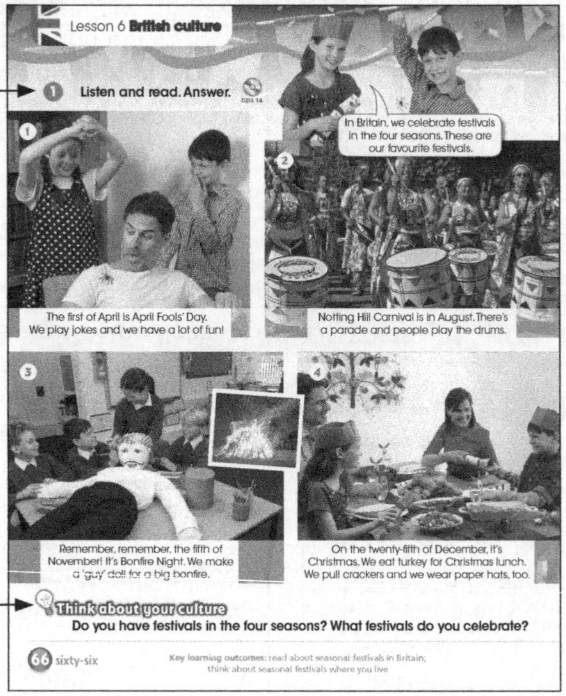

Ending the lesson

- Review the lesson.
- Review the task flashcards.

Extra activity

Extension

- Bonfire rhyme.

Digital resources

Teacher's Digital: Don't forget you can teach this lesson using the Teacher's App on Navio.

Powered By NAVIO

Activity Book

Activity Book

Activity 1

- Look, read and match.

Activity 2: Think about your culture.

- Read and tick (✓). Draw, write and say.

Recycled vocabulary

- Look, remember and write the word.

Starting the lesson

Use the Trinity Exam Practice cards (optional).

- The pupils practise asking and answering questions. (See p31.)

Review Toby's tongue twister.

▶ *CD3 Track 11 p268*

- Ask the class **What sound did you practise in Toby's tongue twister?** *('ir').* Ask if they can remember the tongue twister.
- Talk Partners The pupils practise the tongue twister as a class and then with a Talk Partner. The pairs play *Faster and faster,* reading from the Pupil's Book (page 65) if necessary. A fast pair says the tongue twister for the class.
- Draw a chart with two columns ('ir' and 'ur') on the board. Elicit words with both spellings. Ask the pupils to classify the words, e.g. *'ir': first, third; 'ur': purple, turtle.*

Set learning outcomes using the task flashcards.

- Say **Today we're going to learn about festivals in different seasons.**
- Hold up the task flashcards in turn and elicit the activities. Stick them on one side of the board. Point to them during the lesson to reinforce your instructions.

Background information

- **April Fools' Day:** This is celebrated on 1st April. It is not a national holiday. People play tricks and practical jokes on each other such as placing a whoopee cushion on a chair, hiding a plastic insect inside a bag of crisps and offering them to a friend or sticking a coin to the pavement.
- **Notting Hill Carnival:** This is celebrated on August Bank Holiday weekend. It began in 1966 and is the largest festival celebration of its kind in Europe. It is held in West London. Sunday is Children's day. Link: www.thelondonnottinghillcarnival.com
- **Bonfire Night:** It is celebrated on 5th November every year. Big bonfires are built and lit. A guy (scarecrow-like figure) is placed on the top of the bonfire and burnt. The guy represents Guy Fawkes who tried to blow up the Houses of Parliament with gunpowder in 1605. There are organised firework displays in the evening. Link: www.bbc.co.uk/newsround/15351828
- **Christmas Day:** The main Christmas meal in the UK is eaten at lunchtime on the 25th December. The traditional British Christmas dinner comprises of turkey, roast potatoes, Brussels sprouts, carrots, parsnips, stuffing, bread sauce and cranberry sauce with Christmas pudding for dessert. Crackers are pulled at the table. These usually have paper hats, jokes and a small present inside. People wear the hats during the meal.

Pupil's Book Activity 1

Listen and read. Answer.

▶ *CD3 Track 14 p268*

- (Books open.) Focus the pupils' attention on the photographs and ask **What can you see?** Say **Let's read and listen.**
- Play the CD. At the end, check understanding by pointing to the first photo. Ask **When is April Fools' Day?** Ask about the other photos.

Pupil's Book Think about your culture

Do you have festivals in the four seasons? What festivals do you celebrate?

- Read out the questions and encourage the class to tell you if they celebrate festivals in each season.

Activity Book

Activity 1

Look, read and match.

- (Books open.) Ask **When is Notting Hill Carnival?** *(In August.)* **Can you see a picture from the carnival?** The pupils match each date to the festival and the corresponding illustration.

Answers: **1** Carnival, a **2** Christmas, d **3** Bonfire Night, c **4** April Fools' Day, b

Activity 2: Think about your culture

Read and tick (✓). Draw, write and say.

- Read the question in the speech bubble. Elicit the pupils' answers.
- Read the first sentence as a class and ask the pupils to tick the box if they play jokes on people on the first of April. Repeat with the other sentences.
- Ask the pupils to draw their favourite festival and write a sentence about it. Invite different pupils to show the rest of the class their drawings and read out their sentences.
- Discuss the events with the pupils and compare similar activities with their culture.

Recycled vocabulary

- The pupils look at the picture and write the word.

Answer: play

Ending the lesson

Review the lesson.

- Say **Today you've learnt about festivals in Britain.**

Review the task flashcards.

- Point to the task flashcards. Say **Look at the activities you've done today. Which activity was your favourite?** Elicit the pupils' favourite activities.

Extra activity

Extension

- Bonfire rhyme. Teach a traditional Bonfire Night rhyme: *Remember, remember the fifth of November, Gunpowder treason and plot. We see no reason why gunpowder treason should ever be forgot.*

Key Competences and Key Learning Outcomes

- Identify the months in each season (optional)
- Read for specific information
- Read and understand a traditional rhyme
- Order sentences from a rhyme
- Complete a rhyme

Key language

- *leap year*

Recycled: Months of the year; Ordinal numbers

Recycled: *There are …*

Materials

- Pupil's Book p67; Activity Book p64; Class CD3; Teacher's App on Navio
- Teacher's Resource Bank: Task flashcards: *find, circle, listen, read, number, write, Talk Partners, say*

Optional materials

- Teacher's Resource Bank: Five Trinity Exam Practice cards (selected from the Starter Unit and Units 1, 2, 3, 4 and 5)
- Sheets of paper, coloured pencils and scissors

At a Glance Lesson Plan

Starting the lesson

- Use the Trinity Exam Practice cards (optional).
- Review seasonal festivals.
- Set learning outcomes using the task flashcards.

Before you read: Activity 1

- Look at the rhyme quickly. Find and circle the months.

Activity 2

- Listen and read the rhyme.

▶ *CD3 Track 15 p268*

After you read

Go to page 64 in your Activity Book.

Ending the lesson

- Review the lesson.
- Review the task flashcards.
- Sing a song (optional).

Pupil's Book

Extra activity

Reinforcement

- Draw a Venn Diagram of months.

Cooperative learning

Learning strategies

- Play *The knuckle game.*

Link to Science

The Sun: the months in each season

Activity Book

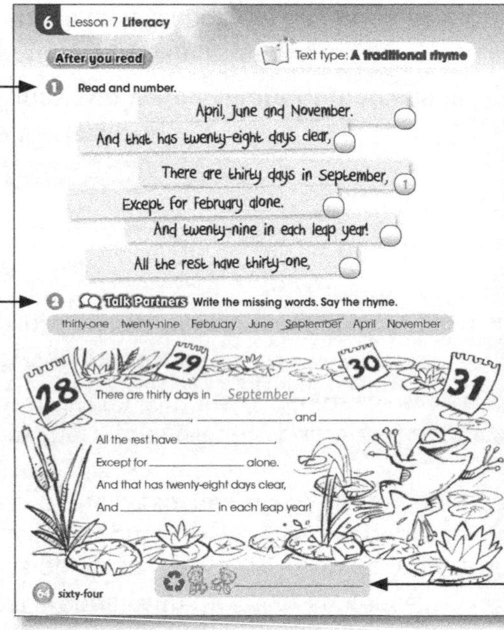

Activity Book

After you read: Activity 1

- Read and number.

Activity 2

- Write the missing words.
- Talk Partners Say the rhyme.

Recycled vocabulary

- Look, remember and write the word.

Digital resources

Teacher's Digital: Don't forget you can teach this lesson using the Teacher's App on Navio.

Pupil's Digital: Encourage your pupils to use the Pupil's App on Navio to practise the vocabulary from this lesson.

Powered By NAVIO

Starting the lesson

Use the Trinity Exam Practice cards (optional).

- The pupils practise asking and answering questions. (See p31.)

Review seasonal festivals.

- Review the seasonal festivals from Lesson 6. Say **When do they play jokes in Britain?** Encourage the pupils to answer with the date. Encourage them to refer back to the lesson if necessary. Repeat with the other festivals. Review the seasonal activities by asking **What do they do on April Fools' Day? Can you remember?** Repeat for all the seasonal activities.

Set learning outcomes using the task flashcards.

- Say **Today we're going to read a traditional rhyme.**
- Hold up the task flashcards in turn and elicit the activities. Stick them on one side of the board. Point to them during the lesson to reinforce your instructions.

Before you read: Pupil's Book Activity 1

Look at the rhyme quickly. Find and circle the months.

- (Books closed.) Tell the pupils that they are going to read a traditional rhyme about the months of the year. Ask them to predict the months that will appear in the rhyme and write them on the board.
- (Books open.) Ask the pupils to scan the text of the rhyme for the names of the months that are mentioned and compare with those they predicted. The pupils circle the months that appear in the rhyme.
- Focus their attention on the two leap years at the top of the page (2018 and 2022). Explain that every four years, February is given an extra day. This is called a leap year.

Pupil's Book Activity 2

Listen and read the rhyme.

▶ *CD3 Track 15 p268*

- Say **Let's read the traditional rhyme.** Play the CD.
- Check understanding by asking **How many days does September have?** *(30)*
- **Which other months have 30 days?** *(April, June and November.)*
- **Which months have 31 days?** (All the rest – elicit the names.) **How many days does February have?** *(28 or 29.)*

Activity Book

After you read: Activity 1

Read and number.

- (Books open.) Focus attention on the first activity. Invite individual pupils to read out the lines from the rhyme in order. The pupils then number the lines.

Answer: 2 5 1 4 6 3

Activity 2

Write the missing words. Say the rhyme.

- Read out the rhyme and ask the pupils to say and write the missing words.
- Talk Partners The pupils practise reading out the rhyme with a Talk Partner.

Answers: **1** September **2** April **3** June **4** November **5** thirty-one **6** February **7** twenty-nine

Recycled vocabulary

- The pupils look at the picture and write the word.

Answer: eat

Ending the lesson

Review the lesson.

- Say **Today you've read a traditional rhyme about the months.** Elicit the names of the months.

Review the task flashcards.

- Point to the task flashcards. **Which activity was your favourite?**

Sing a song (optional).

- Choose a song. The class sings and does the actions. Alternatively, invite the class to choose a song to sing.

Extra activity

Reinforcement

- Ask the pupils to work in groups of three or four. Tell them they will make word cards with the months of the year. Demonstrate how to make the word cards using coloured pencils and scissors.
- Reinforce the number of days in each month by classifying them into a Venn Diagram on the board. Draw two large circles and leave a space in the middle. Write *30* above one and *31* above the other. As the pupils name the months with 30 or 31 days, stick the words cards in the corresponding circle. Stick February in the middle.

Cooperative learning

Learning strategies

- Play *The knuckle game.* Close your right hand into a fist. Start with the first knuckle (right hand, little finger knuckle) and recite the months, while moving a finger along your knuckles and the spaces between them. Say **January** on the very first knuckle. Next, put your finger in between the space between first and second knuckles and say **February**. Move your finger up to the next knuckle for March. The knuckles represent months with 31 days. The spaces between the knuckles represent months with 30 or 28 days. The last knuckle on the right hand represents July. Continue with August on the first knuckle of your other hand. Continue counting along the knuckles and spaces until you get to December.
- Talk Partners Once you have introduced the strategy to the pupils allow quicker learners to help teach the technique to a Talk Partner.

Link to Science

- If you are studying the Science topic of **the Sun** in English, you could review the months that belong to each season with the pupils: Spring: March – May; Summer: June – August; Autumn: September – November; Winter: December – February.

Key Competences and Key Learning Outcomes

- Review language in the unit
- Reflect on own learning
- Sing a cooperative learning song

Key language

Recycled: *celebrate Halloween, eat chestnuts, finish school, go to the beach, open presents, plant seeds, smell flowers, wear warm clothes;* Ordinal numbers; *spring, summer, autumn, winter;* Months of the year

Recycled: *We (go to the beach). They (go to the beach). Do they (celebrate Halloween)? Yes, they do. / No, they don't. What do they do (in winter)? They wear warm clothes. Do you (eat chestnuts) in spring? Yes, we do. When's your birthday? My birthday is on the (eighteenth) of (June).*

Materials

- Pupil's Book p68; Activity Book p65; Class CD3; Teacher's App on Navio
- Seasonal activities flashcards
- Teacher's Resource Bank: Task flashcards: *listen, number, write, say, Talk Partners, sing, stick, think, Think-Pair-Share*
- Teacher's Resource Bank: Traffic light cut-out
- *Give Me Five!* sticker

Optional materials

- Teacher's Resource Bank: Five Trinity Exam Practice cards (selected from the Starter Unit and Units 1, 2, 3, 4 and 5)

At a Glance Lesson Plan

Pupil's Book

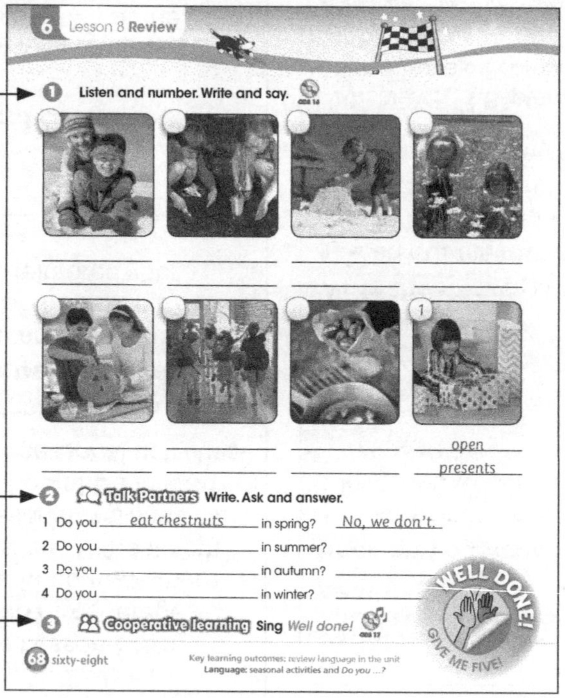

Starting the lesson

- Use the Trinity Exam Practice cards (optional).
- Review the unit vocabulary.
- Set learning outcomes using the task flashcards.

Activity 1

- Listen and number.
- Write and say.
- ▶ *CD3 Track 16 p268*

Activity 2

- Write.
- Talk Partners Ask and answer.

Activity 3 Cooperative learning

- Sing *Well done!*
- ▶ *CD3 Track 17 p268*
- Stick the *Give Me Five!* sticker.
- Go to the Activity Book.

Ending the lesson

- Review the task flashcards.
- Sing a song (optional).

Cooperative learning

Think-Pair-Share

- Remember eight seasonal activities.

Activity Book

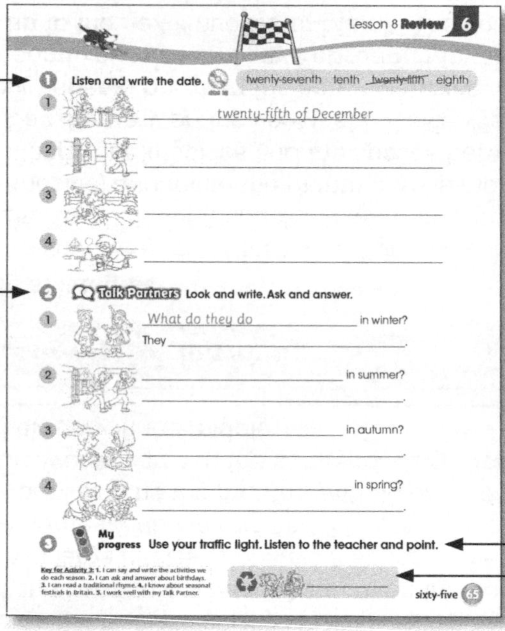

Activity Book

Activity 1

- Listen and write the date.
- ▶ *CD3 Track 18 p268*

Activity 2

- Look and write.
- Talk Partners Ask and answer.

Activity 3 My progress

- Use your traffic light. Listen to the teacher and point.

Recycled vocabulary

- Look, remember and write the phrase.

Digital resources

Teacher's Digital: Don't forget you can teach this lesson using the Teacher's App on Navio.

Pupil's Digital: Encourage your pupils to use the Pupil's App on Navio to practise the vocabulary from this lesson.

Powered By NAVIO

Starting the lesson

Use the Trinity Exam Practice cards (optional).

- The pupils practise asking and answering questions. (See p31.)

Review the unit vocabulary.

- Play *Disappearing words* (see p23) with the unit flashcards to review actions.
- **Option:** Play the game in two teams. The teams take it in turns to remember the words.

Set learning outcomes using the task flashcards.

- Say **Today we're going to remember what we've learnt in Unit 6.**
- Hold up the task flashcards in turn and elicit the words. Stick them on one side of the board. Point to them during the lesson to reinforce your instructions.

Pupil's Book Activity 1

Listen and number. Write and say.

▶ *CD3 Track 16 p268*

- (Books open.) Point to each of the pictures and elicit the words.
- Play the CD. Pause after each sentence. The pupils write the correct number in the circles.
- Play the CD again. The pupils write the correct activity under each picture. Then they say the verbs.

Answers: **1** open presents **2** go to the beach **3** celebrate Halloween **4** plant seeds **5** eat chestnuts **6** wear warm clothes **7** finish school **8** smell flowers

Pupil's Book Activity 2

Write. Ask and answer.

- (Books open.) Ask the pupils to complete the questions and answers.
- **Talk Partners** The pupils practise the questions and answers with a Talk Partner. The pupils then choose other activities from the photographs and continue to ask and answer in pairs.

Pupil's Book Activity 3: Cooperative learning

Sing *Well done!*

▶ *CD3 Track 17 p268*

- Praise the class for their hard work and play the *Well done!* song. The pupils listen. Play the CD again. The pupils join in.

Stick the *Give Me Five!* sticker.

- The pupils stick the *Give Me Five!* sticker on the Pupil's Book page.

Activity Book

Activity 1

Listen and write the date.

▶ *CD3 Track 18 p268*

- (Books open.) Elicit the four activities in the illustrations. The pupils write the date that Jake and Molly do each activity. Pause the CD after each one to give the pupils time to write the dates.

Answers: **1** twenty-fifth of December **2** twenty-seventh of July **3** eighth of April **4** tenth of August

Activity 2

Look and write. Ask and answer.

- Read out the first example. Ask the pupils what the children do. *(They wear warm clothes.)* Ask the pupils to complete the questions and answers individually.
- **Talk Partners** The pupils ask and answer the questions with a Talk Partner.

Answers: **1** What do they do; wear warm clothes **2** What do they do; They finish school **3** What do they do; They eat chestnuts **4** What do they do; They smell flowers

Activity 3 My progress

Use your traffic light. Listen to the teacher and point.

- (Books closed.) Ask the class to take out their traffic light cut-out. Say **Let's think about our work in this unit.** Read the first self-assessment statement. Point to the green circle and say **Yes, I can do this very well.** Point to the orange circle and say **Yes, I can do this**. Point to the red circle, shake your head and say **No, I can't do this.**
- Read the remaining statements. For each one, the pupils point to the colour on their traffic light that shows how they feel about their own learning.

Self-statements assessment

1. I can say and write the activities we do each season.
2. I can ask and answer about birthdays.
3. I can read a traditional rhyme.
4. I know about seasonal festivals in Britain.
5. I work well with my Talk Partner.

Recycled vocabulary

- The pupils look at the picture and write the phrase.

Answer: drink hot chocolate

Ending the lesson

Review the task flashcards.

- Point to the task flashcards. Say **Look at the activities you've done today. Which activity was your favourite?** Elicit the pupils' favourite activity.

Sing a song (optional).

- The class chooses their favourite song from the unit. The class sings and does the actions.

Cooperative learning

Think-Pair-Share

- Ask **Can you remember the eight seasonal activities?** Ask the class to think silently on their own for a minute.
- **Talk Partners** The pupils work with a Talk Partner to remember and name all eight activities.
- Invite a pair to say one of the phrases. Hold up the corresponding flashcard and prompt the class to repeat the phrase.
- Finally, repeat the procedure, asking different pairs of pupils each time, until all eight activities have been named.

Key Competences and Key Learning Outcomes

- Watch and understand a video about the four seasons
- Complete a survey

- Learn to do a survey

Key language

- *summer, autumn, winter, spring;* Months of the year; *chestnuts, do a survey, plant seeds, season*

Materials

- Pupil's Book p69; Activity Book p66; Class CD3; Video; Teacher's App on Navio
- Teacher's Resource Bank: Task flashcards: *tick, read, write, circle, listen, think, say, Talk Partners*
- Twelve sheets of paper

Optional materials

- Teacher's Resource Bank: Trinity Exam Practice cards (selected from Unit 6)

At a Glance Lesson Plan

Pupil's Book

Starting the lesson

- Use the Trinity Exam Practice cards (optional).
- Play a game to review months of the year.
- Set learning outcomes and use the task flashcards.

Pre-watching activity

- Predict what seasonal activities they are going to see.

Activity 1

- Watch the video.
  Unit 6 video 279
- Tick (✓) or cross (✗). Are these activities in the video?

Activity 2

- Watch the video again.
  Unit 6 video
- Read and circle.

Activity 3

- Do a survey. Ask your friends and write.

Go to the Activity Book.

Ending the lesson

- Review the lesson.
- Review the task flashcards. Elicit the pupils' favourite activities.

Extra activity

Extension

- Pupils work together in groups to do an activity.

Digital resources

Teacher's Digital: Don't forget you can teach this lesson using the Teacher's App on Navio.

Pupil's Digital: Encourage your pupils to use the Pupil's App on Navio to practise the vocabulary from this lesson.

Powered By NAVIO

Activity Book

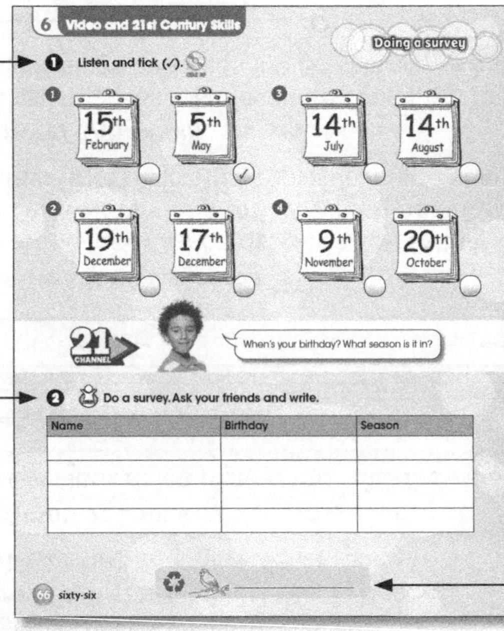

Activity Book

Activity 1

- Listen and tick (✓).
  ▶ *CD3 Track 19 p268*

Activity 2

- Do a survey. Ask your friends and write.

Recycled vocabulary

- Look, remember and write the word.

Starting the lesson

Use the Trinity Exam Practice cards (optional).

- The pupils practise asking and answering questions. (See p31.)

Review months.

- Write the 12 months of the year on separate pieces of paper and stick them around the room. Tell the pupils you are going to ask a question about the months and they have to go and stand next to the correct month. Suggested questions: **What month is Christmas? What month comes after January?**

  Talk Partners Ask **What month is your birthday? When is spring / summer / winter / autumn?**

Set learning outcomes and use the task flashcards.

- Say **Today we're going to watch a video and then ask and answer questions about the four seasons**.
- Hold up the task flashcards, in turn, and elicit the activities. Stick them on the side of the board. Point to them during the lesson to reinforce your instructions.

Pre-watching activity

Think-Pair-Share Ask the pupils what activities they do in the four seasons. Write their answers on the board.

Pupil's Book Activity 1

Watch the video. Tick (✓) or cross (✗). Are these activities in the video? *p279*

- Ask **What's Abby's favourite season?** Play Part 1 and elicit answers.
- Focus the pupils' attention on the video stills. Ask **What seasons can you see? What are the children doing?**
- Play Part 2 and pause the video after the first video still. Ask the pupils to point to the corresponding photo in their book and show the tick in the circle.
- Play the video for pupils to tick and cross the video stills.
- Ask **Which season is the most fun? Why?**

Answers: From left to right: ✓ ✓ ✗ ✓

Pupil's Book Activity 2

Watch the video again. Read and circle.

- Play Part 2 again. Pause after the children plant the seeds. Read out the first sentence in Activity 2. Ask **Do we plant seeds in summer or spring?**
- Play the video all the way through for pupils to check and circle the words.
- Ask the pupils some questions to check understanding. Suggested questions.
  Why is Tom's favourite season summer? *(Because he can go to the beach.)*
  What colour are the flowers in spring? *(Purple.)*
  Who are the children playing football on the beach with? *(With their grandmother and grandfather.)*
  What month is Abby's birthday? *(November.)*
  What clothes do you wear in winter? *(Warm clothes.)*
  What do Tom and Sophie want to do now? *(Ask their friends when their birthdays are. Make a birthday survey.)*

Answers: **1** spring **2** summer **3** autumn **4** winter

Pupil's Book Activity 3

Do a survey. Ask your friends and write.

- Copy the season survey chart on the board. Ask a few pupils **What's your favourite season?** and write their name and tick their answers on the chart.
- Tell the pupils to stand up and ask three friends *What's your favourite season?* and complete the survey.

Answers: Pupils' own answers

Activity Book

Activity 1

Listen and tick (✓).

▶ *CD3 Track 19 p268*

- Focus the pupils' attention on the calendars. Point to each one and ask **What's the date?**
- Tell the pupils they are going to listen to people talking about dates and they have to listen and tick the correct calendar.
- Play the CD, pausing after each exchange, for pupils to tick the dates.

Answers: **1** 5th May **2** 19th December **3** 14th August **4** 9th November

Activity 2

Do a survey. Ask your friends and write.

- Read out the speech bubble. Elicit responses from the pupils. Explain that the pupils are going to do another survey about birthdays and seasons. Say **When's your birthday? What season is it in?**
- The pupils stand up and interview four people for their survey.

  Talk Partners Pupils compare the answers on their survey.

Recycled vocabulary

Answer: bird

Ending the lesson

Review the lesson.

- Ask **Which activity was easy / difficult?**

Review the task flashcards.

- Point to the task flashcards on the board. Say **Look at the activities you've done today. Which activity was your favourite?**

Extra activity

Extension

- Divide the class into groups of four. Ask the pupils to share their survey results from the Activity Book, Activity 2. On the board write sentence starters, for example, *There are (three) birthdays in (July). There are (six) birthdays in (spring).* The pupils collate the results of their four surveys and write sentences to show the results.

My project 2: Jobs

Key Competences and Key Learning Outcomes

- Identify and name different jobs
- Ask and answer questions about jobs
- Say what people do in their job

- Listen for specific information
- Work in small groups to plan a jobs poster

Key language

- *artist, cook, dancer, doctor, firefighter, footballer, pilot, police officer, teacher, vet; boots, helmet, white coat; cook, dance, fly a plane, paint pictures, put out fires*
- *He's / She's a (teacher). He / She wears (a uniform). A (doctor) (helps) (people). A (pilot) (flies a plane). I want to be (a vet).*

Materials

- Pupil's Book p70; Activity Book p68; Class CD3; Teacher's App on Navio
- Teacher's Resource Bank: Task flashcards: *listen, number, Talk Partners, read, write*

Optional materials

- Teacher's Resource Bank: Five Trinity Exam Practice cards (selected from the Starter Unit and Units 1, 2, 3, 4, 5 and 6)

At a Glance Lesson Plan

Pupil's Book

Starting the lesson

- Use the Trinity Exam Practice cards (optional).
- Set learning outcomes using the task flashcards.

Learn: Activity 1

- Listen, point and repeat.

▶ *CD3 Track 20 p269*

Activity 2

- Listen and number. Listen and repeat.

▶ *CD3 Track 21 p269*

Plan your project

- Plan your jobs poster.

Go to page 68 in your Activity Book.

Ending the lesson

- Review the lesson.
- Review the task flashcards.

Extra activity

Vocabulary extension

- *dentist, nurse, postman / woman, shop assistant, singer*

Link to Science

- **Where people work:** jobs in cities and villages.

Activity Book

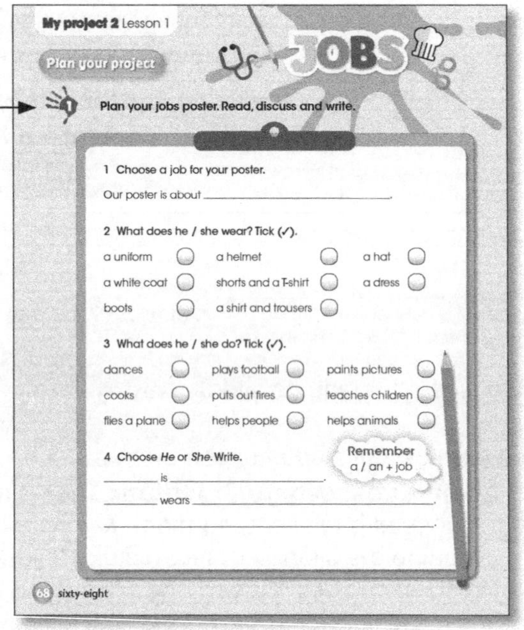

Activity Book: Plan your project

Activity 1

- Plan your jobs poster. Read, discuss and write.

Digital resources

Teacher's Digital: Don't forget you can teach this lesson using the Teacher's App on Navio.

Pupil's Digital: Encourage your pupils to use the Pupil's App on Navio to practise the vocabulary from this lesson.

Powered By NAVIO

Starting the lesson

Use the Trinity Exam Practice cards (optional).

- The pupils practise asking and answering questions. (See p31.)

Set learning outcomes using the task flashcards.

- Explain the aims of the lesson. Say **Today we're going to learn about different jobs.** Check understanding.
- Hold up the task flashcards and elicit the words. Stick them on one side of the board. Point to them during the lesson to reinforce your instructions.

Learn: Pupil's Book Activity 1

Listen, point and repeat.

▶ *CD3 Track 20 p269*

- (Books open.) Focus pupils' attention on the people. Ask **Who can you see?** Ask **Can you see a teacher?** Point to the teacher. **Can you see a footballer?** Point to the footballer. Introduce new vocabulary by pointing to the other people and saying **Look. She's / He's a (firefighter / cook).** Encourage the pupils to point to the different jobs and repeat after you.
- Play the CD. The pupils listen and point to the jobs as they hear them. Play the CD again. The pupils repeat the words, pointing to the different jobs.
- Name different jobs in a random order. The pupils point to the corresponding picture each time.
- Talk Partners The pupils repeat the activity with a Talk Partner, taking turns to say and point to the different jobs.

Pupil's Book Activity 2

Listen and number. Listen and repeat.

▶ *CD3 Track 21 p269*

- Say **Look at the photos.** Play the CD pausing after each sentence for the pupils to number the pictures.
- Play the CD again and the pupils repeat the sentences, pointing to the jobs as they do so.
- Say the jobs in a random order. The pupils point to the corresponding picture and say the sentence each time.
- Encourage the pupils to give similar descriptions about the other jobs on the page.
- Talk Partners The pupils ask and answer questions with a Talk Partner about the job they would like to do when they grow up.
- **Personalisation:** Ask the pupils if their parents or other family members do any of these jobs. Ask **Is your (mother) (a doctor)?** Elicit answers *(My (mother) is a …).*

Plan your project: Activity Book

Activity 1

Plan your jobs poster. Read, discuss and write.

- (Books open.) Explain to pupils that they are going to make a jobs poster. First they need to discuss which job to choose and what information to write on the poster.
- Invite a volunteer to read out the first question. Check that the pupils understand they have to write the name of their chosen job on the line.
- Discuss the other questions with the pupils. They tick the corresponding options and then write to complete question 4.

Ending the lesson

Review the lesson.

- (Books closed.) Say **Today we've talked about jobs. What do you want to be when you grow up? Which is your favourite job?** Encourage the pupils to respond and praise them for their effort.

Review the task flashcards.

- Point to the task flashcards. Say **Look at the activities you've done today. Which was your favourite?** Elicit the pupils' favourite activities.

Extra activity

Vocabulary extension

- Present and practise five additional jobs: *dentist, nurse, postman / woman, shop assistant, singer.*

Link to Science

- If you are studying the Science topic of **where people work** in English, you could review additional jobs the pupils may have learnt in their science lessons *(builder, carpenter, electrician, factory worker, farmer, fisherman, plumber).* Remind the pupils that some people work in cities and others work in villages.

My project 2: Jobs

Key Competences and Key Learning Outcomes

- Write and present your jobs poster
- Follow instructions
- Think about your project
- Sing a cooperative learning song

Key language

Recycled: *artist, cook, dancer, doctor, firefighter, footballer, pilot, police officer, teacher, vet*

Recycled: *He's / She's (a vet). He / She (wears a white coat). He / She (helps animals).*

Materials

- Pupil's Book p71; Activity Book p69; Class CD3; Teacher's App on Navio
- Teacher's Resource Bank: Task flashcards: *Talk Partners, read, sing, listen, think, read, write, colour*
- Coloured pencils, scissors, card, glue

Optional materials

- Teacher's Resource Bank: Five Trinity Exam Practice cards (selected from the Starter Unit and Units 1, 2, 3, 4, 5 and 6)

At a Glance Lesson Plan

Pupil's Book

Starting the lesson

- Use the Trinity Exam Practice cards (optional).
- Play *Guess which job I'm thinking of?*
- Set learning outcomes using the task flashcards.

Create: Activity 1

- Read. Make your jobs poster.

Show and tell: Activity 2
Cooperative learning

- Sing *It's fun to work together!*
- ▶ *CD3 Track 22 p269*

Activity 3: Show and tell

- Listen. Present your jobs poster to the class. Make a class jobs wall display with all the posters.
- ▶ *CD3 Track 23 p269*

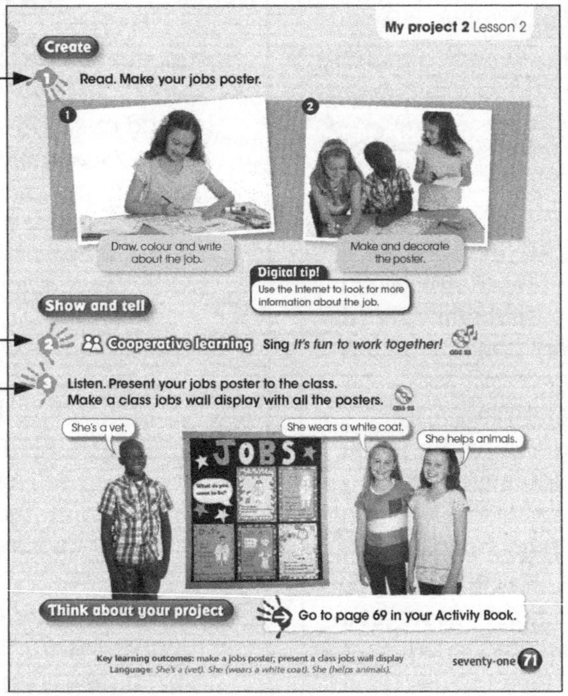
My project 2 Lesson 2
Create
1 Read. Make your jobs poster.
Draw, colour and write about the job.
Make and decorate the poster.
Digital tip! Use the Internet to look for more information about the job.
Show and tell
2 Cooperative learning Sing It's fun to work together!
3 Listen. Present your jobs poster to the class. Make a class jobs wall display with all the posters.

Think about your project Go to page 69 in your Activity Book.
Key learning outcomes: make a jobs poster; present a class jobs wall display
Language: She's a (vet). She (wears a white coat). She (helps animals).
seventy-one 71

Think about your project

- Go to page 69 in your Activity Book.

Ending the lesson

- Review the lesson.
- Sing *Well done!*
- ▶ *CD3 Track 17 p268*
- Review the task flashcards.

Link to Science

- **People who help us:** types of jobs and places of work

Activity Book

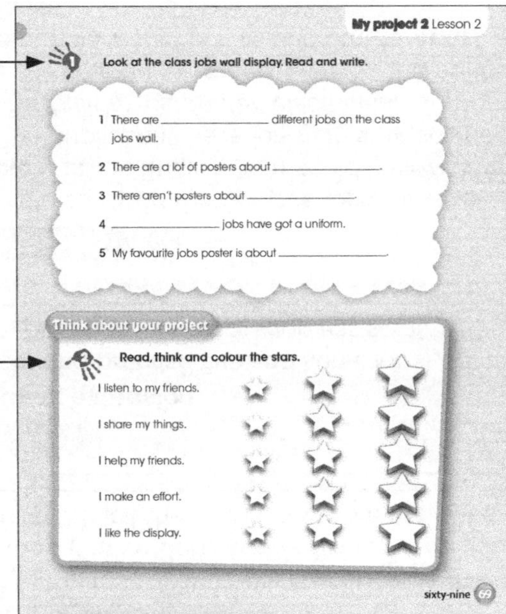
My project 2 Lesson 2
1 Look at the class jobs wall display. Read and write.
1 There are ______ different jobs on the class jobs wall.
2 There are a lot of posters about ______.
3 There aren't posters about ______.
4 ______ jobs have got a uniform.
5 My favourite jobs poster is about ______.
Think about your project
2 Read, think and colour the stars.
I listen to my friends.
I share my things.
I help my friends.
I make an effort.
I like the display.
sixty-nine 69

Activity Book

Activity 1

- Look at the class jobs wall display. Read and write.

Think about your project: Activity 2

- Read, think and colour the stars.

Digital resources

Teacher's Digital: Don't forget you can teach this lesson using the Teacher's App on Navio.

Pupil's Digital: Encourage your pupils to use the Pupil's App on Navio to practise the vocabulary from this lesson.

Powered By NAVIO

Starting the lesson

Use the Trinity Exam Practice cards (optional).

- The pupils practise asking and answering questions. (See p31.)

Play *Guess which job I'm thinking of?*

- Ask the pupils to look at the jobs (Pupil's Book p70). Describe one of the jobs. The pupils guess the job you are describing. **He wears shorts and a T-shirt. He kicks and throws a ball.** *(A footballer.)* **She works in a school. She writes on the board.** *(A teacher.)*
- Talk Partners The pupils play the game with a Talk Partner.

Set learning outcomes using the task flashcards.

- Explain the aims of the lesson. Say **Today we're going to make jobs posters.**
- Hold up the task flashcards and elicit the words. Stick them on one side of the board. Point to them during the lesson to reinforce your instructions.

Create: Pupil's Book Activity 1

Read. Make your jobs poster.

- (Books open.) Ask the class to look at the photos. Explain that they are going to make their jobs posters about the job they would like to do.
- (Books open.) Read out the instructions, or invite different volunteers to read them out. The pupils follow the text.
- Use the internet to find out more information about the jobs they have chosen.
- The pupils then use the clipboard sheet from the previous lesson (Activity Book p68) to help them make their posters.

Show and tell: Pupil's Book Activity 2:
Cooperative learning

▶ *CD3 Track 22 p269*

- In order to build a positive classroom environment, all pupils need to participate and contribute to the lesson. Sing *It's fun to work together!* with the class when you want to remind pupils of the importance of joining in.
- Play the CD. The pupils listen.
- Play the CD again and encourage the pupils to sing.

Pupil's Book Activity 3

Listen. Present your jobs poster to the class. Make a class jobs wall display with all the posters.

▶ *CD3 Track 23 p269*

- (Books open.) When the pupils have completed their posters, focus their attention on the photo. Play the CD, pausing after each sentence for the pupils to repeat.
- Display the pupils' posters on the wall. Encourage different groups to stand up and present their posters to the rest of the class.

Activity Book

Activity 1

Look at the class jobs wall display. Read and write.

- (Books open.) After the presentations, ask the class to look at the class jobs wall display and complete the sentences.
- Talk Partners Encourage the pupils to compare their answers with a Talk Partner.

Think about your project: Activity 2

Read, think and colour the stars.

- Say **Let's think about how we work.** Read each sentence and ask the class to colour the star for how they work. (Small star: sometimes; medium-sized star: usually; big star: always.) Praise the class for their efforts.

Ending the lesson

Review the lesson.

- Ask the class to close their books and say **Today we've worked together. What have we made?** *(A class jobs wall display.)* Praise the class for their hard work and display all the posters in a prominent place.

Sing *Well done!*

▶ *CD3 Track 17 p268*

- (Books closed.) Praise the class for working together and for following instructions well. Play the CD. The pupils sing the song together.

Review the task flashcards.

- Point to the task flashcards. Say **Look at the activities you've done today. Which was your favourite?** Elicit the pupils' favourite activities.

Link to Science

- If you are studying the Science topic of **People who help us** in English, you could remind the pupils that some people help us by providing a service, some people build houses and others work in villages. Ask questions to help the pupils relate the people who help us to the places in the city they have learnt about in their Science class. **Who works at the airport?** *(A pilot works at the airport.)* **Who works in a school?** *(A teacher works in a school.)*

Date: ____________________ **Unit:** __________

1 What did my pupils learn in this unit?

2 How did my pupils work? (✓)

individually ☐ in pairs ☐ in small groups ☐

in large groups ☐ as a class ☐

3 Which key competences did my pupils develop?

- Competence in linguistic communication ☐
- Competence in mathematics, science and technology ☐
- Digital competence ☐
- Learning to learn ☐
- Social and civic competences ☐
- Sense of initiative and entrepreneurship ☐
- Cultural awareness and expression ☐

4 Which lessons / activities were the most successful and why?

5 Which lessons / activities did my pupils find the most difficult and why?

6 What did I try in the classroom for the first time? How did it go?

7 Which resources did I find most useful? (including webpages)

8 What could I do differently next time I teach this unit?

Unit 7 My house

Unit overview

Key Competences and Key Learning Outcomes

- Identify and say ten rooms in the house (Lesson 1)
- Use *There's a / There are / There isn't a / There aren't any* (Lesson 2)
- Read, listen and understand a story about a haunted house (Lesson 3)
- Ask and answer about who objects belong to (Lesson 4)
- Watch and understand a video about unusual houses (Video and 21st Century Skills)

- Use the Pupil's App on Navio

- Use a strategy to practise spelling key words (Lesson 1)
- Say a tongue twister and practise 'ou' and 'ow' spellings (Lesson 5)
- Review language from the unit and reflect on own learning (Lesson 8)
- Practise activity types found in the Cambridge Exams: Pre A1 Starters

- Understand the importance of being kind to your friends (Lesson 3)
- Learn to help at home (Video and 21st Century Skills)

- Work with a Talk Partner to practise and reinforce learning (all lessons)
- Play a communication game about where objects are (Lesson 5)

- Sing three songs (Lessons 1, 4 and 8)
- Understand and act out a story (Lesson 3)
- Learn about children's bedrooms in Britain (Lesson 6)
- Think about what you've got in your bedroom (Lesson 6)
- Read and understand a play script (Lesson 7)
- Complete and act out a conversation from a play (Lesson 7)

Vocabulary

Core vocabulary
bathroom, bedroom, dining room, flat, garage, garden, hall, house, kitchen, living room; box, camera, clock, phone, radio, watch

Extension vocabulary (optional)
chimney, roof, wall, window; upstairs, downstairs; key, lamp, rug, towel

Other vocabulary
floor, shut, watching TV, watering the flowers; armchair, funfair, ghost, haunted, mirror, piano, scared, sofa; board games, bookcase, drum, guitar, pop music, pyjama, stickers, sticker collection, upstairs; dragon, fairy godmother, get married, glass, midnight, play, prince, sad, script, wicked

Recycled vocabulary
bed, bread, door, eating, food, having a shower, mouse, running, shoes; skeleton, witch; bath, bed, run, shower; mess; big, small; books, music; car, dress, horse, mice, phone, pumpkin, sister; clean, dirty, new, old

Structures

Core structures
There's / isn't a (garage). There are / aren't any (bedrooms). Whose is this (watch)? It's mine / yours / his / hers.

Other structures
Let's go inside! I'm not scared. What fun! What do you do in the (living room)? I (watch TV) in the (living room). Come back! What a mess! These shoes are made of glass.

Recycled structures
have a shower, There's a … There are …

Phonics

Alternative vowel spellings **'ou'** / **'ow'** (br**ow**n, c**ow**, l**ou**d, m**ou**se, ar**ou**nd, h**ou**se)

British Culture

Bedrooms

Literacy

Text type: a play script (text to entertain)
Reading skills: predicting from title; scanning for specific information; remembering facts; acting out conversations

21st Century Skills

Living in the world: learn to help at home

Cooperative learning

Songs: *Well done!* (Lesson 8)
Skills: Listening to others (Lesson 3); Working together as a team (Lesson 5); Think-Pair-Share (Lesson 2, Lesson 8)

Values

The importance of being kind to your friends.

Cross-curricular links

Links to Science

Materials: different materials; properties of materials; natural and manufactured materials; the properties of glass

Suggested Arts and Crafts concepts
Observing and identifying lines, shapes, colours, patterns, textures and forms in art and the environment; making and playing a game

Key Competences and Key Learning Outcomes

- Identify and say ten rooms in the house
- Say the vocabulary chant
- Stick the rooms stickers

- Identify different materials (optional)

- Use a strategy to practise spelling key words

- Sing a song about a mouse

Key language
- *bathroom, bedroom, dining room, flat, garage, garden, hall, house, kitchen, living room*

Extension vocabulary
- *chimney, roof, wall, window; upstairs, downstairs*

Recycled: *bed, bread, door, eating, food, having a shower, mouse, running, shoes*

Recycled: *There's … There are …*

Other vocabulary: *floor, shut the door, watching TV, watering the flowers*

Materials
- Pupil's Book p72; Activity Book pp70 and 79; Class CD3; Teacher's App on Navio; Unit 7 stickers
- Rooms flashcards; Seasonal activities flashcards
- Teacher's Resource Bank: Rooms word cards
- Teacher's Resource Bank: Task flashcards: *listen, sing, read, stick, say, match, write, Talk Partners*

Optional materials
- Teacher's Resource Bank: Five Trinity Exam Practice cards (selected from the Starter Unit and Units 1, 2, 3, 4, 5 and 6)

At a Glance Lesson Plan

Pupil's Book

Starting the lesson
- Use the Trinity Exam Practice cards (optional).
- Review seasonal activities.
- Set learning outcomes using the task flashcards.

Vocabulary presentation
- Present the new vocabulary.

Activity 1
- Listen and point.
- ▶ *CD3 Track 24 p269*
- Sing *There's a mouse in my house!*

Word cards
- Read the word cards.
- Match them to the flashcards.

Activity 2
- Read and stick the ten stickers.
- Listen and say the chant.
- ▶ *CD3 Track 26 p269*
- Go to the Activity Book.

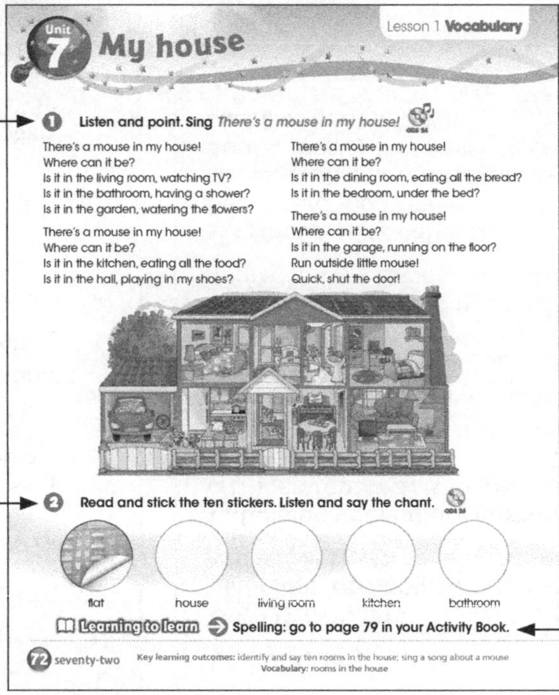

Unit 7 My house — Lesson 1 Vocabulary

1 Listen and point. Sing *There's a mouse in my house!*

There's a mouse in my house!
Where can it be?
Is it in the living room, watching TV?
Is it in the bathroom, having a shower?
Is it in the garden, watering the flowers?

There's a mouse in my house!
Where can it be?
Is it in the kitchen, eating all the food?
Is it in the hall, playing in my shoes?

There's a mouse in my house!
Where can it be?
Is it in the dining room, eating all the bread?
Is it in the bedroom, under the bed?

There's a mouse in my house!
Where can it be?
Is it in the garage, running on the floor?
Run outside little mouse!
Quick, shut the door!

2 Read and stick the ten stickers. Listen and say the chant.

flat house living room kitchen bathroom

Learning to learn → Spelling: go to page 79 in your Activity Book.

72 seventy-two

Ending the lesson
- Review the lesson.
- Review the task flashcards.

Extra activity

Vocabulary extension
- Present six additional vocabulary items.

Link to Science
- **Materials:** different materials

Learning to learn

Spelling
- Practise spelling at any time during this unit (Activity Book p79).

Digital resources

Teacher's Digital: Don't forget you can teach this lesson using the Teacher's App on Navio.

Pupil's Digital: Encourage your pupils to use the Pupil's App on Navio to practise the vocabulary from this lesson.

Powered By NAVIO

Activity Book

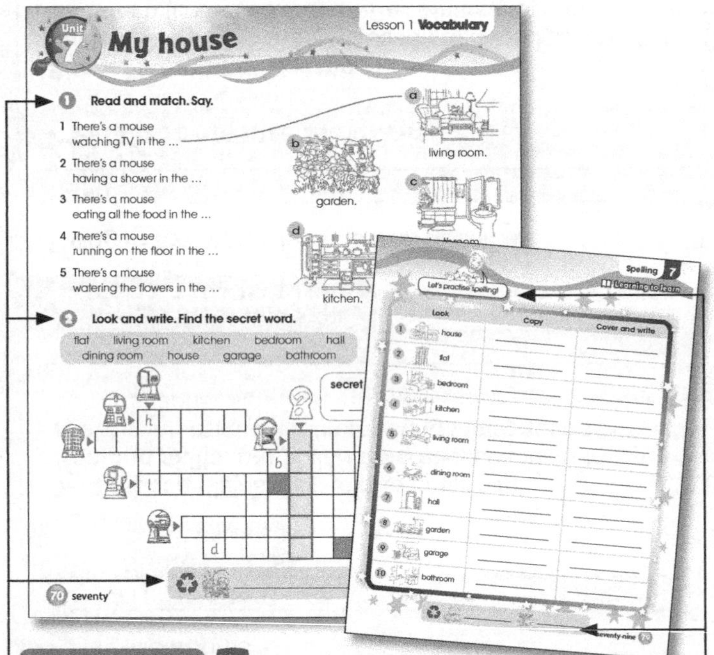

Unit 7 My house — Lesson 1 Vocabulary

1 Read and match. Say.

1 There's a mouse watching TV in the …
2 There's a mouse having a shower in the …
3 There's a mouse eating all the food in the …
4 There's a mouse running on the floor in the …
5 There's a mouse watering the flowers in the …

a living room. b garden. c … d kitchen.

2 Look and write. Find the secret word.

flat living room kitchen bedroom hall dining room house garage bathroom

70 seventy

Spelling 7 — Let's practise spelling! — Look / Copy / Cover and write: house, flat, bedroom, kitchen, living room, dining room, hall, garden, garage, bathroom

Activity Book

Activity 1
- Read and match. Say.

Activity 2
- Look and write. Find the secret word.

Recycled vocabulary
- Look, remember and write the phrase.

Spelling

Let's practise spelling!
- Use the *Look-Copy-Cover-Write* technique.

Recycled vocabulary
- Look, remember and write the words.

Starting the lesson

Use the Trinity Exam Practice cards (optional).

- The pupils practise asking and answering questions. (See p31.)

Review seasonal activities.

- Play *Which one's missing?* (See p23.)

Set learning outcomes using the task flashcards.

- Explain the aims of the lesson. Say **Today we're going to learn the names of different rooms.**
- Hold up the task flashcards and elicit the words. Stick them on one side of the board. Point to them during the lesson to reinforce your instructions.

Vocabulary presentation

Present the new vocabulary.

- (Books closed.) Show the pupils the *house* flashcard and ask **What's this?** Repeat for the *flat* flashcard. Point to either the flat or the house as appropriate and say **I live in a (house / flat).** Ask a pupil **Do you live in a house or a flat?** Encourage the rest of the pupils to ask the question in chorus. The pupil gives the answer as appropriate.
- Talk Partners The pupils ask and answer the question with a Talk Partner.
- Play *Slowly, slowly* (see p23) to introduce the rooms vocabulary.
- (Books open.) Ask **What can you see?** Ask **Can you see a mouse? Where is the mouse?** Elicit the rooms where they can see the mouse. Ask **What's it doing?** Name the actions the mouse is doing in each room. Stick the rooms flashcards on the board in the order they appear in the song.

Pupil's Book Activity 1

Listen and point. Sing *There's a mouse in my house!*

▶ *CD3 Track 24 p269*

- Say **Let's listen to the song.** Play the CD and point to the flashcards of the rooms as you hear them.
- Play the CD again. The pupils sing and do the actions.

Word cards

Read the word cards. Match them to the flashcards.

- (Books closed.) Hold up one of the rooms word cards. The pupils read collectively. A pupil sticks the word card next to the corresponding flashcard on the board. Repeat.
- Point to each word card. The pupils read the words.

Pupil's Book Activity 2

Read and stick the ten stickers. Listen and say the chant.

▶ *CD3 Track 26 p269*

- Ask a pupil to read the first word. The pupils stick the corresponding sticker above the word.
- Talk Partners The pupils find and stick the remaining stickers. Encourage them to use cooperative language. Repeat with the other stickers.
- Play the CD. The pupils listen and say the chant, pointing to the stickers in turn.

Activity Book

Activity 1

Read and match. Say.

- (Books open.) Ask a pupil to read out the first sentence and the name of the corresponding room. Repeat. The pupils match each sentence half to the corresponding room.

Answers: **1** a living room **2** c bathroom **3** d kitchen **4** e garage **5** b garden

Activity 2

Look and write. Find the secret word.

- The pupils complete the crossword. Encourage them to help each other with spelling.

Answers: (down) hall; (across) house, flat, living room, kitchen, dining room, bedroom, bathroom, garage; secret word – garden

Recycled vocabulary

- The pupils look at the picture and write the phrase.

Answer: eat chestnuts

Ending the lesson

Review the lesson.

- Say **Today we've learnt the names of rooms. What words do you remember?** Elicit the words from the pupils.

Review the task flashcards.

- Point to the task flashcards. Say **Look at the activities you've done today. Which was your favourite?** Elicit the pupils' favourite activities.

Extra activity

Vocabulary extension

- Present six additional house words: *chimney, roof, wall, window; upstairs, downstairs.*
- Use the Vocabulary Booster on Navio to practise these new words.

Link to Science

- If you are studying the Science topic of **materials** in English, you could remind the pupils that houses are made of many different materials. Elicit materials you can find in different rooms and write them on the board.
- Ask **What's the sofa made of? What are the windows made of?**

Spelling (Activity Book p79)

Let's practise spelling!

- The pupils can practise spelling the ten rooms using the *Look-Copy-Cover-Write* technique at any time before the Lesson 8 Review.

Recycled vocabulary

- The pupils look at the picture and write the words.

Answers: autumn, winter

Key Competences and Key Learning Outcomes

- Understand and act out a conversation
- Use *There's a / There are / There isn't a / There aren't any*
- Listen for specific information

Key language

- *There's a / There isn't a (hall). There are / There aren't any (plants).*

Recycled: *bathroom, bedroom, dining room, flat, garage, garden, hall, house, kitchen, living room*

Materials

- Pupil's Book p73; Activity Book p71; Class CD3; Teacher's App on Navio
- Rooms flashcards
- Teacher's Resource Bank: Task flashcards: *listen, act out, write, match, number, Talk Partners*

Optional materials

- Teacher's Resource Bank: Five Trinity Exam Practice cards (selected from the Starter Unit and Units 1, 2, 3, 4, 5 and 6)

At a Glance Lesson Plan

Pupil's Book

Starting the lesson

- Use the Trinity Exam Practice cards (optional).
- Review the *There's a mouse in my house!* song.
- ▶ *CD3 Track 24 p269*
- ▶ *CD3 Track 25 p269 (optional karaoke version)*
- Set learning outcomes using the task flashcards.

Activity 1

- Listen and repeat.
- ▶ *CD3 Track 27 p269*
- Talk Partners Act out.

Activity 2

- Listen and write *a*, *b*, *c* or *d*.
- ▶ *CD3 Track 28 p269*
- Go to the Activity Book.

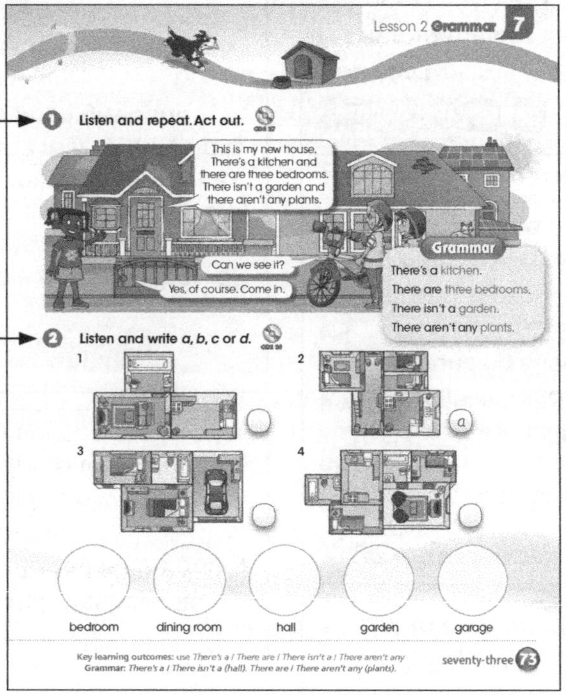

Ending the lesson

- Review the lesson.
- Review the task flashcards.

Extra activity

Reinforcement

- Describe your house or flat.

Cooperative learning

Think-Pair-Share

- Remember ten rooms words.

Activity Book

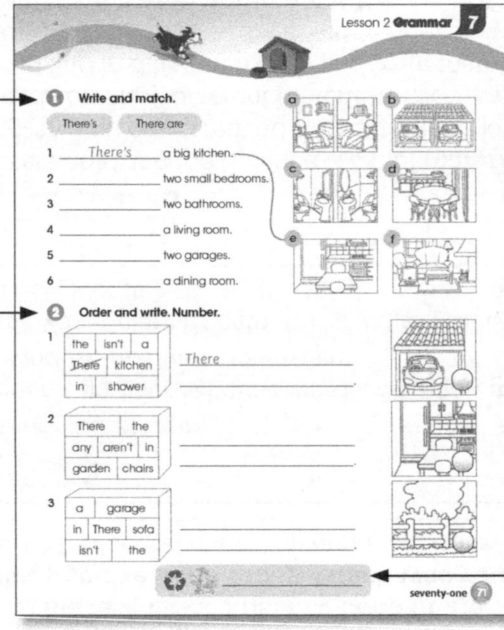

Activity Book

Activity 1

- Write and match.

Activity 2

- Order and write. Number.

Recycled vocabulary

- Look, remember and write the phrase.

Digital resources

Teacher's Digital: Don't forget you can teach this lesson using the Teacher's App on Navio.

Pupil's Digital: Encourage your pupils to use the Pupil's App on Navio to practise the vocabulary from this lesson.

Powered By NAVIO

Starting the lesson

Use the Trinity Exam Practice cards (optional).

- The pupils practise asking and answering questions. (See p31.)

Review the *There's a mouse in my house!* song.

▶ *CD3 Track 24 p269*

▶ *CD3 Track 25 p269 (optional karaoke version)*

- Organise the pupils into two lines facing each other. The lines sing alternate verses in the song. Play the CD and have the pupils act out and sing their part of the song. Play the CD again and have the pupils change roles.

Set learning outcomes using the task flashcards.

- Explain the aims of the lesson. Say **Today we're going to talk about the house.**
- Hold up the task flashcards and elicit the words. Stick them on one side of the board. Point to them during the lesson to reinforce your instructions.

Pupil's Book Activity 1

Listen and repeat. Act out.

▶ *CD3 Track 27 p269*

- (Books open.) Ask **Who can you see?**
- Play the CD. The pupils listen and read the conversation. Check understanding. Ask **Who's moving house? What's Beth's new house like? Is there a (kitchen / living room / bedroom / garden)? How many bedrooms are there?**
- Play the CD again. Pause for the pupils to repeat.
- Talk Partners The pupils practise the conversation with a Talk Partner.

Pupil's Book Activity 2

Listen and write *a*, *b*, *c* or *d*.

▶ *CD3 Track 28 p269*

- (Books open.) Focus attention on the activity and name the rooms in each house.
- Say **Let's listen. Listen and write a, b, c or d.** Play the CD. Pause after each conversation. The pupils number the corresponding home.

Answers: **1** d **2** a **3** b **4** c

Activity Book

Activity 1

Write and match.

- (Books open.) Ask the pupils to look at the sentences and decide whether to write 'There's' or 'There are'. Remind them if necessary that 'there are' is for more than one thing. The pupils then complete the sentences individually and match them to the corresponding illustration.

Answers: **1** e There's **2** a There are **3** c There are **4** f There's **5** b There are **6** d There's

Activity 2

Order and write. Number.

- Encourage a volunteer to look at the words in the bricks and order them to make a sentence. Invite different individual pupils to order and read out the other sentences. The pupils write the sentences in the space provided and number the corresponding illustration.

Answers: **1** There isn't a shower in the kitchen. (middle) **2** There aren't any chairs in the garden. (bottom) **3** There isn't a sofa in the garage. (top)

Recycled vocabulary

- The pupils look at the picture and write the phrase.

Answer: go to the beach

Ending the lesson

Review the lesson.

- Say **Today you've described a house.** Elicit the rooms.

Review the task flashcards.

- Point to the task flashcards. Say **Look at the activities you've done today. Which activity was your favourite?** Elicit the pupils' favourite activities.

Extra activity

Reinforcement

- Describe your house or flat. Elicit all the rooms of the house and stick the flashcards on the board. Describe your own flat or house to the pupils. Use all the target language. Point to the flashcards as you use them in your description. Ask a confident pupil to come to the front and describe his / her house to the class following your model.
- Talk Partners The pupils describe their house or flat and listen to a partner.

Cooperative learning

Think-Pair-Share

- Ask **Can you remember all the rooms of the house?** Ask the class to think silently on their own for a minute.
- Talk Partners The pupils work together to remember and name all ten words.
- Invite a pair to say one of the words. Praise them for their memory, hold up the corresponding flashcard and prompt the class to repeat the word.
- Finally, repeat the procedure, asking different pairs of pupils each time, until all ten words have been named.

Key Competences and Key Learning Outcomes

- Read, listen and understand a story about a haunted house
- Read the story with some fluency
- Identify properties of materials (optional)
- Become familiar with the story through a pre-reading task
- Understand the importance of being kind to your friends
- Understand and act out the story
- Give an opinion on the story

Key language
- *There's a haunted (bedroom). There aren't any (skeletons).*

Recycled: *bathroom, bed, bedroom, dining room, living room, run, shower*

Other vocabulary: *armchair, funfair, ghost, haunted, mirror, piano, scared, skeleton, sofa, witch*

Materials
- Pupil's Book pp74–75; Activity Book p72; Class CD3; Teacher's App on Navio
- Teacher's Resource Bank: Task flashcards: *listen, read, act out, write, draw, Talk Partners*
- Teacher's Resource Bank: Unit 7 Lesson 3 Animated Story

Optional materials
- Teacher's Resource Bank: Five Trinity Exam Practice cards (selected from the Starter Unit and Units 1, 2, 3, 4, 5 and 6)
- Black card and white crayons

At a Glance Lesson Plan

Starting the lesson
- Use the Trinity Exam Practice cards (optional).
- Review the *There's a mouse in my house!* song.
- ▶ ***CD3 Track 24 p269***
- ▶ ***CD3 Track 25 p269 (optional karaoke version)***
- Set learning outcomes using the task flashcards.

Before you read
- Explain the story title.
- Read and answer the question.

Activity 1
- Listen and read.
- ▶ ***CD3 Track 29 p269***
- Act out.
- ***Now watch the animated story!***

After you read: Activity 2
- Go to page 72 in your Activity Book.
- Values: Read and write.

Ending the lesson
- Review the lesson.
- Review the task flashcards

Pupil's Book

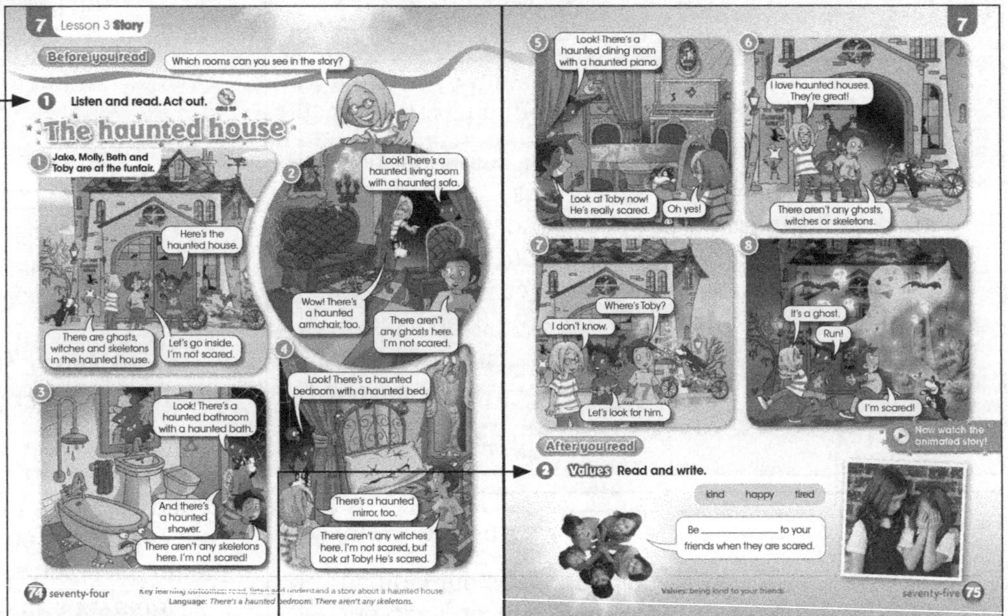

Extra activity
Reinforcement
- Haunted houses.

Cooperative learning
Listening to others
- Play a chain memory game.

Link to Science
Materials: properties of materials

Digital resources
Teacher's Digital: Don't forget you can teach this lesson using the Teacher's App on Navio.

Pupil's Digital: Encourage your pupils to use the Pupil's App on Navio to practise the vocabulary from this lesson.

Powered By NAVIO

Activity Book

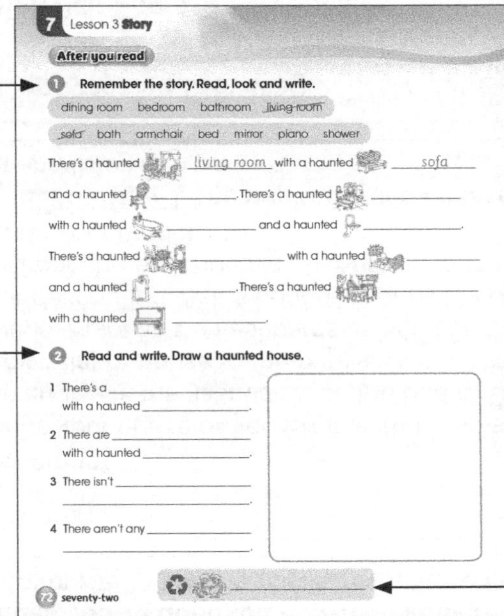

Activity Book
After you read: Activity 1
- Remember the story. Read, look and write.

Activity 2
- Read and write. Draw a haunted house.

Recycled vocabulary
- Look, remember and write the phrase.

Starting the lesson

Use the Trinity Exam Practice cards (optional).

- The pupils practise asking and answering questions. (See p31.)

Review the *There's a mouse in my house!* song.

▶ *CD3 Track 24 p269*

▶ *CD3 Track 25 p269 (optional karaoke version)*

- Play the CD (or use the karaoke version) to sing *There's a mouse in my house!* from Lesson 1.
- Point out the rhyme 'mouse' and 'house'. Ask pupils what animal rhymes with 'flat' ('cat' or 'bat'). Elicit different actions that you can do in each room and substitute them into the song. *(There's a bat in my flat! Where can it be? / Is it in the living room watching TV? / Is it in the bathroom brushing its teeth? / Is it in the kitchen eating all the cheese?)*

Set learning outcomes using the task flashcards.

- Say **Today we're going to listen to a story.**
- Hold up the task flashcards and elicit the words. Stick them on one side of the board. Point to them during the lesson to reinforce your instructions.

Before you read

Explain the story title.

- Ask the class if they like funfairs. Elicit some of the rides they like and explain the meaning of 'haunted'. Read and answer the question.
- (Books open.) Read the speech bubble. Then ask the pupils to scan the story to identify the rooms in the haunted house.
- Talk Partners Ask the pupils to feed back to a partner then invite the class to name the rooms.

Pupil's Book Activity 1

Listen and read. Act out.

▶ *CD3 Track 29 p269*

- (Books open.) Play the CD. The pupils follow the text with their finger. Pause between each frame to check understanding.

Suggested comprehension questions

- Frame 1: **Where are the children going today?** *(To the funfair.)*
- Frame 2: **Which room is this?** *(The living room.)*
- Frame 3: **Where are the children now?** *(The bathroom.)*
- Frame 4: **What is there in the haunted bedroom?** *(A haunted bed.)*
- Frame 5: **Who's scared?** *(Toby.)*
- Frame 6: **Are there really any ghosts and witches in the haunted house?** *(No.)*
- Frame 7: **What's Toby doing? What's going to happen?** *(He's ringing the bell.)*
- Frame 8: **Is there a ghost?** *(Yes.)* **Is it real?** *(No.)*
- Ask **Did you like the story? What part did you like best?**
- Talk Partners The pupils choose their favourite frame.
- Organise the class into three groups (Jake, Molly and Beth).
- Play the CD. Each group joins in when their character speaks. Pause the CD for the pupils to repeat.
- The pupils swap roles and repeat the activity.

After you read

Pupil's Book Activity 2

Go to page 72 in your Activity Book.

Activity Book

After you read: Activity 1

Remember the story. Read, look and write.

- (Books open.) Elicit the haunted items in the living room *(sofa* and *chair)*. The pupils complete the sentences with the words from the box.

Answers: living room, sofa, armchair, bathroom, bath, shower, bedroom, bed, mirror, dining room, piano

Activity 2

Read and write. Draw a haunted house.

- (Books open.) Explain to the pupils that they are going to invent their own haunted house. The pupils complete the activity individually.

Recycled vocabulary

- The pupils look at the picture and write the phrase.

Answer: plant seeds

Activity 2

Values: Read and write.

- Focus attention on the photograph and read the value. Elicit the correct word to complete the sentence.
- Ask the pupils if they are kind to their friends.

Ending the lesson

Review the lesson.

- Say **Today we've listened to a story about a haunted house. Today you've learnt that it's important to be kind to your friends.**

Review the task flashcards.

- Point to the task flashcards. Say **Look at the activities you've done today. Which activity was your favourite?** Elicit the pupils' favourite activities.

Extra activity

Reinforcement

- Using the model from the Activity Book p72, the pupils write their own text about a haunted house. Encourage the pupils to use the extension vocabulary from Lesson 1. Give out black card and white crayons. Ask them to draw their haunted houses on the card and decorate them with spider's webs.

Cooperative learning

Listening to others

- Play a chain memory game to raise pupils' awareness of the importance of listening to others. Say **In the haunted house, there is a haunted bedroom.** The pupil to the left repeats the sentence and adds another room or item. Continue around the class.

Talk Partners The pupils play with a Talk Partner.

Link to Science

- If you are studying the Science topic of **materials** in English, you could review properties of materials with the pupils. Focus on the haunted items from the story. Ask what each is made of and why. **Why is a sofa made of fabric? Why is a chair made of wood?**

Key Competences and Key Learning Outcomes

- Ask and answer about who objects belong to
- Identify natural and manufactured materials (optional)
- Sing a song

Key language

- *box, camera, clock, phone, radio, watch*
- *Whose is this (watch)? It's mine / yours / his / hers. Is it his / hers / yours? There's a (camera) in my (garage).*

Extension vocabulary

- *key, lamp, rug, towel*

Other vocabulary: *mess*

Materials

- Pupil's Book p76; Activity Book p73; Class CD3; Teacher's App on Navio
- Teacher's Resource Bank: Task flashcards: *listen, say, sing, Talk Partners, read, write, find,* colour

Optional materials

- Teacher's Resource Bank: Five Trinity Exam Practice cards (selected from the Starter Unit and Units 1, 2, 3, 4, 5 and 6)

At a Glance Lesson Plan

Pupil's Book

Starting the lesson

- Use the Trinity Exam Practice cards (optional).
- Review the Lesson 3 story.
- Set learning outcomes using the task flashcards.

Vocabulary presentation

- Present the new vocabulary.

Activity 1

- Listen, point and say.
- ▶ *CD3 Track 30 p269*
- Play *Whose is this?*

Activity 2

- Listen and point. Sing *What a mess!*
- ▶ *CD3 Track 31 p270*

Activity 3

- Listen and repeat.
- Talk Partners Ask and answer.
- ▶ *CD3 Track 32 p270*
- Go to the Activity Book.

Ending the lesson

- Review the lesson.
- Review the task flashcards.

Extra activity

Vocabulary extension

- Present four additional vocabulary items.

Link to Science

- **Materials:** natural and manufactured materials

Activity Book

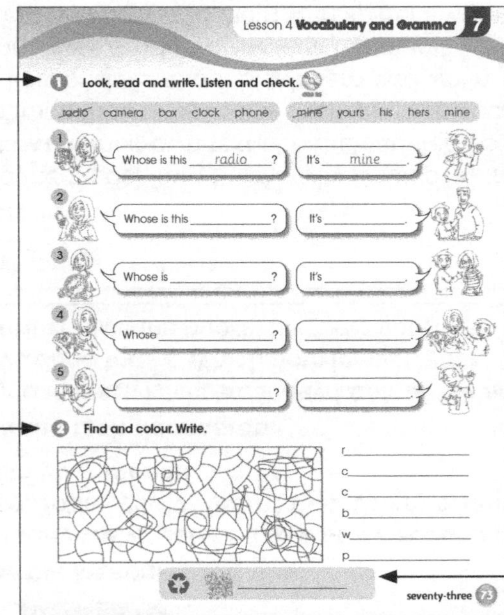

Activity Book

Activity 1

- Look, read and write.
- Listen and check.
- ▶ *CD3 Track 33 p270*

Activity 2

- Find and colour. Write.

Recycled vocabulary

- Look, remember and write the phrase.

Digital resources

Teacher's Digital: Don't forget you can teach this lesson using the Teacher's App on Navio.

Pupil's Digital: Encourage your pupils to use the Pupil's App on Navio to practise the vocabulary from this lesson.

Powered By NAVIO

Starting the lesson

Use the Trinity Exam Practice cards (optional).

- The pupils practise asking and answering questions. (See p31.)

Review the Lesson 3 story.

- Say **In the haunted house, there's a haunted living room. What is there in the haunted living room?** The pupils scan the story and suggest some items. Repeat with the other rooms.

Set learning outcomes using the task flashcards.

- Say **Today we're going to talk about our possessions.**
- Hold up the task flashcards in turn and elicit the words. Stick them on one side of the board. Point to them during the lesson to reinforce your instructions.

Vocabulary presentation

Present the new vocabulary.

- (Books open.) Point to the first picture and say **camera**. Repeat the word and ask the class to say it with you. Ask **Have you got a camera? Let's take a photo!** Repeat with the other items.

Pupil's Book Activity 1

Listen, point and say.

▶ *CD3 Track 30 p269*

- Say **Let's listen and repeat the words.** Play the CD. The pupils repeat each word, pointing to the corresponding photograph each time. Play the CD again and repeat the activity.
- (Books closed.) Play *Whose is this?* Introduce the possessive pronouns by picking up items belonging to you and some of the pupils. Pick up your pencil and say **It's mine.** Encourage all the pupils to pick up their own pencils and repeat *It's mine.* Pick up a pencil belonging to a pupil. Point to the pupil as you say **It's yours.** Encourage the pupils to pick up their friend's pencil and say *It's yours.* Pick up an item belonging to one of the girls and say **It's hers.** Repeat for a boy, saying **It's his.**
- Finally, say the possessive pronouns in random order, encouraging the pupils to point to and look at the corresponding pupils. Say **It's mine.** (The pupils pointto themselves.) **It's yours.** (The pupils look and point to the same person.) **It's his.** (The pupils point to a boy and look at you.) **It's hers.** (The pupils point to a girl and look at you.)

Pupil's Book Activity 2

Listen and point. Sing *What a mess!*

▶ *CD3 Track 31 p270*

- (Books open.) Point to the first picture and elicit the item that Mum is holding. Then say **Let's listen to the song and point to the objects.**
- Play the CD. The pupils listen and point to objects on the page as they appear in the song. At the end of the song ask **Whose is the watch? What does the boy say?** *(It's mine.)* Play the CD again. The pupils sing and point to the people who the items belong to.

Pupil's Book Activity 3

Listen and repeat. Ask and answer.

▶ *CD3 Track 32 p270*

- Play the CD. Play the CD again and ask the pupils to repeat the question and answer. Then, invite a pair of pupils to act out the conversation, miming the objects.
- Talk Partners The pupils practise the conversation naming different objects each time and pointing to different pupils each time.

Activity Book

Activity 1

Look, read and write. Listen and check.

▶ *CD3 Track 33 p270*

- (Books open.) A volunteer reads out the instructions. Prompt the class to read out the words in the box.
- Choose another volunteer to read out the first question and then a different pupil to read out the answer. Repeat for the other questions. The pupils then complete the activity individually.
- Talk Partners The pupils check their answers with a Talk Partner.

Answers: **1** radio, mine **2** phone, his **3** this clock, hers **4** is this camera, It's yours **5** Whose is this box, It's mine

Activity 2

Find and colour. Write.

- (Books open.) The pupils find and colour the hidden objects in the picture. They write the names of the objects in the spaces provided.

Answers: radio, camera, clock, box, watch, phone

Recycled vocabulary

- The pupils look at the picture and write the phrase.

Answer: celebrate Halloween

Ending the lesson

Review the lesson.

- Say **Today we've talked about our belongings.** Elicit some sentences from the pupils.

Review the task flashcards.

- Point to the task flashcards. Say **Look at the activities you've done today. Which activity was your favourite?** Elicit the pupils' favourite activities.

Extra activity

Vocabulary extension

- Use the Vocabulary Booster on Navio and present and practise four additional vocabulary items: *key, lamp, rug, towel.*

Link to Science

- If you are studying the Science topic of **materials** in English, you could review natural and manufactured materials. Ask **What is a (camera) made of?** *(Plastic.)* Remind them that plastic is a manufactured material. Repeat for natural materials.

Key Competences and Key Learning Outcomes

- Say a tongue twister with the 'ou' sound
- Learn and practise 'ou' and 'ow' spellings
- Listen for specific information
- Play a communication game about where objects are

Key language

Recycled: *bathroom, bedroom, dining room, flat, garage, garden, hall, house, kitchen, living room; box, camera, clock, phone, radio, watch; big, small*

Recycled: *Whose is this (camera)? It's mine / yours / his / hers.*

Materials

- Pupil's Book 77; Activity Book p74; Class CD3; Teacher's App on Navio
- Teacher's Resource Bank: Task flashcards: *listen, say, match, cut out, Talk Partners, write, colour*
- Feely bag or shopping bag
- Teacher's Resource Bank: Unit 7 Lesson 5 Activity 3 cut-out
- Scissors

Optional materials

- Teacher's Resource Bank: Five Trinity Exam Practice cards (selected from the Starter Unit and Units 1, 2, 3, 4, 5 and 6)
- Props for the *What a mess!* song
- Glue

At a Glance Lesson Plan

Pupil's Book

Starting the lesson

- Use the Trinity Exam Practice cards (optional).
- Review the *What a mess!* song.
- ▶ ***CD3 Track 31 p270***
- Play *Whose is this?*
- Set learning outcomes using the task flashcards.

Activity 1

- Listen and say.
- ▶ ***CD3 Track 34 p270***
- Go to the Activity Book.
- Go to Magic Phonics.

Activity 2

- Listen and match.
- ▶ ***CD3 Track 35 p270***

Activity 3

- Talk Partners Make and play the game (Teacher's Resource Bank).

Ending the lesson

- Review the lesson.
- Review the task flashcards.

Extra activity

Extension

- Write a description of a house.

Cooperative learning

Working together as a team

- Talk Partners
  Play *Beat the clock.*
- Add to the pronunciation wall display.

Digital resources

Teacher's Digital: Don't forget you can teach this lesson using the Teacher's App on Navio.

Pupil's Digital: Encourage your pupils to use the Pupil's App on Navio to practise the vocabulary from this lesson.

Powered By NAVIO

Activity Book

Activity Book

Activity 1

- Write and say.

Activity 2

- Colour the 'ow' words red and the 'ou' words blue.
- Say.

Go to Magic Phonics.

Activity 3

- Talk Partners
  Play *Snap* in pairs.

Recycled vocabulary

- Look, remember and write the phrase.

Starting the lesson

Use the Trinity Exam Practice cards (optional).

- The pupils practise asking and answering questions. (See p31.)

Review the *What a mess!* song.

▶ *CD3 Track 31 p270*

- If possible, use props for the song (a box, a watch and a bone cut out of paper). Play the parts of the parents by holding up all the items. The pupils play the part of the children in the song, pointing to other pupils to demonstrate *(It's hers / his).* Choose a volunteer to play the dog. Play the CD. All the pupils join in with the whole song.
- Play *Whose is this?* Review the personal pronouns from Lesson 4. Show the pupils your pen and ask **Whose is this?** Point to yourself and ask them to say *It's yours*. Put some of the pupils' objects in a feely bag (or an ordinary shopping bag). Take out an item and ask **Whose is this?** Encourage the owner to say *It's mine!* The rest of the class turn to face him / her and say *It's yours!* Ask the question again and encourage the pupils to face you and say *It's his / hers*, as appropriate. The pupils play the game in groups.

Set learning outcomes using the task flashcards.

- Say **Today we're going to say a tongue twister. We're going to make and play a game.**
- Hold up the task flashcards in turn and elicit the activities. Stick them on one side of the board. Point to them during the lesson to reinforce your instructions.

Pupil's Book Activity 1

Listen and say.

▶ *CD3 Track 34 p270*

- Write the words *house and brown* on the board and ask the pupils which sound they can hear in both words. *('ou')* Circle the target grapheme in each word 'ou' and 'ow' and model the sound. Encourage the pupils to say the sound with you. Check for accuracy.
- *Say* **It's time for Toby's tongue twister! What can you see?**

Go to Magic Phonics.

- Play the CD. The pupils listen and repeat the target sound, then the words and then the entire tongue twister, faster and faster.

Activity Book

Activity 1

Write and say.

- (Books open.) Say **Look at Toby's tongue twister! The letters for 'ou' and 'ow' are missing.** The pupils complete the tongue twister.
- Talk Partners The pupils say Toby's tongue twister and point to the 'ou' sounds.

Answers: brown, cow, loud, mouse, around, house

Activity 2

Colour the 'ow' words red and the 'ou' words blue. Say.

- Ask pupils to say the words then colour 'ow' words red and 'ou' words blue.

Answers: red: cow, clown, crown, owl, shower
blue: mouse, mouth, count, cloud, house

Go to Magic Phonics.

Activity 3

Play *Snap* in pairs.

- Demonstrate the game with a volunteer. You each think of a word, count to three together, point to the picture and say the word. If the words are the same, say *Snap!* If they are different, continue playing the game.
- Talk Partners The pupils play the game with a Talk Partner.

Recycled vocabulary

- The pupils look at the picture and write the phrase.

Answer: smell flowers

Pupil's Book Activity 2

Listen and match.

▶ *CD3 Track 35 p270*

- (Books open.) Explain that Molly and Jake are asking about where some objects are in the house. The pupils draw lines to where the objects are.
- Play the CD. Pause after each sentence to give the pupils time to draw their lines and to check their answers.

Answers: **1** camera, living room **2** radio, dining room **3** clock, hall **4** box, garage **5** phone, bathroom **6** watch, kitchen

Pupil's Book Activity 3

Make and play the game (Teacher's Resource Bank).

- (Books open.) Show the pupils how to cut out the cards. The pupils decorate the house with different objects in each room.
- Talk Partners Both pupils hide the six objects in the house. They place a barrier between them. They take turns to describe the location of the objects. If the items are in different rooms, the pupils turn over the cards. Once they have finished, they remove the barrier to check.

Ending the lesson

Review the lesson.

- Say **Today we've practised a tongue twister**. Ask pupils to say it again.

Review the task flashcards.

- Point to the task flashcards. Ask **Which activity was your favourite?**

Extra activity

Extension

- Once the pupils have finished playing with the cut-outs, they can stick the items on the house with glue. They write a short description of the house following the model *There's … / There are …*

Cooperative learning

Working together as a team

Talk Partners Play *Beat the clock* to practise pronunciation of the 'ou' / 'ow' sound (see p53).

- Add to the pronunciation wall display, adding a cloud ('ou') and a flower ('ow').

Key Competences and Key Learning Outcomes

- Listen for general understanding
- Learn about children's bedrooms in Britain
- Think about what you've got in your bedroom

Key language

- *board games, bookcase, drum, guitar, pop music, pyjamas, stickers, sticker collection, upstairs*

Recycled: *books, music*

Recycled: *There's … There are … There isn't … There aren't any … I've got (a guitar). I love (music). Today, I'm making … We play / listen to …*

Materials

- Pupil's Book p78; Activity Book p75; Class CD3; Teacher's App on Navio
- Teacher's Resource Bank: Task flashcards: *Talk Partners, listen, read, think, match, write, tick, draw, say*

Optional materials

- Teacher's Resource Bank: Five Trinity Exam Practice cards (selected from the Starter Unit and Units 1, 2, 3, 4, 5 and 6)
- Pictures of bedrooms from magazines or catalogues

At a Glance Lesson Plan

Pupil's Book

Starting the lesson

- Use the Trinity Exam Practice cards (optional).
- Talk Partners
  Review Toby's tongue twister.
  ▶ *CD3 Track 34 p270*
- Set learning outcomes using the task flashcards.

Activity 1

- Listen and read. Answer.
  ▶ *CD3 Track 36 p270*

Think about your culture

- What have you got in your bedroom?

Go to the Activity Book.

Ending the lesson

- Review the lesson.
- Review the task flashcards.

Extra activities

Reinforcement

- Talk Partners
  Compare your bedrooms.

Extension

- Talk Partners
  Describe bedrooms.

Digital resources

Teacher's Digital: Don't forget you can teach this lesson using the Teacher's App on Navio.

Powered By NAVIO

Activity Book

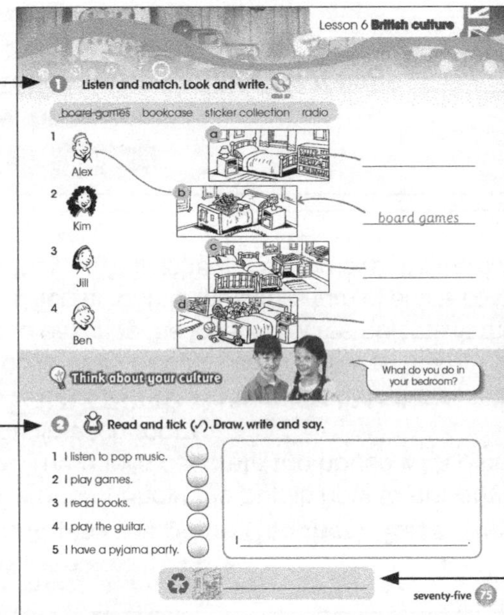

Activity Book

Activity 1

- Listen and match. Look and write.

▶ *CD3 Track 37 p270*

Activity 2: Think about your culture.

- Read and tick (✓). Draw, write and say.

Recycled vocabulary

- Look, remember and write the phrase.

Starting the lesson

Use the Trinity Exam Practice cards (optional).

- The pupils practise asking and answering questions. (See p31.)

Review Toby's tongue twister.

▶ *CD3 Track 34 p270*

- Ask the class **What sound did you practise in Toby's tongue twister?** *('ou').* Ask if they can remember the tongue twister. *(A brown cow and a loud mouse run around the house.)*
- Talk Partners The pupils practise the tongue twister as a class and then with a Talk Partner. The pairs play *Faster and faster,* reading from the Pupil's Book (page 77) if necessary. A fast pair say the tongue twister for the class.
- Draw a chart with two columns ('ou' and 'ow') on the board. Elicit words with both spellings. Ask pupils to classify the words, e.g. 'ou': *house, mouse; 'ow': cow, clown*. Focus the pupils' attention on the words that rhyme and group them together *(house and mouse, flower and shower, loud and cloud, town, down and clown).*

Set learning outcomes using the task flashcards.

- Say **Today we're going to learn about children's bedrooms in Britain.**
- Hold up the task flashcards in turn and elicit the activities. Stick them on one side of the board. Point to them during the lesson to reinforce your instructions.

Pupil's Book Activity 1

Listen and read. Answer.

▶ *CD3 Track 36 p270*

- (Books closed.) Before looking in their books, tell the pupils they are going to listen to Tom and Anna describing their bedrooms. Ask **What do you think is in the bedrooms?** Make a mind map on the board with their suggestions. Write *bedroom* in the centre and bring two separate branches out: one for Tom and one for Anna. Ask the pupils if they think both children have the same things in their bedrooms or if they are different.
- (Books open.) Focus the pupils' attention on the photographs and ask **What can you see? Let's read and listen.** Play the CD. At the end of the text, check understanding by pointing to the second photo. Ask **What is there in Tom's bedroom?** Repeat the question with the other photos.
- Return to the mind map and compare the pupils' suggestions with the children's bedrooms.

Pupil's Book Think about your culture

What have you got in your bedroom?

- Read the question and encourage the class to tell you about their own bedrooms.

Activity Book

Activity 1

Listen and match. Look and write.

▶ *CD3 Track 37 p270*

- (Books open.) Point to the first child on the left and ask **Which is Alex's room?** Then say **Let's listen and find out.** Play the CD, pausing after the first piece of information to check pupils' answers. Repeat the procedure with the other children. The class answers and draws a matching line each time. When they have finished, the pupils label the items in each room.

Answers: **1** b, board games **2** d, radio **3** c, sticker collection **4** a, bookcase

Activity 2: Think about your culture

Read and tick (✓). Draw, write and say.

- (Books open.) Ask the pupils to read the sentences and tick the boxes if they do these activities in their bedrooms. Finally, ask the pupils to draw their own bedroom and complete the sentence. Invite different pupils to show the rest of the class their drawings and describe their bedroom.

Recycled vocabulary

- The pupils look at the picture and write the phrase.

Answer: finish school

Ending the lesson

Review the lesson.

- Say **Today you've learnt about bedrooms in Britain.** Elicit some similarities and differences with their own bedrooms.

Review the task flashcards.

- Point to the task flashcards. Say **Look at the activities you've done today. Which activity was your favourite?** Elicit the pupils' favourite activities.

Extra activities

Reinforcement

- Talk Partners Ask the pupils to read their bedroom description to a Talk Partner. As Pupil A reads the description, Pupil B comments on similarities and differences: Encourage them to say *It's the same! It's different!*

Extension

- Talk Partners Describing bedrooms. Cut some pictures of bedrooms from magazines or catalogues prior to the class. Encourage the pupils to describe them with a Talk Partner.

Key Competences and Key Learning Outcomes

- Learn about the properties of glass (optional)

- Read for specific information

- Read and understand a play script
- Complete conversations from a play
- Act out a play

Key language

- *dragon, fairy godmother, get married, glass, midnight, play, prince, sad, script*

Recycled: *bathroom, bedroom, house, kitchen; clean, dirty, new, old; car, dress, mice, phone, pumpkin, shoe, sister*

Recycled: *There are … Whose is this? It's (mine / yours / hers). Is it yours? She's (cleaning the house).*

Materials

- Pupil's Book p79; Activity Book p76; Class CD3; Teacher's App on Navio
- Teacher's Resource Bank: Task flashcards: *circle, Talk Partners, listen, read, write, act out*

Optional materials

- Teacher's Resource Bank: Five Trinity Exam Practice cards (selected from the Starter Unit and Units 1, 2, 3, 4, 5 and 6)
- Coloured paper

At a Glance Lesson Plan

Starting the lesson

- Use the Trinity Exam Practice cards (optional).
- Review the *What a mess!* song.
- ▶ ***CD3 Track 31 p270***
- Set learning outcomes using the task flashcards.

Before you read: Activity 1

- What's in the play? Look and circle.

Activity 2

- Listen and read the play script.
- ▶ ***CD3 Track 38 p270***

After you read

- Go to page 76 in your Activity Book.

Ending the lesson

- Review the lesson.
- Review the task flashcards.
- Sing a song (optional).

Pupil's Book

Lesson 7 Literacy 7

Text type: **A play script**

Before you read

1 What's in the play? Look and circle.

a pumpkin | a shoe | a clock | a dragon | some mice | a fairy godmother

2 Listen and read the play script.

Cinderella

Scene 1

Cinderella lives in a big house with her two wicked sisters. There are twenty bedrooms, seventeen bathrooms and two kitchens.

Sister 1: Tidy up, Cinderella!
Cinderella: Yes, of course. Whose is this phone?
Sister 2: It's mine.

Scene 2

Poor Cinderella. She's cleaning the house. There's a party tonight, but she can't go.

Cinderella: I'm sad. My dress is old.
Fairy Godmother: Here's a new dress. These mice can be horses. This pumpkin can be a car. These shoes are made of glass. You can go to the party now!

Scene 3

Prince: Do you want to dance?
Cinderella: Yes, please.
Cinderella: Oh no! It's midnight.
Prince: Come back!

Cinderella runs away. Her shoe falls off. The horses are mice again. The car is a pumpkin again. Her dress is old again.

Scene 4

The next day, Cinderella is cleaning the house. The prince visits.

Prince: Whose is this shoe?
Sisters 1 and 2: It's mine!
Prince: Cinderella. Is it yours?
Cinderella: Yes, it's mine. Thank you.

The Prince and Cinderella get married and live happily ever after.

After you read

Go to page 76 in your Activity Book.

Key learning outcomes: read and understand a play script

seventy-nine 79

Extra activity

Extension

- Act out an alternative play script.

Link to Science

- **Materials:** the properties of glass

Activity Book

7 Lesson 7 Literacy

After you read

Text type: **A play script**

1 Read again and circle.

1 Cinderella lives in a flat / (house).
2 There are sixteen / seventeen bathrooms.
3 Cinderella's dress is old / new.
4 Cinderella's new dress is purple / blue.
5 The fairy godmother turns the mice into cows / horses.
6 Cinderella goes swimming / dancing.
7 She loses her phone / shoe.
8 The shoes are made of paper / glass.

2 Talk Partners Write the conversations. Act out.

76 seventy-six

Activity Book

After you read: Activity 1

- Read again and circle.

Activity 2

- Write the conversations.
- Talk Partners Act out.

Recycled vocabulary

- Look, remember and write the phrase.

Digital resources

Teacher's Digital: Don't forget you can teach this lesson using the Teacher's App on Navio.

Pupil's Digital: Encourage your pupils to use the Pupil's App on Navio to practise the vocabulary from this lesson.

Powered By NAVIO

Starting the lesson

Use the Trinity Exam Practice cards (optional).

- The pupils practise asking and answering questions. (See p31.)

Review the *What a mess!* song.

▶ *CD3 Track 31 p270*

- Personalise the song by substituting items from the classroom. Play the parts of the parents by holding up all the items. The pupils sing and point to other pupils to demonstrate. *(It's hers / his.)* All the pupils should join in with the whole song.

Set learning outcomes using the task flashcards.

- Say **Today we're going to read a play script.**
- Hold up the task flashcards in turn and elicit the activities. Stick them on one side of the board. Point to them during the lesson to reinforce your instructions.

Before you read: Pupil's Book Activity 1

What's in the play? Look and circle.

- (Books closed.) Tell the pupils that today they are going to read a play script. Ask if they know what this is. Explain that a play script is used in the theatre. Everybody reads their part and then they learn it and put on a show.
- Tell the pupils that the play script they are going to read is based on the story of Cinderella. Ask the pupils what they can tell you about the story of Cinderella and make a mind map on the board.
- (Books open.) Focus their attention on the pre-reading task.
- Talk Partners Ask the pupils to quickly scan the play, circle the items that appear and compare with a Talk Partner.

Answers: a pumpkin, a shoe, a clock, some mice, a fairy godmother

Pupil's Book Activity 2

Listen and read the play script.

▶ *CD3 Track 38 p270*

- Say **Let's read and listen to the play.** Play the CD. Ask the pupils to follow the text with their finger as they're reading.
- Pause the CD between each scene and scan the room to check that all the pupils are on task. If necessary, ask questions after each scene to help and check understanding.
- Check the pupils' understanding by asking **Who does Cinderella live with? Is her house big or small? How many (bedrooms / bathrooms / kitchens) are there? Is Cinderella happy? Who gives Cinderella a new dress? What happens to the (mice / pumpkin)? Can Cinderella go to the party? What are Cinderella's shoes made of? What happens at midnight? What falls off? Does the prince find her?**
- Explain to the class that they are going to act out the play. Organise the pupils into groups of five and distribute the parts: Cinderella, the two sisters, the fairy godmother and the prince. Play the CD. Each pupil joins in when their character speaks. If the pupils need extra support, pause the CD after each utterance and ask the pupils to repeat the phrase instead.

Activity Book

After you read: Activity 1

Read again and circle.

- (Books open.) Encourage one of the pupils to read out the first sentence and choose between the words 'house' and 'flat'. Say **That's right! Cinderella lives in a house.** Continue for the remaining sentences deciding on the correct answer together.
- Talk Partners Pupils should then circle the correct word in each sentence and check their answers with a Talk Partner.

Answers: **1** house **2** seventeen **3** old **4** blue **5** horses **6** dancing **7** shoe **8** glass

Activity 2

Write the conversations. Act out.

- The pupils complete the conversations from the story.
- Talk Partners The pupils act out the conversations once they have completed them.

Answers: **1** phone, mine **2** dance; Yes, please. **3** Whose is this shoe?; It's mine. **4** yours, it's mine

Recycled vocabulary

- The pupils look at the picture and write the phrase.

Answer: open presents

Ending the lesson

Review the lesson.

- Say **Today we've read a play script.** Ask the pupils to name the characters from the play script.

Review the task flashcards.

- Point to the task flashcards. Say **Look at the activities you've done today. Which activity was your favourite?** Elicit the pupils' favourite activities.

Sing a song (optional).

- Choose a song. The class sings and does the actions. Alternatively, invite the class to choose a song to sing.

Extra activity

Extension

- Replace 'phone' with other objects and encourage the pupils to act out further conversations still playing the characters of Cinderella and her sisters.

Link to Science

- If you are studying the Science topic of **materials** in English, you could ask about the properties of glass, since in the story Cinderella's shoe is made of glass. Ask **Is glass a good material for shoes? Why? Why not? What other materials are shoes made of?**

Key Competences and Key Learning Outcomes

- Review language in the unit
- Reflect on own learning
- Sing a cooperative learning song

Key language

Recycled: *bathroom, bedroom, dining room, flat, garage, garden, hall, house, kitchen, living room; box, camera, clock, phone, radio, watch*

Recycled: *There's (a sofa) in the (living room). There are (socks) in the (bedroom). There is / isn't a (garage). There are / aren't any (bedrooms). Whose is this (box)? It's (mine / yours / his / hers).*

Materials

- Pupil's Book p80; Activity Book p77; Class CD3; Teacher's App on Navio
- Rooms flashcards
- Teacher's Resource Bank: Task flashcards: *listen, number, write, say, sing, stick, follow, Talk Partners, think*
- Teacher's Resource Bank: Traffic light cut-out
- *Give Me Five!* sticker
- Dice and counters

Optional materials

- Teacher's Resource Bank: Five Trinity Exam Practice cards (selected from the Starter Unit and Units 1, 2, 3, 4, 5 and 6)

At a Glance Lesson Plan

Pupil's Book

Starting the lesson

- Use the Trinity Exam Practice cards (optional).
- Review the unit vocabulary.
- Set learning outcomes using the task flashcards.

Activity 1

- Listen and number.
- Write and say.

▶ *CD3 Track 39 p270*

Activity 2

- Look at Activity 1. Write true sentences.

Activity 3
Cooperative learning

- Sing *Well Done!*

▶ *CD3 Track 40 p271*

- Stick the *Give Me Five!* sticker.

Go to the Activity Book.

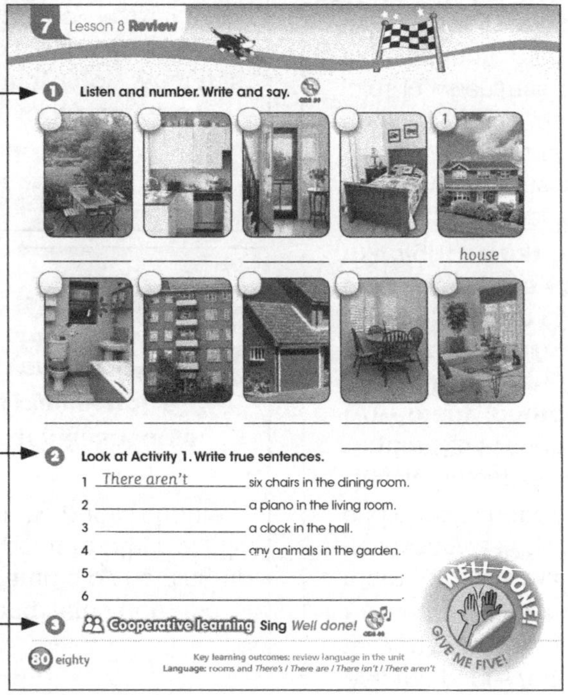

Ending the lesson

- Review the task flashcards
- Sing a song (optional).

Cooperative learning

Think-Pair-Share

- Remember ten rooms words.

Activity Book

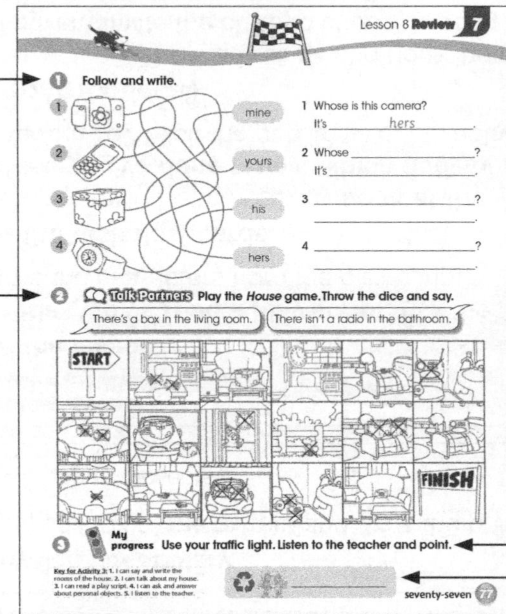

Activity Book

Activity 1

- Follow and write.

Activity 2

- **Talk Partners**
  Play the *House* game.
  Throw the dice and say.

Activity 3 My progress

- Use your traffic light. Listen to the teacher and point.

Recycled vocabulary

- Look, remember and write the phrase.

Digital resources

Teacher's Digital: Don't forget you can teach this lesson using the Teacher's App on Navio.

Pupil's Digital: Encourage your pupils to use the Pupil's App on Navio to practise the vocabulary from this lesson.

Powered By NAVIO

Starting the lesson

Use the Trinity Exam Practice cards (optional).

- The pupils practise asking and answering questions. (See p31.)

Review the unit vocabulary.

- Play *Class chain* (see p23) with the unit flashcards to review rooms.
- **Option:** Play the game in two teams. The teams take it in turns to remember the words.

Set learning outcomes using the task flashcards.

- Say **Today we're going to remember what we've learnt in Unit 7.**
- Hold up the task flashcards in turn and elicit the words. Stick them on one side of the board. Point to them during the lesson to reinforce your instructions.

Pupil's Book Activity 1

Listen and number. Write and say.

▶ *CD3 Track 39 p270*

- (Books open.) Point to each of the photos and elicit the words.
- Play the CD. Pause after each sentence. The pupils write the correct number in the circles.
- Play the CD again. The pupils write the correct room under each picture. Then they say the words.

Answers: **1** house **2** kitchen **3** dining room **4** living room **5** bedroom **6** hall **7** garden **8** bathroom **9** garage **10** flat

Pupil's Book Activity 2

Look at Activity 1. Write true sentences.

- (Books open.) Ask the pupils to look at the photos and complete the sentences. They write their own answers for 5 and 6.

Answers: **1** There aren't **2** There isn't **3** There isn't **4** There aren't **5** & **6** Pupils' own answers

Pupil's Book Activity 3: **Cooperative learning**

Sing *Well done!*

▶ *CD3 Track 40 p271*

- Praise the class for their hard work and play the *Well done!* song. The pupils listen the first time. Play the CD again and encourage the pupils to join in.

Stick the *Give Me Five!* sticker.

- The pupils stick the *Give Me Five! sticker on the* Pupil's Book page.

Activity Book

Activity 1

Follow and write.

- (Books open.) Choose two volunteers to read out the first exchange. Tell them to follow the path from the camera to the word 'hers'. The pupils write questions about each object and then follow the path to determine the answer.

Answers: **1** hers **2** is this phone, mine **3** Whose is this box? It's yours. **4** Whose is this watch? It's his.

Activity 2

Play the *House* game. Throw the dice and say.

- Demonstrate the game with a volunteer. Pupils need a dice and a counter to play. They throw the dice, move their counter and make a sentence about the square they land on. If the items are crossed out, the pupils should make negative sentences. If there is more than one item, the pupils should make plural sentences. *(There's a clock in the kitchen. There isn't a radio in the kitchen.)* The first pupil to the finish line is the winner.
- **Talk Partners** The pupils play the *House* game with a Talk Partner.

Activity 3 My progress

Use your traffic light. Listen to the teacher and point.

- (Books closed.) Ask the class to take out their traffic light cut-out. Say **Let's think about our work in this unit.** Read the first self-assessment statement.
- Point to the green circle, and say **Yes, I can do this very well.** Point to the orange circle and say **Yes, I can do this.** Point to the red circle and say **No, I can't do this.**
- Read the rest of the statements. For each one, the pupils point to the colour on their traffic light that shows how they feel about their own learning.

Self-assessment statements

1. I can say and write the rooms of the house.
2. I can talk about my house.
3. I can read a play script.
4. I can ask and answer about personal objects.
5. I listen to the teacher.

Recycled vocabulary

- The pupils look at the picture and write the phrase.

Answer: wear warm clothes

Ending the lesson

Review the task flashcards.

- Point to the task flashcards. Say **Look at the activities you've done today. Which activity was your favourite?** Elicit the pupils' favourite activity.

Sing a song (optional).

- The class chooses their favourite song from the unit. The class sings and does the actions.

Cooperative learning

Think-Pair-Share

- Ask **Can you remember the ten rooms words?** Ask the class to think silently on their own for a minute. **Talk Partners** The pupils work with a Talk Partner to remember and name all ten words.
- Invite a pair to say one of the words. Hold up the corresponding flashcard and prompt the class to repeat the word.
- Finally, repeat the procedure, asking different pairs of pupils each time, until all ten words have been named.

Key Competences and Key Learning Outcomes

- Watch and understand a video about unusual houses
- Say what you do to help at home
- Understand the importance of helping at home

Key language

- *bathroom, bedroom, bungalow, castle, dining room, flat, hall, house, houseboat, kitchen, living room, windmill*

Materials

- Pupil's Book p81; Activity Book p78; Class CD3; Video; Teacher's App on Navio
- Teacher's Resource Bank: Task flashcards: *number, read, tick, circle, listen, match, draw, Talk Partner*

Optional materials

- Teacher's Resource Bank: Trinity Exam Practice cards (selected from Unit 7)
- Piece of paper for each pupil

At a Glance Lesson Plan

Pupil's Book

Starting the lesson

- Use the Trinity Exam Practice cards (optional).
- **Think-Pair-Share** Talk about favourite rooms.
- Set learning outcomes and use the task flashcards.

Pre-watching activity

- Discuss the types of houses they live in.

Activity 1

- Watch the video.
  Unit 7 video p279
- Number the pictures.

Activity 2

- Watch the video again.
  Unit 7 video
- Read and tick (✓) or cross (✗).

Activity 3

- Read and circle.
  Go to the Activity Book.

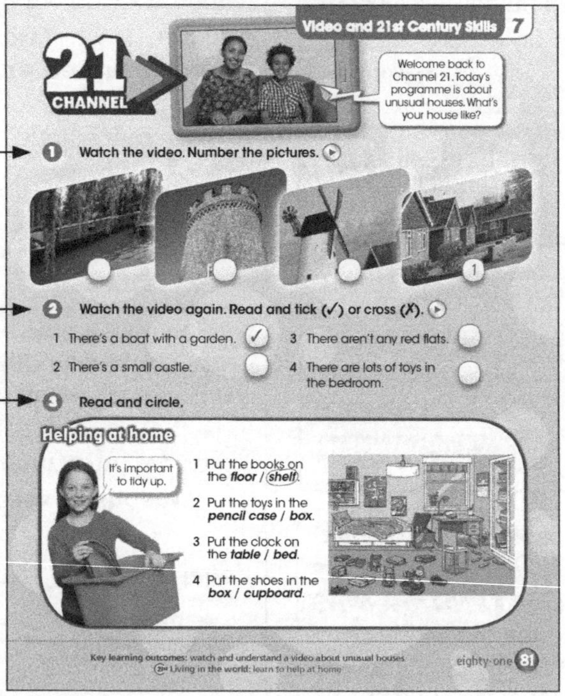

Ending the lesson

- Review the lesson.
- Review the task flashcards. Elicit the pupils' favourite activities.

Extra activity

Extension

- Pupils write sentences to say what they do to help at home.

Digital resources

Teacher's Digital: Don't forget you can teach this lesson using the Teacher's App on Navio.

Pupil's Digital: Encourage your pupils to use the Pupil's App on Navio to practise the vocabulary from this lesson.

Powered By NAVIO

Activity Book

Activity Book

Activity 1

- Where do these things go? Listen and match.
  ▶ *CD3 Track 41 p271*

Activity 2

- Read and tick (✓). Draw and say.

Recycled vocabulary

- Look, remember and write the phrase.

Starting the lesson

Use the Trinity Exam Practice cards (optional).

- The pupils practise asking and answering questions. (See p31.)

Talk about favourite rooms.

- Write the heading *Rooms in the house* on the board. Ask pupils to tell you all the rooms they know and write them under the heading.

  Think-Pair-Share Ask **Which is your favourite room in your house? Why?** In pairs, pupils ask and answer the questions.

Set learning outcomes and use the task flashcards.

- Say **Today we're going to watch a video and then ask and answer questions about unusual houses**.
- Hold up the task flashcards, in turn, and elicit the activities. Stick them on the side of the board. Point to them during the lesson to reinforce your instructions.

Pre-watching activity

- Ask **What type of house do you live in? What type of other houses do people live in?**

Pupil's Book Activity 1

Watch the video. Number the pictures. *p279*

- Play Part 1. Ask **What type of house does Sophie live in?** *(A flat.)*
- Focus the pupils' attention on the video stills. Ask **Which type of house would you like to live in?**
- Play Part 2, pausing after the first video still. Ask the pupils to point to the corresponding photo in their book.
- Play Part 2 for pupils to write the numbers in the order they see the photos.

Answers: From left to right: 3 4 2 1

Pupil's Book Activity 2

Watch the video again. Read and tick (✓) or cross (✗).

- Read out the first sentence in Activity 2. Ask **Has the boat got a garden?** Show the tick in the circle.
- Play the video. Pupils tick or cross the sentences.
- Ask the pupils to look at the sentences they crossed and ask them to correct them.
- Ask the pupils some questions to check understanding. Suggested questions.

  How many floors has the tall house got? *(Seven.)*
  What rooms are there on the houseboat? *(A living room, kitchen, bathroom and bedroom.)*
  Why does Tom think the bedroom in the video is the same as his? *(There are a lot of toys.)*
  What do the children do in the bedroom? *(Tidy up.)*
  What do Tom and Sophie need to do now? *(Tidy up.)*

Answers: 1 ✓ 2 ✓ 3 ✗ 4 ✓

Pupil's Book Activity 3

Read and circle.

- Ask **Is the bedroom tidy?** Ask **When you tidy up, where do you put your books / toys / clothes?**
- Read out number one, including the circled word.
- The pupils read the other sentences and circle the words.

  Think-Pair-Share Read out the speech bubble. Ask **Why is it important to tidy up?**

Answers: **1** shelf **2** box **3** table **4** cupboard

Activity Book

Activity 1

Where do these things go? Listen and match.

▶ *CD3 Track 41 p271*

- Point to each of the pictures to elicit the vocabulary.
- Play the first exchange on the CD. Ask **What thing are they talking about? Where does it go?** Show the matching line.
- Play the rest of the CD, pausing after each exchange, for pupils to match.

Answers: **1** camera on the shelf **2** phone on the table **3** watch in the box **4** radio in the cupboard

Activity 2

Read and tick (✓). Draw and say.

- Ask a few pupils **What do you do to help at home?** Elicit answers.
- The pupils tick the things they do. The pupils draw pictures to illustrate the activities they do.

  Talk Partners Pupils take turns to show their partner their pictures and talk about how they help at home.

Recycled vocabulary

Answer: climbing frame

Ending the lesson

Review the lesson.

- Say **Today we've watched a video about unusual houses. What did we learn about helping out at home?** *(It's important to tidy up especially our own bedrooms.)*
- Ask **Which activity was easy / difficult?**

Review the task flashcards.

- Point to the task flashcards on the board. Say **Look at the activities you've done today. Which activity was your favourite?**

Extra activity

Extension

- Ask the pupils to write a sentence on a piece of paper to say what they do to help in the house. Write a model sentence on the board. *I tidy my bedroom, I make my bed and put my toys in a box.*

Date: ______________ **Unit:** ______________

1 What did my pupils learn in this unit?

2 How did my pupils work? (✓)

individually ☐ in pairs ☐ in small groups ☐
in large groups ☐ as a class ☐

3 Which key competences did my pupils develop?

- Competence in linguistic communication ☐
- Competence in mathematics, science and technology ☐
- Digital competence ☐
- Learning to learn ☐
- Social and civic competences ☐
- Sense of initiative and entrepreneurship ☐
- Cultural awareness and expression ☐

4 Which lessons / activities were the most successful and why?

5 Which lessons / activities did my pupils find the most difficult and why?

6 What did I try in the classroom for the first time? How did it go?

7 Which resources did I find most useful? (including webpages)

8 What could I do differently next time I teach this unit?

Unit 8 All around the town

Unit overview

Key Competences and Key Learning Outcomes

- Identify and say ten places in a town (Lesson 1)
- Use *Is there a …? / Are there any …?* and short answers
- Read, listen and understand a story about a dark night (Lesson 3)
- Ask for and give directions (Lesson 4)
- Read and write about the emergency services in Britain (Lesson 6)
- Watch and understand a video about road safety (Video and 21st Century Skills)

- Act out a conversation giving directions (Lesson 4)

- Use the Pupil's App on Navio

- Use a strategy to practise spelling key words (Lesson 1)
- Say a tongue twister and practise 'y' and 'igh' spellings (Lesson 5)
- Review language from the unit and reflect on own learning (Lesson 8)
- Practise activity types found in the Cambridge Exams: Pre A1 Starters

- Understand the importance of remembering where you put your things (Lesson 3)
- Learn to cross the road safely (Video and 21st Century Skills)

- Work with a Talk Partner to practise and reinforce learning (all lessons)
- Play a communication game giving directions (Lesson 5)

- Sing three songs (Lessons 1, 4 and 8)
- Understand, act out and give an opinion on a story (Lesson 3)
- Think about the emergency telephone number where you live (Lesson 6)
- Read, understand and write an invitation (Lesson 7)

Vocabulary

Core vocabulary
baker's, bank, bus station, car park, chemist's, fire station, museum, police station, post office, train station; go straight on, turn (left / right), from, to

Extension vocabulary (optional)
airport, butcher's, hotel, library, market, university; go along, go past the …, on the corner, opposite

Other vocabulary
dinosaurs, exploring, holidays; dark, hungry, night; doctor, emergency, fire engine, firefighter, helmet, loud, police officer, safety, siren, uniform, wheels; candles, face painting, games, invitation

Recycled vocabulary
Places in the town; Seasons; *between, in front of, next to; balloons, big, birthday, cake, car, party, presents, red, ride a bike, sweets*

Structures

Core structures
Is there a (bank)? Yes, there is. No, there isn't. Are there any (museums)? Yes, there are. No, there aren't. How do I get to the (post office)? Go straight on. Turn left / right. How do I get from the (bank) to the (post office)?

Other structures
Here's / There's the cinema. Call this number if you need … Come to my party. I hope you can come! My (dad)'s a (firefighter).

Recycled structures
It's (between / in front of / next to). Remember! He / She wears / drives / rides …

Phonics

Alternative vowel spellings **'igh'** / **'y'** (fl**y**, l**igh**t, n**igh**t)

British Culture

The emergency services

Literacy

Text type: an invitation (persuasive text)
Reading skills: scanning for specific information; remembering facts

21st Century Skills

Living in the world: learn to cross the road safely

Cooperative learning

Songs: *Well done!* (Lesson 8)
Skills: Listening to others (Lesson 1); Working together as a team (Lesson 5); Think-Pair-Share (Lesson 8)

Values

The importance of remembering where you put your things.

Cross-curricular links

Links to Science
Forces: sources of light and sound; natural and artificial light sources; changing direction

Suggested Arts and Crafts concepts
Observing and identifying movement in sculptures; making and playing a game

Key Competences and Key Learning Outcomes

- Identify and say ten places in a town
- Say the vocabulary chant
- Stick the places in a town stickers
- Identify sources of light and sound (optional)
- Use a strategy to practise spelling key words
- Sing a song about a town

Key language
- *baker's, bank, bus station, car park, chemist's, fire station, museum, police station, post office, train station*

Extension vocabulary
- *airport, butcher's, hotel, library, market, university*

Recycled: *bookshop, café, cinema, hospital, park, restaurant, supermarket, sweet shop, swimming pool, town, toyshop, zoo; behind, between, in front of, next to*

Recycled: *It's (behind / next to) the post office. It's (between) the (bank) and the (museum).*

Other vocabulary: *dinosaurs, exploring, holiday*

Materials
- Pupil's Book p82; Activity Book pp80 and 89; Class CD3; Teacher's App on Navio; Unit 8 stickers
- Places in the town flashcards from Level 1 Unit 7; Places in a town flashcards
- Teacher's Resource Bank: Places in a town word cards
- Teacher's Resource Bank: Task flashcards: *listen, sing, read, stick, say, match, write, Talk Partners*

Optional materials
- Teacher's Resource Bank: Five Trinity Exam Practice cards (selected from the Starter Unit and Units 1, 2, 3, 4, 5, 6 and 7)

At a Glance Lesson Plan

Pupil's Book

Starting the lesson
- Use the Trinity Exam Practice cards (optional).
- Review places in a town.
- Set learning outcomes using the task flashcards.

Vocabulary presentation
- Present the new vocabulary.

Activity 1
- Listen and point.
- ▶ *CD3 Track 42 p271*
- Sing *All around the town.*

Word cards
- Read the word cards.
- Match them to the flashcards.

Activity 2
- Read and stick the ten stickers.
- Listen and say the chant.
- ▶ *CD3 Track 44 p271*

Go to the Activity Book.

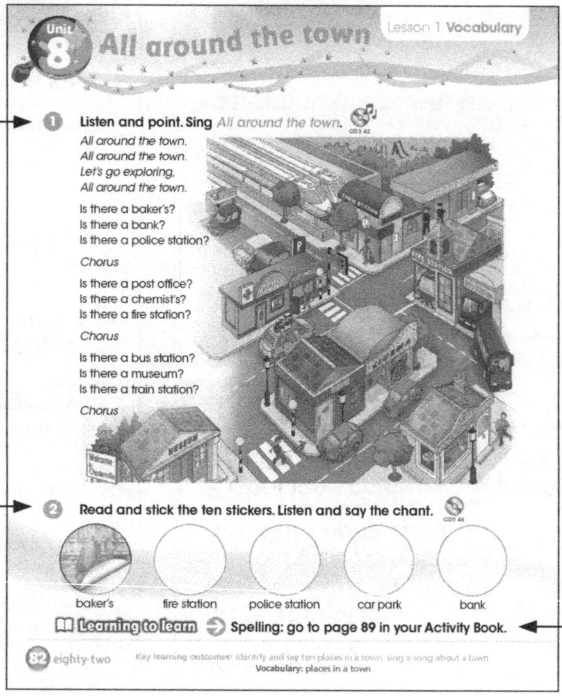

Ending the lesson
- Review the lesson.
- Review the task flashcards.

Extra activity

Vocabulary extension
- Present six additional vocabulary items.

Cooperative learning

Listening to others
- Play *Memory chain.*

Link to Science
- **Forces:** sources of light and sound

Learning to learn

Spelling
- Practise spelling at any time during this unit (Activity Book p89).

Digital resources

Teacher's Digital: Don't forget you can teach this lesson using the Teacher's App on Navio.

Pupil's Digital: Encourage your pupils to use the Pupil's App on Navio to practise the vocabulary from this lesson.

Powered By NAVIO

Activity Book

Activity Book

Activity 1
- Read and match.

Activity 2
- Read, look and write.

Recycled vocabulary
- Look, remember and write the word.

Spelling

Let's practise spelling!
- Use the *Look-Copy-Cover-Write* technique.

Recycled vocabulary
- Look, remember and write the word.

Starting the lesson

Use the Trinity Exam Practice cards (optional).

- The pupils practise asking and answering questions. (See p31.)

Review places in a town.

- Review the places in the town from Level 1. Say **In this place there are (lots of sweets). What place is it?** *(Sweet shop.)* Repeat with all the Level 1 places. Stick the flashcards (Level 1, Unit 7) on the board in a street formation. Position some places *behind, in front of, next to, near* and *between* others to practise prepositions of place. Ask **Where's the (toyshop)?** The pupils answer using the corresponding preposition.

Set learning outcomes using the task flashcards.

- Explain the aims of the lesson. Say **Today we're going to learn the names of more places in a town.**
- Hold up the task flashcards and elicit the words. Stick them on one side of the board. Point to them during the lesson to reinforce your instructions.

Vocabulary presentation

Present the new vocabulary.

- (Books closed.) Introduce the new places in a town one by one by describing them before you show the flashcard. Say **In this place we (buy bread).** Show the flashcard and say **It's a (baker's).** The pupils repeat. Stick the flashcard on the board and repeat with the other cards.

Pupil's Book Activity 1

Listen and point. Sing *All around the town.*

▶ *CD3 Track 42 p271*

- (Books open.) Say **Jake, Molly and Beth are on holiday. What's the name of the town? Can you see the car park?**
- Ask about the other places. Rearrange the flashcards on the board in the order that they appear in the song.
- Play the CD and do the actions. The pupils watch and listen. Play the CD again. The pupils sing and join in.
- At the end of the song, ask the pupils **Which place is not in the song?** *(The car park.)*

Word cards

Read the word cards. Match them to the flashcards.

- (Books closed.) Hold up one of the places in the town word cards. The pupils read collectively. A pupil sticks the word card next to the corresponding flashcard on the board. Repeat.
- Point to each word card. The pupils read the words.
- Indicate the 's in *baker's* and *chemist's*. Tell the pupils that a baker is the person who makes the bread and the baker's is the name of the shop. A chemist is the person and the chemist's is the shop.

Pupil's Book Activity 2

Read and stick the ten stickers. Listen and say the chant.

▶ *CD3 Track 44 p271*

- Ask a pupil to read the first word. The pupils stick the corresponding sticker above the word.
- Talk Partners The pupils find and stick the remaining stickers. Encourage them to use cooperative language.
- Play the CD. The pupils listen and say the chant, pointing to the stickers in turn.

Activity Book

Activity 1

Read and match.

- (Books open.) A pupil reads out the first sentence and points to the illustration of the place. Repeat for the other sentences. The pupils read and match individually.

Answers: **1** b **2** a **3** d **4** c **5** g **6** f **7** e **8** h

Activity 2

Read, look and write.

- Read out the instructions. The pupils look at the map, read the clues and write the name of each place.

Answers: **1** car park **2** fire station **3** chemist's **4** post office **5** bank

Recycled vocabulary

- The pupils look at the picture and write the word.

Answer: house

Ending the lesson

Review the lesson.

- Say **Today we've learnt the names of places in the town.** Elicit the words from the pupils.

Review the task flashcards.

- Point to the task flashcards. Ask **Which was your favourite activity?** Elicit the pupils' favourite activities.

Extra activity

Vocabulary extension

- Present six additional places in town: *airport, butcher's, hotel, library, market, university.*
- Use the Vocabulary Booster on Navio to practise these new words.

Cooperative learning

Listening to others

- Play *Memory chain* (see p67) with places in a town from Lesson 1 and those learnt in Level 1.

Link to Science

- If you are studying the Science topic of **forces** in English, you could review light and sound sources. Ask the pupils what you can see at a fire station or a police station. Explain that police cars and fire engines use light and sound to give warnings.

Spelling (Activity Book p89)

Let's practise spelling!

- The pupils can practise spelling the ten town words using the *Look-Copy-Cover-Write* technique at any time before the Lesson 8 Review.

Recycled vocabulary

- The pupils look at the picture and write the word.

Answer: bathroom

Key Competences and Key Learning Outcomes

- Use *Is there a …? / Are there any …?* and short answers
- Understand and act out a grammar conversation
- Complete and practise a conversation
- Ask and answer questions about places in a town

- Listen for specific information

Key language

- *Is there a (bank)? Yes, there is. / No, there isn't. Are there any (museums)? Yes, there are. / No, there aren't.*

Recycled: *baker's, bank, bus station, car park, chemist's, fire station, museum, police station, post office, train station*

Materials

- Pupil's Book p83; Activity Book p81; Class CD3; Teacher's App on Navio
- Places in a town flashcards
- Teacher's Resource Bank: Places in a town word cards
- Teacher's Resource Bank: Task flashcards: *listen, act out, number, write, think, Talk Partners*

Optional materials

- Teacher's Resource Bank: Five Trinity Exam Practice cards (selected from the Starter Unit and Units 1, 2, 3, 4, 5, 6 and 7)

At a Glance Lesson Plan

Pupil's Book

Starting the lesson

- Use the Trinity Exam Practice cards (optional).
- Review the *All around the town* song.
- ▶ ***CD3 Track 42 p271***
- ▶ ***CD3 Track 43 p271 (optional karaoke version)***
- Play *Memory!*
- Set learning outcomes using the task flashcards.

Activity 1

- Listen and repeat.
- Talk Partners Act out.
- ▶ ***CD3 Track 45 p271***

Grammar focus

- *a* and *any*
- Talk Partners Ask and answer questions.

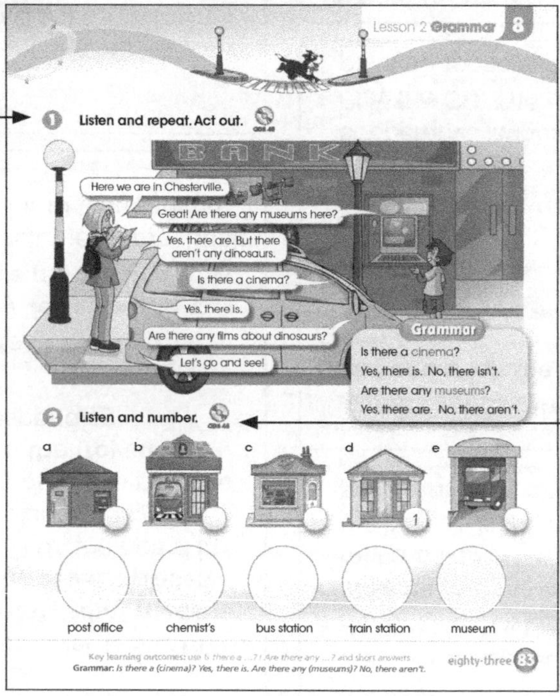

Activity 2

- Listen and number.
- ▶ ***CD3 Track 46 p271***
- Go to the Activity Book.

Ending the lesson

- Review the lesson.
- Review the task flashcards.

Extra activity

Reinforcement

- Talk Partners Ask and answer about the town or neighbourhood where you live.

Activity Book

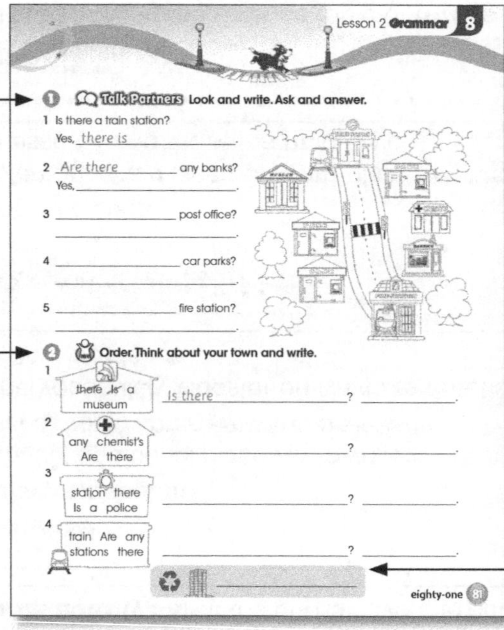

Activity Book

Activity 1

- Look and write.
- Talk Partners Ask and answer.

Activity 2

- Order. Think about your town and write.

Recycled vocabulary

- Look, remember and write the word.

Digital resources

Teacher's Digital: Don't forget you can teach this lesson using the Teacher's App on Navio.

Pupil's Digital: Encourage your pupils to use the Pupil's App on Navio to practise the vocabulary from this lesson.

Powered By NAVIO

Starting the lesson

Use the Trinity Exam Practice cards (optional).
- The pupils practise asking and answering questions. (See p31.)

Review the *All around the town* song.

▶ *CD3 Track 42 p271*

▶ *CD3 Track 43 p271 (optional karaoke version)*
- Give the flashcards from the song to volunteers and ask them to line up in the order of the song. As each place in the town is heard, the pupil holding the corresponding card should hold it up. Play the CD (or use the karaoke version).

Play *Memory!*
- Play *Memory!* (see p23) with the places in the town flashcards and word cards.

Set learning outcomes using the task flashcards.
- Explain the aims of the lesson. Say **Today we're going to ask and answer questions about places in the town.**
- Hold up the task flashcards and elicit the words. Stick them on one side of the board. Point to them during the lesson to reinforce your instructions.

Pupil's Book Activity 1

Listen and repeat. Act out.

▶ *CD3 Track 45 p271*
- (Books open.) Explain that Jake and Molly are on holiday with their family. Beth is with them. Ask **What places can you see?**
- Play the CD. The pupils listen and read the conversation. Check understanding. Ask **Are there any museums? Are there any dinosaurs? Is there a cinema?**
- Play the CD again. Pause for the pupils to repeat.
- Talk Partners The pupils practise the conversation.

Grammar focus

a* and *any
- Focus the pupils' attention on the grammar box. Highlight the use of 'a' when asking about singular places (*Is there a post office?*) and 'any' when asking about plural places (*Are there any banks?*). For oral consolidation, name places in the town, swapping between singular and plural at random.
- Talk Partners The pupils ask a Talk Partner the correct question. Say **Bank** (Pupil A: *Is there a bank?*). Say **Museums** (Pupil B: *Are there any museums?*).

Pupil's Book Activity 2

Listen and number.

▶ *CD3 Track 46 p271*
- (Books open.) Ask the pupils to name the places in the town. Say **Let's listen. Number the places in the order you hear them.**
- Play the CD. Pause after each conversation. The pupils number the corresponding place. Repeat with the remaining conversations, pausing after each one to check the pupils' answers.

Answers: **1** d **2** a **3** e **4** b **5** c

Activity Book

Activity 1

Look and write. Ask and answer.
- (Books open.) Ask the pupils to look at the picture of the town on the right and name the different places. Encourage a pupil to read out the first question. A different pupil looks at the picture and answers the question. Repeat for the remaining questions.
- Talk Partners Pupils write the questions and answers and then practise them with a Talk Partner. Remind them to write 'a' with singular places and 'any' with plural places.

Answers: **1** there is **2** Are there, there are **3** Is there a, No, there isn't. **4** Are there any, No, there aren't. **5** Is there a, Yes, there is.

Activity 2

Order. Think about your town and write.
- Invite a pupil to order and read out the first sentence. Invite a different pupil to think about his / her town and answer the question. The pupils write the question and the short answer for each one.
- Talk Partners The pupils check their answers with a Talk Partner.

Answers: **1** Is there a museum? **2** Are there any chemist's? **3** Is there a police station? **4** Are there any train stations?

Recycled vocabulary
- The pupils look at the picture and write the word.

Answer: flat

Ending the lesson

Review the lesson.
- Say **Today you've asked and answered about places in a town.** Elicit the two questions and the possible answers.

Review the task flashcards.
- Point to the task flashcards. Say **Look at the activities you've done today. Which activity was your favourite?** Elicit the pupils' favourite activities.

Extra activity

Reinforcement
- Ask the pupils **Is there a (museum / fire station) / Are there any (banks / car parks) in your (town / neighbourhood)?**
- Talk Partners Encourage the pupils to work with their Talk Partner to ask and answer about the town / neighbourhood where they live.

Key Competences and Key Learning Outcomes

- Read, listen and understand a story about a dark night
- Read the story with some fluency
- Identify natural and artificial light sources (optional)
- Become familiar with the story through a pre-reading task
- Understand the importance of remembering where you put your things
- Understand and act out the story
- Give an opinion on the story

Key language

- *Is there a baker's? Are there any banks near here? Turn right here.*

Recycled: *baker's, bank, chemist's, police station, post office; car*

Recycled: *The (car) is in front of the (red bank).*

Other vocabulary: *dark, hungry, night, remember*

Materials

- Pupil's Book pp84–85; Activity Book p82; Class CD3; Teacher's App on Navio
- Places in a town flashcards
- Teacher's Resource Bank: Task flashcards: *listen, read, act out, write, number, think, Talk Partners*
- Teacher's Resource Bank: Unit 8 Lesson 3 Animated Story

Optional materials

- Teacher's Resource Bank: Five Trinity Exam Practice cards (selected from the Starter Unit and Units 1, 2, 3, 4, 5, 6 and 7)

At a Glance Lesson Plan

Pupil's Book

Starting the lesson

- Use the Trinity Exam Practice cards (optional).
- Review places in a town.
- Set learning outcomes using the task flashcards.

Before you read

- Explain the story title.
- Read and answer the question.

Activity 1

- Listen and read.

▶ *CD3 Track 47 p271*

- Act out.

Now watch the animated story!

After you read: Activity 2

Go to page 82 in your Activity Book.

- Values: Read and write.

Ending the lesson

- Review the lesson.
- Review the task flashcards.

Extra activity

Extension

- Role-play.

Link to Science

- **Forces:** natural and artificial light sources

Activity Book

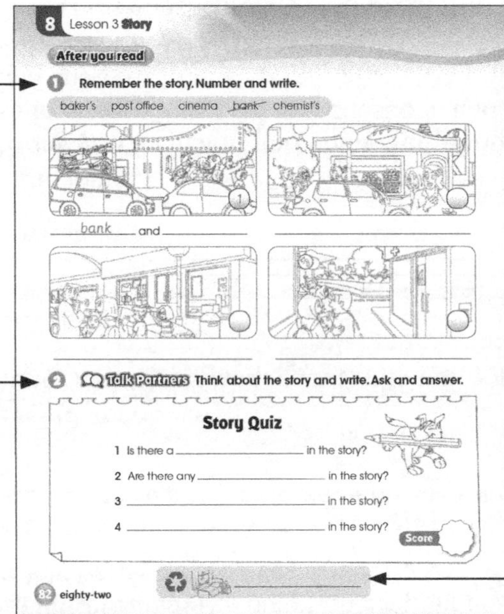

Activity Book

After you read: Activity 1

- Remember the story. Number and write.

Activity 2

- Think about the story and write.
- Talk Partners
Ask and answer.

Recycled vocabulary

- Look, remember and write the word.

Digital resources

Teacher's Digital: Don't forget you can teach this lesson using the Teacher's App on Navio.

Pupil's Digital: Encourage your pupils to use the Pupil's App on Navio to practise the vocabulary from this lesson.

Powered By NAVIO

Starting the lesson

Use the Trinity Exam Practice cards (optional).

- The pupils practise asking and answering questions. (See p31.)

Review places in a town.

- Secretly, give one of the pupils a flashcard and say **This is a place in your town.** The rest of the class asks questions to discover the place *(Is there a bank in the town? / Are there any museums in the town?)*. Repeat with different volunteers, changing the flashcard.

Set learning outcomes using the task flashcards.

- Say **Today we're going to listen to a story.**
- Hold up the task flashcards and elicit the words. Stick them on one side of the board. Point to them during the lesson to reinforce your instructions.

Before you read

Explain the story title

- (Books open.) Ask the class what things they do at night (have a snack, go to bed, etc.). Focus their attention on Frames 1 and 2. Tell them that in the day you can see bright colours (Frame 1), but at night it is dark and you can't see the colours (Frame 2).

Read and answer the question.

- Remind the pupils that Mum, Dad, Jake, Beth and Molly are on holiday in a different town. Elicit the name of the town. *(Chesterville.)*. Read the speech bubble and ask the pupils to scan the story to identify the places in the town.
- Talk Partners The pupils feed back to a Talk Partner and name the places.

Pupil's Book Activity 1

Listen and read. Act out.

▶ *CD3 Track 47 p271*

- (Books open.) Play the CD. The pupils follow the text with their finger. Pause between each frame to check understanding. Ask **Did you enjoy the story? Why? Why not?**

Suggested comprehension questions

- Frame 1: **Where are they going?** *(To the cinema.)* **Is it day or night?** *(Day.)*
- Frame 2: **Is it day or night now?** *(Night.)* **Can they see the car?** *(No.)* **Is the streetlamp on?** *(No.)*
- Frame 3: **Do they know where the car is?** *(No.)*
- Frame 4: **Where does Dad think the car is?** *(Near the baker's.)*
- Frame 5: **Do they know where the car is?** *(No.)*
- Frame 6: **Where does Dad think the car is?** *(In front of the red bank.)*
- Frame 7: **How does the magic bike help them find the car?** *(It turns on the streetlamp.)*
- Frame 8: **Can Mum and Dad see the car now?** *(Yes!)*
- Organise the class into five groups (Mum, Dad, Beth, Molly and Jake).
- Play the CD. Each group joins in when their character speaks. Pause the CD for the pupils to repeat.

Now watch the animated story!

After you read

Pupil's Book Activity 2

Go to page 82 in your Activity Book.

Activity Book

After you read: Activity 1

Remember the story. Number and write.

- (Books open.) Ask the pupils to find the first picture from the story. The pupils write numbers to order the pictures and then label the places.

Answers: **1** bank and cinema **2** chemist's **3** post office **4** baker's

Activity 2

Think about the story and write. Ask and answer.

- (Books open.) Tell the pupils they are going to write a quiz about the story for a Talk Partner. They complete the first two questions by looking back at the story. Then they write two more questions of their own.
- Talk Partners The pupils ask a Talk Partner the questions and write their score in the flash.

Recycled vocabulary

- The pupils look at the picture and write the word.

Answer: bedroom

Pupil's Book Activity 2

Values: Read and write.

- Focus attention on the photograph. Read out the information in the speech bubble and prompt the class to tell you the missing word.
- Ask the pupils if they lose their things. Ask who helps them. Ask if they help their mum and dad find their things like Jake in the story.

Ending the lesson

Review the lesson.

- Say **Today we've listened to a story about getting lost. Today you've learnt that it's important to remember where you put your things.**

Review the task flashcards.

- Point to the task flashcards. Say **Look at the activities you've done today. Which activity was your favourite?** Elicit the pupils' favourite activities.

Extra activity

Extension

- Do a role-play. Choose three pupils to play the roles of Jake, Mum and Dad in the story. The pupils should choose different places for Dad and different directions for Jake.
- Organise the pupils into groups of three and ask them to invent and act out mini-conversations.

Link to Science

- If you are studying the Science topic of **forces** in English, you could review light sources and shadows. Remind the pupils that when there is no light, we can't see. Ask **Is a streetlamp a natural or artificial light source?** Elicit other artificial light sources. Encourage the class to recall natural light sources. Focus attention on the story again and ask them to point out and name the different light sources in the story.
- Remind them that a shadow is formed when an opaque object blocks the light from the light source. Ask them to find the shadows in the story.

Key Competences and Key Learning Outcomes

- Ask for and give directions
- Act out a conversation giving directions
- Sing a song

Key language
- *go straight on, turn left, turn right; from, to*
- *How do I get to the (bank)? How do I get from (here) to (there)? There's the (train station).*

Extension vocabulary
- *go along, go past the …, on the corner, opposite*

Recycled: *bank, fire station, museum, police station, post office, train station*

Materials
- Pupil's Book p86; Activity Book p83; Class CD3; Teacher's App on Navio
- Teacher's Resource Bank: Task flashcards: *listen, say, sing, Talk Partners, act out, read, match, number, write*

Optional materials
- Teacher's Resource Bank: Five Trinity Exam Practice cards (selected from the Starter Unit and Units 1, 2, 3, 4, 5, 6 and 7)
- Places in a town flashcards from this unit and Level 1

At a Glance Lesson Plan

Pupil's Book

Starting the lesson
- Use the Trinity Exam Practice cards (optional).
- Review the Lesson 3 story.
- Set learning outcomes using the task flashcards.

Vocabulary presentation
- Present the new vocabulary.

Activity 1
- Listen, point and say.

▶ *CD3 Track 48 p272*

Activity 2
- Listen and point. Sing *Which way do I go?*

▶ *CD3 Track 49 p272*

Activity 3
- Listen and repeat.
- Talk Partners Act out.

▶ *CD3 Track 50 p272*

Go to the Activity Book.

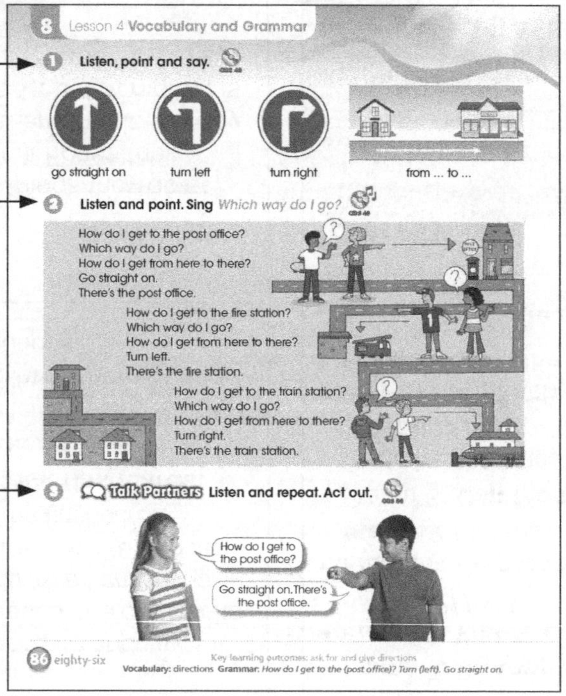

Ending the lesson
- Review the lesson.
- Review the task flashcards.

Extra activities

Reinforcement
- Play *Directions.*

Vocabulary extension
- Present four additional vocabulary items.

Digital resources

Teacher's Digital: Don't forget you can teach this lesson using the Teacher's App on Navio.

Pupil's Digital: Encourage your pupils to use the Pupil's App on Navio to practise the vocabulary from this lesson.

Powered By NAVIO

Activity Book

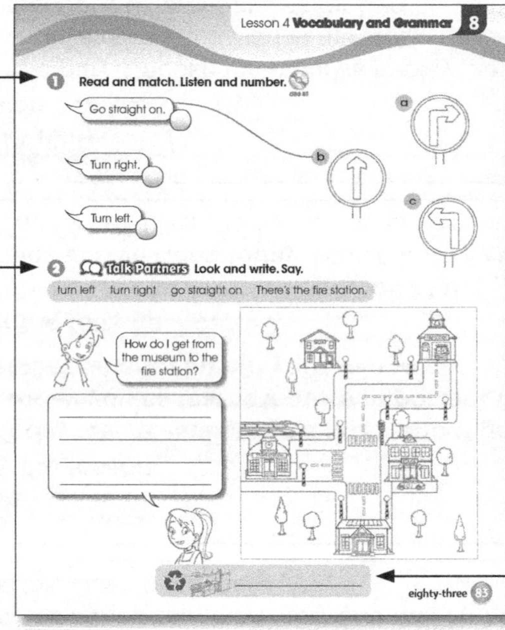

Activity Book

Activity 1
- Read and match. Listen and number.

▶ *CD3 Track 51 p272*

Activity 2
- Look and write.
- Talk Partners Say.

Recycled vocabulary
- Look, remember and write the word.

Starting the lesson

Use the Trinity Exam Practice cards (optional).

- The pupils practise asking and answering questions. (See p31.)

Review the Lesson 3 story.

- Read out statements from the story frames in random order. The pupils scan the story and say which frame. Say, e.g. **I think our car is near the baker's!** *(Frame 4.)*

Set learning outcomes using the task flashcards.

- Say **Today we're going to learn to ask for and give directions.**
- Hold up the task flashcards in turn and elicit the words. Stick them on one side of the board. Point to them during the lesson to reinforce your instructions.

Vocabulary presentation

Present the new vocabulary.

- (Books open.) Point to the first picture on Pupil's Book page 86 and say **Go straight on.** Mime walking straight on and encourage the pupils to copy you. Prompt the class to repeat after you and do the same action. Repeat the process with the other directions. Introduce 'from' and 'to' in the same way. Say **I'm going from (the window) to (the door).**

Pupil's Book Activity 1

Listen, point and say.

▶ *CD3 Track 48 p272*

- (Books open.) Say **Let's listen and repeat.** Play the CD. The pupils repeat each phrase, pointing to the corresponding illustration each time. Play the CD again. This time the pupils repeat and do the action.

Pupil's Book Activity 2

Listen and point. Sing *Which way do I go?*

▶ *CD3 Track 49 pp272*

- (Books open.) Ask **Where do the children want to go?**
- Play the CD. The pupils listen to the song and point to the children. Play the CD again. The pupils sing and do the actions.

Pupil's Book Activity 3

Listen and repeat. Act out.

▶ *CD3 Track 50 p272*

- Play the CD. Play the CD again and ask the pupils to repeat the question and answer. Then, invite a pair of pupils to act out the conversation.
- Talk Partners The pupils practise the conversation with a Talk Partner naming different places from the song each time.

Activity Book

Activity 1

Read and match. Listen and number.

▶ *CD3 Track 51 p272*

- (Books open.) The pupils match each direction with its corresponding sign. Then, they listen to the conversations and number the directions in the order they hear them.

Answers: **1** b Go straight on. **2** c Turn left. **3** a Turn right.

Activity 2

Look and write. Say.

- (Books open.) The pupils read the question, look at the map and write the directions using the phrases in the box.
- Talk Partners The pupils read the finished directions to a Talk Partner.

Answers: Go straight on. Turn right. Turn left. There's the fire station.

Recycled vocabulary

- The pupils look at the picture and write the word.

Answer: kitchen

Ending the lesson

Review the lesson.

- Say **Today we've talked about directions.** Elicit some sentences from the pupils.

Review the task flashcards.

- Point to the task flashcards. Say **Look at the activities you've done today. Which activity was your favourite?** Elicit the pupils' favourite activities.

Extra activities

Reinforcement

- Play *Directions.* Set some obstacles around the centre of the class. Choose a pupil and ask him / her to stand at the starting place and ask the question **How do I get from the door to my desk?** Ask the class to give directions. Encourage the pupils to say *Turn left, Turn right, Go straight on,* as appropriate. The volunteer should only move following the directions given.
- Alternatively, draw a simple map on the board and stick the flashcards from the unit and Level 1 according to the pupils' suggestions. *Put the (baker's) (next to / in front of / near) the (fire station).*

Vocabulary extension

- Use the Vocabulary Booster on Navio and present and practise four additional vocabulary items for giving directions: *go along, go past the …, on the corner, opposite.*

Key Competences and Key Learning Outcomes

- Say a tongue twister with the 'igh' sound
- Learn and practise 'y' and 'igh' spellings
- Listen for specific information
- Review changing direction (optional)
- Play a communication game giving directions

Key language

- *cry, dry, fight, fly, light, night, right, sky*

Recycled: *baker's, bank, bus station, car park, chemist's, fire station, museum, police station, post office, train station*

Recycled: *How do I get from the (school) to the (chemist's)? Go straight on. Then, turn left / right.*

Materials

- Pupil's Book p87; Activity Book p84; Class CD3/4; Teacher's App on Navio
- Teacher's Resource Bank: Task flashcards: *listen, say, draw, cut out, write, colour, Talk Partners*
- Teacher's Resource Bank: Unit 8 Lesson 5 Activity 3 cut-out
- Scissors

Optional materials

- Teacher's Resource Bank: Five Trinity Exam Practice cards (selected from the Starter Unit and Units 1, 2, 3, 4, 5, 6 and 7)

At a Glance Lesson Plan

Pupil's Book

Starting the lesson

- Use the Trinity Exam Practice cards (optional).
- Review the *Which way do I go?* song.

▶ ***CD3 Track 49 p272***

- Set learning outcomes using the task flashcards.

Activity 1

- Listen and say.

▶ ***CD4 Track 1 p272***

Go to the Activity Book.

Go to Magic Phonics.

Activity 2

- Listen and draw lines. Use different colours.

▶ ***CD4 Track 2 p272***

Activity 3

- Make and play the game (Teacher's Resource Bank).

Ending the lesson

- Review the lesson.
- Review the task flashcards.

Cooperative learning

Working together as a team

- Talk Partners
  Play *Beat the clock.*
- Add to the pronunciation wall display.

Link to Science

- **Forces:** changing direction

Digital resources

Teacher's Digital: Don't forget you can teach this lesson using the Teacher's App on Navio.

Pupil's Digital: Encourage your pupils to use the Pupil's App on Navio to practise the vocabulary from this lesson.

Powered By NAVIO

Activity Book

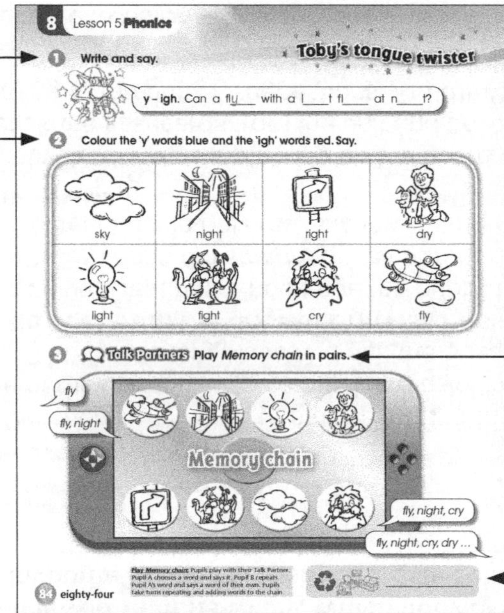

Activity Book

Activity 1

- Write and say.

Activity 2

- Colour the 'y' words blue and the 'igh' words red. Say.

Go to Magic Phonics.

Activity 3

- Talk Partners
  Play *Memory chain* in pairs.

Recycled vocabulary

- Look, remember and write the phrase.

Starting the lesson

Use the Trinity Exam Practice cards (optional).

- The pupils practise asking and answering questions. (See p31.)

Review the *Which way do I go?* song.

▶ *CD3 Track 49 p272*

- Divide the class into two groups and ask them to line up facing each other. Group A sings the question part and Group B sings the direction. Play the CD.

Set learning outcomes using the task flashcards.

- Say **Today we're going to say a tongue twister and we're going to make and play a game.**
- Hold up the task flashcards in turn and elicit the activities. Stick them on one side of the board. Point to them during the lesson to reinforce your instructions.

Pupil's Book Activity 1

Listen and say.

▶ *CD4 Track 1 p272*

- Write the words *fly* and *light* on the board and ask the pupils which sound they can hear in both words *('igh')*. Circle the target grapheme ('y' and 'igh') in each word and model the sound. Encourage the pupils to say the sound with you. Check for accuracy.
- Say **It's time for Toby's tongue twister! What can you see?**
- Play the CD. The pupils listen and repeat the target sound, then the words and then the entire tongue twister, faster and faster.

Go to Magic Phonics.

Activity Book

Activity 1

Write and say.

- (Books open.) Say **Look at Toby's tongue twister! The letters 'igh' and 'y' are missing.** The pupils complete the tongue twister.

Answers: fly, light, fly, night

- **Talk Partners** The pupils say Toby's tongue twister and point to the 'igh' sounds. They play *Faster and faster,* taking turns to say the tongue twister faster each time.

Activity 2

Colour the 'y' words blue and the 'igh' words red. Say.

- Ask pupils to say the words then colour 'igh' words red and 'y' words blue.

Answers: blue: sky, dry, cry, fly;
red: night, right, light, fight

Go to Magic Phonics.

Activity 3

Play *Memory chain* in pairs.

- Demonstrate the game with two volunteers. Pupil A chooses a word and says it. Pupil B repeats Pupil A's word and says a word of their own. The pupils take turns repeating and adding words to the chain until a mistake is made.
- **Talk Partners** The pupils play the game with a Talk Partner.

Recycled vocabulary

- The pupils look at the picture and write the phrase.

Answer: living room

Pupil's Book Activity 2

Listen and draw lines. Use different colours.

▶ *CD4 Track 2 p272*

- (Books open.) Elicit the names of the places on the map. Explain to the pupils that they are going to listen to Beth, Molly and Jake. They should draw lines showing the route each child takes, using a different colour for each set of directions.
- Play the CD. Pause after each sentence to give the pupils time to draw lines and check their answers.

Pupil's Book Activity 3

Make and play the game (Teacher's Resource Bank).

- (Books open.) Explain to the class that they are going to make and play the directions game. Show the pupils how to cut out the game.
- Pupil A asks for directions to one of the places in the town. Pupil B gives the directions while Pupil A moves Molly, Beth or Jake. The pupils then swap roles.

Ending the lesson

Review the lesson.

- Say **Today we've practised a tongue twister**. Ask the pupils to say it again. **Today you've given and followed directions with your cut-out.**

Review the task flashcards.

- Point to the task flashcards. Say **Look at the activities you've done today. Which was your favourite?** Elicit the pupils' favourite activities.

Cooperative learning

Working together as a team

- **Talk Partners** Play *Beat the clock* to practise pronunciation of the 'igh' / 'y' sound (see p53).
- Add to the pronunciation wall display, adding a section of blue paper ('y' – sky) and a large piece of black paper ('igh'– night).

Link to Science

- If you are studying the Science topic of **forces** in English, you could review directionality. Gather the pupils in a group in the centre of the class. Ask them to move forwards, backwards, sideways and to change direction. Remind them that forces make things change direction.
- If you haven't got space in the classroom for the pupils to move, use the characters and the maps from the cut-outs. Say **Move Jake forward three steps. Now move him sideways two steps.**

Key Competences and Key Learning Outcomes

- Read about the emergency services in Britain
- Listen for general understanding
- Think about the emergency telephone number where you live

Key language

- *doctor, emergency, fire engine, helmet, loud, police officer, safety, siren, uniform, wheels*

Recycled: *big, red, ride a bike*

Recycled: (*My dad's*) *a* (*firefighter*). *He / She* (*works / drives / wears / helps …*).

Materials

- Pupil's Book p88; Activity Book p85; Class CD4; Teacher's App on Navio
- Teacher's Resource Bank: Task flashcards: *Talk Partners, listen, read, think, write, tick, draw, say*

Optional materials

- Teacher's Resource Bank: Five Trinity Exam Practice cards (selected from the Starter Unit and Units 1, 2, 3, 4, 5, 6 and 7)
- Photo of a firefighter from the pupils' own country

At a Glance Lesson Plan

Pupil's Book

Starting the lesson

- Use the Trinity Exam Practice cards (optional).
- **Talk Partners** Review *Toby's tongue twister*.
- ▶ *CD4 Track 1 p272*
- Set learning outcomes using the task flashcards.

Activity 1

- Listen and read. Answer.
- ▶ *CD4 Track 3 p272*

Think about your culture

- Do you know the emergency telephone number in your country?
- Go to the Activity Book.

Ending the lesson

- Review the lesson.
- Review the task flashcards.

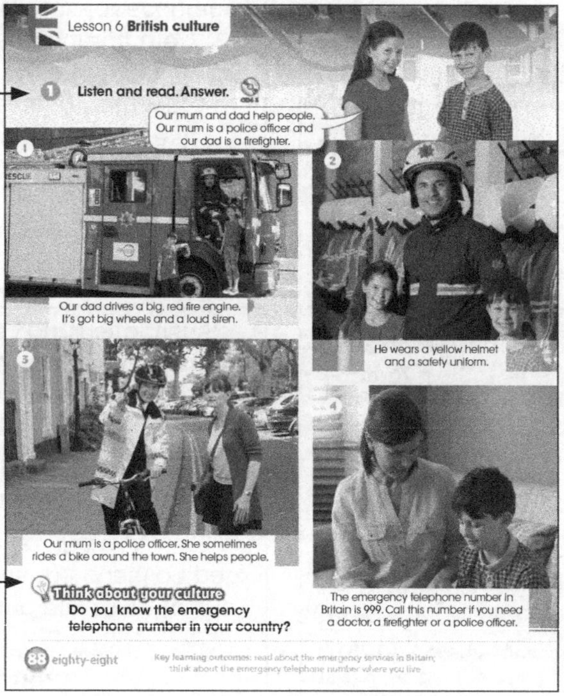
Lesson 6 British culture
1 Listen and read. Answer.
Our mum and dad help people. Our mum is a police officer and our dad is a firefighter.
Our dad drives a big, red fire engine. It's got big wheels and a loud siren.
He wears a yellow helmet and a safety uniform.
Our mum is a police officer. She sometimes rides a bike around the town. She helps people.
Think about your culture
Do you know the emergency telephone number in your country?
The emergency telephone number in Britain is 999. Call this number if you need a doctor, a firefighter or a police officer.
88 eighty-eight

Extra activities

Extension

- Compare British firefighters with firefighters from pupils' own country.
- Compare and contrast firefighters and police officers.

Digital resources

Teacher's Digital: Don't forget you can teach this lesson using the Teacher's App on Navio.

Powered By NAVIO

Activity Book

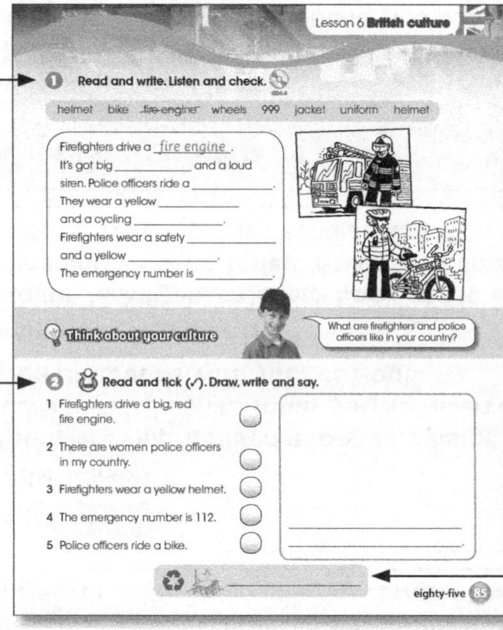
Lesson 6 British culture
1 Read and write. Listen and check.
helmet bike ~~fire engine~~ wheels 999 jacket uniform helmet
Firefighters drive a *fire engine*. It's got big ______ and a loud siren. Police officers ride a ______. They wear a yellow ______ and a cycling ______. Firefighters wear a safety ______ and a yellow ______. The emergency number is ______.
Think about your culture
What are firefighters and police officers like in your country?
2 Read and tick (✓). Draw, write and say.
1 Firefighters drive a big, red fire engine.
2 There are women police officers in my country.
3 Firefighters wear a yellow helmet.
4 The emergency number is 112.
5 Police officers ride a bike.
eighty-five 85

Activity Book

Activity 1

- Read and write. Listen and check.
- ▶ *CD4 Track 4 p272*

Activity 2: Think about your culture

- Read and tick (✓). Draw, write and say.

Recycled vocabulary

- Look, remember and write the phrase.

Starting the lesson

Use the Trinity Exam Practice cards (optional).

- The pupils practise asking and answering questions. (See p31.)

Review Toby's tongue twister.

▶ *CD4 Track 1 p272*

- Ask the class **What sound did you practise in Toby's tongue twister?** *('igh').* Ask if they can remember the tongue twister. *(Can a fly with a light fly at night?)*
- Talk Partners The pupils practise the tongue twister as a class and then with a Talk Partner. The pairs play *Faster and faster,* reading from the Pupil's Book (page 87) if necessary. A fast pair says the tongue twister for the class.
- Draw a chart with two columns ('y' and 'igh') on the board. Elicit words with both spellings. Ask pupils to classify the words, e.g. *'y': fly, sky; 'igh': night, light.*

Set learning outcomes using the task flashcards.

- Say **Today we're going to learn about firefighters and police officers in Britain.**
- Hold up the task flashcards in turn and elicit the activities. Stick them on one side of the board. Point to them during the lesson to reinforce your instructions.

Pupil's Book Activity 1

Listen and read. Answer.

▶ *CD4 Track 3 p272*

- (Books open.) Focus the pupils' attention on the photographs and ask **Who can you see?** *(A firefighter and a police officer.)* Then say **Let's listen and read.** Play the CD. At the end of the text, check understanding by pointing to the first photo and asking **What does a firefighter drive? What has a fire engine got?** Look at the third photo and ask **What does a police officer wear?** Look at the fourth photo and ask **What is the emergency number in Britain?**

Pupil's Book Think about your culture

Do you know the emergency telephone number in your country?

- Read out the question and encourage the class to tell you the emergency telephone number in their country.

Activity Book

Activity 1

Read and write. Listen and check.

▶ *CD4 Track 4 p272*

- (Books open.) The pupils listen and write the missing words. Play the CD again to check answers.

Answers: fire engine, wheels, bike, jacket, helmet, uniform, helmet, 999

Activity 2: Think about your culture.

Read and tick (✓). Draw, write and say.

- (Books open.) Ask the pupils to read the sentences about firefighters and police officers and tick the boxes if they are similar in their own country.
- Finally, ask the pupils to draw a picture of a firefighter or a police officer in their own country. Invite different pupils to show the rest of the class their drawings and describe them.

Recycled vocabulary

- The pupils look at the picture and write the phrase.

Answer: dining room

Ending the lesson

Review the lesson.

- Say **Today you've learnt about firefighters and police officers in Britain.** Elicit some similarities and differences with firefighters and police officers in their own country.

Review the task flashcards.

- Point to the task flashcards. Say **Look at the activities you've done today. Which activity was your favourite?** Elicit the pupils' favourite activities.

Extra activities

Extension

- If possible, find a photo of a firefighter from the pupils' own country to compare with the British firefighter. Draw a Venn Diagram on the board. Encourage the pupils to compare and contrast the firefighters and write the information in note form on the board, e.g. *Britain: wears a yellow helmet. Own country: wears a black helmet,* etc.
- Draw a table on the board with two columns (*firefighter* and *police officer).* Ask questions to encourage the pupils to compare and contrast. Ask **What does a firefighter drive?** Write *fire engine* in the *firefighter* column. Repeat the question for police officer. Ask **Is there a (siren / light)? Where does a firefighter / police officer work? What does a firefighter / police officer wear?** Comment on similarities and differences with the pupils.

Key Competences and Key Learning Outcomes

- Read and understand directions on an invitation
- Read for specific information
- Read and understand an invitation
- Write an invitation

Key language

- *candles, face painting, games, invitation*

Recycled: Months of the year, Ordinal numbers, Seasons; *balloons, birthday, cake, party, presents, sweets*

Recycled: *How do I get to …? From the (school) … Go straight on. Turn left / right. (Partyland) is (between) the (toyshop) and the (café).*

Materials

- Pupil's Book p89; Activity Book p86; Class CD3/4; Teacher's App on Navio
- Teacher's Resource Bank: Task flashcards: *tick, listen, read, write, draw*

Optional materials

- Teacher's Resource Bank: Five Trinity Exam Practice cards (selected from the Starter Unit and Units 1, 2, 3, 4, 5, 6 and 7)
- Card, real party invitations, felt-tip pens or coloured pencils

At a Glance Lesson Plan

Starting the lesson

- Use the Trinity Exam Practice cards (optional).
- Review the *Which way do I go?* song.
- ▶ *CD3 Track 49 p272*
- Set learning outcomes using the task flashcards.

Before you read: Activity 1

- What can you see on the invitation? Tick (✓).

Activity 2

- Listen and read the invitation.
- ▶ *CD4 Track 5 p272*

After you read

Go to page 86 in your Activity Book.

Ending the lesson

- Review the lesson.
- Review the task flashcards.
- Sing a song (optional).

Pupil's Book

Extra activity

Reinforcement

- Make an invitation.

Activity Book

Activity Book

After you read: Activity 1

- Read again. Write.

Activity 2

- Write an invitation. Draw.

Recycled vocabulary

- Look, remember and write the word.

Digital resources

Teacher's Digital: Don't forget you can teach this lesson using the Teacher's App on Navio.

Pupil's Digital: Encourage your pupils to use the Pupil's App on Navio to practise the vocabulary from this lesson.

Powered By NAVIO

Starting the lesson

Use the Trinity Exam Practice cards (optional).

- The pupils practise asking and answering questions. (See p31.)
- Review the *Which way do I go?* song.

▶ *CD3 Track 49 p272*

- Play the CD. The pupils sing and do the actions.
- Extend the song by substituting the places in the song with other vocabulary from the unit and alternating the directions.

Set learning outcomes using the task flashcards.

- Say **Today we're going to read an invitation.**
- Hold up the task flashcards in turn and elicit the activities. Stick them on one side of the board. Point to them during the lesson to reinforce your instructions.

Before you read: Pupil's Book Activity 1

What can you see on the invitation? Tick (✓).

- (Books closed.) Ask **When do you (send / receive) an invitation?** *(For a birthday party.)* Elicit information that is usually on a birthday invitation.
- (Books open.) Focus the class on the pre-reading activity. Ask **What can you see on the invitation?** Ask the pupils to quickly scan the invitation and tick the items that appear. If you have access to any invitations, show them to the class. Encourage the pupils to describe them by asking **What can you see? Is there a (name / telephone number / house / map)?**

Answers: a name, a day, a date, a map, a phone number, directions

Pupil's Book Activity 2

Listen and read the invitation.

▶ *CD4 Track 5 p272*

- Say **Let's read and listen to the invitation.** Play the CD.
- Check the pupils' understanding by asking **Who is the invitation for? Is the invitation from Jane? What day is the party? What date is the party? Where is the party? How do I get from the school to Partyland?**

Activity Book

After you read: Activity 1

Read again. Write.

- (Books open.) Focus the pupils' attention on the comprehension questions and read out the instructions. Then, read out the first question and prompt the class to give the answer. Repeat the procedure with the other questions. Alternatively, invite different pupils to read out and answer each question.

Answers: **1** Jane **2** Sam **3** Saturday, 9th May **4** Partyland **5** 691345

Activity 2

Write an invitation. Draw.

- Explain to the class that they are going to write a birthday invitation for a friend. Then ask the pupils to fill in the information. They should include directions to the place of the party and complete the map. When the class have finished, encourage individual pupils to show their invitation to the rest of the class and read out the directions.

Recycled vocabulary

- The pupils look at the picture and write the word.

Answer: hall

Ending the lesson

Review the lesson.

- Say **Today you've read an invitation and you've written an invitation.** Elicit the information you see on a party invitation.

Review the task flashcards.

- Point to the task flashcards. Say **Look at the activities you've done today. Which activity was your favourite?** Elicit the pupils' favourite activities.

Sing a song (optional).

- Choose a song. The class sings and does the actions. Alternatively, invite the class to choose a song to sing.

Extra activity

Reinforcement

- Hand out pieces of card and felt-tip pens or coloured pencils.The pupils make their own party invitation out of card. Display the finished invitations in a prominent place.

Key Competences and Key Learning Outcomes

- Review language in the unit
- Reflect on own learning
- Sing a cooperative learning song

Key language

Recycled: *baker's, bank, bus station, car park, chemist's, fire station, museum, police station, post office, train station; from, to, go straight on, turn (left / right)*

Recycled: *Is there a (bank)? Yes, there is. / No, there isn't. Are there any (museums)? Yes, there are. / No, there aren't. How do I get from the (fire station) to the (post office)? Turn (left / right). / Go straight on.*

Materials

- Pupil's Book p90; Activity Book p87; Class CD4; Teacher's App on Navio
- Places in a town flashcards
- Teacher's Resource Bank: Task flashcards: *listen, number, write, say, Talk Partners, sing, stick, think*
- Teacher's Resource Bank: Traffic light cut-out
- *Give Me Five!* sticker

Optional materials

- Teacher's Resource Bank: Five Trinity Exam Practice cards (selected from the Starter Unit and Units 1, 2, 3, 4, 5, 6 and 7)

At a Glance Lesson Plan

Pupil's Book

Starting the lesson

- Use the Trinity Exam Practice cards (optional).
- Review the unit vocabulary.
- Set learning outcomes using the task flashcards.

Activity 1

- Listen and number.
- Write and say.
- ▶ *CD4 Track 6 p272*

Activity 2

- Listen. Look at Activity 1.
- ▶ *CD4 Track 7 p272*
- Talk Partners Ask and answer.

Activity 3 Cooperative learning

- Sing *Well Done!*
- ▶ *CD4 Track 8 p273*
- Stick the *Give Me Five!* sticker.
- Go to the Activity Book.

Ending the lesson

- Review the task flashcards.
- Sing a song (optional).

Cooperative learning

Think-Pair-Share

- Remember the ten places in a town.

Digital resources

Teacher's Digital: Don't forget you can teach this lesson using the Teacher's App on Navio.

Pupil's Digital: Encourage your pupils to use the Pupil's App on Navio to practise the vocabulary from this lesson.

Powered By NAVIO

Activity Book

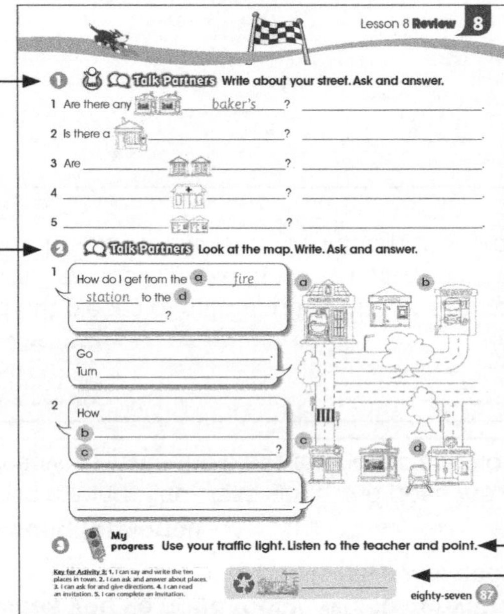

Activity Book

Activity 1

- Write about your street.
- Talk Partners Ask and answer.

Activity 2

- Look at the map. Write.
- Talk Partners Ask and answer.

Activity 3 My progress

- Use your traffic light. Listen to the teacher and point.

Recycled vocabulary

- Look, remember and write the word.

Starting the lesson

Use the Trinity Exam Practice cards (optional).

- The pupils practise asking and answering questions. (See p31.)

Review the unit vocabulary.

- Play *Quick flash* (see p23) with the unit flashcards to review places in a town.
- **Option:** Play the game in two teams. The teams take it in turns to remember the words.

Set learning outcomes using the task flashcards.

- Say **Today we're going to remember what we've learnt in Unit 8.**
- Hold up the task flashcards in turn and elicit the words. Stick them on one side of the board. Point to them during the lesson to reinforce your instructions.

Pupil's Book Activity 1

Listen and number. Write and say.

▶ *CD4 Track 6 p272*

- (Books open.) Point to each of the photos and elicit the words.
- Play the CD. Pause after each sentence. The pupils write the correct number in the circles.
- Play the CD again. The pupils write the correct place under each picture. Then they point and say the words.

Answers: **1** post office **2** chemist's **3** fire station **4** baker's **5** bank **6** bus station **7** train station **8** museum **9** police station **10** car park

Pupil's Book Activity 2

Listen. Look at Activity 1. Ask and answer.

▶ *CD4 Track 7 p272*

- (Books open.) Ask a confident pair of pupils to read out the questions and answers. Play the CD.
- **Talk Partners** The pupils ask and answer questions about their town or neighbourhood with a Talk Partner.

Pupil's Book Activity 3: Cooperative learning

Sing *Well done!*

▶ *CD4 Track 8 p273*

- Praise the class for their hard work and play the *Well done!* song. Encourage the pupils to join in.

Stick the *Give Me Five!* sticker.

- The pupils stick the *Give Me Five!* sticker on the Pupil's Book page.

Activity Book

Activity 1

Write about your street. Ask and answer.

- (Books open.) Invite individual pupils to use the illustrated clues to complete each question. The pupils answer about their own street. The pupils should work on their own to complete the questions and write their own answers.
- **Talk Partners** When they have finished, they practise the questions and answers with a Talk Partner.

Answers: **1** baker's **2** post office **3** there any museums **4** Is there a chemist's **5** Are there any banks

Activity 2

Look at the map. Write. Ask and answer.

- Read the instructions. The pupils complete each question with two places by looking at the map and then complete the answer with the corresponding directions.
- **Talk Partners** The pupils ask and answer with a Talk Partner.

Answers: **1** fire station, train station? Go straight on, turn left, then turn right. **2** How do I get from the bus station to the police station? Go straight on, turn right, then turn left.

Activity 3 My progress

Use your traffic light. Listen to the teacher and point.

- (Books closed.) Ask the class to take out their traffic light cut-out. Say **Let's think about our work in this unit.** Read the first self-assessment statement. Point to the green circle and say **Yes, I can do this very well.** Point to the orange circle and say **Yes, I can do this.** Point to the red circle and say **No, I can't do this.**
- Read the remaining statements. For each one, the pupils point to the colour on their traffic light that shows how they feel about their own learning.

Self-assessment statements

1. I can say and write the ten places in town.
2. I can ask and answer about places.
3. I can ask for and give directions.
4. I can read an invitation.
5. I can complete an invitation.

Recycled vocabulary

- The pupils look at the picture and write the word.

Answer: garden

Ending the lesson

Review the task flashcards.

- Point to the task flashcards. Say **Look at the activities you've done today. Which activity was your favourite?** Elicit the pupils' favourite activity.

Sing a song (optional).

- The class chooses their favourite song from the unit. The class sings and does the actions.

Cooperative learning

Think-Pair-Share

- Ask **Can you remember the ten places in a town?** Ask the class to think silently on their own for a minute.
- **Talk Partners** Then, the pupils work together to remember and name all ten words.
- Invite a pair to say one of the words. Hold up the corresponding flashcard and prompt the class to repeat the word.
- Finally, repeat the procedure, asking different pairs of pupils each time, until all ten words have been named.

Key Competences and Key Learning Outcomes

- Watch and understand a video about important places in town and road safety
- Say what you do to cross the road safely

- Learn to cross the road safely

Key language

- *baker's, bank, bus station, car park, chemist's, fire station, museum, police station, post office, train station, zebra crossing*

Materials

- Pupil's Book p91; Activity Book p88; Class CD4; Video; Teacher's App on Navio
- Teacher's Resource Bank: Task flashcards: *tick, read, circle, think, listen, number, write, draw, say, Talk Partners*
- Places in a town flashcards

Optional materials

- Teacher's Resource Bank: Trinity Exam Practice cards (selected from Unit 8)

At a Glance Lesson Plan

Pupil's Book

Starting the lesson

- Use the Trinity Exam Practice cards (optional).
- Review places in town.
- Set learning outcomes and use the task flashcards.

Pre-watching activity

- Say what important places are in their town.

Activity 1

- Watch the video.
  Unit 8 video
- Tick (✓) or cross (✗). Which places are in the video?

Activity 2

- Watch the video again.
  Unit 8 video p280
- Read and answer.

Activity 3

- Read and think. Tick (✓) or cross (✗).

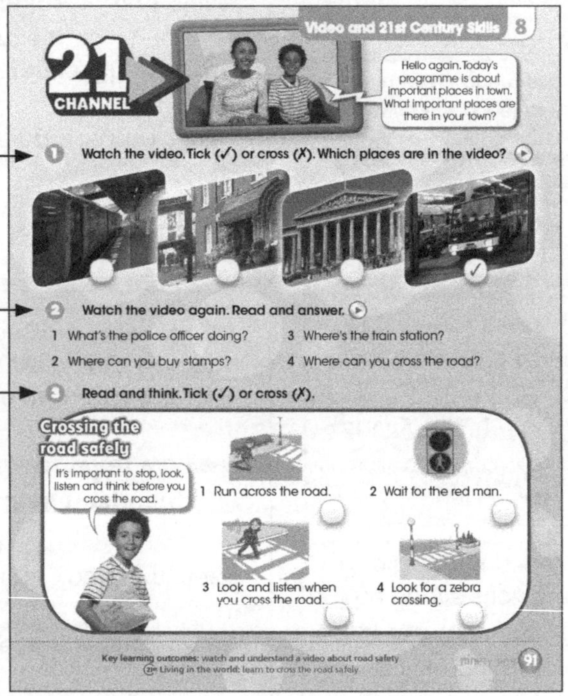

Ending the lesson

- Review the lesson.
- Review the task flashcards. Elicit the pupils' favourite activities.

Extra activity

Extension

- Making a sign for road safety.

Digital resources

Teacher's Digital: Don't forget you can teach this lesson using the Teacher's App on Navio.

Pupil's Digital: Encourage your pupils to use the Pupil's App on Navio to practise the vocabulary from this lesson.

Powered By NAVIO

Activity Book

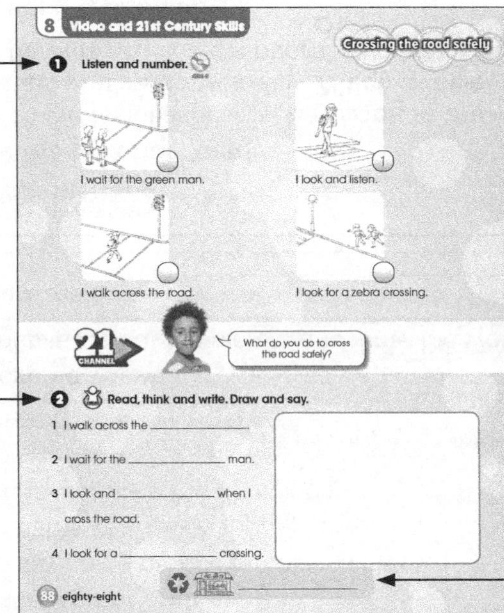

Activity Book

Activity 1

- Listen and number.
  ▶ *CD4 Track 9 p273*

Activity 2

- Read, think and write. Draw and say.

Recycled vocabulary

- Look, remember and write the word.

Starting the lesson

Use the Trinity Exam Practice cards (optional).

- The pupils practise asking and answering questions. (See p31.)

Review places in town.

- Divide the class into ten groups. Give each group a places in town flashcard. Say **I want to buy some bread.** Encourage the group with the baker's flashcard to hold up the card and stand up. Repeat the activity with all the flashcards.

Set learning outcomes and use the task flashcards.

- Say **Today we're going to watch a video and then ask and answer questions about important places in town and road safety.**
- Hold up the task flashcards, in turn, and elicit the activities. Stick them on the side of the board. Point to them during the lesson to reinforce your instructions.

Pre-watching activity

- Ask **What important places are there in your town?**

Pupil's Book Activity 1

Watch the video. Tick (✓) or cross (✗). Which places are in the video? *p280*

- Ask **What places do Sophie and Tom think are in the video?** Play Part 1. Elicit answers.
- Focus the pupils' attention on the video stills. Ask **What are the places?**
- Play Part 2. Pause the video after the first video still. Ask the pupils to point to the corresponding photo in their book.
- Play the video again for pupils to tick and cross the photos.
- Ask **Which of the places in the video are in your town?**

Answers: From left to right: ✓ ✓ ✗ ✓

Pupil's Book Activity 2

Watch the video again. Read and answer.

- Play Part 2 again. Pause after Sophie says, *He's working.* Read out the first question in Activity 2 to elicit the answer. Pupils say *He's working.*
- Play the video all the way through for pupils to check and write their answers.
- Ask the pupils some questions to check understanding. Suggested questions.
  Why do the lights on the fire engine flash? *(To tell people to be careful.)*
  Are all the police cars blue and yellow in Abby's town? *(No.)*
  What do you do when you find a zebra crossing? *(Push the button.)*
  When can you cross the road at a zebra crossing? *(When you see the green man.)*
  What is it important to do when you cross the road? *(Look and listen.)*
  Where does Sophie need to go? *(The post office.)*
  Where is it? *(Straight on and turn left.)*

Answers: **1** He's working. **2** At the post office. **3** Behind the post office. **4** At a zebra crossing.

Pupil's Book Activity 3

Read and think. Tick (✓) or cross (✗).

- Read out the first sentence. Ask **Is this safe to do? Do you tick or cross?**
- Read out the rest of the sentences for the pupils to follow. Pupils tick or cross the sentences.
- Ask **Why is it important to stop, look, listen and think before you cross the road?** *(To check for traffic, think if it's safe to cross and not take a risk, look for a zebra crossing, wait for the green light, listen for any emergency vehicles travelling fast.)*

Answers: 1 ✗ 2 ✗ 3 ✓ 4 ✓

Activity Book

Activity 1

Listen and number.

▶ *CD4 Track 9 p273*

- Ask **What are the children doing?**
- Play the first exchange on the CD and ask **Which picture?** Show the number one in the circle.
- Play the rest of the CD, pausing after each exchange, for the pupils to number the pictures.

Answers: Top row: 4 1; Bottom row: 2 3

Activity 2

Read, think and write. Draw and say.

- Elicit responses from the pupils. Read out the sentence starters for the pupils to follow. The pupils complete the sentences with good road safety advice. The pupils draw pictures to illustrate their advice.

Recycled vocabulary

Answer: toyshop

Ending the lesson

Review the lesson.

- Say **Today we've watched a video about road safety and important places in town. What do we know about road safety?** *(Find a zebra crossing. Wait for the green man. Look, listen and think.)*
- Ask **Which activity was easy / difficult?**

Review the task flashcards.

- Point to the task flashcards on the board. Say **Look at the activities you've done today. Which activity was your favourite?**

Extra activity

Extension

- Divide the class into small groups. Tell them to choose a piece of advice about road safety. They draw a sign to illustrate the advice to use to teach other children.

Date: ____________________ **Unit:** __________

1 What did my pupils learn in this unit?

____

____

____

____

2 How did my pupils work? (✓)

individually ☐ in pairs ☐ in small groups ☐

in large groups ☐ as a class ☐

3 Which key competences did my pupils develop?

- Competence in linguistic communication ☐
- Competence in mathematics, science and technology ☐
- Digital competence ☐
- Learning to learn ☐
- Social and civic competences ☐
- Sense of initiative and entrepreneurship ☐
- Cultural awareness and expression ☐

4 Which lessons / activities were the most successful and why?

____

____

____

____

5 Which lessons / activities did my pupils find the most difficult and why?

____

____

____

____

6 What did I try in the classroom for the first time? How did it go?

____

____

____

____

7 Which resources did I find most useful? (including webpages)

____

____

____

____

____

8 What could I do differently next time I teach this unit?

____

____

____

____

Unit 9 Holiday fun

Unit overview

Key Competences and Key Learning Outcomes

- Identify and say ten holiday places (Lesson 1)
- Use past simple: 'I' and 'you' (Lesson 2)
- Understand and act out a conversation (Lesson 2)
- Ask and answer questions about where you were yesterday (Lesson 2)
- Read, listen and understand a story about a magic trip (Lesson 3)
- Use irregular plurals (Lesson 4)
- Read and learn about summer holidays in Britain (Lesson 6)
- Read, understand and write a diary extract (Lesson 7)
- Watch and understand a video about weekend activities (Video and 21st Century Skills)

- Use the Pupil's App on Navio
- Learn to use a digital camera (Video and 21st Century Skills)

- Use a strategy to practise spelling key words (Lesson 1)
- Say a tongue twister and practise 'ear' and 'air' spellings (Lesson 5)
- Review the language from the unit and reflect on own learning (Lesson 8)
- Practise activity types found in the Cambridge Exams: Pre A1 Starters

- Understand the importance of playing outside with your friends (Lesson 3)

- Work with a Talk Partner to practise and reinforce learning (all lessons)
- Play a communication game about where you were (Lesson 5)

- Sing three songs (Lessons 1, 4 and 8)
- Understand, act out and give an opinion on a story (Lesson 3)
- Think about what you do in your summer holidays (Lesson 6)

Vocabulary

Core vocabulary
aquarium, castle, chocolate factory, circus, funfair, safari park, science museum, sports centre, theatre, water park; child, children, man, men, woman, women

Extension vocabulary (optional)
amusement arcade, art gallery, climbing wall, ice rink, royal palace, skateboard park, person, people, parent, grandparent

Other vocabulary
dolphin; bored, magic, tower, trip; arts and crafts, butterfly house, giant chess, hide and seek, maze, paint a cup / plate, summer holidays; badge, clown, diary, roller coaster, stilts, ticket

Recycled vocabulary
Places in the town, Describing hair and eyes, Family members, Days of the week; *fish, fly, holiday, hungry, slide; birthday, games, garden; cloudy, cold, hot, sunny; fast, tall*

Structures

Core structures
Where were you yesterday / last weekend? I was at the (circus). We were at the (chocolate factory). Were you at the (castle)? Yes, I was. No, I wasn't. Who's that (man / woman)? He's / She's my (uncle / aunt). Who are those men / women)? They're my (uncles / aunts).

Other structures
It was fun / great! Yesterday was (Saturday). It was (sunny).

Recycled structures
Let's go to … Where's (Beth)? Here I am. He's / She's got (short) (hair). There is / are … He's / She's my (cousin). They're my (grandparents). We can (play hide and seek). We love (the maze). Our favourite place is … In this photo, we're playing …

Phonics

Alternative vowel spellings **'air' / 'ear'** (b**ear**, p**ear**, st**air**s, funf**air**)

British Culture

Summer holidays

Literacy

Text type: a diary (text to retell events)
Reading skills: scanning for specific information; remembering facts

21st Century Skills

Digital skills: learn to use a digital camera

Cooperative learning

Songs: *We can do it!* (Lesson 7); *Well Done!* (Lesson 8)
Skills: Listening to others (Lesson 1); Working together as a team (Lesson 5); Think-Pair-Share (Lesson 8)

Values

The importance of playing outside with your friends.

Cross-curricular links

Links to Science
Electricity: machines that use electricity.

Suggested Arts and Crafts concepts
Observing and identifying the effect of colour and light and dark in art; making and playing a game

Key Competences and Key Learning Outcomes

- Identify and say ten holiday places
- Say the vocabulary chant
- Stick the holiday places stickers

- Identify machines that use electricity (optional)

- Use a strategy to practise spelling key words

- Sing a song about a holiday

Key language
- *aquarium, castle, chocolate factory, circus, funfair, safari park, science museum, sports centre, theatre, water park*
- *We're on holiday. We're having a great time. Let's go to the …*

Extension vocabulary
- *amusement arcade, art gallery, climbing wall, ice rink, royal palace, skateboard park*

Recycled: Places in the town from Levels 1 and 2; *fish, fly, holiday, hungry, play, slide*

Other vocabulary: *dolphin*

Materials
- Pupil's Book p92; Activity Book pp90 and 99; Class CD4; Teacher's App on Navio; Unit 9 stickers
- Holiday places flashcards; Places in a town flashcards
- Teacher's Resource Bank: Holiday places word cards
- Teacher's Resource Bank: Task flashcards: *listen, sing, read, stick, say, match, write, Talk Partners*

Optional materials
- Teacher's Resource Bank: Five Trinity Exam Practice cards (selected from the Starter Unit and Units 1, 2, 3, 4, 5, 6, 7 and 8)

At a Glance Lesson Plan

Pupil's Book

Starting the lesson
- Use the Trinity Exam Practice cards (optional).
- Review places in a town. Play *Slowly, slowly.* (See p23.)
- Set learning outcomes using the task flashcards.

Vocabulary presentation
- Present the new vocabulary.

Activity 1
- Listen and point.

▶ *CD4 Track 10 p273*
- Sing *We're on holiday.*

Word cards
- Read the word cards.
- Match them to the flashcards.

Activity 2
- Read and stick the ten stickers.
- Listen and say the chant.

▶ *CD4 Track 12 p273*

Go to the Activity Book.

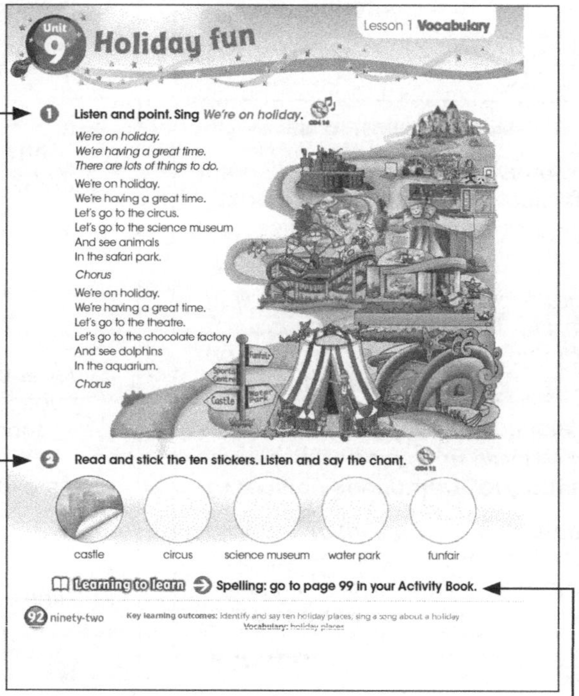

Ending the lesson
- Review the lesson.
- Review the task flashcards.

Extra activity

Vocabulary extension
- Present six additional vocabulary items.

Cooperative learning

Listening to others
- Play *Memory chain.*

Link to Science
- **Electricity:** machines that use electricity

Learning to learn

Spelling
- Practise spelling at any time during this unit (Activity Book p99).

Digital resources

Teacher's Digital: Don't forget you can teach this lesson using the Teacher's App on Navio.

Pupil's Digital: Encourage your pupils to use the Pupil's App on Navio to practise the vocabulary from this lesson.

Powered By NAVIO

Activity Book

Activity Book

Activity 1
- Read and match.

Activity 2
- Look and write.

Recycled vocabulary
- Look, remember and write the phrase.

Spelling

Let's practise spelling!
- Use the *Look-Copy-Cover-Write* technique.

Recycled vocabulary
- Look, remember and write the phrase.

Starting the lesson

Use the Trinity Exam Practice cards (optional).

- The pupils practise asking and answering questions. (See p31.)

Review places in a town.

- Review the places in a town from Unit 8. Play *Slowly, slowly* (see p23) with the Unit 8 flashcards and stick them up on the board as the pupils guess them.

Set learning outcomes using the task flashcards.

- Explain the aims of the lesson. Say **Today we're going to learn the names of fun holiday places.**
- Hold up the task flashcards and elicit the words. Stick them on one side of the board. Point to them during the lesson to reinforce your instructions.

Vocabulary presentation

Present the new vocabulary.

- (Books closed.) Ask **Where do you like to go for a day out?** Accept any suggestions and introduce the new vocabulary by showing the flashcards one by one.
- Play *Which one's missing?* (See p23.)

Pupil's Book Activity 1

Listen and point. Sing *We're on holiday.*

▶ *CD4 Track 10 p273*

- (Books open.) Ask **Where are Molly, Jake and Toby? What places can you see?** The class point to and name the different places. Stick the flashcards on the board in the order that they appear in the song.
- Play the CD and do the actions. Play the CD again. The class sing and do the actions.

Word cards

Read the word cards. Match them to the flashcards.

- (Books closed.) Hold up one of the holiday places word cards. The pupils read collectively. A pupil sticks the word card next to the corresponding flashcard on the board. Repeat.
- Point to each word card. The pupils read the words.

Pupil's Book Activity 2

Read and stick the ten stickers. Listen and say the chant.

▶ *CD4 Track 12 p273*

- Ask a pupil to read the first word. The pupils stick the corresponding sticker above the word.
- **Talk Partners** The pupils find and stick the remaining stickers. Remind them to use cooperative language.
- Play the CD. The pupils listen and say the chant, pointing to the stickers in turn.

Activity Book

Activity 1

Read and match.

- (Books open.) A volunteer reads the first sentence segment and the matching second half. Read the complete sentence together. Repeat.
- **Talk Partners** The pupils read and match individually and check their answers with a Talk Partner.

Answers: **1** to see fish **2** to play on the slides **3** to make chocolate **4** to play sport **5** to see a play

Activity 2

Look and write.

- Name the holiday places at random. The pupils point to each one. A pupil reads out a place name and points to the place. Repeat. The pupils write the names of the places individually.

Answers: **1** water park **2** funfair **3** safari park **4** castle **5** circus **6** science museum

Recycled vocabulary

- The pupils look at the picture and write the phrase.

Answer: bus station

Ending the lesson

Review the lesson.

- Say **Today we've learnt the names of holiday places.** Elicit the words from the pupils.

Review the task flashcards.

- Point to the task flashcards. Say **Look at the activities you've done today. Which was your favourite?** Elicit the pupils' favourite activities.

Extra activity

Vocabulary extension

- Present six additional holiday places: *amusement arcade, art gallery, climbing wall, ice rink, royal palace, skateboard park.*
- Use the Vocabulary Booster on Navio to practise these new words.

Cooperative learning

Listening to others

- Play *Memory chain* (see p67) with places in a town from Lesson 1 and those learnt in Level 1.

Link to Science

- If you are studying the Science topic of **electricity** in English, discuss the attractions at the funfair and explain to the pupils that they use electricity. Think about the funfair rides in turn and discuss those which use electricity for light, sound, motion or heat.

Spelling (Activity Book p99)

Let's practise spelling!

- The pupils can practise spelling the ten words using the *Look-Copy-Cover-Write* technique at any time before the Lesson 8 Review.

Recycled vocabulary

- The pupils look at the picture and write the phrase.

Answer: post office

Key Competences and Key Learning Outcomes

- Use past simple: 'I' and 'you'
- Understand and act out a conversation
- Ask and answer questions about where you were yesterday

- Listen for specific information

Key language

- *Where were you (yesterday)? I was at the (circus). Were you at the (castle)? Yes, I was. No, I wasn't.*

Recycled: *aquarium, castle, chocolate factory, circus, funfair, safari park, science museum, sports centre, theatre, water park*

Materials

- Pupil's Book p93; Activity Book p91; Class CD4; Teacher's App on Navio
- Holiday places flashcards
- Teacher's Resource Bank: Task flashcards: *listen, act out, match, write, draw, Talk Partners*

Optional materials

- Teacher's Resource Bank: Five Trinity Exam Practice cards (selected from the Starter Unit and Units 1, 2, 3, 4, 5, 6, 7 and 8)
- Small pieces of paper (one per pupil)

At a Glance Lesson Plan

Pupil's Book

Starting the lesson

- Use the Trinity Exam Practice cards (optional).
- Review the *We're on holiday* song.

▶ ***CD4 Track 10 p273***

▶ ***CD4 Track 11 p273 (optional karaoke version)***

- Play *Where are you?*
- Set learning outcomes using the task flashcards.

Activity 1

- Listen and repeat.

▶ ***CD4 Track 13 p273***

- Talk Partners Act out.

Activity 2

- Listen and match.

▶ ***CD4 Track 14 p273***

Go to the Activity Book.

Ending the lesson

- Review the lesson.
- Review the task flashcards.

Extra activity

Reinforcement

- Play *Friend match.*

Digital resources

Teacher's Digital: Don't forget you can teach this lesson using the Teacher's App on Navio.

Pupil's Digital: Encourage your pupils to use the Pupil's App on Navio to practise the vocabulary from this lesson.

Powered By NAVIO

Activity Book

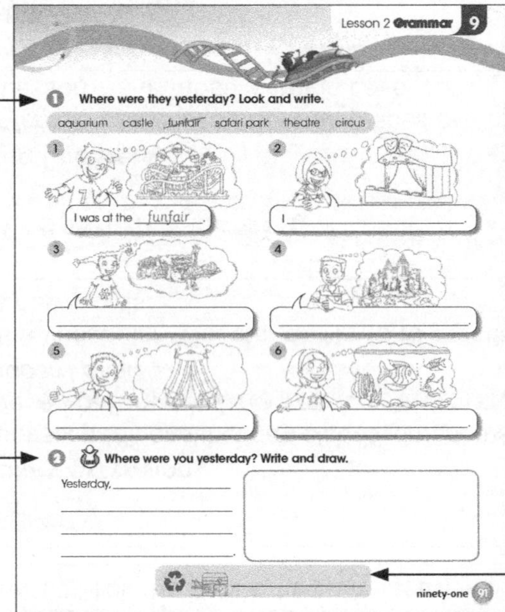

Activity Book

Activity 1

- Where were they yesterday? Look and write.

Activity 2

- Where were you yesterday? Write and draw.

Recycled vocabulary

- Look, remember and write the phrase.

Starting the lesson

Use the Trinity Exam Practice cards (optional).

- The pupils practise asking and answering questions. (See p31.)

Review the *We're on holiday* song.

▶ *CD4 Track 10 p273*

▶ *CD4 Track 11 p273 (optional karaoke version)*

- Stick the flashcards from the song in different places around the room. Ask the pupils to stand up in the centre of the classroom. Play the CD (or use the karaoke version). The pupils do the actions and sing the song. When they hear the holiday places they turn towards them and walk on the spot. For the chorus, everyone turns and faces you again.

Play *Where are you?*

- Choose a volunteer and secretly show him / her one of the holiday places flashcards. Ask the pupil to mime the activity. The rest of the class asks questions until they guess the place *(Are you at the circus? Are you at the water park?).* Change the volunteer and play again.

Set learning outcomes using the task flashcards.

- Explain the aims of the lesson. Say **Today we're going to ask and answer questions about the past.**
- Hold up the task flashcards and elicit the words. Stick them on one side of the board. Point to them during the lesson to reinforce your instructions.

Pupil's Book Activity 1

Listen and repeat. Act out.

▶ *CD4 Track 13 p273*

- (Books open.) Ask **What can you see?**
- Play the CD. The pupils listen and read the conversation. Check understanding. Ask **Where was Beth yesterday? Was Jake at the funfair? Was Jake at the aquarium?**
- Play the CD again. Pause for the pupils to repeat.
- Talk Partners The pupils act out the conversation with a Talk Partner.

Pupil's Book Activity 2

Listen and match.

▶ *CD4 Track 14 p273*

- (Books open.) Ask the pupils to name the holiday places in the illustrations. Say **Let's listen. Match Molly, Jake and Beth to the places they were at yesterday.**
- Play the CD. Pause after each conversation for the pupils to match each child to the corresponding place. Pause after each one to check the pupils' answers.

Answers: **1** c **2** b **3** a

Activity Book

Activity 1

Where were they yesterday? Look and write.

- (Books open.) Ask the pupils to look at and name the holiday places inside each thought bubble. Ask **Where were you yesterday?** Encourage a confident pupil to answer. Repeat for the remaining questions. The pupils write the answers individually.

Answers: **1** funfair **2** was at the theatre **3** I was at the safari park. **4** I was at the castle. **5** I was at the circus. **6** I was at the aquarium.

Activity 2

Where were you yesterday? Write and draw.

- Personalise this activity by asking individual pupils **Where were you yesterday?** The pupils reply with true answers. They may use recycled vocabulary from previous units or Level 1 if they were not at one of the holiday places from Unit 9. The pupils write a sentence and draw themselves and a place where they were yesterday.
- Talk Partners The pupils read out their sentences and show their pictures to a Talk Partner.

Recycled vocabulary

- The pupils look at the picture and write the phrase.

Answer: train station

Ending the lesson

Review the lesson.

- Say **Today you've asked and answered about the past.** Elicit some questions and answers.

Review the task flashcards.

- Point to the task flashcards. Say **Look at the activities you've done today. Which activity was your favourite?** Elicit the pupils' favourite activities.

Extra activity

Reinforcement

- Play *Friend match.* Give each pupil a small piece of paper. Ask the pupils to choose one of the holiday places and write it on the piece of paper. The pupils stand up and walk around the room asking each other *Where were you yesterday?* Encourage the pupils to answer using full sentences: *I was at the (circus).* If they find a pupil who was at the same place, they form a group.

Key Competences and Key Learning Outcomes

- Read, listen and understand a story about a magic trip
- Read the story with some fluency
- Become familiar with the story through a pre-reading task
- Understand the importance of playing outside with your friends
- Understand and act out the story
- Give an opinion on the story

Key language

- *Where were you? We were at a (chocolate factory).*

Recycled: *aquarium, castle, chocolate factory, water park; fly, holiday, hungry, summer*

Recycled: *Lets go to … Where's (Beth)? Here I am.*

Other vocabulary: *bored, magic, tower, trip*

Materials

- Pupil's Book pp94–95; Activity Book p92; Class CD4; Teacher's App on Navio
- Holiday places flashcards
- Teacher's Resource Bank: Task flashcards: *listen, read, act out, write, Talk Partners*
- Teacher's Resource Bank: Unit 9 Lesson 3 Animated Story

Optional materials

- Teacher's Resource Bank: Five Trinity Exam Practice cards (selected from the Starter Unit and Units 1, 2, 3, 4, 5, 6, 7 and 8)

At a Glance Lesson Plan

Pupil's Book

Activity Book

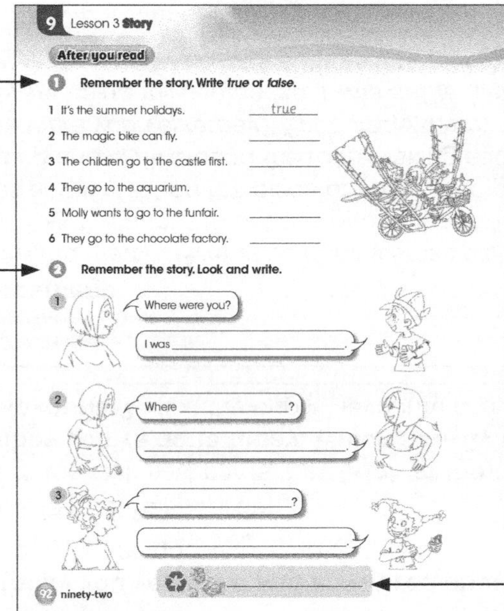

Starting the lesson

- Use the Trinity Exam Practice cards (optional).
- Review the song *We're on holiday.*

▶ ***CD4 Track 10 p273***

▶ ***CD4 Track 11 p273 (optional karaoke version)***

- Going on a day trip. Play *Quick flash.*
- Set learning outcomes using the task flashcards.

Before you read

- Read and answer the question.

Activity 1

- Listen and read.

▶ ***CD4 Track 15 p273***

- Act out.

Now watch the animated story!

After you read: Activity 2

Go to page 92 in your Activity Book.

- Values: Read and write.

Ending the lesson

- Review the lesson.
- Review the task flashcards.

Extra activity

Extension

- Role-play.

Digital resources

Teacher's Digital: Don't forget you can teach this lesson using the Teacher's App on Navio.

Pupil's Digital: Encourage your pupils to use the Pupil's App on Navio to practise the vocabulary from this lesson.

Powered By NAVIO

Activity Book

After you read: Activity 1

- Remember the story. Write *true* or *false.*

Activity 2

- Remember the story. Look and write.

Recycled vocabulary

- Look, remember and write the phrase.

Starting the lesson

Use the Trinity Exam Practice cards (optional).

- The pupils practise asking and answering questions. (See p31.)

Review the song *We're on holiday.*

▶ *CD4 Track 10 p273*

▶ *CD4 Track 11 p273 (optional karaoke version)*

- Play the CD (or use the karaoke version).
- Extend the song by adding a new verse with other unit vocabulary (funfair, water park, sports centre, etc.).

Going on a day trip.

- Play *Quick flash* to review holiday places.
- Select a volunteer to 'go on a day trip'. Ask him / her to step outside the classroom for a moment and secretly show him / her one of the places. The pupil says *Goodbye! I'm going on a day trip!* When he / she comes back in, the class asks *Where were you?* The pupil answers *I was at (the castle).* Repeat with different volunteers, changing the flashcard each time.

Set learning outcomes using the task flashcards.

- Say **Today we're going to listen to a story.**
- Hold up the task flashcards and elicit the words. Stick them on one side of the board. Point to them during the lesson to reinforce your instructions.

Before you read

Read and answer the question.

- (Books open.) Read the speech bubble, then ask the pupils to think of places we go on a day trip to. Scan the story to identify the places from the magic trip.
- Talk Partners The pupils feed back to a Talk Partner and name the places.

Pupil's Book Activity 1

Listen and read. Act out.

▶ *CD4 Track 15 p273*

- (Books open.) Play the CD. The pupils follow the text with their finger. Pause between each frame to check understanding.

Suggested comprehension questions

- Frame 1: **What are Jake, Molly and Beth doing?** *(Nothing.)*
- Frame 2: **What happens to the magic bike?** *(It can fly.)* **Where does Jake want to go?** *(The castle.)*
- Frame 3: **Where are they now?** *(At the castle.)* **Do they like it?** *(Yes.)*
- Frame 4: **Where does Molly want to go?** *(The water park.)*
- Frame 5: **Where are they now?** *(At the water park.)* **Is it fun?** *(Yes.)*
- Frame 6: **Where does Beth want to go? Why?** *(To the chocolate factory. She's hungry.)*
- Frame 7: **What does Mum say? What does (Jake / Molly / Beth) say?** *(Where were you? We were at a chocolate factory … and a castle … and a water park.)*
- Frame 8: **Does Mum think they've got a magic bike?** *(No.)*
- Organise the class into four groups (Mum, Beth, Molly and Jake).
- Play the CD. Each group joins in when their character speaks. Pause the CD for the pupils to repeat.
- Ask the pupils if they enjoyed the story. Why? Why not?

Now watch the animated story!

After you read

Pupil's Book Activity 2

Go to page 92 in your Activity Book.

Activity Book

After you read: Activity 1

Remember the story. Write *true* or *false*.

- (Books open.) Encourage a confident pupil to read the first sentence. Ask the class to decide if the statement is correct or incorrect by answering 'true' or 'false'. Repeat with the remaining statements.
- Talk Partners The pupils write 'true' or 'false' individually. Then they check their answers with a Talk Partner.

Answers: **1** true **2** true **3** true **4** false **5** false **6** true

Activity 2

Remember the story. Look and write.

- (Books open.) Encourage a volunteer to read Mum's first question. The pupils look at the illustration and answer with the corresponding place. They write questions and answers about the story.
- Talk Partners The pupils read their questions and answers with a Talk Partner.

Answers: **1** at the castle **2** were you, I was at the water park. **3** Where were you? I was at the chocolate factory.

Recycled vocabulary

- The pupils look at the picture and write the phrase.

Answer: car park

Pupil's Book Activity 2

Values: Read and write.

- Ask the pupils if they have fun playing outside with their friends. Read the value and prompt the class to choose the correct word to complete the sentence.
- Ask the pupils what they like to play with their friends.

Ending the lesson

Review the lesson.

- Say **Today we've listened to a story about a magic trip. Today you've learnt that it's important to play outside with your friends.** Elicit activities the pupils enjoy doing with their friends.

Review the task flashcards.

- Point to the task flashcards. Say **Look at the activities you've done today. Which activity was your favourite?** Elicit the pupils' favourite activities.

Extra activity

Extension

- Role-play. Stick the holiday places flashcards on the board. Choose a volunteer to play the part of Mum in the story. Choose another volunteer to play the part of Jake, Molly or Beth. Mum asks *Where were you?* The pupil playing Jake, Molly or Beth answers with any of the holiday places: *I was at the (circus).*
- Talk Partners The pupils role-play the exchange with a Talk Partner, taking turns to be Mum.

Key Competences and Key Learning Outcomes

- Use irregular plurals
- Ask and answer about groups of people
- Sing a song

Key language

- *child, children, man, men, woman, women*
- *Who's that (man / woman)? He's / She's my (uncle / aunt). Who are those men / women)? They're my (uncles / aunts).*

Extension vocabulary

- *person, people, parent, grandparent*

Recycled: *aunt, cousin, uncle; eyes, hair; long, short; black, blonde, blue, brown, green*

Recycled: *He's / She's got (short) (hair).*

Materials

- Pupil's Book p96; Activity Book p93; Class CD4; Character flashcards; Teacher's App on Navio
- Teacher's Resource Bank: Task flashcards: *listen, say, sing, Talk Partners, write, read, match*
- Pupils' family photos or drawings

Optional materials

- Teacher's Resource Bank: Five Trinity Exam Practice cards (selected from the Starter Unit and Units 1, 2, 3, 4, 5, 6, 7 and 8)

At a Glance Lesson Plan

Pupil's Book

Starting the lesson

- Use the Trinity Exam Practice cards (optional).
- Review the Lesson 3 story.
- Review how we describe people's hair and eyes.
- Set learning outcomes using the task flashcards.

Vocabulary presentation

- Present the new vocabulary.

Activity 1

- Listen, point and say.
- ▶ *CD4 Track 16 p273*

Activity 2

- Listen and point. Sing *Who's that?*
- ▶ *CD4 Track 17 p273*

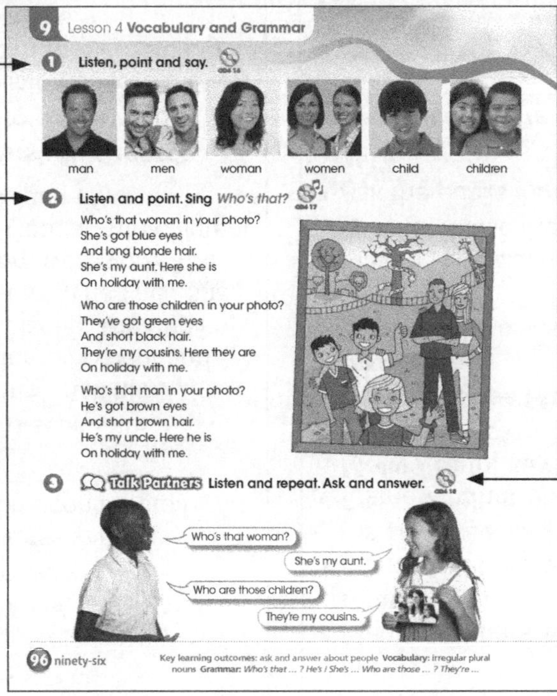

Activity 3

- Listen and repeat.
- ▶ *CD4 Track 18 p274*
- Talk Partners Ask and answer.
- Go to the Activity Book.

Ending the lesson

- Review the lesson.
- Review the task flashcards.

Extra activities

Reinforcement

- Singular or plural?
- Play *One or two?*

Vocabulary extension

- Present four additional vocabulary items.

Activity Book

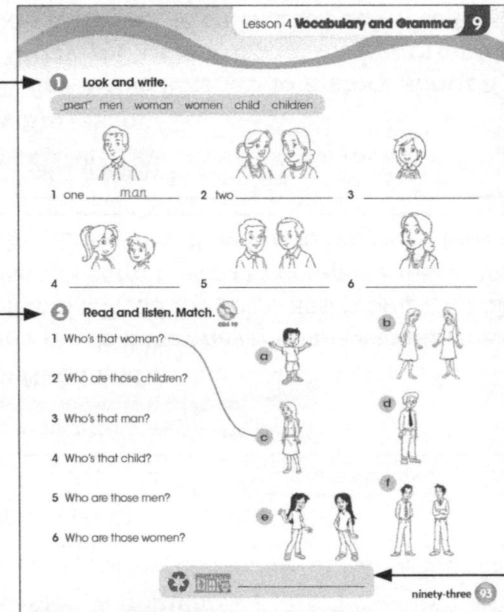

Activity Book

Activity 1

- Look and write.

Activity 2

- Read and listen. Match.
- ▶ *CD4 Track 19 p274*

Recycled vocabulary

- Look, remember and write the phrase.

Digital resources

Teacher's Digital: Don't forget you can teach this lesson using the Teacher's App on Navio.

Pupil's Digital: Encourage your pupils to use the Pupil's App on Navio to practise the vocabulary from this lesson.

Powered By NAVIO

Starting the lesson

Use the Trinity Exam Practice cards (optional).

- The pupils practise asking and answering questions. (See p31.)

Review the Lesson 3 story.

- Say statements about the children's activities in the story in random order. The pupils scan the story and say which frame the activity appears in. Say, e.g. **They were at the water park.** *(Frame 5.)*

Review how we describe people's hair and eyes.

- Use the character flashcards to review physical descriptions. Stick them on the board and say **She's got brown eyes.** *(Beth.)* **He's got blonde hair.** *(Jake.)*

Set learning outcomes using the task flashcards.

- Say **Today we're going to ask and answer about people.**
- Hold up the task flashcards in turn and elicit the words. Stick them on one side of the board. Point to them during the lesson to reinforce your instructions.

Vocabulary presentation

Present the new vocabulary.

- (Books closed.) Draw a mouse on the board and remind the pupils that we say 'one mouse'. Draw another mouse next to it and elicit *two mice*. Remind the pupils that sometimes the word is different for plural items. Elicit other examples the pupils know *(tooth / teeth, foot / feet).*
- (Books open.) Point to the first photo and say **man**. Repeat the word and ask the class to say it with you. Say **One man, two men!** and point to the second picture. Repeat with the other photos.

Pupil's Book Activity 1

Listen, point and say.

▶ ***CD4 Track 16 p273***

- (Books open.) Say **Let's listen and repeat.** Play the CD. The pupils listen to each word, pointing to the corresponding photo each time. Play the CD again. This time the pupils repeat.

Pupil's Book Activity 2

Listen and point. Sing *Who's that?*

▶ ***CD4 Track 17 p273***

- (Books open.) Point to the illustration in the activity and ask **What can you see?** *(A family.)* **Who can you see in the picture?** *(A woman, a man and some children.)* Ask the pupils to predict which members of the family they are.
- Play the CD. The pupils listen to the song. Play the CD again. The pupils sing.

Pupil's Book Activity 3

Listen and repeat. Ask and answer.

▶ ***CD4 Track 18 p274***

- Play the CD. Pupils follow the conversation. Play the CD again and ask the pupils to repeat the questions and answers. Then, invite a pair of pupils to act out the conversation.
- Talk Partners The pupils practise the conversation with a Talk Partner naming different family members each time. Ask the pupils to bring in photos of their real family to do this activity, or they can draw a picture of their family beforehand.

Activity Book

Activity 1

Look and write.

- (Books open.) Ask the pupils to decide if they need to use a singular word (for one person) or a plural word (for more than one person). Look at the first picture and ask **Is there one or more than one?** Establish that there is one person and the pupils should use the singular word (one man). Pupils complete the activity individually.

Answers: **1** one man **2** two women **3** one child **4** two children **5** two men **6** one woman

Activity 2

Read and listen. Match.

▶ ***CD4 Track 19 p274***

- (Books open.) Choose a volunteer to read the first question. Play the CD. The pupils read and listen. Play the CD again. The pupils match the questions to the illustrations.
- Talk Partners The pupils check their answers with a Talk Partner.

Answers: **1** c **2** e **3** d **4** a **5** f **6** b

Recycled vocabulary

- The pupils look at the picture and write the phrase.

Answer: police station

Ending the lesson

Review the lesson.

- Say **Today we've talked about different people.** Elicit some words from the pupils.

Review the task flashcards.

- Point to the task flashcards. Say **Look at the activities you've done today. Which activity was your favourite?** Elicit the pupils' favourite activities.

Extra activities

Reinforcement

- Draw a chart on the board. Write *one* at the top of one column and *more than one* at the top of the other column. Write singular words in the left-hand column and ask the pupils to provide the plural words for the right-hand column.
- Play *One or two?* (a version of *Simon says*). Say singular and irregular plural words the pupils know at random. Say **Stand up if it's more than one.** Then say **Man**. The pupils remain seated and say *One man.* Say **Women.** The pupils stand up and say *Two women.* Alternate singular and plural words randomly *(foot, feet, man, men, tooth, teeth, mouse, mice, woman, women, child, children).*

Vocabulary extension

- Use the Vocabulary Booster on Navio and present and practise four additional words: *person, people, parent, grandparent.*

Key Competences and Key Learning Outcomes

- Say a tongue twister with the 'air' sound
- Learn and practise 'ear' and 'air' spellings
- Listen for specific information

- Play a communication game about where you were

Key language

- *air, airport, bear, chair, funfair, hair, pear, stairs, wear*

Recycled: *aunt, brother, cousin, family, father, grandfather, grandmother, mother, sister, uncle; eyes, hair; black, blond(e), curly, long, short, white*

Recycled: *Where were you (last weekend)? I was at the (science museum). Who's that (man / woman / child)? Who are those (men / women / children)? He's / She's / They're my …*

Materials

- Pupil's Book p97; Activity Book p94; Class CD4; Teacher's App on Navio
- Teacher's Resource Bank: Task flashcards: *listen, say, match, cut out, write, colour, Talk Partners*
- Teacher's Resource Bank: Unit 9 Lesson 5 Activity 3 cut-out
- Scissors

Optional materials

- Teacher's Resource Bank: Five Trinity Exam Practice cards (selected from the Starter Unit and Units 1, 2, 3, 4, 5, 6, 7 and 8)
- Pupils' family photos

At a Glance Lesson Plan

Pupil's Book

Starting the lesson

- Use the Trinity Exam Practice cards (optional).
- Review the *Who's that?* song.
- ▶ *CD4 Track 17 p273*
- Set learning outcomes using the task flashcards.

Activity 1

- Listen and say.
- ▶ *CD4 Track 20 p274*
- Go to the Activity Book.
- Go to Magic Phonics.

Activity 2

- Listen and match.
- ▶ *CD4 Track 21 p274*

Activity 3

- Make and play the game (Teacher's Resource Bank).

Ending the lesson

- Review the lesson.
- Review the task flashcards.

Extra activity

Reinforcement

- Family photos.
- **Talk Partners** Ask and answer questions about your family.

Cooperative learning

Working together as a team

- **Talk Partners** Play *Beat the clock.*
- Add to the pronunciation wall display.

Activity Book

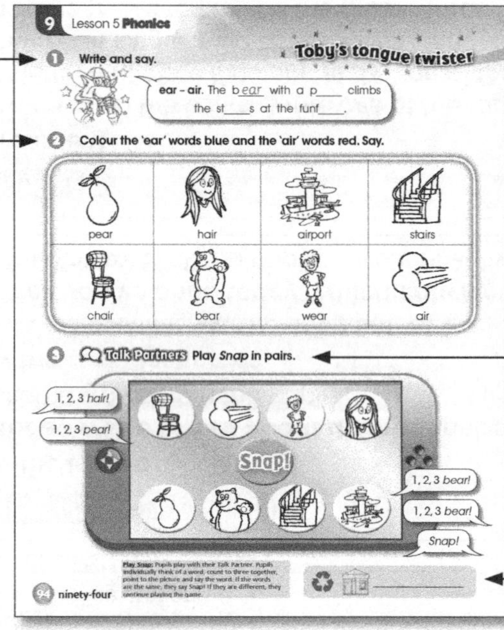

Activity Book

Activity 1

- Write and say.

Activity 2

- Colour the 'ear' words blue and the 'air' words red. Say.

Go to Magic Phonics.

Activity 3

- **Talk Partners** Play *Snap* in pairs.

Recycled vocabulary

- Look, remember and write the phrase.

Digital resources

Teacher's Digital: Don't forget you can teach this lesson using the Teacher's App on Navio.

Pupil's Digital: Encourage your pupils to use the Pupil's App on Navio to practise the vocabulary from this lesson.

Powered By NAVIO

Starting the lesson

Use the Trinity Exam Practice cards (optional).

- The pupils practise asking and answering questions. (See p31.)

Review the *Who's that?* song.

▶ *CD4 Track 17 p273*

- Divide the class into two groups. The pupils line up facing each other. Group A sings the question part and Group B sings the answer. Play the CD.

Set learning outcomes using the task flashcards.

- Say **Today we're going to say a tongue twister. We're going to play a communication game about where you were.**
- Hold up the task flashcards in turn and elicit the activities. Stick them on one side of the board. Point to them during the lesson to reinforce your instructions.

Pupil's Book Activity 1

Listen and say.

▶ *CD4 Track 20 p274*

- Write the words *pear* and *funfair* on the board and ask the pupils which sound they can hear in both words *('air')*. Circle the target grapheme in each word ('air' and 'ear') and model the sound. Encourage the pupils to say the sound with you. Check for accuracy.
- *Say* **It's time for Toby's tongue twister! What can you see?** *(A bear, a pear, stairs and a funfair.)*
- Play the CD. The pupils listen and repeat the target sound, then the words and then the entire tongue twister, faster and faster.

Go to Magic Phonics.

Activity Book

Activity 1

Write and say.

- (Books open.) Say **Look at Toby's tongue twister! The letters for 'air' and 'ear' are missing.** The pupils complete the tongue twister.
- Talk Partners The pupils say Toby's tongue twister and point to the 'air' sounds. They play *Faster and faster,* taking turns to say the tongue twister faster each time.

Answers: bear, pear, stairs, funfair

Activity 2

Colour the 'ear' words blue and the 'air' words red. Say.

- Ask pupils to say the words and then colour the 'ear' words blue and 'air' words red.

Answers: blue: pear, bear, wear
red: hair, airport, stairs, chair, air

Go to Magic Phonics.

Activity 3

Play *Snap* in pairs.

- Demonstrate the game with a volunteer. You each think of a word, count to three together, point to the picture and say the word. If the words are the same, say *Snap!* If they are different, continue playing the game.
- Talk Partners The pupils play the game with a Talk Partner.

Recycled vocabulary

- The pupils look at the picture and write the phrase.

Answer: bank

Pupil's Book Activity 2

Listen and match.

▶ *CD4 Track 21 p274*

- (Books open.) Explain to the pupils that they are going to listen to Molly and Beth asking and answering questions about Beth's family photo. They match the family words to the corresponding person in the photo.
- Play the CD. Pause after each sentence to give the pupils time to draw the lines and to check their answers.

Answers: (from left to right in photo) father and brother, cousin and aunt, grandmother, grandfather

Pupil's Book Activity 3

Make and play the game (Teacher's Resource Bank).

- (Books open.) Explain to the class that they are going to make the cut-out. Show them how to cut out the frame.
- The pupils draw their family members on a day trip. Revise any other family words they need for the activity.
- Talk Partners The pupils ask and answer questions about the family with a Talk Partner. *(Where were you last weekend? I was at the … Who's that woman? That's my mother. Who are those women? They're my aunts.)*

Ending the lesson

Review the lesson.

- Say **Today we've practised a tongue twister.** Ask the pupils to say it again. Say **Today you've talked about your family with your cut-out.**

Review the task flashcards.

- Point to the task flashcards. Say **Look at the activities you've done today. Which was your favourite?** Elicit the pupils' favourite activities.

Extra activity

Reinforcement

- Family photos. Ask the pupils to bring in photos of their family. Ask one of the pupils to show the photo to the class while the other pupils ask questions: *Who's that man? Who are those children?*, etc.
- Talk Partners The pupils ask and answer questions about their families using the vocabulary and question structures from the lesson.

Cooperative learning

Working together as a team

- Talk Partners Play *Beat the clock* to practise pronunciation of the 'air' / 'ear' sound (see p53).
- Add to the pronunciation wall display, adding a pear ('ear') and a chair ('air').

Key Competences and Key Learning Outcomes

- Read about summer holidays in Britain
- Listen for general understanding
- Think about what you do in your summer holidays

Key language

- *arts and crafts, butterfly house, giant chess, hide and seek, maze, paint a cup / plate, palace, summer holidays*

Recycled: *birthday, games, garden*

Recycled: *Yesterday, we were at (Blenheim Palace). There is … / There are … We can (play hide and seek). We love (the maze). Our favourite (place) is (the arts and crafts studio). In this photo, we're (playing giant chess).*

Materials

- Pupil's Book p98; Activity Book p95; Class CD4; Teacher's App on Navio
- Teacher's Resource Bank: Task flashcards: *Talk Partners, listen, read, think, number, write, tick, draw, say*

Optional materials

- Teacher's Resource Bank: Five Trinity Exam Practice cards (selected from the Starter Unit and Units 1, 2, 3, 4, 5, 6, 7 and 8)

At a Glance Lesson Plan

Pupil's Book

Starting the lesson

- Use the Trinity Exam Practice cards (optional).
- **Talk Partners** Review *Toby's tongue twister*.
  ▶ ***CD4 Track 20 p274***
- Set learning outcomes using the task flashcards.

Activity 1

- Listen and read. Answer.
  ▶ ***CD4 Track 22 p274***

Think about your culture

- What do you do in the summer holidays?

Go to the Activity Book.

Ending the lesson

- Review the lesson.
- Review the task flashcards.

Extra activity

Extension

- Summer holiday activities in Britain.

Activity Book

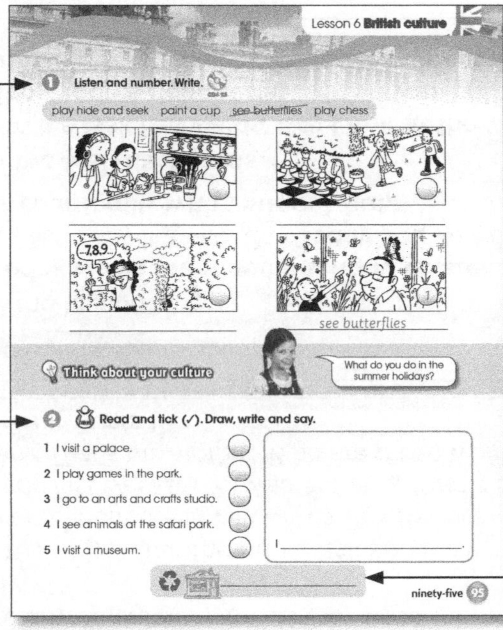

Activity Book

Activity 1

- Listen and number. Write.
  ▶ ***CD4 Track 23 p274***

Activity 2: Think about your culture.

Read and tick (✓). Draw, write and say.

Recycled vocabulary

- Look, remember and write the word.

Digital resources

Teacher's Digital: Don't forget you can teach this lesson using the Teacher's App on Navio.

Powered By NAVIO

Starting the lesson

Use the Trinity Exam Practice cards (optional).

- The pupils practise asking and answering questions. (See p31.)

Review Toby's tongue twister.

▶ *CD4 Track 20 p274*

- Ask the class **What sound did you practise in Toby's tongue twister?** *('air').* Ask if they can remember the tongue twister. *(The bear with a pear climbs the stairs at the funfair.)*
- Talk Partners Practise the tongue twister as a class and then with a Talk Partner. The pairs play *Faster and faster,* reading from the Pupil's Book (page 97) if necessary. A fast pair says the tongue twister for the class.
- Draw a chart with two columns ('air' and 'ear') on the board. Elicit words with both spellings. Ask pupils to classify the words, e.g. 'air': *hair, chair; funfair; 'ear': bear, pear.*

Set learning outcomes using the task flashcards.

- Say **Today we're going to learn about summer holidays in Britain.**
- Hold up the task flashcards in turn and elicit the activities. Stick them on one side of the board. Point to them during the lesson to reinforce your instructions.

Pupil's Book Activity 1

Listen and read. Answer.

▶ *CD4 Track 22 p274*

- (Books open.) Focus the pupils' attention on the photographs and ask **What can you see?** Then say **Let's listen and read.**
- Play the CD. At the end of the text, check understanding by pointing to the first photo and asking **What can you see here?** Repeat the question with the other photos.

Pupil's Book Think about your culture

What do you do in the summer holidays?

- Read out the question and encourage the class to tell you what they do in the summer holidays.

Activity Book

Activity 1

Listen and number. Write.

▶ *CD4 Track 23 p274*

- (Books open.) Explain to the class that they will listen to different children talking about their summer holiday experiences. Ask **What can you see?** Encourage the pupils to name the different activities.
- Play the CD, pausing after each exchange to check the pupils have numbered the illustration. Then, the pupils write the correct word on the line.

Answers: **1** see butterflies **2** play hide and seek **3** play giant chess **4** paint a cup

Activity 2: Think about your culture

Read and tick (✓). Draw, write and say.

- (Books open.) Read out the first sentence as a class and ask the pupils to tick the box if they visit a palace in the summer holidays. Repeat the procedure with the other sentences.
- Finally, ask the pupils to draw and write about their favourite summer holiday activity.

Recycled vocabulary

- The pupils look at the picture and write the phrase.

Answer: baker's

Ending the lesson

Review the lesson.

- Say **Today you've learnt about summer holidays in Britain.** Elicit some similarities and differences with holiday activities in their own country.

Review the task flashcards.

- Point to the task flashcards. Say **Look at the activities you've done today. Which activity was your favourite?** Elicit the pupils' favourite activities.

Extra activity

Extension

- If you have access to the Internet, show the pupils some other places they can visit in the summer in Britain, e.g. Legoland, Thorpe Park, Alton Towers, Cadbury World, Madame Tussauds and the Tower of London. Explain some of the activities you can do in these places.

Key Competences and Key Learning Outcomes

- Read and understand a diary
- Write a diary extract
- Read for specific information

Key language

- *badge, clown, diary, funfair, ride, roller coaster, stilts, ticket*

Recycled: Days of the week; *cloudy, cold, hot, sunny; fast, tall*

Recycled: *Yesterday was (Saturday). It was (sunny). I was (at the circus). It was (great / fantastic / fun / terrible).*

Materials

- Pupil's Book p99; Activity Book p96; Class CD3/4; Teacher's App on Navio
- Teacher's Resource Bank: Task flashcards: *find, circle, listen, read, think, write, draw, Talk Partners*

Optional materials

- Teacher's Resource Bank: Five Trinity Exam Practice cards (selected from the Starter Unit and Units 1, 2, 3, 4, 5, 6, 7 and 8)
- Sheets of paper stapled together for each pupil

At a Glance Lesson Plan

Pupil's Book

Starting the lesson

- Use the Trinity Exam Practice cards (optional).
- Play *Yesterday I was at the circus.*
- Set learning outcomes using the task flashcards.

Before you read: Activity 1

- Look at the diary quickly. Find and circle the days.

Activity 2

- Listen and read the diary.
- ▶ *CD4 Track 24 p274*

After you read

- Go to page 96 in your Activity Book.

Ending the lesson

- Review the lesson.
- Review the task flashcards.
- Sing a song (optional).

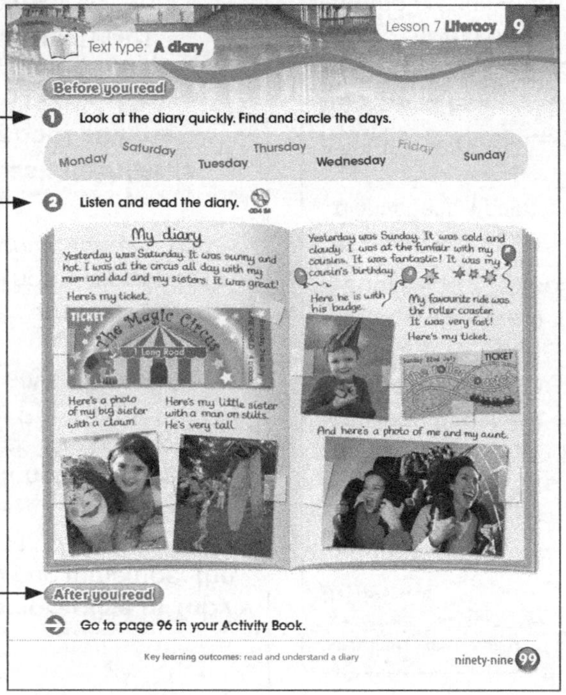

Extra activity

Reinforcement

- Keep a diary.

Cooperative learning

Sing *We can do it!*

▶ *CD3 Track 12 p268*

Activity Book

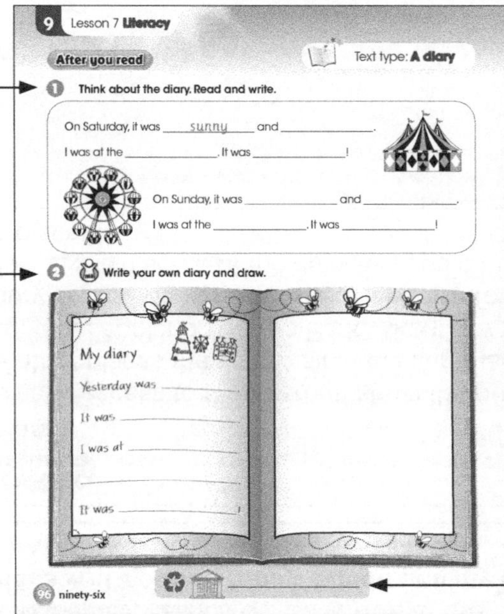

Activity Book

After you read: Activity 1

- Think about the diary. Read and write.

Activity 2

- Write your own diary and draw.

Recycled vocabulary

- Look, remember and write the phrase.

Digital resources

Teacher's Digital: Don't forget you can teach this lesson using the Teacher's App on Navio.

Pupil's Digital: Encourage your pupils to use the Pupil's App on Navio to practise the vocabulary from this lesson.

Powered By NAVIO

Starting the lesson

Use the Trinity Exam Practice cards (optional).

- The pupils practise asking and answering questions. (See p31.)

Play *Yesterday I was at the circus.*

- Say **Yesterday, I was at the circus.** Choose a pupil to repeat your statement and add another place. (*Yesterday, I was at the circus and the chocolate factory.*) The next pupil repeats both statements and adds another. Repeat until a mistake is made.
- Talk Partners The pupils continue playing with one or more Talk Partners. They may include holiday places from Unit 9 and also the places in a town from Unit 8 and Level 1.

Set learning outcomes using the task flashcards.

- Say **Today we're going to read a diary extract.**
- Hold up the task flashcards in turn and elicit the activities. Stick them on one side of the board. Point to them during the lesson to reinforce your instructions.

Before you read: Pupil's Book Activity 1

Look at the diary quickly. Find and circle the days.

- (Books open.) Explain that they are going to read an extract from a diary. Explain that people write things that happen in a diary so that they don't forget. Ask **Do you write in a diary?**
- Focus the pupils' attention on the pre-reading activity. Ask them to scan the diary pages and find the days in the text and circle them.

Pupil's Book Activity 2

Listen and read the diary.

▶ *CD4 Track 24 p274*

- Say **Let's read the diary extract.** Play the CD. The pupils follow the text in their Pupil's Books.
- Check the pupils' understanding by asking **What was the weather like on (Saturday)? Where was she on (Sunday)? Who was she with?**

Activity Book

After you read: Activity 1

Think about the diary. Read and write.

- (Books open.) Read out the instructions. Then, read the first sentence and prompt the class to complete it by looking for the information in the diary pages in the Pupil's Book (p99). Repeat with the other sentences. Alternatively, invite different pupils to read out and complete each sentence.

Answers: **1** sunny **2** hot **3** circus **4** great **5** cold **6** cloudy **7** funfair **8** fantastic

Activity 2

Write your own diary and draw.

- (Books closed.) Explain to the class that they are going to write their own diary extract. Copy the frame onto the board and elicit suggestions from the class to make a collective diary entry. First, brainstorm the days of the week and different types of weather. Then brainstorm holiday places they can choose to write about and expressions, e.g. *It was (great / fantastic / fun / terrible).* Build up an example on the board by collectively choosing a day to write about. Read the collective example together, then rub it off.
- (Books open.) Ask the pupils to write their own fictional diary entry in their Activity Books. The pupils illustrate their diary entry.
- Talk Partners Encourage the pupils to read and show their diary entry to a Talk Partner or to the whole class.

Recycled vocabulary

- The pupils look at the picture and write the phrase.

Answer: museum

Ending the lesson

Review the lesson.

- Say **Today you've read a diary extract. You've written a diary extract, too. Did you like writing a diary?** Elicit some responses.

Review the task flashcards.

- Point to the task flashcards. Say **Look at the activities you've done today. Which activity was your favourite?** Elicit the pupils' favourite activities.

Sing a song (optional).

- Choose a song. The class sings and does the actions. Alternatively, invite the class to choose a song to sing.

Extra activity

Reinforcement

- Encourage the pupils to keep a diary themselves. Staple some pages together for each pupil and ask them to write the title and decorate the cover. For the remaining lessons, start the class by reviewing the questions *What day was it yesterday? What was the weather like? Where were you?* Encourage the pupils to write the answers in their diaries.

Cooperative learning

Sing *We can do it!*

▶ *CD3 Track 12 p268*

- It can be difficult for young learners to sustain concentration and motivation, especially when a task is challenging. In a cooperative classroom, children help, support and encourage each other as they learn. Sing *We can do it!* (from Unit 6) when the class or individual members are finding a task difficult.
- Play the CD. The pupils listen. Play the CD again. The pupils sing.

Key Competences and Key Learning Outcomes

- Review language in the unit
- Reflect on own learning
- Sing a cooperative learning song

Key language

Recycled: *aquarium, castle, chocolate factory, circus, funfair, safari park, science museum, sports centre, theatre, water park; child, children, man, men, woman, women; aunt, brother, cousin, grandfather, mother*

Recycled: *Where were you (yesterday)? I was at the (circus). Who's that (man)? He's my (uncle). Who are those (men)? They're my (uncles).*

Materials

- Pupil's Book p100; Activity Book p97; Class CD4; Teacher's App on Navio
- Holiday places flashcards
- Teacher's Resource Bank: Task flashcards: *listen, number, write, say, Talk Partners, sing, stick, find, circle, read, Think-Pair-Share*
- Teacher's Resource Bank: Traffic light cut-out
- *Give Me Five!* sticker

Optional materials

- Teacher's Resource Bank: Five Trinity Exam Practice cards (selected from the Starter Unit and Units 1, 2, 3, 4, 5, 6, 7 and 8)

At a Glance Lesson Plan

Pupil's Book

Starting the lesson

- Use the Trinity Exam Practice cards (optional).
- Review the unit vocabulary.
- Set learning outcomes using the task flashcards.

Activity 1

- Listen and number.
- ▶ *CD4 Track 25 p274*
- Write and say.

Activity 2

- Listen. Make a fun holiday diary.
- ▶ *CD4 Track 26 p274*
- Talk Partners Ask and answer.

Activity 3 Cooperative learning

- Sing *Well Done!*
- ▶ *CD4 Track 27 p274*
- Stick the *Give Me Five!* sticker.
- Go to the Activity Book.

Ending the lesson

- Review the task flashcards
- Sing a song (optional).

Cooperative learning

Think-Pair-Share

- Remember ten holiday places words.

Activity Book

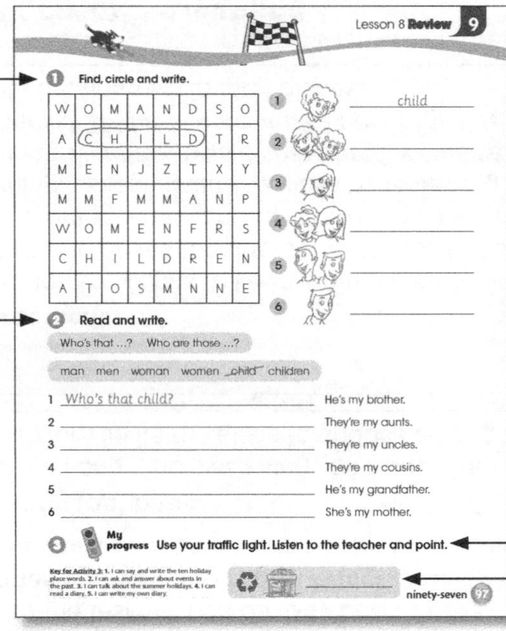

Activity Book

Activity 1

- Find, circle and write.

Activity 2

- Read and write.

Activity 3 My progress

- Use your traffic light. Listen to the teacher and point.

Recycled vocabulary

- Look, remember and write the phrase.

Digital resources

Teacher's Digital: Don't forget you can teach this lesson using the Teacher's App on Navio.

Pupil's Digital: Encourage your pupils to use the Pupil's App on Navio to practise the vocabulary from this lesson.

Powered By NAVIO

Starting the lesson

Use the Trinity Exam Practice cards (optional).

- The pupils practise asking and answering questions. (See p31.)

Review the unit vocabulary.

- Play *Definitions game* (see p23) with the unit flashcards to review holiday places.
- **Option:** Play the game in two teams. The teams take it in turns to guess the words.

Set learning outcomes using the task flashcards.

- Say **Today we're going to remember what we've learnt in Unit 9.**
- Hold up the task flashcards in turn and elicit the words. Stick them on one side of the board. Point to them during the lesson to reinforce your instructions.

Pupil's Book Activity 1

Listen and number. Write and say.

▶ *CD4 Track 25 p274*

- (Books open.) Point to each of the photos and elicit the words.
- Play the CD. Pause after each sentence. The pupils write the correct number in the circles.
- Play the CD again. The pupils write the correct place under each picture. Then they say the words.

Answers: **1** science museum **2** circus **3** castle **4** safari park **5** sports centre **6** theatre **7** water park **8** aquarium **9** funfair **10** chocolate factory

Pupil's Book Activity 2

Listen. Make a fun holiday diary. Ask and answer.

▶ *CD4 Track 26 p274*

- (Books open.) Ask a confident pair of pupils to read the questions and answers. The pupils use their diaries from Lesson 7 or make new entries if you have time.
- Talk Partners The pupils ask and answer questions about their activities from their diaries with a Talk Partner.

Pupil's Book Activity 3: **Cooperative learning**

Sing *Well done!*

▶ *CD4 Track 27 p274*

- Praise the class for their hard work and play the *Well done!* song. The pupils listen the first time. Play the CD again. The pupils sing along.

Stick the *Give Me Five!* sticker.

- The pupils stick the *Give Me Five!* sticker on their book.

Activity Book

Activity 1

Find, circle and write.

- (Books open.) Read out the instructions. First, ask the pupils to name all the people words in the illustrations. Then say **Can you find the words?** The pupils work individually to circle the words and write them next to the corresponding illustration.
- Talk Partners The pupils check their answers with a Talk Partner.

Answers: **1** child **2** children **3** woman **4** women **5** men **6** man

Activity 2

Read and write.

- Choose a confident pupil to read the example question and answer. The pupils read the answers and choose the corresponding question and people words. The pupils work individually to write the questions.
- Talk Partners The pupils act out the mini-conversations with a Talk Partner.

Answers: **1** Who's that child? **2** Who are those women? **3** Who are those men? **4** Who are those children? **5** Who's that man? **6** Who's that woman?

Activity 3 My progress

Use your traffic light. Listen to the teacher and point.

- (Books closed.) Ask the class to take out their traffic light cut-out. Say **Let's think about our work in this unit.** Read the first self-assessment statement. Point to the green circle and say **Yes, I can do this very well.** Point to the orange circle and say **Yes, I can do this.** Point to the red circle and say **No, I can't do this.**
- Read the remaining statements. For each one, the pupils point to the colour on their traffic light that shows how they feel about their own learning.

Self-assessment statements

1. I can say and write the ten holiday place words.
2. I can ask and answer about events in the past.
3. I can talk about the summer holidays.
4. I can read a diary.
5. I can write my own diary.

Recycled vocabulary

- The pupils look at the picture and write the phrase.

Answer: fire station

Ending the lesson

Review the task flashcards.

- Point to the flashcards. Say **Look at the activities you've done today. Which activity was your favourite?** Elicit the pupils' favourite activities.

Sing a song (optional).

- The class chooses their favourite song from the unit. The class sings and does the actions.

Cooperative learning

Think-Pair-Share

- Ask **Can you remember the ten holiday place words?** Ask the class to think silently on their own for a minute.
- Talk Partners Then, the pupils work with a Talk Partner to remember and name all ten words.
- Invite a pair to say one of the words. Hold up the corresponding flashcard and prompt the class to repeat the word.
- Finally, repeat the procedure, asking different pairs of pupils each time, until all ten words have been named.

Key Competences and Key Learning Outcomes

- Watch and understand a video about weekend activities
- Say what you take photos of
- Learn to use a digital camera

Key language

- *aquarium, castle, chocolate factory, circus, forest, funfair, museum, safari park, sports centre, theatre, water park*

Materials

- Pupil's Book p101; Activity Book p98; Class CD4; Video; Teacher's App on Navio
- Teacher's Resource Bank: Task flashcards: *number, read, tick, circle, listen, think, write, draw, say, Talk Partners*

Optional materials

- Teacher's Resource Bank: Trinity Exam Practice cards (selected from Unit 9)
- Pupils' holiday photos

At a Glance Lesson Plan

Pupil's Book

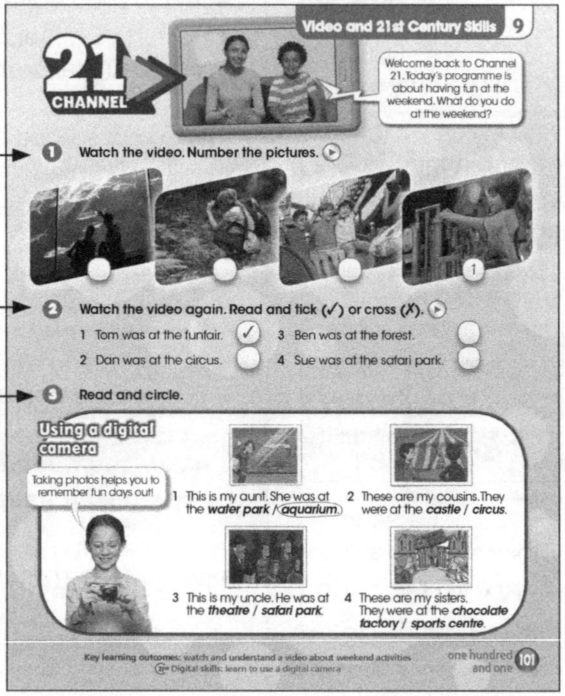

Starting the lesson

- Use the Trinity Exam Practice cards (optional).
- Set learning outcomes and use the task flashcards.

Pre-watching activity

- Talk about what they do at the weekend.

Activity 1

- Watch the video.
- *Unit 9 video p280*
- Number the pictures.

Activity 2

- Watch the video again.
- *Unit 9 video*
- Read and tick (✓) or cross (✗).

Activity 3

- **Think-Pair-Share** Read and circle.
- Go to the Activity Book.

Ending the lesson

- Review the lesson.
- Review the task flashcards. Elicit the pupils' favourite activities.

Extra activity

Extension

- Sharing holiday photos.

Digital resources

Teacher's Digital: Don't forget you can teach this lesson using the Teacher's App on Navio.

Pupil's Digital: Encourage your pupils to use the Pupil's App on Navio to practise the vocabulary from this lesson.

Powered By NAVIO

Activity Book

Activity Book

Activity 1

- Listen and tick (✓).
- *CD4 Track 28 p275*

Activity 2

- Think and write. Draw and say.

Recycled vocabulary

- Look, remember and write the phrase.

Starting the lesson

Use the Trinity Exam Practice cards (optional).

- The pupils practise asking and answering questions. (See p31.)

Set learning outcomes and use the task flashcards.

- Say **Today we're going to watch a video and then ask and answer questions about weekend activities**.
- Hold up the task flashcards, in turn, and elicit the activities. Stick them on the side of the board. Point to them during the lesson to reinforce your instructions.

Pre-watching activity

- Ask **What activities do you do at the weekend?**

Pupil's Book Activity 1

Watch the video. Number the pictures. *p280*

- Play Part 1. Ask **Where was Sophie last weekend?** *(At the theatre.)*
- Focus the pupils' attention on the video stills. Ask **Where are the children?**
- Play Part 2, pausing after the first video still. Ask the pupils to point to the corresponding photo in their book. Point out the number one.
- Play the video again for pupils to write the numbers in order of the photos.

Answers: From left to right: 3 2 4 1

Pupil's Book Activity 2

Watch the video again. Read and tick (✓) or cross (✗).

- Read out the first sentence in Activity 2. Ask **Was Tom at the funfair?** Show the tick in the circle.
- Play Part 2. Pupils tick or cross the sentences.
- Ask the pupils to look at the sentences they crossed and ask them to correct them.
- Ask the pupils some questions to check understanding. Suggested questions:
  What can you learn about at the science museum? *(Water.)*
  What was the weather like in the forest? *(Cloudy.)*
  Where was Sophie's friend Alex? *(At the castle.)*
  Who was at the aquarium? *(Sophie's cousin.)*
  What's Sophie's good idea? *(To make a slide show of holiday photos.)*
  What does Abby ask you to do on your summer holiday? *(Take lots of photos.)*

Answers: 1 ✓ 2 ✗ 3 ✓ 4 ✗

Pupil's Book Activity 3

Read and circle.

- The pupils read the sentences and circle the correct answer.
  Think-Pair-Share Ask **What do you like to take photos of? Do you have your own camera?**
- Ask **What other things can you do to help you remember fun days out?** *(Write a diary. Draw pictures. Look at family photos. Make a video.)*

Answers: **1** aquarium **2** circus **3** theatre **4** chocolate factory

Activity Book

Activity 1

Listen and tick (✓).

CD4 Track 28 p275

- Ask **Where are the children?**
- Tell the pupils to listen to the people talking about the photos and tick the correct pictures.
- Play the first exchange on the CD. Ask **Where is the boy?** Show the example tick.
- Play the rest of the CD for pupils to tick.

Answers: **1** safari park **2** water park **3** circus **4** funfair

Activity 2

Think and write. Draw and say.

- Ask a few pupils, **What do you take photos of?**
- Choose one of the pupils' answers and on the board, write an example sentence, *I take photos of my family in the forest.*
- The pupils write sentences about what they take photos of and then draw pictures to illustrate their sentences.
  Talk Partners Pupils take turns to show their partner their pictures and talk about the photos.

Recycled vocabulary

Answer: sun hat

Ending the lesson

Review the lesson.

- Say **Today we've watched a video about weekend activities. What did we learn about fun activities?** *(It's important to take photos to remember the trip.)*
- Ask **Which was your favourite activity today? Which activity was easy / difficult?**

Review the task flashcards.

- Point to the task flashcards on the board. Say **Look at the activities you've done today. Which activity was your favourite?**

Extra activity

Extension

- Ask pupils to bring photos. Make sure that each group has at least one pupil who has some photos. The pupils take turns to show their photos and talk about them. Encourage the groups to ask questions about the photos, too.

My project 3: Time

Key Competences and Key Learning Outcomes

- Ask and answer about the time
- Read and write the time
- Associate time with daily routines
- Follow instructions
- Work together to practise the time
- Make a clock

Key language

- *It's (eight) o'clock. It's a quarter past (eight). It's half past (eight). It's a quarter to (nine). I (get up) at (seven) o'clock. What time do you (get up)?*

Recycled: *get dressed, get up, go to bed, go to school, have breakfast, play*

Materials

- Pupil's Book p102; Activity Book p100; Class CD4; Teacher's App on Navio
- Teacher's Resource Bank: Task flashcards: *listen, find, Talk Partners, tick, write*
- Teacher's Resource Bank: clock cut-out

Optional materials

- Teacher's Resource Bank: Five Trinity Exam Practice cards (selected from the Starter Unit and Units 1, 2, 3, 4, 5, 6, 7, 8 and 9)

At a Glance Lesson Plan

Pupil's Book

Starting the lesson

- Use the Trinity Exam Practice cards (optional).
- Set learning outcomes using the task flashcards.

Learn: Activity 1

- Listen, point and repeat.
- ▶ *CD4 Track 29 p275*

Activity 2

- Listen.
- ▶ *CD4 Track 30 p275*
- Talk Partners
  Play *Find the clock.*

Activity 3

- Listen, point and repeat.
- ▶ *CD4 Track 31 p275*

My project 3 Lesson 1

TIME

Make a clock and talk about your daily routine

Learn

1 Listen, point and repeat.

2 Listen. Play *Find the clock.*

It's a quarter to nine.

It's number four. It's my turn.

3 Listen, point and repeat.

1 I get up at half past seven.

2 I get dressed at a quarter to eight.

3 I have breakfast at a quarter past eight.

4 I go to school at nine o'clock.

5 I play at half past six.

6 I go to bed at half past nine.

Plan your project

Practise the time. Go to page 100 in your Activity Book.

102 one hundred and two

Key learning outcomes: identify and talk about times

Plan your project

- Practise the time.
- Go to page 100 in your Activity Book.

Ending the lesson

- Review the lesson.
- Review the task flashcards.

Extra activity

Vocabulary extension

- *It's (five / ten / twenty / twenty-five) past / to …*

Link to Science

- **Time:** clocks in the past; measuring time

Activity Book

My project 3 Lesson 1

Plan your project

TIME

1 What time is it? Look and tick (✓).

1 It's a quarter past ten. ✓ It's a quarter to ten.

2 It's three o'clock. It's half past three.

3 It's half past two. It's half past one.

4 It's a quarter to eleven. It's a quarter to nine.

5 It's six o'clock. It's seven o'clock.

6 It's a quarter past seven. It's a quarter to seven.

2 What time is it? Write.

1 It's eight o'clock.

2

3

4

5

100 one hundred

Plan your project: Activity Book

Activity 1

- What time is it? Look and tick (✓).

Activity 2

- What time is it? Write.

Digital resources

Teacher's Digital: Don't forget you can teach this lesson using the Teacher's App on Navio.

Pupil's Digital: Encourage your pupils to use the Pupil's App on Navio to practise the vocabulary from this lesson.

Powered By NAVIO

Starting the lesson

Use the Trinity Exam Practice cards (optional).

- The pupils practise asking and answering questions. (See p31.)

Set learning outcomes using the task flashcards.

- Explain the aims of the lesson. Say **Today we're going to learn how to tell the time and practise.**
- Hold up the task flashcards and elicit the words. Stick them on one side of the board. Point to them during the lesson to reinforce your instructions.

Learn: Pupil's Book Activity 1

Listen, point and repeat.

▶ *CD4 Track 29 p275*

- (Books open.) Point to the first clock and say **It's eight o'clock.** The pupils repeat after you. Tell them that when the long hand is pointing up, it's *something o'clock*. Point to the next clock. Say **It's a quarter past eight.** Tell them that when the long hand is on the three it's *a quarter past* something. Continue with the remaining clocks.
- Use your own copy of the photocopiable clock to show pupils further examples.
- Play the CD. The pupils listen and point to the clocks as they hear the time.
- Play the CD again. The pupils repeat the time, pointing to the different clocks.
- State the different times in a random order. The pupils point to the corresponding clock each time.

Pupil's Book Activity 2

Listen. Play *Find the clock.*

▶ *CD4 Track 30 p275*

- Play the CD, pausing after each sentence for the pupils to repeat. If necessary, demonstrate the game further with a volunteer.
- Talk Partners The pupils play the game with a Talk Partner.

Pupil's Book Activity 3

Listen, point and repeat.

▶ *CD4 Track 31 p275*

- Play the CD. The pupils listen and point to the photos.
- Play the CD again. The pupils repeat the sentences, pointing to the photos.
- Say the jobs in a random order. The pupils point to the corresponding picture and say the sentence each time.
- Encourage the pupils to give similar descriptions about the other routines.
- **Personalisation:** The pupils talk with a Talk Partner about the times they do the different daily routines. Elicit answers (*I (get up) at …*).

Plan your project: Activity Book

Activity 1

What time is it? Look and tick (✓).

- (Books open.) Ask a confident pupil to read the two times next to the first clock. Ask **Which is correct?** Repeat with the remaining clocks. The pupils then tick the correct times individually.

Answers: **1** It's a quarter past ten. **2** It's three o'clock. **3** It's half past one. **4** It's a quarter to eleven. **5** It's six o'clock. **6** It's a quarter to seven.

Activity 2

What time is it? Write.

- Say **Look at the clock in number 1. What time is it?** The pupils read out the example. Ask about the remaining clocks. The pupils then write the times.

Answers: **1** It's eight o'clock. **2** It's half past seven. **3** It's four o'clock. **4** It's a quarter past nine. **5** It's a quarter to eight.

Ending the lesson

Review the lesson.

- (Books closed.) Say **Today we've talked about the time.** Set your own clock to different times and ask **What time is it?** Encourage the pupils to respond and praise them for their effort.

Review the task flashcards.

- Point to the task flashcards. Say **Look at the activities you've done today. Which was your favourite?** Elicit the pupils' favourite activities.

Extra activity

Vocabulary extension

- If you have a confident class, introduce the remaining time expressions: *It's (five / ten / twenty / twenty-five) past and (five / ten / twenty / twenty-five) to.*

Link to Science

- If you are studying the Science topic of **time** in English, you could remind the pupils that there are different types of clocks. People in the past used sand, sun and water clocks to tell the time. Ask them if they can remember anything else that was different in the past in the town and in the home.
- Discuss different expressions of time: *minute, hour, day, weekend, week, month, season* and *year.* Remind the pupils that there are 60 minutes in an hour and 24 hours in a day. Make a two-column chart on the board (clock and calendar) and ask them to classify the different time expressions.

My project 3: Time

Key Competences and Key Learning Outcomes

- Make a clock and talk about your daily routine
- Present your project
- Think about your project
- Ask and answer about the time other pupils do things
- Sing a cooperative learning song

Key language

- *I (have breakfast) at (half past eight).*

Recycled: *get dressed, get up, go to bed, go to school, have breakfast, play*

Recycled: *It's (eight) o'clock. It's a quarter past (eight). It's half past (eight). It's a quarter to (nine). What time do you (go to bed)?*

Materials

- Pupil's Book p103; Activity Book p101; Class CD4; Teacher's App on Navio
- Teacher's Resource Bank: Task flashcards: *read, sing, listen, Talk Partners, write, think, colour*
- Teacher's Resource Bank: clock cut-out
- card, coloured pencils, butterfly clips, scissors

Optional materials

- Teacher's Resource Bank: Five Trinity Exam Practice cards (selected from the Starter Unit and Units 1, 2, 3, 4, 5, 6, 7, 8 and 9)

At a Glance Lesson Plan

Pupil's Book

Starting the lesson

- Use the Trinity Exam Practice cards (optional).
- Review the time. Play *Living clocks*.
- Set learning outcomes using the task flashcards.

Create: Activity 1

- Read. Make your clock.

Show and tell: Activity 2
Cooperative learning

- Sing *Listen to others.*
- ▶ *CD4 Track 32 p275*

Activity 3

- Listen. Tell the class about your day.
- ▶ *CD4 Track 33 p275*

Think about your project

- Go to page 101 in your Activity Book.

Ending the lesson

- Review the lesson.
- Sing *Well done!*
- ▶ *CD4 Track 27 p274*
- Review the task flashcards.

Link to Science

- **Time:** timelines

Activity Book

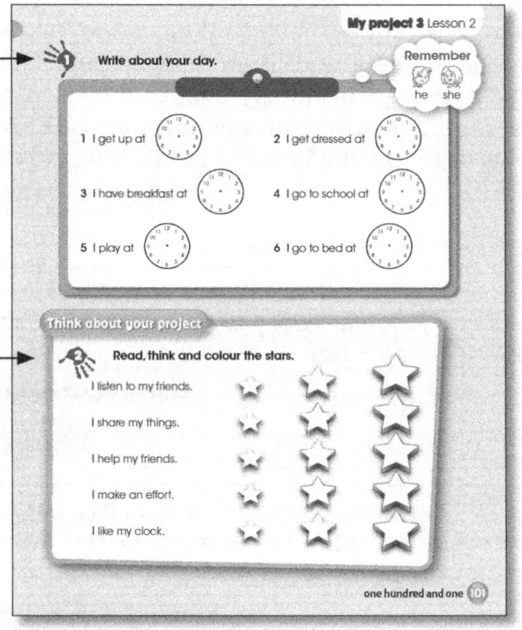

Activity Book

Activity 1

- Write about your day.

Think about your project: Activity 2

- Read, think and colour the stars.

Digital resources

Teacher's Digital: Don't forget you can teach this lesson using the Teacher's App on Navio.

Pupil's Digital: Encourage your pupils to use the Pupil's App on Navio to practise the vocabulary from this lesson.

Powered By NAVIO

Starting the lesson

Use the Trinity Exam Practice cards (optional).

- The pupils practise asking and answering questions. (See p31.)

Review the time. Play *Living clocks.*

- Ask the pupils to pretend they are clocks. State a time and ask them to move their arms to represent the time you say.

Set learning outcomes using the task flashcards.

- Explain the aims of the lesson. Say **Today we're going to ask and answer about the time we do our daily routines.**
- Hold up the task flashcards and elicit the words. Stick them on one side of the board. Point to them during the lesson to reinforce your instructions.

Create: Pupil's Book Activity 1

Read. Make your clock.

- (Books open.) Explain that the pupils are each going to make a clock.
- Read out the instructions, or invite different volunteers to read them out. The pupils follow the text.
- Give each pupil a clock cut-out (See Teacher's Resource Bank). Also hand out scissors and coloured pencils.
- Help each pupil to attach the clock hands to the dial using a butterfly clip.

Show and tell: Pupil's Book Activity 2:
Cooperative learning

Sing *Listen to others.*

▶ *CD4 Track 32 p275*

- In order to work well together, all pupils need to listen carefully to what other people are saying. Sing *Listen to others* with the class when you want to remind pupils of the importance of listening to their classmates.
- Play the CD. The pupils listen and do the actions with you. Play the CD again and encourage the pupils to sing and do the actions.

Pupil's Book Activity 3

Listen. Tell the class about your day.

▶ *CD4 Track 33 p275*

- Focus on the photo. Play the CD. The pupils listen and follow the text.
- Invite pupils to present to the class. Encourage the pupils to read out the information about their day, moving the hands of the clock to the corresponding time.
- Record the pupils' presentations on video. Play these back at a later date or share them with parents.

Activity Book

Activity 1

Write about your day.

- Explain to the pupils that they are going to think about their daily routine and draw the times they talked about.
- Pupils draw to complete the clocks with the times they do each daily routine.
- Talk Partners The pupils take turns to ask and answer questions about the time they do each activity. Elicit the questions they will need to ask for each activity, e.g. *What time do you have breakfast?* and *What time do you go to school?*

Think about your project: Activity 2

Read, think and colour the stars.

- (Books open.) Say **Let's think about how we work.** Read out each sentence and ask the class to colour the star for how they work. (Small star: sometimes; medium-sized star: usually; big star: always.) Praise the class for their efforts.

Ending the lesson

Review the lesson.

- Ask the class to close their books and say **Today we've worked together. What routine activities have we learnt?** Elicit them. Praise the class for their hard work and display all the clocks in a prominent place.

Sing *Well done!*

▶ *CD4 Track 27 p274*

- (Books closed.) Praise the class for working together and for following instructions well. Play the CD. The pupils sing.

Review the task flashcards.

- Point to the task flashcards. Say **Look at the activities you've done today. Which was your favourite?** Elicit the pupils' favourite activities.

Link to Science

- If you are studying the Science topic of **time** in English, you could remind the pupils that we can use a timeline to sequence routine events. Draw a timeline on the board and write the events of your daily routine on it in the order you do them. Encourage the pupils to draw a timeline and talk about the events they do every day using the timeline to help them.

Harvest Festival

Key Competences and Key Learning Outcomes

- Listen, read and say a poem

- Learn about traditional Harvest Festival activities in Britain
- Think about food festivals in your country
- Make a harvest basket

Key language
- *autumn, baskets, celebrate, cheer, food, fruit, ground, grow, harvest, moon, round, summer, vegetables*
- *We celebrate (Harvest Festival). We make (big baskets).*

Materials
- Pupil's Book p104; Class CD4; Teacher's App on Navio
- Food flashcards (Unit 2)
- Teacher's Resource Bank: Task flashcards: *listen, read, match, say, Talk Partners, draw*
- Teacher's Resource Bank: Cut-out
- Scissors, coloured pencils or crayons

Optional materials
- Teacher's Resource Bank: Trinity Exam Practice cards

At a Glance Lesson Plan

Starting the lesson
- Use the Trinity Exam Practice cards (optional).
- Play *Which one's missing?* (See p23.)
- Set learning outcomes using the task flashcards.

Activity 1
- Listen and read.
- ▶ *CD4 Track 34 p275*

Activity 2
- Listen and read. Match. Say the harvest poem.
- ▶ *CD4 Track 35 p275*

Think about your culture
- Do you celebrate Harvest Festival?

Pupil's Book

Teacher's Resource bank
- Make a harvest basket.

Ending the lesson
- Review the lesson.
- Review the task flashcards.
- Say the poem again.

Digital resources

Teacher's Digital: You can also teach this lesson using the Teacher's App on Navio.

Pupil's Digital: Encourage your pupils to use the Pupil's App on Navio to practise the activities from this lesson.

Powered By NAVIO

Starting the lesson

Use the Trinity Exam Practice cards (optional).

- The pupils practise asking and answering questions. (See p31.)

Play *Which one's missing?*

- Play *Which one's missing*? (see p23) with the food flashcards from Unit 2.

Set learning outcomes using the task flashcards.

- Say **Today we're going to talk about Harvest Festival.**
- Ask the pupils if any of them know anything about Harvest Festival.
- Hold up the task flashcards, in turn, and elicit the activities. Stick them on the side of the board. Point to them during the lesson to reinforce your instructions.

Pupil's Book Activity 1

Listen and read.

▶ *CD4 Track 34 p275*

- Say **Let's find out about Harvest Festival.**
- Focus the pupils' attention on the photographs. Ask **What can you see? Which fruit and vegetables do you know? Which season do you think it is?** Then say **Let's listen and read.**
- Play the first part of the CD pausing after the first photograph. Ask **What season is it?** *(Autumn.)*
- Play the rest of the CD for pupils to follow in their books.
- Ask the pupils some questions to check understanding. Suggested questions.
  When is Harvest Festival? *(Autumn.)*
  What is Harvest Festival for? *(To say thank you for all the food.)*
  What do the children do? *(Make baskets of fruit and vegetables.)*

Pupil's Book Activity 2

Listen and read. Match. Say the harvest poem.

▶ *CD4 Track 35 p275*

- Point to each photo and ask **What can you see?**
- Play the CD for the pupils to listen and read. Point out the example matched with the photo. Ask **Why does this sentence match the photograph?**
- The pupils match the sentences and the photos.
- Ask the pupils some questions to check understanding. Suggested questions.
  What season is before autumn? *(Summer.)*
  What does the moon look like? *(It's big and round.)*
  What do they say thank you for? *(All the fruit and vegetables.)*
- Play the poem again, line by line, for the pupils to repeat.
- Divide the class into four groups and assign each group two lines from the poem. The groups say their part of the poem. Change the lines for the group and repeat the activity. For variety, ask the groups to say their lines quietly, loudly, whispering, happily. Encourage the pupils to cheer when they hear the line *Give a cheer!*
- **Talk Partners** The pupils practise reading the poem with their partner.

Answers: Section 1: autumn trees photo
Section 2: the children cheering Section 3: the moon
Section 4: the carrots

Teacher's Resource Bank

Make a harvest basket.

- Ask pupils to cut out and colour their basket.
- They then cut out, colour and stick on the fruit and vegetables.
- At the end of the class, stick their baskets on the wall under the heading 'Harvest festival' to make a class display.

Think about your culture

Do you celebrate Harvest Festival?

- Read the question and ask the pupils what they do if they celebrate Harvest Festival. If they don't celebrate Harvest Festival ask if they have a similar festival about food.
- **Think-Pair-Share** Ask **What's it called? What do you do? Would you like to go to a Harvest Festival? Why? Why not? What food would you say thank you for?**

Ending the lesson

Review the lesson.

- Say **Today you've learnt about Harvest Festival. What did we learn?** *(It's in autumn. People say thank you for the food. Children make big baskets of fruit and vegetables.)*
- Ask **Which activity was easy / difficult?**

Review the task flashcards.

- Point to the task flashcards on the board. Say **Look at the activities you've done today. Which activity was your favourite?**

Say the poem again.

▶ *CD4 Track 35 p275*

- Play the CD. The pupils say the poem again, holding up their basket and pointing to the food.

Carnival

Key Competences and Key Learning Outcomes

- Listen, read and say a rhyme
- Talk about dressing up

- Learn about carnival
- Make a carnival mask

Key language

- *cape, carnival, competition, costume, face, mask, paint, parade, wig*
- *Put on (your costume). Paint (your face). Wear (a wig).*

Materials

- Pupil's Book p105; Class CD4; Teacher's App on Navio
- Teacher's Resource Bank: Task flashcards: *listen, read, say, number, Talk Partners*
- Teacher's Resource Bank: Cut-out
- Scissors, coloured pencils or crayons, string
- Dress up clothes

Optional materials

- Teacher's Resource Bank: Trinity Exam Practice cards

At a Glance Lesson Plan

Starting the lesson

- Use the Trinity Exam Practice cards (optional).
- Set learning outcomes using the task flashcards.

Activity 1

- Listen and read. Say the carnival rhyme.

▶ *CD4 Track 36 p275*

Activity 2

- Read the rhyme again. Find the names of these things in the rhyme.

Activity 3

- Listen and number.

▶ *CD4 Track 37 p275*

Think about your culture

- What do you do for carnival?

Pupil's Book

Festivals

Carnival

1 Listen and read. Say the carnival rhyme. CD4 36

Put on your **costume**.
Paint your face.
Wear a **wig** or a hat.
A **mask** or a **cape**.
Join the **parade**.
Dance and have fun.
It's time for the competition.
Hooray! I won!

2 Read the rhyme again. Find the names of these things in the rhyme.

1 2 3 4 5

3 Listen and number. CD4 37

Think about your culture
What do you do for carnival?

Teacher's Resource Bank: Festivals

Key learning outcomes: say a carnival rhyme
Language: Put on (your costume). Paint (your face). Wear (a wig).

one hundred and five 105

Teacher's Resource bank

- Make a carnival mask.

Ending the lesson

- Review the lesson.
- Review the task flashcards.
- Say the rhyme again.
- Dress up for a class carnival.

Digital resources

Teacher's Digital: You can also teach this lesson using the Teacher's App on Navio.

Pupil's Digital: Encourage your pupils to use the Pupil's App on Navio to practise the activities from this lesson.

Powered By NAVIO

Starting the lesson

Use the Trinity Exam Practice cards (optional).

- The pupils practise asking and answering questions. (See p31.)

Set learning outcomes using the task flashcards.

- Say **Today we're going to talk about carnival.**
- Ask the pupils if they know anything about carnival.
- Hold up the task flashcards, in turn, and elicit the activities. Stick them on the side of the board. Point to them during the lesson to reinforce your instructions.

Pupil's Book Activity 1

Listen and read. Say the carnival rhyme.

▶ *CD4 Track 36 p275*

- Say **Let's find out about carnival**.
- Focus the pupils' attention on the photographs. Ask **What can you see? What are the people wearing? Which costume do you like the best? Why? Does carnival look fun?** Then say **Let's listen and read.**
- Play the CD for the pupils to follow and read in their books. Ask **What do the people do at carnival?** *(Wear costumes. Paint their faces. Dance and have fun.)*
- Say the highlighted words for the pupils to point to the pictures.
- Say the words again for the pupils to repeat.
- Play the CD again. Ask the pupils some questions to check understanding. Suggested questions.
  What colour is the woman's costume? *(Blue and orange.)*
  What is a wig? *(Hair that isn't real.)*
  What is a cape? *(A coat with no arms.)*
  What superhero wears a cape? *(Superman.)*
  What do you think the competition is for? *(The best costume.)*
- Play the rhyme again, line by line, for the pupils to repeat.
- Divide the class into seven groups and assign each group a line from the rhyme. The groups say their lines and everyone joins in with *Hooray! I won!* Change the lines for the groups and repeat the activity.

Pupil's Book Activity 2

Read the rhyme again. Find the name of these things in the rhyme.

- Point to each photo and ask **What is it?**
- The pupils find the words for the pictures from the rhyme.

Answers: **1** mask **2** cape **3** costume **4** parade **5** wig

Pupil's Book Activity 3

▶ *CD4 Track 37 p275*

Listen and number.

- Point to each photo and ask **What can you see? Which costume do you like? Why?**
- Play the first exchange on the CD for the pupils to point to the picture. Tell them to write *1* in the circle.
- Play the rest of the track for the pupils to number the pictures.
- **Think-Pair-Share** Pupils compare their answers.
- Play the CD a final time for pupils to check their answers.

Answers: 3 1 2

Teacher's Resource Bank

Make a carnival mask.

- Ask pupils to cut out and colour their mask.
- They can also decorate it with coloured paper, sequins, etc.
- They then make a hole at each side and tie string to each end, long enough to go round their heads and tie at the back

Think about your culture

What do you do for carnival?

- Read the questions and ask the pupils what they do for carnival. Ask if they would like to go to a carnival.
- **Think-Pair-Share** Ask **What costume would you wear? Would you make a costume? How? How would you paint your face?**

Ending the lesson

Review the lesson.

- Say **Today you've learnt about carnival. What did we learn?** *(People wear costumes for carnival and paint their faces. They dance and have fun and there's a parade.)*
- Ask **Which activity was easy / difficult?**

Review the task flashcards.

- Point to the task flashcards on the board. Say **Look at the activities you've done today. Which activity was your favourite?**

Say the rhyme again.

▶ *CD4 Track 36 p275*

- The pupils say the rhyme again.

Dress up for a class carnival.

- If it's appropriate, you could bring in some dress up clothes and/or ask the pupils to bring in some costumes to have a mini carnival in the class. Sing some of the songs from the unit, have a parade with the pupils wearing their masks, and a competition.

Cambridge Exams Practice and Vocabulary Practice answers

Key Competences and Key Learning Outcomes

- Practise for the Starters Listening Part 3 and Speaking Part 4
- Practise for Reading and Writing Parts 4 and 2

Key language

Recycled: *baseball, basketball, cycling, football, hockey, rollerblading, skateboarding, swimming, tennis, volleyball; bounce, catch, hit, jump, kick, throw*

Recycled: *Do you like (tennis)? Does (Pat) like (hockey)? I play (tennis). I go (rollerblading) (on Saturday). Do you (go skateboarding)? Yes, I do. No, I don't. Does (Anna) (play baseball)? Yes, she does. No, she doesn't. What's your favourite sport? My favourite sport is (football). There is … There are … has got*

Materials

- Pupil's Book p106; Activity Book pp102 and 111; Class CD4; Teacher's App on Navio
- Sports flashcards
- Teacher's Resource Bank: Task flashcards: *listen, tick, Talk Partners, read, write*

Optional materials

- Teacher's Resource Bank: Five Trinity Exam Practice cards (selected from Unit 1)
- Teacher's Resource Bank: External Exams Video

At a Glance Lesson Plan

Starting the lesson

- Review sports and actions.
- Set learning outcomes using the task flashcards.

Activity 1

- Listen and tick (✓). There is one example.

▶ *CD4 Track 38 p275*

Activity 2

- Listen and repeat.
- Talk Partners Ask and answer.

▶ *CD4 Track 39 p275*

Go to the Activity Book.

Ending the lesson

- Review the lesson.
- Review the task flashcards.

External Exams Video

- Additional Cambridge Exams Practice Video: A1 Starters.

Pupil's Book

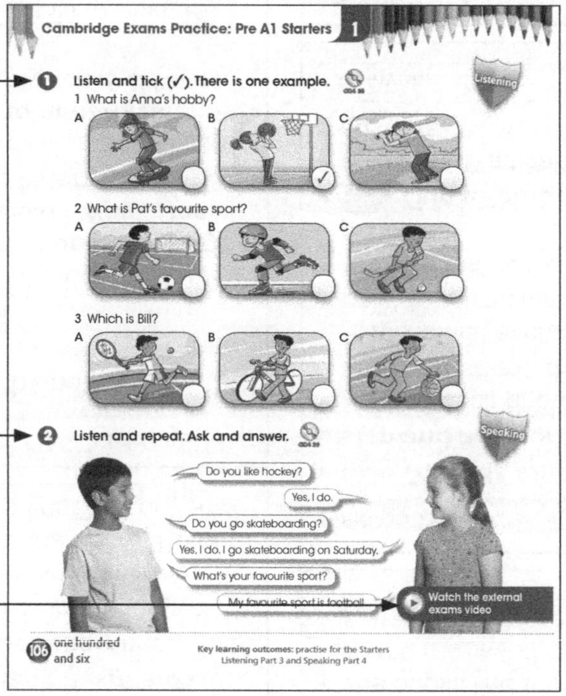

Activity Book

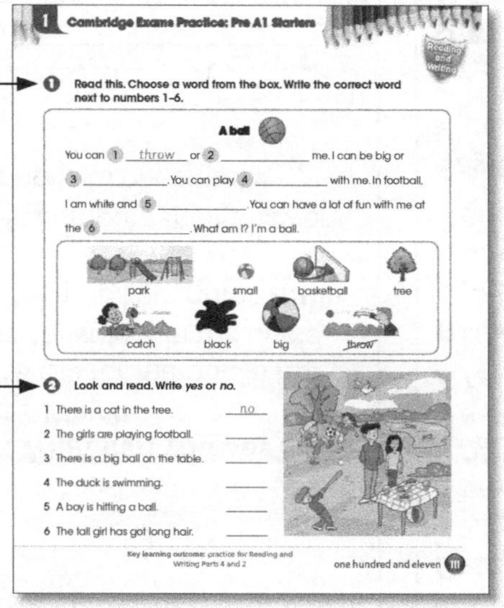

Activity Book

Activity 1

- Read this. Choose a word from the box. Write the correct word next to numbers 1–6.

Activity 2

- Look and read. Write *yes* or *no*.

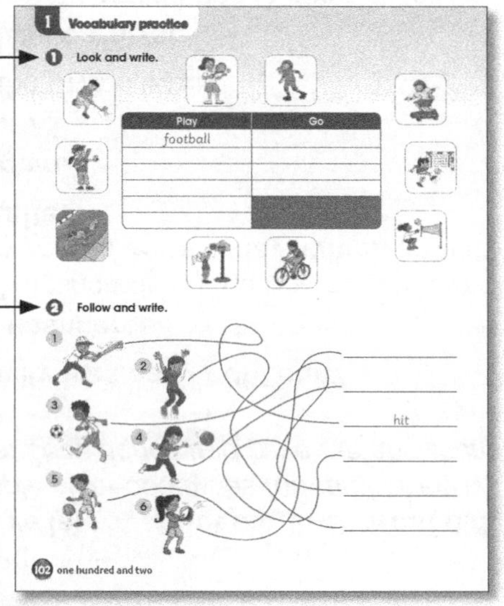

Activity Book

Activity 1

- Look and write.

Activity 2

- Follow and write.

Digital resources

Teacher's Digital: You can also teach this lesson using the Teacher's App on Navio.

Pupil's Digital: Encourage your pupils to use the Pupil's App on Navio to practise the activities from this lesson.

Powered By NAVIO

Starting the lesson

Review sports and actions.

- Choose a game from the Flashcards and Word cards games bank to review the unit vocabulary. (See p23.)

Set learning outcomes using the task flashcards.

- Say **Today we're going to practise activities for an external exam.**
- Hold up the task flashcards in turn and elicit the words. Stick them on one side of the board. Point to them during the lesson to reinforce your instructions.

Pupil's Book Activity 1

Listen and tick (✓). There is one example.

▶ *CD4 Track 38 p275*

- (Books open.) Play the CD. Pause after each conversation to check the answer and to give pupils time to tick the correct picture.

Answers: **1** B **2** A **3** B

Pupil's Book Activity 2

Listen and repeat. Ask and answer.

▶ *CD4 Track 39 p275*

- Play the CD as a model. If necessary, practise the exchange as a class several times. Then invite two confident pupils to act out the conversation with your support. Repeat the procedure with other pairs of pupils.
- **Talk Partners** The pupils practise asking and answering questions with a Talk Partner about the sports they do.

Activity Book

Activity 1

Read this. Choose a word from the box. Write the correct word next to numbers 1–6.

- Read the text and ask the pupils to supply the missing words from the box below.

Answers: **1** throw **2** catch **3** small **4** basketball **5** black **6** park

Activity 2

Look and read. Write *yes* or *no*.

- Point to the illustration and elicit some of the things in the picture. Read the first sentence and ask the pupils to look at the illustration and read the answer.
- Pupils continue on their own reading the sentences and looking at the picture to find the answer.

Answers: **1** no **2** yes **3** no **4** no **5** yes **6** yes

Ending the lesson

Review the lesson.

- (Books closed.) Say **Today we've practised activities for an exam. What questions did you learn?**

Review the task flashcards.

- Point to the task flashcards. Say **Look at the activities you've done today. Which activity was your favourite?** Elicit the pupils' favourite activities.

External Exams Video

Additional Trinity and Cambridge Exams practice (optional).

- Additional external exams preparation material, including videos, worksheets and practice tests can be found in the Teacher's Resource Bank on Navio.

Activity Book page 102: Vocabulary Practice

Answers: **1** Play: football, volleyball, basketball, baseball, hockey, tennis Go: rollerblading, skateboarding, cycling, swimming
2.1 hit **2.2** jump **2.3** kick **2.4** throw **2.5** bounce **2.6** catch

Key Competences and Key Learning Outcomes

LEARN
- Practise for the Starters Listening Part 2 and Speaking Part 3
- Practise for Reading and Writing Parts 3 and 1

Key language

Recycled: *bread, carrots, green beans, lemons, peaches, pineapples, potatoes, sweets, tomatoes, yoghurt*; Numbers 1–50

Recycled: *What's your name? My / His / Her name's … How do you spell that? How old are you / is (Lucy)? What have you got in the bag? We've got (nineteen) apples. What are these? These are (lemons). This is (an egg).*

Materials

- Pupil's Book p107; Activity Book pp103 and 112; Class CD4; Teacher's App on Navio
- Food flashcards
- Teacher's Resource Bank: Task flashcards: *read, listen, write, Talk Partners*

Optional materials

- Teacher's Resource Bank: Five Trinity Exam Practice cards (selected from Unit 2)
- Teacher's Resource Bank: External Exams Video

At a Glance Lesson Plan

Starting the lesson

- Review foods and numbers.
- Set learning outcomes using the task flashcards.

Activity 1

- Read the questions. Listen and write a name or a number. There is one example.

▶ *CD4 Track 40 p275*

Activity 2

- Listen and point.
- Talk Partners Ask and answer.

▶ *CD4 Track 41 p276*

Go to the Activity Book.

Ending the lesson

- Review the lesson.
- Review the task flashcards.

External Exams Video

- Additional Cambridge Exams Practice Video: A1 Starters.

Pupil's Book

Cambridge Exams Practice: Pre A1 Starters 2

1 Read the questions. Listen and write a name or a number. There is one example.

Listening

1 What is the boy's name? Alex
2 What is the girl's name?
3 How old is the boy?
4 How old is the girl?
5 How many apples are there?
6 What is the dog's name?

2 Listen and point. Ask and answer.

Speaking

Key learning outcomes: practise for the Starters Listening Part 2 and Speaking Part 3

one hundred and seven 107

Activity Book

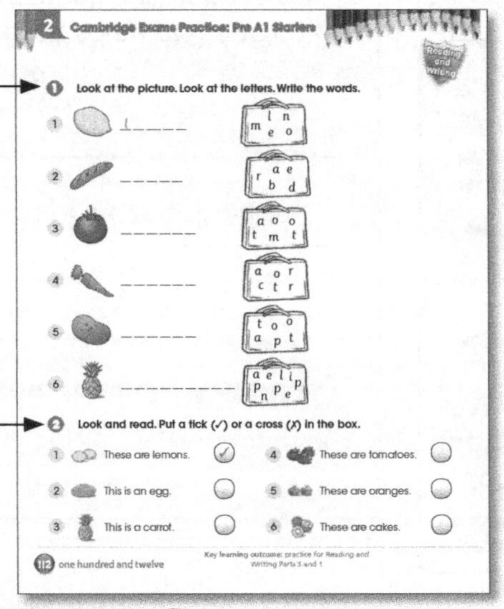
2 Cambridge Exams Practice: Pre A1 Starters

1 Look at the picture. Look at the letters. Write the words.

2 Look and read. Put a tick (✓) or a cross (✗) in the box.

1 These are lemons. ✓
2 This is an egg.
3 This is a carrot.
4 These are tomatoes.
5 These are oranges.
6 These are cakes.

112 one hundred and twelve

Key learning outcome: practise for Reading and Writing Parts 3 and 1

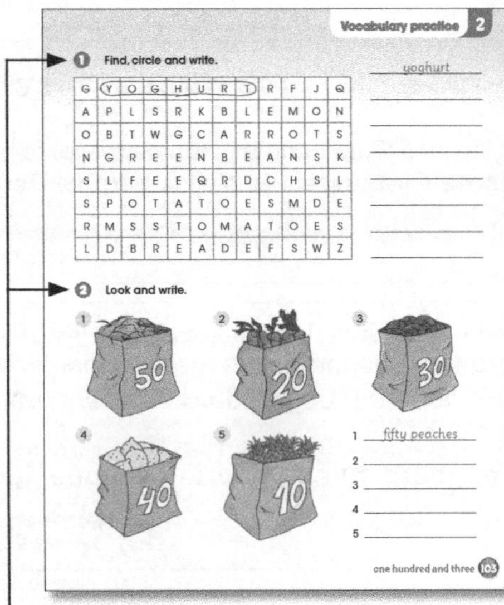
Vocabulary practice 2

1 Find, circle and write.

G	Y	O	G	H	U	R	T	R	F	J	Q
A	P	L	S	R	K	B	L	E	M	O	N
O	B	T	W	G	C	A	R	R	O	T	S
N	G	R	E	E	N	B	E	A	N	S	K
S	L	F	E	E	Q	R	D	C	H	S	L
S	P	O	T	A	T	O	E	S	M	D	E
R	M	S	S	T	O	M	A	T	O	E	S
L	D	B	R	E	A	D	E	F	S	W	Z

yoghurt

2 Look and write.

1 fifty peaches
2
3
4
5

one hundred and three 103

Activity Book

Activity 1

- Look at the picture. Look at the letters. Write the words.

Activity 2

- Look and read. Put a tick (✓) or a cross (✗) in the box.
- Talk Partners Point, ask and answer.

Activity Book

Activity 1

- Find, circle and write.

Activity 2

- Look and write.

Digital resources

Teacher's Digital: You can also teach this lesson using the Teacher's App on Navio.

Pupil's Digital: Encourage your pupils to use the Pupil's App on Navio to practise the activities from this lesson.

Powered By NAVIO

Starting the lesson

Review foods and numbers.

- Choose a game from the Flashcards and Word cards games bank to review the unit vocabulary. (See p23.)

Set learning outcomes using the task flashcards.

- Say **Today we're going to practise activities for an external exam.**
- Hold up the task flashcards in turn and elicit the words. Stick them on one side of the board. Point to them during the lesson to reinforce your instructions.

Pupil's Book Activity 1

Read the questions. Listen and write a name or a number. There is one example.

▶ *CD4 Track 40 p275*

- (Books open.) Read the questions together. Play the CD. Pause after each conversation to give pupils time to write the answer.

Answers: **1** Alex **2** Lucy **3** seven **4** eight **5** 19 **6** Socks

Pupil's Book Activity 2

Listen and point. Ask and answer.

▶ *CD4 Track 41 p276*

- Focus the pupils' attention on the conversation and the food items illustrated and play the CD as a model. Invite two confident pupils to act out the conversation with your support. Encourage them to point to different foods each time.
- Talk Partners The pupils practise asking and answering the questions with a Talk Partner.

Activity Book

Activity 1

Look at the picture. Look at the letters. Write the words.

- (Books open.) Focus attention on the first activity. Ask a pupil to name the first food item. Ask **How do you spell that?** Write the letters on the board as the pupil says them. Ask **Is that right?** Repeat for the other foods. Pupils write the food words on the lines.

Answers: **1** lemon **2** bread **3** tomato **4** carrot **5** potato **6** pineapple

Activity 2

Look and read. Put a tick (✓) or a cross (✗) in the box.

- Focus the pupils' attention on the second activity. Ask a pupil to read the first sentence. Ask **Is that true or false?** Point out the tick in the box.
- Pupils read the remaining sentences and put a tick or cross in the boxes.

Answers: **1** ✓ **2** ✗ **3** ✗ **4** ✓ **5** ✗ **6** ✗

Talk Partners The pupils check their answers with a Talk Partner.

Ending the lesson

Review the lesson.

- (Books closed.) Say **Today we've practised activities for an exam. What questions did you learn?**

Review the task flashcards.

- Point to the task flashcards. Say **Look at the activities you've done today. Which activity was your favourite?** Elicit the pupils' favourite activities.

External Exams Video

Additional Trinity and Cambridge Exams practice (optional).

- Additional external exams preparation material, including videos, worksheets and practice tests can be found in the Teacher's Resource Bank on Navio.

Activity Book page 103: Vocabulary Practice

Answers: **1** yoghurt, lemon, carrots, green beans, potatoes, tomatoes, bread, sweets
2.1 fifty peaches **2.2** twenty carrots **2.3** thirty tomatoes **2.4** forty lemons **2.5** ten pineapples

Cambridge Exams Practice and Vocabulary Practice answers

Key Competences and Key Learning Outcomes

- Practise for the Starters Listening Part 1 and Speaking Part 3
- Practise for Reading and Writing Parts 4 and 3

Key language

Recycled: *bird, crocodile, elephant, fish, giraffe, hippo, lion, lizard, monkey, penguin, snake, tiger; beak, body, face, tail, teeth, wings; behind, between, in, in front of, next to, on, under*

Recycled: *What are these? They're (elephants). What's this? It's a (crocodile). What colour are they? They're (grey).*

Materials

- Pupil's Book p108; Activity Book pp104 and 113; Class CD4; Teacher's App on Navio
- Animal flashcards
- Teacher's Resource Bank: Task flashcards: *listen, draw, Talk Partners, read, write*

Optional materials

- Teacher's Resource Bank: Five Trinity Exam Practice cards (selected from Unit 3)
- Teacher's Resource Bank: External Exams Video

At a Glance Lesson Plan

Starting the lesson

- Review a song from Unit 3.
- Play *Disappearing words.*
- Set learning outcomes using the task flashcards.

Activity 1

- Listen and draw lines. There is one example.

▶ *CD4 Track 42 pp276*

Activity 2

- Listen and point.
- Talk Partners Ask and answer.

▶ *CD4 Track 43 p276*

Go to the Activity Book.

Ending the lesson

- Review the lesson.
- Review the task flashcards.

External Exams Video

- Additional Cambridge Exams Practice Video: A1 Starters.

Pupil's Book

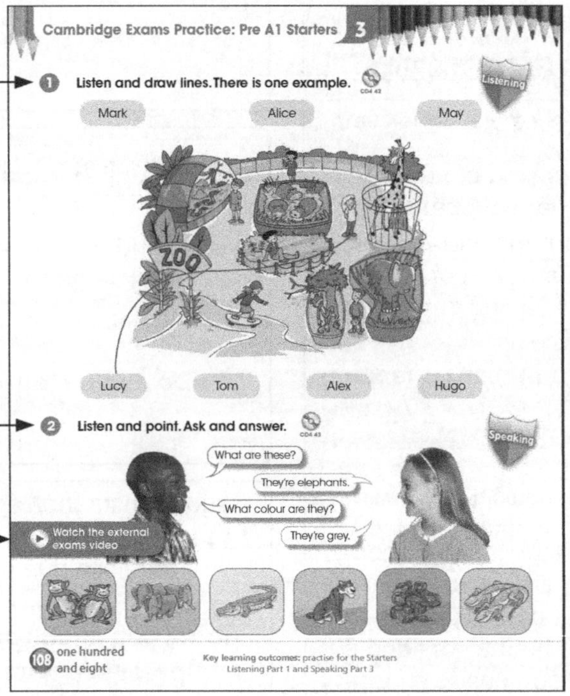

Activity Book

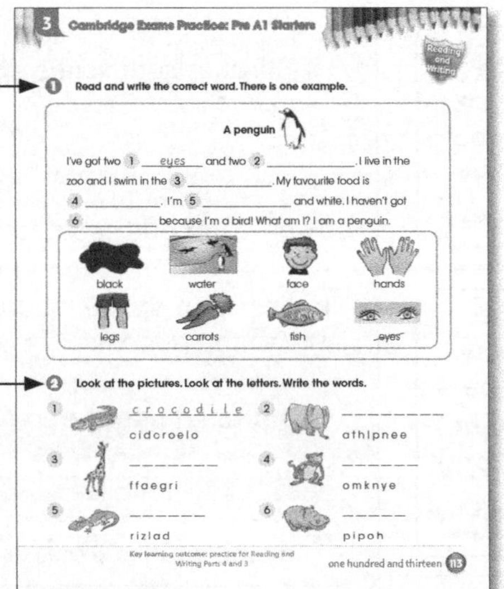

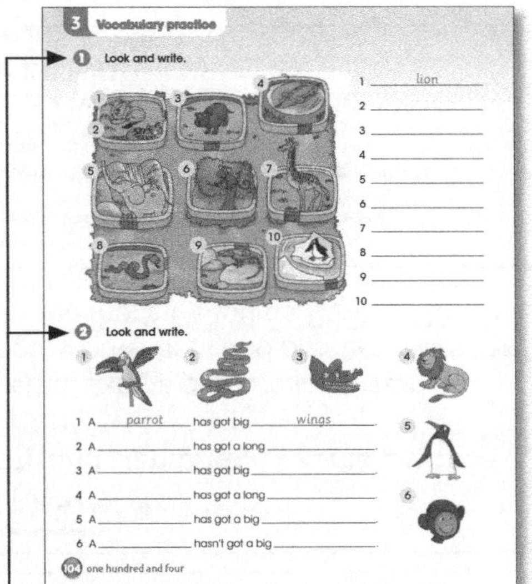

Activity Book

Activity 1

- Read and write the correct word. There is one example.

Activity 2

- Look at the pictures. Look at the letters. Write the words.

Activity Book

Activity 1

- Look and write.

Activity 2

- Follow and write.

Digital resources

Teacher's Digital: You can also teach this lesson using the Teacher's App on Navio.

Pupil's Digital: Encourage your pupils to use the Pupil's App on Navio to practise the activities from this lesson.

Powered By NAVIO

Starting the lesson

Review a song from Unit 3.

- Invite the class to choose one of the songs from the unit (Lessons 1 and 4) to review the unit vocabulary. The pupils sing along and do the corresponding actions.

Play *Disappearing words.*

- Play the *Disappearing words* game (see p23) with all ten animal words from the unit.

Set learning outcomes using the task flashcards.

- Say **Today we're going to practise activities for an external exam.**
- Hold up the task flashcards in turn and elicit the words. Stick them on one side of the board. Point to them during the lesson to reinforce your instructions.

Pupil's Book Activity 1

Listen and draw lines. There is one example.

▶ *CD4 Track 42 p276*

- (Books open.) Say **Look at the zoo. What can you see in the zoo?** Elicit the names of the animals and objects in the zoo. Then elicit the names of the children around the scene.
- Play the CD. Pause after each conversation to check the answer and to give the pupils time to draw the matching lines. There's one extra child.

Answers: **1** Lucy: next to giraffe **2** Alex: looking at the snakes **3** May: eating an ice cream, behind hippos **4** Hugo: blue T-shirt, next to flowers **5** Alice: skateboarding **6** Mark: between elephant and monkey

Pupil's Book Activity 2

Listen and point. Ask and answer.

▶ *CD4 Track 43 p276*

- Focus the pupils' attention on the conversation and play the CD as a model. If necessary, practise the exchanges as a class several times.
- Invite two confident pupils to act out the conversation with your support. Prompt them to point at and talk about the animals illustrated, asking and answering questions about its characteristics. Repeat the procedure with other pairs of pupils.
- **Talk Partners** The pupils practise asking and answering the questions with a Talk Partner.

Activity Book

Activity 1

Read and write the correct word. There is one example.

- (Books open.) Read the text and ask the pupils to supply the missing words from the box. Pupils then fill in the gaps individually.

Answers: **1** eyes **2** legs **3** water **4** fish **5** black **6** hands

Activity 2

Look at the pictures. Look at the letters. Write the words.

- Look at the first picture and ask **What is it?** Ask **How do you spell crocodile?** The pupils look at each picture and use the letters to spell the words.

Answers: **1** crocodile **2** elephant **3** giraffe **4** monkey **5** lizard 6 hippo

Ending the lesson

Review the lesson.

- (Books closed.) Say **Today we've practised activities for an external exam. What questions did you learn?**

Review the task flashcards.

- Point to the task flashcards. Say **Look at the activities you've done today. Which activity was your favourite?** Elicit the pupils' favourite activities.

External Exams Video

Additional Trinity and Cambridge Exams practice (optional).

- Additional external exams preparation material, including videos, worksheets and practice tests can be found in the Teacher's Resource Bank on Navio.

Activity Book page 104: Vocabulary Practice

Answers: **1.1** lion **1.2** tiger **1.3** hippo **1.4** crocodile **1.5** elephant **1.6** monkey **1.7** giraffe **1.8** snake **1.9** lizard **1.10** penguin

2.1 parrot, wings **2.2** snake, body **2.3** crocodile, teeth **2.4** lion, tail **2.5** penguin, beak **2.6** monkey, face

Key Competences and Key Learning Outcomes

- Practise for the Starters Listening Part 2 and Speaking Part 2
- Practise for Reading and Writing Parts 2 and 5

Key language

Recycled: *bridge, forest, grass, hill, lake, leaves, path, river, road, sand; across, along, down, up; basketball, kite; playing, riding (a bike), swimming, walking*

Recycled: *There's … There are … What's he / she doing? He's / She's (running) (up the hill). Is he / she running up a hill? Yes, he / she is. No, he / she isn't.*

Materials

- Pupil's Book p109; Activity Book pp105 and 114; Class CD4; Teacher's App on Navio
- Countryside flashcards
- Teacher's Resource Bank: Task flashcards: *read, listen, write, Talk Partners*

Optional materials

- Teacher's Resource Bank: Five Trinity Exam Practice cards (selected from Unit 4)
- Teacher's Resource Bank: External Exams Video

At a Glance Lesson Plan

Pupil's Book

Starting the lesson

- Review a song from Unit 4.
- Set learning outcomes using the task flashcards.

Activity 1

- Read the questions. Listen and write a name or a number. There is one example.

▶ *CD4 Track 44 p276*

Activity 2

- Listen.
- Talk Partners
Ask and answer.

▶ *CD4 Track 45 p276*

Go to the Activity Book.

Ending the lesson

- Review the lesson.
- Review the task flashcards.

External Exams Video

- Additional Cambridge Exams Practice Video: A1 Starters.

Cambridge Exams Practice: Pre A1 Starters 4

1 Read the questions. Listen and write a name or a number. There is one example.

1 What is the boy's name? Bill
2 What is the girl's name?
3 How many dogs has the boy got?
4 How many cats has the girl got?
5 What is the name of the boy's favourite animal?

2 Listen. Ask and answer.

Key learning outcomes: practise for the Starters Listening Part 2 and Speaking Part 2

one hundred and nine 109

Activity Book

4 Cambridge Exams Practice: Pre A1 Starters

1 Look and read. Write yes or no.

1 A girl is swimming in the water. yes
2 A girl is playing basketball.
3 The frog is in front of the rabbit.
4 A boy is riding a bike.
5 There are three birds.
6 A boy is playing in the sand.

2 Look at the pictures and read the questions. Write one-word answers.

1 Where's the helmet? on the girl's head
2 How many children are there?
3 What's the boy doing? He's
4 What's the girl riding? a
5 Where's the fish? in the

114 one hundred and fourteen

Key learning outcomes: practise for Reading and Writing Parts 2 and 5

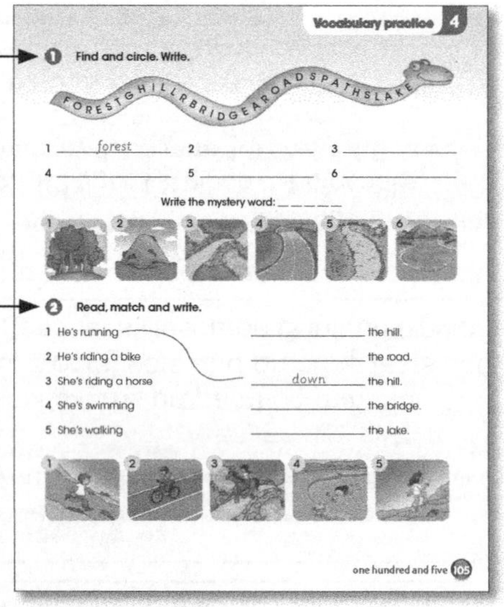
Vocabulary practice 4

1 Find and circle. Write.

1 forest 2 3
4 5 6

Write the mystery word:

2 Read, match and write.

1 He's running — the hill.
2 He's riding a bike — the road.
3 She's riding a horse — down the hill.
4 She's swimming — the bridge.
5 She's walking — the lake.

one hundred and five 105

Activity Book

Activity 1

- Look and read. Write *yes* or *no.*

Activity 2

- Look at the pictures and read the questions. Write one-word answers.

Activity Book

Activity 1

- Find and circle. Write.

Activity 2

- Read, match and write.

Digital resources

Teacher's Digital: You can also teach this lesson using the Teacher's App on Navio.

Pupil's Digital: Encourage your pupils to use the Pupil's App on Navio to practise the activities from this lesson.

Powered By NAVIO

Starting the lesson

Review a song from Unit 4.

- Invite the class to choose one of the songs from the unit (Lessons 1 and 4) to review the unit vocabulary. The pupils sing along and do the corresponding actions.

Set learning outcomes using the task flashcards.

- Say **Today we're going to practise activities for an external exam.**
- Hold up the task flashcards in turn and elicit the words. Stick them on one side of the board. Point to them during the lesson to reinforce your instructions.

Pupil's Book Activity 1

Read the questions. Listen and write a name or a number. There is one example.

▶ *CD4 Track 44 p276*

- Read the questions together. Play the CD. Pause after each conversation to give pupils time to write the name or number.

Answers: **1** Bill **2** Kim **3** two **4** one **5** Ben

Pupil's Book Activity 2

Listen. Ask and answer.

▶ *CD4 Track 45 p276*

- Play the CD. The pupils listen and follow in their books. Play the CD again, pausing after each sentence so that the pupils can repeat. Invite two confident pupils to ask and answer about the illustration.
- Talk Partners The pupils practise describing the picture with a Talk Partner.

Activity Book

Activity 1

Look and read. Write *yes* or *no*.

- (Books open.) Ask the pupils to describe what they can see in the illustration. Then, invite a pupil to read out the first sentence and prompt the class to give the answer. Repeat with the other sentences.

Answers: **1** yes **2** no **3** yes **4** no **5** no **6** yes

Activity 2

Look at the picture and read the questions. Write one-word answers.

- Ask the pupils to describe what they can see in the illustration. The pupils then work on their own to answer the questions.

Answers: **1** head **2** two **3** running **4** bike **5** water

Ending the lesson

Review the lesson.

- (Books closed.) Say **Today we've practised activities for an exam. What questions did you learn?**

Review the task flashcards.

- Point to the task flashcards. Say **Look at the activities you've done today. Which activity was your favourite?** Elicit the pupils' favourite activities.

External Exams Video

Additional Trinity and Cambridge Exams practice (optional).

- Additional external exams preparation material, including videos, worksheets and practice tests can be found in the Teacher's Resource Bank on Navio.

Activity Book page 105: Vocabulary Practice

Answers: **1.1** forest **1.2** hill **1.3** bridge **1.4** road **1.5** path **1.6** lake Mystery word: grass
2.1 down the hill **2.2** along the road **2.3** across the bridge **2.4** across the lake **2.5** up the hill

Key Competences and Key Learning Outcomes

- Practise for the Starters Listening Part 3 and Speaking Part 3
- Practise for Reading and Writing Parts 2 and 5

Key language

Recycled: *dance, drink, eat, listen to music, make a snowman, play, skate, smile, take a photo, wave; clean, dirty, fat, short, tall, thin; animals; food*

Recycled: *What's he / she doing? He's / She's (eating an apple). We're (drinking). They're (eating). Are you (eating)? Are they (drinking)? Yes, we / they are. No, we / they aren't.*

Materials

- Pupil's Book p110; Activity Book pp106 and 115; Class CD4; Teacher's App on Navio
- Action verbs flashcards
- Teacher's Resource Bank: Task flashcards: *listen, tick, Talk Partners, read, write*

Optional materials

- Teacher's Resource Bank: Five Trinity Exam Practice cards (selected from Unit 5)
- Teacher's Resource Bank: External Exams Video

At a Glance Lesson Plan

Pupil's Book

Starting the lesson

- Review a song from Unit 5.
- Set learning outcomes using the task flashcards.

Activity 1

- Listen and tick (✓). There is one example.

▶ *CD4 Track 46 p276*

Activity 2

- Listen and point.
- Talk Partners Ask and answer.

▶ *CD4 Track 47 p276*

Go to the Activity Book.

Ending the lesson

- Review the lesson.
- Review the task flashcards.

External Exams Video

- Additional Cambridge Exams Practice Video: A1 Starters.

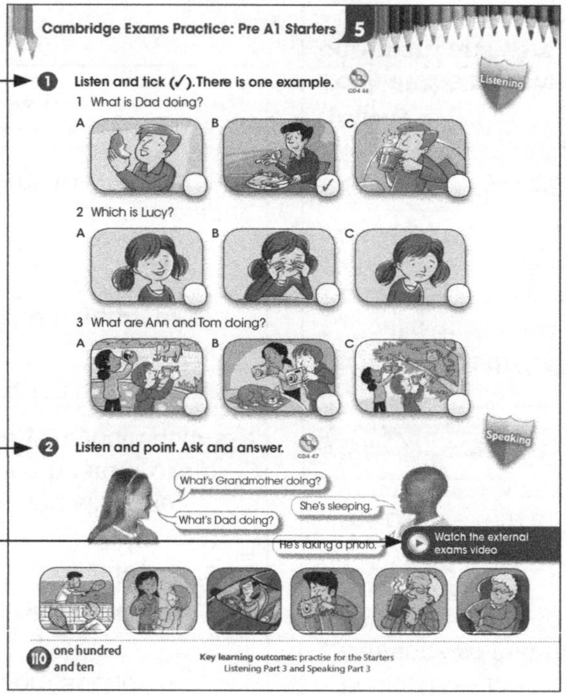

Activity Book

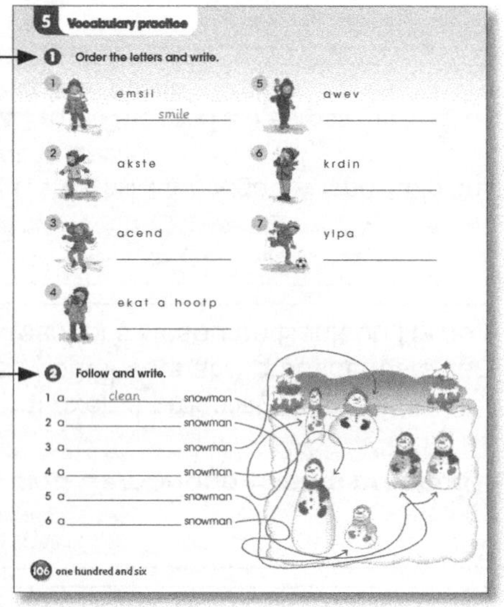

Activity Book

Activity 1

- Look and read. Write *yes* or *no.*

Activity 2

- Look at the pictures and read the questions. Write one-word answers.

Activity Book

Activity 1

- Order the letters and write.

Activity 2

- Follow and write.

Digital resources

Teacher's Digital: You can also teach this lesson using the Teacher's App on Navio.

Pupil's Digital: Encourage your pupils to use the Pupil's App on Navio to practise the activities from this lesson.

Powered By NAVIO

Starting the lesson

Review a song from Unit 5.

- Invite the class to choose one of the songs from the unit (Lessons 1 and 4) to review the unit vocabulary. The pupils sing along and do the corresponding actions.

Set learning outcomes using the task flashcards.

- Say **Today we're going to practise activities for an external exam.**
- Hold up the task flashcards in turn and elicit the words. Stick them on one side of the board. Point to them during the lesson to reinforce your instructions.

Pupil's Book Activity 1

Listen and tick (✓). There is one example.

▶ *CD4 Track 46 p276*

- Look at the illustrations together and ask each question in turn. Elicit words in English.
- Play the CD. Pause after each conversation to give pupils time to tick the correct picture.

Answers: **1** B **2** A **3** C

Pupil's Book Activity 2

Listen and point. Ask and answer.

▶ *CD4 Track 47 p276*

- Focus the pupils' attention on the illustrations and elicit the family members (boys, girls, Mum, Dad, Grandfather, Grandmother). Play the CD. Pause after the first question to elicit the answer. Continue, pausing to elicit a response from the class after each exchange.
- Invite two confident pupils to read out the speech bubbles. Prompt them to ask and answer a question about a different picture. Repeat the procedure with different pairs of pupils.
- Talk Partners The pupils practise the exchanges with a Talk Partner, using the six illustrations as a prompt.

Activity Book

Activity 1

Look and read. Write *yes* or *no*.

- (Books open.) Ask the pupils to describe what they can see in the illustration. Read out each sentence together. The pupils decide if the statements are true or false and write 'yes' or 'no'.

Answers: **1** no **2** yes **3** no **4** yes **5** yes **6** yes

Activity 2

Look at the picture and read the questions. Write one-word answers.

- The pupils read the questions and answer them by looking at the illustration.

Answers: **1** photo **2** carrot **3** dog **4** dancing **5** three

Ending the lesson

Review the lesson.

- (Books closed.) Say **Today we've practised activities for an exam. What questions did you learn?**

Review the task flashcards.

- Point to the task flashcards. Say **Look at the activities you've done today. Which activity was your favourite?** Elicit the pupils' favourite activities.

External Exams Video

Additional Trinity and Cambridge Exams practice (optional)

- Additional external exams preparation material, including videos, worksheets and practice tests can be found in the Teacher's Resource Bank on Navio.

Activity Book page 106: Vocabulary Practice

Answers: **1.1** smile **1.2** skate **1.3** dance **1.4** take a photo **1.5** wave **1.6** drink **1.7** play
2.1 clean **2.2** thin **2.3** fat **2.4** big **2.5** dirty **2.6** small

Key Competences and Key Learning Outcomes

LEARN
- Practise for the Starters Listening Part 3 and Speaking Part 4
- Practise for Writing Parts 4 and 2

Key language

Recycled: *celebrate Halloween, eat chestnuts, finish school, go to the beach, open presents, plant seeds, smell flowers, wear warm clothes;* Ordinal numbers; *actions, clothes, months, seasons, sports; cold, donkey, grass, hot*

Recycled: *Where are …? What …? Who …? He's / She's (wearing a hat). They're (playing in the sand). How old are you? When's your birthday? My birthday is on the (second) of (August).*

Materials
- Pupil's Book p111; Activity Book pp107 and 116; Class CD4; Teacher's App on Navio
- Seasonal activities flashcards
- Teacher's Resource Bank: Task flashcards: *listen, tick, Talk Partners, read, write*

Optional materials
- Teacher's Resource Bank: Five Trinity Exam Practice cards (selected from Unit 6)
- Teacher's Resource Bank: External Exams Video

At a Glance Lesson Plan

Starting the lesson
- Review a song from Unit 6.
- Set learning outcomes using the task flashcards.

Activity 1
- Listen and tick (✓). There is one example.

▶ *CD4 Track 48 p276*

Activity 2
- Listen and repeat.
- **Talk Partners** Ask and answer.

▶ *CD4 Track 49 p276*

Go to the Activity Book.

Ending the lesson
- Review the lesson.
- Review the task flashcards.

External Exams Video
- Additional Cambridge Exams Practice Video: A1 Starters.

Pupil's Book

Activity Book

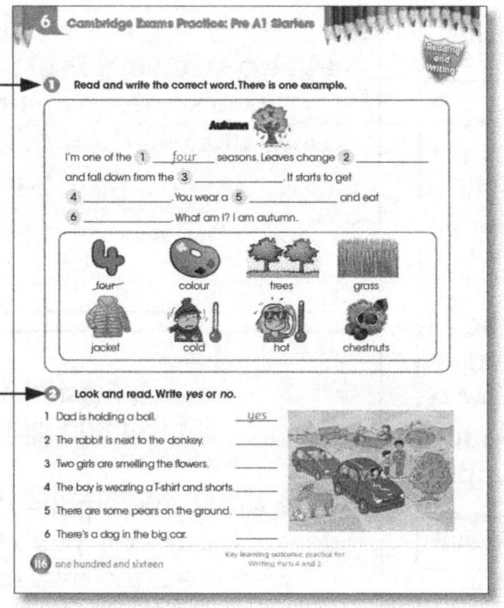

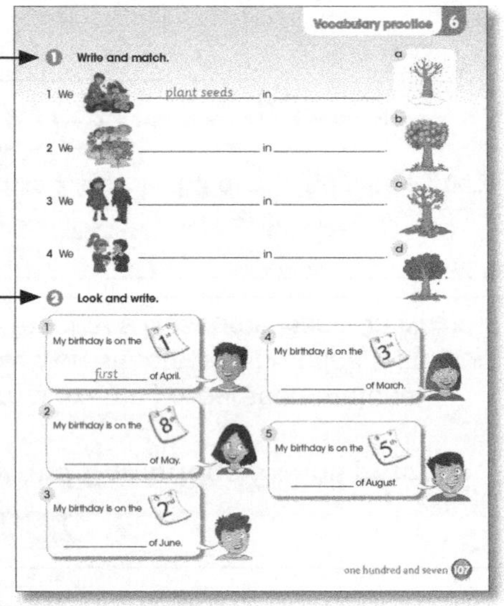

Activity Book

Activity 1
- Read and write the correct word. There is one example.

Activity 2
- Look and read. Write *yes* or *no*.

Activity Book

Activity 1
- Write and match.

Activity 2
- Look and write.

Digital resources

Teacher's Digital: You can also teach this lesson using the Teacher's App on Navio.

Pupil's Digital: Encourage your pupils to use the Pupil's App on Navio to practise the activities from this lesson.

Powered By NAVIO

Starting the lesson

Review a song from Unit 6.

- Invite the class to choose one of the songs from the unit (Lessons 1 and 4) to review the unit vocabulary. The pupils sing along and do the corresponding actions.

Set learning outcomes using the task flashcards.

- Say **Today we're going to practise activities for an external exam.**
- Hold up the task flashcards in turn and elicit the words. Stick them on one side of the board. Point to them during the lesson to reinforce your instructions.

Pupil's Book Activity 1

Listen and tick (✓). There is one example.

▶ *CD4 Track 48 p276*

- Look at the illustrations together and ask each question in turn. Elicit words in English.
- Play the CD. Pause after each conversation to give the pupils time to tick the correct picture.

Answers: **1** B **2** A **3** A

Pupil's Book Activity 2

Listen and repeat. Ask and answer.

▶ *CD4 Track 49 p276*

- Focus the pupils' attention on the conversation. Play the CD. If necessary, practise the exchange as a class several times. Then invite two confident pupils to act out the conversation. Repeat the procedure with other pairs of pupils.
- Talk Partners The pupils practise asking and answering questions about their age and birthday with a Talk Partner.

Activity Book

Activity 1

Read and write the correct word. There is one example.

- (Books open.) Read the text and ask the pupils to supply the missing words from the box below.

Answers: **1** four **2** colour **3** trees **4** cold **5** jacket **6** chestnuts

Activity 2

Look and read. Write *yes* or *no*.

- (Books open.) Ask the pupils to describe what they can see in the illustration. Then, invite a pupil to read out the first sentence and prompt the class to give the answer. Repeat with the other sentences.

Answers: **1** yes **2** yes **3** no **4** no **5** no **6** no

Ending the lesson

Review the lesson.

- (Books closed.) Say **Today we've practised activities for an exam. What questions did you learn?**

Review the task flashcards.

- Point to the task flashcards. Say **Look at the activities you've done today. Which activity was your favourite?** Elicit the pupils' favourite activities.

External Exams Video

Additional Trinity and Cambridge Exams practice (optional).

- Additional external exams preparation material, including videos, worksheets and practice tests can be found in the Teacher's Resource Bank on Navio.

Activity Book page 107: Vocabulary Practice

Answers: **1.1** plant seeds, b spring **1.2** go to the beach, d summer **1.3** wear warm clothes, a winter **1.4** eat chestnuts, c autumn
2.1 first **2.2** eighth **2.3** second **2.4** third **2.5** fifth

Key Competences and Key Learning Outcomes

- Practise for the Starters Listening Part 4 and Speaking Part 4
- Practise for Reading and Writing Parts 5 and 3

Key language

Recycled: *bathroom, bedroom, dining room, flat, garage, garden, hall, house, kitchen, living room; box, camera, clock, phone, radio, watch; between, in, next to, on, under; colours*

Recycled: *Do you live in a house or a flat? I live in a (flat). What's your favourite room? My favourite room is … What's in (your bedroom)? There's a … There are …*

Materials

- Pupil's Book p112; Activity Book pp108 and 117; Class CD4; Teacher's App on Navio
- Rooms flashcards
- Teacher's Resource Bank: Task flashcards: *listen, colour, Talk Partners, read, write*

Optional materials

- Teacher's Resource Bank: Five Trinity Exam Practice cards (selected from Unit 7)
- Teacher's Resource Bank: External Exams Video

At a Glance Lesson Plan

Starting the lesson

- Review a song from Unit 7.
- Set learning outcomes using the task flashcards.

Activity 1

- Listen and colour. There is one example.

▶ *CD4 Track 50 pp277*

Activity 2

- Listen and repeat.
- Talk Partners Ask and answer.

▶ *CD4 Track 51 p277*

Go to the Activity Book.

Ending the lesson

- Review the lesson.
- Review the task flashcards.

External Exams Video

- Additional Cambridge Exams Practice Video: A1 Starters.

Pupil's Book

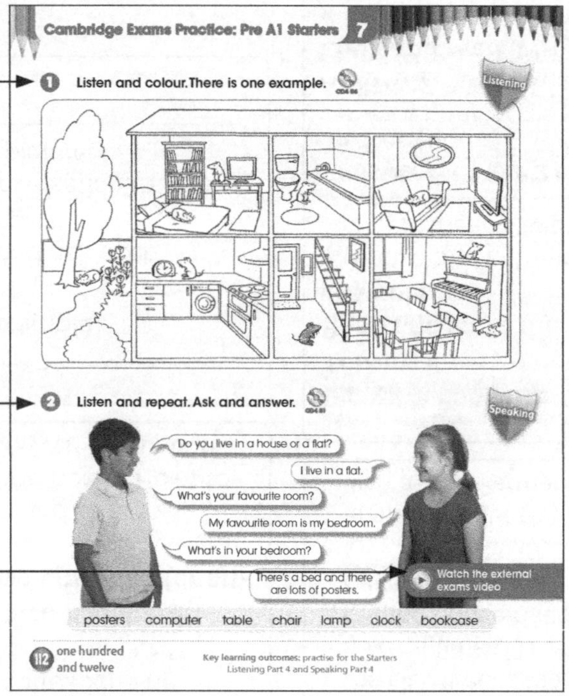

Activity Book

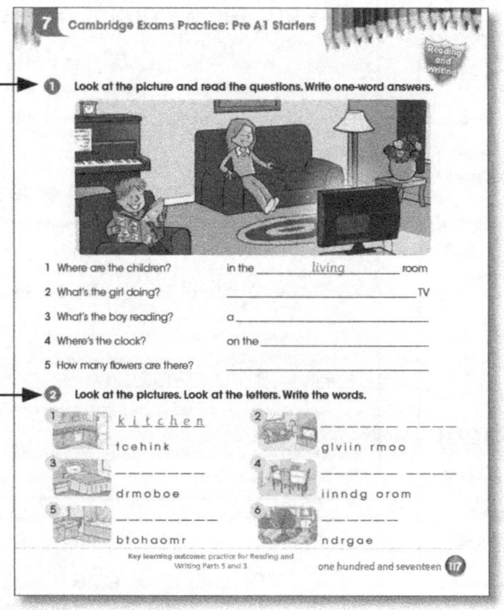

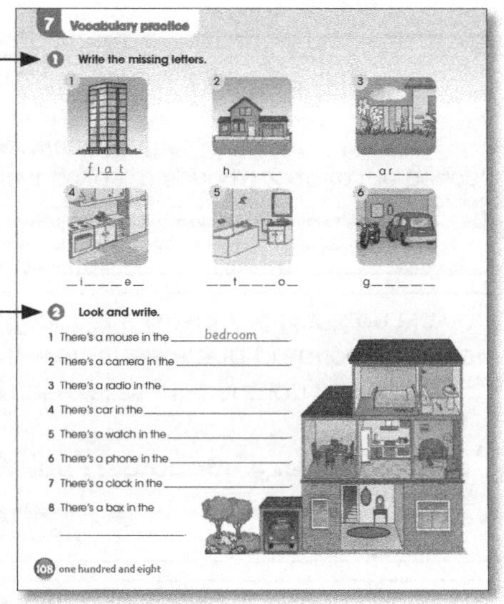

Activity Book

Activity 1

- Look at the picture and read the questions. Write one-word answers.

Activity 2

- Look at the pictures. Look at the letters. Write the words.

Activity Book

Activity 1

- Write the missing letters.

Activity 2

- Look and write.

Digital resources

Teacher's Digital: You can also teach this lesson using the Teacher's App on Navio.

Pupil's Digital: Encourage your pupils to use the Pupil's App on Navio to practise the activities from this lesson.

Powered By NAVIO

Starting the lesson

Review a song from Unit 7.

- Invite the class to choose one of the songs from the unit (Lessons 1 and 4) to review the unit vocabulary. The pupils sing along and do the corresponding actions.

Set learning outcomes using the task flashcards.

- Say **Today we're going to practise activities for an external exam.**
- Hold up the task flashcards in turn and elicit the words. Stick them on one side of the board. Point to them during the lesson to reinforce your instructions.

Pupil's Book Activity 1

Listen and colour. There is one example.

▶ *CD4 Track 50 p277*

- Focus on the illustration and elicit what colour the mouse in the hall is. *(Blue.)*
- Play the CD. Pause after each conversation to give the pupils time to colour the correct mouse.

Answers: **1** blue mouse in hall **2** brown mouse on bed **3** pink mouse next to clock **4** purple mouse under piano **5** orange mouse between tree and flowers **6** red mouse on sofa

Pupil's Book Activity 2

Listen and repeat. Ask and answer.

▶ *CD4 Track 51 p277*

- Focus the pupils' attention on the conversation. Play the CD. If necessary, practise the exchanges as a class several times. Then invite two confident pupils to act out the conversation with your support. Repeat the procedure with other pairs of pupils and write any new vocabulary the class need on the board.
- Talk Partners The pupils then practise asking and answering questions about their house or flat with a Talk Partner.

Activity Book

Activity 1

Look at the picture and read the questions. Write one-word answers.

- (Books open.) Ask the pupils to describe what they can see in the illustration. Then, invite a pupil to read the first sentence and prompt the class to give the answer *(living)*. Repeat with the other sentences.

Answers: **1** living **2** watching **3** comic **4** piano **5** seven

Activity 2

Look at the pictures. Look at the letters. Write the words.

- Look at the first picture and ask **What is it?** Ask **How do you spell kitchen?** The pupils look at each picture and use the letters to spell the words.

Answers: **1** kitchen **2** living room **3** bedroom **4** dining room **5** bathroom **6** garden

Ending the lesson

Review the lesson.

- (Books closed.) Say **Today we've practised activities for an exam. What questions did you learn?**

Review the task flashcards.

- Point to the task flashcards. Say **Look at the activities you've done today. Which activity was your favourite?** Elicit the pupils' favourite activities.

External Exams Video

Additional Trinity and Cambridge Exams practice (optional).

- Additional external exams preparation material, including videos, worksheets and practice tests can be found in the Teacher's Resource Bank on Navio

Activity Book page 108: Vocabulary Practice

Answers: **1.1** flat **1.2** house **1.3** garden **1.4** kitchen **1.5** bathroom **1.6** garage
2.1 bedroom **2.2** kitchen **2.3** dining room **2.4** garage **2.5** bathroom **2.6** living room **2.7** hall **2.8** garden

Key Competences and Key Learning Outcomes

- Practise for the Starters Listening Part 4 and Speaking Part 3
- Practise for Reading and Writing Parts 2 and 3

Key language

Recycled: *baker's, bank, bus station, car park, chemist's, fire station, museum, park, police station, post office, school, train station, zoo; between, in, in front of, next to; colours*

Recycled: *Where's the (bookshop)? It's here. Is there a (bookshop) near your school? Yes, there is. No, there isn't. There's a (bank) next to the (chemist's). There are (three trees). There aren't any (museums).*

Materials

- Pupil's Book p113; Activity Book pp109 and 118; Class CD4; Teacher's App on Navio
- Places in town flashcards
- Teacher's Resource Bank: Task flashcards: *listen, colour, Talk Partners, read, write*

Optional materials

- Teacher's Resource Bank: Five Trinity Exam Practice cards (selected from Unit 8)
- Teacher's Resource Bank: External Exams Video

At a Glance Lesson Plan

Starting the lesson

- Review a song from Unit 8.
- Set learning outcomes using the task flashcards.

Activity 1

- Listen and colour. There is one example.

▶ *CD4 Track 52 p277*

Activity 2

- Listen and point.
- Talk Partners
  Ask and answer.

▶ *CD4 Track 53 p277*

Go to the Activity Book.

Ending the lesson

- Review the lesson.
- Review the task flashcards.

External Exams Video

- Additional Cambridge Exams Practice Video: A1 Starters.

Pupil's Book

Activity Book

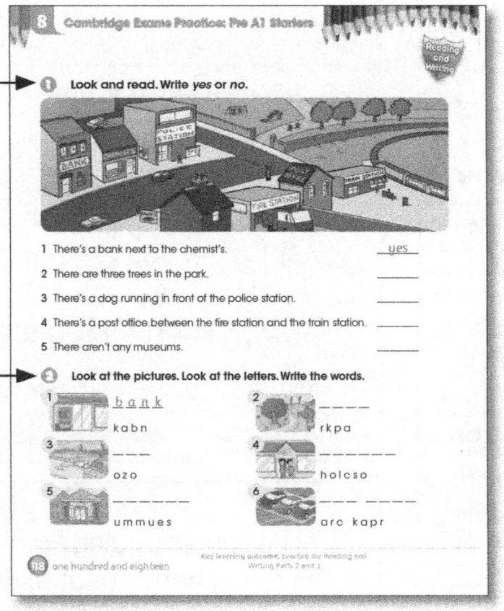

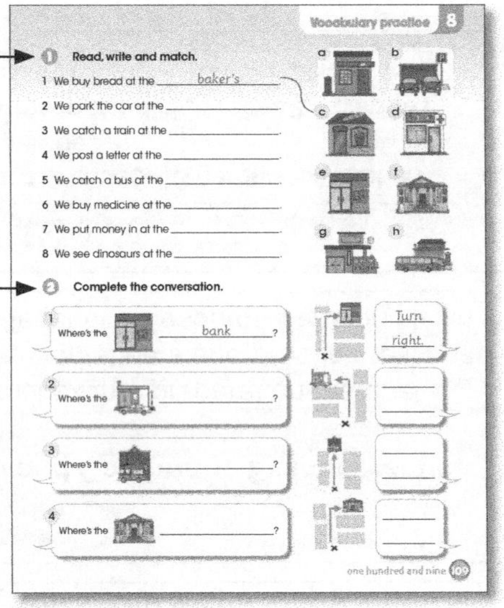

Activity Book

Activity 1

- Look and read. Write *yes* or *no*.

Activity 2

- Look at the pictures. Look at the letters. Write the words.

Activity Book

Activity 1

- Read, write and match.

Activity 2

- Complete the conversation.

Digital resources

Teacher's Digital: Don't forget you can teach this lesson using the Teacher's App on Navio.

Pupil's Digital: Encourage your pupils to use the Pupil's App on Navio to practise the vocabulary from this lesson.

Powered By NAVIO

Starting the lesson

Review a song from Unit 8.

- Invite the class to choose one of the songs from the unit (Lessons 1 and 4) to review the unit vocabulary. The pupils sing along and do the corresponding actions.

Set learning outcomes using the task flashcards.

- Say **Today we're going to practise activities for an external exam.**
- Hold up the task flashcards in turn and elicit the words. Stick them on one side of the board. Point to them during the lesson to reinforce your instructions.

Pupil's Book Activity 1

Listen and colour. There is one example.

▶ *CD4 Track 52 p277*

- Focus on the illustration and elicit the number of birds in the picture.
- Play the CD. Pause after each conversation to give the pupils time to colour the correct bird.

Answers: **1** orange bird next to flat **2** pink bird next to ball **3** blue bird in the tree **4** red bird in front of bookshop **5** brown bird in the water **6** green bird between the flowers

Pupil's Book Activity 2

Listen and point. Ask and answer.

▶ *CD4 Track 53 p277*

- Focus the pupils' attention on the conversation. Play the CD. If necessary, practise the exchange as a class several times.
- Talk Partners The pupils practise asking about the places in the illustrations with a Talk Partner.

Activity Book

Activity 1

Look and read. Write yes or *no*.

- (Books open.) Ask the pupils to describe what they can see in the picture. Read out each sentence together. The pupils decide if the statements are true or false and reply 'yes' or 'no'. The pupils write the answers.

Answers: **1** yes **2** no **3** no **4** yes **5** yes

Activity 2

Look at the pictures. Look at the letters. Write the words.

- Look at the first picture and ask **What is it?** Ask **How do you spell bank?** The pupils look at each picture and use the letters to spell the words.

Answers: **1** bank **2** park **3** zoo **4** school **5** museum **6** car park

Ending the lesson

Review the lesson.

- (Books closed.) Say **Today we've practised activities for an external exam. What questions did you learn?**

Review the task flashcards.

- Point to the task flashcards. Say **Look at the activities you've done today. Which activity was your favourite?** Elicit the pupils' favourite activities.

External Exams Video

Additional Trinity and Cambridge Exams practice (optional).

- Additional external exams preparation material, including videos, worksheets and practice tests can be found in the Teacher's Resource Bank on Navio.

Activity Book page 109: Vocabulary Practice

Answers: **1.1** baker's c **1.2** car park b **1.3** train station g **1.4** post office a **1.5** bus station h **1.6** chemist's d **1.7** bank e **1.8** museum f

2.1 bank, Turn right. **2.2** police station, Turn left. **2.3** fire station, Go straight on. **2.4** museum, Turn right.

Key Competences and Key Learning Outcomes

- Practise for the Starters Listening Part 1 and Speaking Part 4
- Practise for Reading and Writing Parts 5 and 1

Key language

Recycled: *aquarium, castle, chocolate factory, circus, funfair, safari park, science museum, sports centre, theatre, water park; child, children, man, men, woman, women; behind, between, in, in front of, next to; ball, juice, running, tree*

Recycled: *Who's that (man) (next to the car)? That's … Who are those (women)? They're … Have you got any brothers or sisters? Yes. I've got … What's his / her / your sister's / brother's name? His / Her name's … How many …? What's he / she doing?*

Materials

- Pupil's Book p114; Activity Book pp110 and 119; Class CD4; Teacher's App on Navio
- Holiday places flashcards
- Teacher's Resource Bank: Task flashcards: *listen, draw, Talk Partners, read, write, tick*

Optional materials

- Teacher's Resource Bank: Five Trinity Exam Practice cards (selected from Unit 9)
- Teacher's Resource Bank: External Exams Video

At a Glance Lesson Plan

Starting the lesson

- Review a song from Unit 9.
- Set learning outcomes using the task flashcards.

Activity 1

- Listen and draw lines. There is one example.

▶ *CD4 Track 54 p277*

Activity 2

- Listen and repeat.

▶ *CD4 Track 55 p277*

- Talk Partners Ask and answer.

Go to the Activity Book.

Ending the lesson

- Review the lesson.
- Review the task flashcards.

Extra activities

Reinforcement

- Play *Disappearing words.*
- Play *Which one's missing?*

External Exams Video

- Additional Cambridge Exams [illegible]

Pupil's Book

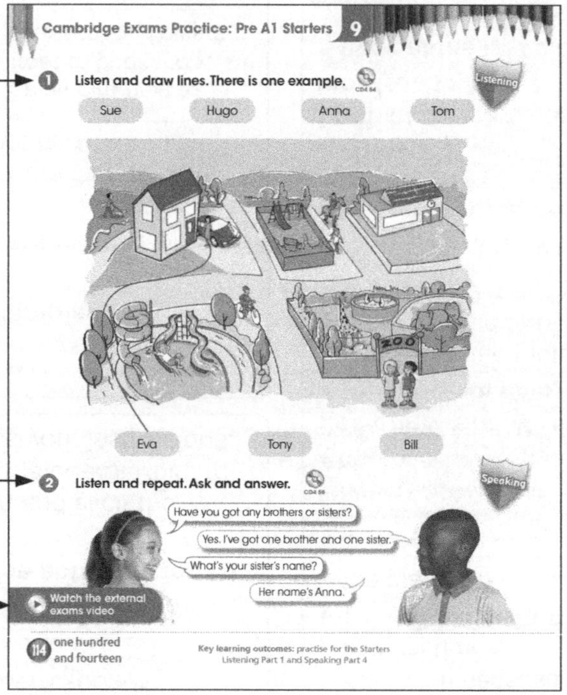

Activity Book

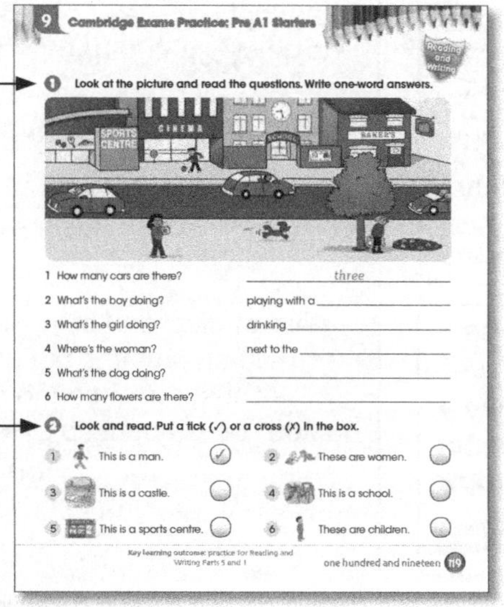

Activity Book

Activity 1

- Look at the picture and read the questions. Write one-word answers.

Activity 2

- Look and read. Put a tick (✓) or a cross (✗) in the box.

Activity Book

Activity 1

- Write the holiday places. Where was Toby yesterday?

Activity 2

- Look and write.

Digital resources

Teacher's Digital: You can also teach this lesson using the Teacher's App on Navio.

Pupil's Digital: Encourage your pupils to use the Pupil's App on Navio to practise the activities from this lesson.

Powered By NAVIO

Starting the lesson

Review a song from Unit 9.

- Invite the class to choose one of the songs from the unit (Lessons 1 and 4) to review the unit vocabulary. The pupils sing along and do the corresponding actions.

Set learning outcomes using the task flashcards.

- Say **Today we're going to practise activities for an external exam.**
- Hold up the task flashcards in turn and elicit the words. Stick them on one side of the board. Point to them during the lesson to reinforce your instructions.

Pupil's Book Activity 1

Listen and draw lines. There is one example.

▶ *CD4 Track 54 p277*

- Play the CD. Pause after each conversation to give the pupils time to draw the matching lines.

Answers: **1** Eva: next to red car **2** Hugo: man with dog **3** Sue: woman on horse **4** Bill: in water park **5** Tom: on bike **6** Anna: yellow T-shirt, eating an apple

Pupil's Book Activity 2

Listen and repeat. Ask and answer.

▶ *CD4 Track 55 p277*

- Focus the pupils' attention on the conversation. Invite two confident pupils to read out the questions and answers. Play the CD. If necessary, practise the exchanges as a class several times.
- **Talk Partners** The pupils practise asking and answering questions about their family with a Talk Partner.

Activity Book

Activity 1

Look at the picture and read the questions. Write one-word answers.

- (Books open.) Ask the pupils to describe what they can see in the illustration. Ask **What can you see?** Read out each sentence collectively.
- **Talk Partners** The pupils describe the scene with a Talk Partner.
- The pupils complete the sentences individually by writing one-word answers.

Answers: **1** three **2** ball **3** juice **4** tree **5** running **6** nine

Activity 2

Look and read. Put a tick (✓) or a cross (✗) in the box.

- Ask a pupil to read the first sentence. Ask **Is it true or false?** Point out the tick in the box.
- Pupils read the remaining sentences and put a tick or cross in the boxes.

Answers: **1** ✓ **2** ✗ **3** ✗ **4** ✗ **5** ✗ **6** ✗

Ending the lesson

Review the lesson.

- (Books closed.) Say **Today we've practised activities for an external exam. What questions did you learn?**

Review the task flashcards.

- Point to the task flashcards. Say **Look at the activities you've done today. Which activity was your favourite?** Elicit the pupils' favourite activities.

Extra activities

Reinforcement

- Play *Disappearing words* (see p23) with the holiday places flashcards.
- Optional: Play again with the additional extension vocabulary from Lesson 1.
- Play *Which one's missing?* Stick all the flashcards on the board. Point to each one in turn and ask the pupils to name them as you do so. Ask the pupils to close their eyes. Secretly remove one of the flashcards and say *Which one's missing?* The pupils name the missing card by asking questions: *Is it the (circus)?*

External Exams Video

Additional Trinity and Cambridge Exams practice (optional).

- Additional external exams preparation material, including videos, worksheets and practice tests can be found in the Teacher's Resource Bank on Navio.

Activity Book page 110: Vocabulary Practice

Answers: **1.1** circus **1.2** aquarium **1.3** sports centre **1.4** theatre **1.5** chocolate factory **1.6** water park Toby: Yesterday I was at the castle.

2.1 science museum **2.2** chocolate factory **2.3** sports centre **2.4** castle **2.5** funfair **2.6** safari park

Audioscript

Starter Unit Lesson 1

Pupil's Book

CD1 TRACK 1

PB page 4 Activity 3

***We've got our school bags* song**

We've got our school bags. [Mime putting a school bag on.]
We're ready for school. [Thumbs up.]
We're on our way. [Walk on the spot.]
Let's go! [Beckon to the class.]

We're ready to listen. [Cup a hand behind your ear.]
We're ready to sing. [Mime singing into a microphone.]
We're ready to speak English. [Mime a talking motion with your hand.]

We've got our school bags. [Mime putting a school bag on.]
We're ready for school. [Thumbs up.]
We're on our way. [Walk on the spot.]
Let's go! [Beckon to the class.]

We're ready to read. [Open your hands like a book and look at them.]
We're ready to write. [Mime holding a pencil.]
We're ready to speak English. [Mime a talking motion with your hand.]

We've got our school bags. [Mime putting a school bag on.]
We're ready for school. [Thumbs up.]
We're on our way. [Walk on the spot.]
Let's go! [Beckon to the class.]

CD1 TRACK 2

PB page 4 Activity 3

Karaoke version: *We've got our school bags* song

CD1 TRACK 3

PB page 4 Activity 4

Boy: What's his name?
Beth: His name is Jake.
Boy: What's her name?
Beth: Her name is Molly.

Starter Unit Lesson 2

Pupil's Book

CD1 TRACK 4

PB page 5 Activity 1

The school subjects chant

Music, English, Spanish, Arts and Crafts, Maths, ICT, Science, PE

CD1 TRACK 5

PB page 5 Activity 2

Girl: What's your favourite subject?
Boy: My favourite subject is Maths. What's yours?
Girl: My favourite subject is English.

CD1 TRACK 6

PB page 5 Activity 3

1
What's your favourite subject?
Boy: My favourite subject is …
Boy: Music.
2
What's your favourite subject?
Girl: My favourite subject is …
Girl: English.
3
What's your favourite subject?
Boy: My favourite subject is …
Boy: Maths.
4
What's your favourite subject?
Girl: My favourite subject is …
Girl: PE.

Starter Unit Lesson 3

Pupil's Book

CD1 TRACK 7

PB page 6 Activity 1

A – B – C – D – E – F – G – H – I – J – K –
L – M – N – O – P – Q – R – S – T – U – V –
W – X – Y – Z

CD1 TRACK 8

PB page 6 Activity 2

Beth: Let's say the alphabet. Say it with me!
Beth, Molly, Jake: A B C D E F G H I J K L M N O P Q R S T U V W X Y Z. That's the end. Let's start again!

CD1 TRACK 9

PB page 6 Activity 3

Boy: How do you spell English?
Girl: E-n-g-l-i-s-h.
Boy: Well done!

Activity Book

CD1 TRACK 10

AB page 4 Activity 1

1 M-a-t-h-s. Maths.
2 S-p-a-n-i-s-h. Spanish.
3 E-n-g-l-i-s-h. English.
4 S-c-i-e-n-c-e. Science.
5 M-u-s-i-c. Music.
6 S-c-h-o-o-l. School.

Starter Unit Lesson 4

Pupil's Book

CD1 TRACK 11

PB page 7 Activity 1

Frame 1
Narrator: Jake and Molly arrive home from school.
Jake: It's very sunny today.
Molly: Yes, it is. It's very hot, too. I'm thirsty.
Jake: Let's go inside and have a drink.
Frame 2
Narrator: Later that evening …
Molly: Is it raining?
Jake: Yes, it is. Listen. It's stormy, too.
Frame 3
Narrator: The next morning, Beth arrives before school.
Beth: Oh no! Look! The bike is wet and dirty.
Jake: I can't ring the bell.
Molly: I know. Let's clean it!
Frame 4
Molly: Ring the bell now, Jake.
Beth: Wow! That's better.
Jake: It's beautiful!
Frame 5
Narrator: The next day, Jake and Molly arrive home from school again.
Jake: It's cloudy today.
Molly: Yes, it is. Let's put the bike inside.
Frame 6
Narrator: Later that evening …
Dad: Oh dear! It's raining again.
Jake: Don't worry, Dad. The magic … the bike is inside.

Unit 1 Lesson 1

Pupil's Book

CD1 TRACK 12

PB page 8 Activity 1

Do you play any sports? song

Do you play any sports? [Point to two different children and raise your shoulders.]
Do you play any sports? [Point to two different children and raise your shoulders.]
I play volleyball and basketball. [Mime hitting a ball along the ground and throwing a basketball into a net.]

Indoors, outdoors, [Gesture down and then open arms wide.]
anywhere is fun. [Punch arms up in the air on fun.]
Come and play with us! [Gesture towards you.]

Do you play any sports? [Point to two different children and raise your shoulders.]
Do you play any sports? [Point to two different children and raise your shoulders.]
I play football and tennis. [Mime kicking a ball and hitting a tennis ball with a racket.]

Indoors, outdoors, [Gesture down and then open arms wide.]
anywhere is fun. [Punch arms up in the air on fun.]
Come and play with us! [Gesture towards you.]

Do you play any sports? [Point to two different children and raise your shoulders.]
Do you play any sports? [Point to two different children and raise your shoulders.]
I go swimming and rollerblading. [Mime overarm swimming and rollerblading.]

Indoors, outdoors, [Gesture down and then open arms wide.]
anywhere is fun. [Punch arms up in the air on fun.]
Come and play with us! [Gesture towards you.]

Do you play any sports? [Point to two different children and raise your shoulders.]
Do you play any sports? [Point to two different children and raise your shoulders.]
I go cycling and skateboarding. [Mime riding a bike and skateboarding: put one arm out in front and the other behind as if balancing on a skateboard.]

Indoors, outdoors, [Gesture down and then open arms wide.]
anywhere is fun. [Punch arms up in the air on fun.]
Come and play with us! [Gesture towards you.]

CD1 TRACK 13

PB page 8 activity 1

Karaoke version: ***Do you play any sports?*** **song**

CD1 TRACK 14

PB page 8 Activity 2

football, basketball, tennis, baseball, skateboarding, cycling, volleyball, rollerblading, hockey, swimming

Unit 1 Lesson 2

Pupil's Book

CD1 TRACK 15

PB page 9 Activity 1

Beth: Molly! Look at this mess! Do you play tennis and basketball?
Molly: Yes, I do. And I go rollerblading.
Beth: Do you go swimming, too?
Molly: Yes, I do. Where are my goggles?
Beth: Here they are!
Molly: Thanks, Beth!

CD1 TRACK 16

PB page 9 Activity 2

1
Beth: Do you play football?
Molly: Yes, I do. I love football!
2
Molly: Do you play tennis?
Beth: No, I don't. I don't like tennis. I like volleyball.
3
Beth: Do you go skateboarding?
Jake: Yes, I do. I love skateboarding!
Beth: Me too! I've got a new skateboard.
Jake: Let's go skateboarding now. Come on!

Unit 1 Lesson 3

Pupil's Book

CD1 TRACK 17

PB page 10 and 11 Activity 1

The very busy week

Frame 1
Narrator: Molly loves sport. Every day, she goes to the sports centre. Every day, she plays a different sport.
Jake: Come on, Molly. Let's go!
Molly: I'm ready!
Frame 2
Narrator: Today is Monday. Molly plays tennis on Monday.
Molly: Come on, Beth. Run!
Beth: I can't hit the ball.
Frame 3
Narrator: Today is Tuesday. Molly plays football on Tuesday.
Molly: Come on, Jake. Kick the ball! Watch out, Beth!
Frame 4
Narrator: Today is Wednesday. Molly plays basketball on Wednesday.
Jake: Molly! Today is basketball.
Molly: Oh no! This is my swimsuit.
Beth: You can't play basketball in a swimsuit.
Frame 5
Narrator: Today is Thursday. Molly goes rollerblading on Thursday.
Beth: Where are your rollerblades, Molly?
Molly: Oh no! These are my football boots.
Beth: Oh dear! You can't go rollerblading in football boots.
Frame 6
Narrator: Today is Friday. Molly goes swimming on Friday.
Jake: Where's your swimsuit, Molly?
Molly: Oh no! This isn't my swimsuit. It's my tennis racket.
Beth: Oh dear! You can't go swimming today, Molly.
Frame 7
Narrator: After the swimming lesson …
Molly: What a mess!
Jake: Don't worry, Molly.
Beth: I know. Magic Bike, please can you help Molly organise her things?
Frame 8
Beth: Look! A tidy box.
Molly: On Saturday, I play baseball and here's my baseball bat. Fantastic!
Jake: Now you can organise your things, Molly.

Unit 1 Lesson 4

Pupil's Book

CD 1 TRACK 18

PB page 12 Activity 1

hit, jump, kick, bounce, throw, catch

CD1 TRACK 19

PB page 12 Activity 2

He's a superstar! **song**

Jump! Kick! Hit the ball!
Throw! Catch! Bounce the ball!

He's a superstar!
He runs like the wind.
He runs and he jumps
And he kicks the ball.
He's a superstar!

Jump! Kick! Hit the ball!
Throw! Catch! Bounce the ball!

She's a superstar!
She runs like the wind.
She throws and she catches
And she bounces the ball.
She's a superstar!

Jump! Kick! Hit the ball!
Throw! Catch! Bounce the ball!

CD1 TRACK 20

PB page 12 Activity 3

Girl: She bounces the ball.
Boy: It's basketball!

Activity Book

CD1 TRACK 21

AB page 9 Activity 1

1
Girl: He bounces the ball. He catches the ball. He throws the ball. He plays basketball!
2
Boy: She kicks the ball. She catches the ball. She throws the ball. She plays football!
3
Girl: He bounces the ball. He throws the ball up in the air. He hits the ball very hard with his racket. He plays tennis!

Unit 1 Lesson 5

Pupil's Book

CD1 TRACK 22

PB page 13 Activity 1

Toby: ai – ay – ai – ay
snails – play – rain – day
Snails play in the rain all day.
Snails play in the rain all day.
Snails play in the rain all day.

CD1 TRACK 23

PB page 13 Activity 2

1
Jake: Beth plays tennis on Monday.
2
Jake: Beth goes swimming on Tuesday.
3
Jake: Beth goes rollerblading on Wednesday.
4
Jake: Beth plays baseball on Thursday.
5
Jake: Beth goes cycling on Friday.
6
Jake: Beth plays hockey on Saturday.
7
Jake: Beth plays football on Sunday.

Audioscript

Unit 1 Lesson 6

Pupil's Book

CD1 TRACK 24

PB page 14 Activity 1

Tom: Hello! I'm Tom.
Anna: And I'm Anna. We go to primary school in England. At school, we have a Sports Day every year. Look at the sports we do.
Tom: This is the egg and spoon race. We put an egg on a spoon and we run to the finish line.
Anna: This is the sack race. We get in a sack and we jump very fast.
Tom: This is the wheelbarrow race. My friend holds my legs and I walk on my hands.
Anna: This is the balloon toss. We throw and catch balloons. Be careful! The balloons contain water.

Activity Book

CD1 TRACK 25

AB page 11 Activity 1

1: What sports do you do on Sports Day?
Boy: I do the sack race. I jump and jump and sometimes I fall over.
2: What sports do you do on Sports Day?
Girl: I do the egg and spoon race. I run to the finish line with the egg on my spoon!
3: What sports do you do on Sports Day?
Boy: I do the wheelbarrow race. I hold my friend's legs and he walks on his hands.
4: What sports do you do on Sports Day?
Girl: I do the balloon toss. My friend throws the balloon and I catch it.

Unit 1 Lesson 7

Pupil's Book

CD1 TRACK 26

PB page 15 Activity 2

Ball! [Cup both hands together in the shape of a ball.]
Big ball, [Open arms wide.]
Small ball, [Hold finger and thumb close together.]
Hockey ball. [Mime hitting a hockey ball.]
Football, [Mime kicking a ball.]
Basketball, [Mime shooting a basket.]
Volleyball, [Mime punching a ball up into the air with two fists.]
Any ball! [Arms out.]
Catch me! [Mime catching a ball.]
Bounce me! [Mime bouncing a ball on the floor.]
Kick me! [Mime kicking a ball.]
Throw me! [Mime throwing a ball.]
Underarm, [Mime an underarm throw.]
Overarm. [Mime an overarm throw.]
BALL! [Cup both hands together in the shape of a ball.]

Unit 1 Lesson 8 Review

Pupil's Book

CD 1 TRACK 27

PB page 16 Activity 1

1
Boy: I play football.
2
Girl: I play basketball.
3
Boy: I go swimming.
4
Girl: I play volleyball.
5
Boy: I play baseball.
6
Girl: I go cycling.
7
Boy: I go rollerblading.
8
Girl: I play tennis.
9
Boy: I play hockey.
10
Girl: I go skateboarding.

CD1 TRACK 28

PB page 16 Activity 2

Girl: Do you play tennis?
Boy: Yes, I do.
Girl: Do you go skateboarding?
Boy: No, I don't.

CD1 TRACK 29

PB page 16 Activity 3

***Well Done!* song**

Well done!
Well done!
Well done everyone!
Let's do a high five!
Well done everyone!
(Repeat)

Unit 1 Video and 21st Century Skills

Activity Book

CD1 TRACK 30

AB page 14 Activity 1

1
Girl: Look, there's Grace! She joins in with all different sports.
Boy: She throws and she catches the ball.
Girl: That's right. She plays volleyball.
2
Girl: Do you play any sports?
Boy: Yes, I do. I play on Monday and Wednesday.
Girl: What sports do you play?
Boy: I play hockey. I'm in a team.
3
Boy: Do you go swimming?
Girl: No, I don't. I go cycling.
4
Girl: Do you join in with sports?
Boy: Yes, I do. I love all sports.
Girl: What's your favourite sport?
Boy: My favourite sport is skateboarding.

Unit 2 Lesson 1

Pupil's Book

CD1 TRACK 31

PB page 18 Activity 1

***Let's go shopping!* song**

Let's go shopping [Mime swinging your arms as if marching off to the shops.]
And buy some food! [Mime paying.]

Bread and meat. [Point to the flashcards.]
Put them in the bag! [Mime putting the food
Yoghurt and peaches, [Continue pointing to all the flashcards and miming putting the food in the bag.]
Bread and meat.
Put them in the bag!

Green beans and carrots,
Yoghurt and peaches,
Bread and meat.
Put them in the bag!

Tomatoes and potatoes,
Green beans and carrots,
Yoghurt and peaches,
Bread and meat.
Put them in the bag!

Sweets and lemons,
Tomatoes and potatoes,
Green beans and carrots,
Yoghurt and peaches,
Bread and meat.
Put them in the bag!

Let's go shopping
And buy some food!

CD1 TRACK 32

PB page 18 Activity 1

Karaoke version: *Let's go shopping!* song

CD1 TRACK 33

PB page 18 Activity 2

bread, pineapples, carrots, potatoes, green beans, tomatoes, yoghurt, sweets, peaches, lemons

Unit 2 Lesson 2

Pupil's Book

CD1 TRACK 34

PB page 19 Activity 1

Shopkeeper: Hello. Can I help you?
Jake: Can I have an apple and a peach, please?
Shopkeeper: Here you are.
Jake: Thank you. And can I have some bread and some carrots, please?
Shopkeeper: Yes, of course.
Jake: Thank you very much. I love carrots. They're delicious!

CD1 TRACK 35

PB page 19 Activity 2

1
Boy: Can I have some green beans, please?
Shopkeeper: Yes, here you are.
2
Girl: Can I have some potatoes, please?
Shopkeeper: Yes, here you are.
3
Boy: Can I have some sweets, please?
Shopkeeper: Sweets aren't good for your teeth! I've got some nice carrots. Carrots are good for you!
Boy: Yes, I like carrots. OK, can I have a carrot, please?
Shopkeeper: Here you are.
Boy: Thank you!
4
Girl: Can I have a yoghurt, please?
Shopkeeper: Yes. Do you want a peach yoghurt or a lemon yoghurt?
Girl: Ooh! A peach yoghurt, please!
Shopkeeper: Here you are.

Unit 2 Lesson 3

Pupil's Book

CD1 TRACK 36

PB pages 20 and 21 Activity 1

The naughty parrot

Frame 1
Narrator: Mum wants Jake and Molly to go to the shop to buy some food for breakfast, lunch and dinner.
Mum: Can you go shopping for me, please? Here's the shopping list and here's some money.
Jake and Molly: OK. Thanks, Mum.
Frame 2
Narrator: Jake and Molly go to the shop on their bike.
Jake: Can I have some bread and some potatoes, please?
Shopkeeper: Yes. Here you are.
Molly: Thank you.
Frame 3
Molly: And can I have some carrots, some tomatoes and a yoghurt, please?
Shopkeeper: Yes. Here you are.
Molly: How much are these green beans?
Shopkeeper: They're 25 cents.
Frame 4
Molly: We've got bread and a peach yoghurt for breakfast.
Toby: Woof!
Jake: Shh, Toby!
Narrator: A naughty parrot takes the bread and the yoghurt.
Frame 5
Molly: We've got green beans and carrots for lunch.
Toby: Woof!
Jake: Toby, stop it!
Narrator: The naughty parrot takes the green beans and the carrots, too.
Frame 6
Molly: We've got potatoes and tomatoes for dinner.
Toby: Woof!
Jake: Toby, what's the matter?
Narrator: The naughty parrot takes the potatoes and the tomatoes. There isn't any food in the bag now.
Frame 7
Jake: Oh no! Where's the food?
Molly: Look! There's a parrot in the tree. It's got our food!
Molly: Magic Bike, can you help?
Frame 8
Jake: Here you are, Mum. We've got all the food for breakfast, lunch and dinner.
Mum: Thank you!

Unit 2 Lesson 4

Pupil's Book

CD1 TRACK 37

PB pages 22 Activity 1

ten, twenty, thirty, forty, fifty

CD1 TRACK 38

PB page 22 Activity 2

***How much is this?* song**

How much is this lemon? [Shrug shoulders and point.]
Ten, twenty, thirty, forty, fifty cents.
It's ten cents. [Show hands in tens.]
Great! I'll take it.

How much is this bread? [Shrug shoulders and point.]
Ten, twenty, thirty, forty, fifty cents.
It's twenty cents. [Show hands in tens.]
Great! I'll take it.

How much are these carrots? [Shrug shoulders and point.]
Ten, twenty, thirty, forty, fifty cents.
They're thirty cents. [Show hands in tens.]
Great! I'll take them.

How much are these sweets? [Shrug shoulders and point.]
Ten, twenty, thirty, forty, fifty cents.
They're forty cents. [Show hands in tens.]
Great! I'll take them.

CD1 TRACK 39

PB page 22 Activity 3

Girl: How much are these?
Boy: They're thirty-six cents.

Activity Book

CD1 TRACK 40

AB page 19 Activity 1

1
Boy: How much are these apples, please?
Shopkeeper: They're fifty cents.
Boy: Thank you.
2
Girl: Hello, how much are these potatoes, please?
Shopkeeper: They're thirty-nine cents.
Girl: Thank you.
3
Shopkeeper: Can I help you?
Boy: How much are these green beans, please?
Shopkeeper: They're twenty-three cents.
Boy: Great! I'll take them.
4
Shopkeeper: Good morning. Can I help you?
Girl: Good morning. How much are these carrots, please?
Shopkeeper: They're thirty-two cents.
Girl: Can I have three carrots, please?
Shopkeeper: Yes, of course.
5
Boy: How much is this peach, please?
Shopkeeper: It's thirteen cents.
Boy: Thank you.
Shopkeeper: Anything else?
Boy: That's all, thank you.
6
Girl: How much is this lemon, please?
Shopkeeper: It's forty-seven cents.
Girl: Thank you.
7
Boy: How much are these tomatoes, please?
Shopkeeper: They're thirty cents.
Boy: Can I have two?
Shopkeeper: What's the magic word?
Boy: Can I have two, please?
Shopkeeper: Here you are.
Boy: Thank you.

Unit 2 Lesson 5

Pupil's Book

CD1 TRACK 41

PB page 23 Activity 1

Toby: ee – ea – ee – ea
Queen – Jean – eats – meat – green – sheep – eats – cheese
Queen Jean eats meat and the green sheep eats cheese.
Queen Jean eats meat and the green sheep eats cheese.
Queen Jean eats meat and the green sheep eats cheese.

CD1 TRACK 42

PB page 23 Activity 2

1
Shopkeeper: Hello. Can I help you?
Boy: Hello. How much is this, please?
Shopkeeper: It's twenty cents.
Boy: Thank you! I'll take it!
2
Girl: How much are these?
Shopkeeper: They're fifty cents.
Girl: Great! I'll take them. Thank you.
3
Boy: How much are these?
Shopkeeper: They're forty-seven cents.
Boy: Great! I'll take them. Thank you!

Audioscript

4
Girl: How much is this?
Shopkeeper: It's thirty cents.
Girl: Thank you! I'll take it!

CD1 TRACK 43

PB page 23 Activity 3

***What do I need to do?* song**

What do I need to do? [Shrug shoulders.]
What do I need to do? [Shrug shoulders.]
Read instructions, [Mime reading.]
They help you. [Wag finger.]

What do I need to do? [Shrug shoulders.]
What do I need to do? [Shrug shoulders.]
Listen to instructions, [Put your hand to your ear.]
They help you. [Wag finger.]

Unit 2 Lesson 6

Pupil's Book

CD1 TRACK 44

PB page 24 Activity 1

Anna: In Britain, there's a special day called Pancake Day. We make pancakes and we have races with them!
Tom: We help Mum make the pancakes. We put flour, milk and two eggs in a bowl. Then, we mix it.
Anna: Mum cooks the pancakes. She tosses a pancake in the air. Then, she catches it again.
Tom: We eat our pancakes. I put chocolate on my pancake. My sister puts sugar and lemon on hers.
Anna: At school, we have pancake races. We run and toss the pancake at the same time. It's good fun!

CD1 TRACK 45

AB page 21 Activity 1

1
Girl: I help Mum make the pancakes.
2
Girl: Mum tosses the pancake in the air.
3
Girl: I put sugar and lemon on my pancake.
4
Girl: At school, we have pancake races.

Unit 2 Lesson 7

Pupil's Book

CD1 TRACK 46

PB page 25 Activity 2

Girl:
Funny face sandwich
This sandwich is easy and fun to make. It's delicious, too!
To make this sandwich you need:
one slice of bread
three slices of cheese
two slices of egg
three olives
one piece of carrot
some salad
Ask an adult to help you.
Instructions:
1 First, put the slices of cheese on the slice of bread.
2 Then, add the eggs for eyes. Put an olive in the centre of each egg.
3 Now, add an olive for the nose and a piece of carrot for the mouth.
4 Finally, add the salad for the hair.

Unit 2 Lesson 8 Review

Pupil's Book

CD1 TRACK 47

PB page 26 Activity 1

1
Boy: Can I have some bread, please?
Shopkeeper: Yes, here you are.
2
Girl: Can I have some tomatoes, please?
Shopkeeper: Yes, here you are.
3
Boy: Can I have a yoghurt, please?
Shopkeeper: Yes, here you are.
4
Girl: Can I have some green beans, please?
Shopkeeper: Yes, here you are.
5
Boy: Can I have some potatoes, please?
Shopkeeper: Yes, here you are.
6
Girl: Can I have some peaches, please?
Shopkeeper: Yes, here you are.
7
Boy: Can I have some pineapples, please?
Shopkeeper: Yes, here you are.
8
Girl: Can I have some lemons, please?
Shopkeeper: Yes, here you are.
9
Boy: Can I have some carrots, please?
Shopkeeper: Yes, here you are.
10
Girl: Can I have some sweets, please?
Shopkeeper: Yes, here you are.

CD1 TRACK 48

PB page 26 Activity 3

***Well Done!* song**

Well done! [Put a left thumb up.]
Well done! [Put a right thumb up.]
Well done everyone! [Put both thumbs up.]
Let's do a high five! [Do a high five with a partner.]
Well done everyone! [Put both thumbs up.]
(Repeat)

Unit 2 Video and 21st Century Skills

Activity Book

CD1 TRACK 49

AB page 24 Activity 1

1
Boy: I'm hungry. Let's cook something for lunch.
Girl: Here's a recipe on my tablet.
Boy: What do we need?
Girl: We need tomatoes, cheese and peppers.
Boy: Pizza! Great! Let's make it.
2
Girl: Let's make something for breakfast.
Boy: Have you got a recipe?
Girl: Let's look on the computer.
Boy: First add the flour and milk.
Girl: Then add the eggs and mix.
Boy: Delicious pancakes.
3
Boy: Let's make a snack.
Girl: Have you got a recipe?
Boy: Here's one on my computer. It's got carrots, eggs, cheese and tomato.
Girl: Great! A funny face sandwich.
4
Girl: Let's make a fruit salad.
Boy: What's in a fruit salad?
Girl: I don't know. Let's look on your phone for a recipe.
Boy: Good idea. Here's one with pineapple, apple, peaches, grapes and pears.
Girl: Let's make it.

Unit 3 Lesson 1

Pupil's Book

CD1 TRACK 50

PB page 28 Activity 1

***I'm a wild animal* song**

I'm a wild animal. I'm dangerous! [Point to yourself and make a scary face.]
I live in the jungle. [Gesture around you.]
I've got four legs [Point to your legs.]
And I'm orange and black. [Point to your body.]
Grrr! I'm a tiger! [Roar and look fierce.]

I'm a wild animal. I'm dangerous! [Point to yourself and make a scary face.]
I live in the grasslands. [Wave your arms from side to side.]
I've got long hair [Point to your hair.]
And I'm yellow and brown. [Point to your body.]
Grrr! I'm a lion! [Roar and look fierce.]

I'm a wild animal. I'm dangerous! [Point to yourself and make a scary face.]
I live in the water. [Mime water.]
I've got a big mouth [Point to your mouth.]
And I'm long and green. [Gesture long.]
Snap! Snap! I'm a crocodile! [Snap your arms together.]

I'm a wild animal. I'm dangerous! [Point to yourself and make a scary face.]
I live in the trees. I've got long arms [Gesture upwards.]
And I climb and climb. [Point to your arms.]

CD1 TRACK 51

PB page 28 Activity 1

Karaoke version: *I'm a wild animal* song

CD1 TRACK 52

PB page 28 Activity 2

crocodile, lion, snake, monkey, penguin, elephant, lizard, giraffe, hippo, tiger

Unit 3 Lesson 2

Pupil's Book

CD1 TRACK 53

PB page 29 Activity 1

Beth: Can you guess my favourite animal?
Jake: Has it got big ears?
Beth: Yes, it has.
Jake: It's an elephant. It's my turn. They're yellow and brown.
Beth: Have they got four legs?
Jake: Yes, they have.
Beth: They're lions.

CD1 TRACK 54

PB page 29 Activity 2

1
Girl: They're small. They've got four legs. They're green and brown.
Boy: Have they got a long tail?
Girl: Yes, they have.
2
Boy: It's long and green. It lives in the water.
Girl: Has it got a big mouth?
Boy: Yes, it has.
3
Boy: It's very long. It's got a long tongue.
Girl: Has it got any legs?
Boy: No, it hasn't.
4
Girl: They're brown and they climb in the trees.
Boy: Have they got long arms?
Girl: Yes, they have.

Unit 3 Lesson 3

Pupil's Book

CD1 TRACK 55

PB page 30 and 31 Activity 1

The mysterious egg

Frame 1
Narrator: Jake, Molly and Beth are at the zoo today.
Jake: I love the zoo! We can see giraffes, elephants and monkeys.
Beth: Come on!
Frame 2
Narrator: Inside the zoo, Beth sees something on the ground.
Beth: Look! What's this?
Jake: I think it's an egg.
Molly: Listen! There's something inside it.
Frame 3
Narrator: The egg hatches and a strange animal appears.
Jake: Wow! What is it?
Molly: I don't know. Let's find out.
Beth: Let's help it find its mum.
Frame 4
Jake: Look. Here's a sign. Giraffe … long neck … eats leaves. Has it got a long neck?
Molly: No, it hasn't.
Beth: It isn't a giraffe. Come on. Let's go this way.
Frame 5
Beth: Look! Here are some eggs.
Molly: These are crocodiles. This baby animal hasn't got big teeth. It's got feathers. It's a bird.
Frame 6
Jake: Look! There's a bird up in the tree.
Molly: How can we get up there?
Beth: Magic Bike, please can you help?
Frame 7
Molly: Oh dear! This bird is very different. This isn't your mum.
Jake: Molly! Beth! Come down! It's a penguin!
Frame 8
Zookeeper: Thank you for helping our lost penguin.
Beth, Jake & Molly: You're welcome.

Unit 3 Lesson 4

Pupil's Book

CD2 TRACK 1

PB page 32 Activity 1

body, teeth, face, wings, tail, beak

CD2 TRACK 2

PB page 32 Activity 2

The animal song

Face, body, teeth and tail. [Point to your face, body and teeth, mime a tail.]
Beak and wings! [Mime a beak and wings.]
A tiger hasn't got a beak. [Shake your finger and mime a beak.]
A tiger hasn't got wings. [Shake your finger and mime wings.]

Face, body, teeth and tail. [Point to your face, body and teeth, mime a tail.]
Beak and wings! [Mime a beak and wings.]

Monkeys haven't got a big face. [Shake your finger and point to your face.]
Monkeys haven't got a big body. [Shake your finger and and point to your body.]

Face, body, teeth and tail. [Point to your face, body and teeth, mime a tail.]
Beak and wings! [Mime a beak and wings.]

A penguin hasn't got a long tail. [Shake your finger and mime a tail.]
A penguin hasn't got teeth. [Shake your finger and mime teeth.]

Face, body, teeth and tail. [Point to your face, body and teeth, mime a tail.]
Beak and wings! [Mime a beak and wings.]

CD2 TRACK 3

PB page 32 Activity 3

Adam: It hasn't got a beak. It's got a long neck.
Libby: It's a giraffe.
Libby: They haven't got wings. They've got big teeth.
Adam: They're crocodiles.

Activity Book

CD2 TRACK 4

AB page 29 Activity 1

1 It hasn't got a beak.
2 It hasn't got a tail.
3 It hasn't got a body.
4 It hasn't got a face.
5 It hasn't got teeth.
6 It hasn't got wings.

Unit 3 Lesson 5

Pupil's Book

CD2 TRACK 5

PB page 33 Activity 1

Toby: oo – ui – oo – ui
kangaroo – goose – swimsuit – fruit – juice – pool
A kangaroo and a goose in a swimsuit drink fruit juice by the pool.
A kangaroo and a goose in a swimsuit drink fruit juice by the pool.
A kangaroo and a goose in a swimsuit drink fruit juice by the pool.

CD2 TRACK 6

PB page 33 Activity 2

1
Boy: It's got four legs. It hasn't got a beak. It's got a tail. It's big. It's black and orange.
Girl: Is it a tiger?
Boy: Yes, it is.
2
Girl: They haven't got hair. They've got a beak and wings, but they can't fly.
Boy: Are they penguins?
Girl: Yes, they are.
3
Girl: It's got a long body. It hasn't got legs. It's got a long tongue!
Boy: Is it a snake?
Girl: Yes, it is.
4
Boy: They haven't got hair. They haven't got a beak or wings. They've got four legs and they are small. They're green.
Girl: Are they lizards?
Boy: Yes, they are.

Audioscript

5
Boy: It's got long legs and a very long neck. It hasn't got a beak. It's got a long black tongue.
Girl: Is it a giraffe?
Boy: Yes, it is.
6
Girl: They've got long hair around their face. They haven't got a beak or wings. They've got a long tail. They're very dangerous!
Boy: Are they lions?
Girl: Yes, they are.

CD2 TRACK 7

PB page 33 Activity 3

***Let's take turns!* song**

Let's take turns.
Let's take turns.
Come on everybody.
Let's take turns.
It's my turn.
It's your turn.
Let's have fun!

Unit 3 Lesson 6

Pupil's Book

CD2 TRACK 8

PB page 34 Activity 1

Tom: Our house has got a big garden. Lots of wild animals come to visit.
Anna: Lots of different birds come into our garden. We put seeds and nuts on a table for the birds.
Tom: Hedgehogs come into the garden, too. We can see them at night.
Anna: Sometimes, a fox comes into the garden. It plays on the grass. We put water in a dish for it.
Tom: Squirrels climb the trees in our garden. They've got a long tail. They're naughty. They eat the bird food.

Activity Book

CD2 TRACK 9

AB page 31 Activity 1

1
Boy: Look at the birds. There's a robin on the bird table.

2
Girl: Look! Next to the pond!
Boy: What can you see?
Girl: It's a hedgehog. Oh! There are two! Can you see them?
Boy: Yes, I can see them now!
3
Boy: Can you see the fox? It's drinking water from the dish.
Girl: Yes! I can see it now.
4
Girl: What's in the tree?
Boy: There are two squirrels.
Girl: Look at their tails!
Boy: Yes! They're really long!

Unit 3 Lesson 7

Pupil's Book

CD2 TRACK 10

PB page 35 Activity 2

Name: Gorilla
Habitat: Gorillas live in the rainforest.
Colour: Gorillas are black.
Size: Gorillas are big.
Characteristics: They've got black hair, small ears and very long arms. Gorillas haven't got a tail. They've got ten fingers and ten toes.
Food: They eat leaves and fruit. Some gorillas eat insects, too.

Name: Polar bear
Habitat: Polar bears live on snow and ice.
Colour: Polar bears are white.
Size: Polar bears are big.
Characteristics: They've got white hair, a big body and four legs. Polar bears have got small ears and a small tail. They've got 42 teeth.
Food: They eat fish and meat.

Unit 3 Lesson 8 Review

Pupil's Book

CD2 TRACK 11

PB page 36 Activity 1

1
Girl: It's got four legs and a big mouth.
Boy: It's a crocodile!

2
Boy: It's got two legs, a beak and wings.
Girl: It's a penguin!
3
Boy: It hasn't got legs. It's got a long body.
Girl: It's a snake!
4
Girl: It's got long legs and a long neck.
Boy: It's a giraffe!
5
Girl: It's got a big body and a very big mouth.
Boy: It's a hippo!
6
Boy: It's got very big ears and a big body.
Girl: It's an elephant!
7
Boy: It's got a long tail and long arms!
Girl: It's a monkey!
8
Girl: It's got a long tail and a lot of hair.
Boy: It's a lion!
9
Girl: It's got short legs. It hasn't got a beak.
Boy: It's a lizard.
10
Boy: It's got a long tail. It hasn't got wings.
Girl: It's a tiger!

CD2 TRACK 12

PB page 36 Activity 3

***Well Done!* song**

Well done! [Put a left thumb up.]
Well done! [Put a right thumb up.]
Well done everyone! [Put both thumbs up.]
Let's do a high five! [Do a high five with a partner.]
Well done everyone! [Put both thumbs up.]
(Repeat)

Unit 3 Video and 21st Century Skills

Activity Book

CD2 TRACK 13

AB page 34 Activity 1

1
Boy: Look at these animals. They've got legs and they've got two eyes.
Girl: ...

Boy: Yes, they have. They haven't got feathers.
Girl: They're monkeys.
2
Girl: Look at these animals. They've got four legs and long tails.
Boy: Have they got sharp teeth?
Girl: Yes, they have. And they're big and dangerous.
Boy: Have they got black and orange stripes?
Girl: Yes, they have.
Boy: Are they tigers?
Girl: That's right!
3
Boy: Look at these animals. They've got four legs. They haven't got beaks and they haven't got feathers.
Girl: Have they got ears?
Boy: Yes. They've got big ears.
Girl: I know! They're elephants.
4
Girl: These animals can swim, but they can't fly.
Boy: Hmmm. Hippos and penguins can swim, and hippos and penguins can't fly.
Girl: They've got tails and two eyes.
Boy: Have they got beaks and feathers?
Girl: No, they haven't.
Boy: They're hippos!

My Project 1 Lesson 1

Pupil's Book

CD2 TRACK 14

PB page 38 Activity 1

1 These are cats.
2 This is a dog.
3 This is a guinea pig.
4 This is a hamster.
5 These are birds.
6 These are turtles.
7 These are stick insects.
8 These are goldfish.
9 These are rabbits.
10 These are spiders.

My Project 1 Lesson 2

Pupil's Book

CD2 TRACK 15

PB page 39 Activity 2

***Listen to others* song**

Listen to others. [Put hand behind right ear.]
Listen, please.
Listen with your ears. [Put hand behind left ear.]
Listen, please.
Listen to others. [Put hand behind both ears.]
Listen, please.
Listen, everybody.

CD2 TRACK 16

PB page 39 Activity 3

Boy: This is my dog. Its name is Bob. Its favourite food is meat. Its favourite toy is a ball. It's brown. It's got four legs and short hair. It lives in my house.
Girl 1 and Girl 2: It's lovely!

Unit 4 Lesson 1

Pupil's Book

CD2 TRACK 17

PB page 40 Activity 1

***I'm going on a nature trail* song**

I'm going on a nature trail. [Swing your arms and march on the spot.]
I'm having lots of fun! [Throw your arms up in the air.]
I can run, run, run in the long, green grass. [Run on the spot.]
I can jump, jump, jump in the leaves. [Jump on the spot.]

I'm going on a nature trail. [Swing your arms and march on the spot.]
I'm having lots of fun! [Throw your arms up in the air.]
I can walk, walk, walk in a big, dark forest. [Walk on the spot.]
I can climb, climb, climb a hill. [Climb on the spot.]

I'm going on a nature trail. [Swing your arms and march on the spot.]
I'm having lots of fun! [Throw your arms up in the air.]
I can swim, swim, swim in the deep, blue lake. [Mime swimming.]
I can play, play, play in the sand. [Mime playing.]

CD2 TRACK 18

PB page 40 Activity 1

Karaoke version: *I'm going on a nature trail* song

CD2 TRACK 19

PB page 40 Activity 2

forest, hill, grass, river, leaves, lake, sand, road, path, bridge

Unit 4 Lesson 2

Pupil's Book

CD2 TRACK 20

PB page 41 Activity 1

Beth's mum: Hello, Beth! What are you doing?
Beth: Can you guess?
Mum: Are you running along a path?
Beth: No, I'm not.
Mum: Oh, Beth! Are you climbing a tree?
Beth: No, I'm not. Don't worry, Mum. I'm climbing a big hill.

CD2 TRACK 21

PB page 41 Activity 2

1
Molly: What are you doing, Beth?
Beth: Can you guess?
Molly: Are you jumping in the leaves?
Beth: No, I'm not.
Molly: Are you playing in the sand?
Beth: Yes, I am!
2
Beth: What are you doing, Molly?
Molly: Can you guess?
Beth: Are you climbing a hill?
Molly: No, I'm not!
Beth: Are you running in the grass?
Molly: Yes, I am!
3
Beth: What are you doing, Jake?
Jake: Can you guess?
Beth: Are you swimming in the lake?
Jake: No, I'm not.
Beth: I don't know! What are you doing?
Jake: I'm walking along the path.

Unit 4 Lesson 3

Pupil's Book

CD2 TRACK 22

PB page 42 and 43 Activity 1

What's Toby doing?

Frame 1
Jake: Let's go on the nature trail.
Molly: Yes, come on!
Beth: Let's go!
Frame 2
Molly: Look! A cycle path. Let's ride along here.
Jake: Good idea!
Beth: What's Toby doing?
Jake: He's running up the hill.
Frame 3
Beth: What's Toby doing now?
Jake: He's rolling down the hill.
Molly: Why's he doing that?
Frame 4
Jake: Now he's jumping in the lake.
Molly: He's a crazy dog!
Beth: What's the matter with Toby today?
Frame 5
Jake: Oh no! He's chasing the sheep!
Beth: Toby! What are you doing? Come here!
Frame 6
Beth: Look at Toby now! He's running in the flowers.
Molly: He's coming this way.
Jake: Catch him!
Frame 7
Jake: Toby has got something in his nose.
Molly: They're spines from a hedgehog.
Beth: Magic Bike, please can you help Toby?
Frame 8
Jake: That's better!
Beth: Poor Toby.
Molly: Thank you, Magic Bike!

Unit 4 Lesson 4

Pupil's Book

CD2 TRACK 23

PB page 44 Activity 1

He's running up the hill.
He's running down the hill.
He's running along the path.
He's running across the bridge.

CD2 TRACK 24

PB page 44 Activity 2

***What's he doing?* song**

What's he doing? [Hold your arms out questioningly.]
He's running up the hill. [Mime running.]
Is he running down the hill? [Point down.]
No! He's running up the hill! [Shake your head and point up.]

What's she doing? [Hold your arms out questioningly.]
She's walking along the path. [Mime walking.]
Is she walking along the road? [Move both arms in a parallel motion.]
No! She's walking along the path! [Shake your hand and wiggle your hand around like a windy path.]

What's he doing? [Hold your arms out questioningly.]
He's sailing across the lake. [Mime pulling at sailing ropes.]
Is he sailing across the river? [Mime a river by separating your hands slowly.]
No! He's sailing across the lake. [Mime a big lake by throwing your arms out wide.]

What's she doing? [Hold your arms out questioningly.]
She's rolling down the hill! CRASH! [Roll one arm over the other and cover your eyes.]

CD2 TRACK 25

PB page 44 Activity 3

Girl: What's she doing? Is she jumping in the leaves?
Boy: No, she isn't.
Girl: Is she running down a hill?
Boy: Yes, she is. Well done!

Audioscript

CD2 TRACK 26

PB page 44 Activity 4

***Calm down* song**

Let's calm down. [Put your palms face down, lower your hands.]
Let's calm down. [Put your palms face down, lower your hands.]
Breathe in, breathe out. [Breathe in and out deeply]
Now let's count.
1, 2, 3, 4, 5 [Count on your fingers.]
Let's calm down. [Put your palms face down, lower your hands.]

Activity Book

CD2 TRACK 27

AB page 41 Activity 1

1
Girl: He's riding a horse across the sand.
2
Boy: She's walking down the hill.
3
Girl: He's running up the hill.
4
Boy: She's riding a bike along the road.
5
Girl: She's swimming across the lake.

Unit 4 Lesson 5

Pupil's Book

CD2 TRACK 28

PB page 45 Activity 1

Toby: or – al – or – al
horse – shorts – walks – talks – storm
The horse in shorts walks and talks in a storm.
The horse in shorts walks and talks in a storm.
The horse in shorts walks and talks in a storm.

CD2 TRACK 29

PB page 45 Activity 2

1
Girl: Where's Sally?
Boy: She's walking along the path.
Girl: Thank you.
2
Boy: Where's Ben?
Girl: He's running down the hill.
Boy: Thank you.
3
Boy: Where's May?
Girl: She's jumping in the leaves.
Boy: Thank you.
4
Girl: Where's Sue?
Boy: She's climbing a tree.
Girl: Thank you.
5
Girl: Where's Bill?
Boy: He's sailing along the river.
Girl: Thank you.
6
Boy: Where's Nick?
Girl: He's swimming in the lake.
Boy: Thank you.

Unit 4 Lesson 6

Pupil's Book

CD2 TRACK 30

PB page 46 Activity 1

Tom: We sometimes go on school trips. Today, we're at a forest school. It's great fun!
Tom: We learn how to make a den from tree branches, twigs and leaves.
Anna: My favourite activity is exploring a tree. I can touch and smell the tree, but I can't see it.
Tom: We make mud pies and decorate them with flowers and leaves.
Anna: We go on a minibeast hunt. We count all the animals we see in the forest.

Activity Book

CD2 TRACK 31

AB page 43 Activity 1

1
Girl: We're at a forest school. It's great fun. We make a den from branches, twigs and leaves.
2
Boy: We make mud pies. We decorate our pies with leaves and flowers. They look delicious, but you can't eat them!
3
Girl: It's great fun to go on a minibeast hunt. We look under rocks and leaves for animals that live in the forest. Sometimes we see caterpillars, butterflies and worms.

Unit 4 Lesson 7

Pupil's Book

CD2 TRACK 32

PB page 47 Activity 2

The adventures of Adam Jones

Frame 1
Narrator: Adam Jones is walking along the beach. He finds an old map in the sand.
Adam: What's this?
Frame 2
Narrator: He sails across the lake to find the treasure.
Frame 3
Narrator: He crosses an old rope bridge.
Frame 4
Narrator: He isn't afraid of the big, dark cave.
Adam: What's in here?
Frame 5
Narrator: There's a secret passage!
Frame 6
Narrator: Mummies chase Adam. At last, he escapes.
Frame 7
Narrator: There are giant spiders. Adam shines his torch and the spiders run away.
Frame 8
Narrator: Finally, he finds the treasure …
Adam: Fantastic. And another map!
Narrator: Next time, read about Adam and the pirate ship.

Unit 4 Lesson 8 Review

Pupil's Book

CD2 TRACK 33

PB page 48 Activity 1

1
Boy: What are you doing?
Girl: I'm sailing across the river!
2
Girl: What are you doing?
Boy: I'm walking across the bridge.
3
Girl: What are you doing?
Boy: I'm playing in the sand.
4
Boy: What are you doing?
Girl: I'm walking across the road.
5
Boy: What are you doing?
Girl: I'm running down the hill.
6
Girl: What are you doing?
Boy: I'm walking along the path.
7
Girl: What are you doing?
Boy: I'm playing in the leaves.
8
Boy: What are you doing?
Girl: I'm sailing across the lake.
9
Boy: What are you doing?
Girl: I'm running in the grass.
10
Girl: What are you doing?
Boy: I'm walking in the forest.

CD2 TRACK 34

PB page 48 Activity 2

Boy: Are you climbing up a hill?
Girl: No, I'm not.
Boy: Are you swimming across a lake?
Girl: Yes, I am.

CD2 TRACK 35

PB page 48 Activity 3

***Well Done!* song**

Well done! [Put a left thumb up.]
Well done! [Put a right thumb up.]
Well done everyone! [Put both thumbs up.]
Let's do a high five! [Do a high five with a partner.]
Well done everyone! [Put both thumbs up.]
(Repeat)

Unit 4 Video and 21st Century Skills

Activity Book

CD2 Track 36

AB page 46 Activity 1

1
Boy: Where are you going today?
Girl: I'm going to the forest.
Boy: Don't walk on the plants!
Girl: Don't worry. I walk on the path in the forest.
2
Girl: Where are you going?
Boy: I'm going to the lake.
Girl: Do you want to take some nuts for the squirrels?
Boy: No. I don't feed wild animals at the lake.
3
Boy: Where are you going to today?
Girl: I'm going to the park.
Boy: There are lots of signs in the park.
Girl: That's right. It's important to respect the signs in the park.
4
Girl: Where are you going?
Boy: I'm going to the river. We're having a picnic today.
Girl: Don't leave your rubbish there.
Boy: Don't worry. I put my rubbish in the bin at the river.

Unit 5 Lesson 1

Pupil's Book

CD2 TRACK 37

PB page 50 Activity 1

***We're going to the lake* song**

We're going to the lake. [Swing your arms back and forth to imply movement.]
We're skating on the ice. [Pretend to skate.]
Wave and smile! [Wave and put a finger either side of your mouth.]
Are you ready? [Put your hands out questioningly.]
Take a photo. [Mime taking a photo.]
That's nice! [Thumbs up.]
We're going to the lake. [Swing your arms back and forth to imply movement.]
We're making a snowman. [Mime patting down the snow.]
Wave and smile! [Wave and put a finger either side of your mouth.]
Are you ready? [Put your hands out questioningly.]
Take a photo. [Mime taking a photo.]
That's nice! [Thumbs up.]

We're going to the lake. [Swing your arms back and forth to imply movement.]
We're drinking hot chocolate. [Mime drinking.]
Wave and smile! [Wave and put a finger either side of your mouth.]
Are you ready? [Put your hands out questioningly.]
Take a photo. [Mime taking a photo.]
That's nice! [Thumbs up.]

CD2 TRACK 38

PB page 50 Activity 1

Karaoke version: *We're going to the lake* song

CD2 TRACK 39

PB page 50 Activity 2

drink, skate, wave, smile, dance, make a snowman, eat, take a photo, play, listen to music

Unit 5 Lesson 2

Pupil's Book

CD2 TRACK 40

PB page 51 Activity 1

Molly: Jake! Look at us!
Jake: What are you doing?
Beth: We're skating on the ice. Take a photo. Quickly!
Jake: Are you dancing?
Beth: Yes, we are. Look!
Jake: That's a great photo.

CD2 TRACK 41

PB page 51 Activity 2

1
Beth: Jake! Molly! What are you doing?
Molly: We're making a snowman. Come and help!
2
Mum: Jake! Molly! What are you doing?
Molly: We're listening to music.
3
Mum: Where are Beth and Jake?
Dad: There they are. Look! They're waving!
4
Molly: Guess what we're doing!
Beth: Are you eating cakes?
Jake: No, we aren't.
Beth: Are you drinking hot chocolate?
Molly: Yes, we are.

Unit 5 Lesson 3

Pupil's Book

CD2 TRACK 42

PB page 52 and 53 Activity 1

The snowman

Frame 1
Narrator: Jake and Molly are playing in their garden.
Beth: Hello! What are you doing?
Jake: We're making a snowman.
Molly: Look! He's got a fat tummy.
Frame 2
Jake: These are his arms.
Molly: And these are his eyes.
Beth: And here's a carrot for his nose.
Frame 3
Molly: Let's go to the park!
Jake: We can't go on the bike. It's snowing.
Beth: Magic Bike, can you help?
Frame 4
Jake: Wow! It's a sledge.
Molly: We can go to the park now.
Beth: Fantastic!
Frame 5
Molly: Look at the snowman.
Beth: He's moving.
Jake: He's alive!
Frame 6
Jake: What's he doing?
Molly: He's taking the magic bike.
Beth: Stop!
Frame 7
Narrator: Jake, Molly, Beth and Toby run after the snowman.
Beth: Come back!
Molly: That's our bike.
Jake: Stop!
Frame 8
Narrator: The snowman goes back for the children. They go sledging down the hill.
Molly: This is fun!
Jake: Wheee!

Unit 5 Lesson 4

Pupil's Book

CD2 TRACK 43

PB page 54 Activity 1

a fat snowman, a thin snowman, a short snowman, a tall snowman, a clean snowman, a dirty snowman

CD2 TRACK 44

PB page 54 Activity 2

***What are they doing?* song**

What are they doing?
They're playing in the snow.
Are they making a snowman?
I don't know.

He's got a dirty hat.
He's got a fat tummy.
His nose is a big, orange carrot.
He's got thin arms.
He's got a clean scarf.
His eyes are small, black stones.

What are they doing?
They're playing in the snow.
Are they making a snowman?
I think so!

CD2 TRACK 45

PB page 54 Activity 3

Girl: He's got a fat tummy. He's got a dirty hat. He's a short snowman.
Boy: Is it number 2?
Girl: Yes, it is.

Activity Book

CD2 TRACK 46

AB page 51 Activity 1

1
Girl: What are they doing?
Boy: They're making a snowman! He's a tall snowman. He's got a big carrot for a nose and small black stones for his eyes.

Audioscript

2
Boy: What are they doing?
Girl: Look! They're making a snowman! He's got a fat tummy and long, thin arms.
3
Boy: What are they doing?
Girl: They're making a snowman. Look! He's got a clean scarf and a clean hat. He's a short snowman!
4
Girl: What are they doing?
Boy: They're making a big snowman! He's got a fat tummy and a dirty hat.

Unit 5 Lesson 5

Pupil's Book

CD2 TRACK 47

PB page 55 Activity 1

Toby: ow – oa – ow – oa
snowman – goat – coat – row – yellow – boat – rainbow
A snowman and a goat in a coat row a yellow boat to the rainbow.
A snowman and a goat in a coat row a yellow boat to the rainbow.
A snowman and a goat in a coat row a yellow boat to the rainbow.

CD2 TRACK 48

PB page 55 Activity 2

1
Boy: They're dancing.
2
Girl: They're drinking hot chocolate.
3
Boy: They're listening to music.
4
Girl: They're taking a photo.
5
Boy: They're skating on the ice.
6
Girl: They're eating.

CD2 TRACK 49

PB page 55 Activity 3

***Sharing is a good thing to do* song**
Pencils, rubbers, scissors, too.
You share with me,
I share with you.
Sharing is a good thing to do.
Yes! Sharing is a good thing to.

Unit 5 Lesson 6

Pupil's Book

CD2 TRACK 50

PB page 56 Activity 1

Tom: In Britain, we can do winter activities all year. We go to a snow centre.
Anna: My brother and I go skating on the ice rink with our friends. Lots of people come here all year round.
Tom: There's a dry ski slope. We go skiing here.
Anna: We go tubing on the dry ski slope, too. It's great fun.
Anna: We can ride on a toboggan here, too. It's our favourite activity!

Activity Book

CD2 TRACK 51

AB page 53 Activity 1

1
Girl: Let's go skiing
Boy: We can't go skiing today, it isn't snowing.
Girl: We can go skiing on a dry ski slope.
Boy: Oh, yes! Fantastic!
2
Boy: What can we do today?
Girl: Let's ride on a toboggan.
Boy: Let's try it.
Girl: Fantastic!
3
Boy: That looks fun!
Girl: What are they doing?
Boy: They're tubing down a hill.
Girl: Let's try it!
4
Boy: Look at those boys.
Girl: They're dancing on the ice.
Boy: Let's go skating.
Girl: Yes, come on. I love the ice rink!

Unit 5 Lesson 7

Pupil's Book

CD2 TRACK 52

PB page 57 Activity 2

The ants and the grasshopper
It's summer. A grasshopper sees some ants. The grasshopper is singing and dancing. The ants are working.
"Hello, ants! What are you doing?" asks the grasshopper.
"We're working. We're collecting food for winter," answer the ants.
"You're silly!" says the grasshopper. "It's summer! Come and play."
"No," answer the ants. "Winter is coming."

In autumn, the grasshopper is still singing and dancing. The ants are still working.
"Hello, ants! What are you doing?" asks the grasshopper.
"We're working. We're collecting food for winter," answer the ants.
"You're so silly!" says the grasshopper.
In winter, the ants are happy. They're eating their food. The grasshopper is cold and hungry.
"I'm hungry!" says the grasshopper. "Can I have some food?"
"No," answer the ants. "Go and look for food in the snow!"

Unit 5 Lesson 8 Review

Pupil's Book

CD2 TRACK 53

PB page 58 Activity 1

1
Girl: Are they playing in the snow?
Boy: Yes, they are.
2
Boy: Are you making a snowman?
Girl: Yes, we are.
3
Boy: Are they drinking hot chocolate?
Girl: Yes, they are.
4
Boy: Are you taking a photo?
Girl: Yes, we are.
5
Girl: Are they skating?
Boy: Yes, they are.
6
Boy: Are you waving?
Girl: Yes, we are.
7
Boy: Are they dancing?
Girl: Yes, they are.
8
Girl: Are you listening to music?
Boy: Yes, we are.
9
Boy: Are they eating?
Girl: Yes, they are.
10
Boy: Are you smiling?
Girl: Yes, we are.

CD2 TRACK 54

PB page 58 Activity 2

Boy: Are you skating on the ice?
Girl 1 and Girl 2: No, we aren't.
Boy: Are you waving and smiling?
Girl 1 and Girl 2: Yes, we are.

CD2 TRACK 55

PB page 58 Activity 3

***Well Done!* song**
Well done!
Well done!
Well done everyone!
Let's do a high five!
Well done everyone!
(Repeat)

Unit 5 Video and 21st Century Skills

Activity Book

CD2 TRACK 56

AB page 56 Activity 1

Boy: My snowman is tall and thin. He's got twigs for arms and leaves for hair. He's got an apple for a nose.
Girl: He's fantastic.
2
Girl: My snowman is big. He's got a fat tummy. He's got twigs for arms and a carrot

Boy: Ha ha.
3
Boy: My snowman is clean. He's got a hat and a scarf. He's got an orange for a nose.
Girl: He's funny.
4
Girl: My snowman is short. He's got long arms and short legs. He's got grass for hair and a lemon for a nose.
Boy: Cool!

Unit 6 Lesson 1

Pupil's Book

CD3 TRACK 1

PB page 60 Activity 1

***What's your favourite season?* song**

What's your favourite season? [Shrug your shoulders.]
Is it spring? [Point to the spring flashcard.]
Spring, when it's warm outside. [Rub your arms and smile as if you are warm.]
We smell flowers. [Put your hand to your nose and mime smelling a flower.]
We plant seeds. [Mime planting seeds.]
My favourite season is spring. [Turn around full circle.]

What's your favourite season? [Shrug your shoulders.]
Is it summer? [Point to the summer flashcard.]
Summer, when it's hot outside. [Fan yourself.]
We finish school. [Gesture around you.]
We go to the beach. [Walk on the spot.]
My favourite season is summer. [Turn around full circle.]

What's your favourite season? [Shrug your shoulders.]
Is it autumn? [Point to the autumn flashcard.]
Autumn, when it's cool outside. [Rub your arms and huddle into yourself as if you are cool.]
We eat chestnuts. [Mime eating.]
We celebrate Halloween. [Pretend to be a ghost.]
My favourite season is autumn. [Turn around full circle.]

What's your favourite season? [Shrug your shoulders.]
Is it winter? [Point to the winter flashcard.]
Winter, when it's cold outside. [Pretend to shiver.]
We wear warm clothes. [Mime putting on a scarf.]
We open presents. [Mime opening a present.]
My favourite season is winter. [Turn around full circle.]

CD3 TRACK 2

PB page 60 Activity 1

Karaoke version: *What's your favourite season?* song

CD3 TRACK 3

PB page 60 Activity 2

smell flowers, plant seeds, finish school, go to the beach, eat chestnuts, celebrate Halloween, wear warm clothes, open presents

Unit 6 Lesson 2

Pupil's Book

CD3 TRACK 4

PB page 61 Activity 1

Beth: Look! I've got a postcard from my cousins Dan and Grace.
Jake: Where do they live?
Beth: They live in America.
Jake: Fantastic! What do they do in summer in America?
Beth: They go to the beach.
Jake: We go to the beach, too. Do they celebrate Halloween?
Beth: Yes, they do.

CD3 TRACK 5

PB page 61 Activity 2

1
Beth: What do you do in autumn?
Molly: We eat chestnuts in autumn.
2
Jake: What do you do in spring?
Beth: We smell flowers in spring.
3
Molly: What do your cousins do in winter?
Beth: They open presents in winter.

Unit 6 Lesson 3

Pupil's Book

CD3 TRACK 6

PB page 62 and 63 Activity 1

The four seasons

Frame 1
Narrator: Beth's cousins are visiting from America. Jake, Molly and Beth are doing a project for school.
Jake: We're doing a project about the seasons.
Dan: We can help you.
Molly: Great!
Grace: We've got our camera.
Frame 2
Molly: How can you take photos of all the seasons in one day?
Beth: That's impossible.
Jake: Be careful with the bike, Dan. You're pedalling backwards.
Frame 3
Narrator: Suddenly …
Jake: Look at the tree! The magic bike can change the seasons.
Beth: Yes. It's spring. I can smell flowers.
Grace: Let's take a photo.
Frame 4
Narrator: The wheels of the magic bike go faster and faster.
Beth: What's happening?
Molly: It's summer now. Look at the green leaves.
Jake: Don't stop, Dan!
Frame 5
Narrator: It's autumn now.
Molly: There are chestnuts on the tree.
Jake: Do you eat chestnuts in America, too?
Dan: Yes, we do.
Frame 6
Narrator: It's winter now.
Molly: Brr! It's cold.
Beth: Look at the tree. It hasn't got leaves now.
Jake: The bike is stopping.
Frame 7
Molly: Let's go and make a poster together.
Beth: Yes. We've got lots of photos for our project now.
Frame 8
Narrator: The next day …
Jake: Look at our project.
Beth: What do you think?
Beth's Dad: It's amazing!
Beth's Mum: Well done, children.

Unit 6 Lesson 4

Pupil's Book

CD3 TRACK 7

PB page 64 Activity 1

first, second, third, fourth, fifth, sixth, seventh, eighth, ninth, tenth, eleventh, twelfth, thirteenth, fourteenth, fifteenth, sixteenth, seventeenth, eighteenth, nineteenth, twentieth, twenty-first

CD3 TRACK 8

PB page 64 Activity 2

***When's your birthday?* song**

My birthday is my favourite day.
Cake and presents.
Hooray!

When's your birthday?
When's your birthday?
My birthday is on the ninth of May.
Do you want to come to my party?

When's your birthday?
When's your birthday?
My birthday is on the eighth of June.
Do you want to come to my party?

When's your birthday?
When's your birthday?
My birthday is on the twelfth of July.
Do you want to come to my party?

CD3 TRACK 9

PB page 64 Activity 3

Boy: When's your birthday?
Girl: My birthday is on the twenty-first of February.

Activity Book

CD3 TRACK 10

AB page 61 Activity 1

1
Boy: How old are you?
Girl: I'm six.

Audioscript

Boy: I'm seven. When's your birthday?
Girl: My birthday's on the fourteenth of May.
2
Boy: My birthday's on the seventeenth of August. When's yours?
Girl: My birthday's on the seventeenth of August, too!
3
Girl: When's your birthday?
Boy: It's in October.
Girl: What date?
Boy: My birthday is on the sixteenth of October. Do you want to come to my party?
Girl: Oh! Yes, please!
4
Girl: When's your birthday?
Boy: My birthday's on the thirteenth of January.
Girl: The thirtieth or the thirteenth?
Boy: The thirteenth of January.

Unit 6 Lesson 5

Pupil's Book

CD3 TRACK 11

PB page 65 Activity 1

Toby: ur – ir – ur – ir
purple – turtle's – birthday – first – third
Is the purple turtle's birthday on the first or the third?
Is the purple turtle's birthday on the first or the third?
Is the purple turtle's birthday on the first or the third?

CD3 TRACK 12

PB page 65 Activity 2

***We can do it!* song**

We can do it!
We can do it!
Yeah!
We can do it!
We can do it!
Yeah!
Come on everybody!
Come on everybody!
We can do it!
We can do it!
Yeah!

CD3 TRACK 13

PB page 65 Activity 3

1
Boy: When's your birthday, Ann?
Girl: My birthday is in May. It's on the 27th of May.
Boy: May? OK. How do you spell your name?
Girl: A – N – N.
Boy: Thanks.
2
Boy: When's your birthday, Tony?
Boy: My birthday is in April. It's on the 7th of April.
Boy: April? OK. How do you spell your name?
Boy: T – O – N – Y.
Boy: Great! Thanks.
3
Boy: Hello, Lucy. When's your birthday?
Girl: My birthday is in March. It's on the 31st of March.
Boy: March? OK. How do you spell your name?
Girl: L – U – C – Y.
Boy: Thank you.
4
Girl: When's your birthday, Nick?
Boy: My birthday is in January. It's on the 29th of January.
Girl: Great! How do you spell your name?
Boy: N – I – C – K.
Girl: Thanks.

Unit 6 Lesson 6

Pupil's Book

CD3 TRACK 14

PB page 66 Activity 1

Anna: In Britain, we celebrate festivals in the four seasons. These are our favourite festivals.
Tom: The first of April is April Fools' Day. We play jokes and we have a lot of fun!
Anna: Notting Hill Carnival is in August. There's a parade and people play the drums.
Tom: Remember, remember, the fifth of November! It's Bonfire Night. We make a guy doll for a big bonfire.
Anna: On the twenty-fifth of December, it's Christmas. We eat turkey for Christmas lunch. We pull crackers and we wear paper hats, too.

Unit 6 Lesson 7

Pupil's Book

CD3 TRACK 15

PB page 67 Activity 2

There are thirty days in September,
April, June and November.
All the rest have thirty-one,
Except for February alone.
And that has twenty-eight days clear,
And twenty-nine in each leap year!

Unit 6 Lesson 8 Review

Pupil's Book

CD3 TRACK 16

PB page 68 Activity 1

1
Girl: They open presents in winter.
2
Boy: We go to the beach in summer.
3
Girl: They celebrate Halloween in autumn.
4
Boy: We plant seeds in spring.
5
Girl: They eat chestnuts in autumn.
6
Boy: We wear warm clothes in winter.
7
Boy: They finish school in summer.
8
Girl: We smell flowers in spring.

CD3 TRACK 17

PB page 68 Activity 3

***Well Done!* song**

Well done!
Well done!
Well done everyone!
Let's do a high five!
Well done everyone!
(Repeat)

Activity Book

CD3 TRACK 18

AB page 65 Activity 1

1
Molly: We open our presents on the twenty-fifth of December.
2
Jake: We finish school on the twenty-seventh of July.
3
Beth: We plant seeds on the eighth of April.
4
Jake: We go to the beach on the tenth of August.

Unit 6 Video and 21st Century Skills

Activity Book

CD3 TRACK 19

AB page 66 Activity 1

1
Girl: What's your favourite season?
Boy: My favourite season is spring.
Girl: Why?
Boy: My birthday is in spring.
Girl: When's your birthday?
Boy: It's on the 5th of May.
2
Boy: When's your birthday?
Girl: My birthday is in winter.
Boy: What date?
Girl: My birthday is on the 19th of December.
3
Girl: Where are you going to on holiday?
Boy: I'm going to England.
Girl: Fantastic! Are you going in summer?
Boy: Yes. I'm going on the 14th August.
4
Boy: What's your favourite season?
Girl: My favourite season is autumn because it's my birthday.
Boy: When's your birthday?
Girl: It's on the 9th of November.
Boy: That's my sister's birthday, too.

My Project 2 Lesson 1

Pupil's Book

CD3 TRACK 20

PB page 70 Activity 1

1
Woman: footballer
2
Woman: pilot
3
Woman: doctor
4
Woman: vet
5
Woman: dancer
6
Woman: teacher
7
Woman: firefighter
8
Woman: artist
9
Woman: cook
10
Woman: police officer

CD3 TRACK 21

PB page 70 Activity 2

A police officer wears a uniform.
A doctor helps people.
A pilot flies a plane.
A teacher teaches children.
A vet helps animals.
A firefighter puts out fires.

My Project 2 Lesson 2

Pupil's Book

CD3 TRACK 22

PB page 71 Activity 2

***It's fun to work together!* song**

Together, together,
It's fun to work together.
You and me,
Me and you.
It's fun to work together.
(Repeat)

CD3 TRACK 23

PB page 71 Activity 3

Child 1: She's a vet.
Child 2: She wears a white coat.
Child 3: She helps animals.

Unit 7 Lesson 1

Pupil's Book

CD3 TRACK 24

PB page 72 Activity 1

***There's a mouse in my house!* song**

There's a mouse in my house! [Wiggle two fingers like a mouse.]
Where can it be? [Shrug your shoulders.]
Is it in the living room, watching TV? [Mime changing channel.]
Is it in the bathroom, having a shower? [Mime washing yourself in the shower.]
Is it in the garden, watering the flowers? [Mime watering flowers.]

There's a mouse in my house! [Wiggle two fingers like a mouse.]
Where can it be? [Shrug your shoulders.]
Is it in the kitchen, eating all the food? [Mime eating.]
Is it in the hall, playing in my shoes? [Mime putting shoes on.]

There's a mouse in my house! [Wiggle two fingers like a mouse.]
Where can it be? [Shrug your shoulders.]
Is it in the dining room, eating all the bread? [Mime eating.]
Is it in the bedroom, under the bed? [Mime looking under a bed.]

There's a mouse in my house! [Wiggle two fingers like a mouse.]
Where can it be? [Shrug your shoulders.]
Is it in the garage, running on the floor? [Gesture outside.]
Run outside little mouse! Quick, shut the door! [Mime closing a door.]

CD3 TRACK 25

PB page 72 Activity 1

Karaoke version: *There's a mouse in my house!* song

CD3 TRACK 26

PB page 72 Activity 2

flat, house, living room, kitchen, bathroom, bedroom, dining room, hall, garden, garage

Unit 7 Lesson 2

Pupil's Book

CD3 TRACK 27

PB page 73 Activity 1

Beth: This is my new house. There's a kitchen and there are three bedrooms. There isn't a garden and there aren't any plants.
Molly: Can we see it?
Beth: Yes, of course. Come in.

CD3 TRACK 28

PB page 73 Activity 2

a
Boy: There's a hall and a big kitchen. There are three small bedrooms. There isn't a dining room. There are lots of plants.
b
Girl: My flat is small. There are two bedrooms and there's one bathroom. There aren't any plants. There's a garage.
c
Boy: There are two bedrooms and two bathrooms. There's a kitchen and there's a living room. There isn't a garage and there isn't a garden.
d
Girl: There's one bathroom and there's a kitchen. There's a living room, too. There aren't any bedrooms and there isn't a garden.

Unit 7 Lesson 3

Pupil's Book

CD3 TRACK 29

PB page 74 and 75 Activity 1

The haunted house

Frame 1
Narrator: Jake, Molly, Beth and Toby are at the funfair.
Beth: Here's the haunted house.
Molly: There are ghosts, witches and skeletons in the haunted house.
Jake: Let's go inside. I'm not scared.
Frame 2
Beth: Look! There's a haunted living room with a haunted sofa.
Molly: Wow! There's a haunted armchair, too.
Jake: There aren't any ghosts here. I'm not scared.
Frame 3
Beth: Look! There's a haunted bathroom with a haunted bath.
Molly: And there's a haunted shower.
Jake: There aren't any skeletons here. I'm not scared!
Frame 4
Beth: Look! There's a haunted bedroom with a haunted bed.
Molly: There's a haunted mirror, too.
Jake: There aren't any witches here. I'm not scared, but look at Toby! He's scared.
Frame 5
Beth: Look! There's a haunted dining room with a haunted piano.
Jake: Look at Toby now! He's really scared.
Molly: Oh yes!
Frame 6
Molly: I love haunted houses. They're great!
Jake: There aren't any ghosts, witches or skeletons.
Frame 7
Jake: Where's Toby?
Molly: I don't know.
Beth: Let's look for him.
Frame 8
Molly: It's a ghost
Beth: Run!
Jake: I'm scared!

Unit 7 Lesson 4

Pupil's Book

CD3 TRACK 30

PB page 76 Activity 1

camera, clock, radio, box, phone, watch

Audioscript

CD3 TRACK 31

PB page 76 Activity 2

***What a mess!* song**

What a mess! [Raise your hands in the air.]
Whose is this? [Shrug your shoulders.]
Whose is this box? [Mime holding a box.]
Is it his? [Point to a boy and shrug your shoulders.]
No. It's mine. [Point to yourself.]

What a mess! [Raise your hands in the air.]
Whose is this? [Shrug your shoulders.]
Whose is this watch? [Point to your wrist.]
Is it hers? [Point to a girl.]
No. It's mine. [Point to yourself.]

What a mess! [Raise your hands in the air.]
Whose is this? [Shrug your shoulders.]
Whose is this bone? [Mime holding a bone with a disgusted face.]
Is it yours? [Point to and look at one of the children and shrug your shoulders.]
No. It's mine. [Point to yourself.]

CD3 TRACK 32

PB page 76 Activity 3

Boy: Whose is this watch?
Girl: It's mine.

Activity Book

CD3 TRACK 33

AB page 73 Activity 1

1
Jake's mother: Whose is this radio?
Jake: It's mine.
2
Jake's mother: Whose is this phone?
Jake: It's his.
3
Jake's mother: Whose is this clock?
Jake: It's hers.
4
Jake's mother: Whose is this camera?
Jake: It's yours.
5
Jake's mother: Whose is this box?
Jake: It's mine.

Unit 7 Lesson 5

Pupil's Book

CD3 TRACK 34

PB page 77 Activity 1

Toby: ow – ou – ow – ou
brown – cow – loud – mouse – around – house
A brown cow and a loud mouse run around the house.
A brown cow and a loud mouse run around the house.
A brown cow and a loud mouse run around the house.

CD3 TRACK 35

PB page 77 Activity 2

1
Boy: There's a camera in the living room.
2
Girl: There's a radio in the dining room.
3
Boy: There's a clock in the hall.
4
Girl: There's a box in the garage.
5
Boy: There's a phone in the bathroom.
6
Girl: There's a watch in the kitchen.

Unit 7 Lesson 6

Pupil's Book

CD3 TRACK 36

PB page 78 Activity 1

Anna: My brother and I have got our own bedrooms. His is big. Mine is small, but I like it. Come and see.
Tom: We live in a house with a big garden. Our bedrooms are upstairs.
Tom: I've got a lot of books, so there's a bookcase in my bedroom. I love music. I've got a guitar and drums.
Anna: I've got a sticker collection in my bedroom. Today, I'm making a book of animal stickers with Alice.
Anna: Sometimes, we have a pyjama party with our friends. We play board games and we listen to pop music.

Activity Book

CD3 TRACK 37

AB page 75 Activity 1

1
Boy: Hi! I'm Alex. My bedroom's great! It's a small bedroom. There isn't a computer or a television, but there are board games.
2
Girl: My name's Kim. My bedroom is big. There's a bed, a bookcase and a radio. There are lots of toys. My favourite toy is my scooter.
3
Girl 1: My name's Jill. I share a room with my sister. I've got a sticker collection on my desk. There are two beds in the bedroom.
Girl 2: Whose is the big bed?
Girl 1: It's mine.
Girl 2: Whose is the small bed?
Girl 1: It's my sister's.
4
Boy: Hi! I'm Ben. My bedroom's small. There's a bed next to the window. There's a bookcase and there are a lot of books.

Unit 7 Lesson 7

Pupil's Book

CD3 TRACK 38

PB page 79 Activity 2

Narrator: Cinderella, Scene 1
Narrator: Cinderella lives in a big house with her two wicked sisters. There are twenty bedrooms, seventeen bathrooms and two kitchens.
Sister 1: Tidy up, Cinderella!
Cinderella: Yes, of course. Whose is this phone?
Sister 2: It's mine!
Narrator: Scene 2
Narrator: Poor Cinderella. She's cleaning the house. There's a party tonight, but she can't go.
Cinderella: I'm sad. My dress is old.
Fairy Godmother: Here's a new dress. These mice can be horses. This pumpkin can be a car. These shoes are made of glass. You can go to the party now!
Narrator: Scene 3
Prince: Do you want to dance?
Cinderella: Yes, please.
Cinderella: Oh no! It's midnight.
Prince: Come back!
Narrator: Cinderella runs away. Her shoe falls off. The horses are mice again. The car is a pumpkin again. Her dress is old again.
Narrator: Scene 4
Narrator: The next day, Cinderella is cleaning the house. The prince visits.
Prince: Whose is this shoe?
Sisters 1 & 2: It's mine!
Prince: Cinderella. Is it yours?
Cinderella: Yes, it's mine. Thank you.
Narrator: The Prince and Cinderella get married and live happily ever after.

Unit 7 Lesson 8 Review

Pupil's Book

CD3 TRACK 39

PB page 80 Activity 1

1
Boy: I live in a house.
2
Girl: There's a kitchen in my house.
3
Boy: There's a dining room in my house.
4
Girl: There's a living room in my house.
5
Boy: There are posters in my bedroom.
6
Girl: There's a hall in my house.
7
Boy: There are plants in the garden.
8
Girl: There's a bathroom in my house.
9
Boy: There's a car in the garage.
10
Girl: My friend lives in a flat.

CD3 TRACK 40

PB page 80 Activity 3

***Well Done!* song**

Well done!
Well done!
Well done everyone!
Let's do a high five!
Well done everyone!
(Repeat)

Unit 7 Video and 21st Century Skills

Activity Book

CD3 TRACK 41

AB page 78 Activity 1

1
Boy: What a mess! Whose is this camera?
Girl: It's mine. Can you put it on the shelf, please?
Boy: Next to the books?
Girl: Yes, please.
2
Girl: Let's tidy up.
Boy: Whose is this phone?
Girl: It's mine.
Boy: Where can I put it?
Girl: Can you put it on the table, please?
Boy: Next to the lamp?
Girl: Yes.
3
Boy: Oh no! There's a watch on the floor.
Girl: It's mine. Can you put it in the box, please?
Boy: OK.
4
Boy: Here's a radio.
Girl: That's mine, too.
Boy: Where shall I put it?
Girl: It goes here in the cupboard. Next to the school bag.

Unit 8 Lesson 1

Pupil's Book

CD3 TRACK 42

PB page 82 Activity 1

***All around the town* song**

All around the town. [Gesture around you with your left hand.]
All around the town. [Gesture around you with your right hand.]
Let's go exploring, [Mime looking all around with interest.]
All around the town. [Gesture around you with both hands.]

Is there a baker's? [Shrug and point to the flashcard.]
Is there a bank? [Shrug and point to the flashcard.]
Is there a police station? [Shrug and point to the flashcard.]

All around the town. [Gesture around you with your left hand.]
All around the town. [Gesture around you with your right hand.]
Let's go exploring, [Mime looking all around with interest.]
All around the town. [Gesture around you with both hands.]

Is there a post office? [Shrug and point to the flashcard.]
Is there a chemist's? [Shrug and point to the flashcard.]
Is there a fire station? [Shrug and point to the flashcard.]

All around the town. [Gesture around you with your left hand.]
All around the town. [Gesture around you with your right hand.]
Let's go exploring, [Mime looking all around with interest.]
All around the town. [Gesture around you with both hands.]

Is there a bus station? [Shrug and point to the flashcard.]
Is there a museum? [Shrug and point to the flashcard.]
Is there a train station? [Shrug and point to the flashcard.]

All around the town. [Gesture around you with your left hand.]
All around the town. [Gesture around you with your right hand.]
Let's go exploring, [Mime looking all around with interest.]
All around the town. [Gesture around you with both hands.]

CD3 TRACK 43

PB page 82 Activity 1

Karaoke version: *All around the town* song

CD3 TRACK 44

PB page 82 Activity 2

baker's, fire station, police station, car park, bank, post office, chemist's, bus station, train station, museum

Unit 8 Lesson 2

Pupil's Book

CD3 TRACK 45

PB page 83 Activity 1

Mum: Here we are in Chesterville.
Jake: Great! Are there any museums here?
Mum: Yes, there are. But there aren't any dinosaurs.
Jake: Is there a cinema?
Mum: Yes, there is.
Jake: Are there any films about dinosaurs?
Mum: Let's go and see!

CD3 TRACK 46

PB page 83 Activity 2

1
Jake: Is there a museum in the town?
Mum: Yes, there is. There's a big museum with lots of interesting things to see.
Jake: Great!
2
Jake: Are there any banks in the town?
Mum: Yes, there are.
3
Dad: Is there a bus station?
Mum: Yes, there is. We can catch a bus to the mountains.
4
Jake: Is there a fire station?
Mum: Yes, there is.
Jake: Can we go and see it?
Mum: Yes, of course!
5
Molly: Are there any baker's?
Mum: Yes, there are. We can buy a big cake tomorrow.
Molly: Mmmm … delicious!

Unit 8 Lesson 3

Pupil's Book

CD3 TRACK 47

PB page 84 and 85 Activity 1

The dark night

Frame 1
Narrator: Jake, Molly and Beth are on holiday with Mum and Dad.
Mum: Here's the cinema.
Jake: Look! There's a film about dinosaurs.
Molly: Great!
Dad: Remember! The car is in front of the red bank.
Frame 2
Narrator: Later …
Beth: It's dark now.
Mum: It's night.
Dad: Let's go back to the car.
Frame 3
Mum: Where's the car?
Jake: It's this way. Turn left here.
Frame 4
Molly: Oh no! That isn't our car.
Dad: I think our car is near the baker's.
Mum: Is there a baker's near here?
Frame 5
Mum: It's very dark. Where's the car?
Jake: It's this way. Turn right here.
Frame 6
Molly: Oh no! This isn't our car.
Dad: I know! Our car is in front of the red bank.
Mum: Are there any banks near here?
Frame 7
Molly: Here's our car.
Jake: It's in front of the red bank.
Beth: It's next to the cinema!

Audioscript

Frame 8
Dad: There's our car!
Jake: Thank you, Magic Bike.
Molly: I'm hungry. Let's have dinner.

Unit 8 Lesson 4

Pupil's Book

CD3 TRACK 48

PB page 86 Activity 1

Go straight on, Turn left, Turn right,
From … To

CD3 TRACK 49

PB page 86 Activity 2

***Which way do I go?* song**

How do I get to the post office? [Point to the post office flashcard.]
Which way do I go? [Shrug your shoulders.]
How do I get from here to there? [Point to yourself and then away from yourself.]
Go straight on. There's the post office. [Walk straight on and then point to the post office flashcard.]

How do I get to the fire station? [Point to the fire station flashcard.]
Which way do I go? [Shrug your shoulders.]
How do I get from here to there? [Point to yourself and then away from yourself.]
Turn left. There's the fire station. [Turn left and walk a few paces and point to the fire station flashcard.]

How do I get to the train station? [Point to the train station flashcard.]
Which way do I go? [Shrug your shoulders.]
How do I get from here to there? [Point to yourself and then away from yourself.]
Turn right. There's the train station. [Turn right and walk a few paces and point to the train station flashcard.]

CD3 TRACK 50

PB page 86 Activity 3

Girl: How do I get to the post office?
Boy: Go straight on. There's the post office.

Activity Book

CD3 TRACK 51

AB page 83 Activity 1

1
Boy: How do I get from the bank to the chemist's?
Girl: Go straight on. There's the chemist's.
2
Girl: How do I get from the fire station to the police station?
Boy: Turn left.
3
Boy: How do I get from the car park to the post office?
Girl: Turn right.

Unit 8 Lesson 5

Pupil's Book

CD4 TRACK 1

PB page 87 Activity 1

Toby: y – igh –y – igh
fly – light – fly – night
Can a fly with a light fly at night?
Can a fly with a light fly at night?
Can a fly with a light fly at night?

CD4 TRACK 2

PB page 87 Activity 2

1
Jake is going from the school to the fire station. Listen to the directions and draw a line.
Jake: How do I get to the fire station?
Beth: Turn right and go straight on. There's the fire station.
Jake: Thank you!
2
Beth is going from the bank to the post office. Listen to the directions and draw a line.
Beth: How do I get to the post office?
Molly: Turn left. Turn right. Go straight on. There's the post office.
Beth: Thank you!
3
Molly is going from the car park to the police station. Listen to the directions and draw a line.
Molly: How do I get to the police station?
Beth: Turn right. Turn left. Go straight on. Turn right and go straight on. There's the police station.
Molly: Thank you!

Unit 8 Lesson 6

Pupil's Book

CD4 TRACK 3

PB page 88 Activity 1

Anna: Our mum and dad help people. Our mum is a police officer and our dad is a firefighter.
Tom: Our dad drives a big, red fire engine. It's got big wheels and a loud siren.
Anna: He wears a yellow helmet and a safety uniform.
Tom: Our mum is a police officer. She sometimes rides a bike around the town. She helps people.
Anna: The emergency telephone number in Britain is 999. Call this number if you need a doctor, a firefighter or a police officer.

Activity Book

CD4 TRACK 4

AB page 85 Activity 1

Firefighters drive a fire engine.
It's got big wheels and a loud siren.
Police officers ride a bike.
They wear a yellow jacket and a cycling helmet.
Firefighters wear a safety uniform and a yellow helmet.
The emergency number is 999.

Unit 8 Lesson 7

Pupil's Book

CD4 TRACK 5

PB page 89 Activity 2

Sam: It's party time!
Sam's 8th birthday
To: Jane
Come to my party on Saturday the 9th of May.
Face painting and games.
Lots of fun!
Cakes and sweets, too.
I hope you can come!
Phone number: 691345
The party is at Partyland.
From the school: Go straight on and turn left. Then, turn right. Partyland is between the toyshop and the café.
See you there!

Unit 8 Lesson 8 Review

Pupil's Book

CD4 TRACK 6

PB page 90 Activity 1

1
Girl: Is there a post office in the town?
Boy: Yes, there is.
2
Girl: Is there a chemist's in the town?
Boy: Yes, there is.
3
Girl: Are there any fire stations in the town?
Boy: Yes, there are.
4
Boy: Is there a baker's in the town?
Girl: Yes, there is.
5
Boy: Is there a bank in the town?
Girl: Yes, there is.
6
Boy: Is there a bus station in the town?
Girl: Yes, there is.
7
Girl: Is there a train station in the town?
Boy: Yes, there is.
8
Boy: Are there any museums in the town?
Girl: Yes, there are.
9
Boy: Is there a police station in the town?
Girl: Yes, there is.
10
Girl: Are there any car parks in the town?
Boy: Yes, there are.

CD4 TRACK 7

PB page 90 Activity 2

Girl: Are there any museums in your town?
Boy: Yes, there are.
Girl: Is there a train station?
Boy: No, there isn't.

CD4 TRACK 8

PB page 90 Activity 3

***Well Done!* song**

Well done!
Well done!
Well done everyone!
Let's do a high five!
Well done everyone!
(Repeat)

Unit 8 Video and 21st Century Skills

Activity Book

CD4 TRACK 9

AB page 88 Activity 1

1
Girl: Be careful when you cross the road.
Boy: Yes. I look and listen when I cross the road.
Girl: Good.
2
Boy: Where are you going?
Girl: I'm going to the museum.
Boy: Don't run across the road.
Girl: No. I walk across the road.
3
Girl: Let's cross the road here.
Boy: No. This isn't a good place to cross the road. Let's look for a zebra crossing.
Girl: Good idea.
4
Boy: Let's cross the road.
Girl: We can't cross the road now. Look at the red man. That means stop.
Boy: Oh yes.
Girl: Wait for the green man and then we can cross the road.

Unit 9 Lesson 1

Pupil's Book

CD4 TRACK 10

PB page 92 Activity 1

***We're on holiday* song**

We're on holiday. [Hold out your hands.]
We're having a great time. [Thumbs up.]
There are lots of things to do. [Gesture all around you.]

We're on holiday. [Hold out your hands.]
We're having a great time. [Thumbs up.]
Let's go to the circus. [Point to the corresponding flashcards on the board.]
Let's go to the science museum [Point to the corresponding flashcards on the board.]
And see animals
in the safari park.

We're on holiday. [Hold out your hands.]
We're having a great time. [Thumbs up.]
There are lots of things to do. [Gesture all around you.]

We're on holiday. [Hold out your hands.]
We're having a great time. [Thumbs up.]
Let's go to the theatre.
Let's go to the chocolate factory
And see dolphins
in the aquarium.

We're on holiday. [Hold out your hands.]
We're having a great time. [Thumbs up.]
There are lots of things to do. [Gesture all around you.]

CD4 TRACK 11

PB page 92 Activity 1

Karaoke version: *We're on holiday* song

CD4 TRACK 12

PB page 92 Activity 2

castle, circus, science museum, water park, funfair, chocolate factory, aquarium, sports centre, safari park, theatre

Unit 9 Lesson 2

Pupil's Book

CD4 TRACK 13

PB page 93 Activity 1

Jake: Hi, Beth. Where were you yesterday?
Beth: I was at the circus with my mum and dad.
Jake: Lucky you! I love the circus.
Beth: Where were you?
Jake: I was at the science museum with Molly.
Beth: Fantastic!

CD4 TRACK 14

PB page 93 Activity 2

1
Beth: Hi, Jake! Were you at the castle yesterday?
Jake: No, I wasn't.
Beth: Were you at the aquarium?
Jake: No, I wasn't.
Beth: Were you at the safari park?
Jake: Yes, I was! It was great!
2
Beth: Hi, Molly! Where were you yesterday?
Molly: I was at the theatre.
Beth: Great. I love the theatre!
Molly: Me too!
3
Jake: Hello, Beth! Where were you yesterday?
Beth: I was at the science museum!
Jake: Fantastic!

Unit 9 Lesson 3

Pupil's Book

CD4 TRACK 15

PB page 94 and 95 Activity 1

The magic trip

Frame 1
Narrator: It's the summer holidays. Jake, Molly and Beth aren't at school.
Jake: I'm bored.
Molly: Me too.
Beth: Magic Bike, can you help?
Frame 2
Molly: Wow! The bike can fly! Where can we go?
Jake: Let's go to the castle!
Beth: There's a place for me, too!
Frame 3
Narrator: The magic bike takes Jake, Molly and Beth to the castle.
Jake: Castles are brilliant!
Molly: Where's Beth?
Beth: Here I am. I'm up in the tower.
Frame 4
Narrator: Jake, Molly and Beth fly on the magic bike again.
Beth: That was fun!
Jake: Where can we go now?
Molly: I know. Let's go to the water park!
Frame 5
Narrator: The magic bike takes Jake, Molly and Beth to the water park.
Jake: Look at me! Wheeee!
Beth: Here I go.
Molly: This is fun.
Frame 6
Narrator: The children fly on the magic bike again.
Jake: That was great!
Molly: Where can we go now?
Beth: I'm hungry. Let's go to the chocolate factory!
Frame 7
Narrator: The magic bike takes the children to the chocolate factory. Then, they fly home.
Mum: Hello, children. Where were you?
Beth: We were at a chocolate factory …
Jake: … and a castle …
Molly: … and a water park.
Frame 8
Jake: We were on our magic bike.
Molly: Shh! Jake!
Mum: Magic bike? Really?

Unit 9 Lesson 4

Pupil's Book

CD4 TRACK 16

PB page 96 Activity 1

man, men, woman, women, child, children

CD4 TRACK 17

PB page 96 Activity 2

***Who's that?* song**

Who's that woman in your photo?
She's got blue eyes
And long blonde hair.
She's my aunt. Here she is
On holiday with me.

Who are those children in your photo?
They've got green eyes
And short black hair.
They're my cousins. Here they are
On holiday with me.

Who's that man in your photo?
He's got brown eyes
And short brown hair.
He's my uncle. Here he is
On holiday with me.

Audioscript

CD4 TRACK 18

PB page 96 Activity 3

Boy: Who's that woman?
Girl: She's my aunt.
Boy: Who are those children?
Girl: They're my cousins.

Activity Book

CD4 TRACK 19

AB page 93 Activity 2

1
Boy: Who's that woman?
Girl: She's my aunt. She's got long blonde hair.
2
Boy: Who are those children?
Girl: They're my cousins. They've got long black hair.
3
Boy: Who's that man?
Girl: He's my father. He's got short blonde hair.
4
Boy: Who's that child?
Girl: He's my brother. He's got short black hair.
5
Boy: Who are those men?
Girl: They're my uncles. They've got short black hair.
6
Boy: Who are those women?
Girl: They're my aunts. They've got long blonde hair.

Unit 9 Lesson 5

Pupil's Book

CD4 TRACK 20

PB page 97 Activity 1

Toby: ear – air – ear – air
bear – pear – stairs – funfair
The bear with a pear climbs the stairs at the funfair.
The bear with a pear climbs the stairs at the funfair.
The bear with a pear climbs the stairs at the funfair.

CD4 TRACK 21

PB page 97 Activity 2

1
Molly: Hello, Beth. Where were you last weekend?
Beth: Hi, Molly. I was at the science museum. Look, this is a photo of my family.
Molly: Who's that man?
Beth: This man?
Molly: Yes. The man with black hair.
Beth: He's my father.
2
Molly: And who's that child?
Beth: The boy with my father?
Molly: Yes.
Beth: He's my little brother.
Molly: How old is he?
Beth: He's two years old.
3
Molly: And who's that woman?
Beth: Which woman?
Molly: The woman with short blonde hair.
Beth: She's my grandmother.
4
Molly: Who's that baby?
Beth: She's my cousin. Her name's Sue.
5
Molly: Who's the woman holding your cousin?
Beth: The woman with the long, curly hair?
Molly: Yes.
Beth: She's my aunt.
6
Molly: Who's the man with white hair?
Beth: He's my grandfather.
Molly: Where's your mum?
Beth: She's taking the photo!

Unit 9 Lesson 6

Pupil's Book

CD4 TRACK 22

PB page 98 Activity 1

Tom: It's the summer holidays. Yesterday, we were at Blenheim Palace. There are lots of fun things to do in the gardens.
Tom: We love the maze. It's very big. We can play hide and seek here. Where are Dad and Anna?
Anna: There are some giant games! In this photo, we're playing giant chess. Mum and Tom are winning.
Tom: Our favourite place is the arts and crafts studio. In this photo, we're painting a plate and a cup for Dad. It's his birthday on the fourteenth of August.
Anna: There's a butterfly house here, too. We can see butterflies from all around the world. They're beautiful.

Activity Book

CD4 TRACK 23

AB page 95 Activity 1

1
Boy: I love the butterfly house. We can see lots of butterflies. Look! There's a big butterfly on your head, Dad! It's beautiful!
2
Girl: … 5 … 6 … 7 … 8 … 9 …10 … Ready or not, here I come! Mmmm … Where's Ben?
3
Boy: Look! What's that?
Girl: It's giant chess! Come on! Let's play!
4
Woman: What are you painting, Jill?
Girl: I'm painting a cup. It's a birthday present for my mum.

Unit 9 Lesson 7

Pupil's Book

CD4 TRACK 24

PB page 99 Activity 2

Boy: My diary
Yesterday was Saturday. It was sunny and hot. I was at the circus all day with my mum and dad and my sisters. It was great!
Here's my ticket.
Here's a photo of my big sister with a clown.
Here's my little sister with a man on stilts.
He's very tall.
Yesterday was Sunday. It was cold and cloudy. I was at the funfair with my cousins.
It was fantastic! It was my cousin's birthday.
Here he is with his badge.
My favourite ride was the roller coaster. It was very fast!
Here's my ticket.
And here's a photo of me and my aunt

Unit 9 Lesson 8 Review

Pupil's Book

CD4 TRACK 25

PB page 100 Activity 1

1
Boy: I was at the science museum yesterday.
2
Girl: I was at the circus yesterday.
3
Boy: I was at the castle yesterday.
4
Girl: I was at the safari park yesterday.
5
Boy: I was at the sports centre yesterday.
6
Girl: I was at the theatre yesterday.
7
Boy: I was at the water park yesterday.
8
Girl: I was at the aquarium yesterday.
9
Boy: I was at the funfair yesterday.
10
Girl: I was at the chocolate factory yesterday.

CD4 TRACK 26

PB page 100 Activity 2

Girl: Where were you on Monday?
Boy: I was at the castle.
Girl: Where were you on Tuesday?
Boy: I was at the safari park.

CD4 TRACK 27

PB page 100 Activity 3

***Well Done!* song**
Well done!
Well done!
Well done everyone!
Let's do a high five!
Well done everyone!
(Repeat)

Unit 9 Video and 21st Century Skills

Activity Book

CD4 TRACK 28

AB page 98 Activity 1

1
Girl: Do you like taking photos?
Boy: Yes, I do. Look at this photo. It's my brother. He was at the safari park at the weekend.
Girl: What fun!
2
Boy: Who's this?
Girl: This is my cousin.
Boy: What's she doing?
Girl: She's playing on the slide. She was at the water park yesterday.
3
Boy: Who's that woman?
Girl: That's my aunt. She was at the circus yesterday.
4
Boy: Where were you yesterday?
Girl: Can you guess?
Boy: At the chocolate factory?
Girl: No. I was at the funfair.

My Project 3 Lesson 1

Pupil's Book

CD4 TRACK 29

PB page 102 Activity 1

1
Girl: What time is it?
Boy: It's eight o'clock.
2
Boy: What time is it?
Girl: It's a quarter past eight.
3
Boy: What time is it?
Girl: It's half past eight.
4
Girl: What time is it?
Boy: It's a quarter to nine.

CD4 TRACK 30

PB page 102 Activity 2

Boy: It's a quarter to nine.
Boy: It's number four. It's my turn. It's a quarter past eight.
Boy: It's number two.

CD4 TRACK 31

PB page 102 Activity 3

1
Boy: I get up at half past seven.
2
Boy: I get dressed at a quarter to eight.
3
Girl: I have breakfast at a quarter past eight.
4
Girl: I go to school at nine o'clock.
5
Girl: I play at half past six.
6
Boy: I go to bed at half past nine.

My Project 3 Lesson 2

Pupil's Book

CD4 TRACK 32

PB page 103 Activity 2

***Listen to others* song**

Listen to others. [Put your hand behind your right ear.]
Listen, please.
Listen with your ears. [Put your hand behind your left ear.]
Listen, please.
Listen to others. [Put your hands behind both ears.]
Listen, please.
Listen, everybody.

CD4 TRACK 33

PB page 103 Activity 3

Girl: I get up at a quarter past eight. I have breakfast at half past eight and I go to school at a quarter to nine.

Festivals: Harvest Festival

Pupil's Book

CD4 TRACK 34

PB page 104 Activity 1

Girl: British children celebrate Harvest Festival in autumn.
Boy: We say thank you for all the food that grows in summer.
Girl: We make big baskets of fruit and vegetables.

CD4 TRACK 35

PB page 104 Activity 2

Summer is over.
Autumn is here.
It's Harvest Festival.
Give a cheer!
The harvest moon
is big and round.
We say 'Thank you' for the food
that grows in the ground.

Festivals: Carnival

Pupil's Book

CD4 TRACK 36

PB page 105 Activity 1

Put on your costume.
Paint your face.
Wear a wig or a hat,
A mask or a cape.

Join the parade.
Dance and have fun.
It's time for the competition.
Hooray! I won!

CD4 TRACK 37

PB page 105 Activity 3

1
Boy: It's carnival time! I'm wearing my costume. I'm wearing a big, red cape. I'm superwoman!
2
Girl: I'm ready for the parade. I'm wearing a hat and boots. I'm a pirate!
3
Boy: I love carnival time. I'm wearing a wig and a hat. I've got a big, red nose. I'm a clown

Unit 1 Cambridge Exams Practice

Pupil's Book

CD4 TRACK 38

PB page 106 Activity 1

1
Narrator: What is Anna's hobby?
Boy: Does Anna play baseball?
Girl: No, she doesn't.
Boy: Does she go skateboarding?
Girl: No, she doesn't. Anna's hobby is basketball.
2
Narrator: What is Pat's favourite sport?
Girl: Does Pat like sport?
Boy: Yes, he loves hockey.
Girl: Is hockey his favourite sport?
Boy: No, it isn't. His favourite sport is football.
3
Narrator: Which is Bill?
Boy: Is that Bill with the tennis racket?
Girl: No, it isn't. Bill has got his bike today.
Boy: Oh yes. I can see him now. What a cool bike!

CD4 TRACK 39

PB page 106 Activity 2

Boy: Do you like hockey?
Girl: Yes, I do.
Boy: Do you go skateboarding?
Girl: Yes, I do. I go skateboarding on Saturday.
Boy: What's your favourite sport?
Girl: My favourite sport is football.

Unit 2 Cambridge Exams Practice

Pupil's Book

CD4 TRACK 40

PB page 107 Activity 1

1
Man: Hello. What's your name?
Boy: My name's Alex.
Man: How do you spell that?
Boy: A-L-E-X.

Audioscript

2
Man: Is this your friend in the picture with you?
Boy: No. This is my sister. Her name's Lucy.
Man: And how do you spell that?
Boy: L-U-C-Y.
3
Man: How old are you, Alex?
Boy: I'm seven.
Man: Seven?
Boy: Yes.
4
Man: And how old is Lucy?
Boy: She's eight.
5
Man: What have you got in the bag?
Boy: Apples.
Man: Have you got a lot of apples in there?
Boy: Yes! We've got nineteen!
Man: Nineteen apples!
Boy: Yes. They're for my dad. He loves cooking!
6
Man: Is this your dog, Alex?
Boy: Yes, it is. His name is Socks.
Man: And how do you spell that?
Boy: S-O-C-K-S.
Man: That's a good name.

CD4 TRACK 41
PB page 107 Activity 2
Girl: What are these?
Boy: They're potatoes
Girl: Do you have potatoes for lunch?
Boy: Yes, I do.

Unit 3 Cambridge Exams Practice

Pupil's Book
CD4 TRACK 42
PB page 108 Activity 1
1
Boy: Here is a photo of me and my friends at the zoo.
Woman: Oh yes! Who's that girl? She's next to the giraffe.
Boy: Her name's Lucy. Lucy's in my class at school.

Narrator: Can you see the line? This is an example. Now you listen and draw lines.
2
Woman: There's a boy there, too. He's looking at the snakes.
Boy: Oh yes! That's Alex.
Woman: Does Alex like snakes?
Boy: Yes. He loves them.
3
Boy: Can you see my friend May?
Woman: Is May behind the hippos?
Boy: Yes, that's right. She's eating an ice cream.
Woman: Oh yes. I can see her.
4
Woman: Look at that boy sitting next to the flowers.
Boy: The boy in the blue T-shirt?
Woman: Yes.
Boy: That's Hugo. Hugo's my best friend.
5
Woman: And what's that girl's name? The girl with the long hair.
Boy: That's Alice.
Woman: What's Alice doing?
Boy: She's skateboarding.
6
Woman: Who's that boy? He's between the elephant and the monkey.
Boy: That's Mark.
Woman: What's in his hand?
Boy: That's Mark's favourite teddy.

CD4 TRACK 43
PB page 108 Activity 2
Boy: What are these?
Girl: They're elephants.
Boy: What colour are they?
Girl: They're grey.

Unit 4 Cambridge Exams Practice

Pupil's Book
CD4 TRACK 44
PB page 109 Activity 1
1
Woman: Hello. What's your name?
Boy: My name's Bill.
Woman: How do you spell that?
Boy: B-I-L-L.
2
Woman: Is this your sister?
Boy: No. This is my friend. Her name's Kim.
Woman: And how do you spell that?
Boy: K-I-M.
3
Woman: Do you like animals, Bill?
Boy: Oh yes! I love dogs.
Woman: Have you got a dog?
Boy: I've got two dogs!
4
Woman: Has Kim got a dog?
Boy: No, she hasn't. Kim likes cats.
Woman: How many cats has Kim got?
Boy: She's got one cat.
5
Woman: What's your favourite dog's name?
Boy: His name's Ben.
Woman: That's nice!

CD4 TRACK 45
PB page 109 Activity 2
Boy: Where's the girl?
Girl: Here.
Boy: What's she doing?
Girl: She's flying a kite.
Boy: Tell me about the picture.
Girl: There is a big house. There is a girl. She's flying a kite.

Unit 5 Cambridge Exams Practice

Pupil's Book
CD4 TRACK 46
PB page 110 Activity 1
1
Narrator: What is Dad doing?
Boy: Is he eating?
Girl: Yes, he is.
Boy: Is he eating a pear?
Girl: No, he isn't. He's eating some fish.
Narrator: Can you see the tick? Now you listen and tick the box.
2
Narrator: Which is Lucy?
Boy: Is she sad?
Girl: No, she isn't.
Boy: Is she happy?
Girl: Yes, she is. Look! She's smiling.
3
Narrator: What are Ann and Tom doing?
Girl: Are they taking a photo?
Boy: Yes, they are.
Girl: Is it a photo of a cat?
Boy: No, it isn't. It's a photo of a monkey!

CD4 TRACK 47
PB page 110 Activity 2
Girl: What's Grandmother doing?
Boy: She's sleeping.
Girl: What's Dad doing?
Boy: He's taking a photo.

Unit 6 Cambridge Exams Practice

Pupil's Book
CD4 TRACK 48
PB page 111 Activity 1
1
Woman: Hugo and Jill are playing.
Boy: Are they playing at the park?
Woman: No, they're playing in the sand.
Boy: Of course! They're at the beach.
2
Woman: Can you see Eva?
Girl: No, I can't. Is she wearing a hat?
Woman: Yes, she is. It's blue.
Girl: Ah! I can see her now.
3
Woman: Where are Tony and Sue?
Boy: They're at the park.
Woman: Are they sitting down?
Boy: No, they aren't. They're playing baseball.

CD4 TRACK 49
PB page 111 Activity 2
Girl: How old are you?
Boy: I'm seven.
Girl: When's your birthday?
Boy: My birthday is on the second of August.

Unit 7 Cambridge Exams Practice

Pupil's Book

CD4 TRACK 50

PB page 112 Activity 1

1
Woman: Find the mouse in the hall.
Boy: Here it is.
Woman: Good. Colour it blue.
Boy: OK. The mouse in the hall is blue.

2
Woman: Can you see the mouse on the bed?
Boy: Yes!
Woman: Good. Colour it brown.
Boy: OK. The mouse on the bed is brown.

3
Woman: Colour the mouse next to the clock pink.
Boy: Next to the clock?
Woman: Yes. Colour it pink.
Boy: OK. I'm colouring it pink now.

4
Woman: Find the mouse under the piano.
Boy: I can see it.
Woman: Good. Colour it purple.
Boy: OK. The mouse under the piano is purple.

5
Woman: Find the mouse between the tree and the flowers.
Boy: Here it is.
Woman: Good. Colour it orange.
Boy: OK. The mouse between the tree and the flowers is orange.

6
Woman: Can you see the mouse on the sofa?
Boy: Yes, I can.
Woman: Good. Colour it red.
Boy: OK. The mouse on the sofa is red.

CD4 TRACK 51

PB page 112 Activity 2

Boy: Do you live in a house or a flat?
Girl: I live in a flat.
Boy: What's your favourite room?
Girl: My favourite room is my bedroom.
Boy: What's in your bedroom?
Girl: There's a bed and there are lots of posters.

Unit 8 Cambridge Exams Practice

Pupil's Book

CD4 TRACK 52

PB page 113 Activity 1

1
Adult: Can you see the bird next to the flat?
Girl: Yes, I can.
Adult: Colour the bird next to the flat orange.
Girl: Orange?
Adult: Yes, that's right.
Narrator: Can you see the orange bird next to the flat? This is an example. Now you listen and colour.

2
Adult: Can you see the bird next to the ball?
Girl: Yes, I can.
Adult: Colour the bird next to the ball pink.
Girl: Pink?
Adult: That's right.

3
Adult: Look at the bird in the tree.
Girl: OK, I can see it. Can I colour it?
Adult: Yes. Colour it blue.
Girl: OK. A blue bird in the tree.

4
Adult: Can you see a bird in front of the bookshop?
Girl: OK, I can see it. Can I colour it?
Adult: Yes. Colour it red.
Girl: OK. A red bird in front of the bookshop.

5
Girl: Look, there's a bird in the water.
Adult: Yes, there is. Colour it brown.
Girl: OK. A brown bird in the water.

6
Adult: Can you see the bird between the flowers?
Girl: Yes, I can.
Adult: Colour it green.
Girl: A green bird between the flowers?
Adult: That's right.

CD4 TRACK 53

PB page 113 Activity 2

Boy: Where's the bookshop?
Girl: It's here.
Boy: Is there a bookshop near your school?
Girl: Yes, there is.

Unit 9 Cambridge Exams Practice

Pupil's Book

CD4 TRACK 54

PB page 114 Activity 1

1
Man: Look down there! Can you see all those people?
Girl: Yes! Who's that woman next to the red car?
Man: That's Eva. Eva drives a red car.
Girl: My dad's got a red car!

2
Girl: Who's that man behind the house?
Man: The man with a big dog? That's Hugo.
Girl: Is that Hugo's dog?
Man: Yes, it is.

3
Girl: Can you see those two women between the playground and the school.
Man: Yes. The woman on the horse is Sue.
Girl: Does Sue like riding a horse?
Man: Yes. She loves horses.

4
Man: Look at that boy!
Girl: The boy in the water park? What's his name?
Man: That's Bill. Bill loves playing in the water.
Girl: Me too.

5
Girl: Look at that fantastic bike!
Man: Yes. That's Tom's bike.
Girl: Does Tom ride his bike every day?
Man: Yes. He rides to school on his bike, too.

6
Man: There are two children in front of the zoo.
Girl: What's the girl's name? The girl in the yellow T-shirt.
Man: That's Anna. She's eating an apple.
Girl: That's good for you.

CD4 TRACK 55

PB page 114 Activity 2

Girl: Have you got any brothers or sisters?
Boy: Yes. I've got one brother and one sister.
Girl: What's your sister's name?
Boy: Her name's Anna.

Videoscript

Unit 1 21st Century Video

PB page 17 Activities 1 and 2

Abby: Hello, everybody. Welcome back to Channel 21. My name's Abby.
Sophie: Hello! I'm Sophie.
Tom: Hi! I'm Tom.
Abby: Today's programme is about Sports Day.
Tom: Do you like sports, Sophie?
Sophie: Yes, I do. I love football and basketball.
Tom: It's Sports Day at school on Monday. Let's watch the video and see what different activities we can do.
Tom: What's this game?
Sophie: This is a Tug of war. The children pull the rope.
Tom: Oh, yes. The boys pull on one side and the girls pull on the other side.
Sophie: That's right. They work together as a team.
Tom: The boys are winning.
Sophie: The girls are winning now.
Tom: Come on, boys.
Sophie: Come on, girls.
Sophie: This is a skipping race!
Tom: There are lots of different races!
Tom: Do you like the sack race?
Sophie: I don't know.
Tom: It's fun to join in with all the different activities.
Sophie: Yes, that's right.
Sophie: This is the three-legged race.
Tom: The children walk together.
Sophie: It's important to walk slowly.
Tom: And wait for your friend!
Tom: Everyone's joining in here.
Sophie: Who's the winner?
Tom: The girl in the blue and white top.
Sophie: This is the egg and spoon race.
Tom: It looks fun!
Sophie: It looks difficult!
Abby: The children are having a lot of fun, aren't they?
Sophie: Yes! They're all joining in with the games.
Tom: Let's try the egg and spoon race.
Sophie: Oh, I don't know …
Abby: Come on, it's fun!
Abby: Come on! Join in!
Abby: Don't forget to join in with the activities on your Sports Day!
Sophie: You can have a lot of fun!
Tom: See you next time.

Unit 2 21st Century Video

PB page 27 Activities 1 and 2

Abby: Hello, again. Welcome back to Channel 21.
Sophie: Hello!
Tom: Hello!
Tom: Do you like pizza?
Sophie: Yes, I do. I love pizza!
Tom: Let's make a pizza for lunch!
Sophie: Great idea. But how do you make pizza?
Tom: You need lots of delicious ingredients to put on top of the pizza.
Abby: Today's video is about making pizza.
Tom: Perfect. Let's watch it.
Sophie: First, you make the pizza base.
Tom: Yes, look! You need flour.
Sophie: That's right. Then you add water.
Tom: Next you push and pull the mixture.
Sophie: That looks fun!
Abby: Make sure you wash your hands before you start.
Sophie: Look! Now it looks like a pizza.
Tom: Yes. Roll and roll the pizza base.
Sophie: It's flat now.
Tom: Yes. What's next?
Sophie: Next, add the tomatoes.
Tom: And now, add the cheese …
Tom: Oh look! You can get the recipe online!
Sophie: That's a good idea.
Sophie: You can get ideas for different ingredients online, too.
Tom: Yes! We can add tomatoes, peppers and onions.
Sophie: We can use our tablets to help us!
Tom: Put the ingredients on top of the pizza base and then put the pizza in the oven.
Tom: Cook the pizza for ten minutes.
Sophie: Mmmm!
Tom: Delicious!
Abby: I'm hungry now!
Sophie: Me too!
Tom: Let's make a pizza. Here's the flour.
Sophie: Oh no! We haven't got any tomatoes or cheese. There's some milk and there are some eggs.
Tom: What can we make with flour, milk and eggs?
Abby: You can make pancakes.
Sophie: How do you make pancakes?
Abby: Let's look online.
Abby: You can find information in an online recipe book.
Tom: You can make anything!
Sophie: Come on!
Tom and Sophie: Bye!

Unit 3 21st Century Video

PB page 37 Activities 1 and 2

Abby: Hello, everyone. Welcome back to Channel 21. Is there a zoo in your town?
Sophie: There's a zoo in our town! What's your favourite animal?
Tom: My favourite animal is a penguin. What's yours?
Sophie: My favourite animal is a parrot.
Abby: Penguins and parrots are both birds and I've got a video about them right here.
Sophie and Tom: Great! Let's watch it.
Sophie: Parrots are different colours. Look! These parrots are red, green, blue and yellow.
Tom: They've got small eyes.
Abby: They've got big, strong beaks. Look.
Sophie: Parrots have got big wings.
Abby: That's right. Look at this parrot's feathers.
Tom: Can they fly?
Sophie: Yes, they can. Look. They fly very well.
Tom: Oh yes! Can they swim?
Abby: No. Parrots can't swim. They are flying over the water to the rocks.
Sophie: They've got long tails, too.
Tom: Where do parrots live?
Abby: Parrots live in trees in the rainforest.
Tom: Look! Here are the penguins now.
Abby: Penguins can swim, but they can't fly.
Sophie: Penguins can walk, too.
Tom: Are all penguins black and white?
Abby: These penguins are black, white and yellow.
Sophie: They've got beaks, too.
Tom: That's right. Penguins have got long beaks.
Sophie: Where do penguins live?
Abby: They live in the snow and ice.
Tom: Here they are with their chicks.
Sophie: Oh! Baby parrots are called chicks, too.
Sophie: Lots of things about parrots and penguins are the same.
Tom: Yes, but some things are different.
Abby: You can draw a diagram to help you see what's the same and what's different. Look.
Tom: We can put the things that are the same in the middle!
Sophie: Parrots and penguins have a beak. We can put that in the middle.
Tom: Penguins can swim.
Sophie: We can put that here.
Tom: And parrots can fly.
Sophie: We can put that here.
Abby: That's great!
Tom: See if you can find things that are the same and different about some other animals!
Sophie: Have fun!

Unit 4 21st Century Video

PB page 49 Activities 1 and 2

Abby: Hello, again. Welcome back to Channel 21.
Tom and Sophie: Hello!
Tom: Do you like natural places, Abby?
Abby: Yes, I do. I love going on a nature trail.
Tom: Me too. And I love the beach! Today's programme is about nature.
Sophie: Great. Let's watch it.
Sophie: Look! What's that? Is it a lake or a river?
Abby: It's a river. You can see it now.
Tom: I can see a big forest, too.
Tom: You can walk along the path in the park.
Sophie: Oh yes! And jump in the leaves.
Sophie: Here's a bridge. Look! It goes over the river.
Tom: What's he doing?
Sophie: He's riding his bike over the river.

Tom: Here's his family.
Sophie: Look at the lake. It's lovely and clean.
Tom: I can see a forest, too.
Sophie: They're having a picnic by the lake.
Sophie: Oh no! Look at all the rubbish.
Tom: There are bottles and cans.
Abby: It's important to put your rubbish in the bin.
Tom: What's she doing?
Sophie: She's putting empty bottles in the bin.
Sophie: What are they doing?
Tom: They're tidying up.
Abby: They're helping to keep the park clean and tidy.
Tom: It's a good idea to have signs in the park.
Sophie: And lots of bins, too.
Tom: Let's make a poster to tell people to tidy up!
Abby: Good idea! It's important to look after the environment. Animals and plants live there.
Sophie: Let's draw a big bin in the park.
Tom: Let's write 'Tidy up!'
Tom: You can make a poster, too.
Sophie: And remember to put your rubbish in the bin.
Tom: See you next time on Channel 21!
Sophie: Goodbye!

Unit 5 21st Century Video

PB page 59 Activities 1 and 2

Abby: Hello, everybody! Welcome back to Channel 21.
Tom and Sophie: Hello!
Sophie: It's snowing today!
Abby: Is it snowing where you live?
Tom: What do you like doing in the snow?
Sophie: I like making snowmen.
Abby: Today's video is about making snowmen.
Sophie: Great! Let's watch it.
Tom: Look! It's snowing.
Sophie: The girl is rolling the snow into a big ball.
Abby: She's making a snowman.
Tom: That's its body.
Tom: Now she's making the face.
Sophie: The eyes … nose … and mouth.
Tom: This snowman is wearing a hat.
Sophie: It's funny!
Tom: This snowman is wearing a scarf and a hat, too.
Sophie: And it's got a carrot for a nose!
Tom: These snowmen are all different! This one has got a blue scarf.
Sophie: And that one has got a pink scarf and a pink hat.
Sophie: This snowman has got twigs for hair!
Tom: Wow! That's really creative!
Abby: Yes! You can think and make a really interesting and different snowman.
Sophie: Oh! This one has got a red nose …
Tom: And long eyelashes.
Tom: This is a big snowman!
Sophie: It's got a hat and a scarf.
Tom: And twigs for arms.
Tom: Here are lots of snowmen.
Sophie: They're really small.
Sophie: I want to make a snowman with an orange for its nose.
Tom: I want to make a snowman with leaves for its hair.
Abby: Your snowmen sound really different and creative!
Tom: Come on, let's go outside!
Sophie: Wait for me!
Abby: See you next time on Channel 21!
Tom and Sophie: Bye!

Unit 6 21st Century Video

PB page 69 Activities 1 and 2

Abby: Hello, everybody. Welcome back to Channel 21.
Tom and Sophie: Hello!
Abby: What's your favourite season, Sophie?
Sophie: My favourite season is spring, because I like planting seeds. What's your favourite season, Tom?
Tom: My favourite season is summer, because I go to the beach. What about you Abby?
Abby: My favourite season is autumn, because it's my birthday in autumn. Let's watch a video about all four seasons.
Sophie: It's spring. Look at all the purple flowers.
Tom: There are leaves growing on the trees, too.
Tom: What are they doing?
Sophie: They're planting seeds. Look, their mum is helping them.
Abby: What do you think they're planting?
Sophie: I think they're planting sunflowers!
Tom: I think they're planting tomatoes.
Tom: Look at those spring flowers.
Abby: Flowers grow when it's warm.
Sophie: I love smelling flowers in spring. Ahhhh.
Tom: We finish school in summer. Then we go to the beach! Do you like the beach, Abby?
Abby: Not really. I prefer cool weather.
Sophie: You can have a lot of fun at the beach.
Tom: We can play in the sand.
Abby: Look! They're playing football with their grandmother and grandfather.
Sophie: Now it's autumn.
Abby: Yes. I love autumn leaves.
Tom: When's your birthday?
Abby: My birthday is on the seventh of November.
Tom: We eat chestnuts in autumn, too.
Abby: Do you like chestnuts?
Tom: Yes, I do.
Abby: It's winter now.
Tom: We can play in the snow in winter.
Sophie: It's cold outside! Brrrr.
Abby: That's right. We can wear warm clothes and make different shapes in the snow!
Tom: Abby, your favourite season is autumn because it's your birthday. Sophie, when's your birthday?
Sophie: My birthday is on the 25th of March. I know! Let's find out when our friends have their birthdays.
Tom: We can add all the birthdays to our calendar.
Sophie: We can make a survey on our tablet. Name …? Tom.
Sophie: When's your birthday?
Tom: My birthday is on the 20th of June.
Sophie: Come on! Let's go and ask our friends.
Tom: Bye!
Sophie: Bye!
Abby: See you next time on Channel 21.

Unit 7 21st Century Video

PB page 81 Activities 1 and 2

Sophie: Hello, everybody!
Tom: Hello!
Abby: Welcome back to Channel 21.
Tom: Sophie, do you live in a house or a flat?
Sophie: I live in a flat.
Tom: And what about you, Abby?
Abby: I live in a bungalow.
Sophie: Great! A house with no stairs!
Abby: That's right. Everything is on the ground floor. There are some unusual houses in today's video.
Tom: Let's watch it.
Abby: Look. These are bungalows. Just like mine.
Tom: Wow! They look great!
Abby: Some people live in windmills.
Sophie: That's interesting.
Tom: Is it small inside?
Abby: Yes, it is. The rooms are round, too.
Sophie: This house is very tall.
Tom: Yes! It's got seven floors.
Sophie: It's got a big garden.
Sophie: Do people live on boats?
Abby: Yes, they do. This is a houseboat.
Tom: It's very long.
Abby: There's a bedroom, a living room and a bathroom inside.
Sophie: Is there a kitchen?
Abby: Yes, of course.
Tom: Look at this one! It's very short.
Tom: This houseboat has got a garden, too!
Abby: Oh yes!
Tom: Wow! It's a castle.
Sophie: It's a very small castle.
Tom: Yes. It's very small.
Sophie: These are all different colours!
Tom: Are they flats?
Abby: Yes, they are. They are small inside.
Sophie: This one is really big!

Videoscript

Abby: It's got lots of rooms inside.
Tom: How many bedrooms has it got?
Sophie: I don't know. Maybe 6!
Tom: Cool!
Tom: I've got a lot of toys, too. That bedroom is like mine!
Sophie: Oh no!
Sophie: They've got a lot of toys!
Tom: What a mess!
Abby: They're tidying up.
Tom: Yes. They're putting all the toys away.
Sophie: Look. They're putting the books on the shelf …
Tom: And the jigsaw pieces in the box.
Sophie: Now the bedroom is tidy again.
Tom: Yes! They can play now.
Sophie: It's important to tidy up after you play.
Tom: That's right.
Abby: I think it's time for you two to tidy up!
Sophie: Oh, yes. Come on.
Tom: Bye!
Abby: Don't forget to tidy your bedroom! Goodbye.

Unit 8 21st Century Video

PB page 91 Activities 1 and 2

Abby: Hello, everybody. Welcome back to Channel 21.
Tom and Sophie: Hello!
Abby: Today's video is about important places in the town.
Abby: What places do you think are on the video?
Tom: Maybe a bank?
Sophie: Or a police station.
Tom: Oh, I know! A fire station!
Sophie: Oh yes! That's very important.
Abby: Let's watch the video and see if you're right.
Sophie: Look! Here's the fire station.
Tom: There's a fire. Look! The lights are flashing.
Abby: The traffic stops to let the fire engine go past.
Tom: Yes. The lights and siren tell people to be careful.
Sophie: Is there a police station in your town, Abby?
Abby: Yes. Here it is.
Tom: Are all police cars blue and yellow?
Abby: No, they aren't, but they are bright colours so that people can see them.
Tom: Here's a police officer, too.
Sophie: He's working.
Sophie: Is this the post office in your town?
Abby: Yes, it is. You can buy stamps, newspapers and lots of things there.
Sophie: And you can post letters!
Tom: Here's the train station.
Sophie: Yes. It's behind the post office.
Sophie: It's on the main road. There's a lot of traffic going to and from the train station.
Abby: Be careful when you cross the road here.
Sophie: You can cross the road at a zebra crossing.
Tom: Yes! Find a zebra crossing and push the button.
Sophie: When you see the green man, you can cross the road.
Tom: That's right.
Sophie: Wait for the cars and buses to stop.
Tom: Look and listen when you cross the road.
Sophie: Don't run.
Abby: It's important to be safe when you go into town.
Sophie: It's my aunt's birthday next week. I've got a present for her.
Tom: Let's go to the post office and post it!
Sophie: How do we get to the post office?
Abby: Go straight on. Then turn left.
Sophie: Can we go on foot?
Abby: Yes.
Tom: But be careful when you cross the road.
Tom and Sophie: Remember! Stop, look, listen and think.
Abby: Let's all go together.
Tom: Good idea.
Abby: See you next time on Channel 21.
Sophie: Bye.

Unit 9 21st Century Video

PB page 101 Activities 1 and 2

Sophie: Hello, everybody!
Tom: Hello!
Abby: Welcome back to Channel 21.
Abby: Where were you last weekend?
Tom: I was at the funfair. Where were you, Sophie?
Sophie: I was at the theatre.
Tom: All our friends were at different places.
Sophie: Let's look at their photos.
Sophie: Who's this?
Tom: This is my friend Dan.
Sophie: Was he at the Science museum?
Tom: Yes, he was. It's a special museum all about water.
Sophie: That's interesting!
Tom: Who are those children?
Sophie: That's my friend Alice and those are her cousins. They were at the sports centre on Saturday.
Sophie: This is my friend Ben. He was at the forest.
Tom: Who's that girl?
Sophie: That's his sister Eva.
Tom: Was it sunny?
Sophie: No. It was cloudy all weekend.
Tom: My friend Jill was at the forest, too.
Sophie: What's she doing?
Tom: She's taking a photo of a squirrel. She loves taking photos with her digital camera.
Sophie: My friend Alex loves taking photos, too.
Tom: Was he at the castle last weekend?
Sophie: Yes, he was. He was at the castle with his aunt.
Tom: Who's that girl?
Sophie: That's my cousin Sue. She was at the aquarium with her mum and dad.
Tom: The aquarium is a great place to take photos!
Abby: It's a good idea to take photos of your family, too.
Tom: That's right! Here's my friend Hugo taking a selfie with his mum and dad and his sister, Ann.
Abby: You can take a lot of great photos at the funfair, too.
Tom: Yes! I've got lots of photos on all the rides.
Tom: And some videos, too! Look!
Sophie: Let's make a slide show with all of our photos.
Tom: Great idea!
Abby: Have you got any photos of the theatre?
Sophie: Yes, I have.
Tom: Let's get the camera!
Abby: Don't forget to take lots of photos of your summer holiday.
Tom: That's right!
Sophie: Have a good holiday and see you next year.
All three: Bye!